MORAL TASTE:
AESTHETICS, SUBJECTIVITY, AND SOCIAL POWER
IN THE NINETEENTH-CENTURY NOVEL

MARJORIE GARSON

# Moral Taste

## Aesthetics, Subjectivity, and Social Power in the Nineteenth-Century Novel

UNIVERSITY OF TORONTO PRESS
Toronto Buffalo London

© University of Toronto Press Incorporated 2007
Toronto Buffalo London
Printed in Canada

ISBN: 978-0-8020-9138-3

Printed on acid-free paper

**Library and Archives Canada Cataloguing in Publication**

Garson, Marjorie Joyce
    Moral taste : aesthetics, subjectivity and social power in the
    nineteenth-century novel / Marjorie Garson.

    Includes bibliographical references and index.

    ISBN-13: 978-0-8020-9138-3
    ISBN-10: 0-8020-9138-5

    1. Aesthetics in literature.    2. Literature and society – Great Britain – History –
    19th century.    3. English fiction – 19th century – History and criticism.    I.
    Title.

    PR878.A385G37 2007      823'.809355      C2006-904770-7

University of Toronto Press acknowledges the financial assistance to its
publishing program of the Canada Council for the Arts and the Ontario
Arts Council.

University of Toronto Press acknowledges the financial support for its
publishing activities of the Government of Canada through the Book
Publishing Industry Development Program (BPIDP).

*For Matt*

# Contents

# Acknowledgments

It is a pleasure to thank those whose interest and affection have sustained me during the writing of this book and whose ideas and suggestions helped shape its argument. In particular, I am grateful to Ann McWhir, whose interest in the topic encouraged me at the very first stages of its composition; to the late Norman Feltes, who pointed me to key sources; to Sara Beam and Matt Beam, whose queries and observations helped me refine many of my arguments; to Judith Williams, who read much of the material with creative and critical attention; to Peter Fairley and Jordan Richards, for their loving support during computer crises; and to Arthur Ripstein, for editorial and practical help at the 'pitching' stage. It has been a pleasure to work with the University of Toronto Press, and I particularly want to thank Jill McConkey for the practical and moral support she offered throughout the whole process of publication, and Jim Leahy for his astute and detailed consideration of the manuscript. I am grateful to Jill Matus, for her continuing friendship and for her encouragement and advice throughout, and to Ed Pechter, Lesley Pechter, and Karen Weisman, for affection, laughter, and gossip. I rejoice to acknowledge the constant inspiration of Iris Fairley-Beam and Emile Fairley-Beam, whose own tastes and accomplishments have provided continual evidence of the centrality of aesthetics in human experience. Above all I thank my husband Paul Richards, whose generosity and devotion almost always overcame the challenges this project presented to his patience.

# MORAL TASTE

# Introduction

The eighteenth-century habit of using the word 'taste' in paired constructions – 'taste and elegance,' 'taste and resources,' 'taste and merit,'
'taste and judgment,' 'taste and accomplishments' – assimilates aesthetic response to a wide range of sometimes contradictory mental and
moral qualities, and the breadth of reference is not dropped in the
decades that follow. The term 'taste' carries more weight in this period
and is applied in a wider variety of situations than it is today. It often
means no more than gentility or manners, but it can mean *mores* (one of
Burney's characters declares that in 'the taste of the present day' young
men think themselves wiser than their fathers). It is commonly used to
describe what we would now tend to call compatibility (a heroine sizing
up a suitor will assess 'the similarity of his taste and turn of mind with
her own,' their 'concordance of taste and humour').[1] Well into the
nineteenth century the word is used of sexual attraction, particularly of
the transgressive kind (the friends of Trollope's Emily Wharton deplore
'her vitiated taste and dreadful partiality' for Lopez, 'the Portuguese
adventurer').[2] George Eliot, who has a great investment in taste of various kinds, uses the word on one occasion in a peculiar moral sense, sati-
rizing her erstwhile friend Mary Sibree for the 'bad taste' of unreflective
self-interest:

> Sibreeanism is that degree of egotism which we call bad taste but which
> does not reach to gross selfishness – the egotism that does not think of oth-
> ers, but would be very glad to do them good if it did think of them – the
> egotism that eats up all the bread and butter and is ready to die of confu-
> sion and distress after having done it.[3]

That Darwin can attribute taste to the female Argus pheasant, who, just like a human being, he says, is able to appreciate ornament, suggests how ready to hand is the term in this period, how easily it can be applied to a variety of ethical, psychological, and social impulses.[4] The prestige of the term and its breadth of application, the sense that the quality of character towards which it points is the *sine qua non* of moral identity, suggests that 'taste' in the widest sense is likely to be an informing principle of novels that focus on development of the 'deep,' developmental self and on moral choice. The subject of this study is the ideological work done by the equation of good taste and moral refinement in a selection of nineteenth-century writings, and I hope to show that the contradictions in the discourse of taste account for a wider range of meanings in even the best-known texts than has always been recognized.

Aesthetics has been a vibrant, even explosive topic in cultural and literary analysis in recent years. Volumes of material dealing with taste have been appearing at a steady pace: specialized monographs on such topics as colour, architecture, speech and elocution, theatre and fashion,[5] as well as more radical or wide-ranging analyses. Allan Megill, for example, suggests that from the study of aesthetics was born, in the early eighteenth century, historical thought itself; Daniel Cottom documents the usefulness of the notion of taste as a way of endorsing the 'natural' power of whoever is at the top of a hierarchical society; Terry Eagleton argues that the work of art emerged as a kind of subject (and the subject emerged as a work of art) at the moment when modern subjectivity was needed to serve the moral and ideological purposes of the bourgeoisie in an emerging capitalist society. The importance of the work of Walter Benjamin for the study of patterns of consumption has been fully acknowledged, and such consumption itself has become an important topic in Victorian studies. The transgressive potential of style has been explored by feminist scholars such as Luce Irigaray, Hélène Cixous, and Judith Butler, who, taking account of Lacan and his theory of specularity, have explained female subjectivity in terms of masquerade, role-playing, and performativity. As influential in recent nineteenth-century studies as Butler is the work of Pierre Bourdieu, whose concept of 'cultural capital' has seemed particularly relevant to the novels of Jane Austen. In addition to these more broadly theoretical approaches, a number of scholars dealing with the late eighteenth and nineteenth centuries have investigated individual aesthetic discourses of the period – John Barrell, painting and art criticism, for example; Rachel Crawford, landscape; Penny Gay, Austen and the theatre; Delia da Sousa Correa, George Eliot and music; Patricia Howell Michaelson, reading aloud – as well as analogous topics having to do with the construction of middle-class female subjectivity: Elizabeth Langland, the treatment of servants; Mary Ann O'Farrell, blushing; Ruth Yeazell, feminine modesty. I shall be drawing on the work of many of these scholars in the discussion that follows. Nevertheless, despite this impressive and indeed overwhelming body of scholarship, I believe there is a place for a study that elucidates the total role of 'tastefulness' of various kinds within individual novels. I am aiming at what might be called breadth within depth: that is, I am attempting a thoroughgoing analysis of a limited number of texts on the assumption that it is only by looking at the range of the signs of 'tastefulness' within each one that we can understand how much work the aesthetic discourse tends to do. Beginning with Scott, whose sense of historical contingency relativizes the discourse of taste on which he nevertheless continues to rely, and with Austen, whose more consistent investment in the equation between good taste and moral discrimination is exemplary for my purposes, I go on to discuss a number of Victorian texts that treat aesthetic refinement as the essential mark of proper middle-class subjectivity.

Every reader is struck by the ineffable tastefulness of so many Victorian novel heroines – Gaskell's Margaret Hale, for example, or Eliot's Dorothea Brooke, who manage to dress stunningly without ever thinking of their wardrobes and furnish their homes with charm even in the absence of material resources, and whose excellent taste asks to be understood not as a result of self-conscious strategy or painstaking effort, but rather as a kind of unmediated emanation of their refinement of spirit. What is the intellectual background of such patently fictional constructions? How do such apparently trivial aesthetic gestures as arranging fruit on a plate (like Margaret) or selecting jewellery (like Dorothea) come to function as an expression of what Bourdieu would call 'charismatic' moral distinction? I shall begin the investigation of this question by sketching out the intellectual history of 'moral taste,' paying particular attention to certain problematic notions that, partly because of their very contradictions, turn out to be wonderfully enabling for novelists throughout the nineteenth century.

The study of aesthetics as a discrete branch of philosophy is founded in the early eighteenth century on classical ideas. The Platonic equation between truth and beauty allows Lord Shaftesbury, a 'devoted disciple of Renaissance neo-Platonism'[6] and the founder of modern aesthetic philosophy, to assert that the philosopher is simply the thorough gentleman.[7] His disciple Francis Hutcheson goes on to postulate not only an innate sense of beauty but also an innate moral sense – 'a moral sense of beauty in actions and affections' – that enables us to choose virtuous actions on the basis of their loveliness (the Author of Nature having 'made virtue a lovely form to excite our pursuit of it').[8] The discourse of sensibility adopts and elaborates on the link between aesthetic responsiveness and social feeling: 'delicacy of taste,' asserts Lord Kames, 'necessarily heightens our sensibility of pain and pleasure; and of course our sympathy, which is the capital branch of every social passion.'[9] Associationist psychology further endorses the connection. Archibald Alison, for example, argues that 'it is by means of this constitution of our nature' – that is, because we form associations between ideas – 'that the emotions of taste are blended with moral sentiment.'[10] It becomes a truism that a taste for natural beauty, for the beauty of the world that God has created, is specifically 'fitted to awaken us to moral emotion.'[11] Mark Akenside, for example, argues that the mind, contemplating the harmonies of nature, seeks a similar harmony within itself – seeks 'to exert within herself this elegance of love' – and thus the passions are chastened and the spirit lifted towards God, who made human beings to 'behold and love / What he beholds and loves.'[12] Alison makes what becomes a conventional connection between a nation's taste, its religious feeling, and its level of evolutionary development: 'In ages of civilization and refinement, the union of devotional sentiment with sensibility to the beauties of natural scenery, forms one of the most characteristic marks of human improvement.'[13] The conviction that taste, 'improved exactly as we improve our judgement,' is 'in reality no other than a more refined judgement,'[14] makes it plausible to believe that 'a man of taste is a man of judgment in other respects'[15] and to take for granted that good taste in one aesthetic field involves good taste in all.

The history of this idea does not however explain how 'moral taste' came to be appropriated by the middle classes and applied to the most banal details of everyday life: why by the time Keats is reminding his readers that Beauty is Truth and Truth Beauty, the word 'taste' can be applied without incongruity to a whole range of behaviours, including diction, elocution, social decorum, manners, style of hospitality, and the right attitude to take towards servants, as well as to more narrowly aesthetic pursuits like drawing and making music. It does not explain why by the 1830s, when J.C. Loudon, the landscape designer, can allude, as if recycling an accepted truth, to 'the rigid disciplines of good taste, which are always in unison with those of good morality,'[16] the word 'taste' can be applied even to modest economy and household order:

> Enter the humblest dwelling under the prudent management of a discreet and rightly educated female, and observe the simplicity and good taste which pervade it. The wise mistress has nothing gaudy in her dress or furniture, for she is superior to the silly ambition of surpassing her neighbours in show. Her own best ornaments are cheerfulness and contentment; her highest displays, those of comfort and a comely gladness; her house is the abode and token of neatness and thrift; of good order and cleanliness; which makes it, and its various divisions, look better than they really are.[17]

This is 'embourgeoisement' indeed.[18] The process by which, at the end of the eighteenth century, the middle classes, while appropriating some elements of aristocratic style, also redefined taste for their own ideological purposes needs to be put into the context of a wider story.

Terry Eagleton sketches out the background of this story – the historical motives for the turn to the aesthetic in the eighteenth century – in his recent study *The Ideology of the Aesthetic*, theorizing it from a Marxist perspective. Eagleton's argument, in brief, is that at the historical moment when methods of production have turned out 'artefacts [that] become commodities in the market place,' these artefacts, which now 'exist for nothing and nobody in particular,' begin to look as if they existed 'gloriously for themselves.'[19] That is, at the moment the commodity floats free of its context, so that it can be 'luminously apprehended as selfbounded and selfcontained upon the immeasurable background of space or time which is not it' (to borrow the words of Joyce's Stephen Dedalus),[20] it begins to seem autonomous, self-regarding, organically unified: indeed, it begins to seem something like a human subject. At the same moment, the human subject begins to look more and more like a work of art. The same mode of production that turns out objects offering themselves for aesthetic consumption requires for its smooth operations the kind of subject attuned to consuming them. 'The idea of autonomy – of a mode of being which is entirely self-regulating and self-determining – provides the middle class with just the ideological model of subjectivity it requires for its material operations.'[21] Hence, aesthetic philosophy, as it is used to stabilize essentially autocratic political regimes, produces 'an entirely new kind of human being – one which, like the work of art itself, discovers the law in the depths of its own free identity, rather than in some oppressive external power.'[22]

Eagleton deals with individual philosophers in this text, not with the social patterns that emerge as a result of the turn towards the aesthetic, nor with the literary productions of the period. Other scholars and critics have been documenting, with different kinds of historical and sociological precision, the ways in which this conceptual shift plays out in society: the turn towards middle-class values at the end of the eighteenth century and the consolidation of middle-class cultural authority. As economic changes placed more wealth in the hands of the middle class and the old signs of status – titles, great estates, luxurious living, aristocratic dress – lost their exclusive prestige, new social lines began to be drawn, and the moral and social authority of the middle class to be justified on the basis of its sensibility, manners, morality, intelligence, and initiative. Brooke's *The Fool of Quality* (1766–72), for example 'puts, on one side, manners, sentiment, feeling, politeness, taste, industry and commerce – and on the other aristocratic landed wealth, fashion, city society, worldliness and corruption.'[23] An aspect of this transformation was the development of the doctrine of separate spheres for men and women. While the aristocratic, patrilineal system privileges men, the middle-class claim to cultural authority involves what has been called the feminization of culture, with a new emphasis on the sanctity of the home and the woman who is its heart, the domestic angel whose purity, modesty, charm, and taste are supposed to make her desirable to a man of any class.[24] Along with this development there is a new valorization of privacy, of interiority, of the individual, of the 'deep' character and the character capable of development, notably, the endlessly explicable, never-to-be-fully-explained characters of Shakespeare; a 'shift from the self as static, metaphysical, and inherited to the rounded, psychological, and self-made subject, one that is capable of the limitless self-improvement valorizing and valorized by the 'open' society and a 'free' economy.'[25] Utilitarianism combines with the evangelical emphasis on personal moral responsibility to endorse the ideology of self-control, self-examination, self-help, and also self-improvement: the cultivation of the enriched, many-faceted subjectivity that testifies to fully civilized human nature. Though aping and attempting to appropriate certain elements of gentry culture, the bourgeoisie redefine taste in terms of their own priorities, forging a fresh connection between good taste and moral sensitivity and distinguishing their true gentility both from the decadence of the aristocracy and from the 'violence' of the working class.[26]

Central to the task of drawing such distinctions is the notion of 'natural taste,' a phrase found everywhere at the end of the eighteenth century. 'Natural taste' is evidently an oxymoron: since what is considered tasteful at any particular historical moment is always a cultural construct, anyone who has taste has already been cultivated. Edmund Burke begins his investigation of taste by attempting to trace aesthetic judgments back to the most basic and universal human responses, the love of pleasure and the fear of pain: for example, the enjoyment of sweet tastes and fear of the dark. But he discovers that nature as an explanatory principle must soon be supplemented by culture. Burke has to explain differences of taste by attributing them not only to the kind of physiological or temperamental differences that might be understood as inborn or merely 'natural,' such as defective sensory equipment or the dullness or sensuality that makes 'base' individuals unable to respond to 'the delicate and refined play of the imagination,'[27] but also to education and experience. Reflecting this tension, 'the words 'nature' and 'natural' in Burke,' though they 'appear sometimes to connote inborn, and therefore predetermined and uniform, characteristics,' at other times 'suggest acculturated, and therefore normative, qualities and habits.'[28] Since the highest kind of taste, the ability to respond appropriately to artworks that deal with 'the manners, the characters, the actions, and designs of men,' depends on 'our skill in manners, and [on] the observances of time and place, and of decency in general' – that is, derives from our attendance at 'the schools of philosophy and the world'[29] – education and experience turn out to be hugely important. Though Burke wants to insist that taste is 'common to all,' or at any rate 'nearly common to all,' and though much of his analysis of aesthetic responses focuses on the most basic kinds of sensory response – for example, on the shapes of sugar crystals and their resulting effect on the tongue – he does point out that it is only 'so far as taste is natural'[30] that it is universal. Despite the interest Burke takes in universal psychological and emotional responses, he does not finally endorse the 'natural taste' of any but the most highly developed individuals. Deeply distrusting Rousseauvian sensibility as a guide to moral action, Burke believes that 'natural' feelings, to be reliable, have to be embodied in institutions and turned into enlightened prejudices, and he sees the great landowner, whose taste has been cultivated within a privileged environment, as the one most likely to judge and act rightly on social issues.[31]

In fact, as the phrase 'natural taste' is actually used at this time, it functions not to connect the individual to whom it is attributed to the rest of humanity by virtue of the common human nature she shares with them, but rather to mark out the exceptional individual who deserves social advancement because she already possesses the refinement her new position would demand. When Scott in 1814 judges his blonde heroine Rose Bradwardine as having 'the natural taste that requires only cultivation' on the basis of a piece of needlework she happens to be holding in her hand as she comes to receive her father and Waverley into her apartment, he evidently does not mean by 'natural taste' anything as specific as talent in textile design: he is simply signalling that Rose is worthy of Waverley's romantic interest because, despite her provincial Scottish upbringing, she is already a thorough gentlewoman in her demeanour. The phrase 'natural taste' attributes to nature what is in reality the work of class, thus reinforcing class lines while pretending to be open to their crossing. It is only as an oxymoron that 'natural taste' can do the ideological work that it does.

'The natural taste that requires only cultivation' is a formula immensely useful to the novelists of the period. Because needlework is so trivial a sign of so general and lofty a quality as 'natural taste,' when Scott uses the expression here without any sense of its incongruity, he seems to be rehearsing an established cliché. As indeed he was: the idea is found everywhere in the previous century. Hugh Blair asserts, as a mere truism, that nature sows the seeds of taste, but cultivation is needed to make them grow; Alexander Gerard observes that 'it is only in the few who improve the rudiments of taste which *nature* has implanted, by *culture* well chosen, and judiciously applied,' that taste is perfected, but that it is, 'like delicate plants, liable to be checked in its growth and killed, or else to become crooked and distorted by negligence, or improper management.'[32] The figure has a long life: Akenside's lines advocating such 'culture' in 1744, if only because they are reprinted in Enfield's *The Speaker*, continue to represent cultural orthodoxy to unfortunate schoolboys like Tom Tulliver well into the nineteenth century.[33]

The opening of *Waverley* is full of Spenserian allusions, and Rose Bradwardine's floral name, reviving the almost-dead metaphor of the blossoming plant, also awakens Spenserian echoes: it reminds the reader not only of Belphoebe, whose 'honour' is described as a rose that opens up but then closes again if threatened by the noon sun or 'the sharpe Northern wind' (an image obviously applicable to Rose Bradwardine), but also of the flower of courtesy, 'which though it on a lowly stalke doe bowre, / Yet brancheth forth in braue nobilitie.'[34] The relevance of Spenser's metaphors to Scott is a reminder that such formulations arise in the sixteenth century, at the time when self-fashioning for social advancement first comes to seem a possibility. Castiglione in *The Courtier*, discussing not natural taste but natural *grace* – a term that, like Spenser, he uses with a full sense of its theological associations[35] – employs, along with images from horse-breeding, the botanical metaphor that becomes an almost inevitable feature of this discourse. 'Natural grace' – especially as initially used in *The Courtier*, to refer to physical, bodily grace – is not so evidently self-contradictory as 'natural taste,' and Castiglione's botanical imagery expresses not so much the possibilities of cultivation as the determinative effect of heredity: in human beings, as in trees, he says, 'the shoots ... nearly always resemble the trunk,'[36] and he is willing to acknowledge that, just as there are exceptional individuals apparently 'fashioned by the hand of some god,' there are also 'inept and uncouth' individuals who will 'yield little fruit even with constant diligence and good care.'[37] For Castiglione, the corollary of 'natural grace' is what might be called 'natural dis-grace': the condition of the individual whom no amount of cultivation can improve. What to think about such individuals (or about such classes of individuals) is an issue that can prove more of an embarrassment in the eighteenth century than it seems to be to Castiglione, who simply assumes that none of the genteel participants in his conversation is defective in this way.

If the 'grace' of aesthetic refinement is understood not as personal charm and attractiveness but as the ability to respond with appropriate reverence to the beauty of God's creation, the stakes are higher, and how to situate those who lack taste becomes a stickier problem. In a theological rather than courtesy-book context, the notion of grace, which Castiglione uses as a rather throwaway metaphor, raises a more embarrassing issue. It is embarrassment of this kind that complicates the rhetoric of Mark Akenside over two hundred years after *The Courtier*, when he finds himself obliged to generalize about this class of fruitless plants. Attempting in 'The Pleasures of Imagination' (1744) to undo the traditional association between taste and aristocratic inheritance – to make clear that taste is not the exclusive province of those 'above' the middle class – Akenside asserts that aesthetic feeling is bestowed not by wealth but by 'God alone.' He then goes on, however, to qualify this statement so as to exclude those 'below.' It is at this point that the botanical metaphor begins to blur and shift:

> But though Heav'n
> In every breast hath sown these early seeds
> Of love and admiration [of beauty], yet in vain,
> Without fair Culture's kind parental aid,
>                     ... in vain we hope
> The tender plant should rear its blooming head,
> Or yield the harvest promis'd in its spring.

Cultivation is necessary – but cultivation does not always work:

> Nor yet will ev'ry soil with equal store
> Repay the tiller's labour ...[38]

There are some shifty if not exactly mixed metaphors here. The plant is not the individual psyche, apparently, but the individual's capacity for aesthetic response: the seed is the seed of tastefulness, and it is the soil that is the psyche. The 'tiller' turns out to be neither God who sows the seeds nor the individual who receives them, but a female personification – 'fair Culture' – whose baffled maternal concern softens the unhappy fact that whatever attempts the truly inferior individual makes towards his own self-development are doomed not to pay off. The ability to develop taste is located apparently not in the seed – Heaven dispenses, one assumes at this point, only good seeds – but in the soil. However this only displaces the problem. If the seeds are sown in every breast, but not every 'breast' is of the required quality – if some seeds do not grow because some breasts are stony ground – why can heaven, which evidently desires culture in everybody, not do more to control the process? And what, exactly, are the seeds themselves, those seeds that Heaven sends down? They seem to be some mysterious entity, potential-taste-that-might-never-develop. Yet seeds are evidently species-specific. If, as Akenside adds, the tiller does not control what species of plant comes up, neither surely does the soil. Can bad soil turn an olive pit into a laurel seed? And what about the more undesirable species? The olive and the laurel, though different in associations and prestige, are both desirable plants, whereas the relevant distinction would seem to be between desirable plants and undesirable ones. What if the seed develops into neither an olive nor a laurel but a weed? Akenside slides from the olive/laurel comparison into an analogous polarity that equally sidesteps the question. Different minds have different preferences, he says: Shakespeare thrives in storm, Waller prefers calm. But what of those who are neither a Shakespeare nor a Waller? Happy the man, says Akenside, ringing changes on an old topos, who is not seduced by money or honour, for such a man can appreciate beauty, the beauty of both the 'city's pomp' and country pleasures. Gliding from one polarity to another, Akenside drifts away from the issue of differential ability, until all of a sudden 'Nature' is treating people equally. Though she does not distribute pomp and honour to all, she does provide equal access to aesthetic pleasure 'to all her children':

> Nature's care, to all her children just,
> With richer treasures and an ampler state
> Indows at large whatever happy man
> Will deign to use them.[39]

The question now is not whether one has the power to respond to the beauty that Nature offers free to all but whether one 'deigns' to use it. We have still not heard what happens to the bad seeds destined from the beginning to develop into plants that nobody wants – into the kind of taste that prefers beer and skittles to Mozart.

The stony-ground metaphor, linking taste to grace through the allusion to the Bible, implies a more absolute distinction than Akenside seems to want. Taste is evidently like grace in the Calvinist sense: those who can respond to beauty are the elect; those who cannot, the reprobate. The difference is not between olive and laurel, Shakespeare and Waller, but between sheep and goat, wheat and chaff. But it is one thing to acknowledge that people are different, another to admit that some are damned, and in the context of liberal discourse about Nature's universal gifts this is a conclusion Akenside prefers not explicitly to reach.

In a theological context, then, taste is a competence that philosophers have begun to find necessary to attribute to all human beings. If, as Burke argues, everyone's sensory equipment is more or less the same, everyone must be at least potentially able to respond to beauty. Indeed, if such appreciation is linked with reverence for God, it would be theologically incorrect to hold that some are by nature denied it. Yet, given these premises, how to explain the difference between the refined taste that characterizes 'us' and the vulgarity that marks 'them'? If Heaven really has sown seeds of aesthetic responsiveness in *every* breast, why has it made some soils unable to receive them, some breasts unable to respond? Why does God permit most people to remain so vulgar? If one brackets the theological dimension of the problem, the alternatives perhaps become clearer, though still not ideologically unproblematic. Either one has to devise an explanatory model that privileges 'our' environment – for example, Burke's claim that the poor do not have as many experiences as the wealthy and thus cannot develop aesthetic principles by means of comparison[40] – or one must, however tactfully, postulate some kind of innate difference.[41]

The formula 'the natural taste that requires only cultivation' has such a long life I think because it finesses such problems. It manages to imply innate difference without insisting on it. The word 'natural' is tactfully ambiguous. It sounds rather liberal, subliminally suggesting that taste is natural to all human beings – that everyone has it and need only 'cultivate' it; yet, as I have suggested, the tag 'the natural taste that requires only cultivation' is invariably applied to the single exceptional individual who has hitherto been denied the requisite nurture. That is, the formula, while implying equality, is consistently used to distinguish between those who are innately capable of cultivation and those who are not. Or is it between those who, when cultivated, develop into a plant worth cultivating and those who, even if nurtured 'with diligence and good care,' do not? The botanist can use good soil and good seed, but if what he plants is not a desirable species, the result will be second-rate. All plants are subject to cultivation, but not all plants are equal in aesthetic prestige. The (English) rose is more tasteful than the dahlia (associated with the working class) or the bougainvillea (the colours of tropical flowers, implies Ruskin, are vulgar).[42]

Talking about flowers avoids talking straight about class and race. The expression 'the natural taste that requires only cultivation' acquires new currency at the historical moment when the middle class is beginning to build its case for cultural authority. Implying that 'taste,' which is never going to blossom in the stony ground of the lower orders, is fully available to non-aristocratic, middle-class individuals but that these individuals must 'cultivate' themselves in order to acquire it, the metaphor speaks to the ambition of those who feel they have both the energy to undertake such cultivation and the innate superiority that will make their efforts pay off. While postulating inner value as innate rather than as a product of class, the cliché apparently also valorizes earnest effort and so can be used to rationalize moral judgment. As it is used in the novels of Austen, for example, this paradigm, which both demands and promises to reward efforts at self-improvement, draws a line between those superior spirits who have the responsibility (and deserve the credit) for their self-culture and the ineluctably inferior, who, though they lack the natural taste that could be cultivated, can somehow nevertheless be blamed for failing to cultivate it. That taste is a gift of nature but that the vulgar can nevertheless be contemptuously dismissed for their vulgarity are the contradictory premises behind many of Austen's character constructions.

My title is taken from *Mansfield Park*, where Henry Crawford is said to have the 'moral taste' properly to appreciate Fanny Price.[43] The phrase is not Austen's alone – it turns up fairly often in various texts of the period – but her characters are a good place to start, not only because her influence can be seen throughout the century but also because of such exemplary contradictions. Austen never uses the formula 'a natural taste that requires only cultivation,' which had no doubt become too hackneyed for her own fastidious taste, and in the figure of Harriet Smith she seems to be making fun of the idea. Emma Woodhouse, determined against all evidence to believe that Harriet Smith has natural taste, thinks that she can cultivate her (as well as marry her off). But she turns out to be wrong. Harriet can be persuaded to give up Robert Martin for Mr Elton, but she cannot learn to value Martin's manly prose, decode a charade, ironize a gothic romance, or evaluate a performance on the pianoforte. Light-mindedly vulgar herself, she cannot detect vulgarity in others: her admiration for Augusta Elton makes clear that it was not Emma's own good taste, as Emma imagines, that induced Harriet to value Emma herself.

In *Emma* Austen seems to be sending up the cultivation-of-natural-taste formula. Yet in her previous novel, *Mansfield Park*, 'the natural taste that requires only cultivation' is the founding premise of the heroine's characterization. Fanny Price, mentored and tutored by her cousin Edmund, turns out to be just the ready pupil that Emma anticipates in Harriet. Though Fanny comes from a household utterly lacking in culture or even order, she emerges almost from the moment she arrives at Mansfield Park as superior both in taste and in character not only to Maria and Julia Bertram but to everyone in the family except Edmund. The Bertrams, expecting the worst in Fanny, are relieved to find that 'her air, though awkward, was not vulgar; her voice was sweet; and when she spoke, her countenance was pretty' (49). How can such a family as the Prices have produced a child with none of the 'very distressing vulgarity of manner' (47) that the Bertrams reasonably anticipate? As time goes on, 'gradually' in the fictional time though instantly in the text, 'the little rusticities and awkwardnesses which had at first made grievous inroads on the tranquillity of all' – awkwardnesses that are never awkwardly specified – 'wore away' (53). 'Rusticities' in Portsmouth? The uncharacteristic sloppiness of diction here suggests that Austen's concession is only perfunctory. Rusticities in Fanny? The Fanny we know is not capable of a rusticity: she is always already refined. 'No one grasps what he has not possessed from birth,' says Thomas Mann's Felix Krull, cited by Cottom to support his argument that in the eighteenth century the discourse of taste was used to mark an unbridgeable gap between the aristocracy and everyone else.[44] Austen would agree with Felix Krull, and Fanny, though from a degraded family, is a natural aristocrat. So indeed are many of the naturally tasteful characters I shall be discussing in the readings that follow.

The examples from *Waverley* and *Mansfield Park* illustrate another useful function of the 'natural-taste-that-requires-only-cultivation' formula at this particular historical moment: it sets up what becomes a stock novelistic scenario, the romance between the unawakened heroine and the tutor/'pedagod' who 'cultivates' her and makes her bloom.[45] Indeed, the longevity of the horticultural metaphor might be explained merely in terms of its happy fitness to the topic of female education. Like Scott's Rose Bradwardine, Monimia, the gentle heroine of Charlotte Smith's *The Old Manor House*, has a 'pure and elegant taste' that exists to be cultivated by a discriminating lover. The hero, Orlando, who has early on 'given her a taste for reading, and cultivating her excellent understanding,' is seen at the end of the novel imagining her perusing a literary passage he had taught her to appreciate and musing hopefully about that 'understanding' of Monimia's that is still 'uncultivated' after all his efforts and about 'the delightful task of improving it': a lifetime project, apparently.[46] This *maître-de-sa-maîtresse* topos,[47] a staple of turn-of-the-century fiction, has been dismissed as a type of Foucauldian discipline, an authoritarian male fantasy,[48] but the way it is used by female novelists suggests that it has a perennial appeal for women as well, and it continues to turn up regularly in Victorian fiction, notoriously in a fraught and problematic form in the fiction of Charlotte Brontë and George Eliot, and even, in a twisted parody, in James's *The Awkward Age*. Its resilience can perhaps be explained in terms of its function in a period when relationships between the genders were being renegotiated in ways that made everyone uneasy. Just at the moment when the woman was being given a kind of moral and spiritual authority that made her the centre of the household – at the moment when the middle-class domestic angel was promoted as the new social ideal – this reassuring topos continued to acknowledge masculine cultural authority.

'What man should be to woman ever,' muses Disraeli's Sybil Gerard, is 'gentle, and yet a guide.'[49] The tutor–pupil scenario allows for a period of masculine guidance, even if only the gentlest is needed to enable the heroine to blossom as 'nature' intends.

In the context of this discourse, such blossoming – a wholly natural process, if one is a flower – tends to be represented as joyful, as liberating, indeed as almost pure pleasure. A significant (and ideologically useful) contradiction in the taste/cultivation formula is that while it claims to valorize systematic effort, it actually dramatizes 'natural' ease. The emphasis on 'nature' makes sure that 'cultivation' can never be represented as onerous. Novelistic heroines who demonstrate their taste through their literary and artistic pursuits are characterized by their ardour and receptivity rather than by hard work – the actual labour of mastering a field of study is rarely dramatized – while those who demonstrate it in other ways, for example by their clothing and personal demeanour, are exempted from any effort at all.[50] Indeed, despite the period's emphasis on earnest application and steady effort, systematic practice often becomes problematic in these texts. In a novel like *Middlemarch* it is the vulgar Rosamond Vincy who works on her self-image (practising her singing, for example) and the unworldly and utterly unselfconscious Dorothea who miraculously dresses like a goddess without any effort (and whose voice is the text's only real music). Since the notion of 'natural taste' represents both personal beauty and cultural accomplishment as the unmediated manifestation of spiritual distinction, any emphasis on the work that goes into cultivating them would be counterproductive. Practice indeed becomes a defining issue in an Austen novel. Since both embracing instruction and resisting it become signs of a lack of natural quality, the reprobate characters, the vulgar individuals who lack natural taste, are in a double bind. The Bertram sisters are satirized for practising their music, Augusta Elton for abandoning the practice of hers; Harriet Smith is represented as naturally incapable of absorbing instruction yet ironized for her refusal to learn. It is contradictions such as these, contradictions that often go to the heart of the novel's moral judgments, that I wish to investigate in the study that follows.

I have approached the texts I discuss with the help of explanatory systems developed by the sociology of aesthetics. Aesthetic theory as a branch of philosophy attempts to explain beauty and aesthetic response, but it does not attempt to explain the social function of its

explanations or the ideological work that they perform. The associationists to be sure are willing to admit what might be called a proto-sociolog-
ical explanation of certain aesthetic responses – they notice, for
example, that beauty is attributed to objects owned by the wealthy
classes – but they do not attempt to formulate an overarching theory
linking taste and class. It is only at the end of the nineteenth century,
with the development of sociology, that theorists begin to frame the
whole aesthetic discourse from the outside – begin to try to explain not
beauty itself, in which they do not always seem to believe, but 'tastefulness' as a social phenomenon. Writers such as Veblen, Goffman, and
Bourdieu, by treating taste as a social code that derives from, and
announces, social class – by assuming that there is always what Veblen
calls an 'ulterior, economic ground'[51] to what look like aesthetic judgments – may not help us to the experience of beauty, but they can throw
light on the way the discourse of taste is used in the novel. Treating taste
as social performance and its reception as the decoding of that performance can elucidate the implicit rules that govern such performances.

There is a sense, of course, in which the Victorian novelists have nothing to learn about social performance. The period that perused the conduct book was not unaware of the theatrical nature of social interaction
or of the connection between social performance and class. When Goffman cites nineteenth-century conduct books, or when he quotes Adam
Smith on the 'natural' ease and grace of the aristocrat ('His air, his manner, his deportment, all mark that elegant and graceful sense of his own
superiority, which those who are born in inferior stations can hardly
ever arrive at'),[52] he is acknowledging the debt that sociology owes to
the pre-sociological text. No one knows more than the novelists about
front- and backstage personae, about ulterior motives, or about saving
face. George Eliot's two-page analysis of Mr Riley's motives in recommending Mr Stelling as Tom Tulliver's tutor in *The Mill on the Floss* – a
novel, though not a passage, that Goffman cites – long predates Goffman's analysis of the general practitioner's similarly mixed motives for
recommending a specialist to a patient.[53] No doubt the sociologists
learned as much from the novel as we have to learn from them: it might
be argued that they merely systematize and theorize insights already
found everywhere in the earlier period. Nevertheless, system and theory
can help get us 'outside' these nineteenth-century texts, detect their
contradictions, and understand what ideological functions they perform. I shall briefly review the essential ideas of a number of scholars
whose relevance to the issues I am discussing has made them necessary

to this study: Thorstein Veblen's concept of conspicuous consumption and of the role of the middle-class wife as vicarious consumer; Erving Goffman's distinction between front- and backstage and his sense of the teamwork necessary to stage the performances of everyday life; Judith Butler's theory that gender is largely performative; and the social analysis of Pierre Bourdieu, who has been described as 'sociologizing' Kant and whose critique is founded on the demystification of the notion of 'natural taste' that I have been discussing.

Looking at American society at the end of the Victorian period, Veblen analyses the self-representation of what he calls the leisure classes with a jaundiced eye, characterizing it in ethnographic terms as a throwback to 'honour' cultures, where work is servile and exemption from work is a mark of prestige. In such cultures, status is signalled by what Veblen famously calls 'conspicuous leisure' – the 'unproductive consumption of time'[54] – and the 'conspicuous consumption,' indeed the wanton waste, of material goods. These same patterns of behaviour are just what Veblen sees when he looks around him at contemporary America, which, he implies, is perhaps less civilized than it imagines itself to be. As influential as these two famous notions is Veblen's analysis of the status of women in a society where leisure and consumption are signs of wealth but the businessman who earns the money has no time either to rest or to buy. The role of such a man's wife, Veblen argues, is to consume on his behalf: to display his success not only by dressing well and devising a tasteful home but also by refraining from any kind of useful employment. Women, in contemporary society as in cultures that the contemporary world would consider barbaric, are a form of property; they are ornaments; in fact they are servants, and their costly, uncomfortable, dysfunctional clothing is the equivalent of servants' livery. Constituting as they do 'a vicarious leisure class,'[55] they have to be conspicuously idle and conspicuously useless: hence the premium on female delicacy, on small hands and feet, tiny waists, and debilitating garments like corsets. Veblen argues that the anti-feminists who oppose women's 'emancipation' on the grounds that the middle-class woman is showered with material objects and not allowed to work are identifying as feminine perquisites what are really the signs of woman's servile status – 'marks of the un-free.' He expresses the hope that what he calls 'this 'New-Woman' movement' will effect a return to the utopian state in which 'the ideal human character is a character which makes for peace, good-will, and economic efficiency, rather than for a life of self-seeking force.'[56] In the meantime, however, he observes in the American upper classes what he calls a 'potlatch'[57] of conspicuous waste: the frenetic consumption of products and processes that function as signs of wealth precisely because they involve waste of time, waste of money, and waste of work. Whatever is useless for practical life is supremely useful as a sign of 'the relation of status': a retinue of servants; carefully cultivated manners; fine china; silver spoons; hand-made furniture and craft objects (Veblen has no use for Morris and Ruskin); closely trimmed lawns; decorative bowers and pavilions; topiary work; pet animals, especially dogs;[58] top hats; beautifully bound books (he has a particular animus against the Kelmscott Press and all its works); priestly vestments; academic ritual; college sports; the study of the classical languages; and indeed the humanities in general, the chief purpose of which, he says, is to produce 'a type of character suited to a régime of status.'[59] Whereas Kant sees in the uselessness of the art object the very condition of its aesthetic apprehension, Veblen condemns the consumption of such objects, though without taking on Kant explicitly. Veblen's analytical paradigm, which takes wasteful expense as the sole criterion of the desirable consumer article, is not very nuanced: Pierre Bourdieu, a less surly and more sophisticated analyst, looking, through the perspective that Kant provides, at the same social class – the class that can afford to be disinterested because it has transcended material needs, the class 'habituated' (as Veblen puts it) 'to take no thought for the morrow'[60] – produces a paradigm more useful for defining the qualities an object must have if it is to endow its owner with social prestige. But Veblen's seminal concepts of 'conspicuous leisure' and 'conspicuous taste' and his analysis of the woman's 'vicarious' role have become received ideas in materialist cultural criticism.

Veblen will occasionally describe the practices he analyses in theatrical terms – he refers, for example, to 'a performance of leisure'[61] – but he does not use the theatrical metaphor consistently or heuristically. Erving Goffman does do so, and his distinction between front-stage and backstage behaviour has become another received idea in social analysis. Though Goffman does not concern himself with aesthetics directly, his work is relevant here not only because it influenced Bourdieu, who cites him from time to time, but also because it suggests ways of thinking about certain novelistic scenarios. Goffman is interested in how people maintain the 'face' they want to present to the world in the social and professional encounters of everyday life. Understanding each person-to-person encounter as a complex attempt to project and protect one's self-image while not gratuitously undercutting the self-image of others, he analyses the ways in which individuals work together to produce the hierarchical positions that allow for stable, smooth, and socially productive interactions. The theatrical metaphor is developed with some consistency. Goffman sees individual self-presentation as role-playing and complex group interaction as a theatrical production that involves not only a full cast of characters but also others – a producer, a director, sometimes stage-hands – who work behind the scene to make sure that the performance comes off successfully. Backstage activities produce 'mystification,' which is what Goffman calls the process of projecting an idealized image by concealing the labour and strategizing that goes into the public performance: 'the real secret behind the mystery [being] that there is no mystery; the real problem ... to prevent the audience from learning this too.'[62]

Goffman has little to say about taste specifically, though both costume and 'stage sets' are potentially relevant to his work. He mentions dress in passing, without expanding on the topic, and as for setting, since he is for the most part concerned with the staging of professional competence, the stage-sets he describes tend to be institutional rather than domestic: the doctor's office, for example, or the funeral parlour, though he does remark briefly on the busy effort it may take to produce the impression of domestic serenity. Nevertheless, Goffman is relevant for my purposes insofar as his front- and backstage distinction helps us think about how certain social spaces are handled in novels. Backstage activities – for example, the brutal rudeness of the headwaiter to his subordinates in the kitchen, which switches to debonair courtesy as soon as he goes through the door to the dining room – are posited by Goffman as the messy or degrading reality behind the fine appearance. When the novelist takes the reader 'backstage' to observe the behaviour of characters of whom we are invited to disapprove, her approach may be Goffmanesque: one thinks of the Lydgate marriage in *Middlemarch*, where no one but the reader understands the conflict and tension behind the faces that the Lydgates present to the world (though other characters are credited with empathy to the degree that they guess). But 'backstage' scenes in novels, though they may be deployed with sociological detachment for satiric ends, can also contribute to the mystification of idealized characters. Narratologists have pointed out that one mark of the protagonist in any narrative is (as Mieke Bal puts it) that he or she can 'occur alone'[63] – that only the reader is allowed to follow the hero or heroine into a space closed to the other characters within the fictional world. Goffman's analysis can help refine this rule. The mark of the heroine is not only that we see her alone but that when we do she is even finer than she seemed 'front-stage.' When the move from front- to backstage reveals difference, it signals hypocrisy; but when it reveals consistency, it implies 'depth.' Novelistic scenes of this kind have a strongly theatrical dimension, and Goffman's metaphor, by reminding us how unlikely it is for someone to have no backstage lapses in her life, clarifies how they work to mystify the excellence of the heroine.

Goffman's theatrical metaphor, based as it is on an appearance/reality binary, implies a traditional humanist view of subjectivity: that is, it implies that there is a real person there behind – and before – her performances. The construction of individual subjectivity is not Goffman's central topic. Nevertheless, although some of his remarks suggest that for practical purposes he will take the traditional notion for granted, he is apparently open to a more purely constructivist understanding of subjectivity. Although Goffman makes a sharp theoretical distinction between 'the real, sincere, or honest performance' and 'the false one that thorough fabricators assemble for us, whether meant to be taken unseriously, as in the work of stage actors, or seriously, as in the work of confidence men,'[64] he also says he wishes to reserve the term 'sincere' for 'individuals who believe in the impression fostered by their own performance.'[65] This implies that the boundary line between hypocritical and 'sincere' performance is perhaps more blurred than is usually understood – indeed that it is often hard to draw: 'All the world is not, of course, a stage, but the crucial ways in which it isn't are not easy to specify.'[66] Pointing out that what he calls a 'status, a position, a social place' is nothing but 'a pattern of appropriate conduct' ('Performed with ease or clumsiness, awareness or not, guile or good faith, it is none the less something that must be enacted and portrayed, something that must be realized'),[67] Goffman will sometimes come close to saying that subjectivity itself is nothing more than performance. 'If persons have a universal human nature, they themselves are not to be looked to for an explanation of it. One must look rather to the fact that societies everywhere ... must mobilize their members as self-regulating participants in social encounters ... through ritual.' His somewhat startling conclusion is that 'universal human nature is not a very human thing. By acquiring it, the person becomes a kind of construct, built up not from inner psychic propensities but from moral rules that are impressed upon him from without.'[68] A postmodern gender theorist like Judith Butler, having taken on the insights of Freud and Lacan, goes further, seeing performance as constitutive of gender if not of subjectivity itself.

I cite Butler here not because she owes anything to Goffman and sociology (on the contrary: trained as a philosopher, she situates herself in the line of French feminists reacting to the work of Freud and Lacan) but because her notion of 'performativity' has been seen as particularly relevant to Jane Austen. Judith Butler as her subject of investigation the construction of gendered subjectivity in response to 'the forcible and reiterative practice of regulatory sexual regimes.'[69] Determined to defend and enable individuals who, because their gender is seen as anomalous by society as a whole, are 'condemned to a death within life,' Butler wants to make us understand that the two genders recognized by society are not natural, not 'true and original,' but rather are socially constructed by a semiotic system that ignores all the other positions on the gender spectrum. Butler insists that gender is largely performative: that 'what we take to be an 'internal' feature of ourselves is one that we anticipate and produce through certain bodily acts.' Gender is continually constructed, 'manufactured through a sustained set of acts,'[70] by the individual who, day by day, anticipates what is expected of her and acts the part. Butler's analysis raises the question of whether there is any subject at all before or behind the performance. Sometimes she implies that there is not: for example, she objects to Lacan's idea of the masquerade because it seems to 'postulate a femininity that is prior to mimicry and the mask.'[71] But at other times she says that she does not intend to argue 'that all of the internal world of the psyche is but an effect of a stylized set of acts,' while declaring nevertheless 'that it is a significant theoretical mistake to take the 'internality' of the psychic world for granted.'[72] She admits that she also 'sometimes waffles between understanding performativity as linguistic and casting it as theatrical,' pointing out in her own defence that 'speech itself is a bodily act'[73] – an assertion with which Pierre Bourdieu, who analyses the different ways the mouth is used by speakers of the French language, would certainly agree.[74]

The scope of Butler's analysis is arguably somewhat more limited than those critics who adopt her ideas for literary criticism often imply. Not only does she focus almost exclusively on the performance of gender, she can use the term 'performativity' in quite a restricted sense, to describe not the construction of gender in general, much less the construction of subjectivity itself, but rather just the provocative performances of individuals who 'act up.' Alluding to transgressive theatrics like dressing in drag, she gives a rather narrow definition of performativity as 'this relation of being implicated in that which one opposes, this turning of power against itself to produce alternative modalities of power.'[75] Nevertheless, Butler's work is now routinely invoked by literary critics to apply to subjectivity in general. Austen's *Mansfield Park* is the perfect test case for such a critical approach: its apparent panic about theatricality has been interpreted as Austen's defence against the suspicion that all subjectivity is performative, particularly in a society like hers, where the roles of gentlewoman and gentleman demand ritualized and repetitive acts of self-representation.

The work of Pierre Bourdieu, too, has been felt particularly relevant to Austen, and it is Bourdieu's analytical paradigm that I have found most useful for my purposes. Bourdieu, who studies the social function of the discourse of taste in modern France and whose interest lies less in the way individual subjectivity is constructed than in the way social power is perpetuated, owes more to Goffman, whom he cites from time to time, than to the Lacanian tradition represented by Butler.[76] He is using Goffman's metaphor when he says that those whose time is worth most can display their resources by offering 'a potlatch of time'[77] and sounds very much like him when he says that everyone always tries to 'produce a profit of distinction on the occasion of each social exchange.'[78] But Bourdieu also situates himself within a much broader intellectual tradition. His thesis is that buying into the Kantian doctrine of aesthetic disinterestedness is a way of repudiating those classes of people who, because of their material circumstances, cannot afford to be disinterested. In his practical research, Bourdieu studies the aesthetic choices of the various levels of French society, explaining the elite's supposed preference for high culture (as well as all the other aesthetic preferences that distinguish them from what he calls 'the dominated classes') in terms of a system of polarities underpinned by the interested/disinterested binary.

Bourdieu's most seminal notion for recent critics of the nineteenth-century novel is what he calls 'cultural capital.' Cultural capital is the kind of savoir faire 'inherited from the family'[79] that has had money for a long time. It is an effect of financial capital that has been transformed into culture – 'into better concealed forms of capital, such as works of art and education' – so as to produce 'the detachment of inherited ease.'[80] This detachment, and the 'disinterested' aesthetic attitude that expresses it, feel 'natural' to the people who exhibit them. Those who absorb a set of aesthetic and social preferences as children do not attribute these preferences to their privileged material environment: the 'acquisition of legitimate culture by insensible familiarization within the family circle tends to favour an enchanted experience of culture which implies forgetting the acquisition.'[81] The discourse of taste, Bourdieu argues, mystifies practices that actually derive from social and material wealth by representing them as natural refinement, natural 'evolvedness,' indeed, as 'natural taste': 'The ideology of natural taste owes its plausibility and its efficacy to the fact that ... it *naturalizes* real differences, converting differences in the mode of acquisition of culture into differences of nature.'[82] Members of the dominant class do not pretend but really feel that their aesthetic responses are simply natural and that those who do not share them are essentially vulgar, base, even physiologically inferior. Because the dominant class is the realization of the norm – because in them 'the principles of evaluation and the principles of production coincide perfectly'[83] – members of this class can simply be themselves and at the same time effortlessly embody the criteria of social excellence which they themselves have to power to put in place. For Bourdieu, 'natural taste' is indeed an oxymoron, a vicious delusion that excludes those who can never acquire the 'naturalness' that only a moneyed background can provide.[84] 'Natural taste' is the premise behind what Bourdieu calls the 'charismatic ideology,'[85] the mystified way of thinking that regards good taste, even in dress or interior design, as if it were the spontaneous emanation of personal excellence.

Bourdieu argues that the dominant class likes high culture because, since it can be represented as open to all, it can be the object of merely symbolic appropriation.[86] A person who enjoys listening to a Beethoven symphony, reading a novel by Proust, or attending an exhibition of Picasso paintings can argue that he has not exclusively appropriated the cultural object he contemplates: that his enjoyment of it deprives no one else of pleasure. What he ignores, Bourdieu points out, is that the cultural background that enables one to take pleasure from such aesthetic objects can in fact be exclusively appropriated: that acquiring the taste that transcends money costs money.[87] Analogously, Bourdieu objects to Comte's assertion that 'language forms a kind of wealth, which all can make use of at once without causing any diminution of the store, and which thus admits a complete community of enjoyment.'[88] Bourdieu calls this 'the illusion of linguistic communism'[89] and insists that aesthetic pleasure, the pleasure that Kant argued 'should be able to be felt by every man,'[90] is in fact 'the privilege of those who have access to the conditions (that is to say, the social positions) in which the 'pure' and 'disinterested' disposition is able to constitute itself durably.'[91] This strand of Bourdieu's argument is clearly relevant to some of the ideas I have been discussing: it suggests the naivety or bad faith of those writers who insist that 'Nature' or the landscape is free to all and imply the perversity or innate baseness of those who choose not to take advantage of this 'free' gift. When Austen has Edmund Bertram in *Mansfield Park* respond to Fanny Price's rhapsody on the beauty of the night sky with the observation that 'they are much to be pitied who have not been taught to feel in some degree as you do – who have not ... been given a taste for nature in early life,'[92] his observation can be read as Austen's acknowledgment that nature is not in fact free to all: that a taste for it requires just the material and cultural resources that Bourdieu describes. Indeed, it is this recognition, I shall argue, that motivates her endorsement of Mansfield Park itself.

As Bourdieu differentiates 'cultural capital' from financial capital, so he also distinguishes between cultural capital, absorbed insensibly from the childhood environment, and what he calls 'educational capital,' the learning that is acquired belatedly and by dint of laborious study. The possessors of cultural capital and of educational capital wear their learning with a difference. Because the aristocratic individual possesses the 'embodied cultural capital of the previous generations,' which 'functions as a sort of advance (both a head-start and a credit),' his 'early, imperceptible learning' will be deployed with much more insouciance than the 'belated, methodical learning' of less privileged individuals, who look to him like mere pedants.[93] The autodidact or the middle-brow makes too obvious the history of his acquisition of the kind of knowledge that 'works' only if one has never had to 'learn' it – only if one has acquired it by birth, so that it seems to be part of one's 'nature' or 'essence.'[94] The mark of the social striver is his eagerness to discover the rules of taste and his abject willingness to follow them, whereas the mark of the aristocrat is a style that expresses 'confident relaxation and lofty ignorance of pedantic rules.'[95] Condescension occurs when one is sure enough of one's position to 'deny' hierarchy 'without appearing to be ignorant or incapable of meeting [its] demands.'[96] The 'strategies of condescension,' says Bourdieu, in a passage that could be a gloss upon Austen's Emma Woodhouse, are 'those symbolic transgressions of limits which provide ... the benefits [of] conformity to social definition and the benefits that result from transgression.' Only the 'person who is sure of his cultural identity,' the person endowed with abundant cultural capital, 'can play with the rules of the cultural game,'[97] making playfulness a sign of mastery. The easy grace that Castiglione calls *sprezzatura* and

Montesquieu mystifies as *je ne sais quoi* is, Bourdieu insists, simply the result of inherited privilege.

Central to Bourdieu's system is his concept of 'habitus.'[98] Habitus as I understand it is a sort of fusion of 'habitat' and 'habits': it is the repertoire of responses, the set of behaviours or strategies developed by an individual under the pressure of the lifetime experiences that have given him a sense of where he fits in relative to others, what he can expect from life, and what others expect of him. Bourdieu depicts the individual as co-opted and constructed by his environment. The social strategies such an individual adopts are not calculated or deliberate – Bourdieu distinguishes his position from rational-choice theory on this point – but rather quasi-instinctive. Defining himself in terms of the system which has defined him, he takes as an expression of his personal taste the only products and activities that are open to him: he 'has what he likes' only 'because he likes what he has.'[99] 'Sincerity' is possible only for round pegs in holes made round to receive them, and by which they were in fact shaped. A member of the dominated class, he points out, seizes the pleasures of the present because he has no future worth looking forward to, 'likes' cheap fattening food because this is what he was brought up on, and has the body to correspond – a body that, since it is despised by those above him, condemns him to self-consciousness or even self-hatred, to 'fascination with a self possessed by the gaze of others.'[100]

Bourdieu's notion of the habitus has been praised as a paradigm that not only takes due account of the body but also extricates sociological thinking from the nature/nurture, choice/necessity dilemma.[101] It has even been praised as an acknowledgment of the day-to-day creativity of ordinary people,[102] but this is a minority view. Most of Bourdieu's critics find his theory fairly deterministic. Though the dominated may have a degree of flexibility, they can never it seems extricate themselves from the invidious paradigms into which they are inserted by the overall semiotic system. Indeed the most fundamental charge that is brought against Bourdieu's theory is that it is incapable of accounting for social change.[103] The function of judgments of taste in the system he describes is to make the crossing of social boundaries as difficult as possible: 'to stop those who are inside, on the right side of the line, from leaving, demeaning, downgrading themselves'[104] and to keep those on the wrong side of the line from moving up. The method by which this is done is what Bourdieu calls 'symbolic violence.' This term refers not to overt abuse but to a more insidious form of domination: to the process of keeping people out by making them feel they deserve to be kept out. Bourdieu contends that taste is always negation – that 'tastes are perhaps first and foremost distastes, disgust'[105] – and that the function of judgments of taste is to humiliate the those whose 'base' preferences, whose patterns of consumption, whose way of using the language, whose very bodies have been shaped by economic exigencies. The humiliation is so effective that the dominated are induced to accept the very standards by which they are dismissed as inferior. The person who wants to rise must reject what he once was: he is 'condemned to shame, horror, even hatred of the old Adam, his language, his body and his tastes, and of everything he was bound to, his roots, his family, his peers, sometimes even his mother tongue, from which he is now separated by a frontier more absolute than any taboo.'[106] This rather violent description of the damage done to social strivers might make us reflect with surprise how little pain seems to be felt by many of such characters in novels, where discrimination tends to elevate the dominant class without, apparently, much humiliating the dominated. This is a topic to which I will return in the chapter on Austen. Bourdieu's assertion that 'tastes are perhaps first and foremost distastes, disgust' is also markedly relevant to Charlotte Brontë, who can use the discourse of taste in the service of a fairly vicious racism.

The class division within society grounds a set of binaries which Bourdieu sees as structuring the discourse of taste from Kant to the present. Good taste is defined in negation, as what is not-vulgar. The choices of the dominant group, though they are experienced as free and 'pure,' are actually determined by 'the specific constraints of the economy of symbolic goods, such as explicit or implicit reference to the forced choice of those who have no choice, luxury itself having no sense except in relation to necessity.'[107] In other words, the dominant must, by semiotic necessity, desire and display what the dominated can never have and despise what the dominated find beautiful. Since the taste of the elite must be a sign of their transcendence of material necessity, the dominant class favours the spiritual over the material, form over matter, the abstract over the concrete; since it signals their more developed, evolved state of being, they privilege the difficult over the easy, the subtle over the obvious, chaste austerity over ornament. Since they feel themselves to be unique, special individuals, they select individual sports that have to be learned in childhood within exclusive environments (and that pit the individual against another individual or against himself or 'nature') over team sports, especially those readily acquired on the cheap and those involving bodily contact (each class, Bourdieu says, is obliged to select the sport that 'does not contradict that class's relation to the body at the deepest and most unconscious level').[108] Other antitheses listed by Bourdieu include involvement/detachment, emotion/reason, expansiveness/economy, immediate pleasure/deferred pleasure, forced/free, coarse/fine, heavy/light, flashiness/sobriety, facile/complex, and common/unique. Behind these polarities, Bourdieu argues, lies a threat: a threat to the private spaces of bourgeois exclusivity, the threat of a fall either into decadence or into mass culture. This binary system, along with the concept of habitus, explains why tastes come in sets – why so many eighteenth- and nineteenth-century writers can assume that 'good taste' in one field guarantees 'good taste' in all: the individual's social position is 'bound through a relation of homology to a set of activities (playing golf or the piano) and goods (a vacation home or a masterpiece painting) that can themselves be characterized only relationally.'[109] Because Bourdieu analyses taste not primarily as a response to high art but rather as a wide and overdetermined range of unfree choices that operate, as a set, to define an individual as essentially vulgar or refined, his theory illuminates novels that represent the moral excellence of their heroes and heroines by means of quite trivial stylistic gestures and choices.

Bourdieu's social analysis has been criticized on various grounds. It has been suggested that high culture is not as important in conferring status as Bourdieu suggests, even in France;[110] that in some matters of taste the elite do not differ as much from those they consider below them as Bourdieu implies (and as they would no doubt like to believe);[111] and that the generalizations he formulates do not apply to America, with its many different status groups.[112] But they do apply quite well to some of the nineteenth-century texts I discuss, and though what Bourdieu calls 'legitimate' taste, the appreciation of high culture, is not an important topic in these novels, his argument does illuminate their social transactions. I have found the system of polarized binaries that he draws up useful in understanding the ways in which these novels are organized.

I would like to give one extended example of one such binary at work in eighteenth- and nineteenth-century texts. Bourdieu includes in his list of the binaries that shape aesthetic discourse not only form and matter but also line and colour. These polarized pairs have figured in art-critical discourse for centuries. In philosophy, form has been understood as a primary or essential quality, colour as a secondary or dependent quality; traditionally, form and line are represented as spiritual, masculine, colour as sensual and feminine. The history of these identifications is outlined by Charles Riley,[113] who quotes Charles Blanc's 1870 warning:

> The union of design and color is necessary to beget painting just as is the union of man and woman to beget mankind, but design must maintain its preponderance over color. Otherwise painting speeds to its ruin: it will fall through color just as mankind fell through Eve.

Blanc's statement corroborates Bourdieu's assertion that judgments of taste can be 'terribly violent,'[114] but it is equalled in its animus by any number of other comments in the same period. Indeed, the nineteenth-century discourse about colour emphatically confirms Bourdieu's theoretical paradigm.

The sense that some colours are essentially vulgar and that those who prefer them manifest an essential coarseness of physiological and spiritual organization shapes many a sneer in nineteenth-century discourse. Bourdieu asserts that 'pure pleasure,' that is, 'pleasure purified of pleasure ... become[s] a symbol of moral excellence.'[115] Evidently because colour itself has the taint of the pleasurable, 'colourful colour' consistently has less aesthetic prestige than 'colourless colour.' Throughout the period, subtle, blended shades are consistently privileged over bright, primary hues, which are associated with children, dark-skinned races, the working class, the nouveau riche, and women of dubious breeding and morality. To be sure, the doctrine of associationism itself makes such nailed-down identifications philosophically dubious. Colour is an inevitable topic in associationist analysis, where it became a commonplace that there is nothing essential or necessary about such links. It seems clear to associationists that what we consider beautiful depends almost entirely upon association.[116] Alison for example points out that the colours of the dress of common people never seem beautiful and shrewdly remarks that newly fashionable colours are usually disagreeable until we acquire some positive association with them;[117] years later, James Mill, citing Alison's remark about vulgar dress, repeats his point that fashionable colours seem beautiful simply because they are associated with 'Rank and Elegance.' But though Mill goes on to argue that our feeling that there are certain 'right' colours for objects is mere convention – that taste is always a mere matter of association – he continues to discriminate nevertheless between 'aesthetic' and what he calls the 'lower' pleasures.[118]

The 'demystification potential' of associationism in fact never really does seem to 'take.' Picturesque discourse, though it relies on associationist premises, consistently equates a taste for subdued, subtle colours with an evolved, civilized sensibility. Payne Knight, asserting that 'bright tints of yellow, blue or red' may 'please the infant' but not 'the experienced mind,' praises Rembrandt's 'soft tints' and 'sweetly blended light,' allows that even objects ugly in themselves can be pleasing if depicted in 'Soft varied tints and nicely blended hues,' and rhapsodizes over twilight, the moment when 'glittering colour fades' to leave the scene 'tinged in soft hues and light transparent shades'; Gilpin lauds the English climate for the haze, mist, and fog that allow such subtle visual effects.[119] Aesthetic preferences such as these often corroborate invidious social judgments. Payne Knight deplores paths of 'red-hot gravel, fringed with tawdry green,' objecting waspishly to the 'everlasting green' of Repton's lawns, while Repton for his part characterizes the newly built brick villas of suburban arrivistes as 'scarlet sins' against taste.[120] The red-brick motif occurs for a full century (the association, as in 'red-brick universities,' to this day): Thomas Hardy, though he argues in a poem that people in 'gaudy' brick villas are often more truly tasteful than those in classier stone, nevertheless signals Alex d'Urberville's nouveau-riche status (and moral unreliability) by placing him in a 'crimson brick' mansion that rises 'like a geranium bloom against the subdued colours around.'[121] The suggestion that it takes a civilized mind to appreciate subtle colour is used to endorse discriminations that are overtly based on nationality, class, and race.

Fashion advice well into the Victorian era picks up the same set of values and prejudices. Mrs Alexander Walker, for example, though evidently familiar with associationist discourse – she cites Alison on 'unity of colouring' and on the association between colour and mood[122] – nevertheless does not hesitate to make the most absolute social judgments about colour choice. Women she says who choose to wear 'prettier,' 'that is, more gaudy,' colours make a 'gross and vulgar' mistake.[123] Tropical heat engenders aesthetic crudity: 'A large assembly of the middle classes in tropical countries, presents to the eye more scarlet and bright yellow than in the north.' Indeed, Mrs Walker is willing to generalize that 'in all countries, the civilized woman, whose taste is elevated, likes mixed colours less glaring, because she distinguishes the most fine and delicate shades, in the same way that she prefers fine lines and more difficult proportions to squares and too simple relations.'[124] Walker's language precisely confirms Bourdieu's critique of the notion of 'natural taste,' implying as it does an actual physiological difference between the refined eye that can 'distinguish' these shades and shapes and one that cannot. For Walker, class, race, and nationality can be ranked by colour choice. She despises, even loathes, the French. Gallic fashion, she suggests, is a kind of anti-English conspiracy: the French dressmaker uses 'colours that render our women hideous.' Or is it a mere defensive manoeuvre? 'Does a Frenchwoman adopt the strongest and most glaring colours to overpower the yellow, green, and black horrors of her visage, or the frightful mustaches of her upper lip, or her coarse and dirty black hair, – the Englishwoman assumes the fashionable colour which is equally calculated to make her look ill and the Frenchwoman well, and which renders her exquisite complexion insipid, and gives to her soft and placid features the air of "*un mouton qui rêve!*"'[125] The Englishwoman's more refined complexion is properly set off by 'dove-coloured' costume – the colour name is a favourite of the period[126] – or something equally neutral, and the young man on the prowl is advised to keep Mrs Walker's rule in mind:

> Ladies of the most refined taste are distinguished, especially as to promenade dress, by the simplest and chastest costume, and so surely in this case, that if any one happen to follow a lady whose dress is marked by these characteristics and which presents somber and in themselves less agreeable colours, he may almost certainly predict handsome features and a beautiful complexion, because these colours if judiciously chosen, render almost every complexion striking and brilliant.[127]

Yet there is something very theoretical about all this praise of non-colour if one is actually looking at Mrs Walker's book, which is illustrated with colour plates that are vividly chromatic even by present-day standards. Indeed, her specific practical advice about accent colours – she suggests using a 'relieving colour' of 'natural contrast, as purple of yellow, or blue of orange'[128] – evokes costumes that sound downright garish. Though novels and conduct books consistently argue that true elegance consists in simple lines and modest neutral tones, there is a gap between what the Victorians preached and what they practised. Particularly after the invention of aniline dyes in the late 1850s,[129] but evidently before as well, if Walker's fashion plates are any evidence, Victorian women favoured strong colours. As is well known, Hippolyte

Taine remarked on the harsh hues worn by English women;[130] Evans cites the brilliant clothing of liberated Quakers and alludes to a 'shocking toilette' of Queen Victoria's, 'a mantle and sun-shade of crude green which did not seem to go with the rest of her costume';[131] Burn asserts that it is lucky that Victorian family photos are black and white so that we can't see the 'dreadful clash of colours into which fashion and aniline dyes have led the daughters.'[132] The same chromatic vividness was favoured in interiors from the 1830s on, a trend motivated partly by the discovery that polychrome decoration had been used in the ancient world.[133] Emily Eden, in India in the 1840s, set her native servants to work tearing up cloth and sewing it together in strips so as to devise striped red and white curtains with a red border.[134] J.C. Loudon, whose *Villa Companion* defined what was tasteful in homes and gardens in the 1840s, dutifully lauds simplicity and unity of design while in practice approving not only a wide range of elaborate ornament but also rooms saturated with what sound like vibrant and fussy colour combinations. Nevertheless fictional heroines on both sides of the Atlantic continued to be constrained by the discourse of dullness until the end of the century. An 1884 story in *the Atlantic Monthly* depicts widowed Anice Enlow, a Dorothea Brooke knock-off with a stirringly melodious voice, in an elegant black dress trimmed with dark violet ('a mere accompaniment to her superb figure'), forming a stunning visual contrast to her despised rival, who is decked out 'like some gay tropical bird, in her light dress and bright colours.'[135] And real-life non-heroines continued to be disciplined in the same terms. If servants dress in cheap garish clothes, suggested a sympathetic *Cornhill* article of 1874, it may be because we allow them no way to develop their taste: 'a box of crayons downstairs' might help.[136] The servants of Aurora Floyd, who admire the less-than-chaste colour choices of the sartorially transgressive heroine, confirm the same stereotype: their 'uncultivated tastes,' we are told, 'were a great deal more disposed to recognize splendour of colour than purity of form.'[137] Elizabeth Braddon seems to take for granted in her readers not only condescension towards servants but also a thorough familiarity with the discourse in which colour is subordinated to line. This anti-colour rhetoric, circulated in a whole range of popular texts, no doubt has a paradoxically enabling effect: it allows bourgeois consumers to purchase garish objects while still claiming to value the austerity that testifies to moral seriousness and fitness for cultural authority.

To be sure, this is not the whole story. Rich, brilliant, saturated colour, though distrusted in the dress of the modest lady, can be lauded in art-critical discourse. Though Ruskin insists on purity of line, he also responds ecstatically to pure intense colour:[138] see for example his almost mystical enthusiasm about what might be called holy colour in 'The Twelve Zodiacal Colours.'[139] This element in Ruskin's writing is relevant I think to Eliot's Dorothea Brooke, who though usually garbed in the chastest of hues – grey, black, or white – is defined at the very beginning of *Middlemarch* by her response to the brilliant colour of the emerald in her mother's ring. Ruskin, though in a remark that postdates Eliot's novel, reminds us that Saint Dorothea was associated with colour when he complains that an Academy painting of schoolgirls is chromatically too muted to be either beautiful or realistic: English girls, though 'perhaps not all of them St Dorothys,' are at least, he says, 'good enough to have their rose-leaves painted about them thoroughly,' insisting that 'rich colour may be in good taste, as well as the poorest.'[140] Saint Dorothea was the subject of a brilliantly coloured painting by Burne-Jones, and the Pre-Raphaelites of course favoured deep, intense, and bright colour. To be sure, the Pre-Raphaelites were considered vulgar by many Victorians because of their association with wealthy manufacturers who tended to be their most reliable purchasers. The nineteenth-century discourse about colour, in short, admits a range of values, but all these values have hierarchical social implications.

The topic of colour is relevant to several of the texts I discuss, not only to Eliot's, but also to those of Gaskell and Brontë, whose character constructions are shaped by a disdain or even intense hostility to 'coloured' women.[141] Like such received ideas about colour, so the other notions on which my analyses are founded – 'resources,' 'simplicity,' and 'consistency,' for example – are the merest clichés in the period.[142] Indeed, representations of tastefulness in nineteenth-century texts seem always already conventions, commonplaces deployed so mechanically as to fly beneath the critical radar. In this study I identify a number of these ideas and trace their roots in other writings, both literary and non-literary, in order to show what the notion of tastefulness contributes to a wider cultural agenda. Each of my chapters undertakes a close reading of one or more primary texts, attending to all of the signals of tastefulness and attempting to show how they work together to produce meaning. My method is formalist in that I focus on internal structures of language and imagery, deconstructive in that I demonstrate the contradictions within these patterns and particularly the instability of the conceptual binaries on which they are based, and more broadly cultural in its acknowledgment of the social and economic pressures to which the novelists were responding. Taking account of contemporary anxieties that shape the text's structure or its details – anxieties for example about social mobility (Austen and Loudon), militant Catholicism (Brontë), French competition with British manufacturers (Gaskell), commerce and commodification (Eliot) – I attempt to understand why certain ways of representing and endorsing tastefulness remained serviceable for many decades and how the discourse of taste enables a wider discourse about middle-class subjectivity and entitlement and indeed about national character in the period.

Chapter 1 deals with Walter Scott's *Waverley*, a novel that is central to my concerns for several reasons: its subject matter (the way literary taste shapes a life); its ambiguous treatment of taste and style; its influence on later writers; and its development of the convention – the 'woman's-room' topos – that is the subject of my second chapter. My purpose in the first chapter is both to qualify the current orthodoxy that Waverley is a type of female reader and also to make a wider point about the ways in which the novel deconstructs the tastefulness with which the author feels obliged to endow his hero and heroines. Because Scott slides between a humanist understanding of taste as aesthetic response, constituting a rich, layered, developing subjectivity, and a sociological understanding of taste as a system of signs, identifying members of the dominant class to each other and thus strengthening their political and social alliances, *Waverley* is a particularly good illustration of the contradictions that bedevil the discourse of taste throughout the century.

*Waverley* also develops a topos, the description of the woman's room, that has a long afterlife in nineteenth-century fiction. Chapter 2 deals with way the heroine's room is made into a sign of the moral and aesthetic values she represents and the way this topos is used to negotiate the paradoxes of woman's economic dependency in a patriarchal system. Identifying five essential elements of the conventional scenario, I argue that when these elements are split up, redistributed, or suppressed, the contradictions it attempts to occult are made visible and the positive vision of female autonomy breaks down into irony, satire, and parody. Tracing the woman's-room topos, as well as its demonic parody, the sinister boudoir, through novels by Radcliffe, Disraeli, Dickens, Thackeray, and Braddon, I show how a device that began as an endorsement of modest self-sufficiency turns in the end into a frank fantasy of conspicuous consumption. The fact that the convention is still going strong at the end of the century indicates that there is a perennial attraction to this useful way of characterizing Veblen's 'vicarious consumer.'

The relevance of Jane Austen's novels to the theoretical issues discussed in the preceding pages evidently necessitates a concentrated look at her work. Chapter 3 is organized around two pairs of terms foregrounded in the dialogue of Austen's Augusta Elton – 'resources' and 'accomplishments,' 'taste' and 'performance' – and analyses the relationship between cultivated interiority and social mobility in *Mansfield Park* and *Emma*, two novels linked not only by their chronological propinquity and their tendency to offend readers with their 'violently discriminatory' social and moral judgments[143] but also by their allusions to the slave trade. While in *Mansfield Park* the difference between taste and performance cannot be sustained, it is in *Emma* that performance is finally rejected in the interests of propriety and property. Documenting a gothic undernote that is both evoked and repressed in these texts, I argue that for Austen 'natural taste' always requires for its development abundant material resources.

While the writing of John Ruskin would seem to be an obvious choice for a study of this kind, I have chosen instead to deal with the topic of architecture and landscape design by looking at the work of John Claudius Loudon, a critic of Humphry Repton and a noted landscape gardener and horticultural writer, not only because he is less well known than Ruskin but also because he illustrates how high-culture aesthetic ideas were filtered and qualified in the light of practical aspirations and marketplace realities. Chapter 4 analyses Loudon's *Suburban Gardener and Villa Companion* (1838), a practical handbook that adapts received ideas about taste and art to the resources of the Victorian bourgeoisie. Repton's contention that even a modest property provides all the benefits of the largest estate, a statement that sounds strained even when addressed to the substantial gentry, becomes positively paradoxical when echoed by Loudon. But the way the paradox is developed, in a lengthy text replete with advice for solving practical problems of home construction and estate design, offers fascinating insight into the self-representation of the middle and upper-middle classes. Dickens no doubt knew of Loudon and would have had good reason to be interested in his advice, and though I cannot document direct influence, the ideals popularized by such arbiters of middle-class taste certainly shape the way Dickens represents some of the properties in his novels. Looking at houses in *Bleak House, A Tale of Two Cities, Dombey and Son, Great Expectations,* and *Our Mutual Friend,* I conclude this chapter with a discussion of Dickens's parodic adaptations of the Repton–Loudon discourse.

The way Charlotte Brontë grounds judgments of character in sometimes quite violent judgments of taste makes her central to this study. Chapter 5 deals with *The Professor, Jane Eyre,* and *Villette,* the three novels linked by the governess theme and shaped by Brontë's Belgian experience. Brontë's female protagonists stake their sense of themselves on their own good taste, which is developed around three related themes – plagiarism, displacement, and surveillance – all of which involve problematic doubling. I demonstrate how the tenuous identity of the Brontë heroine is deconstructed along with the system of signs by which her good taste is signalled – notably the 'fashion system' on which, in her very repudiation of it, she rather desperately relies – and how she is trapped into resisting pleasure by the system of signs by which she is produced.

*North and South* is a notoriously problematic text. From the beginning, criticism has focused on the way Elizabeth Gaskell links the private love story with the public issue of industrialization. There is no better way of getting at the complex ideological work that the discourse of taste can do than by examining how it is used to finesse a number of issues that Gaskell is unable really to resolve. In chapter 6 I argue that the notion of 'stately simplicity' shapes both strands of the novel in such a way as to privilege the genteel values of the heroine, dramatize what middle-class taste has to offer to the British industrialist, and endorse the cultivated woman's entitlement to the luxury goods England imports and manufactures. Most importantly, it is deployed to negotiate class relations, offering a reassuring vision of working-class desire bound and tamed by the mystique of bourgeois femininity.

Perhaps the most 'sociological' of the Victorian novelists is George Eliot, who is always willing to explain the attitudes and the style of her characters in terms of their economic and class position. Yet her attempt to bring this hermeneutic to bear on her heroine Dorothea Brooke soon breaks down, as has often been pointed out, into something close to idealization. I argue that Dorothea's 'natural taste' is an expression – sometimes acknowledged, but often not – of her class position, and that the way Eliot constructs her is an index of her own anxiety about commercialism and about the threat to organic subjectivity that it seems to pose. Chapter 7 focuses on the word 'consistency' as it is used in *Middlemarch.* When Eliot has Mrs Ned Plymdale praise her friend Harriet

Bulstrode's 'consistency' in having the feather in her hat dyed lavender, the irony is in line with her association of the Plymdale-Bulstrode-Vincy group as a whole with the manufacturing, buying, and selling of textiles. Dorothea Brooke, on the other hand, who has the 'deep' consistency we are asked to admire, is thoroughly etherealized, raised above the material exigencies of everyday life. But Dorothea too is a commercial product, albeit a classy one, and Eliot can only construct her heroine by repressing the commodification in which the novel as a form is involved. My discussion documents the novel's efforts at sociological objectivity and the collapse of this objectivity in the mystified representation of Dorothea's taste and beauty.

In the Conclusion I look forward to what happens to the theme of tastefulness in the last quarter of the century, specifically to the split between what might be called sociological relativism, in the work of writers like George Gissing and Thomas Hardy, and aestheticism, represented by Henry James. These three writers continue to draw upon the woman's-room topos discussed in chapter 2, and I use their treatment of it as a way of marking both what they owe to the century's discourse of taste and their difference from earlier writers.

Literary criticism attempts to look at what texts know but (as it were) do not know they know: at particular issues and insights, meaningful to the critic now, that are adumbrated, though necessarily unselfconsciously, by writers who saw their world in terms of different values, different preoccupations, and a different understanding of human subjectivity. The purpose of this study is to complicate the reading of many nineteenth-century texts, not just the ones I have singled out for attention, by alerting readers to the kinds of mystification accomplished by the discourse of tastefulness throughout the century.

# 1 The Discourse of Taste in *Waverley*

Assuming a reader for whom good taste is the necessary mark of the novelistic hero or heroine, Scott takes care to establish the equal taste-fulness of both of the women in whom Edward Waverley has a romantic interest. In the amusing chapter 54, where the protagonist, attempting to decide which lady deserves his love, undertakes a systematic comparison of Rose Bradwardine and Flora Mac-Ivor at Holyrood House, it is made clear to us if not to him that in point of taste there is nothing to choose between them. The touchstone is Shakespeare. Waverley judges Rose to have the superior taste when she elects to hear Waverley himself reading from *Romeo and Juliet* rather than Fergus playing the flute. He does not realize why Flora votes for music instead of poetry, but the reader, who is made privy to her motive – she does not want to encourage Waverley in any way – also perceives that she at least equals Rose in her appreciation of Shakespeare. When Flora says, on behalf of Romeo, that it makes perfect sense to move on to a second lady if one is getting nowhere with the first, she is to be sure hinting that Waverley should transfer his affections to Rose, but she is also defending the consistency of Shakespeare's characterization. Quite different though they are in most of their tastes, Rose and Flora are united in their appreciation of Shakespeare's genius, as they must be if they are to be worthy objects of the protagonist's attentions.

This chapter, endorsing as it does both the discourse of taste and the humanist model of subjectivity that this discourse implies, neatly exemplifies the way Scott links taste and character in *Waverley*. The characters judge each other on the basis of taste, and we are invited to do the same. In women, an appreciation for Shakespeare is predictably associated with a range of positive qualities, just the qualities that a proper female education is supposed to inculcate: reverence for masculine genius, dignity, modesty, tact, the ability to join gracefully in intelligent conversation. Most important, it is associated with insight into the character of others. It is taken for granted that appreciating Shakespeare means responding to his characters, and that human character is both developmental and 'deep,' requiring insight and empathy for its interpretation. The depth model of subjectivity that Flora implies in her analysis of Romeo (her assumption that behind what seem like contradictory actions there can be found a principle that will reduce them to unity) – the depth model that she herself exemplifies here, where only the reader is aware of her true motivation – is the model Scott takes for granted as he constructs his own characters. Implying that human character is an organic whole, consistent and coherent – that there can always be found, underlying its various manifestations, a deeper theme in terms of which they can be understood – *Waverley* begins with the account of the education of the hero. The adolescent's taste for romance is represented as the significant determinant of his subsequent decisions, the constant factor that underlies and can explain if not justify his wavering commitments.

The protagonist's taste must of course be differentiated from that of the women he loves. 'Everybody' loves Shakespeare, at least everybody in whom the novel-reader could be expected to take an interest. The hero of a *Bildungsroman*, which is what this novel looks like for the first hundred or so pages, needs more than a taste for Shakespeare to define him.[1] The 'education-of-the-hero' convention always represents the protagonist as different from and more distinguished than the other characters. Scott has every reason to take adolescent literary passion seriously – after all, his account of Waverley's self-education is based on his own youthful reading – and the 'reading-list' topos he inherits from Rousseau and Wordsworth and passes on to writers such as George Eliot and Thomas Hardy always establishes the superiority of the solitary reader.[2] Though Shakespeare and Milton are the first two authors on Waverley's list, mentioned first probably less to indicate that he read them first than to suggest that a gentleman's familiarity with them goes (almost) without saying, it is his more idiosyncratic taste for romance and romanticized history that dominates his bibliography and that suggests he is an individual interesting enough to be the subject of the history to follow.

It is a commonplace of criticism that Waverley's taste for romance feminizes him, and though this has been convincingly demonstrated, I would argue that there is a kind of structural necessity to such feminization. If the hero's reading is to distinguish him from those around him, unless they are illiterate and the habit of reading itself is distinction enough (perhaps David Copperfield's case at Mr Creakle's school), it has to be markedly different: more obsessive, wide-ranging, dreamy, idealistic; more 'feminine,' if the protagonist is a man (perhaps more masculine if she is a woman).[3] It is by suggesting that Waverley is fascinated by an unfashionable genre that Scott can show that his hero is superior both in taste and intelligence to his more ordinary friends and relatives. Waverley's literary preferences, formed without their guidance, must be understood as original – wholly his own. There is nothing particularly select about the family library, 'a miscellaneous and extensive collection of volumes ... assembled together, during the course of two hundred years, by a family which had been always wealthy, and inclined ... as a mark of splendour, to furnish their shelves with the current literature of the day, without much scrutiny or nicety of discrimination' (13). But from this heterogeneous collection, Waverley, alone and without adult supervision, chooses a set of texts of some distinction. Apparently this taste has done him harm, rendering him intellectually undisciplined as well as something of a social misfit. It has become a commonplace that Waverley's unguided reading 'leads to romantic excesses which can only be cured by harsh and near fatal experience.'[4] Yet it is that very enthusiasm for romance that exposes Waverley personally to the Cause his family reveres, so that, unlike the parental generation, who remain fixed in antagonistic and anachronistic postures, he is able, while appreciating both sides of the question, ultimately to choose the progressive model. Considering that Waverley functions as a transition figure, it is hard to see his literary taste, the very mark that differentiates him from the parental generation, as a merely negative trait.[5]

Nor is it a merely femininizing trait. Though Scott is drawing on a familiar satirical stereotype, that of the female reader of romances who obtains the unwholesome or even poisonous novels she devours through problematic channels, from her friends or from lending libraries, he is himself in the process of rehabilitating – that is, masculinizing – romance,[6] and he makes clear that his hero is more cultivated, more discriminating, and more virile than such a reader. There is nothing promiscuous about the volumes Waverley devours. Unlike the newspapers that arrive at Waverley-Honour, they have not been passed hand to hand; they do not circulate, like novels, among women, but have come as it were 'straight' down to him through the male line: indeed, rather than implicating Waverley in a subversive youth culture, they insulate him from it. Moreover, there is nothing relaxed or effete about the way he reads. His appetite is vigorous; his efforts are focused – he will 'throw himself with spirit upon any classical author' suggested to him, 'make himself master of the style so far as to understand the story' (12), and if he likes it, read to the end. And his choices, though they may be sweets, are not drugs or poison. Waverley does consume books as he would consume food, but his reading is described in terms that suggest less indiscriminate gorging than passionate selectivity. He is not a 'glutton of books' (350)[7] but a gourmet, an 'epicure who only deign[s] to take a single morsel from the sunny side of a peach' and who 'read[s] no volume a moment after it ceased to excite his curiosity or interest' (13).

A lusty but limiting appetite of this kind is required to produce unity out of the diversity of the family collection. The formation of gentlemanly taste requires the *copia* to which Waverley is exposed, but *copia* demands discrimination. Only rigorous selectivity can distill out of this mass a coherent whole analogous to the coherent, integrated subject it is helping to form. Waverley's pickiness also has aristocratic associations. Scott actually presents as a bit déclassé the earnest studiousness that Waverley shirks. By referring, though with apparent respect, to the educational capital laboriously acquired by 'the poor student,' who, 'limited to a narrow circle for indulging his passion for books,' 'must necessarily make himself master of the few he possesses,' the narrator in effect makes the 'erudition' of such a reader just the mark of a member of 'the lower ranks' (13) that Bourdieu insists it will always be.[8] The suggestion is that the inheritor of a centuries-old family library can well dispense with earnest scholarship. Waverley may not be interested in formal literary analysis, but his taste itself imposes form upon the corpus of his reading matter. Unlike a woman's commonplace book – for example, his Aunt Rachel's patchwork of 'choice receipts for cookery and medecine, favourite texts, and portions from high-church divines, and a few songs, amatory and jacobitical, which she had caroll'd in her younger days' (22) – Waverley's selection of beloved narratives has a coherence analogous to the unity of the personality that has drawn it up.

In short, the protagonist's literary preferences may be one-sided, but they are presented as no unwholesome female craving but rather as a vigorous masculine appetite: the idiosyncratic taste of an intelligent and cultivated young gentleman, not the self-indulgent reading of an unbalanced girl. Moreover, these masculinizing notes are quietly strengthened as the novel progresses. Readers tend to focus on Waverley's taste for romance – understandably, since it is romance that is emphasized in chapter 3. But alongside the very obvious allusions to the romancers lies another set of allusions to less romantic writers, allusions that, emerging more gradually and coming to the fore as the political and military action becomes more serious and Waverley begins to realize its serious-ness, subtly normalize his taste by assimilating it to that of the implied reader.

This normalization is accomplished in several ways. Even when Waver-ley's perspective is not in question, the narrator peppers his own prose with Waverley-like allusions, implying a cultivated reader who is his (the narrator's) cultural equal. When the narrator, for example, alludes to *The Faerie Queene*, observing that young Waverley is not under 'the irre-sistible influence of Alma' (12) – that is, that he does not care for sports – the bluff periphrasis, directed to the reader, evokes not a shared taste for romance but simply a shared cultural literacy. Because the same kind of allusion is used when it is a question of Waverley's point of view, the protagonist's perspective is subtly assimilated to our own. When for example we are told that Fergus's voice, '"loud as a trumpet with a silver sound"' (99), reminded Waverley 'of a favourite passage in the descrip-tion of Emetrius,' whereas 'that of Flora, on the contrary, was soft and sweet, "an excellent thing in a woman"' (100), the first allusion is explic-itly assigned to Waverley, but the second belongs equally to character, narrator, author, and reader. This kind of slippage elides the gentle-manly perspectives of reader, narrator, and protagonist, linking Waver-ley's taste with ours and thus qualifying the distancing effect of the earlier emphasis on his adolescent romanticism – though also qualify-ing, necessarily, the impression of Edward's individuality by assimilating him to a wider group, that group of which we as cultivated readers are also members.[9]

Indeed, many of Waverley's own explicit literary associations turn out to be more 'masculine' than might have been expected from the initial emphasis on romance. Fergus believes that Waverley's favourite poet is not Spenser or Ariosto but Shakespeare, and the impression is corrobo-rated not only by his dramatic reading from *Romeo and Juliet*, performed in a social, femininized setting, but by a number of other allusions that suggest a more manly taste for the heroic and historical plays. A Scottish legend reminds Waverley of 'a rhyme quoted by Edgar in *King Lear*' (59); regretting his dilatoriness in joining the Jacobite cause, he quotes 'to himself' three lines from *King John* (166); and the night before bat-tle, he compares Bradwardine to Fluellen, quoting to Fergus two more lines from *Henry V* (222). Though Waverley's reference to a comic minor character from this play is local and trivial enough, Scott follows it up immediately with a description of the army the night before battle, triggering memories both of the fourth act of Shakespeare's play and also of the sixth book of *The Iliad*.[10] The result is that, when in the next paragraph the narrator, describing the sleeping soldiers '"thick as leaves in Valambrosa"' (223), goes on to allude to *Paradise Lost*, evoking, back through Milton's epic, Dante and Virgil as well,[11] Waverley's casual allusion is positioned retrospectively as emerging out of a great (masculine) literary tradition, a tradition the reader shares with him. By the time he has become aware of the seriousness of his predicament and properly critical of his revolutionary companions, the impression of Waverley's literary romanticism has been tempered and qualified by allusions to thoroughly canonical authors, allusions which, emerging as they do gradually and under pressure, seem to proceed from a 'deeper' level of his psyche. The true, essential Waverley is, at least in his literary taste, apparently one of 'us.'

The process is a subtle one, more subtle than the pointed discussion of romance reading at the beginning of the novel and less dramatic than Waverley's rather sudden revulsion with the Jacobite cause for which it helps to prepare, but it subliminally links development in taste with development in character. This process of normalization is indeed an unobtrusive solution to another structural problem. Waverley has to be characterized as an individual, but individuality and taste are always in tension. Since 'good taste' is group taste, taste cannot be truly individual without ceasing to be 'good.' Scott defines his hero in relation to two groups: the group of romance readers, on the one hand, and the group of 'English gentlemen' on the other. Without ever denying or cancelling Waverley's affection for the romances of his youth, Scott quietly strengthens the 'gentlemanly' notes to bring him in line with the implied reader as he matures into political wisdom.

The masculine/feminine binary also gives the hero the depth and sensitivity required for the construction of bourgeois subjectivity at this moment in time. The romance of Waverley's life is over when what is under – his fundamental good sense and good taste, guaranteed by his inwardness with Shakespeare – has emerged in a way naturalized by the understated way Scott handles it. The depth model of character, which allows an individual to exist at the nexus of two discourses – masculine/feminine, Spenserian/Shakespearean, romantic/historical – as long as one of them is 'deeper' than the other, facilitates the construction of an undisturbing androgyny appropriate to the polished civility of a feminized culture. It also anticipates the happy ending of the novel, Waverley's withdrawal into an aestheticized realm of private domestic life.[12]

Scott's treatment of Waverley's literary taste, then, is in line with the premises of the *Bildungsroman* as a genre: that taste is character, that character development is the novel's proper topic, and that character is destiny. Yet as the second half of the novel unfolds, these generic expectations are to a degree disappointed. In the end it is less character than pure luck that determines our hero's fate. Specifically, it is another set of writings, different in every respect from the books that have helped to shape Waverley's imagination, yet, I would argue, parodically analogous to them. The way these documents operate puts 'individual character' into a more ironic context than might have been expected from the *Bildungsroman* cues at the beginning of the novel.

The very foregrounding of the romantic elements in Waverley's seduction by the Mac-Ivors allows Scott ingeniously to construct, behind the story of this seduction, a complicated pattern of accident and intrigue that will surprise the reader as much as it does the hero when the trap is sprung – a pattern that depends, even more heavily than Scott's plots usually do, on pieces of paper that circulate without the hero's knowledge and behind his back.[13] The texts that almost do Waverley in are not, despite the emphasis on his literary education, the ones he has chosen but the ones that have in effect chosen him: the two bundles of paper which first implicate him in and then exonerate him of treason. On the one hand, there are the incriminating papers that come together during the authorities' investigation of Waverley; on the other, there is the packet filched, at Rose's request, from Donald Bean Lean by his daughter Alice.[14] The way in which these two sets of texts fight it out, as it were, on Waverley's behalf and decide his legal fate not only illustrates Scott's taste for ingenious plotting, it sidelines 'individual character' as the determinant of destiny.

When he is apprehended at Cairnvreckan, Waverley's belongings at Dundee and at Tully-Veolan have already been searched and found to contain two sets of writings, both from his Jacobitical tutor Pembroke. At Dundee are the two copies of the treatise that Pembroke insisted on giving to Waverley on his departure from England; at Tully-Veolan, pamphlets that he forwarded later. The investigation of Waverley's conduct has caused these two packets of paper to be brought together for the first time and their gist communicated to Major Melville. On his person Waverley is carrying four letters: three from home, bitterly complaining about his father's supposed mistreatment by an ungrateful king and urging him to be true to the principles of his family, and a fourth from Fergus containing Flora's poem about Captain Wogan, who supported a Jacobite rebellion with English cavalry and whose exploit, as Melville observes, 'the writer seems to expect you should imitate' (158). All these documents come together for Melville's perusal, and all of them seem to tell the same story.

The farcical way in which some of these papers are connected with both ladies' literary accomplishments seems almost to parody the notion of subject formation via literature. Rose's literary education becomes tangled up with politics when Waverley commissions Houghton to fetch from Waverley-Honour 'some books ... elegant literature ... designed for a lady's perusal' (157) and Pembroke takes the opportunity to enclose the unsolicited pamphlets; Flora's enthusiasm for poetic composition is exploited by Fergus, who affects to despise such effusions but who has a shrewd sense of the effect they are likely to have on Waverley. Flora's verses on Captain Wogan may seem slighter and less significant to us than they do to Melville, but Fergus has evidently forwarded them to Waverley with a political motive, and Melville, recognizing his handwriting, finds in them simply evidence of revolutionary intention. The novel, while consistently drawing on an established discourse of taste, makes clear the great gap between literary taste and the texts of real life: between what texts are supposed to do culturally in the privacy of the study and in an aesthetic context and what they do in the real world of social and political action, where 'character' matters less than the network that links the 'individual' to other people and their agendas and where mere taste cannot plead its innocence.

Autonomous choice, the cornerstone of taste, is irrelevant here. Waverley does not need even to have read these writings to be condemned by them. His tutor's 'dull compositions' (157), 'quickly consigned ... to a corner of his travelling trunk' (30), have, he swears, scarcely been looked at, but Melville assumes, with some logic, that their very dullness implies his sympathy with their contents ('can you suppose any thing but value for the principles they maintain would induce a young man of his age to lug such trash about with him?'). Melville's summary of the evidence against Waverley makes us suddenly aware of how these writings – 'pestilent jacobitical pamphlets, enough to poison a whole country' and 'letters ... expressing high rancour against the house of Brunswick' (164) – would look in a court of law. For those who distrust him, Waverley is nothing more than the sum of these texts. When Melville orders Gilfillan to take Waverley to Stirling and to 'deliver him, with these papers' to the governor (173), he speaks as if Waverley himself were continuous with the documents – as if the prisoner and the papers were part of the same package – as indeed, from the point of view of the bureaucrat who has to deal with them, they are.

The second bundle of papers is the one that is passed on to Waverley by Alice Bean Lean as he is leaving the cabin of Janet Gellatley and heading on to Holyrood – the packet he cannot secure until his arrival in Edinburgh. This packet, which contains the letters from Waverley's military superiors that were intercepted by Donald Bean Lean as well as Houghton's letter to 'Ruffin' making clear how he was misled by Donald, is eventually passed on to Talbot, who carries it with him back to London to prove that Waverley was not responsible for the treason done under his name. The appeal is successful, and Waverley is exonerated. But the very fact that the one bundle cancels out the other, as if they, not he, were the autonomous agents, suggests how completely they are outside of Waverley's control and places in ironic perspective the notions of autonomy, selectivity, and free choice on which both taste and the concept of individual character depend.

The effect of this random series of events is to suggest that historical contingency makes the highly developed individual subject irrelevant, except as an unwitting conduit for social forces (and discursive trajectories) over which he has no control. Though to himself – from the inside, so to speak – Waverley feels like the product of a *Bildungsroman*, an individual with complex, nuanced motivations, and though we are by and large invited to respond to him in the same way, the 'Waverley' both his enemies and his allies cobble together is merely a node through which other texts have circulated. Waverley's accusers are wrong: the texts do not prove what they seem to prove about the protagonist's motivations. Yet the purity of his motives does nothing to alleviate the suffering of his victims, as Waverley comes to realize, and the way events to which he has unwittingly contributed unroll behind his back suggests that the kind of 'individual character' privileged by the novel may be almost irrelevant to historical process. However innocent and well-meaning Waverley may be personally, structurally, once he has stumbled into unfolding political events, he functions merely as a social pressure point through which harm can be done. What is more politically important than an individual's rich inner life is the discursive networks he sets humming because of his very position – because of his social class, his nationality, his associations and allegiances – in ways he cannot begin to control.

There is a sense, then, in which the novel subverts its own generic premises. The literary texts Waverley chooses are only a tiny subset of the texts whose circulation he enables just by occupying a certain position. The notion of autonomous character is endorsed by focusing, as the *Bildungsroman* does, on that subset and blanking out the wider discursive network. A postmodern, constructivist view of human personality, which sees the subject as indeed nothing but a flow of texts, high and low, literary and non-literary, would insist that any paradigm that freezes this flow and subdivides it – that draws a line between the texts a person chooses and those that choose him, and moreover founds a 'subjectivity-constructing' genre on that line – is the specious construction of a humanist discourse with a passionate but blinkered investment in notions like individuality, coherence, and freedom of choice. Scott's novel, while by no means endorsing this view, nevertheless teasingly enacts it and partly for this reason remains an endlessly suggestive object of analysis for readers who do not subscribe to the humanist program. *Waverley*, while replicating the bourgeois investment in 'individual character,' also invites a critique of such investment as narcissistic and anticommunitarian – as the self-pleasing illusion of a class whose members can afford to cultivate their individuality.

The plot function of the circulating documents does not to be sure mean that taste and character have nothing to do with Waverley's final fate. For the happy ending to come about, Waverley has to realize that he has been led down the wrong political path, and he has to acquire powerful English allies who are eager to defend him. Taste plays a role in both these developments, but it is taste understood from a sociological perspective, taste as a system of signs that link like with like to maintain class solidarity, not taste as a set of aesthetic responses that enrich individual subjectivity.

The turning point of the novel is a kind of recognition scene: Waverley's revulsion, on the battlefield, at what he suddenly realizes is the crudity and vulgarity of the group of Highlanders with whom he has associated himself. When Waverley observes the demeanour of Colonel Gardiner and particularly when he hears his word of command 'in the English dialect' and in a 'well-distinguished voice,' it comes suddenly upon him that his involvement with men of 'wild dress and appearance' who speak 'an uncouth and unknown language' has been not only wrong but vulgar and that 'his own dress, so unlike that which he had worn from his infancy,' is equally uncouth. It is Waverley's taste as much as his reason that makes him realize he has backed the wrong horse and that the group he has been opposing are gentlemen whose values he ought to support. He presently goes on to save the life of Talbot, whom he has recognized immediately as 'a man of extended knowledge and cultivated taste' (246) even before they discover the link that connects them personally.

As he recognizes the quality of such people, so they recognize his. Just when things look blackest for him, Waverley is saved by the intercession of two influential gentlemen who are won over to his side by the realization that he is one of their own. At the very nadir of his fortunes, when he has been delivered into the custody of Major Melville, Waverley suddenly turns into a suave and witty conversationalist. His 'ease and gaiety' and 'remarkable natural powers of conversation' generate 'very lively discourse' (171) and demonstrate to the Major how gallantly he can 'sustain his misfortunes' (170). As a result of their interview, Melville, despite his damaging summary of the evidence against the prisoner, is impressed enough by Waverley to reflect that there can be 'criminality' without 'dishonour' (170) and to warn Gilfillan ('bred a grazier,' as he rather unpleasantly observes) to treat the 'gentleman' with whom he is entrusted with 'no ... incivility' (173). Later, restored to England, introduced into the home of Talbot, and encouraged to seek Lady Emily in her parlour, 'where you will find her when you are disposed for music, reading, or conversation,' Waverley is as 'delighted at being restored ... to the society of his own rank' as she is 'pleased with his manners and information' (292). It is Waverley's polished 'civility' that recommends him to the two English gentlemen who pull strings to extricate him from the results of his mistakes. The coming together of these Whig gentlemen is the happy ending towards which the novel moves. Blood loyalty, the novel as a whole suggests, is an inadequate bond in the modern state, and both brotherhood and fatherhood are a questionable basis for community. The bond of shared taste – less personal than that of blood but more personal than that of political belief – turns out to be a flexible, resilient, and inclusive basis of social connection, as Waverley, gradually absorbed into a group of adult men who are his equals, outgrows a series of inadequate father figures to become at once his own man and a member of a rational civic order.[15]

The way Scott brings about this denouement is however perhaps less plausible for us today than for his first readers. While Waverley's flash of distaste on the battlefield is convincingly dramatized, his sudden emergence as a debonair conversationalist is not. Considering the initial emphasis on his inadequate early socialization, the self-possessed charm that wins over Melville is rather a surprise. Where did our hero acquire these impressive and hitherto undemonstrated social skills?[16] Scott's contemporaries, trained to associate 'good taste' with what Montesquieu called the *je ne sais quoi* of social grace, would not ask. Pierre Bourdieu would have an answer: it is Waverley's class-based manner, testifying to the *habitus* in which his reading has been done, that saves him from the matter of that reading.[17] But the novel's refusal to make this distinction – the representation of Waverley's social demeanour as if it were continuous with his education rather than an unexpected development – naturalizes the link between personal sensibility and social *savoir faire* that constitutes taste at this historical moment. Waverley's allies support him of course not because of the individual literary taste that differentiated him from his family but simply because they recognize him as one of their own. Truly individual taste would be socially impotent. Even as the novel endorses good taste as a reliable sign of good character, it also illustrates Bourdieu's thesis: the real function of taste is as a social code that enables the dominant class to close ranks against those who would threaten its solidarity. The tension between taste as personal aesthetic choice and taste as social semiotic may help account for the dissatisfaction that readers have always felt with Scott's hero, who has seemed a somewhat conventional construction, lacking the autonomy and individuality promised at the beginning of the novel.

While Waverley's taste is constructed in opposition to that of his family on the issue of individuality, it is constructed in relation to Fergus and Flora Mac-Ivor on the issue of sincerity. The tension between sincerity and artifice is generically overdetermined in a narrative about seduction, and here again the discourse of taste is structurally useful to Scott. The stylish Mac-Ivors are not only aestheticized figures in themselves but also active connoisseurs with an interest in aesthetic issues, and the way their tastes are represented as mere fashion underlines the threat that they pose to the naive and idealistic hero. At the same time, however, it also problematizes the equation between good taste and good moral character on which so many of the reader's judgments are apparently to be based.

Waverley's literary taste is markedly 'sincere.' He reads the books he loves against the pressure of his environment because they give him pleasure. The privacy of his reading in the early chapters and its antisocial nature guarantee the authenticity of his taste as an expression of his real self. When that self turns out to be more complex than it seemed to be at the beginning – when deeper layers emerge – the sincerity of his response to romance seems to guarantee as well the genuineness of these subsequent layers. Taste can be a reliable sign of personal character if it is authentic in this way. The fact that Waverley's deeper responses *now* connect him with other cultivated Englishmen simply demonstrates that good taste does have the universality the philosophers want to claim for it: that the semiotic system is working as it should to bind good people together.

What would make this semiotic unreliable is 'personal taste' that does not flow from personal feeling: a pose contaminated by fashion or affectation, an aesthetic gesture that expresses not one's own responses but one's anticipation of the responses of others. If there is a code, it can be learned; if there are signs, they can be faked; if there is a fashion, it can be adopted, self-consciously or not. Taste has a rhetorical potential that Waverley himself is apparently too innocent to think of invoking but that his more sophisticated Jacobite hosts are always ready to exploit. In Fergus and Flora the rhetorical function of taste is quietly foregrounded, so as finally to call in question the link between taste and moral character to which, even as he exposes its dubiousness, Scott continues to appeal.

Unlike Waverley, who is rooted in England and for whom the repudiation of the Jacobite cause means returning to his roots, Fergus and Flora, more sophisticated, self-conscious, and relativistic, are the split and deracinated products of two very different cultures. Their situation shapes their sense of taste in a way that brings them perhaps closer than Waverley to the intuitions of Scott himself, with his historicizing interest in cultural difference, and that accounts for their sense of personal style, their awareness of audience, and their readiness to select, combine, and compare. Taste is the topic of a surprising number of the pages allotted to the Mac-Ivor siblings, who not only assess and exploit Waverley's aesthetic enthusiasms but also discuss and display their own, and the issue of performativity is central to the characterization of this pair, who are developed around the overlapping binaries of sincerity/ theatricality, nature/artifice, and taste/fashion. The way Fergus is aligned with theatricality, art, and fashion – with the second term of each set – in the end destabilizes, I shall argue, not only the characterization of his supposedly more sincere sister but also the very notion of good taste by which he himself is constructed.

Fergus Mac-Ivor understands taste as a system of signs that can be deployed to manipulate other people. A romantic Highlander in his more attractive attributes – his personal courage, his flashes of generosity, even his superstition – Fergus in his sophistication is continental, specifically French, a man 'of whom a Frenchman might have said ... "*Qu'il connoit bien ses gens*"' (89), and his shrewd calculation of aesthetic effect is one mark of his dubious Frenchness. By temperament Fergus is self-dramatizing and even theatrical, but his theatricality is also a pose, and he knows enough not to assume it at the wrong time. Evan Dhu, conducting Waverley to Fergus's lodge, anticipates that his chief will not fail to appear there with 'his tail on'; Fergus, on the other hand, knowing that such a display is likely to seem to 'an English young man of fortune ... rather ludicrous than respectable' and 'cautious of exhibiting external marks of dignity, unless at the time and in the manner where they were most likely to produce an imposing effect' (89), defers to what he understands as the English taste for modesty and understatement and saves the show instead for a fitter occasion, the 'solemn hunting' (116) of the stag. The reader, encouraged by Evan Dhu's remarks to anticipate a colourful display of Highland pageantry, registers not only the anticlimax but also the canny calculation behind it and is alerted to the public-relations dimension of every subsequent show put on by the brother and sister. While complaining to Waverley of the crudity of the Highlanders and Highland scenery, Fergus carefully stage-manages its manifestations so that that crudity will attract rather than offend him, offering Waverley a romantic image of the Highlands mediated by a sophisticated European notion of decorum – a decorum that Scott's implied reader has been taught to approve. The effect is complex: registering Fergus's disingenuousness, we nevertheless identify with his aesthetic principles, even as they frustrate our own, as well as Waverley's, romantic desire.

Since before we have been allowed to catch a glimpse of it, we are made to regard Highland spectacle as a kind of masquerade rather than as an authentic expression of a tribal identity, by the time Waverley is induced to become part of the spectacle – by the time Fergus induces him to don 'your new costume' (196) that he has assembled and purchased – he seems, whatever his own intentions, to be playing a game of dress-up. Critics usually discuss Waverley's assumption of the tartan in terms of his own subjectivity, making a point of its inauthenticity and his narcissism,[18] but the commercial associations of the dress are equally suggestive. The costume is first described by Fergus, ordering Shemus of the Needle to collect its various elements. Most of the garments Waverley is to wear will be borrowed – the Prince 'has given Mr Waverley broad-sword and pistol' and Fergus offers his own 'short green coat, with silver lace,' 'handsome target,' and 'dirk and purse' – but some will have to be bought: he begins by telling Shemus to 'Get a plaid of Mac-Ivor tartan, and sash ... and a blue bonnet of the Prince's pattern, at Mr Mouat's the haberdasher' (197). Both the elegance and the provenance of the articles – some handed down, others purchased – make clear that identity, as Fergus conceives it, is a matter of style and fashion: at once theatrical and commodified.

We are reminded that this flurry of display has immediate economic implications. By recalling the effect, on the lives of ordinary people, of the cause espoused (and the poses struck) by the rebels, the reference to Mouat the haberdasher connects the personal projects of the principal characters with the local and national economy, and the real interests of the ordinary people of Edinburgh with those of the citizens of Dundee, who are 'chiefly engaged in mercantile pursuits' (31). Though the billeting of this glamorous group at Holyrood is apparently good for local business in the short run, such business, which might go on and quietly thrive (as does Widow Flockhart's), through changes in political leadership, might also be threatened by the Jacobite invasion, as both Scottish and English merchants assumed it would be.[19] From the longer historical perspective, however, the Cause will prove to be a boon to Scottish industry. The sartorial impact of the whole Jacobite phenomenon – what the narrator will later refer to as 'tartan fever' (339), an ersatz enthusiasm to the development of which the Waverley novels themselves largely contributed – is its most enduring legacy.[20] This kind of taste is not an expression of either individual discrimination or authentic national character, but a fashion promoted by canny marketing. Both historical romance and national costume are marketable products, like the Waverley novels that helped to endow them with value. By associating Fergus with mere shopping, Scott underlines the factitiousness and calculation of his Highland persona; by writing into his novel an allusion to the commodification in which it partakes, he also foregrounds the bogus nature of Highland glamour in general, always already stage-managed and commodified.

The way Fergus frames his sister's taste for Highland scenery also produces an odd and intriguing ambiguity. There is a series of layered ironies here that end up subverting not just Fergus's taste, which is to be expected, but the very discourse by which he is ironized.

Fergus sets up Flora's recitation of Mac-Murrough's verses on the assumption that her performance will act powerfully on the young Englishman's imagination. Nevertheless, he finds it politic to rally her on her Scottish enthusiasms, implying to Waverley, as one gentleman to another, their own more refined standards. Fergus lightly mocks the Highland landscape his sister loves by contrasting it to the products of more developed cultures: 'A simple and unsublimed taste now, like my own, would prefer the jet d'eau at Versailles to this cascade, with all its accompaniments of rock and roar; but this is Flora's Parnassus ... and that fountain her Helicon' (109). Fergus's art/nature binary implies his own solidarity with Waverley, whose answering sophistication he pretends to assume, while it also aligns Flora with sublime nature in terms guaranteed to increase her glamour for Waverley.

It does the same for Scott's reader, though at Fergus's expense. For readers familiar with the writing of Picturesque theorists like Richard Payne Knight and Uvedale Price, the fountains of Versailles have sinister associations.[21] Fergus's comparison is simply a cliché of Picturesque discourse. Exponents of the Picturesque represented the formal style favoured by continental monarchs as the expression of the kind of tyranny that invited revolution and regarded both the British countryside itself and the style of landscape gardening based on it as an expression of the spirit of English liberty that was the best defence against civic disorder. Gilpin comments on the self-styled 'King of Patterdale' that 'the prince of Windsor and Versailles would shrink in a comparison with the magnificence of his dominions.'[22] Evidently, Fergus in 1745 cannot have read Gilpin, but the allusion reverberates with Scott's implied reader, who has, and whose associations with Versailles are both richer and darker than his. In his preference for Versailles and his denigration of the Picturesque, Fergus unwittingly situates himself, for us at least, on the side of European tyranny. The effect is to endorse Flora's taste rather than devalue it, though her own association with the Picturesque also has its ironies, as we shall see.

The remark that Fergus makes right after his allusion to Versailles calls in question, however, the very semiotic by which we have been evaluating all these characters. Elaborating on the theme of Flora's artless simplicity, Fergus compares her to one of the Highlanders, joking that her taste for water would complement the taste for whiskey of 'her coadjutor' Mac-Murrough, who 'has just drank a pint of usquebaugh to correct, he said, the coldness of the claret' (109). His implication is not only that Mac-Murrough claims to find claret 'cold' merely as an excuse for getting at the whiskey but that his preference for whiskey over claret, like Flora's preference for things Scottish over things continental, is rather barbaric. His disingenuous complaint is designed not only to draw attention to his retainers' large appetites and to his own largesse but also to make flatteringly clear that the sophisticated taste that he and Waverley share is superior to both a woman's romanticism and a Highlander's crudity. The remark, concise, witty, and allusive, is proffered not only as a description of his taste but as a sample of it. As Fergus judges Flora and Mac-Murrough, so the reader judges him, making a moral equation between his somewhat gratuitous condescension and his continental pretensions.

A proleptic echo of his remark ironizes this shared hermeneutic, however, as it were behind Fergus's back. We know, because the narrator has told us only a few pages earlier, exactly why the Highlanders have not developed a taste for wine. Having been made to understand that their 'taste was to be formed according to ... rank ... held at table,' they obediently call, 'apparently out of choice, for the liquor which was assigned to them from economy,' claiming to find the wine to which they are not entitled 'too cold for their stomachs' (96). Burke held that superior taste is the product of 'superior knowledge':[23] that the cultivated gentleman has simply been exposed to a wider range of experiences than the menial, and that for this reason, if no other, his taste is bound to be better. But lack of exposure is not the problem here. Fergus's followers know perfectly well the difference between claret and whiskey, whiskey and water. It is not ignorance of wine that makes them learn, or pretend, to prefer whiskey, but lack of social and economic power. As Bourdieu points out, those who cannot get what they like have to like what they get, and the taste so formed is not an index of personal sensibility but simply a class marker.[24]

The rhyming of the two remarks exposes the disingenuousness of Fergus, who must know the reasons for his followers' vulgar choices. More than that, however, it admits an analogy between lower-class taste, which is understood as nothing but a sign of social class, and the taste of the gentleman, which is supposed to have everything to do with individual discrimination and moral character. Demystifying the taste of Mac-Murrough and his fellows threatens to demystify that of the principal characters as well.[25] Autonomous disinterested taste is a myth, the figure of Fergus makes clear, and if a myth in relation to the low and vulgar characters, so also perhaps in relation to the high and cultivated. The narrator, characterizing the taste of a member of the lower orders, can be permitted a cynical reductiveness unthinkable in relation to his principal characters, but the effect of his remark, connecting as it does to Fergus's cheerfully relativistic satire, weakens the link between taste and essential nature upon which their own characterization is in part based. To Fergus, Mac-Murrough's taste is no taste at all; but from the perspective that the narrator's remark suddenly makes available, no more perhaps is that of Fergus, Flora, Rosa, or Waverley himself.

Yet even in making these connections, we are registering Fergus's own vulgarity – the tastelessness of his display of taste, so mannered, so disingenuous, so different from English understatement – and judging him by a more genteel standard. The text continues to appeal to our own 'good taste' even at the moment when it suggests that taste is relative. Addressing readers shaped by the notion of taste on which he relies, Scott simply exploits the discourse for his own local purposes and lets the contradictions stand. Leavening the sometimes rather lumpish discourse of taste with the odd flash of sociological scepticism, *Waverley* exhibits some of the contradictions that will continue to shape nineteenth-century novels with an investment in the same discourse.

As a novelistic character Flora Mac-Ivor is more of a puzzle than her brother. Critics disagree about how to read her. Evidently a more idealized figure than Fergus, purer in her motives, more ardent in her enthusiasm,[26] she is nevertheless compared to the dangerous enchantresses of romance. Her romanticism has a self-delusional aspect, yet the poses she strikes seem to have an element of calculation. Since she improves on her brother's proposal by staging in a particularly impressive way the recitation of bardic verse that he sets up, we do get the impression that the pair are working together. Yet though she represents both deception and self-deception, she also speaks the truth, even beyond her own understanding.[27] As a lady she is chivalrously protected by Scott himself from the kind of scrutiny to which Fergus is subjected, and as a romantic heroine she consistently exhibits the good taste that has become a generic imperative. The contradictions in the way her taste is represented account I think for some of the ambiguities that have puzzled readers.

Scott differentiates Flora from Rose by assigning her more vigorous and idiosyncratic tastes. Though both ladies revere Shakespeare and both, like Scott, are interested in folk poetry, Flora is more active in the pursuit of her enthusiasms, more individual in her preferences, and more self-conscious in the projection of her personal image. But individualizing Flora means assigning her particular aesthetic interests, and the very particularity inevitably locates these interests at a specific historical moment. Flora is linked more closely than Rose to the fashions of a particular time and place, and such particularity not only threatens the notion of generalized tastefulness by which a heroine is conventionally constructed, it locates Flora in a nexus of discourses with sometimes contradictory implications.

Flora's dress is described without irony and in generalized clichés appropriate to the representation of a romantic heroine. We are told that her costume,

> which was in texture elegant, and even rich, [was] arranged in a manner which partook partly of the Parisian fashion, and partly of the more simple dress of the Highlands, blended together with great taste. (99)

In the discourse of taste, 'simple' is almost obligatory after 'elegant and rich,' and the otherwise problematic French/Scottish polarity here functions simply to provide a historically particular way of grounding the predictable oxymoron. Indeed, Scott uses Highland custom as a pretext for catering to the reader's assumed taste for 'simplicity' in female appearance. Flora's hair, we are told,

> was not disfigured by the art of the friseur, but fell in jetty ringlets on her neck, confined only by a circlet ... (99)

The French 'friseur,' linked as it is with 'disfigured,' makes clear that Flora, though Parisian in elegance, avoids Parisian artificiality; but the notion of simplicity is qualified by the value of the circlet, which is 'richly set with diamonds' (99). Neither the rhetorical aspect of Flora's costume – her evident desire to make a political statement with her carefully balanced fusion of styles – nor the ethnographic gesturing of the narrator is allowed to undercut the overall impression of elegance and quality. Given that he is describing not one but two national fashions, no single detail of which he enables us to visualize, Scott does all he can to exempt Flora from specificity and endow her with an aura of timeless glamour. The rhetoric is carefully controlled to maintain, in the face of Flora's exoticism, the complete tastefulness of the romance heroine. Taste trumps politics, imposing aesthetic unity on political difference.

Like Fergus's, however, Flora's self-presentation is blandly ironized by a parodic lower-class figure. The sartorial glamour of the French connection has already been undercut by Donald Bean Lean, who only shortly before received Waverley with 'a profusion of French politeness and Scottish hospitality' (80) in 'an old blue and red uniform, and a feathered hat' (80) left over from his service in the French army. The outlaw has laid aside Highland dress as a compliment to Waverley, but in his makeshift get-up he looks 'so incongruous' that instead of being impressed the Englishman is 'tempted to laugh' (80). What will count more than the way in which Flora's and Donald's costumes differ is what they have in common. Both their outfits are emblematic of the unviable political project in which they are caught and in which they are catching Waverley. The similarity in dress exposes Flora's serene fashion sense as another form of dress-up, even of *bricolage*: more elegant than Donald's but no less constrained; less factitious than Waverley's but equally inauthentic as an expression of 'self.' The aesthetic realm to which Flora is largely confined by Scott himself is no escape from the exigencies of history: the Cause she espouses will be ruined by the tensions that in her costume she has so pleasingly reconciled.

Flora's theatricality is more restrained than Fergus's, or, at least, the impression we are allowed to form of it is more muted, but there is always something self-conscious and often something problematic about the display of her tastes and accomplishments. Her enthusiasm for bardic verse is an example. This taste is apparently no affectation: the narrator has already established her pleasure in Highland 'researches' (101), and though when her brother asks her to translate Mac-Murrough's tribute to Waverley she demurs – 'even if I could translate them as you pretend' (103) – Flora evidently has enough knowledge of Gaelic to render Mac-Murrough's lines in praise of Waverley into English verse, if allowed to withdraw for a time in order to do it. But her withdrawal can also be seen as a manoeuvre designed to whet Waverley's curiosity and enflame his desire, since it gives her time to set up the scene in the glen. It is noteworthy that we never hear the results of her work: her recitation is interrupted by Fergus's dog just at the moment when she would have been getting to the inserted stanzas, and she is reduced to paraphrasing them. The effect is mildly disconcerting. It is impossible to believe that Flora's linguistic claims – or the claims made by her brother on her behalf, which she only half disavows – are to be understood as simply fraudulent, yet hard to ignore her failure to deliver precisely the verses she is supposed to have translated.[28] Fergus has suggested that Flora consults with Mac-Murrough about his compositions, even collaborates in writing them: indeed, he believes this specific song to be 'your joint composition, for I insist you had a share in it' (103). If what Mac-Murrough sings were a translation back into Gaelic of an English text composed by Flora, she would of course be quick to render the prepared verses in English but would need time to do the same for a truly bardic improvisation. Are we to believe that the singer's reference to Waverley caught Flora herself by surprise? The payment Fergus gives Mac-Murrough, his last silver cup, is perhaps owed to his sister. There is just a suggestion here that researches like hers might taint and cheapen an authentic oral culture – that the researcher's efforts to enrich her own subjectivity will end up commodifying the culture she values for its primitive purity.

Flora's songs indeed 'are not so much the effusions of a native sensibility as the accomplishments of a highly-cultivated taste, fashionably, if anachronistically, tinctured with the late eighteenth-century fad for the sentimental Ossian.'[29] Her taste for nature, exemplified by the glen to which she has Waverley conducted, is equally time-bound and artificial. Here again there is a parallel with Donald Bean Lean that tends to ironize Flora's self-presentation. It has often been pointed out how Waverley's romantic images of the Highlands are subsequently deflated by the reality of the rough countryside, once he has entered it.[30] In the representation of Flora's glen, the sequence is reversed: the natural scene precedes and ironizes the artificial one. Waverley is drawn towards Flora very much the way he had, shortly before, been drawn towards Donald – led forward in a state of excitement and anticipation into a landscape that is rough, wild, and mysterious, full of twists, turns, surprises, and revelations. A human figure signals the climax of each journey – a short man 'in a silly French uniform'[31] on the one hand, a fascinating lady high on a perilous rustic bridge on the other – and though the difference between the figures marks Flora's space as that of romance and Donald's as that of reality, the similarity between the two settings also implies an analogy between Donald and Flora, positioning her as the public-relations branch of a project that is larger, more unwieldly, and more morally problematic than she understands.[32] Her glen, though natural in contrast to the kind of court setting that her brother prefers, is artificial in comparison with the real Highland country, to which it bears the same relation as Waverley's classy costume does to ordinary Highland dress. The effect is to mark off and trivialize the aesthetic realm itself, in which Flora is situated, and to imply, even as she exercises it, that the kind of control she has is limited and delusory.

What kind of control does she have? How negative a judgment of

Flora is implied by her entrancing performance in the glen? Flora is compared to an 'enchantress of Boiardo or Ariosto' (106), and it has been suggested that Waverley should have read her as if she were a figure in Spenserian allegory.[33] But the question is not how Waverley reads Flora but how we do. A questing knight in an allegorical romance always has trouble reading correctly. It is Spenser's reader, not his perennially bemused protagonist, upon whom the burden of interpretation rests. The fact that Scott's reader has more difficulty decoding Flora than Spenser's reader has in decoding Acrasia makes clear the problem of using taste as a sign of human character.

If Flora were in fact an Acrasia, her 'taste' would represent her, for the reader if not for the errant quester, in an unproblematic and transparent way: it would be understood as just the spontaneous emanation of her real nature that novelists often assume taste to be. A reader who interprets the details of the Bower of Bliss will find them continuous with everything else about Acrasia. As an allegorical figure, Acrasia has no 'character' except that of the temptation she stands for: hence there is an exact fit between the female figure and the physical space in which she is located. Taste is a reliable sign of character in an allegory, but only in an allegory. In real life there can be no such transparent signs.

The novel knows this, despite its (sometime) reliance on such signs. If Flora's glen did express her nature in this reliable way, she would be more sinister and seductive than she is otherwise made out to be.[34] In fact Scott goes out of his way to emphasize that the space that Flora occupies is not, like Acrasia's, a transparent emanation of her nature. Waverley may feel that Flora's glen has been created at her 'nod,' but the narrator points out that it has simply been constructed according to her orders – 'decorated with trees and shrubs, some of which had been planted under the direction of Flora, but so cautiously, that they added to the grace, without diminishing the romantic wildness of the scene' (106). Moreover, the glen is no generalized 'Eden in the wilderness' but a deliberately planned landscape – planned according to Picturesque principles recognizable by the 1790s (if not by the 1740s when the planning was supposedly going on) as those of writers like Gilpin, Price, and Knight,[35] who suggest the specific structure Flora has devised – the artfully natural bridge, the 'two pine-trees laid across, and covered with turf' (105)[36] – and commend just the kind of 'variety' and 'intricacy' that dilate Waverley's progress and enhance his suspense.[37] Scott's description of the glen is a catalogue of the features that Picturesque theorists demand: the rocks of 'a thousand peculiar and varied forms'

(105) the paths carefully cultivated to produce unexpected and charming views, the water in lively motion – 'rapid and stony torrents and cataracts'; the apparently natural pathway, as if 'shaped by the mere tread of passengers and animals ... as unconstrained as the footsteps that formed it'[38] but actually smoothed out for easier walking. This is not just 'nature' but nature distilled and reconfigured according to a well-developed contemporary program. It is, in fact, a fashion – a fashion that belongs not to the timeless world of romance but to a specific cultural moment. If the romantic landscapes from Waverley's adolescent reading seem to have materialized in Flora's glen, it is not because he has stepped into the world of romance but because his taste, like hers, is the product of a particular period. The style Flora chooses already has a particularly rich set of historical associations, all of which contribute to the ambiguity of her character.

The Picturesque is a gendered style, and it is the gender associations that Scott chiefly exploits. The desirable landscape characterized by writers like Price has a teasingly feminine character: it is seductive, riveting but baffling the eye of the entranced visitor who moves through it. The apparently natural but actually deliberate 'disposition of objects which, by a partial and uncertain concealment, excites and nourishes curiosity'[39] is given an emphatically erotic charge. Like the landscapes Price approves, Flora's glen 'invite[s] the eye to penetrate ... yet keep[s] its curiosity alive and unsatisfied' – 'leads the eye (according to Hogarth's expression) a kind of wanton chace.'[40] The way Waverley's wandering eye is fixed by Flora's startling entrance high above his head is just the kind of effect recommended by Picturesque writers. The word 'burst' is a favourite in this discourse: the house itself, says Knight, should be so situated as to seem to be 'bursting from some deep-embowered shade' and 'rising to the view' to surprise the visitor.[41] Scott's narrator notes 'the wild beauty of the retreat, bursting upon him as if by magic' (106), and Flora literally rises before Waverley, emerging onto the 'precarious eminence' (105). The Picturesque, says Price, 'is the coquetry of nature.'[42] Waverley's enchantment by the landscape may have more to do with his romantic expectations than with Flora's intentions, but her willingness to play along with the erotics of the Picturesque seems to implicate her in its code.

Yet Scott quickly pulls back from this suggestion as well. Flora, the narrator assures us, is not being intentionally seductive: she takes no credit for the impression she sees the situation is making on Waverley and quickly shifts his attention to her song. The glen, cited by her brother as an expression of her personal feeling for nature, is ordinarily her private retreat, and the narrator's observation that the paths have been 'rendered easy in many places for Flora's accommodation' (105) endorses the impression that she is often alone in it. Yet her supposed love of solitude seems incompatible with the flamboyant way she dramatizes herself on this occasion. Indeed, far from exemplifying the spirit of solitude to which she refers, Flora makes a theatrical spectacle of herself. The glen feels like a Spenserian trap and she seems to be using herself as bait. On the other hand, common sense prevents us from postulating that she has devised the landscape, like Acrasia's Bower, in anticipation of whatever naive young Englishman happens along. We are told indeed that Flora does not want to enlist Waverley in the Cause at all.

The fudging here is the recourse of a writer who, wanting to heighten the erotic suspense of the moment yet also to exonerate his heroine of deliberate mischief, displaces her seductiveness onto the landscape and then denies the displacement. But by choosing a semiotically 'loaded' style and then having to back away from its full range of associations, Scott raises a wider issue. Can there exist in any historical period any style that does not come imbued with social and (in the widest sense) political associations – any aesthetic object one might adopt as an expression of one's own personal taste that is not already semiotically loaded? Beauty does not exist in a social and historical vacuum but is attributed to particular objects and styles by means of particular codes developed in particular times and places (and, many theorists would add, to promote particular interests). Defining Flora in terms of an aesthetic that has a particularly strong historical charge not only makes her unreadable (which perhaps is to Scott's advantage) but also testifies to the problem of using 'personal style' as a sign of individual character.

The political associations of the Picturesque were as familiar as the erotic and are equally problematic in relation to Flora. As has been pointed out, Picturesque landscape was associated by its proponents with freedom but by its opponents with revolutionary licence. As Price describes it, such a landscape is analogous to the Burkean commonwealth – as English as 'the old rugged oak, or knotty wych elm' that in their sturdy roughness serve as its emblems.[43] Picturesque landscape is like an organically developing society, made up of a multitude of individuals, each following his own path of development but linked to others in a complementary and 'natural' way. Insisting that various kinds of trees and bushes be allowed to grow up together as they naturally would and that a brook or river be 'allowed its liberty' to follow its own course, Price associates the style with individuality and freedom and its alternative with despotism. Arbitrarily 'clumping' trees like 'Capability' Brown, he says, makes them like 'bodies of men drilled for the purposes of formal parade'; planting groves solely of larches that look like 'scattered platoons of spearmen' on 'one of the old military plans' makes the countryside look as if it were 'en herisson.'[44] Political rebellion is the likely result of the kind of despotic rigidity expressed by the formal garden, whereas the Picturesque, with its respect for nature and the individual, is the appropriate emblem of an old-growth commonwealth. Such inflammatory metaphors as these, however, seemed to conservatives dangerously revolutionary. Walpole satirized Knight as 'Jacobinically' willing to destroy the 'purity' of the landscape, and Anna Seward confessed that his 'system appears to me the Jacobinism of taste.'[45] As a result of the paper war between Repton and Price and their supporters, the analogy 'between picturesque composition and political confusion'[46] was as well established as that between the Picturesque and Whig liberalism.

It would seem at least ironic that Flora is using her glen to enlist Waverley in the subversion of the very English values with which the Picturesque is associated. If the Mac-Ivors were to have their way the countryside would indeed be 'en herisson.' While she may allow the effervescent little stream the liberty to follow its own downward course, Flora draws Waverley against his English nature uphill and into a movement that would divest him of his own autonomy and threaten the liberty of the nation as a whole. Yet just what weight we are to give to this set of associations is not clearly signalled by the text. Scott's first readers might – or they might not – be aware that the Picturesque had been made to stand for both the English constitution that Flora would destroy and the revolutionary energies that threaten that freedom.[47] Is Scott simply updating his Spenserian and Ariostan allusions by assuming his readers' acquaintance with Picturesque discourse? Or if, as Barrell has suggested, Picturesque focalization quickly became so thoroughly naturalized that it ceased to be thought of as a fashion at all and became just the right way of looking at landscape, is he representing her glen as simply 'nature' itself as opposed to Fergus's sinister 'culture'?[48] Flora of course could have no discursive associations of the kind available to us, since, though as a contemporary of Gilpin's she would have been responding to the same cultural currents that shaped him, in 1745 the Picturesque texts that generated the controversial metaphors had not been written.[49] The anachronism tends to protect her from the imputa-

tion of faddishness and to make her feeling for the glen, which anticipates an aesthetic not yet articulated, the sign of an innate tastefulness
that transcends time and fashion. But just as Fergus's remark about Versailles, which immediately follows the scene in the glen, tends retroac-
tively to activate political meanings not foregrounded in the scene itself,
so Flora's own subsequent satire of Waverley's country-house aesthetic
raises the issue of fashion and its subversion of individual taste.

When Flora describes Waverley's abandonment of revolutionary
action in favour of a 'domestic happiness, lettered indolence, and elegant enjoyments,' the terms in which she does it – picturing his readiness to 'refit the old library in the most exquisite Gothic taste, ... draw
plans and landscapes, and write verses, and rear temples, and dig grot-
toes' (250) – suggest that she sees his taste merely as a popular fashion
and mocks it as such. Flora is speaking to Rose Bradwardine, and Rose is
allowed to have the last word – to express her desire for withdrawal into
this private, aestheticized domain. Indeed, Flora supports Rose: the two
women work together to get the domestic heroine the home she
desires.[50] Yet Flora's caricature remains on record, ironizing the very
denouement it adumbrates. Personal taste, as Flora makes clear, turns
out not to be particularly personal at all. Seen through Flora's eyes,
Waverley suddenly looks a good deal less like an individual and more
like a follower of a fashion that is already thoroughly predictable, and
the Waverley-Honour he will shape less an expression of his individual
taste than the mirror-image of dozens of similar estates dotting the
English countryside. By the same token, however, Flora's glen looks less
like either a sinister Bower of Bliss or an authentic expression of her
feeling for nature than a fashionable cliché. In hindsight, from the perspective of 1814 or any date in the future, no one's taste looks either
universal or individual. It can only seem a transitory fashion, adopted at
a particular moment by members of a particular social class. Hence the
problem of using it, as Scott nevertheless insists on doing, as a mark of
personal moral refinement.

On the whole the suggestion that Flora has excellent taste helps to
insulate her from the critique of romantic Jacobitism, so that she can
remain an appealing figure: dark but not undecorous; passionate, political, yet still refined. It is partly no doubt the emphasis on their tasteful
refinement that makes Scott's dark heroines so acceptable to his Victorian readers. Yet the awareness that taste can never function as a simple
emanation of character – that it is always shot through, contaminated,
with social meanings – is also implied in Flora's representation. As the

tasteful individual withdraws into private life, it has already been made clear that such individuality is itself an illusion.

As the defeat of the Jacobite cause is on the whole a happy ending in the political sphere, so Waverley's retirement into contented domesticity is apparently a happy ending in the personal. Yet it is a commonplace of criticism that the novel's denouement is too pat and that certain details in the final pages seem positively parodic. The impression of parody derives not only from the way in which Waverley is extricated from the consequences of his actions or from the predictable pairing of hero and blonde heroine but also from the way the domestic space that they will inhabit is represented. Specifically it comes from the narrator's account of the quasi-magical restoration of Tully-Veolan and his ekphrastic description of the painting of Fergus and Waverley that will be hung in its dining room.

The novel ends with the restoration of both the houses that had been threatened by the rebellion and with the assurance that they will descend to Rose and Waverley.[51] As his uncle's heir, Waverley, who will no doubt have heirs of his own, will restore the wavering honour of Waverley-Honour, maintaining and 'improving' the estate and passing it along to a new generation firmly attached to the new order and the Whig polity. Waverley-Honour will not be Waverley's and Rose's only home, however: as the heirs of Baron Bradwardine, they will presumably in due time take possession of Tully-Veolan. The renewed Waverley-Honour is a household that, except in the proleptic vision of Flora, we never get to see. What we do see, to our astonishment, is the magical restoration of the Scottish mansion that will one day be the young couple's holiday retreat.

In chapter 71 this property, purchased for Bradwardine by Colonel Talbot,[52] suddenly appears restored so quickly and completely to its former state as to erase its violent past almost entirely. Only fifty pages earlier, in chapter 63, Scott had depicted the mansion wrecked, burned, and defiled. Now, risen from its ashes, it seems never to have witnessed the violence that has torn up so much of the rest of the country:

> The pigeon-house was replenished; the fountain played with its usual activity, and not only the Bear who predominated over its bason, but all the other Bears, whatsoever, were replaced upon their stations, and renewed or repaired with so much care, that they bore no tokens of the violence which had so lately descended upon them. (334)

Despite a bit of tactful modernization – new stables 'of a lighter and more picturesque appearance' to replace the unhealthy old building fortunately demolished by the fires of war, and 'a new green-house stocked with the finest plants' – the house and gardens have been reconstructed 'with the strictest attention to maintain the original character of both' (334); in the dining room, 'where new moveables had been necessary, they had been selected in the same character with the old furniture' (338). Unlike the fashionable gothic additions Flora predicts at Waverley-Honour, the repairs to Tully-Veolan reach back into the past only to restore what had already been there, creating a deliberate illusion of undisturbed continuity. Apparently, though improbably, someone entering the house for the first time would not be able to tell that the rising of 1745 had ever touched this property – would not even realize that the building had been reconstructed.[53]

The characters' purpose in so thoroughly erasing the signs of the rebellion is, presumably, to soften the Baron's memories of his own sufferings. On the one hand, this seems to be a rational approach to the trauma of war, less morbid than that of the Jacobites, who treasure the scars of conflict and the legends that explain them. Aunt Rachel's story about young William Waverley, mortally wounded in the Civil War, encouraged Edward to trace, as William's fiancée does before she dies, 'the drops of his blood, from the great hall-door, along the little gallery, and up to the saloon, where they laid him down to die at his mother's feet' (18). The restoration of Tully-Veolan, on the other hand, by making the past blend seamlessly into the present, refuses to memorialize the violence or allow the imagination to linger on it. The tasteful melding of old and new allows the inhabitants to move beyond the past and its quarrels so that they will not have to be re-fought. The past is restored to build a foundation for the future; the Baron's life is put back together so that the next generation can move forward. 'Good taste' in architecture – careful stylistic homogeneity – seems to line up with sound mental and political hygiene. That it also lines up with a sort of historical amnesia puts this tastefulness, however, into a somewhat ironical perspective.

Duncan raises the issue of 'Property as theft' in connection with Tully-Veolan: 'in the romance of property,' he says, 'possession is marked off from the historical forces of its acquisition.'[54] The issue for the property owner is how to represent (or erase) the violence on which his ownership is founded. The violence done *against* him can of course be remembered and memorialized in material objects. Though drawing attention to bloody stains on one's floor may be in questionable taste by the standards of 1814 – and Scott makes us feel this – it is also a sort of pedigree. But the violence by which the property has been acquired – the violence done by the owner's ancestors, or the violence from which the owner, though personally blameless, has profited – has to be occluded or erased. It is true that the damage to Tully-Veolan was done not by the Baron but by his enemies; yet his secure repossession of it nevertheless depends on their annihilation. The Highlanders were dispossessed and destroyed by the process that gave the Baron back his property. It has been pointed out that Scott's novels fail adequately to take account of this process, which was to culminate in the Highland Clearances.[55] But one could argue that in the treatment of Tully-Veolan the process of erasure is in fact critiqued, if in a backhanded and oblique way. By suggesting the magical and patently bogus nature of the restoration, the narrative ironizes a happy ending that installs a wealthy English gentleman complacently on a tasteful Scottish estate.

Pursuing his argument that the past can exist now only as a commodity, Duncan points out that the house as described by Scott announces itself as a restoration.[56] The description of Tully-Veolan might be cited as another example of the heritage-industry kitsch that Clara Tuite attributes to the great houses fantasized by Austen, were it not for Scott's own signals about its speciousness.[57] His choice of words underlines the synthetic aspect of the restored mansion, suggesting that it has become less a dwelling than a stage-set, where the servants, for example, serve dinner 'in full costume' (338). The way this seamless illusion was funded by English capital is also relevant to its meaning. The Baron points out that it is money, 'the *Diva Pecunia* of the Southron – their tutelary deity, he might call her,' that has so speedily 'removed the marks of spoliation' (333). This is not the only English money that is flowing northward. The English are already busy collecting Highland mementos: Talbot has been able to retrieve the Baron's drinking cup because Frank Stanley, possessed by 'tartan fever,' has been overheard describing the vessel by a servant who tracked it down in an ad hoc antiques market fuelled by 'the spoil of half the army' (339). Though Tully-Veolan is not going to serve as a vacation home for its English buyer Talbot, who promptly restores it to its Scottish owner, it will no doubt function as one for the English Waverleys who will inherit it, and we are reminded of the way English gentlemen less altruistic than Talbot would in time obtain possession of the Scottish countryside and parcel it out into private vacation estates, tastefully decorated with 'authentic' artifacts.[58] The Highlands and their history are becoming commodities, a process facilitated by Scott's own poems and novels, and their dwelling places merely a chapter in the history of taste. Despite its accent on the positive, the novel's ending allows us to register this process. Tully-Veolan, insofar as it 'stands in' both for a Waverley-Honour we never see and for the Scottish estates that rich Englishmen were beginning to acquire, makes the hero's retirement into domesticity seem not only an act of appropriation but also rather like the entry into a theme-park dream world, while its sudden metamorphosis, so clearly a wish-fulfillment fantasy, parodies the facile satisfactions that the novelist is obliged to supply.[59]

The picture of Fergus and Waverley, which is the focal point of the restored dining room, is problematic in a similar way. The historical past, so carefully erased in the house itself, is apparently preserved only in this painting, which, more cheerfully and tastefully than trails of blood under the carpet, memorializes the '45:

> It was a large and spirited painting, representing Fergus Mac-Ivor and Waverley in their Highland dress, the scene a wild, rocky, and mountainous pass, down which the clan were descending in the background. It was taken from a spirited sketch, drawn while they were in Edinburgh by a young man of high genius, and had been painted on a full length scale by an eminent London artist. Raeburn himself, (whose Highland Chiefs do all but walk out of the canvas) could not have done more justice to the subject; and the ardent, fiery, and impetuous character of the unfortunate Chief of Glennaquoich was finely contrasted with the contemplative, fanciful, and enthusiastic expression of his happier friend. Beside this painting hung the arms which Waverley had borne in the unfortunate civil war. (338)

The picture, like the historical romance itself, is a generic hybrid – Scott's ekphrastic description draws on two genres, portraiture and battle painting – and like the romance, it tends to turn 'history' into picturesque background, divesting it of causality and violence.[60] As a mirror-text that freezes into an epitomizing image the narrative we have just read, the picture demands interpretation. But as such an epitome it is manifestly misleading, and as a decorous and tactful falsification of the complex process that the novel as a whole has just delineated, it tilts the narrative towards a romance of private life.[61]

Scott compares the painting to a Raeburn portrait, but such a portrait would not depict troops in the background. Anonymous groups of small

military figures are, on the other hand, characteristic of a battle painting, which ordinarily represents colourful principals engaged in a violent confrontation in the foreground and undifferentiated commoners
involved in various skirmishes in the distance. Yet this is not a battle
painting, either. There is no military action here: the clans file elegia-
cally down the pass, while Fergus and Waverley simply stand facing
the viewer. The fact that there was an art-critical debate about what
'moment' the history painter should choose to depict, a debate to which
Scott contributed, suggests that the static quality of this image is deliberate. Scott argues elsewhere that painting is less truthful than fiction precisely because the painter, confined as he is to a single 'moment,'
cannot convey causality and consequence.[62] But even a single moment
in a battle at least implies causality, in that it demands contextualizing
narrative for its full understanding. The picture of Waverley and Fergus
on the other hand contains no action that calls for interpretation.
There is no single moment from the novel we have just read that is
depicted here – no single moment that could be. In the interests of aesthetic and domestic decorum, the painting misrepresents not only the
personal relationship between the two men but also the relationship
between the leaders and the troops they attempted to lead. The balanced pairing of the two figures implies an unproblematic amity that
never characterized their relationship at any point, while the emphatic
foregrounding of the two leaders and the visual diminution of the clan
in the background suggests a control over the 'minor' characters that
neither of them ever had. The army as we have seen it – motley, chaotic,
sometimes heroic, but never predictable – was quite different from the
contained, rather static group docilely descending the mountain, who
merely serve as a backdrop for the two main characters in whose personal narratives we have become involved.[63] Less a record than piece of
decor, the painting is the kind of domestic article, which, like the reproduction furniture, will as the years pass help give the family that owns
Tully-Veolan what Bourdieu calls 'social power over time.'[64] A generation or two later, when the memories of Waverley and Fergus have
dimmed, the painting will function less to call up specific events than to
testify that the owners of the house, blessed by such a colourfully attractive ancestor, are of genuine 'old family.' The violence to which the family owes its possession of the property is erased even in the object that
memorializes it.

It is not only the background of the painting, it is also the doubling of
the principal figures that makes it unlike the usual Raeburn portrait.

Raeburn produced life-size portraits of Highland chiefs in full dress,[65] and a reader familiar with his work would visualize highly individualized faces, detailed picturesque costume, life-size scale, and an assertive stance. But Raeburn's chiefs always walk out of the canvas one by one. Doubling them up, as Scott's fictional artist does, would almost comically undercut the impression of monumentality and individual presence that is Raeburn's most characteristic effect, suggesting not so much a heroic emblem of national character as two gentlemen in fancy dress.

This doubling of the male figures invites a certain way of reading the novel, what might be called the Maggie Tulliver reading. Maggie is dismayed by the contrasted romantic fates of Scott's fair heroines, who get their men, and his dark heroines, who do not.[66] In the picture the two attractive young men are polarized in the same potentially erotic way. Unlike Raeburn's portrait subjects, who are finely individualized, Waverley and Fergus are represented less as military leaders than as contrasting physical and psychological types: fair and elegant on the one hand, dark and brooding on the other. The triple adjectives used to describe them – 'ardent, fiery, and impetuous,' 'contemplative, fanciful, and enthusiastic' (338) – offer no visual information but instead suggest complementary physiques and sensibilities.[67] The picture announces its suitability as an ornament for private life by seeming to belong to the realm of personal erotic taste.

In its conventionality and decorum, the double portrait falsifies the complex historical situation that Scott has developed in the novel as a whole: by throwing the emphasis on the well-born and attractive individual, it erases the tensions that make the novel interesting to the politically engaged reader, handing it back to the lover of romance.[68] In a canny move, the novel sanctions, while at the same time ironizing, its own thinner and possibly more saleable reading. Scott has a sense of tastes, plural, and is able to appeal along various fronts. But this sense of various reading publics is rather different from the kind of discriminating selective personal taste upon which the *Bildungsroman* had originally seemed to be founded. Scott is constructing a new reading public by addressing the mass-market reader as a cultivated gentleman. The awareness that the novel encodes – that taste cannot be as individual, as apolitical, as disinterested as this model of personal cultivation implies – is cognate with his negotiation of the newly emerging literary marketplace.

I have begun this study with Scott's first historical novel because its subject is the way literary taste can shape a life, because in *Waverley* taste itself sets the plot in motion, and because it exemplifies the theoretical problems involved in using 'moral taste' as a sign of character. But it is also important as a model for readers and writers to come. As one of the most widely read novels of the nineteenth century, appreciatively perused no doubt by every one of the subsequent authors I discuss, Scott's novel illustrates the way the discourse of taste might be used in fiction throughout the century. Though I have foregrounded the elements in *Waverley* that subvert the link between taste and character, it is clear that Scott on the whole takes that connection for granted, and so do many of the writers who follow him. *Waverley* may indeed have transmitted, to novelists who appreciated it, specific 'taste scenarios': particular solutions to perennial fictional problems. One of these scenarios is the topic of my next chapter. Scott was no doubt at least as influential as either Radcliffe or Austen in putting into circulation what I shall call 'the woman's-room topos,' a conventional scene that continues to turn up in fiction, in increasingly qualified and complex forms, until the end of the century. His lengthy and elaborate exploration of this device – his account of Rose Bradwardine's *Troisième Étage*, her private apartment at Tully-Veolan – will be my starting point as I investigate this topos, a convention invented not only to display the good taste of the modest woman but also to negotiate the issue of her dependence on male approval and financial support.

# 2 A Room with a Viewer: The Evolution of a Victorian Topos

While the theatrical encounter between Edmund Waverley and Flora Mac-Ivor in her glen lives on in literature, shaping scenes in later nineteenth-century novels,[1] Waverley's visit to Rose Bradwardine's *Troisième Étage*, though less exciting than this encounter, provides a still more useful model for Scott's successors. The visits to Flora and to Rose seem rather carefully paired. In both cases Waverley is granted access to the lady's private space by a male relative and guided to it by a minor character who functions like the Spenserian porter or gatekeeper, and in both cases he has to make a rather laborious ascent to an elevated spot, a cultivated space that testifies to the taste of the woman who has shaped it.[2] But while the meeting with Flora is a striking scene, one of the imaginative high points of the novel, the visit to Rose and the description of her tasteful apartment sound rather ready-made, as if Scott were rehearsing an already-established convention. It is a convention that will have a long life. When at the end of *The Awkward Age* (1898) Henry James's Vanderbank compares Nanda Brookenham to a heroine in a novel, 'up here ... perched in your tower or what do you call it? – your bower' with 'Flowers and pictures and – what are the other things people have when they're happy and superior? – books and birds,'[3] he is still drawing, albeit facetiously, on the same topos that Scott uses to characterize Rose. The polarities of enclosure and penetration, constriction and expansion on which this topos is based will continue to shape female characterization throughout the century. The following chapter looks at the constituent elements of this topos and its function in texts by Scott, Dickens, Disraeli, Thackeray, and Braddon and argues that it was successful for so long not only because of the ideological issues it manages to finesse but also because of the technical problems it solves.

The chief of these is the problem of putting on display the modest woman who would be properly diffident about displaying herself. Good taste is understood as a legible sign of good character, but to be read it must be visible. While a man's activities offer many opportunities for such social visibility, a proper lady's do not. Architectural sequestration is a traditional sign of female chastity – the unplucked blossom in the walled garden comes to mind – with the result that the more chaste and retiring the tasteful heroine, the more difficult it will be for a lover to observe and appreciate her taste. One problem with interpreting Flora Mac-Ivor is that the showy way in which her personal style is dramatized implies, if not an ulterior motive on her part, at least a dubious theatricality. Self-display of this kind is impossible for a more conventional heroine without a Highland glen at her disposal. But the kind of display that is possible – the display of her polite 'accomplishments,' such as playing and singing, in public – is already the subject of a hostile 'anti-accomplishment' discourse, which sees the exercise of such talents as an incitement to vanity and superficiality.[4] In order to represent the heroine's good taste so that it shall be understood as a sign of her personal self-cultivation rather than of her desire to show herself off to a potential husband, the novelist needs to represent her developing and refining that taste in a private space that testifies to her modesty and interiority – a space no man would ordinarily enter. The problem, then, is to get the hero into what Goffman would call this 'backstage' area so that he can read the signs of her refinement: in other words, so that her taste will do the work that 'accomplishments' are designed to do and win the lady the husband that, by cultivating it, she has earned. The way Scott has Rose's virtues displayed to Waverley is an endorsement not only of the notion of the feminine sphere but also of the homosocial alliances of a patriarchal society.[5]

Rose Bradwardine's private apartment, though in a sense the heart of the household, is also cut off from it: secluded, even isolated, a miniature realm, self-contained and complete. In this *Romance of the Rose*, the domestic heroine's '*sanctum sanctorum*' (58) turns out to be even more difficult to penetrate than Flora's picturesque valley. Like a hero of Spenserian romance, Waverley has to be led a labyrinthine journey 'through one or two of those long awkward passages with which ancient architects studied to puzzle the inhabitants of the houses which they planned' and up the 'perpendicular cork-screw' of 'a very steep, narrow, and winding stair' (58) before he can emerge into the carefully demarcated space where Rose will receive him. This time it is the lady's father rather than her brother who acts as the go-between. While Fergus's role in setting up the meeting between Waverley and his sister has a faintly unpleasant aura, since he is exploiting her sexual charm to achieve a political aim, the Baron's sponsorship of Waverley is an appropriate prelude to the virtuous marriage that will eventually result from it, an affirmation of patriarchal arrangements that make the father the guardian of a woman's safety and virtue until she is handed over to her husband.

Every object and activity in Rose's apartment testifies to her good taste and to the wider virtues that good taste is understood to guarantee. For readers of Spenser, the space is 'templar,' that is, not only special and self-contained – penetrable by the hero only under particular well-controlled circumstances – but also exemplary, embodying feminine values of which the wider narrative needs to take account.[6] Rose's sequestration dramatizes her virginal and protected status: she is the as-yet-unplucked flower in a kind of battlemented garden. But the decor and accessories of the apartment also make clear her creative connection, first with her family, whose outdated allegiances she will transcend, and then with the world outside her window. To signal her family piety, the room, 'hung with tapestry,' is said to be

> adorned besides with two pictures, one of her mother, in the dress of a shepherdess, with a bell-hoop; the other of the Baron, in his tenth year, in a blue coat, embroidered waistcoat, laced hat, and bag-wig, with a bow in his hand.

Bradwardine explains that it was a 'woman's fantasy' of his mother's to have this picture painted, adding that the only other portrait ever made of him was done to celebrate 'his being the first to mount the breach of a fort in Savoy during the memorable campaign of 1709' (58). Both the paintings themselves and his remarks about them underline the distinction between masculine bellicosity and feminine 'fantasy,' while implicitly relegating both to a picturesque past that will turn out to be of limited relevance to the heroine. The presence of her parents' portraits on Rose's wall testifies to her filial affection, but the costume-party imagery of the two pictures marks her difference from them. Distressed rather than exhilarated by military violence, natural and unselfconscious in her demeanour, Rose will be oriented towards a prosaic, pacific future rather than a romantic, self-dramatizing past. In both her respect for and difference from her parents, she represents the potential for the family's translation to modernity.

The natural is the keynote of Rose's own portrait. There is a feeling of the extemporaneous about the men's visit – the Baron goes ahead two steps at a time to announce their arrival – and Rose seems, particularly compared with Flora, modest and anything but artful as she emerges from an interior room to greet them, still holding in her hand the 'little labours in which she had been employed.' Yet nature is immediately linked with art. These little labours – needlework of some kind – are too trivial to be further identified but not to be promptly decoded as the signs of 'a natural taste which required only cultivation' (58). The cliché is already a dead metaphor, but Rose's floral name brings the submerged botanical allusion to life. Like the emblematic flowers in *The Faerie Queene*, the 'bloosme of comely courtesie,' and the rose that closes its petals against the sun and 'sharpe Northern wind' but unfolds them when calm weather returns,[7] Rose is a plant who will receive the cultivation her nature merits when she can be taken out of the north wind by Waverley and transplanted to more fertile southern soil. Scott is able to use this conventional metaphor to anticipate not only Rose's personal future but also the Whig resolution towards which the novel will move.

He also uses it to endorse a predictable relationship between father-in-law and son-in-law, husband and wife. Before Waverley's arrival Rose's attainments have been real but limited. The Baron, classical scholar though he is himself, has taught his daughter two modern languages, French and Italian, and has 'ornamented her shelves' with only 'a few of the ordinary authors in those languages' (58). Rose is found to be 'uninformed' and provincial by Colonel Talbot, who considers her education is 'as ill adapted to her sex or youth, as if she had appeared with one of her father's old campaign coats upon her person for her sole garment' (247). But, as Talbot grants, 'simplicity may be improved' (291). The metaphors of the Scottish thistle and the English rose are implicit. Scott has Rose left uncultivated by her somewhat prickly Scottish father precisely so that her English lover will have the opportunity to make her bloom. Since, as Flora tells Waverley, 'The woman whom you marry ought to have affections and opinions moulded upon yours' (136), Waverley, even before he is aware he is falling in love with her, begins to function as her tutor, and Rose proves to be the exemplary pupil, deferring 'with eagerness to his remarks upon literature' and demonstrating 'great justness of taste in her answers' (64). To perfect her literary education Waverley sends home for copies of the 'best English poets, of every description, and other works on belles letters' (65) and also refines her established taste for romance, helping her with her translations of Tasso and no doubt perusing with her the Ariosto that, after the uprising, will be found beneath her window. Since for a woman these substantial Italian texts are signs not of irresponsible dreaminess but of intellectual effort and culture, Waverley, taking over where her father left off, can blamelessly pass on to Rose the enthusiasm for romance that he himself has to outgrow, depoliticizing it by relegating it to a feminized realm of literary taste.

This is a separate realm, but it is not to be understood as a limited one. On the contrary, Rose's horizons quickly expand as Waverley 'open[s] to her sources of delight of which she had hitherto had no idea' (65). The delicately sexual suggestion is that the domestic heroine, thus cultivated, will unfold and blossom into the 'new pleasures' (65) to which only her lover can introduce her and that she will be able to wander innocently through the landscapes of literal as well as literary romance even as she remains physically sheltered within the patriarchal estate. The discourse of taste is used to underwrite the doctrine of separate spheres by suggesting that the limited physical and social space to which a woman is confined is not really limiting: that through self-culture she can achieve subjective liberation without foregoing male protection.

The image of innocent wandering through an aestheticized landscape has already been adumbrated in the description of the prospect from Rose's window.[8] Her 'Gothic balcony,' a 'bartizan, or projecting gallery, before the windows of her parlour' – a space, 'crowded with flowers of different kinds,' that is itself a walled garden – looks out over the larger garden below, providing 'a most beautiful prospect' of the grounds and the landscape beyond them (59). The narrator's description of the scene as if it were a landscape painting is an ekphrasis that seems masculine in its discursive authority.[9] Aesthetic response offers errancy without error. As the reader's eye is both teased and guided from one plane to another, the image of firm boundaries is artfully played against the notion of willful wandering – scopic desire controlled and chastened by aesthetic form:

> The formal garden, with its high bounding walls, lay below, contracted, as it seemed to a mere parterre; while the view extended beyond them down a wooded glen, where the river was sometimes visible, sometimes hidden in copse. The eye might be delayed by a desire to rest on the rocks, which here and there rose from the dell with massive or spiry fronts, or it might dwell on the noble, though ruined tower, which was here seen in all its dig-

nity, frowning from a promontory over the river. To the left were seen two or three cottages, a part of the village; the brow of a hill concealed the others. The glen, or dell, was terminated by a sheet of water, called Loch Veolan, into which the brook discharged itself, and which now glistened in the western sun. The distant country seemed open and varied in surface, though not wooded; and there was nothing to interrupt the view until the scene was bounded by a ridge of distant and blue hills, which formed the southern boundary of the strath or valley. (59)

The eye, following the gleam of water, is led systematically to the vanishing point of the composition. But it is suddenly brought back at the end of the paragraph to the balcony itself – 'To this pleasant station' – and to Rose's duties as hostess: 'Miss Bradwardine had ordered coffee' (59). This rather abrupt conclusion, which by terminating the descriptive passage allows the narrative to move forward, sustains the paradox of freedom in confinement on which the whole chapter is based. Rose's domestic responsibilities are apparently no trammel on her inner freedom, here dramatized in terms of the reader's own aesthetic responsiveness to the view she enjoys. Rose's room may be small and sequestered, but the suggestion is that her mental landscape is limited only by her taste and sensibility.

Having dealt with the family portraits on Rose's walls, the handiwork on which she spends her time, the books she reads, the flowers she tends, and the view she enjoys, Scott moves on to the topic of her music, as systematically as if working down a list. As indeed he is: the description of Rose's apartment is based on the conventional list of the talents and competencies of the properly educated young lady. These competencies always come in sets, as they must do to preserve the distinction between properly feminine charm, which is consistent with amateur activities in a number of areas, and the achievement of the serious artist: between mere taste, which is pleasingly decorative, and genius, which in a woman would be threatening if not 'unnatural.' The enclosure/ expansion binary on which the description of Rose's singing and playing is based underwrites a second binary – amateur/professional – that is equally important for the construction of the feminine norm. Miss Bradwardine's music is not a public accomplishment: she performs, as Mrs Chapone would have a young woman do,[10] for her family's gratification, singing only when 'called upon' (59) by her father. Since her musical education has been rudimentary, she has 'made no proficiency further than to be able to accompany her voice with the harpsichord,' and though 'even this was not very common in Scotland at that period' (59), her technical skill is deficient by English standards. But her provincialism has compensations. Because Rose is not a skilled technician, she pays extra attention to the words of the song:

> To make amends, she sung with great taste and feeling, and with a respect to the sense of what she uttered that might be proposed in example to ladies of much superior musical talent. (59)

Her musicality, thus differentiated from both superficial feminine accomplishments and serious masculine art, is aligned with 'sense,' and that sense, though 'natural' to Rose herself, is promptly gendered masculine by Scott's management of the metaphor that follows, with its allusion to the 'high authority' of a male poet:

> Her natural good sense taught her, that if, as we are assured by high authority, music 'be married to immortal verse,' they are very often divorced by the performer in a most shameful manner. (59)

In this male-female union, music would seem to be female and words male, if only because the 'immortal verse' quoted here is that of John Milton.[11] The nuptial metaphor suggests both that equality is as desirable in a good marriage as in a good song and that the woman fit for equality – a woman like Rose, whose music defers to male words – demonstrates that fitness by recognizing the principle of subordination.

The words/music polarity will be played out again in chapter 54, and the relationship between feminine taste and masculine genius reiterated, when Rose votes for Waverley's reading of Shakespeare over Fergus's performance on the flute. Her connection with Shakespeare is already established, however, in the scene in her apartment, in a slightly more complicated way, so as to suggest Rose's openness to the world around her. When the conversation turns to a particular peak visible in the distance, the peak popularly known as St Swithin's Chair, and to the 'popular superstition' associated with it, and Waverley is reminded 'of a rhyme quoted by Edgar in King Lear,' Rose is 'called upon to sing a little legend' of an anonymous 'village poet' (59): to supply a folkloric footnote to Waverley's quotation. Her song, enhanced by the 'sweetness of her voice, and the simple beauty of her music' (60), tells of a lady who goes out on All Hallow's Eve to seek from the Night-Hag information about the fate of her husband, only to be found the next morning 'clay-cold upon the grounsill ledge' (61). This embedded narrative, suggesting as it does that, for a woman, venturing out of the home and asking questions can be fatal, turns on the tension between inside and outside, exposure and protection on which the whole chapter is based. Rose apparently rejects its moral. She does not sing the song to its conclusion, and when she laughs at the story and she and her father go on to repudiate the kind of superstition that it expresses, the suggestion is that she feels herself limited by no such gendered prohibition. Indeed, her very familiarity with these legends and ballads implies not Rose's isolation from what is outside the home but rather a sympathetic openness to the folk culture of the surrounding area. Her interest in local folklore is in turn promptly associated with her father's sense of responsibility for the people who depend upon the Bradwardine family, as the talk turns to the Baron's defence of the 'witch' Janet Gellatley, 'born on his estate' (61). Though Rose's own acts of communal benevolence remain merely metaphorical – it is the flowers on her balcony rather than the individuals connected with the estate that she is said to have 'taken under her special protection' (59) – it is made clear that her sheltered existence is not incompatible with an interest in the lives and literary traditions of the local people. The episode not only suggests the complementarity of Shakespeare and ballad, 'high' and folk culture, enlightenment rationality and a taste for local legend, but positions Rose, with her expansive, cultivated taste, as bridging the gap between them.

In her barricaded garden aerie, Rose is, in short, associated in the most positive way with both nature and culture: with music and poetry; with landscape and landscape painting; with flowers; with organic development, social responsibility, and cultural responsiveness. The woman's-room topos allows Scott to develop a series of systematic and nuanced equations between the aesthetic sphere on the one hand and the social, moral, and political spheres on the other, so as to make the implicit claim that the apparent limitations of sheltered feminine life in a constricted space are no limitations at all: that in exercising her taste, the heroine has full scope for her abilities; that she can travel mentally if not physically, unfold and blossom, even as she serves the needs of her family and community. By linking her responses to painting, landscape, gardening, and music both with the development of her own faculties and also with various kinds of social sympathy and service, Scott implies an unproblematic congruence between the aesthetic and the social, between individual self-culture and social obligation. As he presents it, the situation of a cultivated woman is to be understood as bounded only by the horizon.[12] Self-cultivation, anything but solipsistic, is fully compatible with responsiveness to the wider community.

The woman's-room topos in *Waverley* carries another political message as well. The very notion of the landscape prospect, as has often been pointed out, endorses the political and economic hegemony of the landed gentry. The novel as a whole makes clear that the kind of environment in which feminine culture can best unfold is an estate like Waverley-Honour, which has in reality the sunny 'prospect' that Tully Veolan only seems to offer. As Waverley is shortly to discover, the Baron does not control the country Rose's balcony surveys, and her physical security is not assured. The battered copy of Ariosto that, after the uprising, Waverley finds on the ground beneath Rose's balcony makes clear that the domain of feminine taste can remain intact only within a stable social and political order. Rose's apartment looks south, and the south is where her destiny will lie. The promise implied by the view from her balcony can be kept only in a nation that guarantees the security of property and the stability of the landed estate. In such a society, confinement to the female social sphere is, it is suggested, fully compatible with true freedom. In short, Scott's elaborate if conventional presentation of Rose's personal space serves not only to endorse the doctrine of separate spheres but also to connect it with the English constitution.[13] The woman's-room topos is one of the means by which Scott aligns political progressiveness with social conservatism.[14]

If Scott's treatment of Rose's *Troisième Étage* already has the flavour of an established convention, on what model might he have been drawing? It has been suggested that Fanny Price's East room in *Mansfield Park* is based on the apartment of Emily St Aubert, the beleaguered heroine of Anne Radcliffe's *The Mysteries of Udolpho* – not the terrifying room in the castle, but the less memorable one in which she is originally brought up and from which she is ejected by her father's death into a wicked and complicated world[15] – and it is probable that Rose's room also owes something to Radcliffe. Certainly what might be called the carceral boudoir in Scott's *Kenilworth* – the ominously luxurious Cumnor House in which Varney installs Amy Robsart – invites comparison with Philippe de Montalt's magnificent saloon in *The Romance of the Forest*.[16] In both Scott's and Radcliffe's novels, the spaces that define and/or confine the heroines are carefully demarcated and more or less closed off, and in both they function as a refuge (or not) from the wider world of male violence. In a couple of decades at the beginning of the nineteenth century, at the moment when the middle-class values of self-cultivation and feminized gentility were gaining ascendancy and woman's situation in a man's world was being both sensationalized and sentimentalized, we see the emergence of an enduring fictional topos.

*The Mysteries of Udolpho*, which promises escape into the landscape of gothic adventure, starts out in the domestic realm of private taste, a realm from which the heroine will be expelled and to which she is destined to return. In the first few pages the reader is introduced to the cultivated life Emily lives in the family home La Vallée, a comparatively modest structure – originally 'merely a summer cottage,' not a stone of which her father will alter, though 'considerable additions were necessary to make it a comfortable family residence' (2) – and to her own apartment, which is precisely located in the larger building. The front of the house has 'a southern aspect,' looking out on 'the grandeur of the mountains' (4); the library faces west; there is a greenhouse 'adjoining the library' (3); and 'adjoining the eastern side of the greenhouse, looking towards the plains of Languedoc' – that is, facing southeast, where in the sunny morning of her life, she would get the morning sun – is 'the south parlour' (593),

> a room, which Emily called hers, and which contained her books, her drawings, her musical instruments, and some favourite birds and plants. Here she usually exercised herself in elegant arts, cultivated because they were congenial to her taste, and in which native genius, assisted by the instructions of Monsieur and Madame St. Aubert, made her an early proficient.

Emily is destined not to spend very many pages in this apartment, but it remains the standard of virtuous, cultivated innocence against which the world of gothic experience is to be measured and by which its terrors are to be withstood.

Though its situation in the house is carefully spelled out, there is something rather abstract about Emily's room as an architectural space. Though we are told exactly where to find it on the ground floor of the chateau, once we are inside it the chamber has no spatial features. Its emblematic contents – 'her books, her drawing, her musical instruments ... some favourite birds and plants' – are listed rather than located in space and exist only to testify to the stereotypical accomplishments of the novelistic heroine. The paragraph is a tissue of clichés: all these heroines who cultivate their individual taste turn out to be individual in almost exactly the same way. Like Rose Bradwardine, Emily has 'native genius,' but hers has already been thoroughly 'cultivated': the botanical metaphor both implies that she is of good seed and endorses her application and effort. It goes almost without saying that she enjoys caring for birds and plants, activities that endow her with a kind of aestheticized maternal aura, and that she is adept at music, at drawing, and at all the other 'elegant arts': it is an axiom of this discourse that good taste in one field implies good taste in all. Emily is also an avid reader. It is not surprising that she has developed 'in her early years a taste for works of genius' (6), since as the only surviving child she has been lovingly tutored by her father, a considerably more polished gentleman than the Baron Bradwardine:

> St. Aubert cultivated her understanding with the most scrupulous care. He gave her a general view of the sciences, and an exact acquaintance with every part of elegant literature. He taught her Latin and English, chiefly that she might understand the sublimity of the best poets. (6)

This is the kind of rigorous education that feminist writers were advocating for women and produces in the idealized heroine just the balance between sensibility and strength of mind that they hoped it would. Emily has both elegant accomplishments and solid learning – there is no need to choose between them in this novel – and the result is an exemplary feminine character. 'Virtue is little more than active taste' (49), her father believes, condensing Shaftesbury's assertion, and in cultivating her taste he has also established her virtue. Madame Montoni, who despises her niece's fineness of feeling, contemptuously attributes it to her education, but along with this feeling goes a moral and spiritual strength that will sustain the heroine in her adventures outside La Vallée.

Emily's room is precisely located not only within the house but also in relation to the landscape around it. *The Mysteries of Udolpho* is a book of views, and it is in keeping with her emphasis on visual marvels and delights that Radcliffe should describe the view from the chief windows of La Vallée and make clear the way in which the principal rooms relate to the surrounding landscape. M. St Aubert's library looks towards the Pyrenees, and he and his wife often pass days botanizing 'among the neighbouring mountains' (3). The windows of Emily's room, which 'descended to the floor,' are 'particularly pleasant,' and so is the view from them: less sublime than her parents', more beautiful. Like Scott, Radcliffe makes viewing the prospect sound like 'reading' a painting:

Opening upon the little lawn that surrounded the house, the eye was led between groves of almond, palm-trees, flowering-ash, and myrtle, to the distant landscape, where the Garonne wandered. (3)

The axis is horizontal, in contrast to the dizzy verticality of the sublime mountains and castles in which Emily will subsequently be trapped, and the description turns on a gentle tension between stasis and movement: between the rooted plants and the caged birds and the peaceful employments in a private space on the one hand and the unfolding landscape – the wandering river, the moving (though not wandering) eye – on the other. The static quality of the description suggests that aesthetic contemplation is enough: that the shelter and enclosure offered by La Vallée are not constraining and that the mental culture Emily enjoys there provides her with all the exercise she needs. If a woman has a window, she does not need a door: where the eye is led, the foot need not follow. As a gothic heroine Emily is destined to travel, and the reader's impatience to get her out of this sheltered haven and into a more sublime scene and horrid situation is itself perhaps a critique of the ideology of domesticity endorsed by the woman's-room topos. But the implicit claim is that this tasteful domain fully suffices for the heroine's happiness.

It is a domain on which she will continue to draw as her adventures unfold. Emily's culture is portable, and her room travels with her, in that she is always ready to recreate it at a moment's notice. Every time she gets a moment of stability, Emily pulls out her books and sketching materials, and though given her fraught existence she seems unlikely to get much reading done, it is clear that she will happily settle down and live in a room like the one she has left as soon as she gets the chance. The physical space she is brought up in is thus identified, by its portability, with Emily's moral autonomy. At the end of the novel, despite the machinations of her aunt's evil husband, the family estate will be restored to her; but the reason that she can truly possess it is that she has carried it with her all along.

Access to Emily's private space is an issue throughout the novel. Her room at La Vallée is presented as a self-contained unit. The view from the window orients the room to the outside world, but there is no mention of an interior door that communicates with the rest of the house, and we never see Emily inside her room in the company of another person. Indeed, she is never actually seen inside it at all: no individual scene takes place here, her habitual activities being catalogued only in the past continuous tense. Imaginatively, the domestic space seems protected, sealed off in its privacy, in dramatic contrast to her room in the Castle of Udolpho, which has two doors that can never be secured against violent male penetration. But though it is the alarums and excursions of this gothic plot that compel the reader's imagination, Emily's ultimate destiny is in fact being shaped by a less theatrical kind of male penetration: the entry of the two men who love her into spaces where she feels no gothic threat.

In a plot constructed to deliver a happy marriage, the heroine's interiority is of little use if no man takes note of it. Though the implication is that the tastes nurtured within the protected feminine sphere are private resources for her own self-culture, an essential function of the woman's room in a novel is to make these tastes manifest: to display her excellences and accomplishments, not only to the reader, but to the men who will fall in love with her. Emily's admirers need to be given an opportunity to scrutinize and judge Emily's essential nature. As a result, in *The Mysteries of Udolpho*, as in many novels that follow it, the lover is made to penetrate the 'backstage' space that testifies to her taste so that he can peruse it at leisure. Such scenes of inspection are not always easy to manage, and the awkward ways in which novelists solve the problem draw attention to the contradictions it is invented to resolve.

Emily meets her destined husband Valancourt only after she has left La Vallée, and there is no question of his entry into it while she is in residence. But when the two have been separated and Emily detained far from her native countryside, Valancourt is admitted to the house by a sponsor, the family servant Theresa, a woman whom he has saved from destitution and established in residence and who later describes his fascination with the place in terms of the conventional list of female accomplishments. As Theresa will tell Emily:

'Why, when you was away, mademoiselle, he used to come to the chateau and walk about it, so disconsolate! He would go into every room in the lower part of the house, and, sometimes, he would sit himself down in a chair, with his arms across, and his eyes on the floor, and there he would sit, and think, and think, for the hours together. He used to be very fond of the south parlour, because I told him it used to be yours; and there he would stay, looking at the pictures, which I said you drew, and playing upon your lute, that hung up by the window, and reading in your books, until sunset.'
(593–4)

If this is a kind of voyeurism, it is a tempered and mediated kind. Odder and more intense is the somewhat creepy surveillance of Emily's other admirer, Du Pont, a neighbour who, smitten with her from a distance, has been prevented by his father from paying her his addresses. Du Pont in effect stalks Emily, spying on her, following her to the fishing house that is one of her favourite haunts, listening to her music, and leaving behind ardent sonnets that describe his response to

> Her soul-illumin'd eyes,
> The sweet expression of her pensive face,
> The light'ning smile, the animated grace ... (7)

This is an oddly intimate and close-up shot of a face focalized by a hidden voyeur. The point made by this peeping-Tom scenario is that Emily's investment in her music, her books, and her sketching is genuine and unselfconscious. But the need to resort to such a ludicrous and unsavoury situation suggests that the model of sealed-off female autonomy that Radcliffe is constructing is indeed a fictional one.

Later novelists faced with the same problem solve it in less transparent but not always less problematical ways. Though few go so far as to have the lover lurking in the bushes, the need to expedite his intimate exposure to the heroine has generated in some novels, Charlotte Brontë's, for example, scenarios of surveillance that, though they may be technical in origin, seem to have psychological and political implications. The intruder into a woman's private space must be unobserved and/or unexpected so that her inability to prepare for his inspection can testify to the reliability of the evidence he is there to decode. The heroine must be given no chance to strike an artful pose or to devise in advance a scenario that will display her to best advantage. There is an obvious paradox here. The heroine's private chamber must be understood as a space of true privacy, an emblem of her interiority, a space where she can evade the demands made on her by a coercive social environment and cultivate her authentic nature. Charlotte Brontë, for example, who has a deep investment in such notions, has Jane Eyre declare that, when she was alone creating the pictures Rochester inspects, 'I was absorbed ... I was happy. To paint them, in short, was to enjoy one of the keenest pleasures I have ever known' ( 121). But the fact that Jane's assertion is an answer to a question of Rochester's ('Were you happy when you painted these pictures?' 121) has a certain irony, suggesting that the real payoff for these private pleasures comes only when they begin to serve as signs, to a man one wants to impress, of one's intriguing interiority. The woman's-room topos, however suavely it is developed, tends to raise the very questions about a woman's relationship to the wider social order that it is designed to occlude.

Underlying all of these question is the issue of male financial support. The objects in the woman's room – drawings, music, flowers, birds, books – are not, in Scott and Radcliffe, envisaged in terms of their monetary value, which would be modest. They are represented as valuable not in themselves but merely because they allow the heroine to develop her taste and expand her nature. The point of private, amateur activities like needlework, singing, and drawing is not just to produce beautiful objects but to produce, by means of one's cultural activity, an enhanced self of which these objects are the signs. It becomes a truism of the period that one practises drawing less to learn to draw than to learn to see.[17] The worth of the objects in the heroine's room, which is sentimental and moral rather than material, depends on the value added by her cultural work upon them. The role of a woman's male protector is not so much to buy her things as to provide her with the arena in which she can use them for her own self-culture and in the service of her family. The financial cost of these practices (and of the style of life that permits them) is suppressed so that they can be read as the expression of the woman's essential nature rather than of her economic situation.

Insofar as the woman's room is represented as insulated from – as somehow transcending – economic issues, it spiritualizes the proper lady and thus the very property on which her propriety is based.[18] Even though the plot in which Emily St Aubert becomes involved is motivated by her uncle's lust for her family property, Emily herself never has to think about money. Her steadfastness under Montoni's pressure, which is figured as a sexual threat, is the spiritual authority of the virgin, and her fitness to inherit the estate can be demonstrated not by her ability actively to foil his plot but simply by her embodiment of the cultural values for which the property stands. She inherits the property because of her own metonymic relationship to it: she herself is the 'property' that will give the home its value for its male proprietor. The issue negotiated by the woman's-room convention is the heroine's relationship to men (specifically, to the man who has put her into this room, that is, her father or whoever acts for him, and the man who will take her out of it into a home of her own, that is, her prospective husband), her dependence upon them for financial support, and the service she provides in return: the performance of 'vicarious leisure.'

The topos in short offers imaginary solutions to real problems, and when its constituent elements are skewed or rearranged, the speciousness of its solutions is made clear. I find five key elements in this topos: a room, a set of tastes, a view, a voyeur, and a backer – that is, a specific physical space, characterized by its limitedness, which suggests the woman's independence, autonomy, and contentment; a set of tastes, figured as a set of objects, which is practised within this private space and which suggests her multi-faceted (and thus unthreatening) self-development; a view, characterized by its expansiveness, which affirms her connection to the outside world; a male voyeur, whose function is to get into the room, read her taste, perceive her excellence, and engage himself to support it; and a male backer, whose money and property enable the woman to inhabit this space. When these elements are split up, redistributed, suppressed, or foregrounded, the contradictions the topos attempts to occult are made visible, and the positive vision of female autonomy breaks down into irony, satire, or parody.

Dickens, who loves lists, who is fascinated by obsession, and who likes to construct his characters in terms of the bizarre little spaces in which they live, develops these conventions with ebullient ingenuity. Though he can use the woman's-room discourse in a blandly orthodox way, as I shall show in the next chapter, parodying it releases in Dickens a misogynistic energy that produces much more intense comic or dramatic scenarios. What particularly attracts Dickens's satire, as it does that of Jane Austen and many other writers of the period, is the cultivation of female 'accomplishments,' those conventional feminine skills that, when they move out of the lady's private apartment and into the drawing room, are consistently associated with flirtation, attention-seeking, and artistic incompetence. In Dickens such a move becomes not only a sign of vanity but also an act of usurpation: the wife who shows off her talents appropriates for herself the living space that ought to be sanctified to 'family values.' The drawing room of the widowed Mrs Bayham Badger, for example, is spitefully described by Esther Summerson, the domestic angel of *Bleak House*, as littered with evidence of her aesthetic pretensions:

She was surrounded in the drawing-room by various objects, indicative of her painting a little, playing the piano a little, playing the guitar a little, playing the harp a little, singing a little, working a little, reading a little, writing poetry a little, and botanising a little. She was a lady of about fifty, I should think, youthfully dressed, and of a very fine complexion. If I add, to the little list of her accomplishments, that she rouged a little, I do not mean that there was any harm in it. (132)

This woman, who is Richard Carstone's landlady, is a very minor character in *Bleak House*, but Dickens spins out the conceit with comic extravagance. Mrs Badger, who considers herself 'still young' and 'an acquisition to every society' (173), has a pair of deceased husbands to go with her own set of accomplishments, both of whom have provided her with groups of young men to flirt with and each of whom is assigned a single vocational mania. Her first, Swosser, a naval Captain, cannot express himself except in naval language ('when you make pitch hot, you cannot make it too hot'); her second, Professor Dingo, an archaeologist who while on his honeymoon in Devon offended the local people 'by chipping off fragments of the houses and other buildings with his little geological hammer,' 'in his last illness ... (his mind wandering) ... insisted on keeping his little hammer under the pillow, and chipping at the countenances of the attendants' (175). That these two obsessively active men have predeceased her raises the suspicion that Mrs Badger's own even more frenetic self-obsession may have simply worn them out.

While the shallowly versatile Mrs Badger is a comic figure, the single-talent woman tends to be represented as a pathetic yet also somewhat sinister monomaniac. A number of Dickens's most grotesque female figures are characterized in terms of one obsessive feminine activity pursued in a claustrophobically enclosed space. For music, we have the blighted harpist Rose Dartle, cast off and disfigured by James Steerforth, whose silent miming of musical performance enacts her rage both at the man who has ruined her and at his mother, with whom she is forced to live. For aviculture, we have crazy Miss Flite, subsisting in a bare room over Krook's junk shop, who has given her birds names that recapitulate the story of her life: 'Hope, Joy, Youth, Peace, Rest, Life, Dust, Ashes, Waste, Want, Ruin, Despair, Madness, Death, Cunning, Folly, Words, Wigs, Rags, Sheepskin, Plunder, Precedent, Jargon, Gammon, and Spinach' (152). For tasteful needlework, we have Jenny Wren, the doll's dressmaker, who copies the costumes of the rich and fashionable to support herself and her alcoholic father. The compelling caricature of this stunted and prematurely aged child, which reminds us what happens when women's genteel accomplishments are forced into the marketplace, makes clear that the flip side of the woman's room is the seam-stress's garret or the sweatshop. Dickens is savagely aware of how dependent is the woman's sphere on the heterosexual economy in which women have to find their place, but though he may invite our sympathy for these damaged women, who have been wrecked by a social system he critiques, he nevertheless makes them all more or less gro-tesque, drawing on the conventional feminine pursuits to produce the vision of a specifically feminine deformation of personality. In the most extreme and parodic ways, Dickens associates the cultivation of woman's talent with moral and social disorder and the collapse of 'family values.'

These female obsessives, minor or secondary characters, are repre-sented as social victims. When a major character in a Dickens novel affects accomplishments of her own instead of properly nurturing her husband's genius, however, she becomes less a victim than an aggressive parasite. From the moment David Copperfield meets her, Dora Spenlow is consistently associated with flowers and characterized by a childish devotion to trivial decorative arts: flower painting, guitar playing, sing-ing sentimental songs. Though David is impressed, Dora's failure to master the practical domestic arts is the corollary of her complacency with her own accomplishments. Even before her marriage to David, objects associated with her aesthetic pretensions colonize their future home. Like Waverley, David gets a proleptic survey of a space shaped by his future bride:

> Such a beautiful little house it is, with everything so bright and new; with the flowers on the carpets looking as if freshly gathered, and the green leaves on the paper as if they had just come out; with the spotless muslin curtains, and the blushing rose-coloured furniture, and Dora's garden hat with the blue ribbon – do I remember, now, how I loved her in such another hat when I first knew her! – already hanging on its little peg; the guitar-case quite at home on its heels in a corner; and everybody tumbling over Jip's Pagoda, which is much too big for the establishment. (482)

David is enchanted, reading the room as an emblem of Dora herself, of her charm and taste. But this space is not to be Dora's alone, but Dora's and David's, and its ominous code is easy to decipher. It is a kind of gar-den, but an artificial and lifeless garden, with the usual view from the window displaced into leafy wallpaper and the flowers that it is the con-ventional heroine's task to nurture reproduced in the carpet. It is a transparently illusory Eden, which, allowing for no growth, points to an inevitable fall. Once married, Dora nurtures, not her husband, but her little dog Jip, whose miniature but oversize pagoda takes over the parlour, just as her frivolous hobbies, in a monstrous act of usurpation, swell to fill up the whole house. In due time, when David has become frustrated by Dora's inability to run their home efficiently, we get a second view of the same room, a view that makes clear how her light-mindedness has shrunk the house and diminished David's life. Trying to squeeze their dinner guest Tommy Traddles in round the dinner-table, David realizes that

> though there were only two of us, we were at once always cramped for room, and yet had always room enough to lose everything in. I suspect it may have been because nothing had a place of its own, except Jip's pagoda, which invariably blocked up the main thoroughfare. On the present occasion, Traddles was so hemmed in by the pagoda and the guitar-case, and Dora's flower-painting, and my writing-table, that I had serious doubts of the possibility of his using his knife and fork. (491)

As a 'vicarious consumer,' Dora is a failure: not only, as Langland points out, does she fail to portray the family status accurately,[19] but also, by continuing to display the accomplishments she developed when she was supported by her father, she emasculates David by implying that the handover from father to husband is not complete. Dora's refusal to discipline her pet – Jip is 'encouraged to walk about the table-cloth during dinner ... putting his foot in the salt or the melted-butter' – marks the collapse of proper hierarchy here, but more telling, if less graphic and funny, is the fact that her incompetent flower painting claims equal space with the budding novelist's writing, the vocation by which he is beginning to support the household.[20] Because Dora's financial backer is David and she is wasting his substance, she is in a sense a kept woman. The tone in this passage is light, but her vanity and incompetence spell Dora's doom. A woman who cultivates an unworthy notion of female charm rather than the domestic skills that would enable her to serve the household cannot be allowed to survive if her husband's story is to have a happy ending.

When the woman's-room space expands to fill the whole house in *David Copperfield*, the result is unpropitious. But this development may also be presented as a social ideal, one that writers less hostile than Dickens to feminine self-cultivation can eagerly endorse. Disraeli is one such writer.

Predictably, the novelist who declares in *Coningsby* that 'there is no end to the influence of woman on our life' (380) – that 'the continual society of refined and charming women ... refines the taste, quickens the perception, and gives, as it were, a grace and flexibility to the intellect' (226) – represents the domestic spaces he describes not only as permeated by that wholesome feminine influence but also as filled with conventional woman's-room objects and activities.

*Coningsby*, Disraeli's Young England novel, follows the eponymous hero from Eton to the beginning of his political career. The story of Coningsby's political and emotional development is intertwined with that of his school friends, Lord Henry Sydney and Ernest Lyle, ardent idealists who propose to solve the problem of working-class poverty by restoring what they are determined to call 'the order of the peasantry' to 'its pristine condition' and by bringing back its traditional 'manners, customs, ceremonies, rites and privileges' (118). All the major characters in the novel are polarized in terms of their attitude to this solution and, more generally, in terms of their sense of social responsibility. Coningsby's widowed grandfather and guardian, the Marquis of Monmouth, 'the wealthiest noble in England' (7), represents the irresponsible aristocrat who lives 'almost constantly abroad' (12) in 'luxurious retirement in Italy' (12); it is a sign of his lack of interest in his dependants that he leaves Coningsby Castle empty for most of the year. The philanthropic Sydney family, by contrast, who live year-round on their estate ('There was not a country-house in England that had so completely the air of habitual residence as Beaumanoir' [112]), are concerned about the problem of the poor and earnestly looking for ways to solve it. The men of the family use the 'little half hour' (116) after dinner when they withdraw from the ladies to debate political solutions, while the female members of the household, 'deeply sensible of the responsibility of their position,' undertake 'their pilgrimages of charity and kindness' to the underclass with the requisite 'earnestness' and with gratifying results: a visibly 'superior tone' in the 'peasantry' they succour 'to that which we too often witness' (130).

The homes of these two families are polarized along the same lines. The Sydneys' paternalistic relationship with the 'peasants' who depend upon them is analogous to their ardent family feeling. Arriving as a guest at Beaumanoir, Coningsby is impressed by 'a family bound together by the most beautiful affections' (13–14); entering their morning-room, a woman's-room space where men are made welcome, he is smitten with delight. Free indirect discourse aligns the character's values with the narrator's:

How delightful was the morning-room at Beaumanoir; from which gentle-men were not excluded with that assumed suspicion that they can never enter it but for felonious purposes. Such a profusion of flowers! Such a multitude of books! Such a various prodigality of writing materials! So many easy chairs too, of so many shapes; each in itself a comfortable home; yet nothing crowded ... And the ladies' work! How graceful they look bend-ing over their embroidery frames, consulting over the arrangement of a group, or the colour of a flower. The panniers and fanciful baskets over-flowing with variegated worsted, are gay and full of pleasure to the eye, and give an air of elegant business that is vivifying ... Then the morning cos-tume of English women is itself a beautiful work of art. At this period of the day they can find no rivals in other climes. The brilliant complexions of the daughters of the north dazzle in the daylight; the illumined saloon levels all distinctions. (112–13)

This woman's-room space, now moved into the very centre of the home, testifies not only to feminine charm but also to national character, social responsibility, and 'family values,' and its conventional props – books, flowers, needlework, writing materials – function in the conventional way, not as material possessions but as resonant signs of moral taste.

In a second set piece, the narrator pairs this happy home with sterile, decadent Coningsby Castle. 'Nothing,' we are told, 'could present a greater contrast' than these two architectural spaces. While the charm of Beaumanoir derives from its status as a year-round residence, Con-ingsby, the seat of an absentee landlord, is grand but at the same time both cold and vulgar, marred by the aura of impermanence and the tasteless juxtaposition of old and new articles:

Everything, indeed, was vast and splendid; but it seemed rather a gala-house than a dwelling; as if the grand furniture and the grand servants had all come down express from town with the grand company, and were to dis-appear and to be dispersed at the same time. And truly there were mani-fold traces of hasty and temporary arrangement; new carpets and old hangings; old paint, new gilding; battalions of odd French chairs, squad-rons of queer English tables; and large tasteless lamps and tawdry chande-liers, evidently true cockneys, and only taking the air by way of change. (176)

Household articles, unilluminated by love and culture, are rendered demonic: jumbled together without any order or decorum, they announce their status as mere commodities. Disraeli fuses aristocratic decadence with new-money vulgarity and equates them both with shopping. The problem with those cockney lamps and chandeliers, apparently, is that somebody has recently bought them and brought them up from London: their newness and urban origin make them into improbable signs of crude financial power.

Predictably, the female guests at Coningsby fail to fulfill their social responsibilities even to the rest of the company. Their women's-room activities are actively antisocial, characterized by either frivolous dispersal or self-indulgent withdrawal:

> The modes and manners of the house were not rural; there was nothing of the sweet order of a country life. Nobody came down to breakfast; the ladies were scarcely seen until dinner-time; they rolled about in carriages together late in the afternoon as if they were in London, or led a sort of factitious boudoir life in their provincial dressing-rooms. (176–7)

Coningsby is consistently constructed by negation, as the polar opposite of Beaumanoir. Describing its drawing room, Disraeli enumerates yet again the conventional set of morally charged objects, simply to point out that Coningsby lacks them:

> There was ... an absence of all those minor articles of ornamental furniture that are the offering of taste to the home we love. There were no books neither; few flowers; no pet animals; no portfolios of fine drawings by our English artists ... full of sketches by Landseer and Stanfield, and their gifted brethren; not a print even, except portfolios of H.B.'s caricatures. (176)

The absence of these fetishized and feminized *things* in the Coningsby drawing room is congruent with the absence of the decorous activities and wholesome routines that Disraeli identifies with English country life. The 'minor articles of ornamental furniture' at Beaumanoir must also have been purchased, perhaps even in London, but their provenance is elided by their association with what Disraeli sees as productive modes of feminine activity, and the objects mystified as sign of these modes.

The discourse of domestic taste tries to make us forget that objects ever cost money by making them into signs of love and culture. Yet Disraeli's insistent catalogue of desirable objects tilts toward the shopping list, simply because of the specificity of the individual items and their availability to contemporary consumers. The description of the drawing room makes Landseer and Stanfield, artists whose images became clichés of the Victorian middle-class interior, into something like brand names, and these brands into signs of domestic harmony and virtue.[21] The reader, introduced with Coningsby into Beaumanoir's morning room, is expected to read its signs as he does – to spiritualize the objects that Disraeli enumerates. But when particular objects that can be purchased are made to signify values that transcend money, a topos devised to testify to individual mental culture easily becomes a rationalization for consumer display.[22]

Such display becomes the overt theme in *Dombey and Son, Vanity Fair,* and the novels of Mary Elizabeth Braddon, and when it does the woman's-room topos is turned upside down. When the two sets of signs cross – when the luxury items that announce male financial power are moved into the woman's private chamber; the relatively inexpensive things that express the woman's own taste replaced by costly objects (silks, satins, laces, and jewels) that express the taste of the man who gave them to her – the novelistic heroine finds herself inside the demonic parody of the woman's room, the sinister and claustrophobic boudoir.[23]

The description of the boudoir is a complementary novelistic paradigm, emphasizing not the bounty that a woman has to give but the material support she needs to secure. The 'boudoir' topos foregrounds precisely what the 'woman's room' is designed to suppress: that marriage is a market transaction and that what a woman chiefly has to sell is her aesthetic value. It dramatizes not the woman's self-sufficiency but her dependence on a man, not her integrity or moral autonomy but her willingness to sell out – as well as her ability to attract a backer who is willing to buy. A man who finances a woman's feminine charm has purchased her, and her price, whether paid in satins and jewels or in flowers and books and watercolours, is therefore determinate and calculable. But the boudoir emphasizes what the woman's-room topos occludes: the radical dependence of the woman on the man who has provided her with a place to live, the tenuousness of her position, and the limits of her autonomy, particularly her lack of control over her own space and time. Plots that develop around a female 'boudoir' character often make a point of the fact that marriage is a deal between the woman and her backer, a deal that, from his point of view, she is refusing to fulfill. A bargain of this kind has to be demonized in order to occult what it has in common with ordinary marriage.

Like the woman's room, the boudoir is set off from the rest of the house and indeed from the outside world as a whole. But separateness now has a negative rather than a positive valence. Instead of a window with a view, drawing the eye outward, there is likely to be a mirror, fixing the woman within a claustrophobic circle. Despite its self-enclosedness, however, this space is not protected or secure. On the contrary, the woman, dependent on the man who provided her with these costly accoutrements, finds herself unable to keep him out of it. Since this woman has been positioned not as an active subject, a mind, but as a passive object for display, a body, male penetration of the space where that body is groomed for display has sexual implications, and the man who enters it is felt to be an intruder. In an emblematic image that recurs with surprising frequency, his startled face in her mirror, not only suggests his alienation from her but also constitutes, by its rupture, the closed circuit of the lady's narcissism.

As problematic as the backer's own intrusion is the relationship between this backer and the voyeur figure. Often the two functions are fused into one, the husband himself figuring as the intrusive voyeur. Sometimes, however, the husband sponsors the entrance of a second voyeur who functions as his partner or double. Homosocial triangles proliferate in these novels, sometimes in peculiar and arresting ways. It is one thing for Rose Bradwardine's father to introduce Waverley into his daughter's apartment; it is quite another to have Dombey insist on Carker's attendance in his wife's boudoir. Yet the rather insistent parallels that Scott himself sets up between the two scenes of penetration do allow us to register that Baron Bradwardine has in fact achieved, through Rose's liaison with Waverley, what Fergus wanted to achieve through Flora's: the backer has secured, by means of the woman he sponsors, the voyeur's social and financial help. Despite the emphasis on heterosexual love in these novels, the voyeur's willingness to represent or act on behalf of the backer suggests that the woman is merely an object through which men's relationships with each other are played out, and that the real issue is the circulation of patriarchal power and wealth.[24]

Since the gifts with which the lady is surrounded represent tributes that she has secured by her personal charm and accomplishments, the metaphor of prostitution is inevitable if often implicit, and her relationship with her backer is usually disturbed and may be temporary. The silks, satins, jewels, and trinkets are typically scattered about in careless disorder, an image that suggests that she neither owns nor values these things, which have been chosen not by her but for her, by the same man who also chose the woman herself. Like them, she is an acquisition, an object to be displayed. Lacking a window that connects her with the wider world, the lady has to find the door. The plot often turns on her ejection or escape from this room, and once out of it, she cannot reconstitute it. Unlike Emily St Aubert's books and paints, the contents of the boudoir, which are emblems not of her true self but of her alienation from it, cannot be retained. When she leaves the house, not only is she, as a possession, lost to the man who provided them, but she forfeits everything he has given her and is cast out into the world without resources spiritual or material.[25]

The stock scenarios that can be developed around this figure offer a writer like Dickens irresistible opportunities for novelistic melodrama. Edith Dombey, for example, who has acquiesced in the project of her first backer, her shameless mother, and allowed herself to be sold to the wealthiest bidder, feels herself, despite the bonds of legal matrimony, to be a kept woman, and her indifference to the luxury with which her husband showers her is a measure of her self-contempt as well as her resistance to his mastery.[26] Once she has entered his house, Edith cannot deny her husband physical access to her: Dombey has the power to enter her room even against her will. All she can do is display her indifference to the goods that are her purchase price – the goods that are intended to display Edith herself as Dombey's prize acquisition. Though Dombey has physical power over Edith, what he sees when he forces himself into the room in which he has installed her is the evidence of his failure to master her mind:

> He glanced round the room: saw how the splendid means of personal adornment, and the luxuries of dress, were scattered here and there, and disregarded; not in mere caprice and carelessness (or so he thought), but in a steadfast haughty disregard of costly things: and felt it more and more. Chaplets of flowers, plumes of feathers, jewels, laces, silks and satins; look where he would, he saw riches, despised, poured out, and made of no account. The very diamonds – a marriage gift – that rose and fell impatiently upon her bosom, seemed to pant to break the chain that clasped them round her neck, and roll down on the floor where she might tread upon them. (650–1)

When Edith 'turn[s] her back upon him, and ... [sits] down before her glass,' the gesture expresses not so much her vanity as her resistance to her husband. But her hostility is a prison for Edith herself, who is trapped in the sterile circle of the mirror and its reflection, as she is fixed in his baffled and objectifying gaze:

> He looked back, as he went out at the door, upon the well-lighted and luxurious room, the beautiful and glittering objects everywhere displayed, the shape of Edith in its rich dress seated before her glass, and the face of Edith as the glass presented it to him. (657)

It is clear that Edith will eventually flee this room, and when she does her escape is dramatized by Dombey's second visit to the boudoir, schematically paired with the first. This time the reader follows him alone into the room his wife has vacated:

> When the door yielded, and he rushed in, what did he see there? No one knew. But thrown down in a costly mass upon the ground, was every ornament she had had, since she had been his wife; every dress she had worn; and everything she had possessed. This was the room in which he had seen, in yonder mirror, the proud face discard him. This was the room in which he had wondered, idly, how these things would look when he should see them next? (756)

Dombey's powerlessness over Edith confirms her spiritual independence and thus in a way elevates her over her husband, but it also distorts her situation in ways that tell against her. Chiefly, with its emphasis on emotional pathos, it tends to blur the issue of financial dependency. Though it is the husband's insensibility that compels the wife to leave the marriage, these passages, which are all focalized from his point of view, go so far as to hint that his loss, which is affective only, is comparable to her loss, which is both affective and material. Paradoxically, the representation of the abusive husband as a baffled and helpless alien in his wife's boudoir can even suggest that he not she is the real victim of the relationship.

Though Edith, as the dark heroine of her own melodrama, is accorded a good deal of sympathy by the novel, she is at the same time positioned as the sexual transgressor: as the prostitute she feels herself to be. The vignette of the empty room littered with discarded jewels is a conventional Victorian still life, a novelistic *vanitas*, the function of which is to suggest the transience, not only of the marital relationship, but of feminine beauty – indeed of the female body itself.[27] Although

Edith's jewels are cast aside, it is her mother's body, not hers, that decays. But since she and her mother are partners in the same project, the mother's death scene can be read as a displacement of the one her daughter has also 'earned.' In *Dombey and Son* as in *Great Expectations*, a beautiful, dangerous, bejewelled young woman is in league with a senile hag, whose sexualized death takes place with sensational vividness before our eyes. Estella is paired with Miss Havisham, who goes up in flames (but whose decaying body is also figured, in her own 'boudoir,' by her wedding cake); Edith is paired with her mother, a more than usually misogynistic Dickensian grotesque, who shrivels and falls apart as we watch.[28] Though neither Estella nor Edith is actually guilty of an adulterous sexual relationship, both have used their sexuality to torment men, and in both novels, through the imagery of bodily decay, it is as if the consequence of the daughter's sexual transgression, the venereal disease so feared by the Victorians, is displaced upon the mother who expedited it. The composite mother-daughter team victimizes men, and the text avenges itself on woman as the appalled narrator details her dissolution. In Mrs Skewton's extended death scene on the one hand and her daughter's empty *vanitas* room on the other, the novel offers, in modes both melodramatic and gothic, complementary emblems of the temptress' eventual fate.

But, though Edith is fused with her mother on the symbolic level, as a 'realistic' character she is sharply distinguished from her. Insofar as she is also positioned as the tragic heroine of the novel, Edith is capable of insight and a certain degree of redemption. But she must divest herself of her luxurious adornments if she is to survive as a moral being. Since her flight from her husband's home does prove to be the prelude to moral clarity, if not social resurrection (impossible for a fallen woman in a Dickens novel), the vacated boudoir with her discarded garments in it is, within this redemptive context, a kind of empty tomb.[29] Here again, moral clarity lines up with good taste, for Edith Dombey does show herself to be a woman of taste, albeit taste that must manifest itself negatively, in repudiation and resistance. She cringes both at the vulgarity of her mother and at her husband's crude display of purchasing power; she despises her own accomplishments, Dombey for having been impressed by them, and the payoff he has given her. Her discrimination and bitterness are to her credit, for heightened consciousness is the mark of the valuable woman. In the woman's-room woman, heightened consciousness takes the form of self-cultivation; in the boudoir woman, it takes the form of ironic detachment. If such a woman attracts, it is by her mocking relationship to the cultural stereotype by which she is defined, a stereotype that she parodies with contemptuous ease in order to exploit the kind of man who can be duped by it into rewarding her with financial support. Edith can evoke pathos because she is supposed to have been browbeaten into this role against her will. An adventuress like Becky Sharp, on the other hand, who actively engages in self-promotion, exuberantly switching personas to suit her various audiences, invites a more complicated response.

The rule in fiction is that a female character cannot want both love and luxury. Rare indeed is the novelistic heroine who genuinely loves her husband but who at the same time desires and frankly enjoys the goods that he is able to buy her. In order to maintain the spiritualization of the feminine on which the woman's-sphere ideology depends, the discourse of taste needs to work hard at keeping apart in fiction what in real life might plausibly be found together: marital affection and the enjoyment of beautiful things. The woman who wants love but not money, like Edith Dombey, can have potentially tragic status.[30] The woman who wants money and not love, like Rosamond Vincy, is dismissed as morally negligible and incorrigibly vulgar. The woman who goes after money and status but finds that they do not satisfy her – a woman like Becky Sharp – is allowed to be at least morally interesting. In his treatment of Becky and her relationship to desirable commodities Thackeray undertakes a systematic deconstruction of the domestic ideology that spiritualizes the Victorian marriage market and mystifies the domestic angel.

Like Edith Dombey, Becky too is a woman of taste, if only in the sense that she has to be a kind of cultural critic, exploiting and parodying a range of stylistic conventions – literary, theatrical, sartorial, musical – in order to produce whatever image she assumes will sell. The role she plays perhaps most productively is that of the faithful and charming little wife to Rawdon Crawley. Ironically, as long as she finds it advantageous to play this role, she is a much more effective domestic angel than Amelia Osborne, whose devotion to her husband George is heartfelt but sterile, whose maternal affection is positively destructive, and who is quite unable to repay Dobbin for his years of devotion (here the metaphor of prostitution becomes overt). In contrast to Amelia, Becky brings out the best in her husband, transforming Rawdon from a randy roué to a contented husband and a devoted father. The sharp distinction that a writer like Dickens tries to make between the virtuous wife and the 'boudoir' lady like Becky, who is frankly a kept woman, is tenuous, and through Becky's parody Thackeray foregrounds its lack of substance and makes clear that conventional marriage can be an even less honest form of prostitution.

Unlike Edith, Becky by no means despises the loot she collects, which, when we get a glimpse of her boudoir, is not scattered about but tidily ranged in the closet or carefully secreted in hidden drawers. But neither does she look to it for pleasure. Her clothes and jewels are simply instrumental goods, functioning on the one hand as a savings account and on the other as the set of costumes she needs to perform her series of charades. Becky rifles drawers and closets, grabs what she can, squirrels away her treasures, and calculates her inventory, but the objects she acquires are always a means to an end – power, glamour, revenge – rather than ends in themselves: simply props in the game she is playing. Thackeray defers to conventional morality when he insists that the game is not worth the candle: that Becky's most brilliant successes leave her bored and restless. The wicked adventuress despises love and sells herself for loot, and the failure of the loot to make her happy completes a predictable moral pattern. Becky does not get what she wants, or rather, she is not able to want what would give her contentment. But since neither is anyone else in the novel, her situation seems as much emblematic of the human condition, at least 'the way we live now,' as specific to the fallen woman. Alienated from her own experience by her role-playing, compelled to turn even genuine responses into dramatic scenes, Becky systematically makes herself into an object for others' consumption, adjusting her act, if not always successfully, to what she assumes to be their tastes. She may have no stable self, but, the novel suggests, nor do most people, who share her inauthenticity but not her sense of irony – a sense of irony that the text as a whole tends to endorse.

The objects Becky collects do not express her taste, but the taste of those from whom she has wheedled or stolen them, or her sense of the taste of others. Though she is reputed by characters like her husband and Pitt Crawley to have more taste than money – to have the French-woman's gift of making something tasteful out of inexpensive materials – the charming little dinners she whips up for Pitt Crawley are based on partridges from Lord Steyne's estate and wine from his cellar and her attractive toilettes on fine lace stolen from Queen's Crawley. Becky's boudoir, according to convention, is packed with luxury goods purchased with men's money. But in his characterization of his transgressive heroine, Thackeray reworks the boudoir topos in a brilliantly unexpected way, by having Becky's room focalized not by the men who have

funded it but by an uncharacteristically innocent and juvenile voyeur.
The reader sees the boudoir for the first time through the eyes of her
young son Rawdie:

> Sometimes, when she was away, and Dolly the maid was making his bed, he
> came into his mother's room. It was as the abode of a fairy to him – a mystic
> chamber of splendour and delights. There in the wardrobe hung those
> wonderful robes – pink and blue, and many-tinted. There was the jewel-
> case, silver-clasped: and the wondrous bronze hand on the dressing-table,
> glistening all over with a hundred rings. There was the cheval-glass, that
> miracle of art, in which he could just see his own wonderful head, and the
> reflection of Dolly (queerly distorted, and as if up in the ceiling), plumping
> and patting the pillows of the bed. (369)

Dolly seems to be making the child's own bed at the beginning of this
passage and his mother's at the end: the linguistic slippage here, the
ambiguity about whose bed is whose, conveys the ardent oedipal feeling
in which the dazzled Rawdie is caught up. The disorder in this room is
not physical but emotional and is brilliantly suggested by the 'queerly
distorted' mirror reflection both of Dolly and of the little boy whose
place in his mother's affections, as in her vacated boudoir, is so problematic.

As we have learned to expect, the items in this boudoir are signs not
of Becky's own nature but of the desires of the male who constructs her.
The goddess Rawdie worships does not exist: these metonymic objects,
which are about all he sees of his mother, express his desire rather than
hers. These are fetishes in the Freudian sense, glittering icons of eroticized femininity in the eyes of this disempowered child whose 'wonderful head' is cut off by the edge of Becky's mirror and whose masculine
identity is threatened by her narcissistic self-absorption. In a piquant
reversal of the usual endorsement of maternal feeling, however, Thackeray makes Becky's very indifference to her son his salvation. His
mother's failure to reciprocate his passion turns out to be a good thing
for this little voyeur, who, free to displace his jealousy onto his rival
Steyne and so to cleave to his maternal father, is liberated by Becky's
slap from potential fixation and sent on his way to functional adult-
hood. By her combination of erotic glamour and callous indifference,
Becky, it could be argued, brings out the best in her son as well as in her
husband, evoking a tenderness and gallantry that are essential elements
of his developing 'manly' nature and that will have no place to settle

except, appropriately, on a female of his own age, Amelia's daughter Jane. The subversion of conventional Victorian notions of family affection is witty and radical. Nevertheless the note of seduction and betrayal is strong in this scene. The relationship between this little voyeur and Becky's backer, Lord Steyne, is only implicit at this point, but Rawdie will presently come to understand that his mother is deceiving him with the man whose gifts adorn her. Thackeray dramatizes the victimization, not of the woman by her dependency on a patriarchal economy, but of the male child whose erotic feelings are so tantalizingly aroused and so brutally insulted.

The conventional scene of physical disorder in the boudoir is provided later in *Vanity Fair*, when Rawdon has stripped his wife of the gifts she has received from her lover and when Mademoiselle Fifine, who has already scooped up the 'bracelets and rings; and ... brilliants' (515) that 'had been lying on the floor, since Rebecca dropped them there at her husband's orders' (517), systematically loots her room as well, carrying off

> not only ... the trinkets ... and some favourite dresses on which she had long kept her eye, but four richly gilt Louis Quatorze candlesticks, six gilt Albums, Keepsakes, and Books of Beauty, a gold enamelled snuff-box which had once belonged to Madame du Barri, and the sweetest little ink-stand and mother-of-pearl blotting books, which Becky used when she composed her charming little pink notes ... and all the silver laid on the table for the little *festin* which Rawdon interrupted. (527)

Unlike the robes, rings, and jewel case focalized by the little boy, this sounds like an inventory of collectibles. When individual objects are specified, enumerated, and as it were given price tags, the metaphor of the fair is foregrounded, and the notion of prostitution is almost explicit. Like Becky herself, these negotiable items are once again in circulation – on the market and on the move – stage props in a scene that has shifted. Becky's practice of serial impersonation, her method of shoring up her fictitious identities by means of objects, renders her inauthentic, to be sure. But the suggestion is that the woman's-room woman, the Rose or Emily or Amelia, may be equally inauthentic – equally a construction produced to meet the taste of the time – indeed, equally dependent for her identity upon the fetishized objects by which she is metonymically defined. The assumption that the virtuous woman's watercolours, embroidery, flowers, and guitar are also stage props is one that *Vanity Fair* takes for granted. Such objects, as we have seen in Disraeli, are also capable of fetishization.

In the novels of Mary Elizabeth Braddon, the issue of the commodity fetish is taken up in an unexpectedly transparent way. The morally serious novelist of the period is obliged to condemn luxury objects as vanities: signs of materialism, decadence, or social irresponsibility. But the line between condemnation and titillation is a fine one, and a popular writer like Braddon can cannily slide across it to fascinate the middle-class reader with a dazzling vision of covetable things. In Braddon's fiction, visions of tastefulness tend to turn into consumer fantasies. A look at two of her heroines, Aurora Floyd and 'Lady Audley' (an avatar of Thackeray's Becky Sharp), shows how a topos invented to celebrate the culture of the woman's mind and spirit can be used to endorse her role as household consumer of material goods. The famous scene in which Lady Audley's boudoir is entered by not one but three voyeurs, with consequences that shape the rest of the plot, is a melodramatic caricature of the patterns I have been discussing. It is also a tantalizing catalogue of stuff one could buy, if one had a fortune like Sir Michael Audley's.[31]

Lady Audley is apparently a model young wife, the kind of woman a man would want to spoil with expensive gifts. Cheerful, charming, and delightfully beautiful in an ingénue style, with 'large and liquid blue eyes,' 'rosy lips,' 'delicate nose,' and a 'profusion of fair ringlets' (52), she is also preternaturally accomplished: a veritable prodigy of feminine taste and skill. She can sketch; she can paint; she can do needlework, producing at the appropriate moment 'a large piece of Berlin-wool work – a piece of embroidery which the Penelopes of ten or twelve years ago were very fond of exercising their ingenuity upon – the Olden Time at Bolton Abbey' (118); she will 'hover about a strand of hothouse flowers, doing amateur gardening with a pair of fairy-like silver-mounted embroidery scissors' (77); she can play her guitar and sing, as her husband puts it, 'for all the world like one of those what's-its-names, who got poor old Ulysses in trouble' (35); she will '[sit] down to the piano to trill out a ballad, or the first page of an Italian bravura, or [run] with rapid fingers through a brilliant waltz' – or perhaps '[wander] into a pensive sonata of Beethoven's' (87). How a woman with her life history has acquired this dazzling range of talents is never made clear, nor what we are to think of their genuineness. The painting she blots when she suddenly realizes that Robert Audley has guessed her secret – the copy of 'a water-colour sketch of an impossibly beautiful Italian peasant, in an

impossibly Turneresque atmosphere' (117) – is evidently, perhaps deliberately, a hybrid cliché.[32] Judging from the irony in this description, we
might be inclined to regard Lady Audley's other talents as equally insub-
stantial and to assume that it is only from Sir Michael's point of view that
his wife seems so accomplished. On the other hand, most of the observations about her gifts are not his, and when the narrator tells us that
her piano playing is 'brilliant' we are apparently to believe it. The portrait of the accomplished lady is suspended frankly between parody and
daydream: it is a wish-fulfillment fantasy of the way to win a wealthy and
indulgent backer.

To attract such a backer of course has been Helen Talboys's aim.
'Lucy Graham' is a kind of Becky Sharp, skillfully acting the part of the
proper lady in order to secure a man who will support her financially,
and frankly exultant to have succeeded. To be sure, we are told that she
is a woman of 'many paradoxes' (87): her 'love of sombre and melancholy melodies, so opposite to her gay, frivolous nature' suggests that
there is more to her than to Becky, as does the treasure she hides in her
secret drawer – not loot from her lover but a lock of hair from her dead
child.[33] But she is just as materialistic, openly gloating over her gains:
'it's something to wear sables that cost sixty guineas, and have a thousand pounds spent on the decorations of one's apartment' (106).
Unlike Becky, however, Lady Audley seems to take an active pleasure in
the objects themselves. Surrounded by the possessions her husband has
given her, she is 'as happy as a child surrounded by new and costly toys'
(52); in her boudoir, 'with her jewel box beside her, upon the satin
cushions, and Sir Michael's presents spread out in her lap,' she loves to
'[count] and [admire] her treasures' (3). This pleasure in material consumption is a sure sign that she is destined to be expelled from her consumer paradise. But Braddon develops the traditional topos with certain
differences that tend to undercut its moral assumptions.

It is significant that the treasures Braddon enumerates are not only
the usual boudoir articles but also the objects conventionally associated
with woman's-room activities: not just silks and jewels, but also the paints
and brushes, the embroidery materials, and the musical instruments
that allow her to display her private tastes decoratively in public. Instead
of suppressing the issue of money, like Radcliffe or Scott, Braddon
makes a point of how much such activities actually cost. Lady Audley's
eagerness to point out to Robert Audley as she opens her 'her velvet-cov-
ered sketch-book' (116) that 'these colours I am using cost a guinea
each at Winsor and Newton's – the carmine and ultramarine thirty shil-

lings' (117) may be implausible – what motive can she have for flaunting her lowly origins to a man who, even if he had not guessed her secret, might resent a former governess entering his family? – but it shows that she is well aware of what the woman's-room topos works to occlude: feminine self-culture does not transcend economics. By collapsing the distinction between the two sets of imagery – by fusing the luxurious textiles associated with the boudoir with a woman's-room activity, painting – Braddon underscores the point that cultivation costs money: that to do what a proper lady does, at least in the style that will mark her as a proper lady, involves more than merely natural taste and earnest effort.

This is an awareness that Braddon assumes her readers share. Braddon does not mystify tastefulness by denying its material base. Her plotting may be sensational and unrealistic, but in her awareness of the link between wealth and gentility she is quite down to earth. While reproducing the correct moral stance, indeed relying on it as a clue to interpretation – using Lady Audley's love of luxury as a hint that she will be brought low – Braddon plays unashamedly upon the consumer desires of her readers and even directs these desires towards specific objects. In the portrait of Lady Audley, as in that of Aurora Floyd, the eponymous heroine of Braddon's second bestseller, Braddon adumbrates a new identity for the middle-class wife – she who is to be provided with pretty things – and for the successful husband: he who is to provide them.

Helen Talboys has in fact done what Becky Sharp only dreamed of doing: parleyed her situation as governess into marriage with a wealthy old man. She has managed to get Sir Michael to do for her what it is hard to imagine stingy Sir Pitt Crawley doing for Becky, even had she landed him: shower her with personal gifts – priceless paintings, 'Claudes and Poussins, Wouvermans and Cuyps' (29), a 'massive walnut-wood and brass inlaid casket ... full as it can be of diamonds, rubies, pearls, and emeralds' (29), a set of sables, 'the handsomest that can be obtained' (47) in Russia. The visual inventory that Robert Audley takes of her hands alone yields an impressive total:

> He looked at her pretty fingers one by one; this one glittering with a ruby heart; that encoiled by an emerald serpent; and about them all a starry glitter of diamonds ... his eyes wandered to the rounded wrists: the broad, flat, gold bracelet upon her right wrist. (87)

The 'generous baronet' has also constructed a glorified female space in the heart of his noble but rundown estate – 'transformed the interior of the grey old mansion into a little palace for his young wife' (52). As Phoebe explains to her intended, Luke Marks,

> 'it's a tumble-down looking place enough outside; but you should see my lady's rooms, – all pictures and gilding, and great looking-glasses that stretch from the ceiling to the floor. Painted ceilings, too, that cost hundreds of pounds, the housekeeper told me, and all done for her.' (27)

Braddon has split Thackeray's Sir Pitt into two and distributed his distinguishing traits, stinginess with money and susceptibility to female charm, between two characters, the better to endorse masculine generosity. The greedy skinflint type in this novel is not, as in *Vanity Fair*, the decayed aristocrat, but the debased menial Luke Marks, a brute 'by no means troubled with an eye for the beautiful' (111–12), who is equally capable, it is suggested, of murdering his wife Phoebe and of begrudging her silk gowns. The susceptible backer is Sir Michael, who loves to shower trinkets upon the adored spouse. The husband who is not merely willing to inundate his wife with material goods but who finds his life positively empty without a woman to spend money on is Braddon's contribution to romance fantasy.

Within the brilliant 'fairy palace' Sir Michael has prepared for his lady is a smaller and even more brilliant private apartment, her boudoir, which we enter on two separate occasions. Phoebe Marks, who is in some sense Lady Audley's double, is aware of her mistress's past, and the way she becomes so is by mastering the secrets of this boudoir.[34] An interloper and sinister guide, Phoebe not only rifles the chamber herself but also introduces into it not one but three voyeurs: three men who have no business there and who have, or acquire, three different reasons to blackmail Lady Audley. Initially, she shows the apartment to Luke, in the process discovering and taking possession of the incriminating lock of baby hair; later on, she admits her mistress's enemy Robert Audley and her first husband George Talboys, with results that bring about Lady Audley's ruin. The penetrability of this private space supposed to be secure – for before the second of these invasions, Lady Audley has actually locked the door and taken the key to London – is the main method of dramatizing the vulnerability of her position, a vulnerability due, as has been pointed out, not just to Lady Audley's deception of her husband but to her very situation as an economically dependent woman.[35] Phoebe's willingness to act on behalf of men – directly on behalf of her husband Luke, who later exploits Phoebe herself, and indirectly on behalf of Lady Audley's husband, who casts off his own wife – manifests again the substantial dependency of even the most assertive, ruthless, and ingenious woman on a patriarchal system that will reward her highly if she secures male support but disempower and brutalize her if she loses it. Specifically, it illustrates the lack of control over living space of a woman who is dependent on a man to provide it. Lady Audley's boudoir will shortly give way to the prison of which it is a figure: her maid's invasion of her private apartment facilitates Helen Talboys's own eventual incarceration in a genteel lunatic asylum.

The second tour of the boudoir is equally arresting and original: it is an ingenious and exaggerated reprise of the topos as developed by earlier writers. Since the room is emphatically cut off from the rest of the house and secured against penetration, the male voyeurs, both of whom turn out to be acting on behalf of the backer figure, have to enter it even more laboriously than Waverley did Rose's *Troisième Étage*, by 'crawling on ... hands and knees' (68) down a secret passage 'about four feet high' (68): here the suggestion of genital penetration is almost explicit. George Talboys's inspection of the room brings about an important development in the plot, as on seeing her portrait he realizes that Lady Audley is really his wife Helen Talboys and thus has committed bigamy; but his alienation from her is registered even before this, when, like Dombey or little Rawdon, he sees 'his bearded face and tall gaunt figure reflected in the cheval-glass, and wonder[s] to see how out of place he seem[s] among all these womanly luxuries' (69). The luxuries are the conventional objects that mark Lady Audley as a kept woman, a woman who has sold herself for money:

> The whole of her glittering toilette apparatus lay about on the marble dressing-table. The atmosphere of the room was almost oppressive from the rich odours of perfumes in bottles whose gold stoppers had not been replaced. A bunch of hothouse flowers was withering upon a tiny writing-table. Two or three handsome dresses lay in a heap upon the ground, and the open doors of a wardrobe revealed the treasures within. Jewellery, ivory-backed hairbrushes, and exquisite china were scattered here and there about the apartment. (69)

The flat, mechanical writing in the last sentence – how many ivory-backed hairbrushes would one scatter about one's room, and does one really scatter china? – suggests that Braddon simply needs a certain number of nouns to make up the set: the signs of the kept woman are so conventional that she can put her pen on automatic pilot.

But that Braddon has the power to endow even tired conventions with suggestive resonance is demonstrated in her treatment of that staple of gothic fiction, the weirdly ominous portrait. The most spectacular item in the room is the painting, not of anybody's ancestors, for Helen Talboys's project is precisely to cut herself off from her past, but of the lady herself – the lady that she, under her husband's auspices, has almost become. The portrait is on easel rather than on the wall, and in the boudoir rather than in a public room, because it is unfinished – as of course is she. One of the walls of the boudoir serves as its background, and this same wall is already covered with other paintings, which in turn are reproduced in the portrait. The *mise-en-abyme* not only positions Lady Audley herself as another precious object among objects, it also suggests that the most valuable gift Sir Michael has to give his wife is her own transfigured self. This is a makeover that has nothing to do with mere cosmetic changes – 'Lucy Graham,' with her natural beauty, has no need of those – and everything to do with the social status with which her husband's money can endow her. What is supposed to go on in the conventional woman's room is the process of enriching one's subjectivity by cultivating one's taste, but the portrait cynically suggests how the self might really be transformed. Instead of patiently developing a best self, a woman can simply marry a rich man and get herself a financial makeover.

The portrait is an ominous fairy-tale mirror, a magic mirror that offers Helen Talboys an idealized image of herself but also tells her that only so long as she retains his love will 'Lady Audley' be the fairest one of all. But it is also a contemporary production: stylistically, it belongs to Braddon's historical moment. Its style is not only rather gothic, endowing the sitter's 'deep blue eyes' with a 'strange, sinister light' and her mouth with a 'hard and almost wicked look' (70), but also rather vulgar, with its luridly enhanced Pre-Raphaelite colouring and its excessively minute Pre-Raphaelite detail. The gothic details strike a sinister note and suggest that the lady's apotheosis is synthetic and will be transient, but the vulgarity sends a more complicated message. The narrator's dismissive tone flatters the reader, who is expected to know that the biggest patrons of the Pre-Raphaelites were newly moneyed northern manufacturers. This association with new wealth is appropriate to the project of Lady Audley herself, of course, but also significant is the questionable taste of Sir Michael, which he has demonstrated both in choosing his wife and in choosing to have her painted in this way. We are invited to rise above vulgar acquisitiveness even as we are made to envy it: to condescend to Sir Michael's taste but at the same time to be titillated by the vision of his lavish expenditure. We are invited to remember that money cannot buy taste (or a virtuous wife) but at the same time to feel that a wife, even a less than virtuous one, is the right person to spend it on. How wicked of Lady Audley so deviously to get hold of a man who will buy her all this slightly tacky stuff: how wicked the trick, and how enviable the stuff! Braddon's fiction exploits the daydream of an endlessly wealthy, endlessly indulgent husband with transformative financial power.

The fact that Lady Audley enjoys her husband's money and what it buys – that she frankly exults in her paints, her jewels, and her sables – sets her up for a fall, whatever sympathies Braddon may subversively express for her travails. But Braddon counts on a reader who shares her heroine's fascination with material goods. Helen Talboys's transformation is bound to be reversed: midnight will strike, and the fine gown will change back into rags. We await the dissolution of the splendid if sinister persona represented by the picture. But the fact that the portrait has been painted not only of Lady Audley but for her is nevertheless calculated to appeal to a reader titillated not only with the promise of wifely transgression but also with the glittering vision of husbandly largesse.

In Braddon's world, where it is the role and the reward of a rich man to buy things for his wife, the woman's-room topos is reworked as a prescription for husbands and as a wishful fantasy for wives. In her novels the good-hearted man is rightly in thrall to the charms of feminine taste. Though at times he may be duped (as he would consistently be in Dickens), he is nevertheless looking for happiness in the only place where it can be found. Braddon's consistent message is that a man's money is sterile if there is no woman to buy things for. This is Veblen with a complacent twist: a new kind of 'vicarious consumption' that ministers not to the rich man's pride but apparently to the deepest needs of his heart. Alicia Audley's frustrated suitor, Sir Harry Towers, has, when she refuses him, 'very little pleasure ... in returning to the stately mansion hidden among sheltering oaks and venerable beeches,' and muses despairingly, 'What's the good of being rich, if one has no one to help spend one's money?' (126); Aurora Floyd's father is shown realizing how empty a luxurious mansion can be without a woman at its heart:

Archibald Floyd was very lonely at Felden Woods without his daughter. He took no pleasure in the long drawing-room, or the billiard-room and library, or the pleasant galleries, in which there were all manner of easy corners, with abutting bay-windows, damask-cushioned oaken benches, china vases as high as tables, all enlivened by the alternately sternly masculine and simperingly feminine faces of those ancestors whose painted representations the banker had bought in Wardour Street.

People are not so very much happier for living in handsome houses ... Archibald Floyd could not sit beside both the fireplaces in his long drawing-room, and he felt strangely lonely – looking from the easy-chair on one hearth-rug through a vista of velvet-pile and satin-damask, walnut-wood, buhl, malachite, china, parian, crystal, and ormolu, at that solitary second hearth-rug and those empty easy-chairs. (214)

The mandatory assertion that money cannot buy a man happiness is at the same time a tantalizing inventory of luxurious things it can buy. The message is not that these things are worthless, but simply that Floyd lacks a woman with whom he could share them.

Aurora Floyd is that woman. Where Aurora's father leaves off as gallant provider, her husband, the dense but decent John Mellish, stands ready to take over. In the home Mellish provides for his adored wife, we are back in the woman's room, in the cozy, indeed downright kitschy, domestic space of feminine decor and feminine activities:

Mrs Mellish's bedroom, a comfortable and roomy apartment, with a low ceiling and deep bay-windows, opened into a morning-room, in which it was John's habit to read the newspapers and sporting periodicals, while his wife wrote letters, drew pencil sketches of dogs and horses, or played with her favourite Bow-wow. They had been very childish and idle and happy in this pretty chintz-hung chamber ... The shaded lamp was lighted on the morocco-covered writing-table, and glimmered softly on the picture-frames, caressing the pretty modern paintings, the simple, domestic-story pictures which adorned the subdued grey walls. This wing of the old house had been refurnished by Aurora, and there was not a chair or a table in the room that had not been chosen by John Mellish with a special view to the comfort and pleasure of his wife. The upholsterer had found him a liberal employer, the painter and the sculptor a noble patron. He had walked about the Royal Academy with a catalogue and a pencil in his hand, choosing all the 'pretty' pictures for the ornamentation of his wife's room. A lady in a scarlet riding-habit and three-cornered beaver hat, a white, pony, and a pack of greyhounds, a bit of stone terrace and sloping turf, a flower-bed, and a fountain, made poor John's idea of a pretty picture; and he had half-a-dozen variations of such familiar subjects in his spacious mansion. (310–11)

There is no view from these rooms, which, opening onto each other, turn inward, towards the smug comforts of the marital idyll. The world outside is represented only by the paintings on the wall, the sentimentalized images of English country life that Mellish finds 'pretty' enough for his wife's room.[36] Braddon displays her own taste by condescending to the husband's taste in pictures. But what is important is not John Mellish's own taste, which is obviously mediocre, but his willingness to write an open cheque to support what he takes to be hers.

This is downmarket Disraeli. The heart of the house has become the site of lavish masculine tribute to aestheticized femininity; the catalogue of female pastimes has been translated into a list of the things that have to be purchased as signs of the rich and full domestic life. The objects itemized here express, as usual, the lady's personal interests, and though this lady is somewhat unconventional in her passion for dogs and horses – Aurora Floyd is allowed, along with a piquant hint of transvestism, the Squire-Western enthusiasms formerly associated with a certain kind of male character[37] – the note of domesticity nevertheless signals her essential purity. Through the woman's-room topos, the heroine's enjoyment of a charming private space has been so firmly associated with her domestic virtue that it is an easy move to suggest that the indulgence of her taste is a fitting reward for that virtue. In this consumer fairy tale, a woman's appreciation for pretty things in itself comes to serve as the moral justification of her financial support. About all a pretty woman like Aurora Floyd has to do is *not* murder her husband in order to merit the rewards he showers upon her.[38]

If a woman's frank enjoyment of material goods were not to be read as prostitution, a way needed to be found of purifying boudoir consumerism with woman's-room imagery. Braddon finds the way. In developing domestic space as she does in these two novels, Braddon collapses the polarity between woman's room and boudoir. By implicitly admitting that, since every woman who is supported by a man has traded her charm for financial support, luxury objects are not the mark of difference between honest wife and kept woman they have been made out to be, Braddon suddenly moves from Victorian moral earnestness to what sounds like a very modern fantasy of the ideal middle-class home filled with consumer objects. She focuses the reader's attention frankly on the husband's buying power, but by continuing to draw on the woman's-room pieties to define her 'good' woman and the happy home she creates, she teaches the middle-class woman how to rationalize her sense of entitlement.

Money cannot buy happiness, but what it can buy is evidence of one's willingness to spend it on one's wife. The home has become a space of consumer display, and though what is on display is, as ever, private contentment, that private contentment is now expressed by the lavish purchase of material objects. It is now the reader herself who, like a curious household visitor, enters the room as voyeur, eager and able to read its legible signs – the reader for whose covetous eyes these commodities are displayed.[39] When taste turns into conspicuous consumption and objects are fetishized as proclaiming domestic happiness, we are moving into the discursive world of the shelter magazine. Veblen analyses the division of labour within the bourgeois family whereby a woman, by tastefully spending her husband's money, testifies to his earning power. The marital relationship in *Aurora Floyd* conforms to the dynamic that Veblen calls vicarious consumption, but Braddon can sanitize and sentimentalize his paradigm because she has ready to hand a topos that associates genteel taste with moral purity and domestic piety. Good taste is the compensatory fiction that keeps the woman in her place – and makes her place that of the family purchasing agent. A topos established to ground the notion of woman's essential spirituality turns so readily into a vision of feminized consumption because of the contradictions on which it is based from the beginning.

The construction of woman's nature in terms of an aestheticized and enclosed space is a device so economical and versatile that it continues to be used by novelists throughout not only the nineteenth century (as some of the following chapters will illustrate) but also the twentieth, and indeed, with whatever ironies and qualifications, up to this moment. But the function of this topos in the Victorian novel is historically specific, endorsing the notion of femininity to which the century was committed. The 'woman's-room' discourse rationalizes the socioeconomic situation of the middle-class woman by suggesting that the iron bars of the domestic sphere do not a prison make; that good taste, like feminine influence, is essentially spiritual rather than dependent upon material resources; that self-cultivation, anything but self-regarding, is a necessary condition of social responsiveness. At the same time, when the topos is varied, parodied, or turned upside down, it can also serve to ironize such articles of faith and to deconstruct the paradigm of idealized domesticity that they support. In a period of material prosperity and industrial expansion, it can even endorse a program of domestic consumption and suggest a new role for the woman who, confined though she may be to the domestic realm, has the power to direct much of the family's spending. The middle-class Englishwoman's situation at the heart of the household, though it is a kind of impotence, is also, after all, a kind of entitlement, and a topos devised to enumerate her excellences will find such entitlement easy to defend.

As has been suggested, certain moments in Austen's fiction invite analysis in terms of this convention: Fanny Price's white room, for example, has been thought to be directly influenced by Radcliffe's Emily St Aubert. I discuss this room in the chapter that follows, which argues that both *Mansfield Park* and *Emma* are constructed around some of the polarities I have been discussing. The starting point of my discussion of Austen is the dialogue of one of her most obnoxious characters, *Emma*'s Augusta Elton. Staking her claim to 'resources' and 'taste' while decrying her own musical 'execution' and 'performance,' Mrs Elton underlines the tension between modesty and self-display that it is the woman's room's function to resolve and puts a comic spin on the anti-accomplishments discourse that forces good taste, as it were, into the woman's-room closet. Following the clue offered by her strident rhetoric, I examine Austen's treatment of the relationship between interiority and social performance and between material and cultural resources in these two novels. In chapter 3 I argue that *Mansfield Park*, which begins in an anti-accomplishments, anti-theatrical mode, makes a case for social performance, whereas *Emma*, confessedly the livelier and more dramatic of the novels, calls in the end for withdrawal and contemplative aesthetic judgment rather than 'performance' or 'execution' – as a defence, however, against the awareness that such judgment is itself a form of social action. Austen is a novelist to whom the arguments of Pierre Bourdieu have seemed especially relevant, and I shall draw on his notions of 'cultural capital' and 'symbolic violence' in my discussion of the ways in which she endorses the social authority of her truly tasteful characters.

# 3 Resources and Performance: *Mansfield Park* and *Emma*

Mrs Elton in *Emma* is one of those Austen characters whose vulgarity is signalled by the relentless repetition of a limited number of words. One is 'barouche-landau': she manages to work into almost every conversation she joins some allusion to her sister Selina's wealthy husband, her estate Maple Grove, and her fashionable carriage. Another is 'exploring.' Avid for distraction, Mrs Elton urges 'exploring' expeditions, jaunts, she points out, so comfortably accomplished in a barouche-landau. A third is 'resources.' Cravenly dependent on society of any kind – 'No invitation came amiss to her' (224) – Mrs Elton nevertheless proclaims her ability to live to herself alone, supported by inner resources that would make her content with the most complete retirement. Affecting dismay about the flood of invitations she and her husband are receiving as the village's most recently married couple – 'From Monday next to Saturday, I assure you, we have not a disengaged day!' – she makes the point that 'a woman with fewer resources than I have need not have been at a loss' (224). In the funny verbal duel in chapter 39[1] between Mrs Elton, who wants to brag about her sister, and Mr Weston, who wants to brag about his son, she corners him into admitting that the Churchill estate is 'a retired place' so that she can draw the comparison she is setting up:

> 'Aye – like Maple Grove, I dare say. Nothing can stand more retired from the road than Maple Grove. Such an immense plantation all around it! You seem shut out from every thing – in the most complete retirement. – And Mrs Churchill probably has not health or spirits like Selina to enjoy that sort of seclusion. Or perhaps she may not have resources enough in herself to be qualified for a country life. I always say a woman cannot have too

many resources – and I feel very thankful that I have so many myself as to
be quite independent of society.' (239)

The more extensive the estate, the more retired the mansion, the
greater the need for cultivated self-sufficiency. Mrs Elton links ownership of land with interiority to suggest that her inner resources qualify
her for a Maple Grove of her own. But having failed to acquire one, she
is later heard to lament the lack even of a donkey:

> 'In country life I conceive it to be a sort of necessary; for, let a woman have
> ever so many resources, it is not possible for her to be always shut up at
> home.' (278)

Mrs Elton's three favourite words mutually deconstruct: her claim to
'resources' is contradicted by her avidity for 'exploring,' preferably in a
'barouche-landau.' In crudely foregrounding both her inner and her
sister's outer resources, Mrs Elton betrays a lack of cultural capital for
which she is bound to be ironized in a novel by Jane Austen.[2]

The word 'resources' resonates in *Emma* because it is one of the many
details that link Mrs Elton with the heroine herself.[3] Emma Woodhouse
has already assured her protégée, Harriet Smith, that because of her
own resources she will never marry:

> 'If I know myself, Harriet, mine is an active, busy mind, with a great many
> independent resources; and I do not perceive why I should be more in
> want of employment at forty or fifty than one-and-twenty. Women's usual
> occupations of hand and eye and mind will be as open to me then, as they
> are now; or with no important variation. If I draw less, I shall read more; if
> I give up music, I shall take to carpet-work. And as for objects of interest,
> objects for the affections, which is in truth the great point of inferiority, the
> want of which is really the great evil to be avoided in *not* marrying, I shall
> be very well off, with all the children of a sister I love so much, to care
> about. There will be enough of them, in all probability, to supply every sort
> of sensation that declining life can need.' (66)

Emma, quick to detect false notes in discourse, would ordinarily be the
first to mock this kind of speech, which is a proleptic parody of a woman
she will despise. Like Mrs Elton, Emma speaks in terms of quantity
rather than quality – 'too many,' 'so many,' 'a great many,' 'enough' –
offering the kind of inventory that in Austen is the mark of the medio-

cre spirit. Her apparent understanding of the psyche as a zero-sum construction – that more of this means less of that – rather than an organism capable of expansion and development ironizes Emma's assertion even as it endorses the developmental model. This silly monologue both signals that Emma does not 'know herself' – that she will change her mind about marriage – and serves, when the word 'resources' is later echoed by Mrs Elton, to draw attention to the ways in which the two women are alike. It also highlights an issue central less to *Emma*, where 'resources' are dismissed with a laugh, than to *Mansfield Park*, where the notion shapes the construction not only of the heroine but of most of the other major characters.

Both women's speeches are paradoxical. To parade self-sufficiency is evidently to negate it. The contradiction points to a problem both for the character who has more resources than accomplishments and for the novelist who has to represent such a character. In Mrs Elton, Austen provides a monitory example of how not to call attention to one's interiority. How to do it is a more difficult problem, the solution to which shapes a number of scenes in both of these novels. Tasteful self-advertisement is one of the skills that novels like Austen's might teach readers who, like Mrs Elton, aspire to gentility.[4]

In their use of 'resources,' Mrs Elton and Emma are evidently drawing on an established discourse. Originally applied to men in their old age rather than to women in domestic seclusion, the notion of resources goes back to the classical writers. It was Cicero who in his essay on 'Cato and His Friends' had Cato argue

> A person who lacks the means, within himself, to live a good and happy life will find any period of his existence wearisome. But rely for life's blessing on your own resources, and you will not take a gloomy view of any of the inevitable consequences of nature's laws.[5]

This is a compensatory paradigm. Inner wealth makes up for loss or lack: loss of health, loss of prestige, loss of social involvement. Though Cato represents it as adequate compensation, envisaging a range of activities for what Emma calls 'declining life,' later writers tend to suggest that only the quietest pleasures will remain to the elderly man and that he will be able to draw on these pleasures only if he has taken care in his youth to store them up in anticipation of his old age. By the mid-eighteenth century this advice had become a cliché. 'What an unhappy man I must now have been,' writes Lord Chesterfield to his son in 1746,

> if I had not acquired in my youth some fund and taste of learning? What could I have done with myself at this age, without them? ... My books, and only my books, are now left me; and I daily find what Cicero says of learning to be true ... Let me, therefore, let me most earnestly recommend to you to hoard up, while you can, a great stock of knowledge; for though, during the dissipation of your youth, you may not have occasion to spend much of it, yet ... a time will come when you will want it to maintain you.[6]

The monetary metaphor becomes explicit, and the economic model, like Emma's, is a static one, conservative in the literal sense: resources are conserved, banked, like a pension or savings, so that one can draw on them in the future. The wealth is evidently more than metaphorical, however: this sounds like a gentleman who can be spiritually self-sufficient because he is economically self-sufficient. Since he does not need his resources to do anything for him in the wider community, they can be imagined as innocent: not as conferring social power, but rather as compensation for the renunciation of such power.

There comes to be a rather specific deadline for the period of cultural acquisition. 'Remember,' says Chesterfield, 'that whatever knowledge you do not solidly lay the foundation of before you are eighteen, you will never be master of while you breathe. Knowledge is a comfortable and necessary retreat and shelter for us in advanced age; and if we do not plant it while young, it will give us no shade when we grow old.'[7] Chesterfield's advice speaks to the bourgeois investment in timing and scheduling – his systematic laying-up of subjective treasure is in line with other kinds of prudential foresight – while also suggesting a certain aristocratic dignity: Chesterfield supplements the monetary metaphor with one of Fanny Price's favourite symbols of gentry stability, the noble tree that signifies a noble past. In Chesterfield's discourse we already see the 'embourgeoisement' of aristocratic ideals that Clara Tuite analyses as central to Austen's own project.[8]

By the end of the century, novelists had picked up this modified notion of resources and used it in the construction of plot and character. Fanny Burney is alluding to the Ciceronian paradigm when she has Camilla's good-hearted but foolish uncle Sir Hugh, 'uncultivated and self-formed,' who missed the deadline for cultural acquisition, find himself, in his dotage, jealous of the 'constant resources which his brother found in literature' and eager to go back to school with the youngsters.[9] Austen evokes it with a difference when the narrator of *Emma* refers to Harriet Smith's collection of charades as 'the only mental provision she was making for the evening of life' (52). The joke lies in applying the Ciceronian notion of gentlemanly cultivation to a commonplace and incurably sociable young woman. It is clear that no kind of 'mental provision,' much less collecting charades, could for a minute provide the mindless and utterly dependent Harriet with self-sufficient enjoyment.

Yet a woman without resources is no laughing matter. Such self-sufficiency had begun by this period to be felt as even more important for women than for men. What begins in Cicero as a strategy for a time in a man's life is readily applied in the eighteenth century to the place in which a woman is to conduct hers. An aging gentleman will find himself increasingly cut off from active pleasures, but a woman, particularly if she is unlucky in love, may be confined for the whole of her life to an even more retired situation. Mrs Chapone in her *Letters on the Improvement of the Mind* points out that although music and drawing probably will not give much pleasure except to the young woman herself and her family, 'it is of great consequence to have the power of filling up agreeably those intervals of time, which too often hang heavily on the hands of a woman, if her lot be cast in a retired situation' (155) and advocates the cultivation of those pleasures 'which would remain when almost every other forsakes them; which neither fortune nor age can deprive them of, and which would be a comfort and a resource in almost every possible situation in life' (209).[10] The situation to which she delicately alludes (and to which Emma understands resources to be particularly relevant) is dependent spinsterhood. An unmarried woman who has nothing to keep herself innocently entertained may become a social nuisance, like the mischievous Miss Marland in *Camilla*, 'equally void either of taste or of resources.'[11] The desire to remain connected to other people is evidently more compelling for a woman so marginalized than for the retired gentleman envisaged by Cicero or Chesterfield, and this desire needs to be rerouted and contained if society, particularly the young woman to whom her meddling may be especially damaging, is to be protected against her. Burney's view of resources is negative: they are necessary, she suggests, so that 'surplus' women will not meddle with or corrupt other women. But the Ciceronian formula offers a way in which this essentially coercive agenda can be constructed as an ideal of spiritual self-cultivation.

Some of Burney's contemporaries on the other hand emphasize resources as the woman's defence against a dangerous or oppressive society. The reality of patriarchal power, of the way women's lives have to be conducted in the spaces they are allotted within an economic system largely controlled by men, is always relevant to the discourse of female resources. The most fraught representations of the notion that I have come across are in gothic or historical novels, where a plot involving male violence generates the corollary image of a space of resourceful female retirement. Mrs Chapone evidently does not have in mind a wealthy wife like Mrs Elton's sister Selina, but there is gothic potential in the supposed 'seclusion' of Maple Grove, 'retired from the road,' 'shut out from every thing' by an 'immense plantation' of trees, 'in the most complete retirement' – a situation that might turn a woman without Selina's 'health and spirits' into a madwoman in the attic.[12] Emily St Aubert in Radcliffe's *The Mysteries of Udolpho*, beleaguered in a gothic castle, restores her composure by pulling out her books and paints every time she gets a few hours to herself. More relevant than Radcliffe's heroine to *Emma* however is the Italian countess in Mme de Genlis's *Adelaide and Theodore, or Letters on Education*,[13] who, locked for years by her husband into an underground dungeon, retains her sanity by reciting day after day all the poetry she has committed to memory. Since Emma Woodhouse alludes to *Adelaide and Theodore*, Austen probably assumes that her readers know this tale, which gives an unexpected gothic resonance to the image of Maple Grove. The suggestion that life in a country estate might be a form of imprisonment for the unlucky wife is oblique in *Emma* – less so in *Mansfield Park*, where Maria Bertram, even before marriage, is desperate to 'get out' of Sotherton – but in the context of a social reality where a woman's material well-being and chances of happiness depend upon her relationship to men, the notion of 'resources' always has gothic potential.[14]

In view of this power structure, Austen is sceptical about the sufficiency of inner resources to make a woman happy. A critic of *Emma* complains that for all the emphasis on Jane Fairfax's music, it is never represented as an emotional resource for her.[15] This is true, but this is not a criticism of Austen; rather, it speaks to her realism about women's situation. Jane's piano playing does have several functions, and Austen makes them all clear. It is a skill required of a young woman hoping to obtain the position of governess, and if Jane is not lucky enough to marry, she will need it: as Mrs Elton points out, she would be worth still more with the harp. In a social context, her music is an accomplishment, one much valued by Frank Churchill, who is so eager to show off her talent that Mr Knightley complains he threatens her health. Indeed, Frank's investment in Jane's music suggests that perhaps this was one of the features that attracted him to her in the first place, and if so it will have proved not an inner but a material resource, since Jane, in securing Frank, does obtain a home which, in economic terms at least, is much better than she could have hoped for. The novel is frank about the practical advantages for a lady of such visible skills. Jane's music has moral implications as well: her polished execution testifies to her solidity of character and steadfastness of application. It also has class implications: adopted into the Campbell family and educated along with their daughter, Jane has taken advantage of the opportunity to cultivate her natural taste, and so she merits the social advancement that eventually comes her way. But Austen gives us no sentimental vision of Jane comforting herself with tunes as her relationship with Frank falls apart. In *Emma* the efficacy of the kind of resources claimed by Mrs Elton is simply not dramatized at all.

As the treatment of Jane Fairfax suggests, the term 'resources' is implicitly related to 'accomplishments.' The words continue to be paired and polarized throughout the nineteenth century.[16] Accomplishments are for charming an audience in the drawing room: resources are what one turns to in the seclusion of one's own apartment. If resources are reassuring in a married woman because they testify to her capacity for domestic contentment, accomplishments are ominous for the opposite reason, because they whet her appetite for applause and public admiration, satisfactions that, having attracted a husband, she may nevertheless be loath to relinquish. Resources are admired as a sign of interiority, accomplishments decried because they involve immodest self-display. Austen is consistently hard on young ladies who parade their accomplishments, rarely to the pleasure of their captive audiences.

Yet the two terms refer to essentially the same set of feminine activities. Painting, drawing, even embroidery and carpet work may be practised in private but are also displayed in public; music serves for private solace as well as for public recital; even the most private activities, reading and study, have a public dimension, as Austen makes clear in *Mansfield Park*, where reading aloud becomes a topic for discussion and the Bertram children's schoolroom information is 'performed' for admiring adults. The determination to polarize 'resources' and 'accomplishments' draws attention to a cultural pressure point and suggests anxiety about woman's place and her willingness to accept it. It also points to a problem for the modest but resourceful young lady. To make her resources work for her, a marriageable woman has to turn them into accomplishments. The signs of interiority have to be exteriorized if the woman is to get the moral credit she is entitled to. How to publicize the taste for privacy without looking as foolish as Mrs Elton? How can the novelist put on display the modest woman's unwillingness to be displayed? *Emma* and *Mansfield Park* are organized around these questions and, I shall argue, around two pairs of terms that restate and yet eventually destabilize the public/private polarity. One of these pairs is 'resources' and 'accomplishments,' the other 'taste' and 'performance.' Having both these pairs put into play by the loudmouth Mrs Elton ensures that the reader will hear them and register the serious issues to which she parodically points.

The chief resource of which Mrs Elton boasts is her love of the piano, yet when, during their first conversation, Emma politely mentions that 'Highbury has long known that you are a superior performer' (213), Mrs Elton demurs, and with unexpected vigour:

> 'Oh! no, indeed; I must protest against any such idea. A superior performer! – very far from it, I assure you. Consider how partial a quarter your information came from. I am doatingly fond of music – passionately fond; – and my friends say I am not entirely devoid of taste; but as to any thing else, upon my honour my performance is *mediocre* to the last degree.' (213)

Why the emphasis? As the narrator of Burney's *Camilla* points out, the 'slight accomplishments' that characterize a lady have to be 'but slightly pursued' precisely in order to testify to her amateur status – 'to distinguish a lady of fashion from an artist,' that is, from someone who must earn her living by performance.[17] Mrs Elton presumably has never contemplated herself in just this situation. She cannot have anticipated apprenticeship to the governess trade, though her eagerness to seal Jane's doom might suggest that it is a terror she has had to repress. But she has been on the marriage market, trading such talents as she has for a marital establishment. Mr Elton and the home he provides are worse than Selina's but better than nothing, and the alacrity with which she abandons her principal accomplishment testifies to her sense of relief. Accomplishments are for attracting a husband, and now that she has one she can let them slide. As a married lady, she insists, she does not and will never again have the time to practise her music.[18] The truth no doubt is that as a glamorous newcomer to Highbury she has no intention of exposing herself to comparison with the talented Jane Fairfax. Since detached contemplation is the mark of those who are not obliged to make a living, the way to defend her abandonment of her music, she intuits, is to elevate 'taste' over 'performance.' Mrs Elton has a sense of the kind of claim the discourse of taste requires of her, but the clumsy effusiveness with which she deploys this discourse succeeds only in earning her Emma's bemused contempt.

Harriet Smith is evidently apprenticing herself to the same discourse – specifically, perhaps, to Mrs Elton, by whom she is predictably impressed. Flattering Emma for her performance on the piano, Harriet observes:

> 'Mr Cole said how much taste you had: and Mr Frank Churchill talked a great deal about your taste, and that he valued taste much more than execution.'

Harriet is learning to parrot the discourse in which 'taste' is valued over 'performance' or 'execution' and perhaps even to grasp the class assumptions behind it, since she goes on to remark rather callously that Jane had better play well because she is destined to become a governess. Has she heard Mrs Elton making such insinuations about Jane behind her protégée's back? Both women imply that finished execution is the degrading mark of the professional, of the woman who has to rely on her music to support herself.

Austen has her heroine repudiate this hierarchy of judgment. Emma is an expert interpreter of the discourse of taste, which she can explicate or parody with ease, and she perfectly understands what is meant by the men's flattering remarks. She knows that praising her own taste is merely a way of excusing her lack of skill at the keyboard. She also appreciates Jane's musical 'execution,' even though she is a little jealous of it, and she tries to make Harriet understand that taste and performance are complementary rather than mutually exclusive: that Jane, who has both 'taste and execution,' is much the superior musician. Harriet, however, is obtusely sceptical: 'Are you sure? I saw she had execution, but I did not know she had any taste. Nobody talked about it' (179). Harriet's association with Emma has given her enough sophistication to sneer at execution but not enough to negotiate the discourse of taste that is supposed to transcend it. Emma, by her ability to use this discourse, displays just the taste that has been attributed to her, albeit in a wider sense than her flatterers intended.

I would argue, indeed, that in having Emma intervene in this way,

Austen herself is endorsing the very privileging of 'taste' over 'execution' that Emma is teaching Harriet to reject. For Austen's reader, Emma's taste trumps Jane's performance. It is largely because of Emma's good taste that we are aligned with her from the first pages of the novel and inclined to dismiss her failures of execution. Mrs Elton is right: the mark of the gentlewoman is the role of the detached arbiter, not of the expert practitioner. When Emma acts, she often acts badly: the schemes she tries to execute prove abortive and her performances malicious and destructive. But because we are taught by Austen to value taste over performance and to recognize Emma's taste as fundamentally sound, we know that she is capable of reformation. The heroine's specific aesthetic judgments, which are usually invested with authority by the text and which appeal to the standards with which the implied reader is expected already to identify by class position and literary experience, make us complicit with Emma from the beginning in a way that is never entirely undercut by her subsequent errors of will and feeling. That these judgments also endorse the social stratification towards which the novel is moving demonstrates the ideological function of this powerful discourse. 'Every body has their level,' says Mr Elton (102), one of those characters who, like Mary Crawford, is demonized for expressing openly the impulses of the text as a whole,[19] and when everybody finds it the novel can end with Emma's and Knightley's critique of Frank Churchill's epistolary prose. Emma's taste is in fact a form of cultural capital, which confers real and potentially sinister social power, but Austen does not want to tell us this: she wants to insist that it is not taste but the refusal to heed it that does social harm.

Emma's efforts to make Harriet understand what the men really mean by their remarks apparently reflect well on her. There is something generous not only in her willingness to give Jane credit for superior skill but also in her attempt to initiate Harriet into the language of the group she is trying to join. This kind of missionary work – of cultural outreach to the discursively challenged – figures in both *Emma* and *Mansfield Park*. In contrast to Burney, whose elite characters tend simply to mock their vulgar inferiors, Austen postulates a positive way of closing the gap between social classes. Hazlitt objected that Burney's heroines are just as vulgar as the people they despise, because they are constructed as their polar opposites, simply to despise them:

> Of the two classes of people, I hardly know which is to be regarded with most distaste, the vulgar aping the genteel, or the genteel constantly sneering at and endeavouring to distinguish themselves from the vulgar ... To be

merely not that which one despises, is a very humble claim to superiority: to despise what one really is, is still worse. Most of the characters in Miss Burney's novels, the Branghtons, the Smiths, the Dubsters, the Cecilias, the Delvilles, &c. are well met in this respect and much of a piece: the one half are trying not to be taken for themselves, and the other half not to be taken for the first.

As Hazlitt's distaste suggests, a scenario in which gentlefolk mock the vulgarity of their social inferiors is not serviceable for middle-class self-presentation in the long run, if only because it makes it embarrassingly obvious that social distinction depends upon maintaining an underclass of social inferiors. Overt snobbery testifies less to plenitude than to lack: 'Those who have the fewest resources in themselves, naturally seek the food of their self-love elsewhere' – that is, in making fun of others.[20] It is not by snide hostility to social climbers that the middle class will justify its fitness for cultural leadership. More efficacious, because apparently more generous, is the conversion paradigm developed by Austen, whereby taste is modelled for a wider group than will be able fully to profit from it and a select few are chosen to move up. Clifford Siskin has argued that Austen invents 'developmental' characters as a way of ratio-nalizing the mobility she observes in the society around her. In these narratives of development, educability becomes a key issue. Because Austen's vulgar characters, unlike Burney's, share some traits and dis-cursive mannerisms with the genteel, she is able to make clear what the vulgar could learn from their betters if they would pay attention. Blam-ing those who refuse to internalize the lessons of 'taste' they are offered is a way of linking successful mobility with moral deservingness. Many are called, but that so few are chosen is no doubt a comfort to writers and readers anxious about the fluidity of social boundaries.

I have begun with *Emma* in order to introduce, through the dialogue of Mrs Elton, the polarized terms around which both it and *Mansfield Park* are constructed and to suggest the way these notions are used to mark characters as worthy (or not) of social mobility. I turn now to *Mansfield Park*, the earlier novel, to look in more detail at how these polarities play out within a single complex text. I shall return to *Emma* in the second half of this chapter.

*Mansfield Park* is clearly, even schematically, organized around the two polarities Mrs Elton puts in play: taste and performance, resources and accomplishments. This novel has long been recognized as contributing to the anti-accomplishment discourse discussed in the last chapter. Mary Crawford, in her characterization of the 'accomplished and pleasing' Owens sisters Edmund has been visiting in Peterborough, mocks the conventional caricature of the accomplished woman (or women, for they often come in sets): 'Two play on the piano-forte, and one on the harp – and all sing – or would sing if they were taught – or sing the better for not being taught – or something like that' (293). Though Mary is nervous about Edmund's acquaintance with these potential rivals, she can afford to parody the discourse of accomplishments, for she herself is triumphantly accomplished. The Bertram sisters, however, less talented than Mary, approach their accomplishments without irony. Maria and Julia, taught to take for granted that the point of their education is not intellectual or moral cultivation but 'brilliant acquirements' (68), develop as might be expected. Their educational acquisitions are displayed by the kind of rote performance that requires repetitive drill – they boast of their mastery of 'the chronological order of the kings of England, with the dates of their accession, and most of the principal events of their reign' (54), 'besides a great deal of the Heathen Mythology, and all the Metals, Semi-Metals, Planets, and distinguished philosophers' (55) – and their accomplishments are polished in the same way. The product that results is what their parents had in mind: as Sir Thomas watches his daughters 'exercise their memories, practise their duets, and grow tall and womanly,' he complacently sees them 'becoming in person, manner, and accomplishments everything that could satisfy his anxiety' (56). The narrator's tart chiasmus emphasizes the artificiality of the young women's conditional behaviour by setting it against their natural physical development. All this busy self-fashioning signals the social insecurity of the Bertrams, a *nouveau riche* family anxious to appropriate the prestige of the long-established Rushworths. The main point of the sisters' moral fall is to demonstrate that an educational system founded on a debased understanding of women's potential may result in the dangerous disruption of patriarchal authority, but their expulsion from Mansfield Park also serves to erase an arriviste anxiety that needs to be eliminated if the estate is to serve as the model of gentry culture.

As the heroine destined to be linked with this purified estate, Fanny Price, in her resistance to 'accomplishments,' exemplifies the 'natural taste' the busy Rushworth ladies lack. Fanny is initially constructed as the direct opposite of her female cousins, in terms of her possession of both taste and resources and her opposition to both accomplishments and performance. Her first encounter with Maria and Julia Bertram makes clear she has no accomplishments, no wish to develop them, and no interest in the mediocre display of other people's. In their observation 'that she had but two sashes, and had never learnt French' (51), they themselves are just as vulgar, Austen suggests in a spaced-out chiasmus, as the Portsmouth girls, who, more than three hundred pages later, dismiss Fanny because 'she neither played on the pianoforte nor wore fine pelisses' (388). Maria and Julia are also disgusted to find that she is not particularly 'struck with the duet they were so good as to play' (51). This actually quite implausible independence of mind testifies to an innate tastefulness that transcends any possible genetic or cultural influence. How, we might ask, has this child from a rowdy Portsmouth household so quickly learned to be so discriminating?

As I have argued in the Introduction, it is because Fanny, a 'clever' child, with 'a quick apprehension as well as good sense,' is one of those chosen spirits who possesses, as the cliché has it, the natural taste that requires only cultivation. Fanny's innate superiority is demonstrated by her easy, rapid 'cultivation' under the supervision of her cousin Edmund.[21] Though her tutor must occasionally 'correct her judgment,' he only has to 'encourage her taste' for her ardently to appropriate the cultural treasures that he places before her. Under his guidance, she punctually develops a range of positive tastes, solidly based on 'a fondness for reading which, properly directed, must be an education in itself' (57). This process is summarized in a single short paragraph, glossed over so quickly that we never see any of their lessons, never see the problems of a beginning pupil. Fanny is positioned as the natural aristocrat in the midst of all these bourgeois strivers: not only a Cinderella, but a swan in a nest of female ducklings. Fanny's education is represented, not as drill, practice, or rote memory, but as the pleasurable unfolding of natural propensity. Not only does she love books, specifically the serious literary genres of biography, poetry, and history, and respond passionately and informedly to natural beauty, she also has an intense appreciation of distinguished musical and dramatic performances. Although unimpressed as a child by her cousins' duet, Fanny listens 'full of wonder' to Mary Crawford's harp (220) and, 'alive and enlightened' (336), to Henry's reading of Shakespeare. As Mrs Elton suggests, the role of the gentlewoman is indeed to discriminate, not to perform: Fanny's taste, which is a contemplative rather than an active virtue, resides in her ability to appreciate beauty, not to create it, and has the paradoxical prestige of both interiority and responsiveness to the outside world.

Fanny is also characterized in terms of resources, which, though trivi-
alized in *Emma*, is one of this novel's organizing ideas. Austen dwells on
the inner resources that country life requires and arranges its characters
along a moral spectrum in terms of their ability to sustain rural retirement in a harmless and self-sufficient way. Mrs Grant, a fairly contented
woman, nevertheless welcomes the arrival of her half-siblings because,
'having by this time run through the usual resources of ladies residing
in the country without a family or children; having more than filled her
favourite sitting-room with pretty furniture, and made a choice collection of plants and poultry, [she] was very much in want of some variety
at home' (74). It is because they are hungry for amusement and 'variety'
that Mrs Norris and Mrs Grant, adult authorities who ought to oppose
the theatricals, support the young people's project. Since the interest
that these two women take in the theatricals contributes directly to the
crisis that confronts Fanny – Mrs Norris turning viciously on her when
she refuses to fill in the first time; Mrs Grant, who fails to show up to
play the part of the Cottager's Wife, exposing Fanny finally to even
Edmund's appeal – their culpability is clear and their lack of resources
consequential. In this novel, as in Burney's *Camilla*, women with empty
minds endanger other women if they do not hurt themselves.

With fine comic counterpoint, however, Austen makes the woman
who does possess resources an equally dubious figure. Lady Bertram, 'a
woman who spent her days in sitting nicely dressed on a sofa, doing
some long piece of needlework, of little use and no beauty' (55), needs
no further distraction. Serenely uninvolved with the doings of the young
people, blissfully oblivious to the possible danger of her husband's voyage, 'very anxious' about her guest of honour Mrs Rushworth but
unable to 'spare time to sit down herself' to play cards with her 'because
of her fringe' (145), she is so entirely fulfilled by her occupation that
when Sir Thomas returns, even though she finds herself 'so sensibly animated as to put away her work' (195) for an evening, all she has to say to
him is that 'her own time had been irreproachably spent during his
absence; she had done a great deal of carpet work and made many yards
of fringe' (195). Though women in particular may find themselves at a
loss without inner resources, satisfaction with those usually prescribed
for them argues an almost animal insensibility. Busy with her fringe,
Lady Bertram is all too self-sufficient and no more responsible a parent
than the two ladies who have too little to occupy their time.

Implicitly contrasted with aunt Norris, Lady Bertram is explicitly compared with her other sister, Fanny's mother. The three maternal figures

are polarized in terms of action, representing excessive busyness on the one hand, excessive sloth on the other. Lady Bertram does nothing, while aunt Norris does too much, officiously promoting Maria and Julia and making an intrusive performance of her mean economy. There is a place for such initiative, and it is in a straitened household like the Prices' in Portsmouth: Fanny admits that it would have been better for her mother to display more of her aunt Norris's managerial energy, less of her aunt's inertia. But among gentlefolk, the work a lady is called upon to do is not material but cultural: sympathizing, supporting, comforting, judging, offering moral guidance. In *Mansfield Park* as in *Emma*, busyness is gendered female and given lower-middle-class associations, while the real lady is the heroine who simply responds to the people around her in a perceptive and principled way. It takes 'moral taste,' rather than the kind of superficial accomplishments prescribed for women, to fill the woman's role as the resource of the household.

It is Fanny who fills this role, in a way that emphasizes not only her Christian humility and feminine modesty but also her natural superiority to those who exploit her. For Lady Bertram and Mrs Norris she is a material resource, indeed a kind of servant, a role that emphasizes their coarseness of feeling and her refinement. Forced by Mrs Norris to pick roses under a hot sun, Fanny collapses with a headache, and while it seems tactless to compassionate her heat prostration on the lawn of an estate funded by Antiguan slave labour,[22] it does establish her princess-and-the-pea delicacy: this heroine, consistently associated with whiteness, may be debilitated, but she is never, like Cinderella, blackened by the physical labour she is forced to undertake.[23] The spiritualization continues as Fanny's story unfolds, her role becoming wider and quieter as the demands on her become more complex. During the theatricals, when 'being always a very courteous listener, and often the only listener at hand,' she not only helps the actors learn their parts but listens sympathetically to all their 'complaints and distresses' (184), Fanny is used to make up for their own deficiencies of mind and temper. Indeed, when she attempts to show Rushworth 'how to learn' (186), she is really trying, as Henry points out, 'to give him a brain which nature had denied – to mix up an understanding for him out of the superfluity of your own' (236). Henry's bookkeeping metaphor cheapens a generosity that we are asked to read as Christian charity or noblesse oblige, but his remark also makes clear that Fanny's superiority to those around her is as much a matter of 'nature' as of education: that it is because of the innate richness of her spirit that she can be a resource for others.

Fanny is also notably resourceful herself. Austen places her heroine in just the kind of situation that Hester Chapone had in mind when she advocated cultivated self-sufficiency for women, and her temperament fits her for the self-culture that Chapone recommends. Her experience in the carriage on the way to Sotherton is characteristic of her position in the Bertram household:

> She was not often invited to join in the conversation of the others, nor did she desire it. Her own thoughts and reflections were habitually her best companions; and in observing the appearance of the country, the bearings of the roads, the difference of soil, the state of the harvest, the cottage, the cattle, the children, she found entertainment. (110)

All of Fanny's tastes look like genuine resources, intellectual, imaginative, and spiritual: just the resources for life in the country, for the clergyman's wife she is destined to become. Like Radcliffe, Austen apparently approves of resources for women and attributes moral and spiritual strength to the heroine who possesses them.

Yet it is worth noting that Fanny's resources do not usually work as Chapone and Radcliffe suggest they ought to do. Indeed, except on this single occasion of the lonely ride to Sotherton, their efficacy is far from clear. Consider the ironies of the East room, the room to which Fanny is wont to flee 'after any thing unpleasant below, and find immediately consolation in some pursuit, or some train of thought at hand' (173) This room is an iconic representation of the resources that support the heroine in her virtuous retirement. The catalogue of its effects is conventional – 'Her plants, her books – of which she had been a collector, from the first hour of her commanding a shilling – her writing desk, and her works of charity and ingenuity, were all within her reach' (173) – and Edmund, who knows how this cultural pattern is supposed to play out, imagines Fanny 'taking a trip into China' seated 'comfortably down at your table' as the door closes behind him (177). But Fanny derives only limited solace from her room in the absence of social relationships. Its charm for her is due to its human associations: she 'could scarcely see an object in that room which had not an interesting remembrance connected with it. – Every thing was a friend, or bore her thoughts to a friend' (173). But these friends are so rarely 'within her reach' when she needs them, so distressingly intrusive when they do turn up, that there is something rather theoretical about this kind of comfort. Indeed, no sooner have we read this description than Edmund knocks at her door to try to persuade Fanny to condone his decision to perform in the theatricals, and when he leaves, sentimentally imagining her mental travels, her peace of mind has been destroyed for the rest of the day: 'there was no reading, no China, no composure' for her (177). Fanny finds no pleasure in the prospect of resourceful solitude when everyone else is involved in a common activity. When she watches the actors at the beginning of the rehearsals, she is forlorn to think that she might 'retreat from it to the solitude of the East room, without being seen or missed' by them, feeling indeed that 'any thing would have been preferable to this' (180). The room is repeatedly invaded by the actors, who force Fanny to watch them rehearse their parts or listen to them reminisce about their pleasure. Never for a moment, in any scene dramatized in the novel, does this domestic space actually serve as the 'nest of comforts' it is said to be.[24]

The implicit promise of the discourse of resources is that the supernumerary female, occupying her private time in contented retirement, will not impose on other people. But we never see the contentment, only the pain when other people impose upon her. It is because Fanny has bought into the ideology of resources that she is out of everybody's way when they do not need her and easy to get hold of when they do. A childhood spent providently laying up cultural treasure does not pay off in personal happiness. Like the heroines of gothic novels, Fanny is harassed, oppressed, and finally, at Portsmouth, virtually imprisoned. Because of her inner resources, she does survive and endure – indeed, she is able to provide cultural resources for Susan – but there is no question of emotional fulfillment for her until the male power structure shifts. Austen may ask us to admire the resourceful woman, but she is also aware of how the discourse of inwardness for women plays into a destructive ideological agenda. The only satisfactory solution for a woman of genteel tastes, as all her novels make clear, is the kind of material support a prosperous man can provide.

The woman who knows this and systematically conducts her life campaign in the light of the knowledge is Mary Crawford,[25] who is developed along the accomplishment/resources axis as a complete foil to the heroine. Mary, who lacks interiority, is consistently constructed in terms of her relationship to space. Always conscious of self-positioning and self-display, she is equally eager to 'place' and frame others: she is the one who wants to know whether Fanny is 'out' and who attempts to mark her with the gold chain that would have brought her out indeed, as the object of Henry's affection, without her knowledge.[26] As eager to gain the spotlight as Fanny is to avoid it, an accomplished performer, a witty conversationalist, an impressive musician, a spirited rider, and of course an enthusiastic participant in the theatricals, Mary is fixated on material resources – on money, 'the best recipe for happiness I ever heard of' (226), and the services it will buy, and on other people insofar as they can be used to advance her own interests. Taking inventory of the resources at the parsonage, she is gratified to find 'a sister without preciseness or rusticity – a sister's husband who looked the gentleman, and a house commodious and well fitted up' (74) to serve as a stage on which to display her own beauty and accomplishments. Indeed she envisions herself as the heroine of her own drama, on display as in a theatre:

> A young woman, pretty, lively, with a harp as elegant as herself; and both placed near a window, cut down to the ground, and opening on a little lawn, surrounded by shrubs in the rich foliage of summer, was enough to catch any man's heart ... Mrs Grant and her tambour frame were not without their use; it was all in harmony; ... even the sandwich tray, and Dr Grant doing the honours of it, were worth looking at. (95–6)

But this scene does not prove adequate to sustain her when the weather turns grey. As Austen repeatedly emphasizes, Mary, without Fanny's 'delicacy of taste, or mind, or feeling' (110), lacks the inner resources needed for country living: she responds to 'nature, inanimate nature, with little observation' (110); like Mrs Elton, needs constant social activity to keep from being bored; and objects to Edmund's clerical profession partly because it would mean embracing country life permanently.

What she does have, however, is the ability to 'talk the talk' – to claim both the taste that readers are willing to grant her[27] and the inner resources she so obviously lacks. Mary is an accomplished musician, and it is this talent that critics seem to chiefly have in mind when they credit her with 'taste.' But in a novel, where music can be represented only in words, Mary's musical performance is displaced by her verbal performance, which creates a more ambiguous impression. Mary gets a lot of conversational mileage out of her harp, which, because she cannot rent a cart in the middle of harvest, eventually has to come in a barouche – the word will link her with Mrs Elton – in a journey she ironizes as a chain of rustic gossip:

> 'The truth is, that our inquiries were too direct; we sent a servant, we went ourselves: this will not do seventy miles from London – but this morning we

heard of it in the right way. It was seen by some farmer, and he told the miller, and the miller told the butcher, and the butcher's son-in-law left word at the shop.' (89)

The butt of her irony is the local people who have inconvenienced her, but her witty language also figures her own restless mobility. While her brother can define himself at least partly in relation to his landed estate, Mary has only 'portable property' to bring to the marriage market: her self, her talent, and her harp. Like the instrument, Mary is on the move, so it is important that she not appear to be on the make. The charmingly deft modesty topos with which she introduces her performance on the harp is designed to suggest that her music is not to be understood as a mere shallow accomplishment and to advertise her interiority and capacity for contented withdrawal:

'I shall be most happy to play to you both ... at least, as long as you can like to listen; probably much longer, for I dearly love music myself, and where the natural taste is equal, the player must be the best off, for she is gratified in more ways than one.' (90)

The remark implies that her love of music itself is more important than her love of performing – that music is a true resource for her – while also making clear to her audience that they are in for a polished performance. This is a statement without much content, except the oblique claim of enriched subjectivity. It may be doubted that Mary spends much time in the private pleasure she affects – all the evidence we are given is to the contrary – but she is sufficiently mistress of the discourse to know what stance to affect, and she thoroughly charms Edmund, who takes her at her word. Mary does not have taste in the full, positive sense of the word, but she has mastered the discourse of taste so as to impress not only Edmund but also many of Austen's readers.

Fanny, on the other hand, who does have real taste but lacks this mastery, is painfully unable to advertise the quality of her subjectivity. When she tries to 'outer' her inner resources, Fanny's remarks, leaden with learned allusion, tend to put off not only the characters in the novel but also some readers, who find her tiresome and priggish. The most notorious example of this incapacity is her monologue to Mary on shrubbery, time, memory, the evergreen, and the variety of nature. In contrast to Mary's canny haiku of self-promotion, this extended speech, Fanny's longest in the whole novel, is striking only for what sounds like its desperate invention. Her awkwardness here might be attributed to her uneasiness with Mary, whom she cannot really like; yet Fanny has the same problem with Edmund. Desperate for his attention during the visit to Sotherton, she quotes poetry at him, objecting to the felling of the oaks – 'Cut down an avenue! What a pity! Does it not make you think of Cowper? "Ye fallen avenues, once more I mourn your fate unmerited"' (87) and expatiating on the chapel: 'Here are no aisles, no arches, no inscriptions, no banners. No banners, cousin, to be "blown by the night wind of Heaven." No signs that "a Scottish monarch slept below"' (114). This is the rhetorical equivalent of tugging at his elbow, and the same strain marks the little excursion into the sublime with which she tries to keep him at the window looking at the stars when Mary is called away to sing:

> 'Here's harmony! ... Here's repose! Here's what may leave all painting and all music behind, and what poetry only can attempt to describe. Here's what may tranquillize every care, and lift the heart to rapture! When I look out on such a night as this I feel as if there certainly would be less of both if the sublimity of Nature were more attended to, and people were carried more out of themselves by contemplating such a scene.' (139)

This star-gazing speech, replete with literary allusions, is itself an allusion, a comic-pathetic parody of the stock episode in which a male 'pedagod'[28] uses the starry sky to instill in a young woman a proper sense of wonder at God's creation.[29] We have never seen Edmund teaching Fanny about the stars – indeed, we have never actually seen him teaching her anything – and here Fanny becomes his instructor in a vain attempt to draw him back to the right kind of reverence.[30] But though he replies to her effusion in the tone of a gratified instructor awarding a satisfactory grade ('I like to hear your enthusiasm, Fanny' [139]), he presently turns back to Mary. In a real-life love triangle, a feeling for 'Nature' is neither the resource Fanny claims nor an accomplishment to compete with Mary's music.

Fanny's dialogue is precisely that of someone who is 'not often invited to join in the conversation of others' (110), who has been thrown back upon her own inner resources for hours every day. The chains of association evoked in her by the shrubbery, the chapel, and the stars have a daydreamy coherence that could be attractively rendered in the free indirect discourse Austen is praised for pioneering,[31] if they were represented as Fanny's private thoughts. The problem is saying them out loud, where they tend to sound like the 'hoard' or stockpile Lord Chesterton described. The discourse of taste requires that literary quotations be injected into conversation concisely, obliquely, and probably with some irony, so as to imply that the common culture, 'naturally' possessed by everyone in the group, does not need to be spelled out. But such naturalness takes practice. Fanny's lack of conversational tact makes her tone strained and urgent, and the result is a foot-in-the-mouth awkwardness that cannot evoke erotic desire. In Edmund it evokes – as any remark is likely to do – merely more tutorial discourse: 'You forget, Fanny, how lately all this has been built, and for how confined a purpose, compared with the old chapels of castles and monasteries' (114).

These exchanges dramatize, more vividly than the account of Fanny's room, the flaw in the theory of resources. Talking to oneself for hours on end makes it hard to talk to others. An enriched subjectivity not only serves distressingly little purpose at moments of real-life anxiety, it can positively incapacitate one for social interaction. Critics complain that Austen makes Fanny unattractive, as if she does not know what she is doing. On the contrary, I see such dialogue as part of the sceptical analysis of 'resources' that leads in *Emma* to their ridicule and abandonment.

Unable to perform her resources, Fanny has to rely on her author, who sets her up in a number of scenes so theatrical that they seem at odds with the novel's apparent repudiation of theatricality. It has been pointed out that, although Austen positions her heroine as opposed to acting, she herself as a novelist dramatizes that opposition. Fanny's resistance to the group's demand that she participate in the theatricals puts her in the spotlight. Her distressed appeal – 'I could not act any thing if you were to give me the world. No, indeed, I cannot act' (168) – is a dramatic speech, and her stance, which attracts everyone's attention, turns her momentarily into the star of a dramatic scene. Fanny is made to perform her reluctance to perform; she goes on to steal the spotlight from Henry during the Shakespeare reading; she is brought 'out' visually for us on the evening when she is presented to society, decorously decked with William's cross on Edmund's chain. Austen repeatedly puts her anti-theatrical heroine into theatrical tableaux, and while this paradox might, as certain postmodern critics suggest, be designed to make clear that all identity is performative, it more likely derives from the practical problems of displaying the modest woman. The more self-effacing the heroine, the more theatrical the episodes she generates, since her author is obliged to demonstrate the excellences that she herself is reluctant to display,[32] and this generalization applies to fiction that does not particularly address the issue of performativity. Austen can – indeed must – put Fanny's virtues on stage. But the novelist's solution is not so easily available to the character. It is not I would argue in the scenes where Austen is displaying her heroine that we find her raising the issue of performativity, but rather in the scenes where Fanny is anxiously trying to display herself. Fanny is caught in Mrs Elton's dilemma – how to draw attention to her taste and resources – and the lengths to which she has to go in order to 'perform' them, when she is not made by Austen to do so, help to account for the more awkward moments in her characterization.

Performance is the keynote of the characterization of Henry Crawford, whose theatricality has been the object of much critical attention. Like his sister, and indeed like many of the characters in the novel, Henry is developed in terms of accomplishments and performance. Wild to perform in a play – 'I feel as if I could be any thing or every thing' (149) – he is acknowledged to be 'the best actor of all' (185), and his theatricality is associated with other sinister qualities, chiefly with his predatory duplicity in love. Like Mary, too, he is given clever speeches in which he characterizes his own taste. But while she claims resources she does not have, he flaunts his indifference to the very notion of resources and the model of prudent hoarding that it implies.

While Mary is constructed in terms of space, Henry constructs himself in terms of time, in opposition to the earnest conservative model of systematic cultural acquisition and preservation associated with all three Bertram siblings. Representing his own development in terms of speed, ease, and precocity, Henry claims never to have spent time and never to have saved it. This cavalier attitude has often been remarked and his inconstancy contrasted – for better or worse – to Fanny's static fidelity and reverence for the past. But I would argue that it is not only Fanny who is shown up by Henry's temporal style. His investment in 'natural' ease and speed positions him not only against Fanny and Edmund but also against Maria and Julia, whose laborious drilling and practising look earnestly bourgeois beside his aristocratic *sprezzatura*. In the end, Henry's account of the effortless getting and reckless spending that display his power reads like a sly send-up of the systematic, provident middle-class way of accumulating cultural capital. Indeed, by validating the notion of natural taste, it paradoxically aligns him in a surprising way with Fanny herself.

Henry's mastery of the discourse of taste sometimes enlists the sympathetic amusement of the reader on his behalf. Though Henry's enthusiasm for 'improving' estates, for example, can be understood as a sign of his contempt for the values that Fanny and Edmund revere, nevertheless the speech in which he characterizes the improvements he made to his own estate, mocking as it does the renovations contemplated by Rushworth, aligns him unexpectedly not only with the reader, who is the only one to appreciate his sly wit – his ironies go over the heads of the people he is talking to – but also with the author herself.

This funny rhetorical performance wraps up chapter 6, which begins with Rushworth boasting about his plans to transform Sotherton Court – all 'seven hundred acres' of it – with the help of Repton at a guinea a day; with Edmund's expressed preference for more personal, more gradual alterations, 'acquired progressively' (88) and planned by the owner himself – a metaphor for the kind of bourgeois self-*Bildung* of which the novel on the whole apparently approves; and with Mary's complaint about renovations to the Admiral's cottage, which left the family 'for *three months* ... all dirt and confusion, without a gravel walk to step on, or a bench fit for use' (88).[33] They digress to other topics, but when at the end of the chapter Mrs Grant invites Henry to tell them about the alterations to Everingham, protesting however that it was perfect to begin with, Henry produces a sly riff on the themes of size and speed. Everingham is surprisingly small, and he himself extraordinarily quick to perfect it:

'I fear there would be some disappointment. You would not find it equal to your present ideas. In extent it is a mere nothing – you would be surprised at its insignificance; and as for improvement, there was very little for me to do; too little – I should like to have been busy much longer ... what with the natural advantages of the ground, which pointed out even to a very young eye what little remained to be done, and my own consequent resolutions, I had not been of age *three months* before Everingham was all that it is now. My plan was laid at Westminster – a little altered perhaps at Cambridge, and at one and twenty executed. I am inclined to envy Mr Rushworth for having so much happiness yet before him. I have been a devourer of my own.' (91–2)[34]

While the echo of 'three months' suggests that Henry is contrasting his own powers of renovation to his despised uncle's, the principal object of his mockery is Rushworth and his investment in grandiose size. Henry knows that the vast Brownian park is in disrepute and that the locus of traditional English values is now seen to be the more modest estate.[35] His covert allusion is to Repton, the designer Rushworth proposes to hire for Sotherton. At the beginning of his career, Repton had positioned himself as the successor to Lancelot 'Capability' Brown, whose gargantuan compositions were to be mocked by Uvedale Price as essentially lower middle-class. Price described Brown's design for Blenheim, the product of a little mind working on a large property, as at once too big and too small.[36] The perfect estate, the 'just-right' estate, would apparently be the product of a great mind working on a small property, and Henry implies that his is just such a mind – that Rushworth is an ignorant oaf and his bloated property a poor thing compared with naturally beautiful Everingham brought to perfection by Henry's own exemplary and precocious taste. The issue of size is an ongoing joke of Austen's own. Mr Rushworth, 'a heavy young man' (72) who eventually comes to realize that Henry has designs on Maria, makes a fool of himself by clumsy jibes at his rival's stature ('No one can call such an under-sized man handsome. He is not five foot nine. I should not wonder if he was not more than five foot eight. I think he is an ill-looking fellow' [129]). Henry, in his mockery of his rival, is here aligned with the author herself. Nevertheless, the joke is finally on Henry, who, though he parrots the principles of simplicity and refined scale, does not himself observe them: the gold chain he chooses for Fanny is too ornate to appeal to her and too big to be worn with William's cross. There is a subliminal phallic metaphor here, the suggestion that size doesn't matter as much as a certain kind of man thinks it does. Though Henry speaks for simplicity and restraint, he aims at striking and large-scale effects, and his taste in jewellery is a sign that Fanny, at least at this point in the relationship, is right to resist his advances. Yet the reader cannot fail to be amused at the wit of this self-styled Alexander who so disingenuously laments that he has no more design worlds to conquer.

Henry claims a 'natural' taste, effortlessly 'cultivated' not by study or practice but simply by exposure to the land itself, which 'pointed out even to a very young eye what little remained to be done' (92). While this formula itself is a disingenuous rhetorical move,[37] and while Mary's satire of the Owen sisters, who sing the better 'for not being taught,' tends to expose the claim of natural taste as a familiar affectation, Henry's self-parodic tone comprehends these objections even as he ironizes the projects of other 'improvers.' In the Admiral's mere cottage, renovations involve 'three months' of discomfort and disorder, but a 'small' estate like Everingham can be transformed, apparently, by the fiat of a juvenile god. Henry pretends to defer to Edmund's preference for gradual change by lamenting his own precocity, but his caricature of the bourgeois fantasy of aristocratic ease and entitlement is a subtle mockery of the patience and persistence implied in Edmund's model of home (and self-) improvement. The impetuous creativity Henry has manifested in improving Everingham speaks of masculine potency and appetite: be he ever so industrious in his youth, how, he implies, can a man hoard up inner resources when the world in which he so happily finds himself calls for their immediate discharge? This dynamic alternative to the Bertram model of earnest, systematic acquisition[38] has, interestingly, already been endorsed in Fanny's own rapid development, her 'natural' superiority to the drilled and practised Bertram sisters. I would argue that in possibly endowing Henry with the 'natural taste' that also characterizes her heroine, Austen makes him in some respects not just her opposite but also her complement.

Henry makes the same kind of claim about his mastery of Shakespeare. The scene in which he reads selected speeches from *Henry VIII* to a dazzled Fanny is a pivotal one in our interpretation of his potential for reformation. While Henry's conquest of Fanny begins as a frank power game, once he has begun to fall in love with her Austen teases us with the possibility that he is capable of real change. But from the time this possibility is articulated – not only by Henry himself, but by Mary, who suggests that Fanny might 'save' him – Austen carefully handles point of view so as to maximize the ambiguity about his motives and morals. From chapter 33 on we have little access to Henry's thoughts and feelings. The Shakespeare reading in chapter 34 is presented largely from Edmund's perspective, and we do not see Henry again until he turns up unexpectedly in Portsmouth in chapters 41 and 42, which are presented primarily from Fanny's. Our judgment of his moral potential turns partly on whether we take his performance of Shakespeare as an example of genuine taste and whether we read his behaviour at Portsmouth as merely a polished performance. The clues Austen supplies are relentlessly ambiguous and in the end undecidable.

Henry's effectiveness as an actor is not in doubt, but Austen frames the scene to problematize the moral significance of this talent, partly by having Henry himself comment on it. He exhibits both theatrical flair and literary intuition, the 'power of jumping and guessing' that allows him to 'light, at will, on the best scene, or the best speeches of each' character (334–5), the ability to shift readily from one mood to another, 'whether ... dignity or pride, or tenderness or remorse' (335). Whatever we think of these talents – talents that, though they characterize distinguished actors of the period and indeed the genius of Shakespeare himself, can also be read as the sinister signs of unstable selfhood and moral flightiness[39] – our response has to be qualified (for better or worse) by the dialogue between Edmund and Henry that follows the performance:

> 'That play must be a favourite with you,' said [Edmund]. 'You read as if you knew it well.'
>
> 'It will be a favourite I believe from this hour,' replied Crawford; ' – but I do not think I have had a volume of Shakespeare in my hand before, since I was fifteen. – I once saw Henry the 8th acted. – Or I have heard of it from somebody who did – I am not certain which. But Shakespeare one gets acquainted with without knowing how. It is a part of an Englishman's constitution. His thoughts and beauties are so spread abroad that one touches them every where, one is intimate with him by instinct. – No man of any brain can open at a good part of one of his plays, without falling into the flow of his meaning immediately.'
>
> 'No doubt one is familiar with Shakespeare in a degree,' said Edmund, 'from one's earliest years. His celebrated passages are quoted by every body; they are used in half the books we open, and we all talk Shakespeare, use his similies, and describe with his descriptions; but this is totally distinct from giving his sense as you gave it. To know him in bits and scraps, is common enough; to know him pretty thoroughly, is, perhaps, not uncommon; but to read him well aloud, is no every-day talent.' (335–6)

Though Edmund is inclined to overvalue Henry in general and has at this moment a particular motive for drawing attention to his good qualities, his judgment is presumably meant to register positively with the reader. A person who can read Shakespeare with sense and feeling seems in an Austen novel impossible to dismiss as incapable of reformation.

The moral status of Henry's own claim, however, is more ambiguous. Though his talent is genuine, his casualness about it, like his sister's about her music, looks like a carefully calculated performance. Again the emphasis is on his precocity and on taste as the natural birthright of the gentleman. Critics have found fault with Henry's assertion that acquaintance with Shakespeare is simply 'part of an Englishman's constitution' (335). That 'English*man*' is sexist has been pointed out,[40] but the class implications of the remark are equally important. There is the claim to a generous liberalism here: his assertion that Shakespeare's 'thoughts and beauties are so spread abroad that one touches them every where, one is intimate with them by instinct' (335) implies they are equally accessible to everyone. But the suavity of Henry's self-presentation, his elaborate carelessness, makes clear that the kind of person really 'intimate' with Shakespeare, the kind of person for whom he has become an 'instinct' – the kind of person able to *talk* so articulately about his becoming an instinct – is a member of a tiny cultural elite.[41] If he really has not looked at Shakespeare since he was fifteen years old, Henry must have mastered the complete works, along with the principles of architectural 'improvement,' as a mere boy. Such speedy acquisition, parodying the schedule recommended by Cicero and Chesterfield, seems too exemplary to be believed, and his implication that this mastery took no effort at all – that no serious study is necessary for the gentleman, who simply absorbs culture through his pores – looks like an airy pose. Yet apparently Henry is not just bluffing: there is no doubt about either the excellence of the performance or the acuteness of his literary sensibility. If he knows the play better than he pretends – if it is indeed a favourite of his, as Edmund assumes – this testifies to his real appreciation of Shakespeare; if he knows it as little as he claims, that testifies just as impressively to his literary intuition. It is not clear that what Bourdieu would call cultural capital is not being represented in this case, as it is in the case of Emma Woodhouse, as simply 'taste': the kind of 'natural taste' that testifies to moral potential. As Neill suggests, the 'Englishness' Austen admires in *Emma* has everything to do with class.[42]

Since what triggers Henry's performance is Fanny's own reading of the play to Lady Bertram, precocious enthusiasm for Shakespeare is evidently one taste the two potential lovers do have in common. Indeed, Fanny's reluctant enchantment with Henry's performance aligns her with him for a moment, by turning her, again, into a performer. On hearing the gentlemen approach, Fanny puts down Shakespeare, takes up her needlework, and assumes an air of such 'deep tranquillity' that Edmund is moved to comment on it, pretending that 'all her attention was for her work.' But she cannot sustain the act: 'taste was too strong in her ... she was forced to listen' (334). Again, it is Fanny's very inability to act that puts her in the spotlight. The effect of the scene depends on embedded focalization, an unusual technique for Austen:[43] Edmund is watching Fanny watching Henry, and as the reading progresses, her 'eyes which had appeared so studiously to avoid him throughout the day, were turned and fixed on Crawford, fixed on him for minutes, fixed on him in short till attraction drew Crawford's upon her' (335), until everybody except Fanny herself is looking at Fanny, including the reader. The modest heroine steals the scene from Henry, testifying to the power of his performance even as she shows him up. Her inability to maintain her pose of indifference is a tribute primarily to Shakespeare's language but also to Henry's acting. Contemplation trumps 'execution' yet testifies to its effectiveness: self-surrender transcends, yet also valorizes, self-display.

This too after all is a pedagogical moment, a moment of cultural transmission between a maiden with 'natural' taste and a man who awakens it. Fanny's sudden transformation, which figures intellectual and imaginative development as desire, is much more erotic than anything that happens between her and Edmund. The episode tends to corroborate both Edmund's assertion that the two really do 'have moral and literary tastes in common' (345) and the narrator's claim that, had she not already been in love with Edmund, Fanny, 'with so much tenderness of disposition, and so much taste' (241), would probably have found him irresistible.

As if she fears that Henry's easy brilliance might tip the balance too far in his favour, however, Austen frames the Shakespeare reading with two discussions of skills that do take practice: oral reading, and preaching. Both reading well aloud and speaking well are the marks of a gentleman. As Tom disingenuously argues in defending *Lovers' Vows* to Edmund, Sir Thomas had always encouraged 'any thing of the acting, spouting, reciting kind ... in us as boys':[44]

'How many a time have we mourned over the dead body of Julius Caesar, and *to be'd* and *not to be'd*, in this very room, for his amusement! And I am sure, *my name was Norval*, every evening of my life through one Christmas holidays.' (152)

Reciting elegant literary extracts was a prescribed way of developing skill in oral performance. Edmund readily admits that 'my father wished us, as school-boys, to speak well' (152) and that he encouraged such exercises. The art of reading aloud is systematically cultivated in the Bertram household. Fanny 'had long been used' to good reading at Mansfield Park – 'her uncle read well – her cousins all – Edmund very well' (334) – and her appreciation of this masculine 'accomplishment'[45] is apparently to be taken as a mark of her own good taste.[46] As critics who raise the issue of performativity have pointed out, the everyday skills of genteel self-presentation require practice. Austen takes masculine 'accomplishments' more seriously than feminine and apparently approves of the systematic training of young gentlemen so that they can perform their class status as adults, not at special moments, like the harpist in the drawing room, but day in and day out, in 'every private company, and almost every public assembly.'[47] The discussion of reading aloud, insofar as it assimilates Henry's performance of Shakespeare to this gentlemanly accomplishment rather than to his involvement in *Lovers' Vows*, seems to endorse his talent. On the other hand, it could plant the suspicion that the reason he knows these selections so well is that they are the kind of purple passage every schoolboy was exposed to in anthologies like Enfield's.[48]

Another kind of performance we are asked to compare with the Shakespeare reading is the delivery of sermons. When the men first begin to discuss this topic Henry seems to be exhibited in a deliberately unflattering light, complacently laying claim to a whole catalogue of questionable motives and attitudes. His admission that his mind tends to wander during prayers – that he finds himself 'nineteen times out of twenty ... thinking how such a prayer ought to be read, and longing to have it to read myself' (338); his discussion of a good sermon as a mere aesthetic experience, 'a capital gratification' (338); the reasons he gives for wanting to be a preacher, which suggest his vanity, his appetite for power, and his love of praise; the assumption on which these reasons are based, that the raw material of a sermon is so boring, so 'limited, and long worn thread-bare in all common hands' (338), that holding the audience's attention is a piquant challenge; his wariness of 'constancy' (339), a theme Fanny pointedly picks up: the list is so relentless that the author seems to be weighting the dice. Henry apparently sees preaching mainly as an opportunity for effective performance: he would be content to preach, he says, only to a London 'audience' (his word) 'educated' enough to be 'capable of estimating my composition' (338). In his emphasis on rhetorical and dramatic technique rather than conviction or depth of feeling, his sense of how to 'touch and affect' such a 'mass of hearers' (338) is at odds with well-established contemporary advice. 'Would you affect your auditors?' asks Robert Robinson, in an influential commentary on the composition of sermons – 'be affected yourself. Would you excite their grief? weep yourself ... These emotions must not be acted, they must be free and natural. They cannot be acted, they may be affected: but the affectation will be discovered, and it will

excite the contempt of the hearers, they will think the preacher a hypo-
crite, who aims to impose on them.'[49] Read as a gloss on Henry's effusions, Robinson's strictures seem to condemn him for his interest in
mere technique, and this condemnation would be in line with the animus against theatricality in *Mansfield Park* as a whole.

Yet Austen is apparently less rigorous than Robinson. It is, after all,
the morally serious Edmund, not the theatrical Henry, who first introduces the topic of the 'art' of delivering sermons. Edmund focuses not
only on the technique of the preacher – 'the art of reading,' 'a clear
manner, and good delivery' (337) – but on the need for a cultivated
audience: he professes himself pleased with the 'spirit of improvement'
that has lately produced more demanding congregations possessed of
'more general observation and taste ... than formerly' and better able to
'judge and criticize' the preacher's 'performance' (Edmund's word).
This kind of advice is also in the air, in handbooks of elocution like
Enfield's and of rhetoric like Blair's, which emphasize the importance of
self-conscious technique.[50] Indeed, Enfield points out that the kind of
'artificial rules' he is offering are necessary to enable a man to speak
naturally – to 'discover and correct those tones and habits of speaking,
which are gross deviations from Nature.'[51] Naturalness needs to be practised. That such a statement would not register as a paradox at the time
dramatizes how hard Austen has been working to keep apart ideas that
her culture insists on collapsing together. The polarities on which this
novel seems to have been constructed cannot be maintained. In her
own taste for dignity and decorum, Austen tips the balance back in favour of the practice and performance that previously functioned as the
marks of mediocrity and vanity and enlists, on the side of artifice, a character, Edmund, previously constructed in terms of his resistance to it.

Indeed, though Edmund usually speaks for transparency and sincerity
in human relationships, deploring the kind of affectation to which
young women in particular are trained, at his most tactful and attractive
he too is well aware of the function of deliberate performance in everyday social life. Edmund tries for example to persuade his sister Maria to
withdraw from *Lovers' Vows* by appealing to the principle of noblesse
oblige ('it is you who are to lead. You must set the example' [164]) and
by explaining how to do it – not by 'haranguing,' as Maria suggests, but
by example:

> 'let your conduct be the only harangue. – Say that, on examining the part,
> you find yourself unequal to it, that you find it requiring more exertion

and confidence than you can be supposed to have. – Say this with firmness, and it will be quite enough. – All who distinguish, will understand your motive. – The play will be given up, and your delicacy honoured as it ought.' (164)

What he is recommending is a more subtle kind of performance than a 'harangue':[52] this is real-life theatre involving, on the part of the actor, both self-conscious artifice and a particular kind of focused empathy, an ability to calculate audience response. Such social performance is justified, apparently, if it has the appropriate rhetorical effect: if it models moral behaviour and inspires others to right action. But Maria ignores her brother's advice, and it is left to Henry Crawford, when he visits Fanny's home in Portsmouth, to practise what Edmund only preaches.

Henry's visit to Portsmouth makes clear that performance is essential in human relationships. His gentlemanly demeanour with the Prices is the kind of performance Edmund advocates, carried off with a panache and success that neither Edmund nor any of his pupils ever achieves. A perfectly frank response on Henry's part to Fanny's home and family would be as unkind as it would be impolitic. Henry's manners are apparently perfect. It is hard to object to his tactful handling of Fanny's parents or to disagree with Fanny's judgment that 'there was something particularly kind and proper in the notice he took of Susan' (398), even though we know he does wish she were not with them. A particular point is made of the way in which Henry's gentlemanly demeanour brings out the best in the Prices. Mrs Price's unexpectedly decorous behaviour is due partly to her Sunday-best clothes and partly to her assumption that Henry's primary interest is in William but also to her feeling 'that she had never seen so agreeable a man in her life' (393). The metamorphosis of Mr Price is even more striking:

> Her father was a different man, a very different Mr Price in his behaviour to this most highly-respected stranger ... His manners now, though not polished, were more than passable; they were grateful, animated, manly; his expressions were those of an attached father, and a sensible man; – his loud tones did very well in the open air, and there was not a single oath to be heard. Such was his instinctive compliment to the good manners of Mr Crawford. (395)

For all the talk about Henry's responsibility to the tenants on his estate, what the upper classes really have to offer their social inferiors, it appears, is this kind of personal example. This is Austen's answer to Burney. The genteel character, instead of mocking the vulgarians as Hazlitt complains Burney's do, simply models a superior standard of behaviour and raises them up by the example of his own good breeding. To be sure, the transformation is temporary and incomplete: in the end the only resource for Susan is to get her away from her parents. But no doubt their exposure to Henry leaves the Prices with a deepened sense of deference to their 'betters' which can only be a stabilizing influence at a moment of social change. The cultural mission to the Prices is divided, split between two 'social workers': Henry inspires them to respect gentility while remaining at their own level; Fanny rescues Susan from them and raises her above them. If gentlemanliness is a performance, it is a performance that is even more artificial yet even more necessary at the boundaries where the classes touch.

The issue of performance also shapes what has become the most notorious crux in the novel: the moment when Fanny asks her uncle about slavery. Scandalized by Mansfield Park's dependency on slave labour,[53] critics have considered the implications of Fanny's question for her own moral status. Is her interest in the topic a mark of her moral sensitivity, her capacity for renovating social awareness? The consensus seems to be that it is not: that Fanny's question implies no serious objection to slavery on either her part or Edmund's.[54] In fact slavery is not the issue here. It is significant that we do not hear Fanny ask the question, which is mentioned by her and Edmund only in retrospect, in the context of a discussion of Fanny's social demeanour. Edmund wishes she would speak up more in public, and Fanny defends herself by pointing out that she did ask about slavery but because 'there was such a dead silence' (213) she thought it tactless to follow up the query with others and risk looking more interested in their father's experiences than Maria and Julia. The topic that engages Fanny and Edmund is not slavery at all but social performance. There is a necessary link between performance and empathy. Because Fanny is always quick to imagine how others might feel, she is prompt to adjust her behaviour accordingly. If acting involves calculating audience response, so also awareness of audience response – the kind of empathy otherwise endorsed in the novel – necessitates constant acting. Like Maria, Fanny does not want to look like a prig: that is, she does not want her behaviour, which she knows is morally superior, to register as criticism of her cousins'. In refusing to 'perform' socially as Edmund thinks she ought, in backing off and falling silent, she is in fact performing, acting a role – a role, to be sure, that she is only too ready, when given the opportunity, to interpret for Edmund, showing up Maria and Julia to him as she professes her unwillingness to do to the family as a whole. The fact that this vignette can be read either as evidence of Fanny's moral sense or as another example of her monstrous self-righteousness illustrates the instability produced by the theme of theatricality in a text with such a stake in taste and decorum, and problematizes the exemplary female subjectivity that is supposed to restore and redeem the moral culture of Mansfield Park.

The taste/performance polarity on which the novel had seemed to be based cannot be sustained. Though *Mansfield Park* decries certain kinds of 'performance,' it also endorses self-conscious role-playing, both deliberate and unconscious. Postmodern critics, Litvak for example, see the excessive hostility to theatricality in *Mansfield Park* as a repression of the uncomfortable awareness that all subjectivity is ineluctably performative, an awareness which, they argue, creeps back in around the edges of the text.[55] This awareness is not to be located in Austen's own nuanced distinctions. Austen differentiates carefully between various kinds of performance: between the acting of Mrs Norris, who has constructed her whole identity around the role she plays in the Bertram household; of the Bertram sisters, who unreflectively play the social parts they have been taught pay off, but without much self-deception as to their real desires; of the more sophisticated Crawfords, who deliberately deceive but begin 'really' to feel more than they had had in mind; and of Fanny, whose ethos of Christian humility often obliges her to act a part. For critics who see the 'lifelong impersonations'[56] of the characters in a hostile light – who see Fanny internalizing, 'inhabiting,' and acting out unreflectively the very ideology that represses her – the firm distinctions Austen wants to make merely confirm the stake she herself has in the difference between 'self' and mask. If we are to continue to find the novel intellectually respectable, they suggest, such distinctions need to be problematized by elements in the text that subvert the very notion of stable and transparent selfhood. The treatment of Henry Crawford I think is the subtlest and most intriguing of these subversions.

Whatever Fanny's opinion of slavery, it does not undercut her reverence for Mansfield Park. Almost from the beginning, she is prepared to 'love this house and everything in it' (60), and her appreciation is only confirmed by the period of exile with her family in Portsmouth at the end of the novel. I take it that we are to read her response to Mansfield Park as yet another sign of Fanny's good taste and see the estate in somewhat the same terms as she is prepared to do. Her love of the place is in line with her ardent response to male authority in general and to other patriarchal structures and institutions. Not only does Fanny revere individual men: her aesthetic, as has often been pointed out, endorses patriarchal authority. The avenue of oaks she hates to see cut down, the romantic chapel she imagines from her reading of Scott, the practice of family prayers, the sublimity of the starry sky (as viewed from the lawn of a great house), the wonder of human creation and of the universe created by God (as exemplifed by evergreen shrubbery), even the name Edmund, 'a name of heroism and renown – of kings, princes, and knights' (224): these are images of a world ordered by the male word, interpreted by male writers, mediated by a patriarchal social system, and elevated by their association with the English country estate.[57] Like Emma observing Donwell Abbey or Elizabeth Bennet reflecting on Pemberley, Fanny makes a space for herself in a man's world by responding with appropriate aesthetic enthusiasm to spaces ordered by the Word of the Father. All her visualizations, with their tincture of the sublime, have a vertical axis, leading her gaze upward. The idea of such systems of order does not constrain or depress her: on the contrary, it inspires her, liberates her, releases her imagination. Austen makes clear how imperfectly the patriarchal ideal has been realized by Sir Thomas and how badly he needs the kind of taste and moral integrity that Fanny herself represents. Nevertheless she allows Mansfield Park to stand as a positive symbol of wider harmonies – harmonies dependent on male authority and manifested in a commodious country estate, however recently founded or dubiously funded, that offers essential material resources to the cultivated heroine.[58]

Indeed, what does account for Fanny's devotion to Mansfield Park, a devotion that dates to very soon after her arrival, long before anyone but Edmund has shown her any kindness? There is no set-piece description of this estate, as there is of Pemberley and Donwell Abbey, but the scattered vignettes that offer glimpses of comfort, prosperity, and certain kinds of decorum suggest the answer to this question. Looking around the property with Mary Crawford instead of up into the heavens with Fanny, we see 'a park, a real park five miles round, a spacious modern-built house, so well placed and well screened as to deserve to be in any collection of engravings of gentlemen's seats in the kingdom' (80). Mary's inventory is morally placed by her enthusiasm for 'improvement' – she takes for granted that the house needs 'to be completely new furnished' (80) – but her positive appraisal can be read as merely a 'horizontal' and practical version of Fanny's mystified 'vertical' response. Fanny herself has not been at Mansfield long when she passionately claims to 'love this house and every thing in it' (60): every *thing*, not every*one*. She makes the claim when she is contemplating banishment to aunt Norris's, and no doubt she is referring to Edmund himself as well as to material objects. But, since the word 'thing' is repeated in the next sentence ('I shall love nothing there') and indeed picked up in the last sentence of the novel (where the parsonage 'soon grew as dear to her heart ... as every thing else, within the view and patronage of Mansfield Park, had long been'[456]), it is too easy just to say, 'For "thing" read "person."' The value of Mansfield Park is so thoroughly spiritualized by Fanny's literary and aesthetic associations – we are so consistently made to feel that she values it 'not for its luxuries but for its propriety, order, and peace'[59] – that it is left for the reader to fill in the unspoken subtext on which her loyalty to it is grounded.

Unspoken, that is, except by Mary Crawford in *Mansfield Park* and by Augusta Elton in *Emma*, who are frank about a woman's desire for a tasteful and substantial dwelling. It is disconcerting to realize that Fanny's inner resources will be rewarded with access to an estate not unlike Selina's Maple Grove, a modern mansion built partly on the profits of slavery. This is as fascinating as it is opaque: the very weirdness of the parallel renders Austen's take on slavery unreadable. Like Charlotte Brontë in *Jane Eyre*, Austen, after endowing the mansion with symbolic glamour, exempts her heroine of merely materialistic interest in it by situating her contentedly in a much more modest dwelling,[60] but unlike Brontë, she represses the gothic subtext that would link property with hidden crime and make life on the country estate a kind of imprisonment. Mansfield Park is allowed to stand as a potential if not a realized ideal because its material resources allow life to be lived with grace and decorum.

What are a few of Fanny's favourite things? There is ample space at Mansfield Park: 'rooms too large' (51) for Fanny to feel comfortable in when she first arrives, but that, despite her own banishment to inferior chambers, she apparently soon finds more attractive, since her claim to love the place comes less than ten pages later; there is a breakfast room with letter paper and 'everything' (52) for writing letters; a well-stocked library; a room of her own for Fanny, which, however small and inferior by Mansfield Park standards, offers her far more privacy and chance for self-culture than she would have at home; there are horses to ride, even if Fanny's entitlement to one is not as secure as that of other members of the family; there are roses to pick, even if it is sadistic of Aunt Norris to make Fanny pick them in the heat of the day. Presumably there is an army of well-trained servants, whose existence makes Fanny's rose picking a scandal and who provide meals easier to eat and digest than Mrs Price's. We hear the names of a few of them – Baddely with the tea-urn; Christopher Jackson, the carpenter whose skillful construction of the amateur stage is the only praiseworthy feature of the theatricals in Sir Thomas's opinion; Chapman, Lady Bertram's maid, whom she dispatches to Fanny too late to help her dress for the ball – but their relative invisibility, in contrast to the rackety intrusiveness of the servants in Portsmouth, suggests how smoothly the house is run. There is a lawn for stargazing; a ballroom large enough to accommodate 'twelve or fourteen couple' (261); and a carriage, which, on the occasion of the dinner party, is ordered, Fanny feels, 'for herself and herself alone' (233). (Her delight and relief suggest that Mrs Elton was right: inner resources do not make up for the lack of a carriage.) As well as regular instruction in the ordinary feminine curriculum, Fanny has dancing lessons that apparently allow her childhood love of dancing to blossom, though there is no account of the practice it would take to transform Portsmouth jigs into Mansfield Park quadrilles.

Indeed, Fanny does acquire accomplishments. Though the word is never used of her, it sneaks back into Austen's novel from the intertext *Lovers' Vows*, where Agatha, adopted at the age of fourteen by 'the lady of the castle and estate' and eventually married to her son, is instructed by her in 'all kinds of female literature and accomplishments.'[61] Fanny's development is not the result only of the maturing of her own natural physical beauty or the blossoming of her mind under Edmund's tutelage. Sir Thomas has been criticized for the complacency with which he tells himself that he is responsible for her improvement, but in fact he is surely correct. Feminine education in the widest sense – 'coming out' as a woman – takes more than 'natural taste' and a library earnestly expounded by a gentlemanly pedagogue; it takes the full resources of gentry wealth, material resources that inner resources may merit but, as Mrs Elton laments, are unlikely to win, unless by means of a fairy-tale ending engineered by the author. No doubt it also takes some practice.

Critics who are dismayed at Fanny's acceptance of an ideology that oppresses her seem to forget how she would have been oppressed had Sir Thomas never taken her in.[62] Neill defends Maria by arguing that marriage is the only career open to her, but the same point, of course, can be made about Fanny.[63] Her adoption has not only allowed her to develop her intellectual potential, as feminists like Wollstonecraft demanded, but also made her marriageable to two presentable men, either of whom might be preferable, for a woman of Fanny's innate refinement, than suitors she would otherwise have encountered. Despite Sir Thomas's tyrannical treatment when she refuses Henry's offer, his intervention in her life is on the whole positive, and though Fanny's gratitude to him is now conventionally treated with irony,[64] it is 'gratitude she really owes to Mansfield Park.'[65] Nor is Sir Thomas's dismay at her refusal of Henry Crawford difficult to understand. If Edmund had married Mary – as he would have done, had Henry not eloped with Maria – what resource would have been left for Fanny? Would she really have been better off back in Portsmouth for the rest of her life? Or back at Mansfield Park – for no doubt Sir Thomas would eventually have relented – as Lady Bertram's personal companion? Though he impersonates the system that makes women dependent, Sir Thomas does understand the implications of that dependency for the individual women whose welfare depends on his actions; in fact, he is *right* about the resources available to Fanny. Though her identification with the bossy men she adores may be repellent and depressing to a present-day reader, the novel does make clear how stark were a genteel woman's alternatives.

The virtues of Mansfield Park are thrown into sharp relief at the end of the novel in the nightmarish episode in which Fanny is compelled to return to her childhood home in Portsmouth. These scenes link moral and aesthetic deficiency with social class in a way that has often evoked a hostile critical response. As Austen presents it, there is no question of self-cultivation in this vulgar environment. Modern readers who find Fanny's sickliness unattractive have found various ways for accounting for Austen's decision to emphasize it,[66] but one reason might surely be just to make clear that there are exceptional individuals with considerable potential who need the material and cultural resources of a place like Mansfield Park to develop it and who would simply be snuffed out in a home like the Prices'. It has been pointed out that in rejecting her own parents Fanny is a snob: that what ought to appall us is not what the family does to her but what is being done to them by an unfair social system of which they are the victims.[67] But if Fanny is a snob, apparently so is Austen: it is not just Fanny but also the text itself that attributes the disorder in the Price home to flaws in the parents', particularly the mother's, character.

The way the Portsmouth group is depicted is the solution to a tactical problem as well as the expression of an ideological position. Exception has been taken both to Austen's demonization of Fanny's home and to the incestuous nature of the conclusion she has devised, with Fanny marrying a 'brother' who stands in for the 'father' she reveres.[68] These two elements are necessarily linked: they express the limited nature of the social mobility Austen wants to allow. To model the exclusive nature of the in group, Austen keeps it 'all in the family,' yet to dramatize the possibility of social advancement, she needs to position Fanny as 'other' by exaggerating the implausible degradation of her background. Fanny is used, in short, to play a dual role. Although she is related by blood to Lady Bertram, Fanny, because of the vulgarity of the home from which she is taken, can easily be seen as representing the elect among the lower middle classes.[69] Mysteriously superior to her nuclear family, however, she represents a middle-class moral earnestness and cultivated interiority that exceed her adoptive parents' as well and that are needed to supplement the aesthetic qualities of Mansfield Park. Having exploited its material and cultural resources to refine and polish her taste and manners, Fanny can then attempt, like a missionary, to carry its message back to Portsmouth. Fanny thus plays the role of middle-class culture-bringer, both to the class above, the gentry, and to the class below, while also representing the small minority of the lower-middle or working class who can be culled out and 'saved' by education and cultivation. Fanny introduces her sister Susan to books precisely as an inner resource, as a means of withdrawing mentally and emotionally from the racket and conflict around her, but the only real solution to Susan's situation is, while gently reforming Mansfield Park, to find a way of bringing Susan into it.

One by one, the novel suggests, really superior individuals from any class may be selected, apprenticed, tested, and brought into the 'family' of the truly genteel. Fanny, a good seed, cannot be cultivated in the home of her birth; the sign that she belongs in a country estate is her growth and blossoming in it. The claim *Mansfield Park* makes to be a novel of education rationalizes a process of social sifting more arbitrary than Austen makes it seem. Fanny is plausibly represented as acquiring as a child the tastes and values of her tutor-cousin, but the real reason that she can 'pass' among the Bertrams is that she never really has to. Her inborn superiority not only to those from whom she has come but to those who adopt her makes Mansfield Park from the beginning what she understands it to be at the end of the novel: her true home. When she returns to Portsmouth, offering a superior standard of behaviour to her nuclear family, though many are called, only one is chosen: Susan, the one with an 'innate taste for the genteel and well-appointed' (409).[70] It is by their receptivity to the culture of the class they wish to join that newcomers demonstrate their worthiness to be received into it, but their progress involves their leaving behind the values of the class from which they came and to which they are by nature superior. Fanny's elevation is a process that individuals without this natural superiority – individuals like Mrs Elton and Harriet Smith – will never be able to emulate. 'Good taste' is a way of rationalizing social mobility for deserving individuals who can be taught, by novels like Austen's among other things, how to speak this discourse – who can be taught it, however, because of their innate receptivity, refinement, and intelligence.

In *Emma*, resources have become a joke: the woman who boasts of them does not have them, the one who needs them cannot use them, and the heroine does not need them because she already has substantial social and economic power. Emma's speech about resources shows them up for what they are: the poor woman's substitute for the real thing. What gives Emma status and finally happiness is the kind of cultural capital she possesses as a birthright: a set of tastes that align her with Knightley and with gentry values from the first pages of the novel. The 'heroine-must-learn' theme in this novel is not only about what Emma learns – which, I shall argue, is simply not to repress the good taste she has always had – but about what those who would like to rise fail to learn from her.

There are several potential pupils in this novel. We have a Cinderella figure, a Fanny Price figure, in the person of Jane Fairfax. Mysteriously superior to her biological relatives, adopted into a household that offers her the opportunity for self-development, and rewarded with a gentry-level husband for taking advantage of the opportunity, Jane is just in Fanny's situation. But Jane's fortuitous education at the hands of the Campbells is not dramatized in *Emma*. Instead, the young woman who plays the role of pupil is Harriet Smith. Like Fanny, Harriet is of humble origin – just how humble, we do not learn in either novel until close to the end – and is adopted by someone eager to improve her: Emma Woodhouse, who is given the role of pedagod/Pygmalion. In offering Harriet cultural resources that are supposed to help her to rise towards her tutor's level, Emma performs a role usually gendered masculine, though with parodic inadequacy that testifies again to Austen's investment in real patriarchs. Unlike Fanny, however, Harriet is defective in nature and resistant of nurture, complacently refusing to be cultivated when given the chance. Her inability and unwillingness to pick up the discourse into which Emma offers to initiate her convict Harriet both of natural inferiority and of culpable resistance to instruction. It is essential to Austen's ideological agenda that Harriet be satirized for these inadequacies rather than compassionated for her lack of cultural capital.

Critics have found Emma's dismissal of Harriet a scandal,[71] but it is clearly endorsed by the text. The problem is not that Emma disposes of Harriet but that Austen has made her disposable. Clifford Siskin asserts that in an Austen novel knowing oneself means knowing one's own level and recognizing one's equals as well as one's inferiors: Emma has to learn that Knightley is on her level and Harriet is below it.[72] He is right. Harriet's bad taste is a sure sign of her lack of wit, common sense, analytical acuity, and even moral stability (the suggestion is that not only Robert Martin's moral solidity but also the retired situation of his dwelling will be needed to protect her from straying into adulterous crushes).[73] No one who listens to Harriet's tone of voice before and after she has been taken up by Emma can seriously argue that Emma has improved her: had Harriet not been too malleable to take any imprint for long – and had she not figured in a story as fairy-tale-like, in its own way, as Jane's – her corruption at Emma's hands might well have had permanent consequences. It is true, as Knightley says, that Harriet is a better person than Mrs Elton, but this is damning with faint praise, particularly since – whether Knightley knows it or not, which he probably does not – Harriet is thoroughly impressed by this dreadful woman. Critics who defend Harriet (and Emma's scant efforts on her behalf) on the grounds that Knightley admits Emma has improved her are missing a comic pattern. Knightley's gallant concession is analogous to Mr Elton's praise of Harriet's portrait. Both the men who court Emma over-praise the Harriet-product she has made because of their interest in the maker, and both are demonstrably wrong.

One of the first signs of Harriet's ineducability is her failure to negotiate the codes that define taste for Austen and for the cultivated characters she endorses. In exposing Harriet to our laughter because (for example) she does not understand that everyone regards Jane as a better pianist than Emma, Austen is not being entirely fair. Like the charade Harriet is comically unable to solve, the discourse of taste is a language that she has never had the opportunity to acquire, a rhetorical game with rules that no one ever articulates for her.[74] Emma's explication of the remark about her own 'taste' in music looks like a lesson: that is, it convicts Harriet of stupidity when she fails to pick up on it. But what Emma does not do – probably could not do, since, as a 'native speaker,' she has internalized the rules of this discourse without analysing them – is spell out for a provincial teenager unaccustomed to gentry society the principles upon which such remarks are based.

The story of Emma's sponsorship of Harriet parodies contemporary novels of education (like Mme de Genlis's *Adelaide and Theodore*) that imply that anything is possible with the right system. When Emma tries to reshape Harriet as Adelaide's mother shapes Adelaide but gets nowhere, this is evidently because Harriet has no innate quality of mind or character. But it is also true that Emma has no system. Emma cannot analyse the principles of the discourse she uses with such tact and skill because she, as a novelistic construction, is a product of it. Emma's cultural capital is naturalized by Austen as simply 'taste,' the kind of taste that in an Austen novel is a sure sign of the heroine's fundamental moral sense but that cannot be communicated by instruction to anyone innately incapable of rising to it.

As in *Mansfield Park*, the notion of taste is developed in dynamic tension with accomplishments and performance. The way Emma's own accomplishments are dealt with is comically indulgent. It is made clear that Emma is by no means a polished performer in any activity that takes application and commitment. She does not practise her scales, she does not finish her drawings, and she does not get through her reading lists. The narrator is properly judgmental about her lack of commitment, complaining that 'in nothing had she approached the degree of excellence which she would have been glad and ought not to have failed of' (32). But this moralizing does not carry much conviction, because the flaws in Emma's musical and artistic execution are mitigated by her awareness of them.[75] Emma is all the more appealing for the sure taste with which she assesses the mediocrity of her own performance.

The heroine's first extended speech in the novel is the funny monologue in which she represents her 'performances' (32) in portraiture: the portfolio of her drawings of her family. As she displays her sketches to a comically uncritical audience, Emma accounts for their flaws in terms of the character and habits of the model. Her drawings of her father, she explains, are not very like him because he is self-conscious; those of Mrs Weston are good because she is a generous, patient sitter; Isabella's picture is unfinished because she could not wait to have her children drawn; the children are not well done because little children will not sit still; Mr John Knightley's portrait was abandoned because Isabella complained it did not do him justice. This amusing digression, though it testifies to her lack of application, actually presents Emma in a sympathetic light. The impression we are left with is not only that Emma does not take herself very seriously – these are mock excuses, designed to convict rather than exonerate the artist – but also that she is deeply fond of these people and has amused insight into their character. Indeed, in the very act of pointing out why she has failed to capture their physical likeness on paper, Emma captures their essential character in words. In eighteenth-century art criticism, 'idea' is privileged over detailed physical accuracy. Emma no doubt knows that the unfinished sketch has a certain prestige and that genius in painting is held to reside in the informing idea rather than in the mere 'mechanic' reproduction of the material world. In a funny and unexpected way her verbal character sketches meet this key criterion of artistic excellence.

Indeed, Emma is probably alluding specifically to this contemporary discourse when she comments wryly on her accurate depiction of baby George's elaborate bonnet. One of the better-known art-critical anecdotes of the time concerned Timanthes, the Greek painter who solved the problem of depicting Agamemnon's inexpressible grief at the death of Iphigenia by covering his face with a veil.[76] Emma solves a different kind of problem, her mediocre draughtsmanship, in the same way. Since she found the child a difficult subject, Emma says, she took advantage of a moment when he was 'nestled down' in the arm of a sofa to draw his headdress instead, with gratifying results: 'it is as strong a likeness of his cockade as you would wish to see,' she says – 'I am rather proud of young George' (33). The carefully rendered cockade is just the kind of detail of costume that Dutch painters were sneered at for focusing on.[77] Emma knows the conventional criteria of good art, even if she cannot produce it herself, and she knows exactly how lame are her own efforts (and, by implication, those of other female daubers and dabblers as well) in the light of these criteria. She appropriates Reynoldian insights with a graceful *sprezzatura* while humorously putting down mere female accomplishments – albeit her own. In refusing to commit herself to her music and drawing, Emma may or may not be morally wrong, but in recognizing the second-rate result, she is aesthetically right, and her detachment and self-parody suggest both her good taste and her good feeling and differentiate her from the vain and shallow young ladies who take accomplishments seriously.

The charm of Emma's performance suggests that actual accomplishments are not as important as the rhetorical stance one takes towards them. This is the way to 'perform' indifference to performance: with self-deprecating wit and effortless cultural allusion. Like the novelist, Emma performs not with paint or piano but with words. Since verbal art is valued over visual, poetry over painting, Emma's rhetorical talent is arguably 'higher' than artistic or musical skill, as well as less gender-specific. Austen raises the issue of accomplishments to display Emma's more substantial *resources*, resources of language, which, associated as they are with wit, judgment, and self-understanding, are more significant, both to Knightley and to Austen's implied reader, than the feminine accomplishments she has not bothered to master.

But when Emma begins to act instead of to judge – when she produces a new drawing, the flattering portrait of Harriet – she becomes not only dishonest but vulgar. This picture is the very antithesis of the fond but unfinished sketches of her family. Emma is perfectly aware of what she is doing and laughs at Elton when he praises the likeness, but she refuses to recognize that her romantic conception of Harriet as the heroine of a foundling romance is as false as the drawing and that to manipulate her life is not only more dangerous but just as vulgar as to manipulate her visual image. The deliberate debasement of Emma's taste is linked with the coarsening of her judgment. We laugh with Emma as she mocks her own drawing, but we laugh at her when she undertakes Harriet's makeover. Austen assumes a reader who, sharing Emma's own standards of taste, recognizes the perils of her project.

Emma is not only a reliable art critic, she is a good reader.[78] Despite the putative inadequacies of her literary education, her taste is fundamentally sound. When called upon to assess prose and verse, Emma judges according to criteria that the reader is expected to accept. But taste is one thing, execution another. As soon as she begins to execute her own plots she represses her own reliable aesthetic intuitions and makes serious mistakes in judgment.

Emma's first act of literary criticism is her assessment of Robert Martin's letter of proposal. Harriet, who has already taken a mental inventory of Martin's two parlours, eight cows, and summer house 'large enough to hold a dozen people' (18), judges the missive as she judges his worldly goods, in terms of quantity rather than quality, and finds it rather less satisfactory. It is 'but a short letter' (40) in her opinion, for Harriet simply does not know that one is not supposed to want more of a good thing: not having been exposed to the discourse in which elegance is aligned with concision and simplicity, she is not impressed by

the ability to 'say just what you must, in a short way' (58). But Emma recognizes immediately, though with surprise, that the letter, with its 'plain,
... strong and unaffected' language, its 'good sense,' 'propriety,' and
'delicacy of feeling,' is 'better written ... than I had expected' (37),
indeed a model of its kind. She cannot bring herself to say that it is
badly written; she cannot even bring herself to exploit Harriet's 'bad
taste' (40) in wishing it were longer, though it would be to her advantage to do so.[79] Martin is indeed correct to write a short letter, not only
because 'such things in general cannot be too short' as Emma will later
say of the charade, but because a long-winded romantic farmer, usurp-
ing the rhetorical prerogatives of the literary class, would seem rather
comic and contemptible than ardent and sensitive. Martin's plain style is
the sign of his sense of decorum; it demonstrates both that he knows his
place and that, for that very reason, he can be allowed to rise (slightly)
above it. We are invited to regard Emma's approval of his style as correct, both because she has nothing to gain and everything to lose by it
and because it flatters our own liberalism about social mobility.

Like Mr Knightley, Emma instinctively respects 'manliness' and is well
able to detect it. Puzzled to account for the excellence of Martin's letter,
she wonders if his sisters, who are receiving a somewhat genteel education, could have written it, but concludes that this is impossible: the
prose is 'not the style of a woman; no, certainly, it is too strong and concise; not diffuse enough for a woman' (37). In view of the recent critical
hostility to Knightley and what is taken to be his pedagogical bullying, it
is important to notice that Emma's taste aligns her with him from the
very beginning of the novel. It is not a question of being converted to
his standards: her judgment here makes clear that she always really
shares them.[80] As must the reader on this occasion: the clarity and concision Emma admires are not standards it is easy to quarrel with. Early in
the novel Austen cannily enlists the reader's aesthetic judgment in the
service of social advancement rather than social exclusion. Good taste is
aligned with liberal social feeling, and both point in the same direction:
towards the recognition of Martin's worth.

Robert Martin can be allowed this worth precisely because, as Emma
says, he belongs to the class of persons 'with whom I feel I can have
nothing to do' (20). A faithful yeoman farmer is no threat to middle-
class self-identity: it is those with whom cultivated people must have
something to do who cannot be so readily idealized. Those critics who
approve of Robert Martin have not noticed the mystification involved in
his construction. Martin's purity of expression is as inexplicable as it is

unanswerable. It is essential that his letter not be reproduced in the novel, since prose exhibiting the 'good sense, warm attachment, liberality, propriety, even delicacy of feeling' (37) that Emma discerns would be indistinguishable from Knightley's own: it would simply erase the class difference that this episode is devised to negotiate. Austen's strategy is to erase Martin himself. We scarcely see him, and we never hear him speak.[81] This is a novelist's solution, unavailable to the filmmaker. Since on screen the actor playing Martin has to look more yokelish than his letter apparently sounds, the director is then cornered into decisions about how to deal with the class tensions that it is the novel's business to repress.[82] Robert Martin is a novelistic construction cannily calculated to evoke a response like Lionel Trilling's: to position Austen as endorsing a certain kind of social mobility and thus exonerate her from the charge of snobbery when she condemns other kinds.

Emma has the good taste to approve Martin's prose, but she will not allow her taste to guide her behaviour. Despite her covert approval, she pretends to believe that a prose style that 'would not have disgraced a gentleman' (37) could be compatible with an offensively 'clownish manner' (40), affects surprise that Harriet could hesitate to refuse Martin, and claims to consider this suitor inferior to a woman whose vulgarity is signalled by her defensiveness about his prose.[83] She is equally disingenuous in her assessment of Martin's taste in books. When Harriet complains that Robert lacks her love of romance and has even forgotten to pick up the copy of *The Romance of the Forest* that she has suggested he read, we are invited to take Harriet's enthusiasm for romance as another example of her preference for quantity over quality and to relate Martin's indifference not only to his taste for manly brevity but to his proper sense of his social position. Austen's contemporaries might have recalled the story, in *Spectator* #71, of the manservant whose elaborate love letter is attributed to his surreptitious reading of the romances he finds in his master's bedroom. In both texts, taste in novels is associated with taste in letter writing, and in both, elaborate rhetoric signals the crossing of class boundaries. A man who writes the kind of letter Emma would value is not likely to be interested in the romances Harriet admires, and Emma must know that. She must feel that the books Harriet urges on her suitor would be a waste of his time, that his willingness even to propose picking them up when he is in town is a measure of his affection and his readiness to meet her tastes halfway, and that his forgetting to do so is rather a sign of industry and responsibility than illiteracy and coarseness. It is after all because he is committed to his work that Martin will be able to provide Harriet with the material resources she really values more than she does romances – resources she has already evaluated and enumerated. But again, though Emma judges correctly, she acts deceitfully, encouraging Harriet to believe that a man unacquainted with gothic fiction is unworthy of her hand.

Emma's taste, in short, would make her, like Knightley, a reliable promoter of the right kind of social mobility, did she not willfully suppress it.[84] Although the novel is often read as a comedy of Emma's errors, in fact events repeatedly confirm her tasteful intuitions. She recognizes Harriet's bad taste in prose but not what it indicates about her overall mediocrity of character. She knows that Elton's charade is 'a jumble without taste or truth' (104), but she will not let herself read these lapses as reliable clues to his intentions. Her sense that his effusive gallantry is 'a mere error of taste' (104) alerts us to her error: in an Austen novel there is no such thing as a *mere* error of taste. She considers the Coles as 'only moderately genteel' (159), and though we laugh at her discomfiture when she thinks she is not invited to their party, Mrs Cole proves her right by means of the extended monologue about their 'new grand pianoforte in the drawing-room' (166), in which she implies that the real mark of status is the ability to pay for an instrument you canot be bothered to play. Eager though Emma is to defend Frank Churchill to Mr Knightley, she is quick to detect his essential 'inelegance of mind' (152) and never really gives her heart to him. The supposedly limited reading she has done, apparently of novels like Edgeworth's or Burney's, has given her crucial insight into her own feelings, for she senses that she cannot be in love if she does not find herself using the word 'sacrifice' when she refuses him.

But though Emma's literary taste is reliable when she is judging the texts of others, when she herself becomes an author she suppresses it. The genres she chooses are vulgar, and she develops them in a vulgar way. She tries to turn Harriet's life into a foundling romance,[85] imagining that her pretty protégée will turn out to be the daughter of a gentleman, and, like Cherry Wilkinson's irresponsible governess, she inflames the imagination of her pupil with self-aggrandizing fantasies, leading her seriously astray.[86] While Emma's makeover project has an appealing generosity, it involves a serious misreading, as much of the genre as of Harriet. The foundling romance, which attributes excellence of character to good blood, is politically conservative. Harriet's story, which turns out to be a foundling romance in parodic reverse (her father is a tradesman), has already been adumbrated by her mediocrity of mind and character. Emma's self-indulgent fling at transcending class difference leads her sentimentally to misread a genre that endorses it. Abandoning her aesthetic sense, she loses her grip on the literary sensibility that should have taught her better.

The malicious narrative Emma concocts about Jane Fairfax belongs to an equally vulgar but more unpleasant genre: the tale of adultery of the kind found, framed by much disingenuous moralizing, in Mme de Genlis.[87] This kind of story is based on simplistic assumptions: that adulterous feelings immediately follow marriage; that a plain man cannot be truly in love with a plain woman; that if a man saves a woman from danger, they must fall in love. Emma assumes that both Mr Dixon's rescue of Jane from drowning and Frank Churchill's rescue of Harriet from the gypsies point to romantic attraction. It is not until romance reader Harriet demonstrates her readiness to follow these premises to their logical conclusion that Emma, confronted with the loss of Knightley, is made to realize how socially subversive they are. The genres that can be read as encouraging the crossing of class boundaries are represented by Austen as fundamentally vulgar, and Emma's impetuous commitment to their myths links her lapse in literary taste with an unwillingness to make proper social distinctions.

It is only when Emma begins to substitute taste for execution, meditation for meddling, and contemplation for action that she can move towards a happy ending. The two climactic episodes, the strawberry-picking party at Donwell Abbey and the 'exploring' at Box Hill, are paired in just those polarized terms. Emma's private meditation on the view from Donwell Abbey is a demonstration of her moral taste, but her performance with Frank Churchill at Box Hill, the public nature of which makes Emma herself feel deeply uneasy, leads her into spectacular social transgression. It is only when Emma stops executing and performing that she begins to 'know herself' and realize that all her projects were misguided. From this point on she does not act, but simply judges. Judging correctly means understanding that she has always in fact agreed with Mr Knightley.

Indeed, I would argue that performance in *Emma* is coded feminine and true taste masculine; that Mr Knightley, like Emma, is shaped by the polarity between taste and execution; and that because he is aligned from the beginning with reliable taste, we know that the heroine will find her destiny only when she admits that they share the same standards and becomes, not an actor, but an informed arbiter and reliable patron of her social inferiors.

Knightley himself is anything but a performer. Not of course that he leads a life of detached contemplation: as critics who like him are fond of pointing out, Knightley is actively involved in the management of his estate, in a way that we are presumably invited to admire.[88] These activities, however, take place offstage: as Butler puts it, in the middle distance.[89] Seen in close-up, in particular dramatized episodes, he is less an actor than an acute observer. Litvak accuses Knightley of wanting to play detective, but since what he detects is not just that Jane has a secret but that Harriet needs a dance partner, his acuteness might rather be praised as insight than dismissed as an exercise in patriarchal power.[90] Though Knightley is 'made for positive interventions,' as Gard puts it[91] – providing a carriage for Jane and her aunt, asking Harriet to dance – these interventions are as quiet as possible, characterized by a modesty, even a secretiveness, that is recognizably Christian: his left hand does not know what his right hand is doing (though Emma usually finds out). The closest Knightley comes to any kind of performance is in the little scene at the end of chapter 28 where he publicly if not unkindly mocks Miss Bates for praising people within their hearing – a flash of wry exasperation that suggests that he and Emma may not fundamentally disagree about this lady's foolishness.[92] But most of the time Knightley observes rather than acts, and whenever he observes, he judges. To be sure, his judgments tend to be moral rather than aesthetic, and he seems to have no particular aesthetic preferences. He produces his coin collection only to set it out for Mr Woodhouse's enjoyment and refers to dancing only to dismiss it, and the only beauty he seems to register is Emma's. But though he never uses the word 'taste' and no one uses it of him, we are not to imagine, as Harriet does of Jane, that because no one speaks of it he does not have it. Knightley's taste is not expressed, like Emma's, in projects, or like Jane's, in accomplishments, but is read in his manners, reflected in his estate, and used to inform his social criticism.

Like Emma, Knightley is discriminating about language. He equates straightforward prose with masculinity: the words 'man' or 'manly' are profoundly positive ones for him, as we have seen they also are for Emma. When he praises Robert Martin for always speaking 'to the purpose; open, straight forward' (44), we connect his assessment with Emma's evaluation of Martin's letter and read it as a judgment of her as well as of Martin. When Knightley finds the style of Frank's letter repellent, condemning his Gallic suavities ('manoeuvring and finessing') in terms of the distinction between the English 'amiable' and the French 'aimable,'[93] we suspect, even allowing for his personal animus against his rival, that Frank will in fact turn out to be unreliable.[94] When, valuing word games no more than Emma herself, Mr Knightley gives a rapid but measured assessment of Mr Weston's 'M/A' riddle – '*Perfection* should not have come so soon' (291) – he manages at once to flatter Weston for his ingenuity and to chide Emma for her impertinence to Miss Bates, even as he implies a critique of the trivial genre itself. In Knightley as in Emma, linguistic discrimination is firmly associated with reliable moral judgment and proper social discrimination.

Indeed, Emma's perfect comprehension of his witty quibble underscores the significance of their shared taste for language. From the first pages of the novel the compatibility of Emma and Knightley is signalled by their tendency to address each other confidentially, over the heads, as it were, of their inferiors. Their mutual attempt, in chapter 1, to point out to Mr Woodhouse the advantages of Miss Taylor's marriage positions them from the very beginning as two adults managing a child (and thus endorses the co-parenting they undertake when Knightley moves in with Emma at the end of the novel).[95] The fact that the first lesson Knightley purports to teach Emma – 'she knows how much the marriage is to Miss Taylor's advantage' (6) and so on – is really directed at her father suggests their essential equality: he knows that she does know all this, and he also knows that she knows what he is doing in pretending to address his advice to her. The terse exchange in chapter 15, when Knightley discovers that the snowfall they are worried about is negligible and the two agree that the carriages should be called, unites them in the same way: as Butler point outs, 'Emma catches his tone when she talks to him.'[96] Fundamentally aligned as they are from the very first pages of the novel, it is slightly bizarre and yet quite appropriate that the only verbal exchange Emma has with her fiancé after their engagement – indeed, the longest passage of sustained dialogue between them in the whole novel – is their critique of Frank Churchill's letter, to which I shall return at the end of this discussion.

It is not only by way of his acts of judgment that the hero is aligned with good taste. As has often been pointed out, Mr Knightley is metonymically identified with his estate, Donwell Abbey. The strawberry picnic, which gives the reader the first view of this estate, is also set up in terms of the ongoing polarity between taste and execution. The episode locates genuine tastefulness firmly with the hero and his estate while it erases the activities that produced the estate in the first place, genders performance female, and displaces it onto a woman – the

woman whose meddling has made her a demonic parody of the heroine herself.

Performance and execution are associated with Mrs Elton, who sets
the polarities into play at the beginning of the episode. Eager as she
always is to flaunt her connection with Maple Grove – the very name
identifies it as a raw new property built by tenacious arrivistes[97] – she is
yet more eager, when the occasion presents itself, to strengthen her connection with Mr Knightley and insinuate herself into his noble old
estate. The projected afternoon at Donwell Abbey begins in a flurry of
busyness on the part of the lady. Knightley's own low-key proposal to
have his friends 'come, and eat my strawberries' has her immediately
offering not only to lend him her housekeeper but even to draw up his
guest list. Knightley refuses the first offer on behalf of his own employee
and declines the second with a suave finality that puts Mrs Elton in her
place while leaving her self-esteem intact: 'there is but one married
woman in the world whom I can ever allow to invite what guests she
pleases to Donwell, and that one is ... Mrs Knightley' (277). The contrast
between her rhetorical strain and overemphasis and the ease with which
he contains her vulgarity illustrates the social power of the true gentleman. Mrs Elton's pushiness enrages Emma, but Mr Knightley deals with
her with an understated irony that has an aesthetic neatness of its own.
The 'elegance' Mrs Elton values so much is evoked, by her own importunities, in those who have to resist her.

Mrs Elton next has to decide how to present herself on the day of the
party. She chooses to dramatize her taste for the simple and the natural
by donning a straw hat and ribbons and arriving on a donkey. Johnson
identifies the get-up as her 'vapidly fashionable appropriation of Rousseauvian ideas about retirement'; Gard and Gay notice the parallel with
Marie Antoinette. But the source of this characterization is more likely
another novel. Austen no doubt expects her reader to connect Mrs
Elton's self-dramatization with that of a fictional character like Cherry
Wilkinson, who says of one of her own affected costumes, 'My pastoral
garb was appropriate: yes, I would rival an Ida, or a Glorvina, in simple
touches of nature.'[98]

Unlike Mrs Elton, Emma does not have to 'perform' her taste for pastoral simplicity before any of the other characters. Because she is the
protagonist and the narrator is willing to follow her as she moves off
alone, she is displayed to the reader, if not to the people in her fictional
world, in a moment of unselfconscious reverie. Mrs Elton is always picturing herself and the effect she is creating, but Emma, as she contem-

plates the view from Donwell Abbey, is attending, for once, not to her own projects and performances but to what is around her. Meditating on the beauty of the 'prospect' and the dignity of the estate as a whole, Emma aligns herself, unselfconsciously, with Knightley and what he stands for: 'English verdure, English culture, English comfort' (282).[99]

As has often been pointed out, the moment has premonitory force: Emma's responsiveness makes clear to us what she herself does not yet know, that she is destined to be the estate's chatelaine. As she looks out from Donwell Abbey, Emma is like Elizabeth Bennet in *Pride and Prejudice*, who visits Pemberley and learns to value Darcy for the moral and social qualities it reveals without imagining that she will ever live in it.[100] Elizabeth is impressed by the apartment that Darcy has provided for his sister, one of the details that induces Clara Tuite to refer to the description of Pemberley as an example of Austen's 'embourgeoisement' of aristocratic taste.[101] Donwell Abbey however remains 'un-bourgeoised' in that there is no space in it specifically dedicated to a woman. Though the suggestion is that there is a place for everyone – the grounds and public rooms accommodate Knightley's guests, the valley below houses the farmer attached to the estate – we are never shown the rooms a wife might occupy. Nor will we ever see them, since at the end of the novel Emma brings her new husband into her own home. Whatever the psychological and emotional implications of this living arrangement, one of its formal effects is to assure that Donwell Abbey remains a thoroughly patriarchal icon.

But though Emma is not given a space at Donwell in this chapter, she provides one for herself. She inserts herself into the scene, not by inventorying it, as Harriet or Mrs Elton would do, but by aestheticizing it, by looking down from a lofty viewpoint on the prospect below, by assuming a point of view – by exercising her taste. The episode as a whole suggests indeed that the way the gentlewoman makes a place for herself in a patriarchal world is by reading that patriarchal economy, by acceding to it, appreciating it, and responding to it with informed aesthetic feeling.[102] Trilling takes the narrative voice here as a corrective to Emma's snobbery, but Emma's viewpoint is aligned with that of the narrator, whose quotable effusion is sandwiched in between the heroine's approving 'views' of the Abbey itself and of Abbey-Mill Farm,

> with all its appendages of prosperity and beauty, its rich pastures, spreading flocks, orchard in blossom, and light column of smoke ascending. (282)

The participles in this musical sentence, horizontally and vertically expansive, suggest the plenitude of the English countryside; and the easy catalogue, the freedom of Emma's glance as she surveys it. (It is interesting that there are no trees here to block or channel her view – neither Selina's embowering maples nor Fanny's Burkean oaks.) Emma's responsiveness to a landscape that lies open to her response is an index not only of her emotional orientation to Mr Knightley but of her moral orientation to the political and economic system that has produced and constructed both the estate and the prospect she admires.

We are not invited in this episode, however, to look directly at that system. Austen's language obscures the idea of process and intentionality, occulting the history of the estate's development. Donwell Abbey and its grounds are described as if they emerged gradually over the centuries as a spontaneous outgrowth of the countryside itself. The house rambles (280), its lime avenue leads 'to nothing' (282), its gardens stretch down to the meadows, the slope acquires steepness, and Abbey-Mill Farm rises at the bottom, as the river makes 'a close and handsome curve around it' (282), tying it together aesthetically into a stable, bounded whole.[103] The verbs assimilate the Abbey to the countryside of which it is a part, as if it and the landscape that contains it had both developed together naturally without the need for human intervention. Even the 'improvements' which have *not* been made are attributed to abstract nouns rather than to the Knightley family: 'neither fashion nor extravagance,' we are told, has 'rooted up' (the one vigorous verb in the passage) the timber (280). Emma herself comes close to personifying Donwell: feeling that 'it was just what it ought to be' (280), she experiences 'an increasing respect for it, as the residence of a family of such true gentility,' as if the estate deserved credit and gratitude for accommodating the worthy Knightleys, who have always been merely its custodians.

Since the process by which Knightley's family acquired and developed the estate has been erased, he himself has nothing to do but conserve what he has inherited. The house contains collections, but Knightley does not seem to be a collector: we have no sense that he has acquired the coins and medals he sets out to amuse Mr Woodhouse. Paradoxically, Knightley can be identified with Donwell Abbey because nothing we see there is the product of his own individual action or choice. There is nothing he personally needs to do, or could have done, to acquire the taste and the gentlemanliness that distinguish him. This is the kind of status that can only have been acquired for him, generations ago, by his ancestors.[104] There is no need for him to 'perform' his tastefulness because the narrator makes sure that we, along with Emma, can read out his value from the estate that is his metonym.

Meanwhile, Mrs Elton continues frenetically to perform hers, dramatizing her taste for the pastoral by insisting on picking the strawberries herself. Like Fanny Price picking roses, however, she soon wears herself out in the heat, and in the space of a single funny monologue her affected enthusiasm gives way to exhaustion and disgust. A materialist critic might make the point that such a lady's posturing depends upon the patient labour of people who really have to pick those strawberries – might draw attention to the way Austen has displaced onto Mrs Elton the 'execution,' the busyness, the hours of work it must have taken to provide for the activities of this gracious afternoon; to the fact that it is Knightley's housekeeper who has organized the fête and who knows how many working people who have done the real berry picking. This very oblique return, via the theme of heat exhaustion, to the issue of slavery casts a strange light back on *Mansfield Park.* Both novels provide evidence that the comfortable way of life Austen seems to idealize is based on the labour of others, but in both the issue is treated with disconcerting 'taciturnity.'[105] Mrs Elton's loquacious self-pity does tend to reflect ironically back on Fanny's 'slavery,' and it certainly suggests that to compare either woman's situation to that of actual slaves, as do both Austen's feminist contemporaries and today's critics, is a scandalous trivialization.

But the role of servants, although we are made to register it, is not a theme Austen emphasizes. The scene is set up not so much to remind us of Knightley's dependence on anonymous labour as to foreground his own civilized, magnanimous sensibility. His ironic response to Mrs Elton's plan to have everything 'as natural and simple as possible' expresses his good taste, even as it makes clear, in a way that present-day readers have found obnoxious, that he takes this anonymous labour for granted:

> 'My idea of the simple and the natural will be to have the table spread in the dining-room. The nature and the simplicity of gentlemen and ladies, with their servants and furniture, I think is best observed by meals within doors. When you are tired of eating strawberries in the garden, there shall be cold meat in the house.' (278)[106]

Mr Knightley is not interested in the acts of production, the work by which the food is secured, but in the act of consumption: the style in which it is offered and eaten.[107] Austen opposes, to the self-conscious performance of the lady on the make, the mental activity of the gentleman host who disperses refreshments by fiat rather than by physical activity. Her scenario does not call upon Knightley to perform or execute, but tastefully to dispense. In his bounty we have real resources, resources hospitably distributed in the tradition celebrated by the country-house poem, not hoarded up for self-sufficient retirement.

The Donwell Abbey episode, in short, erases from the true gentleman all taint of manual labour, opportunism, greed, personal ambition, and self-fashioning and displaces these onto the woman whose attempts at border crossing are blocked and mocked by Austen. The suggestion is that genuine social distinction cannot be faked: that the Mrs Eltons of the world, because they are rooted in no such landed estate and because their attempts to appropriate the taste of the elite are so clumsy and transparent, will never be able to 'pass.' The novelist keeps the vulgar arriviste firmly in her place and advances the spirited gentlewoman into the patriarchal space to which her good taste entitles her. Her text also instructs the implied reader, more sensitive and intelligent than Mrs Elton or Harriet Smith, how such taste is to be performed.

The novel concludes with Emma's and Knightley's discussion of Frank Churchill's letter, another passage to which critics hostile to Knightley and his patriarchal authority have taken strong exception. It is a misreading of the scene however to argue that Emma is right in finding Knightley's assessment of Frank too harsh.[108] The analysis of the letter is carefully framed to imply the opposite. Under the pressure of their emotion for each other, both Knightley and Emma have initially judged Frank rigorously but correctly and then reversed their judgment and become too easy on him. Emma was ready to condemn Frank when she first learned of his secret engagement, and she approaches his letter indulgently four chapters later simply because, newly engaged in the meantime, she is too happy to think ill of any other lover. Knightley, who has distrusted Frank from the beginning, suddenly feels uncharacteristically benign when he learns that Emma has never loved him. It is with a cooler judgment that when, on Emma's insistence, he assesses the letter, he corroborates the reader's own judgment of Frank's behaviour.[109] Austen uses the letter as a writer of detective fiction uses the criminal's confession, to pick up the clues and retell the story from an insider's point of view, but she also uses it as an occasion for moral and aesthetic analysis, underscoring yet again the alignment between taste and ethics.

The topic of the letter takes up the better part of two chapters. In chapter 50 we get its full text – a rambling, histrionic, faux spontaneous performance, so unlike Frank's ordinary mode of expression that we seem to be hearing his real voice for the first time. Johnson had pointed out that 'a friendly Letter is a calm and deliberate performance in the cool of leisure, in the stillness of solitude, and surely no man sits down to depreciate by design his own character.'[110] Frank's refusal to take advantage of the opportunity for cool self-construction that the epistolary form makes available – his insistence on dramatizing the emotional hiatus in his own composition ('Here, my dear madam, I was obliged to leave off abruptly, to recollect and compose myself'[345]) – is self-depreciation of just the kind Johnson found unimaginable. It is as essential to reproduce this letter in full as to suppress Robert Martin's: if the style is the man, Frank is more narcissistic, self-indulgent, and irresponsible than we might otherwise have realized.[111] Emma is too generous, and Knightley's point-by-point critique, which follows in chapter 51, expresses the objections we will have already been formulating, in the moral vacuum opened up by her refusal to judge. Knightley decides to 'speak my opinion aloud as I read' in order to 'feel that I am near you' – so that 'it will not be so great a loss' (349) of the time he would rather spend discussing their own plans. Emma for her part is the readier to forgive Frank because she finds it hard to forgive herself for her involvement with him. Read in its careful complexity, this episode dramatizes the new and better partnership that has replaced Emma's and Frank's mischievous collusion. Knightley does not mention Frank's prose style explicitly, though his judgment is implicit in his 'What a letter the man writes!' But Austen, who has already let the style do its work on the reader, underlines its weakness by having the narrator praise Knightley's own language, when he is finally free to speak of what has been on his mind (coming to live with her father), as 'plain, unaffected, gentleman-like English' (352). This letter-reading episode recalls not only Emma's and Knightley's first argument over Frank's epistolary prose but also Emma's judgment of Martin's letter. Bookending the novel with these critiques reminds us not only how correct Knightley has always been but also how close Emma was to his values from the beginning.

Frank's behaviour has earned condemnation; if Austen were not giving Jane's story a fairy-tale shape, it would have ended much less happily. Nevertheless, it is important to notice that Knightley's disapproval will have no impact on Frank at all. The analysis of the letter is a private moment between Emma and Knightley, who, though he feels that Frank has gained a much better wife than he deserves, does hope that the couple will be happy. Nor does Emma's and Knightley's contempt for the Eltons do them any harm. The good taste of these two social leaders is represented as pure judgment and not as social action: it is represented as displacing, rather than facilitating, performance and execution. *Emma* raises fewer critical hackles than *Mansfield Park* not only because judgments of taste are more suave than moral judgments but also because the kind of social power that taste does have is smoothly occluded from the text.

Bourdieu's phrase for the kind of damage that judgments of taste can do is 'symbolic violence.' By this he means the methods by which the dominated class are persuaded to acquiesce in their own domination: to feel that they are naturally different from those who condescend to them and that they can never measure up. But in Austen's novels characters like Mrs Elton and Harriet Smith never do feel this. They never acquiesce in their own domination; indeed, they never realize that they are being dominated. What Austen always dramatizes is their inability to grasp that there is a gap between their standards and those of the class they wish to join. The very last paragraph in *Emma* is used to document Mrs Elton's contempt for the understated style of the heroine's wedding – a wedding, opines the narrator, 'very much like other weddings, where the parties have no taste for finery or parade' (381). But although Mrs Elton aspires to friendship with such 'parties,' she is apparently incapable of learning what a tasteful wedding looks like to them: incapable of watching what they do and reflecting on the signs that mark their difference from her. Taking her vulgar sister to represent a social standard to which Emma and Knightley might aspire, she judges them by Selina's standards rather than Selina by theirs: 'Very little white satin, very few lace veils; a most pitiful business! – Selina would stare when she heard of it' (381). To an even unrealistic degree, Austen's vulgarians, who are incapable of learning from the heroine, are also incapable of feeling that they have failed to learn. They are put down twice, first by the characters within the fiction for their incorrigible vulgarity, then by Austen for being so dull as not even to recognize it.

Like poetry in Auden's famous line, taste in *Emma* apparently makes nothing happen.[112] Emma can be seen as snobbish in trying to keep Robert Martin down (and be blamed by Trilling) or modern in trying to raise Harriet up (and be praised by Langland as a 'social semiotician' who understands the new relevance of manners). But when she attempts to patrol the social borders, she always fails. What Langland argues that the middle-class lady does – function as an effective social arbiter – Emma precisely fails to do.[113] Emma wants Mr Elton to marry Harriet but he refuses, and on just the grounds that Langland cites: because, stupidly, he does not see marriage to Harriet as a way of advancing his interests.[114] Yet he is degraded by the marriage he does make only in the eyes of true arbiters like Emma and Mr Knightley, whose thorough dislike of his wife does not prevent the Eltons from doing anything except hobnobbing with them. The gossips of Highbury continue to be impressed by the Eltons; even the Westons tolerate them. Only Knightley and Emma despise them. The mystification here is that the negative judgment of such powerful people has no effect on the opinion of the wider community. Mr Elton presumably can no longer boast of 'my good Knightley's' friendship, but there is no sense that he will lose anything else.[115]

While Highbury's failure to notice the Eltons' vulgarity does demonstrate a new kind of social openness (hopeful or disturbing, depending on one's point of view), the way Austen positions Knightley and Emma as the Highbury's representatives – as representatives of the 'essential' Highbury or of the 'best self' of Highbury – works in the opposite direction, suggesting not only the survival but the continuing dominance of a more refined class whose socio-aesthetic judgments, while rigorous, are also innocent. The discrimination of the two major characters does no one any harm; all it does is facilitate their own happy marriage. The novel presents taste not as a mechanism of social selection but rather as a benign and intimate meeting of minds, endorsing romantic love by implying that Emma, once she has become a happy wife, no longer needs to make things happen in the wider community. Like Mrs Elton, she no longer has any interest in 'execution.' That the good taste of Austen's favoured characters would in real life be a form of efficacious and prejudicial social action is something the novel does not want to acknowledge.

When *Mansfield Park* and *Emma* are paired, it is usually to emphasize the anti-theatricality of the former and the liveliness of the latter: to wonder how a novelist who enjoys an Emma Woodhouse could also endorse a Fanny Price. I initially began to compare the novels because the 'resources' to which Mrs Elton calls attention, apparently mocked in *Emma,* seem to be given such prestige in *Mansfield Park.* Realizing how little good her resources actually do Fanny, however, and how many accomplishments the heroine of this anti-accomplishments novel has to acquire, how many performances she has to give, made me see the two novels as complementary in the way they worry away at the question of social action. Both novels develop the notion of innocent taste to model a possible response to the threat of social mobility. By suggesting that the role of the dominant class is to serve as a good example to those below while admitting to their ranks a select few who are worthy to rise, by suggesting that the social climbers who do not deserve to move up will not learn when they are taught, will not succeed if they try, but will not really be hurt when they fail, Austen has developed a paradigm more comfortable than Burney's for rationalizing their exclusion.

The next chapter begins with a passage from *Fragments* by Humphry Repton, the landscape designer Austen's fictional Mr Rushworth plans to hire for his 'improvements' to Sotherton. Like Austen, Repton in this passage is a social critic who tries to teach the social climber the principles of good taste. Repton had to confront social change for a very material reason: he found himself in the later years of his career having to work not only for large established landowners like the Rushworths but also for clients of more modest means and smaller properties. The gingerly way he negotiates this transition, the rhetoric he devises to suggest tactfully to the newly rich that there are certain aesthetic effects at which they had better not aim, is more ponderous than Austen's but tends to the same ends. Repton's argument, which draws, like the 'woman's-room' topos, on an established discourse of modesty and restraint, is a familiar one: he insists that a restricted space may offer all the beauty and comfort of an unlimited domain. This is an axiom as congenial to the Victorians as to the contemporaries of Austen and Repton – many later nineteenth-century social observers would be willing to agree with Repton that 'the great secret of true happiness' is '*Not to wish for more*'[116] – and it is not surprising to find Repton's assertion reiterated, with more emphasis and less qualification, by the landscape designer John Claudius Loudon, writing two decades later. Loudon's *Villa Companion*, a handbook that offers detailed advice to owners of estates of different sizes about how to develop their homes and gardens, is a much longer and more systematic text than *Fragments*, allowing Loudon to articulate with great precision what effects and accessories are appropriate for properties of different sizes. The ideological premises on which Loudon's discussions are based throw light, in turn, on certain passages in the novels of Charles Dickens, who, whether or not he knew Loudon's writings (the evidence is suggestive but sketchy), represents certain houses and estates in his novels so as to deconstruct Loudon's facile assumptions. Dickens's treatment of both the kind of great estate that Repton originally 'improved' and the tiny properties that parody such estates problematizes the 'small-is-sufficient' discourse developed by Repton, Loudon, and the 'women's-room' writers, and the way it does so is the topic of my next chapter.

# 4 The Improvement of the Estate: J.C. Loudon and Some Spaces in Dickens

Humphry Repton's *Fragments* (1816) is a collection, assembled by the famous 'improver' of landed estates, of his most interesting and impressive projects. In this valedictory volume, prepared at the end of his life in order to preserve 'the memory of an art which had declined,'[1] he published for the first time the text of a number of the Red Books prepared for his grander clients. These books consist of aesthetic assessments of their properties, with his prescriptions for improvement, but also describe a number of the more modest estates on which he had been working in recent years. Repton's market was changing, and his style with it: in response to the needs of his less wealthy clients he had begun moving back to more formal, geometrical effects. Fragment 16, 'Concerning Villas,' registers this development.

Denying that he would have less interest in working with owners of modest villas than with inheritors of great estates, Repton sets up an apparently straightforward analogy. 'Places of small extent,' he asserts, can actually be more challenging to deal with than large estates, as a miniature portrait is more challenging to paint than a full-size portrait, although the aim of both is the same: 'the likeness is the chief object' (68). The implication is that the problem confronting both the designer of the small villa and the painter of miniatures is to condense the same number of features into a much smaller space. This is a point that 'improvers' still make today to defend their proportionately higher billings to owners of modest homes, and it is one Repton himself presently hints at, suggesting that the new villas 'springing up' on the outskirts of towns and cities, though only of 'a few acres, require all the conveniences, comforts, and appendages, of larger and more sumptuous, if not more expensive places' (69).

'All the conveniences and comforts' sounds like a huge overstatement, but Repton's purpose is to urge the acceptance of one's own class position and the home that expresses it. Disingenuously twisting the home/portrait analogy, Repton suggests that tarting up a small property is just as misleading as putting on a costume to have one's portrait painted: 'if the nobleman will be painted as a mail coachman, or the plain country gentlemen in the dress he wore at a masquerade, we shall look for the likeness in vain' (68). The advice is directed, evidently, not to the nobleman, who is scarcely likely to have himself represented as a mail coachman, but rather to the 'plain country gentleman,' who will merely look silly – and deceive no one – if he tries on his modest property to copy effects only possible on a large estate. No reason to repine, however: beauty and contentment are available equally to both nobleman and plain country gentleman. Landscape gardening, Repton points out, is concerned with aesthetics not with economics: it 'does not profess to improve the *value* of land, but its *beauty*'

> does not profess to gratify vanity, by displaying great extent, but to extend comfort, as far as it is feasible; and, if possible, to inculcate the great secret of true happiness – '*Not to wish for more.*' (68–9)

The chiasmus folded into this sentence turns on the words 'extent' and 'extend.' The 'vanity' of the great estate is contrasted with the true 'comfort' of the modest home, which also turns out to be characterized by 'extendedness.' Since real taste abjures vain 'display' – since the estate, Repton pretends, does not exist to *be seen* – the rich man is no better off than the proprietor of modest means.

Aesthetic satisfaction does depend, though, as Repton acknowledges, on what one can *see*, and in this respect the large estate would seem to have an advantage over the small. The confessed ideal of the landscape gardener is the estate 'of vast range of unblended and uninterrupted property, like Longleate or Woburn,' where the sight lines are unimpeded and the owner never needs to look at anything he does not own. But rare indeed, says Repton, is the estate of whatever size that can offer this kind of pleasure:

> for I have often found, in places of the largest extent, that their principal views are annoyed by some patch of alien property, like Naboth's vineyard; some
>
>               'Angulus ille
>     Qui nunc denormat agellum.' —[2]

If all estates, even the greatest, have *essentially* the same inconveniences, the most modest proprietor has access to *essentially* the same remedies as the great. We can all improve our estates – Repton here shifts confidingly into the first person – simply 'by availing ourselves of every circumstance of interest and beauty within our reach, and by hiding such objects as cannot be viewed with pleasure.' The second phrase – 'hiding such objects as cannot be viewed with pleasure' – is specific and technical, referring to a problem to which landscape designers continue to give a great deal of attention. The first is more general and has a moral resonance. 'Availing ourselves of every circumstance of interest and beauty within our reach' is a recipe for contentment. True taste is making the best of what we have, and those of us who understand that our reach should never exceed our grasp have it in our power to do that. ('We' are of course the gentlemen with a classical education who recognize the allusion to Horace, who know that great cultural riches do not require great room, and who understand that the secret of happiness is not to wish for more.)

Repton's general claim sounds like a moral cliché, as of course it is. The assertion that contentment requires few material resources, which goes back to the classical writers and is fully developed in poetry in the seventeenth century, is succinctly if rather negatively expressed by Pope in the 'Epistle to Bathurst':

What Riches give us let us then enquire:
Meat, Fire, and Cloaths. What more? Meat, Cloaths, and Fire.[3]

Rachel Crawford has attributed the inflection of such assertions in the eighteenth century to the growing disapproval of vast landed estates and the valorization of the more modest property, a development, she argues, that, though brought about primarily by the emergence of a mercantile class with the economic resources to purchase landed estates, was shaped by the debates provoked by the parliamentary Acts of Enclosure. Arguing that enclosed spaces became associated with agricultural productivity in these debates, Crawford demonstrates the connection between this association, particularly as exemplified in the eroticized discourse in praise of the cottage garden, and certain poetic genres, notably the georgic and the poetry of the bower. She argues that in reaction to anxieties generated by the 'expansionist fervor' of the eighteenth century there was a discourse of contraction that produced the image of 'compressed magnitude' and 'exhuberance within confined space,' a discourse that finds its expression in poetry, in a certain kind of sublime (she quotes Blake's 'world in a grain of sand') and a certain kind of eroticism.[4] However, though the 'oxymoron of compressed magnitude' certainly characterizes the prose of Repton and particularly Loudon, it is not the note of the sublime, the erotic, or even, really, the exuberant that I detect in these writers, but rather a different kind of rhetorical strain.

The edginess of Repton's introduction, its carefully constructed but slightly slippery analogies, suggests that the writer felt uneasy about the demands and desires of his more recent, less opulent clients. An estate, Repton makes clear, needs to express not only the owner's class position but his acceptance of this position. This is a reactive rhetoric: Repton was writing in the context of a well-established discourse contemptuously dismissing small proprietors with grand ambitions. As far back as the first quarter of the eighteenth century, the class was mocked as pushy and vulgar. Robert Lloyd in 'The Cit's Country Box' makes fun of their shabby aesthetic tricks:

> A wooden arch is bent astride
> A ditch of water, four feet wide,
> With angles, curves and zig-zag lines
> From Halfpenny's exact designs.
> In front a level lawn is seen,
> Without a shrub upon the green
> Where taste would want its first great law
> But for the skulking, sly ha-ha,
> By whose miraculous assistance
> You gain a prospect of two fields distance.[5]

As Ann Bermingham points out, 'such elaborate effects, seen as silly attempts to make up for want of size, were nowhere to be found in the expansive gardens of Capability Brown and Humphry Repton. The indispensable condition for the true landscape gardener was *land*, not simply as the raw material to be worked but as its own ornament and aesthetic effect as well.'[6] Anxious hostility to new money produces a discourse, viciously disciplinary, that puts the purchasers of more modest properties in a double bind. They are apparently supposed to ape the taste of their betters in one way only: by internalizing the principle of decorum that will prohibit aping them in other ways. Any attempt to replicate the decorative elements of great estates themselves is read as a sign of risible (and hopeless) social aspiration.

This kind of satiric discourse lends itself readily to novelistic scenarios. When Fanny Burney in *Camilla* uses it, she makes the association between vulgarity and ambition explicit. In a chapter entitled 'Specimens of Taste,'[7] Lionel takes Camilla and Eugenia to visit Mr Dubster, a wig seller and 'a very mean little man, dressed in old dirty cloaths' (275), who is hankering to show off to his visitors a property worthy, he feels, of a formal tour. The building, 'a small house, just new fronted with deep red bricks,' with 'two little bow windows' on the first floor, 'a little balcony' above, and 'in the attic story, a very small venetian window' (274), is so tiny as to be contemptible. But Mr Dubster 'insist[s] upon shewing them not only every room, but every closet, every cupboard, every nook, corner, and hiding place; praising their utility, and enumerating all their possible appropriations, with the most minute encomiums' (277). Ridiculously small, the property is also faddish and fussy. The party 'were compelled to enter his grounds, through a small Chinese gate, painted of a deep blue' (276); what Dubster calls his lake with its island appears to Eugenia 'nothing but a very dirty little pond, with a mass of rubbish in the middle' (275); his 'arbour' is 'an angle, in which a bench was placed close to the chinese rails' with a syringa on one side, a willow growing 'in a little piece of stagnant water' on the other (279); and his labyrinth, 'a little walk he was cutting, zig-zag, through some brushwood, so low that no person above three foot height could be hid by it' (281). Mr Dubster plans to accent the pastoral character of his estate by acquiring a lamb to graze on the island, at least until it is 'fit for killing' (279), and also a swan – but a wooden one, for, as he cannily remarks, 'there's no end of feeding them things if one has 'em alive' (278). Yet pastoral seclusion is not his real desire: Mr Dubster particularly appreciates what landscape designers are most anxious to avoid, exposure to the world outside his gates.[8] His grotto's 'pretty look out' is designed with a view onto a public road, with 'a sight of people and coaches, and gentlemen's whiskeys and stages, and flys, and wagons' (280) going by, and his summer house overlooks the high road, where 'on market days, the people passed so thick, there was no seeing them for the dust' (282).

Dubster has in fact followed Repton's moral, if not his aesthetic, advice: he has availed himself of every circumstance of interest and beauty within his reach and has produced an 'estate' that he finds comfortable and charming. But his optimism and energy avail him nothing in the eyes of the reader to whose snobbery Burney appeals. His impoverished aesthetic is associated with both the gross crudity that allows him to comment on Eugenia's deformity and his outrageous aspiration to court Camilla herself. Though it would make sense to assume that satisfaction with one's own property is the best guarantee against wanting to rise, Dubster is depicted as avid for social advancement. He is a kind of monster of vulgarity and presumption, and his tacky property becomes an emblem of his hopeless ambition: an emblem, reassuringly legible, that will however definitively mark him for social exclusion. The tiny scale of such properties seems to ensure that their owners will never be accepted by those equipped to assess their vulgarity. But the threat behind the absurdity is suggested by the intensity of contempt that it evokes. The elaborate malice of Burney's caricature testifies to an anxiety about those whose slightly more sophisticated taste might enable them to pass as gentry.

The purveyor of 'improvements' has a problematic role in this social shift. By chastening the taste of the wealthier Dubsters and helping them to present themselves as akin to the great landowners, Repton himself might be understood as facilitating a process that evidently makes a certain class of people – a class that no doubt includes some of his own former clients – uneasy if not hostile, and his elaborately defensive rhetoric in 'Concerning Villas' no doubt reflects his awareness of his ambiguous role.

My purpose in the first part of this chapter is to show how the themes and anxieties articulated by Lloyd, Burney, and Repton were developed later in the nineteenth century by writers offering advice on landscape design. The frankly hostile anti-cockney discourse – the sneering middle-class satire of working-class taste in domestic decor – does not end with Lloyd and Burney; on the contrary, we find it picked up in very much the same terms by a writer like Edward Kemp in 1860, whose remarks I shall cite in their place. More interesting for the understanding of Victorian self-construction, however, and the focus of the first half of this chapter, is the writing of John Claudius Loudon (1783–1843), the well-known landscape gardener and prolific horticultural writer, who, reinterpreting Repton's praise of modest property for a burgeoning capitalist marketplace, 'exerted a huge influence on middle-class domestic taste in the early Victorian period.'[9] Loudon's *The Suburban Gardener and Villa Companion* (1838) is a fascinating example of the way proprietorship is linked with middle-class identity at a moment when the ownership of suburban villas, some modest, some very substantial, was becoming a possibility for a wider group of purchasers and when the marketplace was being flooded with new machines and materials. This substantial text is worth examining as a cultural artifact in its own right, and its ideological premises, often implicit but sometimes surprisingly explicit, will be unfolded in the first half of the discussion that follows. My sense is that Loudon's argument is shaped more by complex and sometimes contradictory anxieties about subjectivity and social order in an expanding, competitive economy than by the eroticized exuberance on which Crawford focuses, though no doubt the rhetorical gestures polished in the debates she discusses helped shape his prose style.

Loudon's text is also worth looking at for the light it throws on certain passages in the novels of Dickens, and the second half of this chapter deals with some houses and properties in *Bleak House, A Tale of Two Cities, Dombey and Son, Great Expectations,* and *Our Mutual Friend.* My argument here does not depend on the claim of direct influence, although such influence is certainly possible. Charles Dickens, as is well known, had a deep emotional stake in his own home, Gad's Hill Place, a house he had admired as a young boy, where he wrote *A Tale of Two Cities, Great Expectations, Our Mutual Friend,* and *Edwin Drood,* and where he died in 1870. Sold to him by Mrs Lynn Linton in 1855, the property underwent a series of 'improvements' as Dickens expanded his estate by buying the lot on the other side of the road: there was one round of renovations and acquisitions in 1864, and in 1869 he was renovating again, adding parquet flooring, a new staircase, and a conservatory.[10] On this property Dickens constructed a Swiss-style chalet/summerhouse that could have come out of one of Loudon's design books (Loudon has a picture of a 'gate lodge in the Swiss style'),[11] and the *Villa Companion* seems to be just the kind of manual Dickens would have consulted. As well, Dickens must have known Loudon by reputation, if only because he must have known of his wife. On 22 February 1850 Dickens wrote to Anne Marsh soliciting from her 'some short stories' for *Household Words,* and on 9 March 1850 Marsh's story 'Lettice Arnold' began serialization in *The Ladies' Companion,* a periodical edited, until May of the same year, by Mrs Loudon.[12] Given Dickens's interest in houses and in home renovation, Loudon's reputation at the time, and Mrs Loudon's involvement in periodical publishing and relationship with writers whose work Dickens admired, it is hard to imagine that Dickens was not aware of Loudon's own productions, though whether he perused them or not is impossible to prove. Certain settings in Dickens's mature novels, most obviously the property of Wemmick in *Great Expectations,* demonstrably pick up the anti-cockney satire of writers like Lloyd and Burney without being directly traceable to any one of them individually. These settings, as well

as certain other passages in Dickens, can also be usefully analysed in
terms of the Victorian attitudes to property ownership that Loudon
articulates and no doubt helps to shape, whether or not Dickens has
Loudon specifically in mind. I argue not that Dickens is offering in
these passages a targeted, deliberate critique of Loudon in particular,
but rather that the way he represents certain homes and properties
exposes the problematic elements of Loudonesque home-and-garden
discourse as well as of the diatribes of the anti-cockney satirists.

The question of Repton's influence on Loudon is much clearer. Loudon of course knew Repton's work intimately. Though early in his
career he vehemently attacked some of Repton's ideas and methods, in
1840 he brought out a cheap edition of his predecessor's works[13] that,
like his own writings, found an audience in the Victorian middle class.[14]
In his voluminous *Villa Companion* – a hulking 752 pages, much of it in
small print, in contrast to Repton's slim, elegant quarto – Loudon replicates Repton's arguments about the adequacy of the modest property,
hammering them in with a dogged directness markedly less nervous and
nuanced than Repton's ingenious analogies. Loudon echoes Repton's
statements not only about the difficulties of a small estate for the
improver – he points out that because the small proprietor cannot
afford to make mistakes, the landscape designer must exercise much
'deep consideration' in order 'to produce the greatest possible result
from very limited means' (131) – but also about the equal pleasures for
the proprietor. Matter-of-factly complacent about the contemporary
British social order – capable of asserting, as a truth 'long seen' by everybody, that 'the poor, by cooperation and self-cultivation, may insure to
themselves all that is worth having of the enjoyments of the wealthier
classes' (11) – Loudon begins his *Villa Companion* with the extraordinary
claim that

all, in the way of household accommodation, that is essential to the enjoyment of life, may be obtained in a cottage of three or four rooms, as well as
in a palace ... a suburban residence, with a very small portion of land
attached, will contain all that is essential to happiness, in the garden, park,
and demesne of the most extensive country residence. Let us briefly make
the comparison. The objects of the possessors of both are the same: health,
which is the result of temperance and exercise; enjoyment, which is the
possession of something which we can call our own, and on which we can
set our heart and affections; and the respect of society, which is the result
of their favourable opinion of our sentiments and moral conduct. No man

in this world, however high may be his rank, great his wealth, powerful his
genius, or extensive his acquirements, can ever attain more than health,
enjoyment, and respect. (8)

Given these premises, the conclusion is obvious. Happiness depends
upon the attitude of the homeowner:

> The difference of the happiness of the parties will therefore depend almost
> entirely on the difference in the degrees of their ambition; for in every
> other respect they are equal. All the necessities of life may be obtained in
> as great perfection by the occupier of a suburban residence in the neigh-
> bourhood of London, who possesses 200*l.* or 300*l.* a year, as by the greatest
> nobleman in England, and at a mere fraction of the expense. (9)

Though Loudon's prose style is very different from Repton's – particularly in the habit of dividing a topic into subcategories and moving systematically through them one at a time, a habit which, when applied to
the four grades of properties, has ideological implications, as we shall
see – he uses the same vague abstractions. Repton's 'comfort' and 'contentment' become Loudon's 'health,' 'enjoyment,' and 'respect.'

This is a lulling rhetoric designed to preclude analysis. That the kind
of 'respect' homeowners desire may depend not merely on others'
'favourable opinion of our sentiments and moral conduct' but also on
others' deference to our financial power is uneasily acknowledged – but
at the same time dismissed – as mere 'ambition,' as if this were a motive
too base to be attributed to his readers. Clearly it is disingenuous to pretend that none of his readers, supposedly interested in the minutely specific rules of taste that he is about to provide – dozens of pages, for
example, on the correct way to decorate every principal room in the
house – feel the kind of ambition that would make a large, spectacular
property what he calls their '*beau ideal.*' Competitive ambition, the
engine of the burgeoning economy Loudon takes for granted, needs to
be bracketed if this innocent paradigm of essential equality is to be
maintained. The 'handbook' method of organization Loudon chooses,
his division of the text into sections and subsections, is a good way of
doing this bracketing, of segregating such flagrantly ideological claims,
which are usually found in the introductions to chapters, from the
lengthy sections of practical advice.

There is an obvious economic motive for Loudon's emphasis on the
essential similarity of properties large and small: he is aiming at the wid-

est possible readership. Loudon's market is both wider and somewhat lower than Repton's: solidly middle-class and upper middle-class. As a successful professional with paying clients, a practical businessman who sets out his fee schedule at the end of the volume, he wants to make clear that because 'every essential component part ... is required in a residence of ten acres, or even one acre, that is found in a residence of a hundred, or even a thousand, acres ... the professional charges for laying out a small place will always be much greater, in proportion to its extent, than those for laying out a large place' (481). He also needs to persuade small homeowners that the advice he is going to give to their betters is equally relevant to them: since 'the mansion is but a more ample development of the cottage, and ... the former should always be kept in view as the *beau ideal* of the latter' (83), even 'the humblest individual' has something to learn from his volume. When Loudon declares sententiously that 'all that is essential to a villa should be found in a cottage' (67), he is adapting the happy-man topos to appeal to Victorian consumers of real estate and of his own services.

However, partly because of a certain earnest exhaustiveness in his methodology, Loudon tends to push this argument to a level of literalness that brings its contradictions into sharper focus. What ownership of a small property means in practice is spelled out with slightly embarrassing concreteness when Loudon gets down to specifying the particular spaces that have to be condensed. He argues that

> though a cottage has not a housekeeper's room, a butler's pantry, a larder, a wine-cellar, a coal-cellar, &c., each separate, and of some size; yet in every comfortable cottage there is a closet, where the mistress of the house keeps her dry stores, such as linen &c., and which supplies the place of a housekeeper's room; and a pantry, where she keeps her cooked provisions, and a safe, in which she keeps her meat ... She has a place, also, for liquors and ale, and another for fuel, &c. In short, there is nothing belonging to the mansion which has not its prototype in the cottage. (67)

Though this is 'compressed magnitude' of a kind, there is nothing erotic, sublime, or even exuberant about it. On the contrary, this modest household is beginning to sound uncomfortably close to Mr Dubster's dwelling, with its closets, cupboards, nooks, corners, and hiding places. At such a scale everyday practical issues become more visible and threaten to expose the broader claims of similitude on which Loudon nevertheless continues to insist. Other analogies between specific spaces strain his argument still further. If the first-rate mansion has its conservatory and the suburban residence its greenhouse, 'the smallest description of suburban houses,' Loudon says, has 'the common substitute for a green-house,' its windowsill; and if that windowsill is enclosed in a bow window and separated from the room by means of glass, and 'if the panes of both windows are large, and kept at all times perfectly clean, the view into this plant cabinet from the interior of the room will ... create an allusion to the green-house of the villa, or the conservatory of the mansion' (109–10). An allusion, not an illusion: since the 'great luxury' of a real conservatory is 'that of looking down its main walk from the drawing room window and feeling as if we were sitting in a bower in an eastern garden' (112), even Loudon cannot quite pretend that the effect is very much the same. What is being bracketed in such passages is the labour of 'the mistress of the house' and her female servants, who have to organize these confined spaces and keep these steamy windows 'perfectly clear.' The contradictions call attention to themselves, yet the assertion of essential identity is one in which Loudon has a considerable stake and on which he continues to insist in various ways throughout this volume.

One of the ways he does this is simply the method of organization he chooses for the text as a whole. Whereas Repton organized his *Fragments* as a more or less miscellaneous collection of accounts of individual properties and their particular aesthetic problems, Loudon, though he does include such descriptions, is writing a practical handbook, and his method is to deal with one class of estate at a time and generalize about the problems presented at each level. Since he adopts as his principle of organization the four 'rates' set out by tax law[15] and works systematically up from the smallest 'fourth-rate' property to the huge 'first-rate' landed estates, the effect is both to divide the mass of English property owners and to unite them. Finely distinguishing between the successive levels while at the same time knitting them together in the same volume, he posits a single enormous class – a class defined by ownership of property and interest in its improvement and united in the love of nature and home – that comes to represent the nation as a whole. The vision of British society that emerges is, paradoxically, one of great stability – inasmuch as the gradations of property are fixed by law – and at the same time of continuous progress and improvement, technological, aesthetic, and personal. The urge to improve, Loudon implies, is as universal as the appreciation of nature and of gardens: 'all mankind,' he declares, loves plants (29). The claim that we all love our homes and that the smallest cottage contains everything one could hope for from the grandest mansion is only one of the means by which Loudon reinforces a vision of middle-class unity of spirit, despite the lines that he reinscribes as he moves punctiliously across them.

Perimeter lines, margins, boundaries, and borders are never far from Loudon's thoughts in the *Villa Companion*. They come to function, both visually (in the many maps and plans of individual estates) and verbally, as a subliminal trope that dominates his thinking. Loudon's landscape aesthetic involves both working within the boundaries of the property, if they are so tight that they cannot be disguised, or moving illusionistically across them, if one has an estate large enough to allow for doing so. Ready though he is to declare the sufficiency of the small property, Loudon, like Repton and other earlier improvers, gives a good deal of thought to methods of making real estate seem larger than it is, particularly to ways of 'appropriating the adjoining grounds' (656). Appropriation had become a technical term for the landscape designer: it refers to the illusionistic rather than the actual extension of one's property – the art of making it look as if the estate continued into the surrounding landscape, preferably as far as the eye can see.[16] Improvers of an earlier era, Loudon points out, had developed, for great estates, the practice of 'harmonizing a residence with the surrounding country ... by the projection into it of a continuation of those avenues and lines of trees which formed part of the residence,' so as to imply 'the possession of the grounds beyond the park fence' (656). Though devised for great estates, the same techniques could profitably be used on considerably smaller properties as well, if not by extending avenues into common lands, at least by planting 'a few trees ... within, of the same kinds as those without' (468). Loudon quotes with approval G.J. Parkins (in his *Six Designs for Laying out Grounds*, 1793), who, to hide the boundary line of the property, introduced an orchard that would 'confine the eye to a ruined tower, to a river meandering through the vale below, and to distant mountains' (561 note d). There are other ways too of 'confining the eye' of the visitor to see only what the owner wants to display. Loudon recommends the construction of carefully calculated walks, arranged so 'that more than one walk shall never be seen at a time' (419) and screened so that people on one cannot be seen by those on the other. In a smallish estate, he says, the walks should be designed to cover the greatest possible area of ground, looping and reversing so that the visitor will be presented with different views at every turning and different ones again as he is 'required' to retrace his steps in the opposite direction. The aim is frankly illusionistic:

the eye of the spectator is carried twice over the same ground without his knowing it, and without his passing twice over the same walks; and thus he can hardly fail of giving the place credit for a greater extent than it really possesses. (158)

Somewhat larger properties may be shaped by still more elaborate devices, 'their apparent extent to the stranger walking through them ... doubled or trebled by judicious tunneling in some places, and carrying the road or walk over bridges, through a ruin or rockwork, or under an arcade or trellis-work, in others' (523). Loudon admits that 'improvements of this kind cannot be shown with much effect on paper' but insists that 'when judiciously executed they have the effect of enchantment' (523).

Loudon's enthusiasm about such devices has no doubt much to do with the pleasure of exercising his own powers, but the implication is that, whatever he may claim, his own '*beau ideal*' is the great landed estate, where the visitor can be given a more or less formal tour of the property. The impact on the visitor is always kept in mind: the landscape gardener needs to think about how the estate will unfold over the course of a single tour so that each individual vignette will receive due attention. Since 'the eye can only see, and the ear only hear, one thing at a time' (144), Loudon advises 'dispos[ing] of the shady parts of the walks so as generally to form separations between striking scenes, that the one may be forgotten before the other is entered on' (157–8). In his descriptions of individual houses and estates, the 'spectator,' 'visitor,' or 'stranger' is insistently invoked to focalize the 'views,' 'scenes,' 'vistas,' 'effects,' and 'episodes' designed to evoke a 'strong emotion of admiration and astonishment' (723). Despite his dismissal of 'ambition' as a worthy motive for the homeowner, Loudon does not really attempt to deny that the comfort and contentment of a middle-class home depend largely on how effectively that home can be displayed.

Visual illusions of the kind that Loudon recommends for large properties are effects that frankly cannot be achieved, however, on a small city lot. To create scenes and surprises one needs a certain amount of property to work with, and it cannot be visibly 'right-lined' (151), that is, square or rectangular. Loudon admits that the Picturesque style is 'best adapted for grounds of considerable extent' (169) and deplores the 'constant attempts ... to introduce the irregular manner of planting, and serpentine lines, in places where they are altogether unsuitable,' pointing out 'the impossibility of walking with comfort, when, at every five or six steps, the walk makes a turn' and the pointlessness of using such a path, the purpose of which is to present the visitor with ever-changing views, 'where the turns, for some distance before the eye, may be all seen at once' (168). This vulgarity is perpetrated, he says, by a 'class of person, who know just enough of gardening to be aware that there are two styles ... and regret that they cannot, for want of room, indulge in that style which alone they have been taught to esteem as beautiful' (168). This is as close as Loudon comes to the anti-cockney satire of Burney and Robert Lloyd, but his critique, lacking the overt class animus that sharpens their mockery, is couched in aesthetic terms. The first principle of art is consistency, and winding paths, he says, are simply inconsistent with the geometrical regularity of small urban lots. Bowers are another potential problem. 'In large places ... seats in different situations' are useful both for sitting on and for pointing up 'particular points of view, which might otherwise pass unnoticed by a stranger,' but since in 'small places' only one bower can really be needed, they 'require to be introduced with the greatest caution' (157) if they are not to seem like an affectation. Loudon suggests only a couple of ground plans for small city lots, inevitably quite limited in design.

What one clearly cannot have on a small lot is the status that comes from displaying one's property to competitive advantage to the envious observer. Loudon insists, however, that one can have the full garden experience even in a small lot – indeed, even in an attic. The most modest property will provide enough space for the cultivation of a great variety of plants and enough work to fill up all the owner's spare time. These two themes – the value of variety, particularly as manifested in the systematic collection, and the value of labour – are central both to Loudon's ethos and to his vision of an aggressively competitive, yet essentially stable social order, and I shall pursue each of them in turn.

Even at the lowest end of the social scale, working-class men with very limited resources can produce spectacular plants, 'as a proof of which' Loudon cites 'the tulips, auriculas, pinks, heartseases, &c., growing in the small plots occupied by the Spitalfields weavers; and by the Paisley weavers, and those of the manufacturing towns of Lancashire' (270). Persons of this class however tend to focus on developing individual species to grotesque perfection. In characterizing the botanical efforts of working-class gardeners, Loudon focuses on the fad for what he calls 'monstrous productions' (271), the taste for giant dahlias, cucumbers, and melons, which, he opines, 'may be considered as springing more from a love of gambling than of flowers' (272).[17] Nevertheless, the social function of such hobbies is clear. Men of this class could, presumably, find much less innocent ways of spending their time. Although Loudon does not say explicitly about their hobby what he says about gardening for children – that it allows them, 'instead of passing their leisure hours in a manner degrading to human nature, to interest themselves in recreations both agreeable and useful' (8) – the comparison of flower breeding to gambling suggests what kinds of activities gardening displaces in his mind. But his explicit motive for mentioning such gigantic specimens is to illustrate what can be done with even very limited resources.

Developing a giant dahlia has the taint of vulgarity, but more varied and intellectualized botanizing – specifically, the assembling of enormous collections of different species of trees and plants – is an activity Loudon endows with considerable cultural prestige. That such variety is also fully within reach of the small proprietor is one of his constant themes. Insisting that even in 'fourth-rate gardens attached to street houses, every thing may be grown, though on a smaller scale, and even brought to perfection, that is cultivated in the first-rate gardens attached to the mansions and palaces of the nobility' (285), Loudon identifies a number of persons who have assembled astonishingly diverse collections of plants on small city lots (figs. 55 and 72) and 'in even smaller spaces':

> The late R.A. Salisbury had, in 1820, a very choice collection of alpines, in pots, in a small back yard in Queen Street, Edgeware Road; and Miss Kent, about the same time, had a garden of British plants, in pots, on the roof of the house in which she lived in St Paul's Churchyard ... Mr Ward of Wellclose Square, a distinguished botanist, grows a considerable hardy flora, in troughs, or boxes, on the tops of the walls which enclose his back yard, and on the roofs of the out-buildings in it; and in the different rooms of his house, including his own bedroom, he grows upwards of a hundred specimens of ferns, indigenous and exotic. We know a gentleman whose back garden is hardly 30 ft. square; nevertheless he has a dry stove in it, in which he cultivates a collection of succulent plants, one of the richest in species of any in the neighbourhood of London. (284)

Though this is a kind of plenitude, it is not the slightly sexy copia Crawford finds in the kitchen-garden manuals, but has more to do with intellectual mastery of nature. Unlike the dahlia and cucumber breeders, these named individuals, however tiny their properties, are gentlefolk, dignified by their quasi-scientific interest in botanical taxonomy. Loudon himself, albeit with a professional motive, claims to have grown on his own property virtually all the plants available in Britain: he boasts that he assembled '2000 species at one time' and 'might have had 10,000 in our limited space' (349) if he had confined himself to herbaceous plants. A suburban gardener, Loudon says, if he chose to discard a plant the minute it flowered for the first time, might be able 'in the course of a few years ... [to] have had growing in [his garden] all the plants in cultivation in the open air in Britain, with the exception of a few of the larger of the forest trees,' which might be included in the form of bonsai 'in the Chinese manner' (4).

This almost obsessive 'desire ... to render garden scenery botanically as well as pictorially interesting' (562) is represented as both a personal and a national project, a way of acknowledging the richness and variety of the nation and passing it along to one's visitors and children. Loudon suggests that property ownership is a process of education, both practical and liberal, alluding for example to the pleasures of 'astronomy, botany, gardening, and entomology' (33), to the desirability of formal training in the 'fundamental principles of architecture and gardening' (33), and to the value of a garden and a greenhouse for teaching children natural history (he advocates labelling every plant, as he himself does). Developing one's property is analogous to developing one's self. As the garden fills up with specimens, so the intellect expands to encompass more and more pieces of information – to possess and consolidate its vision of the surrounding world. Loudon suggests trimming a rock garden with 'some curious mineral or geological specimen, as a portion of the Giant's Causeway' (288), with 'pieces of antiquity ... such as stones from some celebrated building now taken down; as, for example, from London Wall or London Bridge, or from the cellar in Bishop Atterbury's house in Hammersmith, where the Protestants in 1556 ... were confined' (288–9), or with 'specimens of plumpudding stone, groups of large shells, corals, corallines, madrepores, tufa, lava, petrifactions, ammonites, and different sort of scoria' (289), until the garden, ranging over both space and time, becomes a kind of museum, complementary to the indoor museums often devised on great estates. Our access to variety, Loudon says, is a happy consequence of 'civilization': because we are civilized, we have the choice of all the plants in the world, as well as all the architectural styles (428). He describes Californian and Australian gardens, collections of tropical plants, conservatories that replicate eastern gardens, and an Italian-style villa ornamented with plants native to Italy, and suggests importing 'Turkey oaks,' 'the thorns of Greece and

America,' 'the laurustinus, the arbutus, and the cistus of Italy' (141), indeed, any of 'the trees and shrubs of North America, the Continent of Europe, and the temperate parts of Asia' (163). The notion of the collection spiritualizes the rage for acquisition: the consumer's urge to own more and more things can be rationalized as a desire to expand the mind, even to participate in the ongoing national project of scientific classification. The individual property, like Britain itself, becomes a microcosm, cramming all the world's diversity into a small space, and the cultivated collector models the colonizing mind, expanding ever outward to possess and order that world.

Indeed, the vision of the national economy that emerges from Loudon's text is dynamic and optimistic. Crawford refers to the new value placed, by the discourse of containment, on laboriousness and ingenuity, and Loudon's text offers even better examples than the ones she cites.[18] The botanical and geological variety of the English countryside and the British empire is complemented by the variety of products and processes created by British manufacturers: Budding's mowing machine, for example, Reid's syringe, the locks of Chubb and Mordan, Kyanised wood, Coade's artificial stone, Austin's or Wyatt's cement, Wyatt's ornamental tiles, Joyce's portable smoke-consuming stoves, and Siebe's Self-pressure Cock. These products fall into two categories: they are less costly imitations of natural materials, or ingenious devices for attaining new kinds of control over nature – for cutting grass, heating houses, controlling the flow of air in greenhouses. Loudon's interest seems to be in technical efficacy, not really in saving labour; although he does suggest that the new method of cooking by gas is so clean that a lady in full dress could easily prepare a meal, the ladies he addresses cannot really be imagined doing so. Writing for empowered consumers confronted with new and improved products, Loudon evokes a burgeoning, confident, and creative economy that invites and rewards participation.

The result of such prosperity and innovation sounds like a fantasy land of conspicuous consumption. Loudon describes individual properties crammed with objects, scenes, and 'effects' – statues, flower stands, urns, rock works, birdbaths, fountains, waterfalls, rock arrangements, fanciful outbuildings. Perhaps the most surprising part of the *Villa Companion* for today's reader is the lengths to which Loudon will go to minister to bourgeois fantasies of seigneurial dignity by creating fake but picturesque peasantry. He advocates fictional scenarios in 'the rustic style,' the object of which, he declares, is 'to produce fac-simile imitations of common nature, as to deceive the spectator into an idea that they are real or fortuitous' (161), chiefly by tarting up abandoned gravel pits with turf, nettles, weeds, pools, houses, and even people. He proposes, for example, making use of a pit that has a 'a hovel or rude cottage in the bottom' by replacing native plants with foreign ones and substituting 'a Swiss cottage, or an architectural cottage of any kind that would not be recognized as the common cottage of the country ... for the hovel' (164), and improving another by constructing in the bottom 'a dwelling-place ... for a workman and his wife, with a hovel to serve as a cow-shed, in which cows might be kept for the family,' to be approached by means of a deliberately 'rough winding road' artificially 'covered with grass' as if through 'the lapse of time' (167) and 'entered through an old rickety gate.' 'Though comfortable within,' he says, the hovel 'ought to appear in a half-ruined state without' (167–8). It is hard not to recall, however, Loudon's warning to his own readers not to build in damp hollows and his reminder about the realities of life even in a cottage orné, which include snails, slugs, spiders, flies, worms, newts, beetles, cockroaches, fleas, offensive smells, and rodents (115–16).

Illusionistic effects of every kind are recommended: Loudon describes lintels put together so as to look as if they bear weight, 'even though the real source of strength should be an unseen iron plate or beam let into the soffit' (135); 'casts of ornaments and flowers in papier maché or plaster of Paris, for lamps or chandeliers to hang from' (87); Corinthian columns 'of scagliola marble, in imitation of verd antique' (372); an 'entablature, ceiling, doors, skirtings, dado, architraves, &c., painted to resemble bronze' (372); and a verandah roof made to look like an awning, 'of such a curve as canvass would naturally take,' with a 'turned wooden tassel' (375). He describes a method of painting interiors so as 'to make the room appear higher than it really is' (98); he explains how to turn a pond into what looks like a river running across the front of the property by arranging for a gap in the trees 'which water might be supposed to flow from so as to leave the spectator room to suppose that there is an outlet in the proper place' (631–2); and, most amusingly, he recommends a method of making a newly constructed tunnel look 'weather-stained so as to imitate an arch of great antiquity,' in order 'to prevent suspicion of fakery' (464) and reassure visitors that the tunnel must be safe to walk through precisely because it has stood for a long time. Some of Loudon's allusions to modern gothic, a style he generally admires, underline its make-believe nature. Though he ordinarily insists on uniform chimney pots throughout a single building, he is willing to admit variety in gothic-style houses 'where irregularity is the characteristic of the architecture,' such variety being rationalizable on the grounds of 'there being more flues in some chimneys than in others,' owing to 'the scattered disposition of the apartments, which is supposed to be produced in order to enjoy particular prospects, in some cases; and, in others, to be the additions made by different builders at different times' (53). Houses were apparently sometimes constructed all at once in such a way as to look as if they had developed over the years one addition at a time, and Loudon is not uncomfortable with such affectation.[19] The only fakery Loudon seems to object to in fact is artificial flowers: he reiterates the Coleridgean point that realistic-looking flowers are vulgar, whereas those rendered in wood, stone, or even plaster may be in good taste (137, 162–3).[20]

Theoretically, Loudon is obliged to insist that such variety must always be subordinated to aesthetic unity. The principle of unity, violated though it seems to be by the clutter and excess of many properties he discusses, is ritualistically invoked at measured intervals throughout his text, primarily to confirm the landscape gardener's status as an artist. 'No irregularity in a building or other object can be satisfactory to the mind,' he characteristically declares, 'unless it can be reduced by it, in a short time, to some principle of order and unity of design' (53), 'no landscape can please that does not form a whole' (410). The role of the landscape gardener, he asserts, is to bring 'all the different parts which enter into the composition of a country residence' (444) together:

> It is chiefly in doing this that the artist has an opportunity of showing to what extent he is entitled to be considered as a man of genius and taste. It is easy to conceive that all the different component parts of a piece of music, a picture, or a piece of architecture, may be correctly executed; and yet that the want of due proportion between these parts may be so great, and the whole may be put together with so little connexion and harmony, as to form an object wholly without sentiment or expression, a body unanimated by a soul. (445)

When Loudon attributes the disorder that results from improper subordination both to a building and to a 'soul,' he is making, in an oddly intense way, the analogy that Eagleton finds so crucial to the construction of the modern 'individual': the analogy between the work of art and the human subject.[21] There is also a subliminal political resonance here. The powerful image of a body without a soul tends to evoke Frankenstein's monster, a figure conventionally associated in this period with the threat of revolutionary violence, and thus to suggest perhaps a certain half-repressed anxiety about social and psychological as well as aesthetic disorder.[22] Like a number of Loudon's remarks, this one has metaphorical implications that Loudon himself never spells out.

The corollary of the doctrine of aesthetic unity is the condemnation of meaningless ornament. Loudon quotes Walker on 'the useless, and, very often, tasteless, love of ornament and display' (94), and often makes the point himself:

> Statues, vases, and other architectural ornaments, ought to be very sparingly introduced at a distance from the house, in gardens in any style ... as the mind can only attend to one sensation, and experience one emotion of pleasure, at a time, it becomes distracted among so many. (157)

But such caveats, apparently an obligatory part of aesthetic discourse at this time, do not carry a great deal of conviction. In practice, despite the lip service paid to unity and simplicity, Loudon is ready to allow an extravagant range of aesthetic effects.[23] His text on the whole is a celebration of British consumer plenitude, and Loudon, responding zestfully to the variety he knows he ought to condemn, displaces his unprincipled enthusiasm onto women, whose love of ornament he ritually decries.

Tensions such as these shape Loudon's depiction of 'The Lawrencian Villa, Drayton Green,' the most spectacular of all the specific properties Loudon describes, which epitomizes variety, artifice, sham, and conspicuous display. It is a property of twenty-eight acres, but the 'house, stable offices, and decorated grounds stand on about two acres' (576), which are crammed with objects and 'scenes' (578) – the word is used repeatedly – 'under the direction of Mrs. Lawrence, F.H.S., the lady of the celebrated surgeon of that name' (576). The objects, many of which are illustrated in Loudon's text by black-and-white vignettes, include a collection of 'pedestals and vases'; a collection of baskets; a collection of 'views' – 'the view of the rustic arch and Cupid' (584), 'the view of the rockwork, statue of Fame, &c.' (583), 'a view of a handsome weeping ash' (583); a collection of little structures – 'a rustic archway of rockwork ... from which an interesting view across the lawn is obtained' (581), a 'span-roofed green-house' (582), an 'Orchidaceous house, with miniature rockworks and artificial hillocks' (589); a 'camellia-house' with a 'statue of Mercury in the foreground' (584); waterworks of various kinds – 'two groups of rockwork, with concealed springs' (584); a 'fountain ... supplied from a cistern which forms a small tower on the top of the tool-house' (582); a 'fountain, surrounded by baskets of flowers, with the two garden nymphs' (585); an 'Italian walk,' and a 'French parterre' (582). I use the word collection deliberately: Mrs Lawrence seems to be motivated by the desire to display a sample of every decorative object, natural or artificial, that she can get her hands on. Even her rock gardens are constructed 'of spars, fossil organic remains, and other geological specimens brought from distant parts of the country' (587). Loudon must not have intended this estate to sound as grotesque as it does, but he does hint that Mrs Lawrence may have gone a bit too far. Discovering that he finds the view into the paddock, 'a plain grass field' with some cows on it, 'an agreeable relief from the excess of beauty and variety on the lawn' (581), he eventually admits that less might be more in a place of this size:

> We are aware that there are many persons, of a simple and severe taste, who will think that the Lawrencian Villa is too highly ornamented with statues and sculptures; but allowance must be made for individual taste, for devotion to the subject, and for the limited extent of the place. (590)

This is the closest Loudon ever comes to criticism of an estate he has chosen to describe. One senses that the Lawrencian Villa might have been included chiefly because it was a project too spectacular, and Mrs Lawrence a lady too formidable, to be ignored. But though hinting that the estate may have its aesthetic limitations, nevertheless Loudon concludes with the suggestion that 'the humblest and most economical possessor of a villa residence of two acres may take a lesson from Mrs Lawrence's taste':

> Every one [sic] cannot have so many fountains, or form rockwork of spars, fossil organic remains, and ... geological specimens ... ; but every one may sink in the ground a few small wooden cisterns lined with lead, and supply them with water by hand ... as brilliant spots to attract the eye, and ... as habitats for aquatic plants. (587)

The ingenuity of British manufacturers has provided cheap substitutes for her costly accessories:

> With regard to the statues, vases, &c., though some of these, at Drayton Green, are of bronze, marble, or stone, and have cost considerable sums,

> yet others of composition, equal in point of taste, though far inferior in pecuniary value, may readily be procured, at a moderate cost, of Austin's artificial stone, or of earthenware. (590)

Such suggestions seem positively to invite the kind of cluttered, small-scale ornamentation described by eighteenth-century satirists like Robert Lloyd and Burney and satirized as cockney vulgarity right on through the Victorian period. The plenitude evoked here is very different from that of the cottage garden described by Crawford: it seems to have more to do with conspicuous consumption than with erotic exuberance.

There has to be a way of mediating between the unity Loudon theoretically admires and the variety he nevertheless requires and enjoys, and the 'gardenesque' style, though recommended by him as a modern alternative to the Picturesque, can also be seen as performing this function.[24] Loudon touts the new style as good for 'displaying the numerous foreign trees and shrubs, which at the present day are becoming comparatively common' (655) on private estates, since it positions trees and plants not in clumps or groves but separately, 'so as to keep each plant perfectly distinct from those around it' (433). This style of planting, which both maximizes the full symmetrical development of each individual specimen and shows off the client's whole collection to best advantage, allows for both multiplicity and individuality. The botanical economy Loudon envisions is a competitive one, and the individualism he admires depends upon careful management of this economy. Each plant, though encouraged to develop its own form to the fullest, has been carefully selected both to contrast and to harmonize with all the others in its vicinity. Though Loudon does not make the analogy explicit, this horticultural ideal implies a social vision, a vision that is corroborated by other aspects of his discussion. The gardenesque style is the vegetable equivalent of the kind of individualism endorsed by liberal social discourse. Like the ideal gardenesque tree, the proprietor Loudon addresses is sturdily self-reliant but developed on all sides. At the same time he is part of a social system based on the kind of stable, finely articulated hierarchy also manifested in the aesthetically pleasing estate and already implied in the four-part structure of Loudon's book.

Indeed, it is not hard to read out of what Loudon represents as merely aesthetic advice a paradigm of the good society and the proper place of the individual within it. The ideals of individual development and hierarchical order are in constant, rhetorically productive tension in the *Villa Companion*. Loudon likes the very word 'high' and uses it often. As was conventional, he insists that the house be built on high ground, for 'elevation is dignity, and depression meanness' (29). But he also uses the word in ways that imply the power to command men and matter: 'high service' (in relation to water) means water on the top floors of the house (63); 'high order and keeping' (235) means the kind of extreme neatness and cultivation that in practice requires an army of servants (picking off insects, trimming borders, picking up leaves, transplanting flowers so that every plant in the garden is in bloom at the same time, cutting the grass by hand around the crocuses in Loudon's lawn). The same sense of hierarchy is found in a good architectural design: 'every whole must be composed of parts' and one of those parts 'should prevail in effect over the others, which ought to be subordinate to it, while they cooperated [sic] with it in forming a whole' (144). Yet here too the tension beween hierarchy and individuality shapes his thinking. The simplest kind of house plan – he calls it 'geometric' – involves a central 'main body' and two smaller 'pavilions' (144); but the superior model, 'the modern or irregular, style,' that is, the gothic-inflected building, which 'requires a much greater knowledge of art' (148), incorporates variety to produce a more muscular and dynamic kind of unity:

> Irregular buildings admit of a degree of harmony and intricacy ... of which regular and symmetrical buildings are not susceptible. Hence ... irregular architecture is in a higher style of art than that which is regular. (150)

There is an implied analogy here with the liberal state and the individual subject: whether in nation, psyche, or building, the stronger, more differentiated, and more idiosyncratic the elements that need to be subordinated, the greater the glory of uniting them in a single structure, and the higher the product that results.[25]

Everything Loudon says about social interaction suggests his acceptance of a similar scale of power and prestige in society and in the family. Gender hierarchy is taken for granted. Though the book is, according to its subtitle, written for 'the instruction of the female part of our readers' (7), it is clear that the implied reader of its more practical sections is the man of the family. Woman's role in this text is to have consumer desires, which, however, need to be regulated by advice like Loudon's. Though he flatters 'the ladies' (7) fulsomely from time to time, paying ritual homage to 'the hand of female taste, the superior elegance of which most writers acknowledge' (377), he always insinuates the limitations of this taste. As is conventional in aesthetic discourse, unity, consistency, creative genius, and mind are coded male – variety, ornament, acquisitiveness, and body, female. Though women are fascinated with the acquisition of goods, they lack the fundamentals of taste:

> Almost every lady has a taste for good furniture, rich carpets, bed hangings, and window drapery; and the consequence is, that, unless ladies have some principle to guide them in their choice, they are apt, when their means admit, to bring the most inconsistent things together in the same house, and even in the same room ... to produce a consistent whole, however humble may be the means, and simple the result, is a much greater beauty, and argues a superior degree of mind, than inconsistency, however beautiful or exquisite may be some of the individual parts.

In order to bring shape and pattern to the mass of individual objects covet, Loudon's ladies need to take instruction from him, a male artist with the kind of principled aesthetic genius that can bring order to female chaos. In his discourse it is not the ambitious cockney but the wealthy wife who becomes associated with 'profuse ornamentation.'[26] Loudon's manual is a concrete example of the way the middle-class wife is schooled in the obligations of what Veblen will call vicarious consumption – in the effective display of the property her husband has provided – and the suggestion is that her failure in this role is almost perverse, considering the ready availability of books (like his) that can teach her how.

If female light-mindedness is often implied, not the least in Loudon's most flattering remarks, male rationality and strength of character are also dramatized in his text. All Loudon's practical advice, particularly about the selection, purchasing, draining, and planning of a property, is implicitly addressed to the man of the family. The social and material world Loudon evokes, particularly when he is talking about the selection of the site for the house and its basic construction in the first hundred pages or so of his book, is a threatening environment, where you need to protect yourself by means of careful management from forces that can ruin your property or your pleasure in it or even hurt or kill you. The imagery in this section of the text is of invasion, penetration, and pollution: smoky neighbourhoods, smoky staircases, bad smells from cesspools, disagreeable 'effluvia' rising from the kitchen into the upper storeys of the house and from the stable litter into the hayloft to contaminate the hay; water concealed in the heart of 'soft, half-burnt bricks' (39), insidiously creeping up the walls and covering even the parlour furniture with mould; damp timber that falls prey to 'dry rot, and premature decay,' twisting the house on its foundation (42); thieves, who can enter the large windows of the 'light and cheerful' breakfast room unless 'fastened at night with iron-locking bars, and not, as is most common, by latch bars' (84); and most terrifying of all, fire – fire creeping up through the unfilled partitions or the flues of underbuilt party walls, or darting through the cracks in a 'Sylvester heating apparatus' mismanaged by a careless servant. Health and security depend upon blocking, bounding, or diverting the flow of dangerously mobile elements and circumventing as far as possible the laziness, incompetence, and greed of servants, employees, and suppliers. Loudon's tone is nevertheless sturdily positive. These goals can be achieved by 'proper management,' and it is his role to advise not only about aesthetics but also about such practical matters. The person who supervises the construction of drains and flues and sewers, hires and keeps an eye on the contractors, carpenters, grooms, and gardeners is implicitly male – explicitly so ('he') at one moment when Loudon offers a technical explanation that requires a bit of mathematical calculation (533). When consumption is represented not as self-indulgence but rather as self-mastery and mastery of the environment, the consumer is a prudent, responsible man.

In society as in the garden, Loudon takes for granted the notion of competing interests: the examples he offers make clear that both the safety and the beauty of a property depend upon the owner's control not only over physical matter but also over other people. Evidently the more financial power a man wields, the more aesthetic control he will also have. If the proprietor of a fourth-rate city lot wants to use the top of the walls that divide his lot from his neighbours' to maximize his plant collection, he will have to negotiate with them; whereas Loudon himself, since he owns the 'double-divided' villa in which he lives, can control the appearance of both halves of his lot by 'binding down' his tenant, who is 'precluded in the lease' from cutting down trees or making other changes (340–1). Loudon does register in passing that the competitive capitalism he takes for granted has its harsher aspects, but though these hurt the poor more than the wealthy, it is the problems they present for the middle-class proprietor that he addresses. Competition can be unfortunate when it undermines aesthetics – when a jobbing gardener, to make a profit, subverts the landscape gardener's designs – or when it leads to poor workmanship: he advises the reader to select a responsible contractor who will give a realistic quote, not one 'beaten down to the lowest price by competition' (474). In general, he advises, 'always employ a man who has a character to lose' (550). He takes for granted that the playing field is not level, that working-class initiative cannot and indeed should not always be rewarded, advising, for example, against hiring an undercapitalized contractor or carpenter, even though admitting that refusing to do so will 'prevent the mechanic or tradesman who has no capital from ever bettering his condition' (476). Good workmanship does not always pay, at least for the workman: Loudon refers to a mason renowned for his rockwork who died in the workhouse, not however to lament his lot but simply to point out that the man's services are no longer available.

Loudon is even ready to recognize that there can be competing interests within the family. Though he gives the obligatory paean to the individual household as the heart of the nation ('The cultivation of the fireside is of the greatest import, public and private,' the brightly blazing hearth, 'a scene to kindle, equally, attachment to one's friends, and love of one's country' [95]),[27] he also records with mild irony the C family's negotiations about the plans for their new estate – negotiations that pit the men, Mr C and his landscape designer, against the women, Mrs C and her daughters. The narrative of this little conflict is, however, literally marginalized in Loudon's text – it is recounted in small print in the right-hand margin, opposite the plans of the C estate – and it is promptly resolved by the sheer scale of the Cs' resources, concluding with the daughters' happy anticipation of a new archery ground (447, 451–3). Family harmony is evidently easier to achieve on a handsome income. The competitive economy Loudon takes for granted clearly offers more to the rich than to the poor, if only because the well-off homeowner can provide enough space to accommodate the competing tastes and interests of individual family members, yet Loudon's awareness of this reality is simply not allowed to impinge on the broader assertion of essential equality that underpins his ideology.

Nor are any of these contradictions allowed to qualify Loudon's vision of home as a sanctified space that offers an escape from the capitalist marketplace and the payoff for one's alienated labour in it. Building his house and cultivating his garden, the homeowner is represented as in touch both with the permanence of art and with the organic rhythms of natural life. Loudon describes a domestic property, which consists of two elements, house and garden, as governed by two principles: the principle of permanence and the principle of change or 'progress'

(170). Whereas architect and builder aim for permanence, the landscape gardener has to allow for continual change, 'the perpetual progress of vegetation which is going forward in [a garden] to maturity, dormancy, or decay' (4). Because the garden 'not only changes every year, but changes with every season' (170), the gardening homeowner, dealing as he does with 'living beings ... which grow and undergo changes before our eyes' (2), becomes attuned to natural rhythms. There is an implied analogy with the growth of the human psyche, in that 'every natural change in a garden ... up to a certain point, is a step in its progress towards maturity' (170). Up to a certain point: Loudon cannot quite keep death out of the garden, but his progressive ethos underwrites the analogous myth of the development of the psyche towards spiritual ripeness and maturity. Crawford's remarks about 'temporality within containment' apply well to such rather lyrical passages, and it is easy to believe that they could owe something to the kind of poetry that she sees as shaped by the same paradox.[28] Like the self, though Loudon never makes the analogy explicit, the estate is an ongoing project, an investment of time that will pay off in a perfected whole.

It is also a do-it-yourself project. Loudon never ceases to emphasize the benefits to the proprietor of regular, strenuous physical work on his own estate. Like Locke, Loudon suggests that we confirm our ownership of property by mingling our labour with it. The homeowner

> finds enjoyment ... in his garden, and in the other rural objects which he can call his own, and which he can alter at pleasure, at a trifling expense, and often with his own hands. It is this which gives the charm of creation and makes a thing essentially one's own. (9)

Linking labour and memory in a way that endorses the vision of ripe, integrated subjectivity, Loudon declares that 'our own work is endeared to us by the difficulties we have met with and conquered at every step: every step has, indeed, its history, and recalls a train of interesting recollections connected with it' (9). Grooming one's property makes work for every social class: not only for the small property owner, who is obliged to undertake it for economic reasons, but equally for the wealthy, the sedentary, and the retired. The wealthiest cannot escape: 'no mistake can be greater,' Loudon insists, 'even for the owner of a first-rate estate, than to suppose that there is any enjoyment in retiring to the country and doing nothing there' (623). The landed gentleman's personal involvement in his farm contributes directly to the health and stability of the nation, for since 'farming and the weather, are topics which every countryman can discuss,' agricultural work will enable the substantial landowner 'to keep up a proper degree of social intercourse with his neighbours' (622). Loudon even goes so far as to suggest that the 'delightful and invigorating' (610) pastime of following the plough is not only an admirable recreation in itself but also an excellent preparation for the work of empire: he envisages the younger sons of the landed gentry ploughing contentedly in Australia or North America (623).

Gardening is equally restorative for individuals at the bottom of the social scale. The factory operative can profit from window gardening, even though he may have to carry out some of his operations 'by candle-light' (5), and the city clerk, after a day of work at his desk, can exhaust the remains of the day working at home:

> We know engravers, gentlemen in public offices, and many tradesmen, who have suburban gardens not above 50 ft. in length by 30 ft. in breadth, [who] ... work daily in their gardens before and after their hours of business; rising early in the morning, and remaining in their gardens till it becomes dark. (272)

'Even in winter,' Loudon reassures his reader, 'there is still something to do in every garden' (4). Loudon goes so far as to design a fourth-rate garden with the aim of producing as much work as possible, recommending certain plants and procedures precisely in the interest of 'creating more work for the occupier, and giving him an oppertunity [sic] of exercising his taste, as well as showing his botanical knowledge' (282). He suggests, for example, a double rather than a single trellis, 'in order that it may occasion the more labour' (231). In one such garden, he reassures his reader, the owner's 'labours ... would be incessant' (235):

> Even [in] the smallest-size fourth-rate suburban garden ... there is work enough for one person, every evening, say from six till it grows dark, throughout the spring, summer, and autumn months; besides work that must be done previously to six o'clock, in the months when it is dark at that hour; such as digging and cropping the culinary part of the garden, &c. (247)

Crawford traces the theme of productive work in the small suburban garden back to 1722, but the quotations she cites, one of which is from

Leigh Hunt's sonnet 'To Horatio Smith,' are not characterized by the somewhat frantic note that marks Loudon's prose at such moments.[29] By the time Loudon has worked his way down to the fourth-rate proprietor and to the actual list of tasks he must complete, his tone has subtly changed, and so has the way he measures time. Even at home, this gardener seems back in the world of the factory or office: the aim seems less to get in tune with time as to kill it. There is indeed something very static about the situation of Loudon's homeowner, nailed down to a mandatory schedule of unending work, fixed in place by his obsessive investment in his property and its maintenance. No doubt Loudon's ethic of constant home improvement makes for social stability. No factory worker who tends his plants by candlelight is likely to have much leisure or energy for shaking up the social system. But the middle-class homeowner seems equally immobilized. Self-improvement and self-presentation – they become one and the same – are so onerous and time-consuming that it is not clear when this improved self has time to experience the satisfaction of the perpetually deferred end product.

Work has still another function as Loudon sees it: it helps to unite the family. At perhaps the most lyrical moment in the text Loudon paints a celebratory picture of the family labouring together to make their garden grow. His domestic scenario differentiates individuals along class and gender lines, fixing them in place even as it unites them in a common endeavour.[30] Even the way one waters plants is age-, gender-, and class-specific:

What pleasure have not children in applying their little green watering pans to plants in pots, or pouring water in at the roots of favourite flowers in borders? And what can be more rational than the satisfaction which the grown up amateur, or master of the house, enjoys, when he returns from the city to his garden in the summer evenings, and applies the syringe to his wall trees, with refreshing enjoyment to himself and the plants, and to the delight of his children, who may be watching his operations? ... What more delightful than to see the master or the mistress of a small garden or pleasure-ground, with all the boys and girls, the maids, and, in short, all the strength of the house, carrying pots and pails of water to different parts of the garden? (3)

The servants, for once up to the task assigned them, are here for a moment granted a semi-feudal fusion with their employers: they become part of 'the strength of the house,' as if this were a noble or

royal family. The husband and wife are contentedly united in complementary tasks. The mistress of the house can undertake to influence
and guide the flowers – 'Tying up and trimming flowers are operations
generally undertaken by the ladies of the family' – but it takes a real
man to impose the serious discipline that the more unruly plants
require: 'The pruning of shrubs and trees, and tying up to stakes such as
require it, invite the hand of the master' (609). The family that gardens
together stays together, and stays in place, each individual confirmed in
his or her position by its ritual enactment in the context of shared
labour.

Almost but not quite excluded from Loudon's text is the kind of work
that this often obsessive gardening is an escape from. There are three
groups of workers conspicuously marginalized in the *Villa Companion*:
the woman, the servant, and the factory worker. The work of the
woman, except at this one moment when she happily joins her husband
and children in the summer garden, is erased almost entirely, in ways
that I have already suggested. To argue that a small fourth-rate house
has everything one could want in a mansion ignores the female effort it
would take to cram all of these functions into a small space. Woman's
maternal function is also ignored: although Loudon does mention from
time to time the educational value of gardens and greenhouses, neither
parent is ever envisaged actually tutoring the children. In the *Villa Companion* supposedly addressed to her, woman does not appear very often,
and when she does she is depicted, as I have suggested, largely as a
demanding and aesthetically irresponsible consumer. The real work of
the world goes on without her, the lively economy Loudon implies serving merely to pique, though never satisfy, her material desires. That
such desires, manufactured rather than chastened by discourse like his,
are the engine of the economy Loudon admires cannot be acknowledged if woman is to be kept in her place as the needy and recalcitrant
pupil of male genius.

Servants on the other hand are constantly present in this text, though
chiefly in three sites: in Loudon's warnings about the mishaps their
incompetence can cause; in his assessments of how much the various
estates he describes would cost to keep up; and on the plans of houses
and gardens, where the spaces provided for them become visible on the
page because he wants to make the servants themselves invisible to the
family. It is the servants of course who do most of the real work, particularly the heavy, dirty, or tedious work, on these properties. There are
armies of them: Mrs Lawrence has 'a smaller number of gardeners than

might be expected': only six in summer, as well as 'one or two women for collecting insects and dead leaves' (578), and three in winter; the Rev. Theodore Williams at Hendon Rectory, with only an acre and a half, has four: a head gardener, a man of all work, a man whose only duty is to attend to the 'pine and fir tribe,' a fourth man who 'is solely occupied in propagating by cuttings or otherwise' (482). Plentiful cheap labour is taken for granted. Servants' work is evidently open-ended: Loudon points out that if you keep a man-servant, his labour on your garden is 'free' since he is being paid in any case. For all the discussion of economy in this text, there seems to be no question of saving money by replacing men by machines. The new mechanical devices Loudon describes are designed not so much to save labour (except occasionally for the do-it-yourself homeowner, who Loudon suggests might want to use Budding's mowing machine on his own grass) as to produce a better or safer result. Servants are assumed to be lazy and incompetent, so that if they are put in charge of potentially dangerous devices, like the Sylvester apparatus for heating houses with a hot metal cockle, which Loudon declares to be perfectly safe 'under a proper system of management' (60), the 'difficulty of getting [them] to attend regularly to apparatus of this, or of any other description' (59) might burn down the house; hence Loudon recommends the less efficient but safer old-fashioned stove that only requires them to supply fuel, 'as much as can be expected, in the present state of things, in respect to servants' (62). They are also assumed to be dishonest (so the coal must be locked up), nosy (so the speaking tube in the dining room should have a cover that closes automatically to prevent the kitchen servants from listening to the family's conversation), and lazy (Loudon recommends a high window in the stable, 'to prevent careless or bad grooms from knowing when their master is coming to look after them' [81]).

But though under constant surveillance themselves, servants are supposed to be invisible. It is taken for granted that servants passing the lawn front destroy 'that complete privacy which is generally considered one of the greatest luxuries of a residence in the country' (695); hence Loudon plans networks of hidden roads and private paths and entrances for their exclusive use so that they will have access to their work areas 'without once crossing a single walk of the pleasure-ground, which the family may walk in and enjoy in perfect retirement' (389). It helps that they get up hours before the family: he explains, for example, that a road he plans to run from the mill paddock to the farmyard, which looks on the site plan as if it would come disagreeably close to the family area, will in fact be 'little used, and that only early in the morning, no perceptible marks of it are seen in the elm avenue' (639). The servants' quarters, as far as possible from the family's, are often close to the animals they tend. For his clients Loudon will devise a water closet with two doors, 'so that no person need come out by the same door by which he went in' (497), but modesty and sensitivity are evidently class-specific: his marginal notes to a plan for a first-rate garden identify a 'Pigsty, near which there is a privy for the farm servants' (plate 266, detail #7). The servants' own interests are never directly consulted, except when, as elements of the aesthetic scheme, they are in danger of being consigned to places too small or shabby for human beings to inhabit. Loudon makes the point that gatehouses must be large enough for the gatekeeper's family to live in and decorative hovels should be modern within even if artfully dilapidated without. Evidently he was progressive in this respect: the very need to state this rule suggests that it was often broken. Nevertheless it is anomalous that a book about the intellectual, spiritual, and physical benefits of private property can contemplate with equanimity the employment of human beings not only as labourers but also as decorative accessories, at salaries and under circumstances that would make homes and gardens of their own an impossibility.

Readers of the *Villa Companion* cannot forget about the servants: the need to get them out of the way keeps them constantly in mind. Erased from the text almost entirely however are industrial workers, who of course do not figure in the domestic scenes Loudon constructs. No factory workers confront the homeowner, and few factories are visible from his windows – though Loudon does mention in passing that factories are becoming so much better designed nowadays that at a distance, as part of the vista, their 'magnificent masses' can actually be an aesthetic asset (30). Other than echoing at one point the cliché about the urban worker whose mind 'is continually craving for food' (625), Loudon never mentions industrial workers at all. Yet the way he sets up his tribute to hobby work in the introductory chapter oddly evokes just what he needs to exclude and repress.

Setting out to explain what differentiates gardening from other kinds of labour, Loudon suddenly produces the same kind of unstable figurative language that signalled Repton's embarrassment about social class. Loudon's theme in this paragraph is that whereas gardening is restorative, useless work is demoralizing:

To labour for the sake of arriving at a result, and to be successful in attaining it, are, as cause and effect, attended by a certain degree of satisfaction to the mind, however simple or rude the labour may be, and however unimportant the result obtained. To be convinced of this we have only to imagine ourselves employed in any labour from which no result ensues, but that of fatiguing the body, or wearying the mind: the turning of a wheel, for example, that is connected with no machinery, or, if connected, effects no useful purpose; the carrying of a weight, from one point to another and back again; or the taking of a walk without any object in view, but the negative one of preserving health. Thus it is not only a condition of our nature, that, in order to secure health and cheerfulness, we must labour; but we must also labour in such a way as to produce something useful or agreeable. Now, of the different kinds of useful things produced by labour, those things, surely which are living beings, and who grow and undergo changes before our eyes, must be more productive of enjoyment than such as are mere brute matter; the kind of labour, and other circumstances, being the same. Hence, a man who plants a hedge, or sows a grass-plot in his garden, lays a more certain foundation for enjoyment, than he who builds a wall or lays down a gravel walk; and, hence, the enjoyment of a citizen whose recreation, at his suburban residence, consists in working in his garden must be higher in the scale, than that of him who amuses himself, in the plot round his house, with shooting at a mark or playing at bowls. (2)

This discussion assumes a 'natural' hierarchy, a 'scale' by which the middle-class hobbyist is self-evidently 'higher' than those who labour for a living. Loudon's figurative language is, however, evasive: he is unwilling to look squarely at the kind of work from which gardening offers an escape. The labour that produces 'living beings ... who grow and undergo changes before our eyes' sounds like childbirth, but female generative power is evoked only to be transferred to the male home-owner, the 'man who plants a hedge, or sows a grass-plot in his garden.' This man is laying a foundation, but not as a mason lays one: his foundation is a spiritual one, a 'foundation for enjoyment'; hence he is evidently a more spiritual creature than a mason. The distinction between gentleman and manual labourer is naturalized – one can assume the brutishness of people who work with 'mere brute matter' – and the parallel between them aborted (as it were) before it has a chance to 'grow and change.' When Loudon tries to envisage wholly unproductive work, the sheer implausibility of his hypothetical scenario calls attention to itself. The individual who would have a 'suburban residence' with enough acreage to contain a bowling lawn or an archery range is hardly likely to be discovered turning a wheel 'that is connected with no machinery, or, if connected, effects no useful purpose' or 'carrying ... a weight, from one point to another and back again' – perversely useless efforts that would be prescribed nowhere perhaps but in a prison. The possibility of work being pointless even if the wheel were attached to something – the possibility, too, of work deeply alienating even though not involving literal machinery at all – is repressed as quickly as it arises, and with it the worker condemned to such labour.

In the *Villa Companion* Loudon constructs a vision of the great class of home lovers united in their personal task of family culture and the great communal project of 'improving' a nation: the weaver labours at his loom and grows prize dahlias in his spare time; the great lord follows the plough and his lady delights in her orchids as does the cottager's wife in her scarlet runners.[31] But the assertion of identity can be pushed no further. Loudon's happy vision cannot accommodate work that is by its very nature dehumanizing or sordid dwellings and oppressive work-places over which the individual has no control at all. Both Loudon and Dickens are animated by the vision of home, and Dickens, who was himself deeply interested in home improvement, very likely knew Loudon's work and may even have been influenced by it. But what Loudon represses, Dickens takes as his theme.

Dickens has also clearly been exposed to the anti-cockney satire of writers like Lloyd and Burney. Loudon's skittishness about confronting real class difference or acknowledging class animosity leads him to avoid this kind of satire, but it continues into the second half of the nineteenth century in much the same terms as in the eighteenth. There is a direct line from writers like Lloyd and Burney, for example, to Edward Kemp, who in *How to Lay out a Garden* (written after Loudon's *Villa Companion* and before Dickens's *Great Expectations*) decries 'the vulgarities and irregularities of mere cockneyism' (32) and generalizes about the reaction they evoke:

> There is nothing of which people in general are so intolerant in others, as the attempt, when glaringly and injudiciously made, to crowd within a confined space the appropriate adornments of the most ample gardens. It is invariably taken as evidence of a desire to appear to be and to possess that

which the reality of the case will not warrant; and is visited with the repro-
bation and contempt commonly awarded to ill-grounded assumption. (31)

Expressions like 'invariably' and 'people in general' as well as the passive verbs that blur and universalize agency express as a universal aesthetic principle what is really middle-class contempt for working-class
taste. Invoking the notion of authenticity, Kemp decries fakes and imitations – or at least the kind of fakes and imitations that mark the perpe-
trator as not middle class:

> Everything partaking of the nature of a *sham*, also, that is wanting in real
> excellence, will be discarded by persons desiring to obtain credit for cor-
> rect taste. Artificial ruins, mere fronts to buildings, figures to represent ani-
> mals, bridges that have no meaning, or for which there is no necessity ...
> will commonly be despised when the trick is discovered. (41)

The rock gardens and other rock fantasies so beloved by Mrs Lawrence
and her ilk (and even recommended by Loudon) have evidently been
taken up by Kemp's cockneys: he condemns 'the staringly gross and
peculiar forms sometimes met with in suburban gardens ... A castellated
grotto, for example, with the greatest and most fantastic variety of outline, and numerous turrets' (33). He also mentions for particular condemnation the

> *unsuitable ornaments* ... which many persons who have only a glimmering of
> the requirements of art have a great propensity for placing about gardens
> ... artificial basins of water, ponds, figures, bridges, flag-poles, prospect-tow-
> ers, cannon, groups of stones, spar, or roots, with objects of a similar
> nature, which may or may not be fitting ornaments for a garden in them-
> selves, but which may be so inappropriately disposed, or so entirely unal-
> lied to the prevailing characteristics of a particular spot, as to be wholly
> inadmissible. (39)

Loudon himself had 'admitted' many such ornaments on larger estates,
and Kemp cannot exclude them on principle, only condemn their
'unsuitable' deployment on properties too humble to deserve them.
This last catalogue in particular, which contains a number of the objects
featured on Wemmick's property in *Great Expectations*, suggests that in
developing the Walworth scenes Dickens was drawing not only on actual
properties he would have seen but also on an established satirical dis-

course. The contemptuous imagery of Kemp is clearly relevant to the Walworth home of Wemmick in *Great Expectations,* but equally relevant to this and to a number of other Dickens settings are the more complex discursive structures developed by Loudon.

Dickens is hostile to the discourse of taste in general, which he finds narrowly and invidiously prescriptive. In particular he has no use for the kind of tastefulness that would inhibit the exuberance and vitality of ordinary people. In 'Our French Watering-Place,' he invents 'Bilkins, the only authority on Taste,' to ironize the preference of the English for 'neutral' colours – 'taste is neutral (see Bilkins)' – and their contempt for the 'lively colours' of regional costume, which he himself is prepared to declare charmingly 'picturesque.'[32] Finding the aesthetic dictates of bourgeois correctness narrow, culture-bound, and authoritarian, he celebrates the 'vulgarity' of individuals who ignore them, particularly the costume of cockney men and boys whose garish finery testifies to a buoyant sense of self. The same principles shape the way he depicts architecture and interiors. Fascinated by the fanciful and the grotesque, Dickens tends to represent architectural regularity and correctness as sterile and stultifying. Yet Dickens was intensely interested in the design of his own home as well as in the homes of his fictional characters, who are consistently constructed in terms of the places they inhabit. What makes Loudon particularly relevant to Dickens is his claim about the sufficiency of small properties. Little dwellings are by no means always positive in Dickens, who habitually represents the twisted lives of society's victims in terms of the constricted and often grotesque spaces in which they have to live. Yet the faith that domestic happiness does not take wealth, that the influence of the domestic angel can make the most modest home into a haven of harmony, is also central to Dickens's vision. Since feminine good taste is a staple of this discourse of modesty, Dickens is from time to time cornered, as it were, into representing the cozy, wholesome little home in terms of an orthodox kind of tastefulness in which he does not wholly believe, and this tension contributes to the coy and unconvincing constructions of femininity to which readers have objected. When Dickens can use the discourse of middle-class taste in a parodic or satirical way, or when he can make the aesthetic correctness of the aristocracy a sign of sinister social power, his writing is lively and engaged, but when he needs to take tastefulness seriously the rhetorical temperature often falls, and he lapses into patent sentimentality.

A thorough investigation of architecture in Dickens would take a book in itself. All Dickens's novels involve vividly described architectural settings, and in many of them, notably *Dombey and Son, Little Dorrit,* and *Great Expectations,* a building is the central symbol. Not all such houses, however, are either notably tasteful or indeed notably vulgar: taste is often simply not the issue. It is gothic fiction, rather than anything Loudon has to say about estate design, that provides the most useful context for Satis House or the Clennan house in *Little Dorrit* (or for the structures that parody them, like the prison, for example, in the latter novel). What I am interested in examining here is Dickens's representation of certain properties in which taste and style are the issue: properties to which Loudon's ideas are relevant. Whether or not Dickens read Loudon, the 'small-is-sufficient' discourse so important to the *Villa Companion* shapes the contrast, in *Bleak House* (1853) and *The Tale of Two Cities* (1859), between the modest and happy domestic establishment and the doomed chateau, while the small yet supposedly sufficient properties of James Carker in *Dombey and Son* (1848), John Wemmick in *Great Expectations* (1860–1), and Noddy Boffin in *Our Mutual Friend* (1864–5) are certainly conceived in response to the discursive tradition to which Loudon contributes. In the pages that follow I will try to show both how a Loudonesque home-and-garden discourse inflects the Dickensian gothic and how it shapes the construction of certain of his comic characters who have a touching investment in their own good taste.

*Bleak House,* which begins with the unhappy Lady Dedlock virtually imprisoned at Chesney Wold – one of those great houses so distinguished that it is open to tourists – and ends with her daughter Esther Summerson contentedly installed in a tiny perfect cottage, rich not in money but in wedded bliss, seems to replicate the Repton/Loudon modesty formula with predictable precision. The great house at Chesney Wold is focalized in chapter 18 by Esther herself, who looks down on it from a distance, in terms that underscore, in somewhat stereotyped language, its exemplary aesthetic perfection:

> It was a picturesque old house, in a fine park richly wooded. Among the trees, and not far from the residence, [Mr Boythorn] pointed out the spire of the little church ... O the solemn woods over which the light and shade travelled swiftly, as if Heavenly wings were sweeping on benignant errands through the summer air; the smooth green slopes, the glittering water, the garden where the flowers were so symmetrically arranged in clusters of the richest colours, how beautiful they looked! The house, with gable and chimney, and tower, and turret, and dark doorway, and broad terrace-walk,

twining among the balustrades of which, and lying upon the vases, there was one great flush of roses, seemed scarcely real in its light solidity, and in the serene and peaceful hush that rested on all around it ... On everything, house, garden, green slopes, water, old oaks, fern, moss, woods again, and far away across the openings in the prospect, to the distance lying wide before us with a purple bloom upon it, there seemed to be such undisturbed repose. (187–8)

The prospect is 'picturesque' in the most literal sense, visualized as it would appear in a picture in an album of great estates – Repton's Red Books, for example – and the estate is what Repton would call 'a vast range of unblended and uninterrupted property' with an unimpeded view: the Dedlocks are not obliged to see from their windows, or indeed even from the hills above, any building or object that does not belong to them. The large landowner's absolute control of his own property is a repeated motif in *Bleak House* – Lawrence Boythorn, Esther's guide on this occasion, has a ferocious running feud with Sir Leicester Dedlock, who insists on closing the public right of way that crosses his land – and a reader of Loudon might register the connection between legal and aesthetic control, a connection that makes the gloriously open prospect of Chesney Wold a sign less of admirable taste than of arbitrary social power. Certainly, the aesthetic perfection of the property signals its sterility. The 'undisturbed repose' that Esther imputes to the place is an illusion, the 'dark doorway' a more reliable clue. The reader already knows the house from the inside as a site of pride, dread, and sorrow – has already, in chapter 2, seen Lady Dedlock looking wistfully down on the gatehouse, watching the gatekeeper's little daughter run out in the rain to greet her father as he returns home in the evening. It is not necessary to know that the well-being of families that lived in such miniature structures was often subordinated to the demands of architectural style to appreciate the contrast between the material luxury of Lady Dedlock's situation and the affective wealth of her employee, but the information does sharpen the suggestion that 'correct' taste and full humanity are mutually exclusive.

It is significant that the life and movement that Esther attributes to this scene come from natural phenomena rather from than the house itself – from the flowers, the breeze, and especially the light – for this passage, with its touch of banality (a deliberate banality, I think, designed to suggest the impressionability of Esther, who is penning this description) adumbrates an elegiac set piece later in the novel. The

Dedlocks are an 'old family' in the most negative sense, and chapter 40 opens with a long passage of highly rhetorical description that foreshadows the collapse of the aristocracy as represented by them and their mansion, which is depicted in the light of the setting sun. A long paragraph is devoted to the portrait gallery in Chesney Wold. Dickens describes in some detail the golden later-summer sunlight 'pour[ing] in, rich, lavish, overflowing like the summer plenty in the land,' to 'thaw' the 'frozen Dedlocks' and endow them one by one for a moment with a semblance of vivacity and warmth, only to die out and leave the mansion 'like a body without life' (428). The sun is going down for the last time on the privilege that built this house, and the family's past, embodied not only in the portraits but also in the uncanny sound of footsteps in the Ghost's Walk, is represented as a burden and a curse rather than an honourable heritage. The gothic inflection is obvious, and it ironize Esther's Reptonian perspective. From afar, as seen by her, Chesney Wold is what Loudon would call the *beau ideal* of a country estate. From the inside, however, it is a house of horrors, with its portraits that come to life, its haunted Walk, its madman – the obsessed lawyer Tulkinghorn – in the attic, and its 'waste of unused passages and staircases,' and by the end of the novel it will be 'a place where few people care to go about alone; where a maid screams if an ash drops from the fire' (662). Since it is the deadness of the appropriately named Dedlocks that Dickens wants to dramatize, it is appropriate that their stone building exhibit a cold regularity, that stylistically it seem all of a piece, a single exemplary aesthetic specimen, rather than the living, evolving organism faked by those home builders who, trying to claim 'old family' for themselves, deliberately designed their homes to look as if they had been built in stages over the years. Viewing the estate on a sunny summer day, Esther does not register that the only life it has is borrowed from the sunlight and that the house's dead 'solidity,' etherealized by the hazy light, is the truth about it.

Esther also fails to realize as she looks down on it that this estate is the home of her mother, and though eventually she learns the truth, she never enters the building. The house that is thematically paired with Chesney Wold – the other house conceived in terms of its relationship to Esther and to the past – is the eponymous home of her adoptive father, John Jarndyce, and it is Esther's entry into this space that is Dickens's means of introducing it to the reader. Notoriously, this is the house where Tom Jarndyce has killed himself: hence its grim name. But Bleak House also embodies a more positive, more distant past. Dickens splits his gothic allusions into two sets, assigning to the Dedlock mansion the stony architecture and the 'gothic' narrative devices while constructing Bleak House in terms of the Ruskinian ideal of collective construction and layered history.[33]

Architecturally, Bleak House lacks the static perfection of Chesney Wold. To dramatize the irregularity of its design, Dickens introduces it by means of a 'house tour' conducted by Esther. While the keynote of Esther's description of Chesney Wold is detachment, invited by a 'correct' aesthetic and imposed by distance, the keynote of this passage is involvement. Arriving at night and taken inside the dwelling before she has seen it clearly from the outside, Esther cannot grasp it in a single glance, but rather has to move through it one room at a time, experiencing it much as Loudon wanted his clients' visitors to experience his carefully planned properties. Instead of orienting the reader from the beginning within a coherent space, Dickens makes Esther dramatize her own pleasurable disorientation:

> It was one of those delightfully irregular houses where you go up and down steps out of one room into another, and where you come upon more rooms when you think you have seen all there are, and where there is a bountiful provision of little halls and passages, and where you find still older cottage-rooms in unexpected places, with lattice windows and green growth pressing through them. (50)

The detail of the 'green growth' brilliantly links the 'pressing' vitality of the growing plants with the nervous interconnectedness of the halls and passageways and the insistent yet confused progress of the home's new inhabitant. Energy seems to press and flow through this house to shape the structure through which it moves, as if the building, like the greenery, had an organic life of its own. The floor plan has a pleasing irregularity that both connects rooms and separates them. From the latticed room, which will be her own, Esther moves 'down two steps, into a charming little sitting-room,' 'up three steps, into Ada's bedroom,' then out of this room into 'a little gallery' that takes her to the 'best rooms' of the house, and 'so, by a little staircase of shallow steps, down into the hall.' But just as we seem to be completing the circuit to arrive back on the ground floor, our guide turns around and takes us back the other way:

> But if, instead of going out at Ada's door, you came back into my room, and went out at the door by which you had entered it, and turned up a few

crooked steps that branched off in an unexpected manner from the stairs, you lost yourself in passages, with mangles in them, and three-cornered tables. (50)

The tangled instructions have rather the same effect as the cunningly devised paths recommended by Loudon: they make what is apparently a 'modest' space seem larger than it is. But that the effect here is not the result of deliberate art is precisely its point. Bleak House really has been built in stages: its delightful irregularity is an effect not to be achieved by a builder who deliberately constructs a house all at once but in different styles.

How to represent the movement of a bemused focalizer through a complex, unfamiliar architectural space is a technique Dickens has learned from the gothic – one thinks of Pip in *Great Expectations* entering Satis House for the first time – but this is positive gothic, and Esther's progress models positive family values. There is both a centripetal and a centrifugal dynamic to her description, which circles back to the centre but also keeps branching out in random directions. The way Esther orients herself in relation to her own room is psychologically realistic, but it also serves to make that room the figurative heart of the house. This focus also makes the men's rooms seem rather tangential. Despite Esther's accurate observations – two steps here, three steps there – the other rooms she describes, Jarndyce's and Richard's, are not located in space: connected in a way impossible to visualize by these long hallways, they seem to be separate, private spaces. The effect is to valorize individual privacy, even though the 'individuality' of all these characters is qualified by the essentialized gender differences that shape the rooms they inhabit.

Gender is indeed heavily underlined by decor. The mere decorativeness that Loudon condemns as a sign of unprincipled feminine taste is celebrated by Dickens, the link between ornament and femininity endorsed: Esther's and Ada's pretty, cozy rooms look down on the flower garden; their sitting room is a pastoral green; Ada's room is 'all flowers' in chintz, paper, needlework, and brocade. But rigorous, masculine self-control also has its emblem: 'the plain room where Mr Jarndyce slept, all the year round, with his window open, his bedstead without any furniture standing in the middle of the floor for more air, and his cold-bath gaping for him in a smaller room adjoining' (50). This apartment might be paired with the 'Growlery' Esther has not yet seen, the study to which Jarndyce withdraws when depressed. The program of physical and mental hygiene John Jarndyce has set up for himself testifies to commendable self-control, and the fact there are cold rooms dedicated to repression as well as cozy, flowery rooms dedicated to youthful development illustrates the balanced Victorian values – domestic comfort, stern self-discipline – that the house represents. Time and space are connected: it is successive additions over *time* that have created the *space* for privacy and individual difference.

The second paragraph of Esther's description also registers the passage of time, and in an equally positive way. Most of the articles and objects in the house allude to time: sometimes directly, like the 'oval engravings of the months' on her walls; sometimes by humorously illustrating the sensibility of a bygone period, like the picture of 'four angels, of Queen Anne's reign, taking a complacent gentleman to heaven'; sometimes by memorializing the people who have lived here in the past. As she investigates the various rooms, Esther comes across

> half-length portraits, in crayons, [which] abounded all through the house; but were so dispersed that I found the brother of a youthful officer of mine in the china-closet, and the grey old age of my pretty young bride, with a flower in her bodice, in the breakfast-room. (51)

These pictures are the middle-class equivalent of the portrait gallery in a great house like Chesney Wold, but without its order, sophistication, and arrogance. Instead of being frozen, like the Dedlock ancestors, at a moment in their prime and lined up in a formal collection to testify to the pedigree of the family, these nameless individuals, whose images have over the years been dispersed around the house, are allowed to age on canvas for the record, their changing images testifying to human limitation and mortality, their family connections surviving, if at all, only by chance.

Esther's catalogue of the other objects in Bleak House recalls the collections described by Loudon, but this jumble of belongings is comically random, unselfconscious, and undistinguished. Dickens has enough stake in the tastefulness of his heroine to make clear that she finds many of the items slightly ridiculous or grotesque. The somewhat alien quality of these objects, which are historically limited in their conception, inept or naive in their execution, not only testifies to a certain engaging earnestness in the people who produced or collected them, it also allows Dickens to represent Esther as one of 'us' in her own taste and cultivation. There is a child's sampler with an amusingly arbitrary design ('a composition in needlework, representing fruit, a kettle, and an alphabet'). There is a zoological specimen that testifies to somebody's quasi-scientific interest in British nature (or perhaps to somebody's fishing trip) – 'a real trout in a case, as brown and shining as if it had been served with gravy' (51). There are a number of souvenirs of empire: 'surprised and surprising birds, staring out of pictures'; a picture of 'the death of Captain Cook'; a picture showing 'the whole process of preparing tea in China, as depicted by Chinese artist'; and

> a Native-Hindoo chair, which was also a sofa, and a box, and a bedstead, and looked in every form, something between a bamboo skeleton and a great bird-cage, and had been brought from India nobody knew by whom or when. (50)

Nobody knew. The contrast between the anonymity, the effacement of these generations of decent modest people who took their efforts for granted and quietly did the work of family and of nation and the self-memorializing of families like the Dedlocks valorizes middle-class modesty and decency. We are never told which of Jarndyce's ancestors, if they are indeed his ancestors, are represented by the various articles Esther names, and the effect is to suggest that the house has evolved along with the 'family' of the new middle class itself: to make it a kind of metonym of that class, of the sum of its tastes, however mediocre, and its achievements, however minor individually. Hence the irony of Bleak House's shocking recent past: of the fact that this unassuming, collective social and cultural work has been so tainted and compromised in the present century by the kind of corrupt national institutions that have led Tom Jarndyce to his death.

There is no question in Bleak House of the aesthetic unity that Loudon demanded in home design. The furniture, like the rooms, is a jumble of old and new, useful and castoff, a jumble that a mere cottage could not accommodate: one needs a certain amount of space to preserve the relics of time. It is the unselfconscious, unsystematic nature of the house and its contents, the indifference to good taste for its own sake, that gives the place its charm. Any attempt to impose a single aesthetic in this house would spoil it. To be sure, there is a pervasive atmosphere of warmth and purity: Bleak House is bright, with its 'illuminated windows ... shining out upon the star-light night' (51), clean, with its 'pure white tiles' (50) and 'display of the whitest linen' (51) and drawers scented with 'rose-leaves and sweet lavender' (51), and well cared for, with its busy but invisible servants bustling around, as Loudon would have them do, behind the scenes ('you could hear the horses being rubbed down ... and being told to Hold Up' [50]), and the sounds of dinner being prepared. But this welcoming ambience does not serve to impose unity on the 'quaint variety' (51) of the furnishings, which 'agreed in nothing, but their perfect neatness' (51) and sweet smell. Tastefulness for its own sake is tyranny in Dickens, and it is only in spaces that elude tastefulness that human warmth and vitality can be cultivated.

This house looks like the dwelling of a happy family, and Dickens's point is that it should have been. In view of the overarching theme of the novel, his pessimistic sense of the way evil social institutions corrupt private manners, it is not surprising that the house does not succeed in sheltering and protecting all its children. Jarndyce may practise admirable self-control, but his retreat to the Growlery, which also expresses his unwillingness to face unpleasant facts, while it makes him an unoppressive 'father,' also makes him an ineffective one – at least to Richard, who is given perhaps too much 'space' to develop his individual subjectivity. Richard's own multipurpose room, 'part library, part sitting-room, part bedroom ... a comfortable compound of many rooms,' is described immediately after the multipurpose 'Native-Hindoo' chair, and the echo implies the difference between the mere ingenuity of the East, which dreams up versatile but silly gadgets, and the centred domesticity of the West, which produces a kind of genial, multifaceted subjectivity. But in a corrupt society like the one Richard must be equipped to enter, such multifaceted geniality can lead to ruin. In his dealings with Richard, Jarndyce fails to strike the right balance between permissiveness and discipline, and with Richard's fall Bleak House comes apart. Its very dissolution gives the house, as a symbol, a certain gravitas. Were all the members of the family to turn out as happily as the house deserves, its description would seem a mere example of Dickensian kitsch. The fact that they do not validates it as a domestic ideal that the novel is not pretending can be realized.

Bleak House is a Dickensian chronotope: the Bakhtinian term is beautifully apt for the way its space is shaped by time. This kind of positive social space, *pace* Loudon, is an advantage not offered by a small cottage, particularly a newly built one. It is partly because the original house is so rich an image that it is disconcerting when at the end of the novel John Jarndyce presents Esther and Woodcourt with its namesake, the blandly tasteful little cottage that he has pre-emptively named 'Bleak

House.' The gift of this cottage is disturbing, not only because of the dual father/lover status of Jarndyce, who, having failed to win Esther for a wife, seems to be participating vicariously in her marriage; not only because he tortures her up to the very last moment by continuing to pretend that she is going to marry him; not only because its emphatic miniaturization – it is a 'cottage, quite a rustic cottage of doll's rooms' (648) – suggests that he is still making a doll out of Esther; but also because the house, described with none of the specificity that makes the original Bleak House so complex and positive an icon, is a mere list of clichés:

> As we went through the pretty rooms, out at the little rustic verandah doors, and underneath the tiny wooden colonnades, garlanded with woodbine, jasmine, and honeysuckle, I saw, in the papering on the walls, in the colours of the furniture, in the arrangements of all the pretty objects, *my* little tastes and fancies, *my* little methods and inventions which they used to laugh at while they praised them, my odd ways everywhere. (648)

The imagery here is vague: the nouns, when they are not generic (room, doors, colonnades, walls, furniture, objects), are abstract (arrangement, taste, fancies, methods, inventions, ways), and the 'fancies' and 'methods' are those not of generations of people but rather of the single, idealized, central presence – the domestic angel. The space, apparently devised by Jarndyce to express Esther's individuality, locks her back instead into the same stereotyped position of little housekeeper that she has always occupied. Though Dickens replicates the obligatory discourse endorsing modest, tasteful contentment, the fairy-tale resolution rings false, not only because of the other discordant notes at the end of the novel (like the notorious final sentence), but also because Dickens really believes neither in the adequacy of tiny dwellings, which he consistently uses as the sign of stunted lives, nor in conventional good taste, which he sees as an oppressive kind of social discipline. When Dickens parrots the 'small-is-sufficient' discourse of writers like Repton and Loudon the effect can only be parodic, the deadness of the language ironizing the moral it implies.

*A Tale of Two Cities*, one of the shortest of Dickens's novels, invites comparison with *Bleak House*, one of the longest, if only in that it uses the same two image, the mansion and the cottage, to make the same point about the inevitable eclipse of illegitimate aristocratic power by the domestic values of the modest middle class. Even some of the details

are similar: the sinister great house – here, the chateau of the Marquis
d'Evrémonde – is, like Chesney Wold, developed in terms of the contrast between dead stone and living light. In a few masterful strokes,
Dickens sets up a metaphor of stoniness that is sustained throughout:

> It was a heavy mass of building, that château of Monsieur the Marquis, with
> a large stone court-yard before it, and two stone sweeps of staircase meet-
> ing in a stone terrace before the principal door. A stony business alto-
> gether, with heavy stone balustrades, and stone urns, and stone flowers,
> and stone faces of men, and stone heads of lions, in all directions. As if the
> Gorgon's head had surveyed it, when it was finished, two centuries ago.
> (141)

The perspective is what in a text like Loudon's would be called a front
elevation: we are looking – along with the Gorgon, in fact – straight at
the chateau's façade. But the building, through the stone faces of men
and the stone heads of lions, is looking back, staring down anyone aspiring to enter it. This is a wonderfully effective fusion of Loudon and
gothic to convey the arrogance and callousness of brutal class power.
The impression of guarded impermeability is of course an illusion – the
Marquis' killer will come in through his window – and after he has done
his job Dickens brilliantly reworks the contrast between dead matter and
living light as the sun rises the next morning:

> The fountain in the village flowed unseen and unheard, and the fountain
> at the château dropped unseen and unheard ... through three dark hours.
> Then, the grey water of both began to be ghostly in the light, and the eyes
> of the stone faces of the château were opened.
>   Lighter and lighter, until at last the sun touched the tops of the still
> trees, and poured its radiance over the hill. In the glow, the water of the
> château fountain seemed to turn to blood, and the stone faces crimsoned.
> (151–2)

A contrast that develops over pages in *Bleak House* is distilled to its
essence in this short novel, arguably to greater effect.

Less compelling, however, is the description of the modest bourgeois
home to which this building is implicitly contrasted, the home of
Charles Darnay and his wife in London. This small but idyllic dwelling,
presided over by the charming and virtuous Lucie, features the usual
'woman's-room' objects – the 'best room' contains 'Lucie's birds, and

flowers, and books, and desk, and work-table, and box of water-colours' (89) – and is supposed to be enchanting in just the usual ways. Lucie's French taste has made the most of her modest English resources:

> Although the Doctor's daughter had known nothing of the country of her birth, she appeared to have innately derived from it that ability to make much of little means, which is one of its most useful and most agreeable characteristics. Simple as the furniture was, it was set off by so many little adornments, of no value but for their taste and fancy, that its effect was delightful. The disposition of everything in the rooms, from the largest object to the least; the arrangement of colours, the elegant variety and contrast obtained by thrift in trifles, by delicate hands, clear eyes, and good sense; were at once so pleasant in themselves, and so expressive of their originator, that, as Mr Lorry stood looking about him, the very chairs and tables seemed to ask him, with something of that peculiar expression which he knew so well by this time, whether he approved? (110–11)

He does, of course – Jarvis Lorry is here assigned the role of 'voyeur' whose function it is to enter the woman's room and register the tastefulness of the woman who has shaped it – and those plaintive personified chairs and tables make clumsily clear that the masculine stamp of approval is the essential element of the 'woman's-room' convention. But the reader may not be so easily convinced. As dubious as the extraordinary suggestion that good taste is 'innate' in the most literal sense – not merely a characteristic of the culture of certain nations, but a trait biologically transmitted to a young woman who has never been exposed to the culture – is the rhetorical numbness of the writing here. When Dickens tries to use orthodox taste as an emblem of moral virtue, his imagination dies: he seems too bored by the discourse to visualize a single object in the room. The only compelling details connected with this house are the gothic ones: M. Manette hidden away compulsively making shoes, and the sound of ghostly footsteps that disturbs the inhabitants at significant moments. These two details rework ways of representing the sinister past already developed in *Bleak House* – Manette is another madman in an 'attic,' and the footsteps are like the uncanny noises in the Ghost Walk – but here Dickens shifts the omens away from the site of aristocratic power and locates them instead in the modest home that is threatened by that power. Dealing with the uncanny, Dickens's imagination is exuberant and ingenious; attempting to use good taste as a sign of positive moral values, it fails.

Not so, however, when he wants it to signal smooth hypocrisy and a compulsive will to power. Esther Summerson's pretty cottage bears comparison with that of James Carker, Paul Dombey's conniving lieutenant in *Dombey and Son*, but the two dwellings represent directly opposite values. The association Dickens makes between perfect good taste and sinister social control is never clearer than in the description of Carker's modest little dwelling, which is as smooth and featureless as the image its owner presents to his employer. Like Carker himself, the 'cottage' is perfectly bland and blandly perfect in appearance, a model of modest completeness, and the language in which Dickens describes it is equally bland and facile, especially when it rehearses the theme of the adequacy of a small property. The dwelling, 'situated in the green and wooded country near Norwood,'

> is not a mansion; it is of no pretensions as to size; but it is beautifully arranged, and tastefully kept. The lawn, the soft, smooth slope, the flower-garden, the clumps of trees where graceful forms of ash and willow are not wanting, the conservatory, the rustic verandah with sweet-smelling, creeping plants entwined about the pillars, the simple exterior of the house, the well-ordered offices, though all upon the diminutive scale proper to a mere cottage, bespeak an amount of elegant comfort within, that might serve for a palace. This indication is not without warrant; for, within, it is a house of refinement and luxury. Rich colours, excellently blended, meet the eye at every turn; in the furniture – its proportions admirably devised to suit the shapes and sizes of the small room; on the walls; upon the floors; tingeing and subduing the light that comes in through the odd glass doors and windows here and there. There are a few choice prints and pictures too; in quaint nooks and recesses there is no want of books; and there are games of skill and chance set forth on tables – fantastic chessmen, dice, backgammon, cards, and billiards. (553)

Carker's little property, with the variety of pleasing features prescribed for the happy Victorian home, has the aesthetic unity Loudon insists on, but in this context such conventional perfection is a sign of Carker's amorality, his inhuman coolness, and his ruthless will to control. The 'opulence of comfort' in the cottage is tainted by 'some subtle portion of himself, which gives a vague expression of himself to everything about him' (554). What the property 'expresses' is precisely nothing: with no past that he will acknowledge and no family to accommodate, Carker has a house that in its perfect tastefulness communicates no sense of individual personality. Like Carker's mask of a face, his home presents an opaque image that defies penetration.[34]

This is the kind of dwelling, perfect of its kind and more than adequate to Carker's needs as a solitary bachelor, that ought to prevent its owner from 'wishing for more,' according to the doctrine of Repton and Loudon. The fact that it does not – that, far from being content within his own house, Carker is determined to penetrate and possess both the house of Dombey, by seducing his wife, and the 'House of Dombey,' by getting control of the business – makes clear why Loudon's optimistic formula is inadequate. In a social order structured by capitalist competition and competitive display it is always possible to 'wish for more,' and the figure of Carker dramatizes the reason that a small and perfect property cannot be counted on to suffice. Such a home has little appeal if dominance is what one wants: the determination to win, humiliate, and destroy makes *differential* size the only thing that matters. The nature of Carker's collection – not coins or botanical specimens but games – points to the reality Loudon willfully ignores: that the economic order that produces a Dombey also produces the gamesmanship of a Carker, the determination to overgo and defeat a rival.

Carker's cottage, a mere detail in the novel, never becomes a systematic motif, like his large white teeth and disturbing smile. But its obvious adequacy and exemplary tastefulness make clear that Dickens, who consistently takes aspiration of one kind or another as his theme, has no Loudon-like illusions about facile consumer contentment. The portrait of James Carker has wider implications than Dickens draws. Carker is represented in the novel less as a type than as an inexplicable individual, with a motiveless, arbitrary, almost Iago-like hatred for his employer. If he is read however as the typical product of the capitalist system, he punctures the illusion on which Repton and Loudon base their ideological claims. The figure of Carker also problematizes the suggestion on which *North and South* comes to rest: that providing employees with a 'fair' wage, adequate to provide the necessities of life, will render them tractable and contented. Dickens understands that for an alienated employee confronted daily with the stupendous wealth of the employer class, enough will never be enough. The trouble with a small, perfect property is just that it is small, when other men's are big. Size matters: perfect tastefulness is no compensation for lack of social and financial power. In a competitive economy it is always possible to wish for more.

Dickens's other two 'Loudonesque' characters, Wemmick and Boffin, do not however wish for more: on the contrary, they are largely constructed in terms of their contentment with rather ridiculous 'cockney' properties of just the kind mocked by Burney and Kemp. In his development of these two characters Dickens is evidently drawing on the discourse that has been the subject of this chapter, though not to equal effect. Wemmick and his property in Walworth are complexly developed and fully integrated into *Great Expectations*, whereas the comedy surrounding Boffin and his 'tour' of the mounds is a perfunctory rerun of a conventional topos. But though the allusion does not fully pay off in the later novel, the reiteration itself testifies to the interest Dickens took in this discourse and its contradictions.

The Walworth episodes in *Great Expectations* are so rich and amusing partly because they ask to be read in several interpretative contexts. Wemmick's estate is comparable to the dwellings of all of those characters in this novel (and other novels by Dickens) who lead stunted lives in limited and peculiar places. If we link Wemmick complacently barricaded in Walworth with Miss Havisham sulking in Satis House, with Mrs Pocket dreaming of past glories while she neglects her present duties, or with Pip himself repining at the forge, the pattern yields a familiar Dickensian moral: the virtue of playing cheerfully the hand that fate has dealt you, putting up with the human condition, with bad luck, old age, mortality itself. In their more immediate context, the Walworth scenes also develop the theme of the undesirable father. Pip's second visit to the moated Walworth estate (chapter 37) is followed by the return of the convict, who penetrates his own barricaded rooms at the Temple (chapter 39), and his final visit to Wemmick's home (chapter 45) immediately precedes his introduction to old Bill Barley at Mill Pond Bank (chapter 46). Such juxtapositions invite comparison between the patience of Wemmick and Clara Barley, solicitously caring for difficult fathers, and the snobbery of Pip, who rejects both Joe and Magwitch. In the context of these moral patterns, Wemmick's devotion to his parent and emotional investment in his home signal his willingness to accept with optimism and charity the possibilities of a miniaturized and stultified life.

The meaning of Walworth also depends on a still more localized contrast. Pip's introductory visit to Wemmick's home dramatizes its difference from the mansion of his employer Jaggers (described by Wemmick just pages before he introduces Pip to Walworth, and visited by Pip immediately afterwards, and also establishes a contrast between the attitudes of Wemmick and Jaggers to the domesticity that ought to offer refuge from their professional life. Both men are bachelors working together in a profession they know contaminates them, and both their properties illustrate their fraught relationship with the wider society. Wemmick tries to make home into a separate sphere by splitting himself in two and by defending his castle psychologically, if not physically, with a moat, a rampart, and a canon, but in fact his cottage can be reached by anyone who wants to step across the ditch. Jaggers's house, on the other hand, though he tantalizingly refuses to lock his doors, is invulnerable to criminal penetration; yet he himself has brought a criminal into it (in the person of his housekeeper Molly, Estella's mother),[35] and he brings his legal work home as well (Pip notices a desk in the corner of the drawing room). Jaggers's house is large, but he shuts himself up in only three rooms: Wemmick's property is tiny, but he thinks of it as extensive and joyfully exploits every bit of it. The studied parallel between these two residences seems to endorse Loudon's assertion that a small lot offers all the real values of a large one. But it does so in a complicated and ironic way.

Wemmick's cottage is an example of just the kind of 'cockneyism' that Burney makes fun of in *Camilla* and that Kemp is still sneering at in 1860. If Dubster has a wooden swan, Wemmick has a cottage tricked out in gothic style, punctuated with gothic windows, most of which are 'sham,' and with a 'top ... cut out and painted like a battery mounted with guns' (208). Wemmick proudly points out, however, that his cannon really fires and that he has a 'real flagstaff' and a 'real flag' (208). His pride is comical, yet his claim to authenticity has a certain moral resonance. Despite his comparative wealth and taste, Jaggers's house, too, contains shams. Jaggers refuses to lock his doors against thieves, but he must feel more insecure than he pretends, since though the watch chain he carries on his person is 'real enough' (207), the plate he uses to entertain his guests is not silver but 'Britannia metal, every spoon' (207). Sham can testify, apparently, not only to cockney vulgarity but also to more complicated anxieties and deficiencies. Pip responds uncomfortably, as well, to the 'carved garlands on the panelled walls' (213) in Jaggers's dining room. This particular sham has much greater aesthetic prestige than Wemmick's painted ramparts – Loudon points out that though paper flowers are vulgar, those 'in a material so unlike the texture of flowers as wood or stone' demonstrate 'a superior degree of mind' in the artist who creates them[36] – but Pip finds the pattern of 'loops' disturbingly easy to associate with the noose. Jaggers's house has been built on the proceeds of crime, in that his income derives from his involvement in a corrupt legal system, and its decor signals the connection. In moral terms, everything important about Wemmick's home – the pride, the peace of mind, the hospitality, the family affection – are real, whereas Jaggers's mansion, a reliable emblem of his morally dubious relationship with the outside world, offers sham hospitality and contains fake silver, lifeless flowers, and a servant who is probably a murderess.

If Wemmick's house is a 'real' home, however, the comedy lies in the way it aspires to more. The Walworth property presents itself as at once a medieval 'Castle' ('an Englishman's home is ... '); a military fortress; a farm; and a 'pleasure ground' in the Picturesque style, with walks, views, and waterworks, and a garden. It contains all the elements that would define it, were it not for its tiny scale, as a 'first-rate estate,' but that, because of that scale, merely exemplify the tacky variety mocked by Kemp. Whatever unity the property possesses is conferred not by any aesthetic principle but simply by the physical barriers Wemmick erects around his lot in his determination to cut himself off from the city and the professional activities that dehumanize him. Wemmick has to resort to fortifications because he is not wealthy enough to flee to the fashionable suburbs as others were doing at this time,[37] but he represents himself as a suburban gentleman, modestly inviting Pip down to see his 'little property,' his 'bit of a garden,' his 'two or three curiosities' (a litotes that isn't [203]), offering him a tour of its 'views' and 'scenes,' asking him 'to take a walk with him round the property and see how the island look[s] in winter-time' (299). The details recall Burney and Kemp: Wemmick's moat is a ditch, his drawbridge a plank, his lake small enough to serve as a wine cooler, his island the size of a salad, his fountain just big enough to wet the back of your hand, and his 'museum' (211) a tabletop. Defying Loudon's strictures against winding paths on a small city lot, Wemmick has constructed a miniature 'pleasure-ground' in the Picturesque style, featuring the requisite winding walk with so many 'ingenious twists' that though his bower is only 'about a dozen yards off,' it takes 'quite a long time to get at' (209). But this is kindlier comedy than Burney's: if we are invited to laugh at Wemmick, we are also, apparently, invited to laugh at the discourse that he has appropriated for his own purposes and to serve his own pleasures. If small is not enough, Wemmick does not want to know it: his refusal to understand how his property would look to more sophisticated taste allows him to live his truncated life with optimism and charity.

The work this small property demands from Wemmick is as varied and diverse, and as constant, as even Loudon could wish. Wemmick is himself, as he proudly points out, 'my own engineer, and my own carpenter, and my own plumber, and my own gardener, and my own Jack of all trades' (209). If he is able to read his own unceasing labour as joyful self-expression, it is no doubt partly because of the do-it-yourself discourse of texts like the *Villa Companion*.[38] But this labour does not do the work on subjectivity or on gender that Loudon counts on. Split in half though he is in the interest of domestic wholeness, Wemmick is called upon at home to play a double role. The handyman skills he boasts of are displaced in the text by the tasks we actually see him doing: caring for his deaf and slightly senile father, whom he bibs, feeds, flatters, and amuses with exemplary tenderness and good humour. These are tasks that would usually be performed by the Victorian woman. When domestic life gets compressed into such a small scale, the labour required may not confirm gender distinctions but instead subvert them. It also subverts the distinction between employer and servant that Loudon both takes for granted and perpetuates. Though the expert ease with which Wemmick performs the chore of feeding his father suggests that he does it often, the reason he does it on this particular occasion is that he wants to talk privately to Pip and so has to dismiss the sole servant. We are reminded of how hard it would be not only to obtain any privacy in such a small space but also to maintain the boundary between servant and employer when one has to share their labour. Despite Wemmick's good cheer, middle-class identity can be maintained only with difficulty in a cottage with a single all-purpose room. Dickens's description both derives its physical details from writers like Kemp and challenges the egalitarian fantasy promoted by Loudon.

Oddly enough, with all this emphasis on work, the one activity conspicuously omitted from the Walworth episodes is the one Loudon especially values: the actual work of gardening. Though Wemmick's cottage is 'in the midst of plots of garden' (208), and though he grows vegetables – Pip is served greens grown on the property – we do not see him cultivating plants at home. There is in fact, except for food products that get eaten (the greens, the pig), no growth or development on this estate at all, but only degeneration and decay. The house, the supposedly permanent part of the estate as Loudon describes it, is full of dry rot – Wemmick has not had access to the seasoned timber Loudon insists on – and what he has created is not so much a garden as a set of mechanical devices that can only run down: the windmill, the jet of water, and the flaps with 'John' and 'Miss Skiffens' written on them, which are supposed to be activated on the arrival of a guest but fall spas-

modically into action on their own initiative. These labour-saving
devices stand in for the butler or front hall maid that the establishment
cannot afford: they are just as unsatisfactory as servants in Dickens's
(and Loudon's) households usually are and not nearly as clever as the
patented inventions advertised by Loudon.

It is significant that there is no reference to flowers of any kind on
Wemmick's estate, though cultivation of flowers is supposed to be the
small homeowner's delight. There cannot be a blooming garden in Walworth, for Pip has already had a tour of what Wemmick calls his 'garden,' the prison itself, and has met some of his 'plants,' the condemned
prisoners. No cultivation or development is possible for these plants: the
prisoners are bad seeds in bad ground, and their only change will be
their death. The continuity Loudon celebrates as the special joy of gardening subsists only in the 'portable property' Wemmick is able to sal-
vage as his prisoners succeed one another on the gallows. This sardonic
pastoral metaphor precludes a flower garden at Walworth. A piece of
what ought to be on the Walworth property if it is to function imagisti-
cally as the Eden in which Wemmick is trying to believe has been separated off and displaced into the city from which he is trying to find
refuge.

Pieces of the city have likewise migrated into the home. The Victorian
home may try to keep the world out, but, insofar as it aims at microcos-
mic completeness, in the end it has to contain what it aims to exclude,
including evidence of the economy on which it is based. Like Jaggers's,
Wemmick's establishment is funded by crime and is adorned by remind-
ers of the corrupt profession in which the money that purchased it has
been earned. Like Jaggers's desk, Wemmick's 'museum' – his 'collection
of curiosities,' which includes 'the pen with which a celebrated forgery
had been committed, a distinguished razor or two, some locks of hair,
and several manuscript confessions' (210–11) – brings his professional
life back into the home.

A proper private museum, of the kind that Loudon mentions as a
desirable feature on a large property, ideally requires, as he points out,
if not a separate building at least a separate wing, since the 'stuffed
birds, or other zoological preparations' will emit unpleasant odours.
Since Wemmick's is not a proper museum – since the aspect of national
life he memorializes is not Britain's natural plenitude and variety but
England's corrupt legal system – there is 'no danger from smells' from
this source.[39] The bad smell, though, is imported back into the text not
only by the dry rot that Pip 'tastes' with the supper but by the living ani-

mals Wemmick keeps in his little farm: by the poultry, by the rabbits, and particularly by the pig.

Wemmick's pig is the last of a series of pigs that get eaten in *Great Expectations*, after the pork pie that Pip steals for the convict in the second chapter and the Christmas pig that becomes in the fourth chapter the occasion for Pumblechook's lecture about how grateful Pip should be that he was not born to be eaten himself. Pumblechook's suggestion, resonating for the child with the awful threat of the young man supposed to be yearning after his heart and liver, establishes the motif of consuming and being consumed that is played out in so many different ways in the novel. You could have been born to be eaten. People are like pigs in this respect – and pigs are like people.[40] Like people, too, pigs in *Great Expectations* are consistently associated with cramped and sordid living conditions. The two themes are combined when Joe, inspecting Pip's room in Barnard's Inn, frankly observes that 'I wouldn't keep a pig in it myself – not in the case that I wished him to fatten wholesome and to eat with a meller flavour on him' (223). Less genially, pigs are linked in Victorian social discourse specifically with the Irish, who are consistently described as living with, or like, swine. Carlyle's Sanspotato 'lodges to his mind in any pighutch or doghutch';[41] Engels observes of the Irish immigrant:

> He builds a pig-sty against the house wall as he did at home, and if he is prevented from doing this, he lets the pig sleep in the room with himself. This new and unnatural method of cattle-raising in cities is wholly of Irish origin. The Irishman loves his pig as the Arab his horse, with the difference that he sells it when it is fat enough to kill. Otherwise, he eats and sleeps with it, his children play with it, ride upon it, roll in the dirt with it, as anyone may see a thousand times repeated in all the great towns of England.[42]

A passage like this makes Loudon's discussion of all the functions a house needs to serve sound like a cruel parody of real poverty. The association between the Irish and pigs is often figurative as well as literal: Mayhew describes the Irish brought to England in coal vessels 'huddled together like pigs, and communicating disease and vermin on their passage.'[43] It is the lives of people like this that Loudon has to exclude in order to claim that a small property contains all the real benefits of the largest, and the motif of the pig comically yet poignantly brings them back to hover like unexorcised ghosts behind the text. The smell of the pig is another evocative link. Wemmick's pig stinks, but we are reminded that this would not be the only bad smell hovering around such a cramped cottage by Loudon's map identifying a 'Pigsty, near which there is a privy for the farm servants' (640). Comically though he is treated, Wemmick's pig evokes not only the most hopeless human squalor but also the everyday degradation of the Victorian underclass.

This pig eventually gets turned into sausages and, at the moment of his metamorphosis, he is commended in familiar, almost personal, terms by his owner ('have ... a little bit of *him*. That sausage you toasted was his, and he was in all respects a first-rater. Do try him if it is only for old acquaintance sake' [377]). In Wemmick's household, the motif of food and eating at first looks wholly positive, with the emphasis on general jollity, warm hospitality, and grease: buttered toast, shiny faces, grilled sausage. But the sausage is made of the pig – the pig referred to just at the moment when he is put on the plate as if he had been part of the family – and this comically disquieting fact brings Pumblechook's remarks back into play. It also brings the city back into the home. Wemmick, it seems, not only has to be his own carpenter, plumber, and gardener, he has to be his own slaughterer and butcher; his estate serves not only as castle, pleasure ground, farm, and garden, but also as a miniature Smithfield, an area already evoked, during Pip's almost hallucinatory introduction to the London scene, as a metaphor for contamination and corruption. Having it all – condensing the whole society into one's own private paradise – means bringing into it the very horrors one set out to exclude.

The Walworth episode exposes the Loudon project, demonstrating that even with middle-class values, there are some classes who cannot have everything. Dickens ironizes not only particular themes of Loudon's, like hobby work, but also the very notion of the private self-sufficient estate, insisting that the individual cannot escape the contamination of the society of which he is a part. Yet Dickens is also complicit with the discourse of taste, which he is deploying even as he parodies it. If the reader did not share with the author an aesthetic standard in the light of which Wemmick's looks comical, she would miss the tone of these chapters. Presenting the Walworth episodes in the voice of an at least somewhat ironic narrator is essential to their effect. It is clear that Pip does not see the Walworth property through Wemmick's eyes. He finds it comical and rather uncomfortable, describing 'the crazy little box of a cottage' (210) as 'the smallest house I ever saw' (208) and observing that the ceiling was so thin that 'it seemed as if I had to balance that pole on my forehead all night' (211). These condescending responses are confided, of course, to only the reader: his host remains convinced that Pip shares his enthusiasm for the beauties of his estate. Wemmick's unawareness that his taste differs from Pip's is an essential part of his meaning.[44]

Ruskin idealistically asserts that the man who shares my taste is my equal, belongs to the same class as I do.[45] From his own perspective, Wemmick does share Pip's aesthetic values. Accepting the claims of writers like Repton and Loudon, he believes that a small property is sufficient if one has taste, and he thinks that he does have it and that therefore he has all he could want. It is at a point like this that Ruskin's assurance collides with the realities of a class-bound culture. Wemmick has bought into the home-and-garden discourse by which he would be condemned by a writer like Kemp and has used it to create a positive identity for himself. But this identity needs to be confirmed by others. Taste is not taste unless it is recognized: an estate does not fulfill its function unless the tour offered to the visitor evokes his envy and respect. The flaw in Ruskin's reasoning is dramatized in Dickens's treatment of Wemmick. Taste gives an entrée into a social class only if it is recognized by the members of that class. Wemmick thinks he can 'talk the talk,' but the mere size of his property ensures that he will speak it with a cockney accent. The middle class is not in fact unified, as Loudon's scheme tends to imply, by a shared taste for gardening and home improvement, but is split into finely distinguished layers on the basis of the scale and style in which that taste is displayed. A small property cannot offer its owner everything he might find on a large one because the most important 'thing' comparative wealth provides is precisely the distinction from those of lower economic status.

The narrative voice aligns the reader with Pip in the recognition of the delusory nature of Wemmick's project. Though we are encouraged to condemn Pip's more serious snobberies, we are invited to share his amusement at Wemmick's pretensions. Though he approves of Wemmick's decency and good heart, Pip distinguishes himself from Wemmick on the grounds of taste, and, merely by picking up the irony that serves to demonstrate Pip's own superior standards, we distinguish ourselves as well. We smile at the taste that differentiates Wemmick from us even while responding to the 'universal' moral qualities that connect him with us.[46] Dickens shows how the discourse of taste works to sustain the delusion of classlessness even as he himself uses it to maintain class distinctions.

And to reassure his reader that they will continue to be maintained.

Wemmick is a comic figure because he does not threaten the social hierarchy. Wemmick is no Dubster, and this is perhaps the most important fact about him. Because Wemmick believes in Walworth and values the self he has constructed by means of it, he has no desire to move *up*. Though he is a man in constant motion, that motion is all on the horizontal plane. Shuttling from office to home and back again splits Wemmick into two: maintaining the illusion of coherent personal identity uses up all his energy. The sense of wholeness and completeness that he constructs for himself by means of Walworth is evidently an illusion, but one that neutralizes *social* aspiration, as the horizontal oscillation displaces vertical movement. The moral and psychological split in Wemmick is spelled out by his transits through the streets of London, while the social split (cockney/gentry) is not dramatized in terms of mobility at all.

Indeed, on the vertical axis, so to speak, Wemmick stays put while concrete objects descend to him. The 'portable property' Wemmick is so eager to secure from the prisoners about to be executed – a grotesque parody of the fortune Pip inherits from the convict – 'trickles down' into his hands through criminal intermediaries, but when it reaches Wemmick it stops. There is no sense in this novel, as there is in Loudon, of the healthy circulation of goods in a well-functioning economy. The verbal tag associated with Wemmick, who is always advising Pip to secure 'portable property,' diverts attention from the fact that the real property by which he defines himself is not portable at all. Wemmick in Walworth is the reverse of mobile: his freehold is stationary, dug in defensively like the castles it imitates, and he stays on it – behind his ditch, going nowhere, acquiring things, not unlike Loudon's obsessively labouring consumers. It is because Wemmick sees his estate as complete (even though we see that it is not) that the aspirations of which it serves as an emblem remain blocked off, without outlet in social action. Wemmick is a comic and reassuring figure because he is a wish-fulfillment fantasy: a man who believes in his own taste without claiming the social perquisites that might go with it. The painted ramparts and the encircling ditch construct a comically literal image of encapsulation, of a class socially and politically contained. By buying into the discourse of taste, Wemmick has succeeded in combining the life of a clerk with the self-image of a landed proprietor without ever needing to push up through the class in the middle: without aspiring to marry up into it, as Dubster did.

And as Pip does. Dickens needs to suppress the Dubster in his protagonist, and one of the ways he does it is through Wemmick. Although

Pip's desire for Estella is morally dubious, it is not ridiculous or grotesque. Pip wants a fortune because he sees it as the way to Estella, but
he is never shown as hankering after material possessions in and for
themselves. Pip aspires to social status, but that status is figured by relationships not by objects: or rather, Estella herself is the object by which
it is figured. The starry imagery connected with Estella ironizes Pip's
adoration yet nevertheless elevates his desire: it is the starriness itself he
yearns after, not the things that go with it. Paradoxically, by showing how
it taints Pip's *spirit*, Dickens spiritualizes Pip's ambition. And though his
spirit is tainted, his taste is never corrupted. Though Estella mocks his
dirty hands and Herbert Pocket has to correct his table manners, we
never in fact get the impression that Pip is crude, uncouth, or undis-
criminating. For the reader, Pip is constructed by his – that is, Dickens's
– amused and sophisticated prose, and since as a writer he is already a
finished product when he takes up his pen on the first page of the
novel, we respond to him from the beginning in terms of that acquired
sophistication. A sensitive, curious child who has become a verbally
poised, appropriately rueful adult, he has an aesthetic right to aspire to
Estella because he is our representative in the novel: that is, an individual of true taste and discrimination. Wemmick represents what has to be
repressed in Pip so that we can take Dickens's protagonist seriously.[47]

In the Walworth episode, then, Dickens exploits the very discourse he
mocks. On the level of explicit social satire, he suggests that small is not
enough, that not everybody can have the beauty and security of the middle-class estate just by getting a set of mental attitudes; on the level of
subliminal class reassurance, he shows the discourse working to contain
social anger, reconciling little people to their little lot; and on the level
of rhetoric he uses it himself to maintain the distinction between the ris-
ibility of the naive cockney he himself might have remained and the
pathos of his hero's aspiring mind, constructed by his author's nuanced
and expressive language.

In comparison with this rich and funny tour de force, the home-and-
garden discourse in *Our Mutual Friend* is somewhat thin and arbitrary. Its
many similarities to the Wemmick episodes make clear that it is a rerun
of the material in *Great Expectations*. Once again we have a small, ridiculous estate touted by its proud owner; once again the dirty money that
built it is alluded to in the estate itself, this house being literally built on
top of the 'dust' that funded it; once again the home-and-garden discourse is associated with a radical division in life of its proprietor: as
Wemmick splits himself in two, so Mr and Mrs Boffin divide the room in

which they live, with her vulgarly stylish furniture on a carpet in the middle, his old-fashioned larder surrounding it. And once again the visitor is offered a tour of the estate, a tour structured around just the sites popularized by the 'improvers.' Describing his property to Silas Wegg, Boffin touches on a number of the conventional features:

> 'This is a charming spot, is the Bower, but you must get to apprechiate it by degrees. It's a spot to find out the merits of, little by little, and a new'un every day. There's a serpentining walk up each of the mounds, that gives you the yard and neighbourhood's changing every moment. When you get to the top, there's a view of the neighbouring premises, not to be surpassed. The premises of Mrs. Boffin's late father (Canine Provision Trade), you look down into, as if they was your own. And the top of the High Mound is crowned with a lattice-work Arbour.' (101)

This brisk survey of desiderata – variety, 'views,' 'serpentining' walks, a constantly changing visual perspective, beauties that unfold only over time, the aesthetic appropriation of adjoining land, decorative outbuildings, pastoral motifs – demonstrates not only that Dickens was completely familiar with the Loudonesque discourse but that he still found it a good joke. Morris argues that both *Great Expectations* and *Our Mutual Friend* deal with 'the containment of social discontent in the dreams of consumer plenitude,'[48] but perhaps Dickens's more significant insight is that mere objects need to be mediated by an advertising-type discourse if they are to testify to the 'good taste' that provides self-satisfaction and middle-class identity. The house tour encourages the proprietor to see his own possessions through the eyes of an admiring visitor, and the discourse of taste he feels himself master of transforms the objects he has managed to assemble into status symbols in his own eyes. But Dickens demonstrates how tricky it is for the déclassé to possess themselves of the discourse and use it to their own advantage.

*Our Mutual Friend* is however a less coherent novel than *Great Expectations* and Boffin a less rich character construction than Wemmick. Boffin's very familiarity with the Loudonesque discourse is, to begin with, both implausible and uncharacteristic. The illiterate servant of a mean master isolated in an old-fashioned house known to the neighbours as Harmony Jail, he is uneducated, cannot read (even ballad sheets), and seems to have very little ordinary social contact with the world around him. It is not Boffin himself but his wife, the 'highflyer at Fashion' (100), who has the aesthetic pretensions and who has rechristened Harmony Jail 'Boffin's Bower,' but the expression of her taste is evidently confined to the interior of the house. Boffin's enthusiasm for the 'landscape' outside suggests that it is he who has designed the grounds, yet he is otherwise presented as emphatically indifferent to style and fashion. The monologue to Wegg is amusing and testifies to his optimism and contentment, but it does not connect with anything else he says or does. It functions merely as a local joke, an indication that Dickens found the Loudonesque discourse irresistibly parodyable whether or not the parody served any particular purpose.

The interior of the house is a promising example of Dickensian grotesque, but again the conceit fails to pay off as it might. The Boffins have access to the whole house they have inherited from their former employer, but they confine themselves to a single room on the ground floor, preserving the rest as a memorial to the lost children of the family. The room they live in is oddly divided up between husband and wife:

It was the queerest of rooms, fitted and furnished more like a luxurious amateur tap-room than anything else within the ken of Silas Wegg. There were two wooden settles by the fire, one on either side of it, with a corresponding table before each. On one of these tables, the eight volumes were ranged flat, in a row, like a galvanic battery; on the other, certain squat case-bottles of inviting appearance seemed to stand on tiptoe to exchange glances with Mr Wegg over a front row of tumblers and a basin of white sugar. On the hob, a kettle steamed; on the heart, a cat reposed. Facing the fire between the settles, a sofa, a foot-stool, and a little table, formed a centerpiece devoted to Mrs Boffin. They were garish in taste and colour, but were expensive articles of drawing-room furniture that had a very odd look beside the settles and the flaring gaslight pendent from the ceiling. There was a flowery carpet on the floor; but, instead of reaching to the fireside, its glowing vegetation stopped short at Mrs Boffin's footstool, and gave place to a region of sand and sawdust. Mr Wegg also noticed, with admiring eyes, that, while the flowery land displayed such hollow ornamentation as stuffed birds and waxen fruits under glass shades, there were, in the territory where vegetation ceased, compensatory shelves on which the best part of a large pie and likewise of a cold joint were plainly discernible among other solids. (99–100)

Though the image is far-fetched, the theme of division and self-division, so pregnant an idea for Dickens, remains suggestive. The Boffins' interior is a comic negative example of the tyranny of taste. Since the room would be unified in style only if one of the spouses dominated the other, its aesthetic incoherence oddly enough figures their marital equality. 'These arrangements is made by mutual consent' between them (100): there really is harmony in Harmony Jail, indeed a utopian identity of purpose in this relationship. Unlike the Wilfers's marriage, dominated by the shrewish wife, the Boffins' is affectionate and egalitarian:

> 'she keeps up her part of the room, in her way; I keep up my part of the room in mine. In consequence of which we have at once, Sociability (I should go melancholy mad without Mrs Boffin), Fashion, and Comfort.' (100)

The divided room is a sign of their mutual respect, which is more fundamental than their preference in interiors. Though Henrietta Boffin aspires to taste, she is content to have it terminate at the edge of her carpet. To be sure, her very tolerance on this issue convicts her of vulgarity. Because unity is the hallmark of aesthetic effectiveness, it is not just the ugly furniture she has chosen but her willingness to confine that furniture to only part of the room that marks her tastelessness. The portrait of Mrs Boffin is affectionate but condescending. Like Loudon, Dickens associates the woman with a passion for mere objects and for 'garish' variety and 'hollow ornamentation' and represents her as oblivious to the principle of unity that is the essential condition of true art. But her aesthetic naiveté contributes to marital harmony. By giving an improbably sunny reading of what would usually be at least a somewhat conflicted situation, Dickens in a backhanded way reminds us that taste is usually dictatorial, authoritarian. Only in fiction would a spouse with a stake in style agree to circumscribe it so grotesquely; only in fiction would a couple be so united as to divide a room like this. The very improbability of the scenario testifies to what Loudon also implies: aesthetic unity involves control of other people. It is only with the fairy-tale erasure of egotism, competitiveness, and individual will that differences of taste will not cause tension and conflict.

The Boffins' divided room expresses alternative ways of responding to their class position. Mrs Boffin aspires to prestige via the display of 'tasteful' consumer items, which are actually debased copies of high style (Dickens uses the same sartorial analogy as Lord Kames: Mrs Boffin's furniture is as vulgar as her dress, 'a low evening-dress of sable satin, and a large black velvet hat and feathers' [99]). Her husband on the other hand stays 'in his place' in a larder loaded with food and drink, a sentimentalized exemplum of homely working-class hospitality and cheer. It is clear which response Dickens prefers. The contrast between the Boffins' personal styles illustrates the gap between what the middle class would like the working class to be and what they would like to be themselves.

Yet the conceit turns out to be inconsequential, for in fact the Boffins are both equally good at heart. Mrs Boffin's aspiration to fashion says nothing about her real values, which are identical with his. Boffin complacently acknowledges that the boundary between their territories will shift when their circumstances do:

'If I get by degrees to be a highflyer at Fashion, then Mrs Boffin will by degrees come for-arder. If Mrs Boffin should ever be less of a dab at Fashion than she is at the present time, then Mrs Boffin's carpet would go backarder. If we should both continny, as we are, why then *here* we are, and give us a kiss, old lady.' (100)

When they come into their fortune, he willingly retreats to a single room in their fashionable house. That it is the most comfortable one, the one people seek when they want to be at ease, feminizes Boffin by assigning him the role that usually goes to the woman, of providing domestic warmth and ease in the heart of the household, but without really masculinizing his wife, who remains, now that she has achieved the 'fashion' she sought, the same down-to-earth, good-hearted woman she always was. Indeed, the treatment of Mrs Boffin is as inconsistent as everything else in the Boffin subplot. The narrator makes clear that her manners are unpolished and her dress bizarre, yet her vulgarity, which embarrasses Bella, does not in the least stand in the way of her acceptance by high society. The point that money buys prestige is transparent enough, but the treatment of it is unsubtle and implausible. Bella's embarrassment at Mrs Boffin's vulgarity is dismissed as yet another aspect of the culpable worldliness she has to overcome, even though the narrator agrees with her. With little of the subtlety or complexity of the episodes involving Wemmick, Dickens's treatment of the Boffins, comically promising in its conception, is consistently anticlimactic in its development.

The reader is no doubt surprised, on entering Boffin's single room, the room that has just been characterized as particularly comfortable and inviting, to find it the scene not of the family harmony the narrator seemed to promise but rather of the beginning of Boffin's campaign against 'John Rokesmith,' the campaign designed to convince Bella that Boffin has been corrupted by wealth. In retrospect, this incongruity (between room and project) is the first clue that Boffin is only putting on an act. But his elaborate pretence of being spoiled by riches only underlines the unrealistic degree to which he and his wife are completely uncorrupted by them. Improbably, neither of the Boffins 'wish for more,' even after having had it: 'like single-hearted children' (429), they surrender their new status willingly, even joyfully, when the real heir turns up, resign the mansion that is legally theirs to John Harmon and Bella, and retreat cheerfully back to the Bower, now bereft of its mounds. Their generosity is one of the most sentimental elements in what has often been called a fairy-tale ending. The lengths to which Dickens goes to deny the personal ambition of these loyal servants no doubt reflects contemporary anxiety about 'the servant problem,' but his solution is so patently facile as to be scarcely reassuring.

The desire of the underclass for self-improvement and self-transformation is a potent theme in the novel, but in the Boffin subplot it is developed so innocently that it lacks bite. She wants style, he wants literacy, but neither's desire affects their essential contentment and sweetness of nature. The wish-fulfillment fantasy is a comforting counterpoint to the disquieting portrait of petit bourgeois rage in Bradley Headstone, who will never get what he wants because he lacks, precisely, *style*. Mrs Boffin's travesty of upper-class taste is supposed to be funny, but Headstone's defeat at the hands of the dandyish Eugene Wrayburn is anything but. Dickens is addressing the same issues as Repton and Loudon, and his fiction registers the same anxiety about social ambition in a competitive society. While he can confront this topic brilliantly, as he does with Headstone, nevertheless nearly fifty years after Repton, he still feels the need to create figures like the Boffins as a way of reassuring readers that it is possible for consumers who have less not to wish for more – at least if they can be persuaded to internalize a discourse devised to be used against them. That the reader retains the right to smile at their vulgarity even while appreciating their goodness of heart shows that the discourse has not lost its exclusionary value. Dickens may condemn orthodox tastefulness, but he never fails to make clear that he recognizes vulgarity, which functions precisely to distinguish the sophisticated author from the endearing and comical figures he creates.

It is important for middle-class social critics, contemplating a burgeoning capitalist economy, to believe that material prosperity offers universal contentment without actual social equality: that in industrial England everyone who is willing to work can make enough to secure happiness even while class distinctions remain in place. Repton and Loudon suggest that because good taste is fully compensatory – that because people with more taste than money or land can enjoy all the spiritual and even physical benefits of those with greater material resources – there is no reason for class lines not to be preserved. Dickens exposes the fallacies in this argument. His novels suggest that unless you are a domestic angel constructed to soar above mere material constraints, social and material inequality is likely to mean a more or less warped personality: that even the rationalizations involved in believing in a miniature world largely of your own making produce their own psychological deformations. The novels also demonstrate how these deformations themselves serve to stabilize the power structure that produces them. Socially, characters like Wemmick and Boffin are dependent on the judgments of those who have the power to evaluate them, among whom must be included the novelist who constructs them. Yet psychologically they are independent: they experience their aestheticized properties as self-contained and themselves as sturdily self-sufficient. Dickens invites us to admire their optimism, but he also dramatizes its conservative implications. The society that has produced these individuals is radically corrupt, but, oiled by the dream of proprietorship, even the smallest cogs in the social machine continue to function smoothly. Individual self-respect may stand in the way of social reform, and Dickens shows how aesthetic aspiration, by bolstering self-respect, can keep the machine going.

Charlotte Brontë's novels dramatize how the defensive self-constructions parodied by Dickens feel from the inside. Wemmick and Boffin may not understand how they look to their betters, but Brontë's middle-class protagonists do understand. The Brontë heroine, precisely because she does not have many other resources, has a passionate stake in her own good taste and a passionate desire to believe in its compensatory function. But because she cannot help seeing herself through the eyes of the cultivated observers who are in a social position to condescend to her, she lacks the self-sufficiency that she, too, claims, and with a fierce defensiveness unnecessary for Dickens's comic characters. It is because of this shift of perspective – because we are, so to speak, inside the outsider – that when Brontë uses some of the novelistic topoi I have been discussing she does it with a new intensity. Now we see the connoisseur from the point of view of the woman who longs to be evaluated by him. The small space in which the heroine is constrained to live her life can only be felt as large enough when it is penetrated by his knowing eye and opened up by his material support. Yet the intense way Brontë dramatizes the depravations and humiliations of this female space, her desire for transcendence and release, produces a startlingly original proto-feminist voice. Originality is an important theme in these novels: a Brontë heroine needs to believe that she is authentic and underivative. But because the distinction she craves is by its nature differential, she has to construct the other characters in her world, especially male tutors and female rivals, in ways that will endorse her semiotically unstable identity. The result is a polarized narrative structure in which good taste can only be grounded in a fierce and often venomous repudiation of vulgarity. Locating this polarizing impulse, as well as the prose style in which it is expressed, partly in the influence of Brontë's real-life tutor Heger, I examine how her investment in good taste turns conventional novelistic topoi into fraught parables of identity.

# 5 Charlotte Brontë: Sweetness and Colour

Charlotte Brontë relies on polarity to organize her fictions, positioning her characters against one another in terms of the values they embody: flesh and spirit, frankness and secrecy, acquiescence and rebellion, domination and submission, plainness and beauty, English rectitude and foreign vice. While such polarization is a feature of Brontë's juvenile work,[1] its effect on her prose style was no doubt consolidated by the pedagogy of Constantin Heger, her adored teacher in Brussels, who, by insisting that his students base their French compositions on canonical models, developed in Brontë not only a taste for antithetical parallelism in sentence structure but also a habit of opposing the writers he obliged her to emulate. While not all of the *devoirs* Brontë prepared for Heger are notably binary in structure, much of the rhetoric in these exercises is organized, at the level of the sentence, the paragraph, or the argument as a whole, in terms of antitheses, both imagistic and conceptual.[2]

Heger may also be partly responsible for another idiosyncratic feature of Brontë's style: her extended, elaborate figures of speech – often personifications – which sometimes generate miniature narratives of their own. Lonoff points out that Heger encouraged Charlotte to focus her writing more tightly and in particular to curb her taste for decorative imagery. Under his influence Brontë's metaphors become more complex and extended but at the same time more rigorously thematized. This development continues in Brontë's mature work, where personified abstractions, usually representing a power adversarial to the protagonist, are used to underscore the binaries of the novel as a whole. William Crimsworth, for example, is attacked by Hypochondria with a capital H; Lucy Snowe, challenged to prove that her essays are her own, confronts her tormenters with a portrait of Human Justice as 'a red, random beldame with arms akimbo,' solacing herself with a 'short black pipe, and a bottle of Mrs Sweeny's soothing syrup' (*Villette*, 582, 504).[3] Human Justice sounds rather like a sister of *Jane Eyre's* Grace Poole with her pot of porter. There is a continuum between the frankly figurative characters in Brontë's novels and the literal ones – between, for example, real fat ladies like Bertha Mason and the painted Cleopatra so mercilessly allegorized by Lucy Snowe. Indeed Brontë's actual characters often come close to personification allegory, as her narrators read their own experience quasi-allegorically, in terms of self-justifying moral patterns, and slot the other figures in their personal drama into categories that confirm their own understanding of themselves.[4]

Though neither Vulgarity nor Good Taste is personified in any of Brontë's novels, they are both represented by characters so narrowly constructed as to function almost as personifications. Tastefulness is incarnated in *Jane Eyre*, for example, not only in major figures like the Rivers sisters, who love German literature and dress with quiet elegance ('all delicacy and cultivation,' in their 'deep mourning,' which, as mourning tends so happily to do in Victorian novels, 'singularly set off their very fair necks and faces' [424]), but also in the 'ladylike' Mrs Colonel Dent, 'whose black satin dress ... scarf of rich foreign lace, and ... pearl ornaments, pleased me better,' Jane says, 'than the rainbow radiance' (214–15) of Rochester's titled guests and who exists merely to make that point. Such figures are one-dimensional, relentlessly moralized, and insistently readable, and Brontë never abandoned them. In the opening of 'Emma,' for example, a fragment of a novel left incomplete at her death, Brontë characterizes a headmistress Miss Wilcox and her 'smart and shewy' sisters in terms of their taste in colour: 'Bright stone-blue is a colour they like in dress – a crimson bow rarely fails to be pinned on somewhere to give contrast – positive colours generally grass-greens – red violets – deep yellow'; whereas 'greys and fawns – all harmonies are at a discount.' We scarcely need to be told that although 'many people would think Miss Wilcox – standing there in her blue merino dress and pomegranate ribbon a very agreeable woman,' the narrator is not among them. Miss Wilcox 'never in her life knew a refinement of feeling or of thought'; 'she could not be delicate or modest because she is naturally destitute of sensitiveness.'[5] It is clear from the outset that a woman who dresses in bright blue and pomegranate is bound to make trouble for the character with whom we are invited to identify. It is not clear yet who this is going to be – the fragment is so brief that its patterns of meaning only begin to reveal themselves – but already Brontë's polarities have begun to generate the template for a delicate, modest, sensitive, and refined heroine who will oppose this vulgar lady.

For whatever else they represent, Brontë's heroines always personify Good Taste: good taste in clothing, in food, in interior decor, in reading, in painting, in writing, in art criticism – in whatever aesthetic area they enter. Brontë is equally invested in feminine elegance and 'masculine' genius. Anxious to establish the cultural and intellectual distinction of her protagonists and their striking originality (much is made of Frances's *devoirs*, of Jane's drawings, and of Lucy's intense responses to painting and theatre), she also has an investment in sartorial taste of the most conventional kind. Brilliantly or extravagantly dressed women are condemned, modest elegance extolled. Frances, Jane, and Lucy may be small and plain, but their dark, demure, and well-fitted costumes not only expose the frivolity and sensuality of their rivals but make a piquant contrast to the energy and individuality of their inner life. Cultural and sartorial taste are complementary, and both contribute to the polarities by which the heroine is constructed. The modest, specifically English decorum of her dress and demeanour distinguish her from decadently aristocratic or vulgarly foreign women, while the range and vitality of her mind distinguish her from other Englishwomen of her own class.

Though critics have pointed out the class assumptions that underlie Jane Eyre's progress towards Proper-Lady status, arguing that the novels express 'not the rage of the Romantic radical who wants justice, but the rage of the outsider who just wants to get in,'[6] Brontë's obsession with good taste, particularly sartorial good taste, demands more systematic analysis. One technical reason for her emphasis on costume is no doubt the problem of representing the sex appeal of the plain heroine. Most of Brontë's novels depend on the premise that a virtuous and brilliant but physically unprepossessing woman can evoke romantic love. But since it may be hard to believe that superiority of character can alone endow a woman with erotic power, the novelist needs to make her heroine's virtue not only compellingly and plausibly readable but also sexually attractive: to find a way in which inner beauty can manifest itself in material form. One way of linking character with appearance is by means of physiognomical and phrenological theory, which allows character traits to be read out from the shape of the skull, the stature, the posture, and the expression of the mouth and eyes.[7] This works efficiently, if, to the modern reader, disquietingly, as a way of dismissing inferior characters: it is easy to make outward and visible ugliness signal inner and spiritual blight. The problem comes with signalling inner beauty in a heroine who is supposed to be outwardly plain. Describing the facial features that suggest generosity, sensitivity, and imagination can make a woman sound physically beautiful in a fairly conventional way. It is hard, after listening to Rochester's description of Jane's eye, 'soft and full of feeling' and shining 'like dew' (251); of her mouth, 'mobile and flexible' (251); of the brow that testifies to 'inward treasure, born within' (252), to retain a lively sense of the plainness Brontë wants to insists on. Such remarks cannot be repeated too often or the founding premise of the narrative will be undercut.

The heroine's good taste, however, is a topic that can be developed in a range of detailed and nuanced ways to impute to her a strong and specifically aesthetic appeal. Her trim figure, her simply arranged hair, her simple, elegant costume, her chaste ornament, her graceful movement, her soft voice, her 'pure and silvery' articulation (*The Professor* 126): these matter so much in a Brontë novel not only because they spiritualize the heroine's body but because they are the only claim to physical beauty that she is supposed to have. Though Brontë's protagonists are small, thin, and plain, they apparently delight not only the mind but the senses of the man who is observing them.

Brontë's investment in feminine good taste has implications both for plot and for characterization. The man capable of appreciating such tastefulness must be a particular kind of individual: someone who has the power and the opportunity to watch the heroine closely as well as the insight to decode the signs of her excellence. Since the plainness of the heroine requires the hero's penetrating eye, the voyeuristic 'masters' who observe and test her are a kind of structural requirement of Brontë's paradigm. While these bullying men have been taken as father figures and the fictional pattern seen as an expression of Charlotte Brontë's feelings about her own father,[8] it is not necessary to resort to a biographical explanation to account for this scenario, which simply takes to its logical conclusions the encounter between the percipient voyeur and the tasteful lady that is already, for wider social and cultural reasons, a staple in the fiction of the period.

The focus on taste also has implications for the narrative voice. Taste is a social code. Its advantage, particularly for a woman, is that it silently displays her excellence without attributing to her any desire to display herself. But for the code to work, the signs must be stable, the interpreter receptive, and the woman credibly unselfconscious. In the fragment from 'Emma,' there is no question about the connection between vulgar taste in colour and poverty of spirit: Miss Wilcox's character is simply read out from her dress by an apparently reliable third-person narrator. When Brontë uses a first-person narrator, however, and especially when the heroine records another person's response to her taste, the situation becomes more complicated. If the woman herself has to bear witness to the impact of her tastefulness on others, she may sound coy and disingenuous. If she is the heroine of a Brontë novel, she may also sound snide and malicious. Since Jane Eyre is responsible for all the words in her narrative, she cannot offload onto her author or onto an omniscient narrator the invidious judgments about the vulgar characters who serve as her foils. It is the first-person narration, I shall argue, that helps to deconstruct the very system of signs on which the Brontë heroine bases her sense of identity.

In *The Professor* Brontë invents a narrator she will use again: a first-person narrator, socially and economically marginal and physically diminutive but exquisitely sensitive to any evidence of vulgarity, who assesses others even as he or she is assessed by somebody else. In this novel Brontë doubles the voyeur figure and splits the lowly-teacher figure into two. Androgynous Yorke Hunsden observes and appreciates the narrator, William Crimsworth, a somewhat feminized 'professor,' who in turn observes and appreciates the beleaguered little lace mender Frances Henri. Crimsworth in particular, who is both an English instructor like Charlotte Brontë and an authoritative 'master' like Constantin Heger, is, in his compulsion to rate the refinement or vulgarity of everyone around him, a prototype for central characters in the later novels.[9]

William Crimsworth is a voyeur who fixes his discriminating eye on all the individuals, particularly all the women, he meets. Disappointed when he arrives at M. Pelet's school to find himself unable to observe the pupils at the *pensionnat* next door, he imagines them from a distance as 'half-angels' (85), but a close-up view reveals instead monsters both morally and physically repulsive.[10] Well before Frances Henri appears on the scene, her excellence is proleptically set off by a series of portraits of other women to whom she will prove superior. All these portraits are rigorously judgmental, but those of Mlle Reuter's young ladies are the most gratuitously venomous.

The pupils in this Belgian school are a mixed lot, nationally and racially, and Crimsworth consistently links vulgarity with sensuality, stupidity, phrenological deficiency, and racial degeneracy. The violence of language is startling, particularly since these pupils, after causing Crimsworth some trivial problems of class management, never make another appearance in the novel: tall, fair, insentient Eulalie, distinguishable only by her breathing from a 'figure, moulded in wax' (85); sensual Caroline with her 'colourless olive complexion, clear as to the face and sallow about the neck,' her 'loose ringlets of abundant but somewhat coarse hair,' 'rolling black eyes' and 'lips, as full as those of a hot-blooded Maroon,' (86); 'stout,' 'ungraceful' Hortense, 'her complexion richly coloured' (85); the 'half-breed' Aurelia Koslow, her 'large feet tortured into small bottines, head small, hair smoothed, braided, oiled and gummed to perfection, very low forehead, very diminutive and vindictive grey eyes, somewhat Tartar features, rather flat nose' (98), 'slovenly and even dirty' – 'her neck ... grey for want of washing, ... her hair ... glossy with gum and grease' (99); the Belgian Adèle Dronsart, 'not much above fifteen but full-grown as a stout young English-woman of twenty,' with 'vicious propensities in her eye, envy and panther-like deceit about her mouth' (100): all fill the narrator with disgust. The last and the worst of the group is Juanna Trista, 'of mixed Belgian and Spanish origin' (100), with her 'gaunt visage' and 'fierce and hungry' gaze (101), whose character is analysed in terms of phrenological categories:

> She had precisely the same shape of skull as Pope Alexander the sixth; her organs of benevolence, veneration, conscientiousness, adhesiveness were singularly small, those of self-esteem, firmness, destructiveness, combativeness preposterously large; her head sloped up in the penthouse shape, was contracted about the forehead and prominent behind. (100–1)

The diatribe continues for a full page: Juanna, we are finally told, 'made noises with her mouth like a horse,' 'ejected her saliva,' and evoked 'a swinish tumult' from 'a band of very vulgar, inferior-looking Flamandes, including two or three examples of that deformity of person and imbecility of intellect whose frequency in the Low Countries would seem to furnish proofs that the climate is such as to induce degeneracy of the human mind and body' (101). The discourse of taste supports the discourse of race: innate traits, for which the individual cannot rationally be held accountable, are presented in a continuum with decisions about self-presentation, allowing the women to be blamed for their vulgarity as well as despised for their racial inferiority. Frances's claim to heroine's status needs apparently to be substantiated by a vicious put-down of all the women who are bigger, heavier, richer, dirtier, more sensual, more vulgar, and less English than she.[11]

These pupils are not the only women who fail to live up to Crimsworth's standards. He also takes a dim view of his brother's wife; of M. Pelet's mother, 'ugly, as only continental old women can be' (70), shabby and dishevelled at home but decked out in public in a 'very brilliant coloured dress ... a silk bonnet with a wreath of flowers, and a very fine shawl' (70); of her friend Mme Reuter, equally gaudy, with 'spring-flowers of different hues circl[ing] in a bright wreath the crown of her violet-coloured velvet bonnet' (72); of Zoraïde Reuter, whose appearance at first attracts him but whose scheming he quickly learns to distrust; and indeed of all of the other *maîtresses* in the *pensionnat*. We are invited, I think, to regard his judgments as valid. Crimsworth is a racist, a misogynist, and a voyeur, but he is not an unreliable narrator, not at least when he interprets female appearance: his taste is apparently sound, and it gives him a genuine insight into character. Though there is a hint that Crimsworth is so hard on women because he himself feels unattractive, it is against the vivid and vicious portraits of these women that the exemplary figure of Frances Henri will emerge, and the criteria by which he condemns the other women in the novel are just those by which she will be exalted.

When Crimsworth finally turns his attention to the novel's heroine, her good taste is delineated in terms not only of the English compositions that she writes for 'mon maître' but also of her charming little apartment, her quietly attractive person, and her modest but appealing costume. While Frances Henri is not as emphatically plain as Jane Eyre or Lucy Snowe, she is apparently unremarkable, particularly to the uninitiated eye: it takes a discriminating observer to appreciate her quiet beauty. But her excellence rapidly makes itself known to the fastidious narrator, and under his gaze she blossoms demurely, her 'thoughtful, thin face' taking on 'a bloom ... a plumpness almost embonpoint' (147), her figure becoming 'rounder' (148). Crimsworth takes care to distinguish between an ordinary man's sensual reaction to these pleasing developments and his own more refined response:

As the harmony of her form was complete and her stature of the graceful middle height, one did not regret (or at least *I* did not regret) the absence of confirmed fulness, in contours, still slight, though compact, elegant, flexible – the exquisite turning of waist, wrist, hand, foot and ancle satisfied completely my notions of symmetry, and allowed a lightness and freedom of movement which corresponded with my ideas of grace. (148)

That is, though short and thin by contemporary standards, Frances's body has a particularly refined kind of appeal. Aesthetic terms like 'harmony,' 'elegant,' 'symmetry,' and 'grace' make clear that Crimsworth's reaction is a cultivated, judicious one and that it is only because Frances appeals to his taste that she attracts his senses. The way Frances dresses is equally satisfying. She is

> a model of frugal neatness, with her well-fitting black stuff dress, so accurately defining her elegant bust and taper waist, with her spotless white collar turned back from a fair and shapely neck, with her plenteous brown hair arranged in smooth bands on her temples and in a large Grecian plat behind: ornaments she had none, neither broach, ring nor ribbon; she did well enough without them; perfection of fit, proportion of form, grace of carriage agreeably supplied their place. (72) [12]

Modesty, purity, simplicity, black-and-white or grey-and-white colour scheme, neat elegant fit: some version of this formula will reappear in all three governess novels, where the heroine's decorous costume tells against the flashy, brightly coloured garb of coarser, more trivial women and endows her with a subtler beauty. Although she lacks the immediate and calculating sex appeal of Zoraïde Reuter, Frances Henri's appearance gives, the narrator insists, the most intense and refined pleasure.

As it so often does, good taste serves a compensatory function here. The way Frances's exquisite taste compensates for her lack of material resources is also the theme of Crimsworth's account of her domestic arrangements. The very name of the street where she lives is suggestive: 'Rue Notre Dame aux Neiges' (171). Though the 'Neiges' looks forward to 'Lucy Snowe' in *Villette*, as associated with Frances it connotes not chilly defensiveness but femininity and purity, while 'Notre Dame' implies sanctity and maternal protection. The scenario of masculine penetration into the woman's room is played out in a conventional way in Crimsworth's visit to Frances's apartment, where a point is made of its perfect neatness, its Englishness, its cozy domesticity, and, in particular, its miniature scale. The limitedness of Frances's life is made clear – she cannot afford a fire – but the domestic idyll is otherwise almost entirely spiritualized. There is nothing sordid or degrading about this poverty, no mention of noise or smells from other apartments: in this tiny space, she will effortlessly produce a tasty European-style meal, a meal of which we have no hint until it is put on the table, even as she carries on with Yorke Hunsden a spirited defence of both English and Swiss culture.

Frances at once perfectly fulfills and piquantly transcends the paradigm of the Proper Lady. In maximizing the charm and comfort of her little home she impersonates the virtues of the female sphere; in her independence of mind and vivacity of expression, she is unexpectedly original.[13]

Frances too is a national hybrid, albeit a more hopeful one: she combines the sturdy independence of the Swiss with an ardent love of everything British and initially attracts Crimsworth's attention during the reading lesson by astonishing him – resigned as he is to the 'uncouth mouthing' of the other pupils, who 'lisped, stuttered, mumbled and jabbered' their way through the assignment – with the 'pure and silvery' (126) accent with which she reads a passage from Scott. Her anglophilia is underscored during Crimsworth's first visit by her doll-size tea set, an antique inherited from the English side of the family. It is a significant moment when she serves Crimsworth weak tea from this set: the china itself, dainty, English, and intact, is a suggestive emblem of the virginal, fastidious little hostess, its provenance a sign of her family piety and her national feeling, and the pleasure she takes in the ritual a token of her fitness for domestic contentment. In her modesty, simplicity, and domesticity, Frances impersonates the Victorian ideal of conventional femininity.

In her forceful and original mind, however, she dramatically transcends this model. It is, after all, neither Frances's personal appearance, which he initially refuses even to suggest to the reader, nor the charm of her domestic appointments that first convinces Crimsworth of Frances's distinction, but rather the *devoir* she composes for him about Alfred the Great. Again the encounter is set up within a specific architectural space, but this time it sounds like a sexual meeting. The time is night, the place is Crimsworth's own little room, the emotion 'rising within me' as he picks up her essay is an unusual feeling of pleasurable anticipation. The professor excitedly imagines penetrating the secrets of his pupil's essential being: '"Now," thought I, "I shall see a glimpse of what she really is"' (133). But what he will glimpse is not of course Frances's body but her transcendent spirit, 'the nature and extent of her powers' (133). It is partly his pupil's very modesty and insignificance that have created his excitement. The titillating gap between her demure exterior and her visionary writing constructs her interiority and eroticizes it while at the same time implying the spiritual refinement of the voyeur who can be thus aroused.

A point is made of the originality of Frances's *devoir*. Though the assignment, a variation on the legend of Alfred the Great with the cakes, is somewhat inappropriate, one might think, for a class of European adolescents, Crimsworth, having 'given the subject' to his pupils, has 'not said a word about the manner of treating it' (135). Contemptuously dismissive nevertheless of 'stupid and deceitful' Eulalie for having 'copied the anecdote out fair' from an abridged history of England (132), he is the more deeply impressed by the 'taste and fancy' (137) of Frances, who has developed her ideas 'without a hint from me' (135). To be original in this novel, it is enough apparently for the pupil to see the potential in the topic her 'master' has proposed and surprise him by exceeding his low expectations.

The topic is peculiarly congenial to the patriotic Frances, not only because of its subject matter but also because it allows her to construct a parable of domestic space and its transcendence.[14] Her vision of the beleaguered king, alone in the Saxon peasant's hut in the midst of a 'great, leafless, winter forest' (133), remembering his God, and taking heart, can be read not only as a patriotic tribute to an English national hero but also as an allegory of her own situation.[15] Like both Crimsworth and Frances, Alfred is superior to those with whom he is forced to associate and finds himself alone, surrounded by enemies, in a small, unworthy chamber. The domestic scene is set, however, only to be transcended, first by the peasant wife's evocation of the dangers of the surrounding forest and then by Alfred's own sweeping overview of the situation in his realm as a whole, a realm that he will go on to rally and unite. The little room that expands suddenly into a vast and immeasurable space – the room that will receive its most dramatic expression in Lucy Snowe's allusion to the tent of Peri-Banou – is first envisioned in Frances's *devoir*, which opens out the domestic scene into vast imagined landscapes, material and spiritual, gothic and sublime. Like Alfred's, the mind of the cultivated lady, it is suggested, can burst the bounds of the modest space to which she is confined and move into times and places unlimited by her material circumstances.

Yet though Frances is original, she is not disquietingly so. What Crimsworth remarks on is not the visionary energy of Frances's writing but her Christian feeling – on the way she makes Alfred turn to 'the scriptural Jehovah for aid against the mythological Destiny' (135). Visionary energy is qualified by orthodoxy: the *devoir* remains an exercise in composition, albeit an impressive one, as well as a quietly Protestant document, and Frances's surprising energy of mind does nothing to threaten or challenge the masculine authority of her teacher.

The claim is that reading this text allows Crimsworth reliable insight into Frances herself, into the essential nature of her mind and heart. But 'what she really is' (133) depends on her specular relationship to masculine authority figures – on the alacrity with which she responds to the pedagogical demands of her master, on her obeisance to a paternal God, and on her admiration for an English king. Patriarchal power is a theme to which Frances ardently responds. The contradictions in this paradigm are not resolved in this text, and the relationship between female originality and male culture will be played out in increasingly vexed ways in *Jane Eyre* and *Villette*. It is typical of the slightly brutal demeanour of all of these 'masters' that when Crimsworth discusses the essay with Frances he focuses mainly on its defects. It is equally characteristic that, far from resenting his harshness, she deeply appreciates it. 'I am glad you have been forced to discover so much,' she says, not 'of my weaknesses in written English,' but 'of my nature' (137): her genius, of which she herself is already quietly convinced. Like Jane Eyre and Lucy Snowe, Frances longs to be penetrated and understood; unlike them, though, she seems incapable of feeling anger towards her observer, no matter how arrogantly he behaves towards her. There is a powerful connection in all of these novels between erotic domination and the judgment of the master, whose good taste is confirmed by his interest in the beleaguered heroine and whose intellectual prestige is established not only, apparently, by his cultural authority over her but also by the acerbic, even sadistic, way he expresses it. Brontë has invented a scenario from which, in her first-person novels, she never departs, but on which she rings increasingly complex and conflicted changes.

As Mlle Henri's teacher, Crimsworth has a right to look at the homework he has assigned: the pedagogical situation is no doubt so popular in the fiction of this period not only because it endorses patriarchal power but because it eroticizes it, allowing a woman to be 'known' in a legitimate way. In *Jane Eyre*, however, the relationship between the master and the novel's heroine becomes more complicated. Though as Jane's employer Rochester does have certain socially sanctioned kinds of authority over her, he apparently needs to know more about her than he can by these means. Accordingly, he sets up much more elaborate scenarios of surveillance than Brontë devises in *The Professor*. More than a voyeur, he is also a trickster, and Jane is tested and tormented in a number of bizarre ways. Her response is ambiguous. The ample evidence of displaced rage in the novel makes it possible to argue that she resents his manipulation as many readers think she should. Yet since whenever Rochester observes Jane his conclusions are so gratifying – and since, as a retrospective narrator, Jane must now understand just how gratifying – the way either Jane the narrator or Jane the character feels about his surveillance is not so clear.

Characteristic of the critical emphasis on displaced anger in *Jane Eyre* is Mary Poovey's treatment of the episode in which Rochester, bizarrely disguised as a gypsy woman, reads Jane's mind as a way of predicting her fortune. Poovey sees fury at the way Jane is manipulated in this episode and is interested in the ways Brontë avoids attributing it to Jane. Though the scene is developed in seven of the nine pages of chapter 19, Poovey focuses not on the episode itself but on its frame, and in particular on what happens in the final two pages: on the 'blow' (255) Rochester receives in the news that his brother-in-law Mason has returned from the West Indies.[16] When Jane learns that she has really been talking not to a gypsy woman but to Rochester, she 'voices more rage toward her "master" than at any other time,' Poovey asserts, suggesting that this rage receives its oblique expression when 'Jane suddenly, and with marked carelessness, remembers Mason's presence' and gives Rochester the disturbing news.

> The 'blow' Jane's announcement delivers is then graphically acted out when Bertha, who is Jane's surrogate by virtue of her relation to Rochester, attacks Mason, whose textual connection to Rochester has already been established. As before, anger and violence are transferred from one set of characters to another, revenge is displaced from Jane's character, and agency is dispersed into the text. (139)

The remark Poovey partly quotes to illustrate what she calls Jane's 'rage' – 'It is scarcely fair, sir ... it was not right' (253) – might seem anticlimactically mild for such a violent outcome. Its mildness, however, does not undercut but rather endorses Poovey's argument: the repressed emotion that the character can express only in the quietest terms is just what has to get into the plot.

Nevertheless, the context of this interchange suggests that 'rage' is not quite the right word for what Jane must be feeling at this point. Jane is rather pleased to be summoned out of the drawing room, where she has been exposed to the insults of Blanche Ingram and her party, and curious to see the gypsy. When she makes the retort Poovey quotes, what she has just heard (along with some cutting sarcasm at the expense of her rival Blanche Ingram, and a no doubt disconcerting, though by no means unflattering, assessment of her own pain and stoicism) is the page-long, warmly appreciative description quoted above, of her expressive face, 'illumined' for Rochester by the firelight (247): her eye 'soft and full of feeling,' her 'mobile and flexible mouth' (251). Upset and bewildered though she no doubt is when she discovers the identity of her interlocutor, it is hard to hear 'rage' in her full response: 'I believe you have been trying to draw me out – or in: you have been talking nonsense to make me talk nonsense. It is scarcely fair, sir' (253). Perhaps not fair, but not merely infuriating, either, especially if Jane remembers that she herself, 'on my guard almost from the beginning of the interview' (254), has not been drawn in or out, that she has not talked nonsense but rather deftly parried his probes, and that he has registered her 'pride and reserve' (251) as admirable reticence, 'very correct – very careful, very sensible' (254). 'The eagerness of a listener,' thinks Jane, referring to Rochester, 'quickens the tongue of a narrator' (250). Despite her pain and confusion, Jane too has been an eager listener to Rochester's quickened words as well as a punctilious recorder of his tributes to her own excellence. Jane has every reason to resent many of Rochester's games, but she is unlikely to be merely angry at the gypsy trick, which allows him to assess her inner nature and express his approval of it in the warmest terms. The episode functions, in fact, precisely to confirm the heroine's superiority to her female rivals, in a more subtle and less overly vicious way than William Crimsworth's diatribes against vulgar foreigners. It gives Jane the character a chance to reproach Rochester, as she could not do for exposing her earlier to his guests' insults, but it also allows Jane the narrator to remain opaque about how fully she has registered his compliments.

The first-person narration of incidents like this one threatens to expose the whole Proper Lady paradigm as an elaborate and knowing game. A modest lady is not supposed to notice the admiration she evokes; she is certainly not supposed to repeat in faithful detail the compliments she receives. Having the individual who is observed tell her own story and tell it retrospectively always raises the question of how much she knew and when she knew it. Jane the narrator must now understand what Jane the character may not – or, indeed, may – have understood at the time: she must know that each of the 'gypsy's' remarks testifies to Rochester's admiration. But Brontë must blur and occlude her awareness if she wants her heroine to go on recording, with appropriate innocence and yet in satisfying detail, such expressions of admiration. It is this false modesty that Lady Eastlake is objecting to when she complains of 'the account [Jane Eyre] herself gives of the effect she produces.' What Lady Eastlake is saying here is that she does not find Jane as attractive as Jane's fictional admirers do, but her remarks also suggest that the narrator cannot be as oblivious to the admiring remarks she records as she pretends to be.[17]

The retroactive comprehension of the first-person narrator not only exposes the strains and contradictions of the Proper Lady act, it also makes clear that in the elaborate game of hide and seek that constitutes a Brontë courtship, the heroine desperately wants to be found out. The assumption of critics like Poovey is that Jane resents Rochester's probing (as she ought), that she wants to keep the secrets of her own nature inviolate while penetrating his. Shuttleworth calls both of Jane's courtships 'competitive exercises in interpretative penetration' and argues that in all Brontë's novels 'power resides with the figure who can unveil the hidden secrets of the other whilst preserving the self unread.'[18] This properly Foucauldian conclusion is not however endorsed by the structure of erotic surveillance in Brontë's novels. Far from resenting observation and exposure, the Brontë heroine is desperate to be known by the master who, alone among the mediocrities with which she is surrounded, is capable of fully reading her nature – that is, of course, fully understanding her excellence. Shuttleworth notes that phrenology encourages the 'superior' individual's belief in her own innate genius, but the corollary of such a conviction would presumably be a desire to have one's nature recognized. The Brontë heroine may be proud of her ability to read the nature of others, but she depends upon finding a man who can read hers, not only because their interpretative ability is a bond between them, a mark of their essential equality,[19] but also because both her romantic fulfillment and her very sense of her own identity depend upon his insight.

Rochester not only reads Jane's face, he also reads her taste. But taste is not so straightforward a matter as in *The Professor*. While the same themes are emphasized – the heroine's face and figure, her wardrobe, her compositions (here, drawings) – they are developed in more complex and problematical ways.

Jane dresses much like Frances, but her costume, constructed by a more fully worked out and relentless system of polarities, turns out to be a less secure sign of 'what she really is.' Like Frances, Jane is tidy and neat – her 'Quaker trim ... being too close and plain, braided locks included, to admit of disarrangement' (157). And like her, she is a humble teacher with a limited wardrobe: three gowns, a black stuff, a black silk, and a light grey, as well as 'a single little pearl ornament which Miss Temple gave me as a parting keepsake' (146). The language suggests a woman's calculation of her limited resources, rather than a man's vision of her demure charm. It is made clearer than in *The Professor* that the heroine has almost no choice about what she wears: she owns only these three dresses, and this is virtually a governess's uniform. Yet the novel seems to be trying to give Jane credit for it, nevertheless: to suggest that her sober toilette is morally admirable, an expression of her essential character.

Rochester's attempt to take Jane out of her governess garb and dress her in satin and lace emphasizes the paradox even as it attempts to contain it. Rochester, though intrigued by the 'strange contrasts' (400) between Jane's quiet exterior and her inner fire and piqued by her 'air of a little nonnette; quaint, quiet, grave, and simple' (160), is less impressed than William Crimsworth with his governess's prim costume: a wealthy man of the world, he is not as likely as an obscure school teacher to lyricize over her collars and cuffs. Instead, Rochester believes that distinction of mind ought to be expressed in distinction of dress: a 'circlet on [Jane's] forehead' would testify accurately, he says, to the 'patent of nobility' that nature has stamped on her brow (326).

What the desire to adorn Jane in fine clothing contributes to plot and characterization is clear enough: it is one of the many signs that the situation Rochester would put Jane in is false and unreal, 'a fairy tale – a day-dream' (325), and one of the many challenges that make her determined to control the terms of her own representation. It makes good psychological sense for Jane to resist being dressed up by her master, which would put her in the same position as Céline Varens or indeed as little Adèle, and her stubbornness on this subject prefigures her eventual refusal to live with him in an adulterous relationship. It is indeed Rochester's oppressive gift-giving that facilitates a key development in the plot. It is not just Jane's general sense of financial disparity between herself and Rochester but specifically her realization that she 'never can bear being dressed like a doll' that leads her to write the letter to her uncle that indirectly aborts the bigamous marriage. But what I am interested in here is less the plot or the psychology of the characters than the semiotic reasons for Jane's refusal to abandon her governess garb.

Both Rochester and Jane see clothing almost allegorically, as emblematic of a woman's moral nature. The tiara that Rochester would give

Jane is intended not to align her with the titled ladies in his drawing room but rather to distinguish her from them. His point is that since Jane has the genuine 'nobility' of spirit that they lack, a tiara on her brow would be not a fashion accessory but a reliable emblem.[20] He and Jane speak the same language, and on these points Jane does not really disagree with him. She, too, reads clothing moralistically if not allegorically; she too has registered the spiritual nullity of the ladies who dress in tiaras and has made clear that she believes herself morally superior to them. But as narrator she has already made luxurious ornament into a sign not of nobility but of aristocratic vanity and assigned her own 'nobility' its sartorial mark. Her 'Quaker' costume already expresses her humility, modesty, patience, and willingness to serve, and it is precisely these qualities that constitute the 'nobility' Rochester praises. 'Nobility' is not the name of one trait as distinct from the others but a generalization about all the traits already signalled by Jane's governess costume. The semiotic slot has been filled and there is no room for duplication, thus no room for Jane to allow herself to enjoy what Rochester offers her. She has been trapped in resistance to pleasure by the very system of signs the novel has used to construct her, and she cannot be allowed to back out into bourgeois *luxe*. Lucy Snowe will be cornered in much the same way.

Jane's refusal of fine clothing is needed to give her simple dress a positive moral valence, make it 'tell' as a statement of personal taste in a way that a governess's dress ordinarily could not. 'Simplicity' cannot register except in terms of its opposite: it acquires a moral resonance only within a polarized system of signs, and in the context of choice – only if the woman who chooses a simple costume could have worn an ornate one. Jane's sober dress is merely a badge of her station, as her piano playing is an index of her vocational proficiency. As Rochester remarks, 'Your garb and manner were restricted by rule' (400). Since she would expose herself to ridicule by affecting fashionable or elaborate dress – the governess gussied up in silk and ribbons is a conventional figure of satire in the novel at this time[21] – Jane would seem to deserve no credit for eschewing it. Giving her an opportunity to dress luxuriously and having her insist on simplicity over ornament is a way of making her quiet taste register as an expression of 'what she really is' rather than just as a badge of her office: of allowing it to be read *as* taste, even though she has had little choice in its selection. Jane demonstrates her difference from the ordinary governess by retaining her governess dress when she has the chance to exchange it for something better. The binary system by which she constructs herself allows her, however, no more nuanced alternative, and the paradoxicalness of her position suggests how desperate is the attempt to use taste as a mark of her essential nature.

Jane apparently objects to the wardrobe Rochester proposes not only because it is bright but because it turns her into a doll. But Jane in grey is a doll as surely as Jane in purple satin: a little nonnette, a governess doll, whose piquancy for Rochester consists precisely in its novelty. If female glamour is a male imposition, as Jane seems to feel when she rejects Rochester's offerings, so of course is the female modesty it displaces. Jane's dress cannot be a transparent sign of her essential nature as long as it is being read by an other – a male voyeur – on whom its meaning depends and in terms of its difference from an other – a female rival – on whom its meaning depends. Invested as she is in her physical appearance and dependent on the mirroring gaze of the other, the heroine is constantly being turned inside out. The almost frantic emphasis in Brontë's novels on the authentic inner self registers anxiety about the degree to which that self is constructed by others.

Since sober dress connotes nobility, bright colour must suggest its opposite, however appealing such colour might seem to be to a writer like Brontë, who in her own painting luxuriated in vivid colours and in her early writings described them with gusto and nuance. In one of her juvenile productions, two of her gentlemen square off on the issue of whose coat is the 'prettier,' the 'salmon-coloured' or the 'apple green,'[22] and her high-life ladies are consistently garbed in gorgeous variety. Though rich colours do serve as a sign of sinister character (Alexander points out that Zenobia, the intellectual, is usually dressed in rich crimson velvet and plumes to signal decadence, in contrast to her rival, gentle Marian Hume, who is always in green and white),[23] Brontë's virtuous characters at this point are also allowed colour – 'this deep shaded green and violet,' says one, 'is just the colour his Grace likes' – and there is an appreciative description of a 'dark green silk frock, judiciously shortened' to show an attractive ankle.[24] Brontë's youthful paintings are brightly and deeply tinted, the 'Portrait of a French Brunette,' with pink roses, brilliant 'coral lips,'[25] and a bright blue shawl, being a particularly vivid example.[26] But bright colour repels and distresses Jane Eyre. Something like panic seems to overtake her when Rochester selects 'a rich silk of the most brilliant amethyst dye, and a superb pink satin' (338) as the beginning of her makeover. The legitimacy of her distaste is systematically endorsed by the moral vacuity of the brightly dressed females in the novel: clothes-mad little Adèle, vulgarly got up in 'a dress of rose-coloured satin, very short, and as full in the skirt as it could be gathered' (171); Rochester's guests, who emerge theatrically from the dining room as 'the curtain was swept back from the arch' (213) dressed in gorgeous costumes, Lady Lynn 'in a satin robe of changeful sheen' with 'an azure plume' and a 'band of gems' in her hair (214), and Lady Ingram in a 'crimson velvet robe, and a shawl turban of some gold-wrought Indian fabric, [which] invested her (I supposed she thought) with a truly imperial dignity' (215). In *Jane Eyre*, pink and azure and crimson and gold are as sure a sign of moral nullity as black, white, and grey are of taste and sense. When brightly coloured dress is consistently made a sign of the inferiority of the aristocratic or continental females who outdazzle the plain, modest heroine, one does not need to be Lady Eastlake to detect the class antagonism that fuels the contempt (and desire).

Jane has to reject bright colour and rich gems and textiles as personal adornment, but the fascination with gaudy luxury turns up elsewhere in the text. It is displaced onto Rochester's mansion, where the dining room features 'purple chairs and curtains, a Turkey carpet ... one vast window rich in stained glass' and 'vases of fine purple spar' (125). The drawing room – 'a fairy place' of 'snow and fire' (126), first glimpsed through a theatrical arch 'hung with a Tyrian-dyed curtain' (125) – boasts 'white carpets, on which seemed laid brilliant garlands of flowers,' 'crimson couches and ottomans,' and 'ornaments ... of sparkling Bohemian glass, ruby red' that 'glowed in rich contrast' to the white mantel and ceiling (126). The awkwardness of the writing here – the lumpy rhythm of the sentences into which all these gorgeous objects have to be crammed, the vulgar silver-fork idiom – exposes the heroine's vision as a consumer fantasy. A mansion as patently covetable as this has to burn down so that Jane cannot be suspected of desiring it, or desiring Rochester because of it. But the fascination with colour and sparkle is also more covertly expressed in the creatures of Jane's fantasy who in some way or other stand in for the heroine. Jane likes to draw glamorous females in intense situations: a 'drowned corpse' seen 'through the green water,' her 'fair arm' stripped by a cormorant of its 'gold bracelet, set with gems,' which Jane has 'touched with as brilliant tints as my palette could yield, and as glittering distinctness as my pencil could impart'; a personified Evening Star in 'woman's shape,' her dim forehead ... crowned with a star' (153). The visionary moon-mother who appears 'in the azure' sky and persuades Jane to flee from Thornfield is a similar figure. Making a dramatic entrance through what sound like theatre curtains, her 'hand ... penetrat[ing] the sable folds and wav[ing] them away,' she seems, as she 'inclin[es] a glorious brow earthward' (407), to be crowned with a metaphorical if not material tiara. The glamorous, theatrical lady may be repressed in the drawing room, but she returns in the heavens to make her entrance as the heroine's alter ego. Jane cannot be allowed to shine in gorgeous raiment, but the text makes clear that the sartorial smugness of the prim middle-class lady masks an envy and desire the more consuming for their repression.

What is missing for Jane is any middle position, any sartorial 'third way.' *Jane Eyre* is unique in Brontë's fiction in that, to demonstrate that Jane herself achieves harmonious balance, it organizes a number of her female foils into polarized sister pairs. The quarrelsome Reed sisters, austere Eliza and worldly Georgiana, are set up as different from each another in nature, in life choices, and in taste, so that Jane can explicitly repudiate the extremes they represent. The claim the novel makes is that Jane does eventually achieve the balance she seeks, the balance between flesh and spirit, self-control and self-indulgence. As she moves closer to that goal – closer, that is, to marriage and to social recognition – her progress is signalled by her encounter with a very different pair of female cousins, Diana and Mary Rivers, cultivated, affectionate sisters polarized only in terms of their names. Though Diana is a bit spunkier than Mary and her hair is curlier, the Rivers sisters talk and dress much alike, as the thorough gentlewomen Jane finds them to be.[27] Yet Jane herself is never allowed to dress like them, never achieves the wardrobe that might express the balance in her nature. Even at Ferndean she casts herself as a servant, and though the loving servitude she embraces in her marriage is, the novel claims, a middle way, she never gets the appearance to go with it. Rochester never does dress Jane up and admire her in the clothes he has bought her: indeed by the time she marries him, he can scarcely see.

Once Jane has fled Thornfield, the issue of her own clothing is dropped. But the gap will be filled in her portrait of Rosamond Oliver, the most banal and yet the most problematic of Jane's paintings. It is these paintings I now want to consider.

Unlike Frances Henri, Jane has no space of her own in which she can entertain her employer and impress him with her taste and domestic virtue. The cozy little room in this novel is assigned not to the heroine but to Mrs Fairfax.[28] It would be inappropriate in any case to have Rochester enter Jane's room (as indeed it is inappropriate to have Crimsworth enter Frances's apartment) and unrealistic to imagine a man of his social stature charmed, like William Crimsworth, by such a modest space. In Jane's portfolio of pictures, Brontë invents, however, an ingenious replacement for the heroine's room, a replacement that will manifest to Rochester just the qualities of mind and spirit that her domestic space is supposed to display. Brontë miniaturizes the room, as it were, shrinking Jane's private space into a portfolio – suggesting how pathetically little space she does have to call her own – and then having that space open out, like Frances's essay, into sublime landscapes that exhibit the heroine's original and 'expanded mind.' While it is taboo for the 'master' to enter his governess's room, it is legitimate for him to command her to appear in his drawing room at his convenience, to perform on the piano, and to display her drawings for him. Opening the covers of her portfolio, Rochester enters the secret places of Jane's imagination, more decorously yet also more penetratingly than he might her chamber.

Again, the text makes a point of the startling originality of the heroine's productions. We may be struck by the derivativeness of these images as well as by their somewhat adolescent theatricality, but the worldly and sophisticated Rochester is apparently impressed. Initially intrigued by the power of the sketches Adèle has shown him, it is because he cannot believe that they are hers that he challenges her – 'probably a master aided you?' – and, when she vehemently denies it, orders her to 'fetch me your portfolio, if you can vouch for its contents being original; but don't pass your word unless you are certain: I can recognise patch-work' (152). His skepticism is understandable: Jane's piano playing, which can be tested, has been mediocre, and drawing and painting, which can be faked – novels are full of drawing masters who finish their pupils' pictures – are 'accomplishments' often associated in the nineteenth-century novels with dishonest self-representation. Having examined Jane's, Rochester acknowledges their aesthetic unity – a unity that testifies to the stable coherent subjectivity Brontë wants to insist on for Jane ('I perceive these pictures were done by one hand') – but he continues to doubt their provenance: 'was that hand yours?' (152). The implication is that images of such power could not have been generated by a mere 'school girl' (154). The point is made yet a third time: 'Where did you get your copies?' demands Rochester; 'Out of my head,' Jane replies (152). Jane, who has a great stake in originality – despising Blanche Ingram because, among other things, 'she was not original: she used to repeat sounding phrases from books'[29] –

recounts his inquisition in detail and evidently with some satisfaction. Her drawings are, we are invited to believe, no mere flimsy female 'accomplishments' but the expressions of a truly original mind.

Like Frances Henri's King Alfred, but rather more transparently, the images of death and transfiguration that Jane has produced – the female figure as a drowned and plundered corpse, then risen as the Evening Star, her eyes 'dark and wild,' her 'dim forehead ... crowned' (153) – offer a plaintive allegory of her own situation. Access to her portfolio allows Rochester to enter her psyche in a particularly intimate way. He no doubt intuits their relevance to Jane's inner life, since he asks her how she felt when she painted them, and his comment about the 'meaning' in the 'solemn depth' (154) of those dark, wild eyes suggests that he is ready to read Jane's eyes as well. Nevertheless, the focus of his question is less the pictures' quasi-allegorical content than the artist's technical skill: 'who taught you to paint wind? (154); 'Where did you see Latmos? – for that is Latmos' (155); 'How could you make [the eyes of the Evening Star] look so clear, and yet not at all brilliant? for the planet above quells their rays' (154). Jane, for her part, tells her reader that though the images were indeed visionary – 'I saw them with the spiritual eye' – the pictures themselves 'are nothing wonderful,' being 'but a pale portrait of the thing I had conceived' (153). Since Rochester finds the execution remarkable, however, the implication is not only that her own technical standards are even higher than his but that her conception was sublime indeed. That her reach exceeds her grasp makes Jane the very model of a Romantic/Victorian aspiring mind. Between them, the hero and the narrator make clear that the portfolio represents a genuinely distinguished achievement.

It is an achievement with a masculine inflection, however, since although Jane has depicted female figures, she owes her notion of Death to Milton and her maritime imagery to Bewick. Like Frances Henri's composition, Jane's little portfolio opens out into a sublime space, into the space of male poetry, science, and exploration; they express her yearning to burst boundaries, travel imaginatively into realms invisible to the corporeal eye. Yet at the same time the way they are displayed and the circumstances under which they were prepared work in the opposite direction, testifying not only to Jane's yearning for transcendence but also to her docility and self-abnegation. However visionary Jane may be, it is clear to Rochester that this is a woman who is willing to keep her vision to herself, to cultivate it only in private and on her own time. When, observing that the paintings must have 'taken much time, and some thought,' Rochester queries 'when did you find time to do them?' the reply he gets is reassuring: 'in the last two vacations I spent at Lowood,' says Jane, 'when I had no other occupation' (152). 'Did you sit at them long each day?' he pursues; 'I had nothing else to do,' she repeats, 'because it was the vacation' (154). Instead of taking Rochester into the heroine's modest room, Brontë gives him proof, in the portfolio, of her contented activity in a limited space, her ability to fill up her private time with cultural resources. The most important thing, perhaps, that a prospective husband has to know about a woman's taste is whether she can repress it in his service. Jane's drawings are evidence of her willingness to live in a mental world, of her ability to be 'absorbed ... and happy' even when she has no 'place.' The question Rochester asks – 'Were you happy when you painted these pictures?' (154) – could suggest either that he cares about her well-being or that he is estimating the modesty of her expectations. Her drawings prove both that Jane is an interesting individual and that she would be willing to suppress that individuality and those interests whenever her domestic duties required it.

Jane's personal taste is indeed apparently of little moment to Rochester once she has passed his series of tests: at any rate, we hear no more conversation about pictures or books or indeed about anything except their own relationship. Jane has very specific literary interests – she loves Scott's *Marmion*, for example, which she is given not by Rochester but by St John Rivers,[30] and she is avid to study German along with Mary and Diana – but Rochester's cultural life remains a blank. Though Jane tells us he has a vigorous, expanded mind, it is never exercised in our presence; though, once married, the couple is said to 'talk ... all day long' (576), and though Jane says her husband 'saw nature – he saw books through me' (577) and that she read to him tirelessly, we never have an inkling of what Rochester's interests might be or of what kinds of scenes or books he enjoys. A hero in a novel of this kind has to have just enough cultivation to recognize the taste of the heroine: if he has more, it does not need to be individualized, and indeed must not be if hers is to be foregrounded.

If Rochester never again looks at her pictures, as far as we know, Jane nevertheless continues to produce them. However, for better or worse, she creates no more uncanny landscapes. Instead, she constructs a contrasting pair of portraits of herself and Blanche Ingram; she sketches fairy scenes for her own diversion, then dreamily evokes the face of Rochester; she draws the Reed sisters' portraits to amaze and amuse them, promising as well a watercolour for Georgiana's album; finally, she prepares a portrait of Rosamond and offers to make a duplicate for St John Rivers. Is this change in the focus and function of her art to be read as loss or gain? We can understand it as progress towards or as a surrender to a more social role. On the one hand, Jane's drawings show her growing less solipsistic, less literary, less melancholy, and more responsive to the material world and to other people.[31] On the other hand, her picture making comes to be less an expression of her personal vision and more a kind of therapy or social work. Jane's double portrait of herself and Blanche Ingram, undertaken to convince herself that the man she loves is not within her reach, and the portrait of Rosamond Oliver that she prepares for St John Rivers, intended to persuade him that domestic felicity is within his, are less aesthetic than moral in their motivation: expressions not so much of Jane's taste as of her 'reason,' her stoicism, and her altruism. Jane explains her motivation for quizzing Rivers about his feelings for Rosamond Oliver: because 'I had then temporarily the advantage of him,' she says, she is determined 'to do him some good, if I could' (473). Such therapeutic aggression invites skeptical analysis in terms of the binaries on which these scenes are constructed.

In a novel full of moralized doubles, these two episodes of portraiture replicate the real-life polarities put in play from the very beginning of the novel. I have suggested that the sister figures in *Jane Eyre* are conceived in polarized pairs, in terms of the flesh/spirit, heaven/earth, reason/emotion binaries on which the text as a whole is constructed – binaries that the heroine claims to transcend. In both portrait-painting episodes, however, Jane abandons any attempt at balance, representing herself (in paint) as the plain, darkly costumed governess contrasted to the Blanche-Ingram fine lady and (in words) as the plain little painter contrasted to the stylishly gorgeous sitter Rosamond. Her motive in the first scene is clear and understandable: this is early on in her relationship with Rochester, before she has any evidence that he finds her attractive. Disciplining her imagination seems to make sense at this point (though, significantly, it leads her to the wrong conclusion). The dynamics of the second scene are more problematic, however, and need to be understood in terms of Jane's second encounter, at Lowood, with Brocklehurst, the antetype of St John Rivers.

The polarity between Eliza and Georgiana Reed, played out again in the names, if not the natures, of Mary and Diana Rivers, is also played out at Lowood, in a less obvious and more complex way, in Jane's two school friends, Helen Burns and Mary Ann Wilson. Mary Ann, whose prosaic name aligns her with Jane, is the child with whom Jane plays out-doors in the warm spring weather unaware that Helen lies dying inside: an irony that defines Jane's nature again in terms of the tension between 'natural' bodily pleasure and lofty but possibly morbid spiritu-ality. It is not Mary Ann Wilson alone, however, who is used by Brontë to represent nature and the body at Lowood. Mary Ann is supplemented by Julia Severn, the girl with the naturally curly hair that Brocklehurst orders cut off. This is a figure whose given name both pairs her allitera-tively with Jane and, because of its association with romance, signals the difference between them.[32]

Jane, Helen, and Mary Ann are not differentiated in terms of per-sonal appearance: all three wear the grotesque school uniforms designed to keep them in preadolescent homeliness and underclass humility. It is only when the Brocklehurst family arrives that the sartorial polarity is reasserted, as his elegantly dressed wife and daughters con-front the assembled pupils. It is at this point that Julia enters the narra-tive. Brocklehurst, scanning the group and selecting two pupils, spunky Jane and curly-haired Julia, for special treatment, imposes a new trian-gulation. Julia draws his eye, evidently, because she represents the (juve-nile) female sexuality that lures him but that he has to repress (there is the suggestion of incestuous attraction here): he spots female beauty, declares it transgressive, oppresses and defaces it but thereby acknowl-edges it. Brocklehurst singles out Jane, on the other hand, not for her beguiling body but for her transgressive spirit. By choosing Julia for physical assault and Jane for spiritual – by clipping Julia's hair but Jane's self-esteem – he reinforces Jane's lack of feminine appeal. While his per-secution puts Jane in the spotlight, aligning her with Helen, who is also singled out for public exposure,[33] it also confirms her plainness as not even worth defacing. The male eye, the paternal eye, ineluctably polariz-ing – desiring, or not desiring – always threatens to deny Jane the happy medium for which she longs: her inner balance cannot withstand the categorizing gaze of the father figure who responds only to conven-tional female beauty. The sartorial position Jane never achieves is repre-sented by the Brocklehurst women, the indulged wife and daughters of a well-to-do man who keeps them all beautifully dressed. Their clothing, though too rich and fine for evangelical women, is neither garish nor vulgar in itself; and while it may be inappropriate for the daughters to be dressed as grown-up young ladies, it is less degrading than the hid-eous school uniforms, which infantilize as well as humiliate the charity pupils. When Brocklehurst, in the presence of his female family, orders

Julia's curls cut off, the elaborate scenario of sexual display and male assault splits and displaces the missing middle: the fantasy of completely innocent, because *natural* and unselfconscious, physical beauty ('Julia's hair curls naturally'), rewarded by paternal largesse in the form of elegant costume.

It is this missing middle that is impersonated by the subject of Jane's final painting, Rosamond Oliver. Confronting again the kind of woman that men adore and indulge, Jane is pushed back into the 'Eliza' position of self-righteous, problematic virtue. Acutely aware that St John finds her sexually unattractive, Jane constructs a tableau (plain woman artist painting gorgeous lady) that is just as polarized, just as moralized, as her pair of miniatures. The difference, though, is that Rosamond is no Blanche Ingram, no sneering aristocrat decadently swathed in silk and satin: neither a servant nor a whore, but the charmingly attractive lady that Jane, as a virtuous gentry wife, deserves to be. Sartorially, Rosamond occupies the space of the 'happy medium' and thus usurps the place Jane ought to be able to claim as her own.

For once in the novel, rich colour and luxurious fabric do not signal vulgarity, decadence, or class aggression. Unlike Rochester's elaborately got up but nasty female guests, Rosamond is not only innocent and affectionate but also genuinely beautiful. When Rosamond requests the portrait, Jane claims to be delighted at the opportunity of tackling so congenial a subject, anticipating 'the pleasure of colouring it' (471), of tinting the background, shading off the drapery, and adding 'a touch of carmine ... to the ripe lips – a soft curl here and there to the tresses – a deeper tinge to the shadow of the lash under the azured eyelid' (470). Indeed, the portrait of Rosamond with her glowing complexion and 'chestnut tresses' (471) sounds remarkably like those pictures of beautiful ladies that the young Charlotte Brontë evidently created with loving attention to illustrate her juvenile fiction. The colour here, though lively, is also muted enough to allow Jane vicariously to revel in it without compunction: Rosamond is a tasteful as well as a beautiful figure in her 'dark-blue silk dress' (471). Jane's refined language indeed testifies as much to her tastefulness as to Rosamond's, if only to the reader, who alone can register its nuances: the narrator uses Rosamond's costume as a way of exhibiting her own good taste. Since aesthetic appreciation is 'higher' than self-display, Jane gets credit for the taste of a costume she did not choose, simply by appreciating it so intensely and depicting it so skillfully. But it is Rosamond who gets the costume itself, a costume provided by a prosperous father, who, as a parent and not a lover, has an unproblematic moral right to lavish on his daughter the classy garments that mark her status as a Perfect Lady.[34]

Jane cannot allow Rochester to dress her up in the costumes he selected, but her narrative nevertheless generates the fantasy of a man who will fund the expression of his woman's own good taste: a generous father figure who will provide the money to support her own choices. This never happens for Jane. Though 'naturally' a lady from childhood and now confirmed as one by her inheritance and her marriage,[35] the heroine never looks like a lady in the narrative we are reading. When at the end of the novel she does actually marry Rochester, she is never pictured either wearing the regular bridal gown a lady of her class might don or acquiring the ordinary wardrobe of a gentry wife. The sartorial gap here is in line with the spiritualizing of Jane in her role as servant: in line, too, perhaps, with Brontë's own realism and despair. Thornfield has to burn down not only to punish the principals in the previous marriage but to make clear that what Jane desired was Rochester himself, not his wealth: merely marital affection, not the gorgeous interiors so warmly evoked when she first laid wondering eyes on them. But the thwarted longing, denied by Jane but never fully repressed by her text, to have her spiritual distinction rewarded by tastefully colourful costume expresses itself in the inevitable putdown of Rosamond, who, Jane takes care to tell us, is a fairly commonplace personality. Rosamond is 'child-like' (464); 'a sweet girl – rather thoughtless' (475), as she reminds St John; 'not profoundly interesting or thoroughly impressive' (470). St John agrees: 'deeply impressed with her defects,' he tells Jane that marriage to Rosamond would be a disaster, that 'she could sympathize in nothing I aspired to – co-operate in nothing I undertook' (477).

Since he clearly believes this to be true, Jane's motivation in teasing him with Rosamond's image is equally problematic. St John Rivers is a more civilized (and arguably more demonic) version of Brocklehurst: he represses not only others but also himself. Like Brocklehurst, he has 'de-selected' Jane: marked her as plain and therefore fit to have her 'nature' clipped. Jane has been made to understand that Rivers sees her as 'formed for labour, not for love' (514) and to sense that, were she to marry him, he would use her as a means of disciplining his sexual appetites: that it is precisely because he does not find her attractive that he would 'scrupulously observe' his sexual obligations to her (517). She is evidently hurt that he finds her sexually repulsive; she is more than hurt, she is enraged and appalled by his proposal of a marriage without sexual feeling.[36] The grotesque scenario she orchestrates here can easily be read as revenge. St John can resist Jane's feminine appeal, but he cannot refuse the moral test she imposes on him. To prove that he lacks the power to repress his sexuality in general as he clearly can when faced with her, she attempts to seduce him, using not her own body, for which she knows he has no use, but the body of Rosamond, which she visualizes through his eyes and which she then flaunts, advertises, and tries to 'sell' (the metaphor of the pimp is not far off) in order to compel not merely a local sexual response but a life decision that he himself believes would eternally damn him. Jane in short tries to tempt St John to be a Brocklehurst: to dismiss Jane herself as a sex object but to keep his beautifully dressed, curly-haired domestic mistress.

In this she fails. The portrait painter gets a violent response, an explosion of sexual metaphor that testifies to the vulnerability of St John's body, but she does not get his soul (no more than he hers): it is no surprise when with an extreme act of self-repression, St John extricates himself from the net of domestic associations that he feels is a sensual snare. Whether he triumphs at the end remains ambiguous. Given the death-oriented nature of his Calvinism, his pride, his ambition, and particularly his determination to use Jane and destroy her if necessary in the pursuit of his own salvation, it is hard to read St John either as an impersonation of the vocation Jane has surrendered or as a Christian hero who gets his reward.[37] It is he himself, not anyone else in the text, who assumes he is headed for heaven,[38] and we might well be permitted to doubt his judgment: St John is not after all the only one this novel damns, even in the face of Jane's apparent attempt to 'save' them.[39] The kind of man who loves a woman who looks like Rosamond Oliver needs to be tormented and the woman herself not only dismissed with the faint praise that is Jane's most subtle form of condemnation but also defined as *not* ultimately desirable: no more able than Jane, at least, to shake St John's resolve. There was never of course any chance that St John would give up his Indian scheme for Rosamond. Jane claims to be trying to get St John to surrender to her temptation and stay in England, a happy husband, but she must know that she will fail. By painting the picture and confronting him with it, she corners him into articulating the mediocrity of her rival and the necessity of flight and committing himself definitely to dying in India instead. The wish that beautiful 'coloured' ladies should die, sublimated (or sublimed) in the image of the drowned figure in the picture Rochester examines, is more cagily handled at the end of the novel, where it is not the lady herself but the man who prefers her to Jane who dies instead, by fire (like Bertha) – burnt up in fiery heat of India – rather than by water. But however ingenious she is in displacing her own desires and eliminating those who will not try to fulfill them, Jane never gets the colour she has always eyed with such peculiar intensity. Lacking Rosamond's beauty, she is not even given Rosamond's beautiful clothes, the wardrobe that she might very well, as Rochester's wife, have expected to enjoy. It is the supposedly high-minded heroine's conflicted feelings about 'mere' personal beauty that help to account for both the sexlessness of the ending and the fraught treatment of clothing in the novel.

The narrative about the portrait of Rosamond is contained within the subplot, and this particular painting of Jane's is apparently never seen by Rochester. The cultural productions of Jane and Frances never threaten the male mastery of Rochester and Crimsworth as Jane's picture of Rosamond threatens Rivers'. Though Frances's essays and Jane's drawings transcend, in their spirituality and technical quality, mere feminine accomplishments, nevertheless they function chiefly as accomplishments ordinarily do: to impress and secure a marriageable man. Brontë depicts Frances and Jane as original, but she is not willing to have their originality subvert their feminine appeal.[40] In *Villette*, however, it becomes clear that this is what genuine independence of mind might very well tend to do. In this novel the discourse of taste is pressed into service until the whole system of polarities is derailed and exploded. The fact that as the teller of her own tale Lucy Snowe is possibly somewhat less reliable than Jane Eyre contributes to its collapse.

Though in *Jane Eyre* the language of the narrative is Jane's, the binaries on which it is based are not apparently just her constructions. We are invited to believe that Jane is on the whole an accurate if not dispassionate observer and a truthful recorder of the people and events in her life and that the polarized patterns she describes are not 'all in her mind.' The problem with first-person narration, though, is that it sometimes suggests more self-satisfaction and spitefulness on the part of the heroine than would be compatible with the reader's thorough sympathy. When the narrator's subject is others' recognition of her superiority to everyone around her, the advantages of first-person narration may be offset by a certain liability. In *Villette*, however, by suggesting that Lucy Snowe partly creates the patterns she observes, Brontë turns that liability into an asset.

In this bleaker version of the governess tale, there are signals that the categories into which Lucy is determined to slot others may be at least partly of her own making and that the way she sees the world may be locking her into a destructive position: that she may be creating for herself some of the problems she attributes to fate or to the malice and obtuseness of others. Specifically, I shall argue, there are signals that her intense investment in her own good taste may narrow her life unnecessarily and deny her the comfort and support that she might have had; that she is founding her identify on a set of responses that she might be well to move beyond. That these signals are, however, inconsistent and problematic makes *Villette* an endlessly ambiguous and fascinating text.

The actual word 'taste' is used in *Villette* more often than in any of the other novels. Lucy is as ready as Jane to observe with snide and even brutal distaste the vulgarities of those she so narrowly observes. The contempt begins on her boat trip to the continent, where the stewardess – a completely minor character who serves no other function and who never reappears – is dismissed with a typical sneer, and where Ginevra Fanshawe in her dainty English toilette is used to show up the crassness of the Watsons. When Lucy arrives in Villette, her distaste for those around her reaches sometimes hysterical proportions. The Belgian pupils she has to deal with are as despicable as the ones William Crimsworth encountered, the other teachers serve chiefly as Lucy's foils, and the demonic Mme Walravens is the impersonation of hideous vulgarity. As many critics have pointed out, *Villette* is a text in which the semiotic systems used to ground stable subjectivity break down into contradiction. Foremost among these systems is the code of tastefulness in which Brontë continues to have such a stake.

In *Villette* the way the heroine is looked at becomes a central issue. Lucy Snowe may resist being put on display but she is also pained at being ignored. Though it makes sense to explain the surveillance she experiences in Foucauldian terms, less as a threat to than as the very condition of her subjectivity, I cannot agree with Shuttleworth that it is simply in resisting interpretation that Lucy confirms her own interiority. The real threat to Lucy's sense of herself is not surveillance but indifference – the threat posed by Dr John, who does not have much interest in looking at her at all and whose interpretive efforts, if wrongheaded, are also half-hearted – and it is against the threat of indifference that the Beck/Paul spy team is mobilized. In the rather gothic space in which Lucy finds herself, in this 'strange house, where no corner was sacred from intrusion, where not a tear could be shed, nor a thought pondered, but a spy was at hand to note and divine' (331), the heroine is subjected to increasingly extreme acts of surveillance, which evoke a polarized response. It is by demonizing Mme Beck and canonizing M. Paul that Brontë rationalizes Lucy's passion to be penetrated – the temptation to exhibitionism that has to be denied and repressed.

In *Villette* the observer figure is split into two and the mixed feelings of the narrator are sharply separated out. Mme Beck, whose 'system' of 'surveillance' and 'espionage' (99) make her worthy to be 'a first minister and a superintendent of police' (102), attracts Lucy's resentment exclusively, while M. Paul, 'this male spy' (331) who 'took it upon himself to place [her] under surveillance' (433), 'saw her ... noted her taste for seclusion, watched her well, long before' he even speaks to her (528), eventually evokes her adoration. In view of Lucy's two very different responses, it is worth noting that both observers are used, as the observers always are in these novels, to testify to the narrator's virtues: Mme Beck, 'a little puzzled' though she is by the 'caractère Anglais' (420), learns to respect Lucy's rectitude and to conclude that she does not require surveillance, while M. Paul, who in fact treats Lucy more punitively, recognizes something more significant and profound, the fiery integrity of her spirit. Their teamwork constitutes Lucy as the paradoxical subject Brontë is always struggling to construct: the self-effacing and modest yet utterly fascinating woman, too special to appeal to any but the most discriminating of men – and too special not to attract the venom of bad women.

In *Villette*, as in *The Professor* and *Jane Eyre*, the man the heroine loves observes the heroine, harasses her, instructs her, and enters her private space in a way that testifies to his recognition of her true distinction. The issue of her room is again made central, but the space she controls here is even more claustrophobic. While Frances has a couple of rooms and Jane a portfolio that is not opened except in her presence, Lucy until the very end of the novel has no room of her own at all: the sleeping chamber she must share with other mistresses is entered and even the containers she has been allotted for her meagre possessions are rifled by the two spies who are keeping her under their observation. Mme Beck's disconcertingly phallic keys expose the contents of her drawers to investigation (proving her rectitude). M. Paul's still more clearly phallic hand, described by Lucy as 'on intimate terms with my desk,' enters this unlocked space unopposed – 'raised and lowered the lid, ransacked and arranged the contents, almost as familiarly as my own' (495) – and leaves reading material (testifying to her intellectual distinction). Lucy apparently loathes Mme Beck's interventions, but she welcomes M. Paul's penetration. If Jane Eyre is enraged at her master's machinations, Lucy Snowe apparently is not: the more blatant the surveillance, the more acquiescent the penetrated heroine.

What is found within those vulnerable spaces is quite different from the inner riches represented by the production of Brontë's earlier heroines. When Jane's portfolio and Frances's apartment and essays are opened, there is something important to be discovered and interpreted, something that functions as positive evidence of the women's taste and imagination. When Mme Beck goes through Lucy's drawer, on the other hand, what she finds is – nothing: no evidence of illicit love, no impropriety. After observing her raid – for Lucy, too, is a spy – Lucy weeps, perhaps because she realizes that Mme Beck is jealous of her and is looking for evidence of a relationship with John Graham. There is no impropriety because there is no relationship. Lucy is vindicated, but her propriety turns out to be not so much a positive example of English virtue as a lack, a negation – evidence of emotional emptiness.

The other intruder finds a similar emptiness. When M. Paul enters Lucy's desk with that prying hand, he is presumably paying tribute to the power of her mind: he would not be leaving texts for her unless he believed her capable of appreciating them. Nevertheless, he gives rather than receives. The cultural offering is his, not hers: he enters a figuratively if not literally empty space, sowing seeds of intellectual development. The image of the phallic hand suggests, even as other signals in the text deny, that the heroine's literary culture depends on the seminal male intellect which fertilizes and shapes her mind. When M. Paul enters Lucy's personal space, in short, what we find there is merely what he has put there, a reflection of himself.

Lucy's text resists with all its rhetorical power the recognition of intellectual dependence, vehemently denying the paternity it implies. A particularly striking example of the narrator's strained rhetoric in this novel is her elaborately developed description of her own 'peculiar talent' (506), personified as the newborn baby (boy) that M. Paul adamantly refuses to foster. In the context of the intense relationship between teacher and pupil, the metaphor of childbirth would seem to identify the teacher as the putative father. Lucy's rhetoric, however, resolutely dodges the identification. When M. Paul repudiates the infant, Lucy's language suggests that he is refusing the role not of father but of midwife: 'He watched its struggle into life with a scowl,' she says; 'he held back his hand – perhaps said, 'Come on if you have strength,' but would not aid the birth' (506). Male roles multiply, but they exclude fatherhood. The brutality of a taskmaster, the obsession of a police detective, and the sadism of an interrogator combine with phallic penetration in the startling metaphors that characterize Lucy's intellectual development under M. Paul's eye:

> He watched tearlessly – ordeals that he exacted should be passed through – fearlessly. He followed footprints that ... were sometimes marked in blood – followed them grimly, holding the austerest police-watch over the pain-pressed pilgrim. And when at last he allowed a rest, before slumber might close the eyelids, he opened those same lids wide, with pitiless finger and thumb, and gazed deep through the pupil and the irids into the brain, into the heart, to search if Vanity, or Pride, or Falsehood ... was discoverable. (506–7)

On the one hand, these metaphors assert Lucy's radical individuality: though harassed and persecuted by M. Paul, her little talent pulls itself together and staggers doggedly forward on its own track, her tutor merely following tyrannically behind. On the other hand, the very violence of the master's resistance to this child – and of Lucy's resistance to the metaphor of paternity – suggests that he is indeed the father. While this bizarre passage makes a large claim for the vigour of Lucy's talent, it also suggests that this talent owes its very being to the father who has no interest in it. It is paradoxical that a passage as 'original' as anything Brontë ever wrote, a passage that only she could have conceived, expresses in the most strained and melodramatic terms her anxiety about the possibility of a personal voice.

The issue of originality returns later in more literal, straightforward ways. Evidently Lucy's writing is disturbingly accomplished and forceful. Not only impressed, as Rochester was by Jane's drawings, but actually dismayed by the vigour of her mind, M. Paul doubts that her work is hers. The conflict between the heroine and her master on this point is more heated and specific than in *Jane Eyre*. M. Paul directly accuses Lucy not only of trespassing 'the limits proper to my sex' and of having 'conceived a contraband appetite for unfeminine knowledge' (508) but specifically of committing 'the most far-fetched imitations and impossible plagiarisms' (509) from abstruse texts that she would not even be capable of reading.

His outrage might be variously interpreted. We might conclude that Lucy's work is unusual and distinguished indeed; or that M. Paul, anxious about losing control over her, is neurotically deluded about its power; or somewhere between – that she is fairly talented and he only somewhat deluded. But the weight of the text as a whole seems behind the first interpretation. If we were to read M. Paul's comically violent reaction, which Lucy herself treats with dismissive humour, as testifying primarily to his feelings about her as opposed to the actual quality of her work, what becomes of the structure so carefully erected to imply the distinction of that work? The power of the very novel we are reading presumably testifies to that distinction, as its disconcerting originality does to the narrator's integrity. M. Paul is quite wrong about Lucy's indebtedness, but his error is a tribute to the masculine vigour of his pupil's original mind. His skepticism, though insulting, is also a compliment – a compliment that, characteristically, the narrator refuses to acknowledge, even as she lays it before her reader. At the same time, the lengths Brontë has to go to in order to produce such a fraught and improbable scenario as the 'plagiarism trial' that follows testifies to her heroine's dependency on male response.

The question of originality is raised yet more emphatically when M. Paul is accused by his colleagues of writing Lucy's essays for her, and again it is resolved in a strangely ambiguous way. The essay in question is one into which Lucy has put a huge amount of effort, one that she has researched painstakingly and written with care.[41] To prove that it is her own work, her master proposes to have Lucy write a new composition, under the scrutiny of her accusers. It is consistent with the pattern I have been tracing that when she begins to write, she finds herself producing, almost against her will, a portrait of Human Justice that condemns her accusers, whose rascality has expressed itself not only in their impiety towards M. Paul but in other forms of chicanery as well.

On the one hand Lucy has proven that she is indeed original, much more original than they had had in mind. Unlike the dutiful homily Charlotte Brontë had herself produced for Heger on the same subject – perhaps even in angry repudiation of it, and of him[42] – Lucy draws a gross and vulgar figure with a cynicism and satirical violence none of her tormenters could have expected. The portrait of Human Justice, because it is heartfelt and unexpected, even by Lucy, seems to be an expression of Lucy's 'real' self, her passion and anger, which flashes out to surprise all of them – an expression, indeed, of just the bitter, angry, satirical self the reader has come to know in the novel as a whole. Harassed into unwonted vehemence, Lucy speaks out for once with a passion adequate to her pain and outrage.

On the other hand, the 'originality' of this effusion is problematic. What Lucy finds she has written has not been generated from the fullness of her sympathetic imagination, as Frances's essay seemed to be, but from rage and pain. It speaks not of transcendence, but rather, in its vision of a Justice who distributes 'sugar plums' to the influential and crushes the poor and weak, of subjection to an unjust social order. Most important, it takes its origin not from Lucy's whole self, certainly not from her 'best self,' but rather from the challenge of the other who confronts her and evokes an almost uncontrolled response. It is not an action but a reaction: Lucy's reaction to her fictional tormenters, Brontë's perhaps to Heger himself. The demonic female figure Lucy constructs is intended as a mirror in which her enemies are expected to recognize themselves, a parodic personification of the men who have impugned the integrity of her master. But the more outrageous injustice has been committed by that master himself, who has erased Lucy from the situation, taken his colleagues' challenge as an affront not to her but to himself, and insisted that she redeem *his* honour. Since M. Paul has been as unjust to Lucy as they have been to him, Lucy's caricature is a portrait of him as well. Like Jane Eyre, who finds herself 'sketching a face' and does 'not care or know' (292) whose face it is going to turn out to be, Lucy, in a much more violent and conflicted way, finds herself, to her own surprise, producing an image, albeit a grotesque and parodic image, of the man she loves. Again there is a sense in which what is 'in' Lucy is merely a reflection of M. Paul – her 'originality' merely a response to his provocation.

Lucy is not of course literally a plagiarist, but even as she vehemently denies the accusation, the mirroring imagery covertly suggests that she owes her intellectual and emotional energy to men and her subjectivity to those whose gaze makes her their object. In this novel, which in part owes not only its narrative to Brontë's relationship with Heger but also the mannered quality of its prose to the models Heger had Brontë study, the originality of the heroine's mind is put in question in a way that exposes the latent anxiety in the earlier texts. When Lucy's private space is opened, there is no transcendence, no opening out into a wider realm, but instead, emptiness, constriction, encirclement, harassment, radical dependency. *Villette* is a claustrophobic text in every way: Lucy is not merely caught in architectural spaces that threaten her, she is defined by cultural voices that possess and inhabit her prose. Brontë has as large an investment in individual genius as in good taste, but her own novels, strikingly idiosyncratic though they are, systematically deconstruct the notion of individuality, even as they continue to embody it in their own startling and by no means always tasteful narratives.

The individual self is not wholly responsible for its own productions; neither can it be securely defined in terms of difference from others. In

*Villette* there is the same attempt we have seen in the earlier novels to ground the character of the protagonist in her difference from other female characters, but this time the categories cannot be kept in place and the boundaries cannot be made secure. The Adèle figure from *Jane Eyre*, the charming doll-like child, reappears here in Paulina Mary, who however has real not meretricious charm and a tasteful wardrobe instead of vulgar French flummery, and it is made much clearer that the motive for the heroine's condescension to this child is jealousy.[43] The coquette figure, too, is more fully developed in Ginevra Fanshawe than in Georgiana Reed or Blanche Ingram. She is just as rigorously differentiated from the heroine – the moment when Ginevra poses them both in front of the mirror is a bizarre rerun of the dual-portrait episode in *Jane Eyre* – but the polarities, though repeatedly underlined, are more ambiguous and unstable. Lucy rather approves of Ginevra when she first spots her on the boat to Belgium in a 'costume plain to quakerism' – a 'simple print dress, untrimmed straw-bonnet,' and 'gracefully worn' shawl (71); she sees her initially as decidedly superior to the vulgar 'Watson-group' (73): the pretty women dressed 'richly, gaily, and absurdly out of character for the circumstances' (71) and the 'plain, fat ... vulgar,' greasy men (71). Ginevra's snobbish dismissal of this group ('those odious men and women,' who, she says, 'should be steerage passengers' [73]), though it reveals a spiteful and unfeeling nature beneath the pretty surface, also aligns her with Lucy, who has just characterized Ginevra herself by contrasting her to them. Ginevra's simple print dress however is soon abandoned for the kind of finery always worn by the heroine's rival. Ginevra in satin is a different woman, according to Lucy, from Ginevra in a straw bonnet; yet both Ginevras talk very much alike. Lucy despises Ginevra, but whether Ginevra feels the same animosity towards her is open to question. Her malice towards Lucy seems to be the flip side of her dependence on her: she sometimes seems to care more for Lucy than Lucy, who favours her in some ways, does for her. Ginevra is in the end less easily dismissed than a Georgiana or a Blanche Ingram, less securely positioned as merely the antithesis of the modest, sober, put-upon narrator.

As the issue of Ginevra's toilette implies, differentiation by means of dress is itself problematic. Again, the heroine is dim, demure, and modest in her attire, particularly in comparison with the colourful, glamorous women against whom she defines herself; again, as in *Jane Eyre*, others want to change the way she dresses, and she resists. But there are differences – differences that finally destabilize the whole signifying system.

The problem is the possibility of duplication. How can Proper-Lady taste continue to 'tell' as an index of moral character if improper ladies don it at will? In *Villette* it becomes clear that 'good taste' is merely a social code, which can be appropriated and exploited by the canny individual who has none of the moral qualities to which it ought to point, and which can lead to impersonation, disguise, and deception. Mlle Reuter, for example, Frances Henri's rival and persecutor in *The Professor*, dresses very much like Frances herself, in 'a neat, simple, mousseline-laine gown [that] fitted her compact, round shape to perfection – delicate little collar and manchettes of lace, trim Parisian brodequins [that] showed her neck, wrists and feet to complete advantage' (83). In *The Professor* nothing is made of this similarity: William Crimsworth, who at first finds Zoraïde attractive, simply learns to distinguish the real heroine from her demonic double. In *Villette*, though, there is not just one look-alike but a flurry of doubles, which proliferate until the whole system breaks down. The key of taste, it turns out, opens into a hall of mirrors, where nothing is what it seems and where the heroine's difference from those she detests or despises cannot be maintained.

It begins when Lucy receives a letter addressed 'Pour la robe grise' and realizes that it could be intended for almost anyone in the *pensionnat*: that while she herself 'wore indeed a dress of French gray' (154), 'Madame Beck herself ordinarily wore a gray dress just now; another teacher, and three of the pensionnaires, had had gray dresses purchased of the same shade and fabric as mine' (156); that even Rosine, who happens at this point to glance through the open door, is wearing a dress 'gray, like mine' (158). To preserve the mystery of the affair between de Hamal and Ginevra, Brontë has Lucy omit to mention the woman for whom the letter is in fact intended, but it turns out that de Hamal has mistaken Lucy for Ginevra on this occasion, while on another he apparently mistakes Mme Beck for Lucy. In the literal sense, not only Lucy but almost all of the other women in the *pensionnat* are in fact grisettes.

The word 'grisette,' as applied to a continental working girl, is a metonymy: grisette was a fabric chosen by such women because it was cheap, and Lucy's observation that 'it was a sort of every-day wear which happened at that time to be in vogue' (156) suggests that price has been a factor in their choice as well. Lucy, however, would certainly not be willing to call herself a grisette, a boundary figure who combines the appearance of modesty and trim elegance with sexual availability. When Lucy uses the term it is with the full pejorative connotation. She has always distinguished herself contemptuously from 'smart, trim and pert'

Rosine, 'eyeing Dr. John' with 'a hand in each pocket of her gay grisette apron' (169) and is understandably dismayed when she suspects that it may be Rosine whom John Graham loves. It does not turn out to be, of course: it is reassuring for Lucy to find, as we already suspect, that he is not at all interested in the little grisette. It is not quite so reassuring, though, to realize that he could not be attracted to any grisette at all and that, had he met Paulina herself 'in simple attire, a dependent worker, a demi-grisette, he would have thought her a pretty little creature' (536) but would not have fallen in love with her. The class of grisettes to whom John Graham is indifferent includes, alas, Lucy herself. Her realization about his feelings for Paulina suggests the pathos and futility of taste without wealth or beauty. What a man like John Graham wants is not just demure modesty but demure modesty accompanied by glamour, charm, family position, and money. The little grey dress, it turns out, simply because it *is* a badge of restrained middle-class taste, is no way to capture such a man's attention and win his heart. In this plot line at least, *Villette* marks the failure of the project that has shaped Brontë's heroines from the beginning: the project of parlaying good taste into sex appeal.

Yet though her narrative registers Lucy's connection with the other grisettes, she continues to insist on her distinction from them, making a pathetic issue out of the elegant fit of the grey dress she has chosen for the day of the fête – 'My *tailleuse* had kindly made it as well as she could: because, as she judiciously observed, it was 'si triste – si peu voyant,' care in the fashion was the more imperative' (183) – and of the exact shade of grey she has carefully selected, 'purple-gray – the colour ... of dun mist, lying on a moor in bloom' (182–3).[44] The metaphor is precise and even ardent, testifying to her own subtle tastes, her feeling for natural beauty, indeed her feeling for language. The aim of Lucy's self-constructions is always to distinguish herself: from the insentient by her nuanced language, from the young and frivolous by her quiet garb. But only the reader has access to this verbal description, and Lucy's costume, though indeed differentiating her from the pupils, immediately identifies her with Mme Beck, whose 'dress was almost as quiet as mine' (183) and who glances approvingly at her as she passes her on the stairs. No matter how refined her sense of colour, how precise her language, Lucy cannot draw herself to the attention of the others in her world by dressing in grey of whatever subtle shade or cut. Her system of polarities has not confirmed her individuality: on the contrary, it has become a duplicating machine that she cannot shut off. In her own semiotic universe Lucy suddenly finds nothing but mirror images and the haunting suspicion that she has become a generic figure, a little grisette-doll without even the grisette's sexual charm. The haunting becomes literal in the person of the supposed ghost who frequents the Pensionnat Beck.

The figure behind the grisette is the nun, whose black-and-white costume is similar to the Quaker or Puritan toilettes of the Brontë heroine and her many doubles but who has to be rigorously differentiated from her – demonized, disfigured, and rejected – so that what they have in common will not too tactlessly draw itself to attention. The nun in *Villette* has been read in many ways,[45] but in the context of the sartorial theme in the novel what is intriguing is that 'she' is primarily a set of clothes, a black-and-white habit that, repulsive though it always is to Brontë's narrators, nevertheless invites comparison with the sober costumes of which they always approve: the costumes of Rochester's 'little nonnette,' Jane (160), or of M. Paul's 'little English Puritan,' Lucy (713).

Women who look like nuns are piquantly appealing to the men in these novels – it is because of 'their dark nun-like robes and softly braided hair' that William Crimsworth can imagine from a distance that Mlle Reuter's young ladies are 'half-angels' (85) – but real nuns, we are invited to believe, are repulsively ugly. Expecting, when he is summoned to meet Mlle Reuter, 'a tall, meagre, yellow, conventual image in black, with a close white cap, bandaged under the chin like a nun's head-gear,' Crimsworth is disconcerted to find instead a pretty bare-headed young woman whose 'nut-brown' hair is worn 'in curls' (79). The distinguishing – and disfiguring – mark of the nun is the 'bandaged' head: the shorn hair apparently is a kind of wound. Yet the polarities tend to collapse, the categories to slide together. It is not only Catholics, after all, who cut off women's hair: the Calvinist Brocklehurst in *Jane Eyre* brutally orders the shearing of Julia Severn's curly locks. And it is not only nuns who bind the head: Frances Henri has a constricted coiffure, as do Jane and Lucy. This heroine's hair, though not cut or covered, is as restrained and tightly bound as her trimly fitting garments, and like those garments it is a positive sign of her good taste, modesty, and self-control.

Self-control, apparently, is the crucial mark of difference. English Protestant young ladies control themselves, while Catholics, Brontë's narrators point out, are alternately indulged and repressed by others.[46] The nun is a figure of horror in these novels because the sexual repression internalized by the Proper Lady and decorously signalled in her toilette is imposed on the nun from outside by a sinister institution and given a uniform. Brontë's narrators want to insist that the nun's habit, devised and imposed by others, repels, while the heroine's costume, the badge of her individual taste, attracts. But they protest too much. The Proper Lady is not, apparently, as attractive as she might wish; the nun, on the other hand, may be much more attractive than the Proper Lady would like to believe. As Brontë's exploitation of the gothic genre itself reminds us, the nun, precisely because she evokes a sado-masochistic *frisson* that the 'bondage' of Protestant costume would deny, is a figure of sinister glamour, a figure around whom erotic fantasy can play. The nun in *Villette* fascinates, rivets the astonished gaze: she represents the point at which modesty becomes mystery, fixes the attention, demands penetration. It is the nun who, in her mystery and inaccessibility, invites the gaze that Lucy both longs and fears to have directed at herself.

The 'nonnette' and the 'grisette' are in fact similarly constructed. While the gap between the sober dress and the young body suggests the potential for transgressive energy, the diminutive ('-ette') suggests the subordination of that energy to the use and pleasure of the man who thus characterizes her. The nun, the grisette, and the Proper Lady are all male constructions, and if they titillate the masculine imagination it is because their modest demeanour implies passion that asks to be discerned and exploited even as it needs to be regulated and suppressed. The imagination is piqued by the contrast between modesty and nubility, as Rochester's is by the demeanour of his 'little nonnette,' whose latent exoticism he fantasizes unleashing into purple satin. But the Proper Lady's modest grey garb, however desperately individualized, is all too easy for a man to ignore, while the nun's habit, which erases her individuality completely in a stark, polarized icon of Proper Lady repression, whets fantasy and desire.

Brontë evokes such fantasies only to funnel them into an anticlimactic subplot that she attributes to de Hamal. Lucy's nun, it turns out, though suspected even by Lucy herself to be a figment of her own disordered brain, was not 'in' Lucy's mind after all but in de Hamal's. But it is just because de Hamal's plot was not aimed at Lucy – because she is not the sort of person with whom lively young men tend to arrange assignations – that the nun is relevant to her story. The dream of elopement with a dashing hero has to be denied and displaced (by making Ginevra a selfish flirt, de Hamal a little ass, and the nun a cheap trick) so that it shall not seem to belong to Lucy, so that it shall not, any more than the nun herself, be found 'in' her own imagination. Taken in and then let down by the mystery, the reader may feel that the cheap trick is not so much de Hamal's as the author's own. But the nun is an image Brontë seems unable to let go of. Even at the very end of the novel, well after de

Hamal's charade has been revealed and the disguise discarded, the pretty nonette insists on slipping back into the text, in the form of that 'Justine Marie' M. Paul is said to have loved so sincerely, albeit so long ago.

It is characteristic of the blurred and muffled way in which the figure of the nun is treated that surprisingly little is made of the revelation of M. Paul's first love. Once Lucy knows that the first Justine Marie is safely dead, she evidently dismisses her from her mind, and her attention shifts to the current Justine Marie, whom she fears M. Paul may now be planning to marry. This young woman is no nonette but the very opposite: a bouncy, round-cheeked 'bourgeoise belle,' 'well-nourished, fair, and fat of flesh,' 'good-humoured, buxom, and blooming' (672) – a decent but commonplace young lady, quite lacking in spiritual distinction, who can be no real rival to the narrator. Doubles proliferate to the last pages of the novel: this flesh/spirit duo, this Justine Marie × 2, is the final and the frankest avatar of a composite being earlier incarnated in Eliza and Georgiana Reed, Helen Burns and Mary Ann Wilson, and, in vestigial form, in the names of Diana and Mary Rivers. When Lucy has to steer as it were between two Justine Maries, the nun and the bourgeoise, straight into the arms of the master and the home he has prepared for her – when she has to be defined, even in these last moments of her narrative, in terms of polarized figures both of whom she is *not like* – it is clear that an identity so desperately and compulsively founded on reiterated difference cannot have the originality and the uniqueness she so desperately wants to claim.

Justine Marie turns out of course not to be the rival Lucy fears: it is Lucy, not she, whom M. Paul loves, and it is for Lucy, not for her, that the tiny perfect home has been prepared. The topos of the woman's room returns in the Edenic daydream at the end of *Villette*, in the charming doll's house fitted out just to Lucy's taste and combining the shine and colour of Rochester's mansion with the miniature scale of Frances Henri's apartment. As Lucy and her benefactor tour the premises, we see the tiny parlour, its 'delicate walls ... tinged like a blush, its 'square of brilliant carpet' (700), its shining table, mirror, porcelain, its chiffonière with the 'crimson-silk door' (701), its 'three green flowerpots, each filled with a fine plant glowing in bloom' (604); we see the little kitchen, with its 'diminutive but commodious set of earthenware'; we see 'the six green and white dinner-plates; the four dishes, the cups and jugs to match' and the 'coffee service of china in the salon' (701) in which Lucy is presently invited to serve her lover chocolate. The idiom is that of the shelter magazine or the advertisement. Though the house tour includes a glimpse of the 'two pretty cabinets of sleeping rooms' on the second floor, this looks less like a marital home than like the conventional lady's room of fiction, functioning, just as such a room always does, as a sign of the taste of the woman who resides in it.

Yet though the room pays tribute to Lucy's taste and meets her desires exactly, it is not she who has shaped it. M. Paul has found the means to pay for the house and its contents and a way to help Lucy meet her rent, and M. Paul has apparently selected, with a nicety of discernment one might not have expected from an absent-minded literary scholar, the rug, the china, the plants, and furniture, down to the last tiny coffee cup. There is a sense in which Lucy, like Céline Varens, set up by Rochester in a Paris 'hotel' (173), is a kept woman. But, more important, she is a male construction. This is the space where Lucy's taste is to manifest itself, but in it we find nothing of hers at all: nothing but what her 'backer' has put there. Lucy takes as a sign of their complete compatibility the fact that his tastes jibes with hers, but the incongruity of his role as interior decorator makes too clear that he has been constructed for Lucy to suit his.

The suggestion is that it is M. Paul who has chosen all of these charming objects. Or could he have had some help? Justine Marie, we remember, has been in collusion with him all along in the love affair with Lucy and has heartily volunteered to give him all the help he wants, and the household arrangements do certainly suggest a woman's touch. The text does not, to be sure, invite such a conclusion: the ineffable tastefulness of the little house situates itself almost frankly in the realm of daydream. But it is impossible not to notice the ambiguity always attending any positive expression of the narrator's own taste in this novel. Her own productions repeatedly take their impress from the male imagination, while all the other women she is so anxious to exclude from her carefully constructed persona keep creeping back in around the edges.

It is in this little room where M. Paul and Lucy take their last supper, a luxurious pastoral snack, chocolate brewed in the little chocolate set, delicate 'rolls ... cherries and strawberries bedded in green leaves' (705). How has a Brontë heroine come to the point where she can feast on sweets with a clear conscience? How can the little Puritan delight in a meal that is nothing but dessert? Not only because she has earned a reward – not only because she has drunk her fill from the bitter cup of sorrow – but also, I would argue, because M. Paul has liberated her, in this respect at least, from the prison house of tastefulness and has provided a strategy by which the whole rigid and elaborate structure can be deconstructed.

Lucy has always tended to read food the way she reads clothing, as a sign: to allegorize it, to moralize it. Sometimes her language is frankly figurative: she calls her emotional neediness 'the cravings of a most deadly famine' (221) and generates elaborate metaphors for the means by which this hunger will be satisfied. John Graham's letters are 'the wild savoury mess of the hunter' (342), a 'sweet bubble – of real honey-dew' (350), M. Paul's the 'real food that nourished, living water that refreshed' (713).[47] But she tends to be equally allegorical about real food. Those who love sweets and gorge themselves on starch and treats are characterized as both vulgar and morally suspect. Well-fed Belgians are despised, Mme Beck's greedy pupils sneered at. Though Lucy cannot help admitting that providing growing schoolgirls with a healthy diet is a method that 'many an austere English school-mistress would do vastly well to imitate' (90), the admission inevitably generates a snide corollary about Catholic sensuality: 'the CHURCH strove to bring up her children robust in body, feeble in soul, fat, ruddy, hale, joyous, ignorant, unthinking, unquestioning. "Eat, drink, and live!" she says. "Look after your bodies; leave your souls to me"' (177).[48]

Lovers of food are slaves to sensuality if not depravity – lovers of sweet food, trivial and light-minded as well. Even Paulina does not escape Lucy's implied censure: Paulina who is attracted to the mulled ale because 'it smells of spice and sugar' (404) but is repelled to find it 'anything but sweet; it is bitter and hot' (404) (Lucy herself characteristically prefers the stimulating black coffee of despair). But it is Ginevra Fanshawe whose sweet tooth lays her open to Lucy's most relentless allegorizing. With no capacity for 'work or suffering,' Ginevra has no taste for 'ordinary diet and plain beverage,' but greedily feeds instead upon pleasure, 'on creams and ices like a humming-bird on honey-paste: sweet wine was her element and sweet cake her daily bread' (198). When Ginevra asks Lucy what she thinks of de Hamal, Lucy is able to sneer at her taste in men as well as in food in a simile she knows will be misunderstood: 'As I like sweets, and jams, and comfits, and conservatory flowers,' she said, smugly confiding to the reader, 'Ginevra admired my taste, for all these things were her adoration' (205). It is hard not to be repelled by the sterility and self-righteousness of this response, hard not to feel that Lucy has missed a chance early on in the relationship to speak to Ginevra kindly and seriously about the dangers of her situation.

That is, if they are dangers: Ginevra's marriage is happy enough, apparently, and she herself is one of those survivors who has learned to negotiate the patriarchal system with a finesse the Brontë heroine never acquires. It is no doubt because Ginevra, like Paulina, is one of the lucky ones that Lucy finds it necessary to condemn in such heavily moralized terms even her most superficial preferences.

The allegorizing habit, however, hurts Lucy more than it hurts the people she judges, who remain oblivious to her condemnation. Repudiating the tastes of those one despises may leave little to savour, particularly if one despises almost everybody. The narrative voice of *Villette* makes it increasingly clear the link between 'good taste' and the refusal of pleasure. It is M. Paul who offers Lucy an escape from this habit of ascetic allegorizing, his fusion of bossiness and indulgence that releases her into sweetness. He does it by literalizing the polarized metaphors she uses to make sense of experience.

M. Paul's first intervention is grossly material. On the afternoon of the school play, he starves Lucy, then with amazing intuition – 'How he guessed that I should like a *petit pâté à la crème* I cannot tell' (190) – stuffs her with 'small *pâtés à la crème*, than which nothing in the whole range of cookery seemed to me better' (189), 'almost forc[ing] upon me more than I could swallow' (191). Though in one sense the dainty food is the payoff, the reward Lucy gets for doing her task so diligently and the compensation she gets for missing her lunch, in another sense it is the very missing of the lunch that constitutes the delightful transgression: she gets what every child wants, dessert without having to finish her meal. By his starve-and-treat routine M. Paul metaphorically wipes the slate clean, allowing Lucy to start over as a child who can begin to grow and develop. By literalizing her emotional hunger, he allows her to begin to escape from it: to experience, with senses sharpened by abstinence, the simplest physical pleasure and eventually to accept the emotional nourishment he gives her as well.

It is in this shift from figurative to literal that M. Paul's liberating power lies. The Brontë heroine cannot escape from her miserable judgmentalness as long as she insists on reading every bonbon, sandwich and cup of tea, every collar, cuff, and hair ornament, as a profound sign, a kind of moral litmus test. It is paradoxically just because M. Paul is not unwilling to use the kind of moralized metaphors so congenial to Lucy – because he is able to compare her longed-for letter, for example, to 'a peach whose bloom was very ripe' (346) – that she can eventually allow him to treat her like a spoiled child.

The turning point is the debate between them when M. Paul finds Lucy in despair at John Graham's desertion. Observing what he calls her 'mutinous' (331) demeanour, he accuses her of being 'one who would snatch at a draught of sweet poison, and spurn wholesome bitters with disgust' (332). Although Lucy resents his interference, they speak the same language, and his metaphors are congenial to her. 'I never liked bitters,' she retorts, 'and to whatever is sweet ... you cannot, at least, deny its own delicious quality – sweetness' (332). Their use of figurative language liberates Lucy to formulate a defence of sweetness as a good in itself, a defence one feels she could never allow herself to voice were she referring to jam or bonbons. Lucy does not in fact contest M. Paul's diagnosis. She does not deny that the sweet poison she is imbibing is unwholesome and might kill her: 'Better, perhaps,' she says defiantly, 'to die quickly a pleasant death, than drag on long a charmless life' (332). The debate about sweet poison and bitter medicine, based as it is on two polarized pairs, medicine/poison and bitter/sweet, has opened a space for the category that is missing – sweet medicine – a space that allows M. Paul to supply it and to begin to cure Lucy's anorexic aesthetic.

M. Paul is able to move Lucy beyond her relentless polarizing of flesh and spirit, perhaps because his readiness to insist on the claims of the spirit co-exists cheerfully with his own capacity for bodily enjoyment. There is no contradiction in his mind between nagging Lucy to abjure the sweet poison of grief and feeding her on chocolates and bonbons, and his very ability to use the kind of metaphor so congenial to Lucy enables her both to formulate a defence of sweetness and to trust him when he offers it to her. A man who can talk like this about moral polarities, Lucy may feel, can be allowed to feed you candy: a man with this kind of soul can be trusted with your body. Before long she will be fetching him unforbidden fruit, apples baked with 'a little spice, sugar, and a glass or two of vin blanc' (514), and sharing them with him.

In learning to cater to his tastes, Lucy has not however abandoned her own critical standards. M. Paul likes bright, cheerful colours, sweet, simple food, and sentimental moralized pictures, and she recognizes that his taste is somewhat childish, 'southern, and what we think infantine' (501). Indeed, she initially takes a stance of amused condescension to him not only because he is short, fiery, and eccentric but also on the usual grounds that his taste is inferior to hers. But she eventually comes to realize that this childish taste is accompanied by kindness, passion, and intelligence, and that it is possible to accept from his hand the bonbons of uncomplicated delight, even perhaps to free herself from her addiction to the hot bitter draught of resentment and despair. Eventually she will be able to take the sweet tributes her lover offers and to use them to assert herself against him. When Lucy coolly stonewalls M. Paul's catechism about the Catholic propaganda he has put in her desk while solacing herself 'with the contents of a bonbonnière, which M. Emanuel's gifts kept well supplied with chocolate comfits' (604), her act has metaphoric force. She will allow M. Paul to delight her palate with chocolate; she will not allow him to stuff her mind with propaganda, for that way, she believes, lies spiritual starvation. By offering her both, he has enabled her to make a more nuanced, less hysterical distinction between them, so that she is free both to enjoy real food and coolly to resist dubious ideas. Indeed, M. Paul, who is a maternal as well as a paternal figure, becomes increasingly a provider of food in the last hundred pages of the novel, treating not only Lucy but all the pension's young ladies to 'a huge basket of rolls ... Coffee and chocolate ... cream and new-laid eggs' (552) during their rural outing. By the time she is consuming chocolate from her own little chocolate set in her own little chocolate box of a *maisonnette*, Lucy has accommodated the childish to the pastoral and begun to erect a more cheerful aesthetic paradigm.[49]

I have constructed a narrative of progress, but the text will not allow it to stand. Despite her altered taste for pleasurable foods, Lucy nevertheless continues to despise 'fat women' (371) who overeat. Though the chronology might suggest that her intense distaste for greedy pupils like Mathilde and Angélique – whose consumption of 'household bread, butter, and stewed fruit ... at "second déjeuner"' she characterizes as 'a real world's wonder' (306) – antedates her own access to bonbons, there is nothing to suggest that it ends when she begins to get fed. Indeed, the technique of retrospective narration allows Lucy as it were to have her cake and eat it too: to leave her contempt for food on record even as she seems to have moved beyond it. Certainly her judgment of the 'slug' Cleopatra, that 'pulpy mass' (371) of flesh, which occurs after the cream puffs but before the bonbons, records a revulsion for greedy eating that nothing she says elsewhere in the text serves to qualify.[50] This oscillation, ironizing or at least destabilizing the narrative of progress, is indeed a subversion of narrative itself, which strives towards cure and closure, and of the subjective coherence that narrative struggles to erect.[51] To escape from the prison that a lifetime of thwarted desire has made of the soul takes more than M. Paul can give, even if he returns from his voyage to give it. There is a sense in which the ending of the novel, however ambiguous, is irrelevant. The self-subverting patterns of

Lucy's narrative have already dramatized that in life there are no end-ings, happy or otherwise.

Unlike Frances and Jane, Lucy is a critic as well as a practitioner of the arts, and her distaste for fat ladies shapes not only her social feelings but also her more narrowly aesthetic judgments. Her intense response to the painting of Cleopatra as well as to the performance of the unnamed actress who plays Vashti have been the object of much critical discus-sion.[52] Both figures are commanding presences, heroic in scale, involved in a kind of self-display that scandalizes Lucy, and though they are antithetically related to one another as flesh and spirit – Cleopatra as consumer of food that sustains the body, Vashti as consumed by the passion that erodes it – they are in different ways greedy for life, which they grasp with a single-mindedness that eludes the diffident and depressive narrator. It is pretty clear that Lucy recoils with fascinated horror at what she considers the bad taste of both women because they represent what she desires. What she needs to believe is that the men she desires recoil too.

Though irritated at the notion that she, a freeborn Englishwoman, should not be allowed to look at the painting, Lucy is gratified to find that both M. Paul and John Graham share her distaste for Cleopatra, and that John Graham is as repelled as she by Vashti's performance.[53] She seems to hope not only that their revulsion is a bond between her and John Graham but that, repudiating Vashti and Cleopatra, he might be likely to embrace Lucy, who sees herself as their polar opposite. But the binary does not work out so neatly. Distaste for Cleopatra and Vashti does not mean desire for Lucy. The problem is that though she is the complete antithesis of these women, she is not the only antithesis: John Graham, alas, contrasts Cleopatra not with hopeful Lucy but with his mother and Ginevra. His response exposes the fallacy of polarizing par-adigms. There are more ways than one of not being Cleopatra, and as long as Lucy tries to find a place for herself in terms of such oppositions she is likely to find that someone else has got there first.

When M. Paul reinforces Lucy's moral polarities instead of cheerfully ignoring them, he goads Lucy into taking a sensible middle position. Lucy loathes the painting of Cleopatra, but she is not going let him order her to look at pictures of Catholic womanhood instead. When M. Paul plants her before them, her own more sophisticated taste in art apparently comes to her aid. However Lucy may dislike Rubenesque women, she knows the difference between what the world has agreed to call high art and mediocre genre painting, and she is able to resist her teacher's bullying on aesthetic as well as political grounds. Her resistance to M. Paul's authority on this occasion can be read as a hopeful omen of their future relationship in which Lucy will be allowed a real degree of autonomy, particularly from Catholic categories and practices (M. Paul will in fact eventually give up trying to convert her).[54]

Yet this is a somewhat illusory victory, for Lucy's resistance on this occasion is not as liberating as the rhythm of the scene seems to imply. M. Paul's demand only confirms the pattern of self-suppression in which Lucy is already caught. Lucy herself has already repudiated, with a violence he himself would be hard put to equal, what Cleopatra represents and already constructed herself as its very opposite: a modest, patient, stoical Proper Lady, albeit a Protestant one. She may talk back to M. Paul when he sits her down in front of the moralized pictures, but she will sit herself down and wait for him as patiently and faithfully as the little woman that is their subject. Though she has rejected its Catholic inflection, Lucy cannot reject the model of female piety and suffering he puts before her, and her sense that she has taken a stand on behalf of a specifically English Protestant identity is somewhat undercut by the parallel between the allegory of the pictures and the pattern her own life takes at the end of the novel.

The Catholic/Protestant polarity may be fundamental to Lucy's identity, but the spell of the Church cannot be so pertly thrown off. The very intensity of her animus against it, particularly at the end of the novel, testifies to its continuing power to induce anxiety. Lucy may be able to critique a set of sexist, vulgarly moralized pictures, but she is not immune to the grosser, more splendid vulgarities of Catholic imagery, whose power over her emotions is suggested by her overwrought representation of them. It is to Lucy's intense but in the last analysis ambiguous and conflicted response to the Catholic Church that I wish to turn at the end of this discussion.

The novel's faith in good taste may be shaken, but its horror of bad taste remains adamantly in place. Good taste may be relative, but vulgarity remains absolute, and the ultimate locus of truly bad taste in *Villette* is the institution of Catholicism itself. The Church is presented not only as obscurantist, authoritarian, sensual, and sinister – an evil parent spying on her children with a 'sleepless eye' (592) and a persistence that even Mme Beck cannot emulate – but as utterly vulgar as well. Catholic sentimentalism, we are asked to believe, leads to the kind of third-rate pictures M. Paul has insisted Lucy contemplate; Catholic schoolgirl piety is shaped by the lurid tales Mlle Reuter's pupils are fed at the *lecture pieuses*; Catholic sensuality is expressed in the gross bodies and empty souls of the pupils at the *pensionnat*; Catholic pomp, which unveils the 'painted and meretricious face' (610) of the Church in all its trashy decadence produces the 'flowers and tinsel,' 'wax-lights and embroidery' (611) of ritual and procession. Catholic repression of women generates the nun and her gothic torments. The nun in turn generates, by a process which by the end of the novel has no time to be anything more than automatic, the sinister Scarlet Women, Mme Walraven, who is developed in such graphic detail and then given so little to do that she seems less a real character than a production of the polarities of the text.

The terrible woman in bright-coloured clothing, the woman so consistently demonized in Brontë's novels, makes her final appearance at the end of *Villette* as the Whore of Babylon.[55] What are we to make of the 'witch-like' (666) Mme Walraven, bizarrely aged, so small and twisted that she is like 'a head severed from its trunk, and flung at random on a pile of rich merchandise' (665), yet 'adorned like a barbarian queen' in 'a gown of brocade' (563) 'bright as lapis-lazuli' (586), in golden rings and in jewels 'purple, green, and blood-red' (563), and placed inside a gothic mansion that never does yield the narrative thrills it seems to promise? To think in terms of a process of automatic reproduction or parody helps to explain the otherwise gratuitous elaboration of this enigmatic figure. Mme Walraven seems thrown up by the text to play Duessa to the nun's Una – a Una who herself is already an empty and demonic double. As tastelessly as Spenser himself and with the same anti-Catholic venom, Brontë characterizes the key figure in the 'junta' in visual terms that make her a more sinister and spectacular impersonation of the worldly power of the Church than the creepy little Archimago, Père Silas, who is her partner. The ghastly, dwarfish hag is all the garish, big-bodied rivals and oppressors of the Brontë heroine rolled up into one, then shrunk, squashed, and twisted out of shape. Though she never does anything in particular – other than fetching Desirée Beck a well-deserved rap with her gold-headed cane – she stands as a horrifying if empty sign of inscrutable evil. In the Catholic Church, the animus against gorgeous women that constructs the Brontë heroine has finally found an adequate metaphor, if not an adequate objective correlative.

By the end of the novel, luxury itself has been polarized: the sweet and colourful pleasures of Lucy's *maisonnette* established as innocent and tasteful, the Walraven mansion and colour and gold and jewels dismissed as both vulgar and unenviable. The good parent has manifested himself at last; the bad parent, too, has emerged from the shadows in the mysterious figure of Mme Walraven and been demonized and finally dismissed. The good parent permits pleasure, while the bad parent, it seems, has wealth and power but no pleasure to offer. The bad parent sends the good parent to his death on the high seas. Or was it the Heavenly Father, Lord of Storms, who willed that M. Paul should never return? Or did he come back after all? Brontë's 'little mystery' remains permanently enigmatic, but the flurry of puzzles at the end of the novel serves to distract our attention from an even more terrifying question.

The gratuitous violence of the portrait of Mme Walraven demands interpretation. Lucy's flight into the arms of Père Silas/solace, her Father Confessor, suggests the motive behind the overheated rhetoric. The narrator, if not Brontë herself, needs to demonize the Church because she desperately wants what it claims to offer. While Brontë's earlier protagonists managed without parents – Jane Eyre, by the sheer power of her desperation, calling up the parental figures she needed, Frances Henri somehow secure in herself under the aegis of Notre Dame des Neiges – Lucy Snowe, with no mother or father or lover, is bereft. What if, in her passionate repudiation of Catholicism, she has made a terrible mistake? What if behind the painted face of the Whore of Babylon is hidden the Madonna of the Snow, the loving mother? What if the Church does not, after all, feed the body and starve the soul, but, like Lucy's 'saint,' Paul, feed the body and soul at once? What if Lucy's relentlessly Protestant criteria of tastefulness have led her to reject the vulgar, sensual, delightful pleasures the Church offers her children – those spiritual bonbons and cream puffs that, like M. Paul's, just might prove to be nourishing as well?[56] Lucy needs to repress these suspicions by all the resources at her command, and she does it, in the end, by calling up an allegorical figure that has the authority of a canonical English Protestant poet as well as of the Bible behind it. The caricature she produces is nevertheless wholly personal, idiosyncratic – 'original' – for, though it draws on traditional imagery, it is fuelled not only by the fear and contempt the Brontë narrator has always felt for big and gorgeous and powerful women, but also perhaps by the complicated anxiety about originality and integrity instilled in Brontë by her Belgian experience.

In Brontë's governess novels, the heroine's good taste, which begins as a compensation for her lack of personal beauty, financial resources, and conventional pleasure, turns out instead to be a cause. Taken as a set, the novels suggest that the compensatory tastefulness in which Brontë apparently has such desperate stake may be a destructive delusion. An appetite for life cannot be displaced as efficiently as the more-taste-than-money-or-beauty formula would like to imply. The discourse of taste is used by these novels to rationalize the heroine's lack – the apparently necessary repression of her desires. But repression, though it heightens desire, may also actively block its satisfaction.[57] The defensive investment that the Brontë heroine has in her own good taste obliges her to resist the pleasures she is offered and even perhaps to dim the good looks she dares not imagine she might possess (there is the suggestion that Lucy in opera dress is more attractive than she can believe). Charlotte Brontë's novels are a passionate, anguished (and highly original) deconstruction of the compensatory fiction offered by the discourse of taste.

It is not necessary to know that Elizabeth Gaskell was Charlotte Brontë's biographer to realize that she admired these novels. A reader of *North and South* recognizes at once the Brontëan patterns that shape it. The love story between the passionate heroine Margaret Hale, who, though exceptional and unconventional, always remains an eminently tasteful 'lady,' and the rather Byronic romantic hero John Thornton, a Carlylean captain of industry, is conducted with all the conflictual fireworks that mark a Brontë romance. Gaskell is as invested as Brontë in the discourse of taste and uses it in some of the same ways. Not only does the heroine's good taste compensate for her modest material resources, it also serves to attract potential lovers, who 'read' Margaret's taste and are smitten by her unique excellence in just the Brontëan way.

Nevertheless Gaskell's social vision is very different from Brontë's. Gaskell mobilizes the discourse of taste more conventionally and less critically, with far less sense of its discursive instability than Brontë, and though it would be hard to say that she uses it to do more ideological work, she does apply it to a wider range of issues. Taking for granted the link between taste and judgment that was a staple of eighteenth-century aesthetic discourse, Gaskell suggests the tasteful lady's competence to address not only personal but also social, political, and economic problems. I shall argue in the following chapter that the notion of 'stately simplicity,' formulated early on to define Margaret Hale, is used to frame not only the novel's construction of female character but also Gaskell's handling of the labour issues she addresses. 'Simple' generic Christianity, 'simple' moral principles, 'simple' practical projects, and 'simple' manliness (and womanliness) are offered as an aestheticized way of dealing with – or of denying – the class conflict Gaskell is reluctant to acknowledge. It is a commonplace of criticism that the way the romantic and industrial plots are linked in *North and South* is unsuccessful, and I believe that part of the problem can be located in the discourse of taste that shapes almost every scene in the novel.

Somebody had to die to produce the tableau of tastefulness with which Elizabeth Gaskell introduces her heroine Margaret Hale. While Margaret's pretty cousin Edith Shaw, 'a spoiled child' (36) arrayed like Titania in blue and white and ribbons, snoozes on the sofa, Margaret has climbed up to 'the very top of the house' (38) to return 'laden' (39) with the heavy shawls acquired by Edith's deceased father, 'the General' (37), presumably in the course of his career in India. Now she stands 'right under the chandelier, quite silent and passive, while her aunt Shaw adjust[s] the draperies' (39), her 'tall, finely made figure, in the black silk dress,' setting off the 'brilliant colours' of the oriental textiles. Though the shawls, destined for Edith's trousseau, are expensive enough to evoke sighs of envy from the other girls' mothers, Margaret's pleasure in them is not materialistic but sensuous and aesthetic: she is described 'touch[ing] the shawls gently' and 'snuffing up their spicy Eastern smell' (39). Margaret evidently makes a striking picture.[1] In case we missed it, we are told that large shawls look much better on her statuesque frame than they would have done on her petite cousin, who will later admit that they make her resemble 'mamma's little dog Tiny with an elephant's trappings on' (299). But Margaret is apparently oblivious to her own attractiveness. Gaskell underlines the childlike simplicity of her response to the situation. All she feels is some amusement at being dressed up, 'enjoying it much as a child would do' (40), at the incongruity of seeing in the mirror her 'familiar features in the unusual garb of a princess' (39), and finally, when Henry Lennox is announced, at 'the ludicrousness at being thus surprised' (40) by him.

Henry of course is in love with Margaret. It is clear that he by no means finds her ludicrous; indeed, as she stands looking at him with an amused smile, he thinks she is wonderful. But it is essential, for Gaskell's purposes, that Margaret not realize this.[2] Her unselfconsciousness is signalled by her own purely conventional costume. Under the shawls she wears 'a black silk dress' donned, we are told, 'in mourning for some distant relative of her father's' (39) – a garment, displaying that 'finely made figure' to advantage, that apparently has the excellent fit Gaskell taught her own daughters to insist on.[3] We hear no more about this distant relative, who has lived and died solely to put the heroine into black silk for the introductory tableau: to balance Eastern ornament with English simplicity. The little vignette is so studiedly constructed to adumbrate Margaret's excellences that we are not asked to query whether she can have been dressed entirely in black throughout the 'whirlwind' (41) of prenuptial parties of which she complains to Henry a page later.

That complaint, along with Margaret's wistful vision of 'a calm and peaceful time just before' a wedding, gives Lennox the opportunity explicitly to name the quality that informs the construction of Gaskell's heroine: 'The idea of stately simplicity,' he says, 'accords well with your character' (42). The notion is then worked out in rather insistent detail. Chapter 2 ends with another 'scene' (44) marking the difference between Margaret and her cousin. After Edith, putting on a little 'gypsy-encampment' act to show her fiancé 'how well she should behave as a soldier's wife,' orders the big tea kettle from the kitchen, dirties her gown, bruises her hand, and goes 'like a hurt child' (45) to get a kiss from him, Margaret, with her 'speedily adjusted spirit lamp,' actually heats the water. Chapter 3 begins by emphasizing the difference between Margaret and her own mother, with a discussion of Mrs Hale's refusal to attend 'her only sister's only child's wedding' on the grounds that all she has to wear is 'a grey satin gown ... midway between oldness and newness' (46). Margaret's true simplicity of character is set against the affectation of Edith and the pride of Mrs Hale as her unselfconsciousness is set against their self-regard.[4] Margaret is simple in every good way: the plainness of her dress becomes aligned not only with a virginal naiveté that guarantees sexual purity but also with a whole range of other moral qualities.

The episode with the Indian shawls exemplifies Gaskell's neat solution to a perennial fictional problem. The heroine of a Victorian novel must not deliberately exhibit her own beauty. Margaret is displaying her cousin's shawls to her aunt's friends, not her own good looks to her potential suitor. By having Lennox arrive unexpectedly, Gaskell contrives to show off Margaret while insisting that she is not the kind of lady who shows off. The romance heroine must also dress with consummate taste but never spend a moment thinking about her appearance. It is not easy to put one's protagonist repeatedly into splendid garments without her collusion. Having other characters do it instead is a good way of solving the problem. We see Margaret arrayed in one elegant costume because her mother, too ill to attend Mrs Thornton's dinner party, wants to look at her in evening dress; in another, because Edith wants to show off her cousin at one of her elegant entertainments. This repeated scenario perhaps owes something to *Jane Eyre*, to Rochester's attempts to deck his beloved out in fine clothing, but the implications here are quite different. Jane must resist Rochester in order to preserve her emotional independence and self-respect, but Margaret, 'latent Vashti' (499) though she is, is under no compulsion to resist the women. Since it is an act of generosity, if not charity, for her to submit to their attentions, her acquiescence does not compromise her modesty. It is partly because the Indian shawls are not intended by either Margaret or her aunt to express Margaret's identity that the author can use them to do so.

Ornaments, likewise offered by others, complement the sartorial simplicity that expresses Margaret's own nature. The Indian shawls are rich, gorgeous, and fragrant with spices. Their exoticism serves both to complement the refined English beauty of the heroine and to suggest her capacity for erotic response – a capacity of which she is herself at this point unaware. This kind of incident, in which a basic costume, simple in line, restrained in colour, and chosen by Margaret herself, is completed by an ornamental accessory provided by someone else recurs several times in the novel. Margaret chooses white silk: it is her mother and Dixon who urge her to add coral jewellery, two 'large coral pins, like small arrows for length' to hold up the 'massive coils' of her hair and a necklace of 'heavy coral beads' nestling 'just below the base of her curved and milk-white throat' to give 'just the right touch of colour' (212) to her romantic pallor.[5] Margaret chooses a 'dead gold-coloured' gown: it is Edith, objecting to the 'horrid blue flowers' provided by Dixon ('What taste!' [520]), who supplies scarlet pomegranate blossoms. The offerings of others, warming up Margaret's cool image, also evoke exotic faraway places. Margaret is simple, single, one – Gaskell will invoke Spenser's Una – but her exemplary simplicity involves the perfect balance of opposites. Modest yet queenly, ready to serve but worthy to command, chaste yet sensuous, alert and aware yet quite unselfconscious, Margaret is deftly constructed out of the contradictions that the Victorian lady has to embody. It is appropriate, the poetics of the novel suggest, that the world's goods be laid at her feet. It is curious that in a novel about mass production and the textile industry, where a point is made of cheap offshore imports, this focus on the priceless handwork of India does not point to the conditions or practices of Indian – or for that matter English or Irish – labour but serves simply to construct an icon of British cultivation and entitlement.

Margaret needs to be tall and strong to carry off an Indian shawl, for the sheer weight and bulk of the garment tested a woman's posture and endurance. Shawls became larger and larger as their popularity peaked in the middle of the nineteenth century,[6] their size increasing to 'a square of about sixty-four inches in the 1840s,'[7] and to a rectangle six feet by four by the end of the decade. The result was that the 'correct management of the shawl, indoors and out,' became 'a test of social gentility.'[8] As an imperial product, made by hand, which inspired in Britain the invention of machines that could mass produce it, the Indian shawl potentially has both political and industrial implications. Bermingham observes that the freedom of the fashionable English-woman 'to consume the dress of other countries confirmed Britain's growing international economic and political power, and its proprietary interest in the far east.'[9] The popularity of these shawls was also a spur to British industry, and by the early nineteenth century imitation cashmere shawls were being manufactured by machine, particularly in the town of Paisley in Scotland, which gave them its name.

In fiction of the period, the genuine Indian shawl is consistently used to characterize wealthy, distinguished individuals of both sexes. Mary Beaufort in Jane Porter's *Thaddeus of Warsaw* (1803) wears one;[10] Clara Mowbray in Scott's *Saint Ronan's Well* (1824) appears in the 'splendour and grace of a rich oriental dress,' in a shawl her brother has secured for her;[11] Disraeli's Lady Monmouth wears 'a rich Indian shawl,' and Lord Valentine a morning robe made of shawls. In *Wives and Daughters*, Mrs Gibson owns an Indian shawl and Lady Cumnor wears one, as does a mature Elizabeth Gaskell in an often-reproduced photograph.[12] In the context of modern machine manufacture – a context evoked by *North and South*, where the manufacture of cheap textiles is the business of the romantic hero – the hand-made shawls of India would register as the 'real thing.'[13] So they do in *Saint Ronan's Well*, where a lady jealous of Clara Mowbray's splendid appearance suggests that an imitation would have done as well ('there are braw shawls made at Paisley, that ye will scarce ken fare foreign'), and Clara's defender, Mr Touchwood, spiritedly denies it ('Not to know Paisley shawls from Indian, madam ... why a blind man could tell by the slightest touch of his little finger').[14] Since such a shawl was a sign of conspicuous wealth and of sometimes oppressive or obnoxious social power, it is not surprising that Margaret is not the owner of the shawl in which she originally appears. Since it also connoted authenticity and entitlement, however, it is equally appropriate that the next shawl she turns up in is apparently her own. In both scenes, the plain, simple dress she wears under the gorgeous garment confirms her elegantly modest simplicity.

Margaret deserves to be offered material goods precisely because she does not covet them. The fact that the shawls are not hers but Edith's has been taken as marking her off from her cousin – as suggesting that she is not going to be the traditional heroine of romance.[15] Mark her off it does, but only to make clear from the outset that she will certainly be the heroine of this particular novel. Sartorial transformation (as in *Jane Eyre*, for example, or indeed *Cinderella*) is the mark of such a heroine; indeed, the unconventional heroine – the dark heroine who resists the ordinary domestic destiny – is herself a convention.[16] One aspect of Margaret's resistance is her sublime indifference to the worldly values of her cousin's household. The shawls that to Mrs Thornton and her friends testify to the family's wealth and status evoke no envy in Margaret. She is not 'untouched by their beauty':[17] on the contrary, she responds to pure beauty as the other women do not. But she has no desire to possess them. Taste has been spiritualized by the claim that it transcends mere ownership: one is supposed to be able to 'possess' the beauty of an object without possessing the object itself. For the truly tasteful, evidently, the best things in life really are free.[18] It is because Margaret is devoid equally of vanity and materialism that her author can show off her loveliness and that the other characters in the novel can compete to offer her material gifts. The merely symbolic nature of the gifts (Margaret does not receive the shawls) and their relative triviality (the accessories are of little financial value) do not undercut the emblem of entitlement that Gaskell is constructing. As a visual tableau, the scenario of the beautiful woman being decked out by other women evokes (for example) Cleopatra, to whom Margaret will later be compared, and identifies Gaskell's heroine as someone to whom tribute would be appropriate. The suggestion is that by not coveting things to which she alone is able to respond fully, Margaret earns them. The man who can respond correctly to her true value earns the right to provide her with them.

Gaskell originally called her novel *Margaret Hale*. The altered title, supplied by Dickens, makes clear that this is not only one woman's love story but also an analysis of the condition of England,[19] and the discourse of taste is used to articulate not only the femininity of the heroine but also Gaskell's vision of the relationship between the classes. The social position of all the major characters is carefully spelled out and eventually aligned with their attitudes to beauty, taste, and style. Margaret descends from the aristocratic Beresford family on her mother's side. Mrs Hale has come down in the world socially and financially, while her sister, Edith's mother, who married a wealthy older man, has prospered. But financial prosperity is not identical with cultural riches. On the contrary, Margaret's tastefulness is set against the vulgar prosperity of her London relatives. Both classes that have combined to produce the London branch of the family have apparently degenerated. Edith's mother transmitted the Beresford blood, while her deceased father, 'the General,' acquired the money. But both aristocratic dignity and imperialistic vigour have been sadly attenuated in his merely worldly wife and fashionable daughter. When the kind of energy that founded Indian fortunes degenerates into mere conspicuous consumption, as it does in Edith and her mother, the simpler, truer taste of the modest and cultivated middle class must be called upon to provide a corrective. It is Margaret, with her moral as well as physical stature, who can do justice to the Indian shawls her uncle has secured and who thus merits the spoils that Englishmen like him have taken from India. If the episode, suggesting as it does that English simplicity is needed to put Indian ornament into satisfying aesthetic relief, says something about the relationship between east and west, it also says something about the relationship between classes as English society itself shifts and changes. Margaret, a kind of Cinderella in the household of the late General, will choose as her husband a man whose ambition is to found a new kind of global empire. The vitality and refinement she exhibits against the backdrop provided by the Shaws suggests that she is marked out to succeed them.

Vitality is an important motif in *North and South*, as it is in the novels of Charlotte Brontë by which Gaskell was so clearly influenced.[20] Sheer energy and power – physical, sexual, financial – have a post-Romantic, Carlylean prestige here, and the contrasts between individuals as well as between classes are worked out in terms of this value. It is significant that Edith, who spends her time amusing herself, is first seen sleeping.[21] Her prospective brother-in-law, Henry Lennox, the plain, sardonic one who holds himself somewhat apart from a good-looking and frivolous family, makes a point of his own professionalized commitment to hard work, contrasting the 'ladies' business' of trying on shawls with 'my business – which is the real and true law business' (41). Henry apparently regards both his in-laws and Margaret's clerical family as elegant but ineffectual drones. His disingenuous compliment to the Hales – that 'twenty years' hard study of law would be amply rewarded by one year of such exquisite serene life' as they enjoy at Helstone, by 'such skies ... such crimson and amber foliage' (60) – though it is intended to flatter, nevertheless associates the aesthetic with the feminine and with the private life of retirement and opposes it to the real world of significant, masculine work in which he sees himself involved.

Gaskell too values earnest work, but she draws the lines rather differently, associating force and vitality with a lively capacity for aesthetic response instead of positing them as opposites. Margaret's physical vigour – her erect posture, her height, her readiness to run upstairs, and ability to carry (and carry off) the heavy shawls – is given an aesthetic inflection in the opening scene, and the association is confirmed when she leaves London and returns to the simplicity of pastoral Helstone. Here, Margaret's taste for nature is described in rather Brontëan terms that link the sensuous, almost sensual pleasure she takes in her rural rambles with her physical strength and energy. As usual, her excellences are developed by means of contrast with other, usually weaker, people who serve as her foils. Margaret tries to tempt her semi-invalid mother 'forth on to the beautiful, broad, upland, sun-streaked, cloud-shadowed common' (49), but Mrs Hale, demoralized and discontented, will hardly leave the house, and it is not surprising when her obsession with 'the unhealthiness of the place' (49) is translated into mortal illness. It is 'at her father's side,' with almost virile energy, that Margaret is accustomed 'to tramp along ... crushing down the fern with a cruel glee, as she felt it yield under her light foot, and send up a fragrance peculiar to it' (48). Her sensuous delight is assimilated to her capacity for social sympathy. If in her walks Margaret loves to feel herself in the company of a 'multitude of wild, free, living creatures' (48), she is equally at home with the common people of the forest and equally energetic in her response to them, caring for their children, reading to them, nursing them, planning to teach in the school.

The association between physical strength, aesthetic responsiveness, and desire to be of service to others is a useful one for Gaskell. In Milton, with her mother ill and their income reduced, Margaret's strength is needed for relatively menial tasks within the home. On the one hand, Gaskell wants to show her heroine rising magnificently to the occasion; on the other, she needs to protect Margaret's social status, even as she irons, clear-starches, and whips up coconut cakes for her visitors. The aestheticization of Margaret's physical energy from the beginning of the novel helps to preserve its cultural prestige even when it manifests itself in actual housework.[22] Both Margaret's physical hardiness and her feeling for beauty distinguish her sharply from the exhausted and damaged people who rely on her. In this novel, poor bodily health serves as an outward and visible sign of spiritual debility, whereas aesthetic sensibility is aligned not only with mental and physical health but also with social sympathy and good works.

To be sure, Gaskell allows us to see that Margaret, though she is sentimentally attached to Helstone, has not taken due account of the realities of southern agricultural work. When it is made clear that unfortunate people actually live in the ruinous cottages Margaret loves to sketch and that the commons, available to Margaret for Brontëan walks, is not available to the village people for food (the area is full of poachers), we realize that Helstone can seem to Margaret like 'a village in a poem' (42) only because she has read more Wordsworth and Tennyson than Crabbe, and that her response to nature needs to be complemented by a sharper awareness of economic realities.[23] It is only much later, when Margaret has to advise the Higginses against moving south, that she is able to articulate what she finds she knew all along: the real brutality of the farm labourer's existence. Yet Margaret's sentimentality about nature and the common people in the Helstone section of the novel is not allowed to undercut in a very radical way the value of her orientation to them. Rather, in the energy of that feeling lies the key to the correction of the sentimentality. Margaret's intense relish for nature and for beauty of all kinds testifies to a capacity for openness and human sympathy that will facilitate her social and political re-education when she meets the man whose forcefulness matches her own and who has the good taste to respond rightly to hers.

It is clear from the beginning that Henry Lennox is not that man. His urban sophistication and professional hustle are no substitute for the spiritual vitality Margaret deserves. Moreover, although, like virtually all the men in the novel, he ardently admires Margaret, his taste in other respects is subtly faulty. To display its limitations, as well as to give us a glimpse of Margaret's Helstone home, Gaskell has Lennox decide to pay Margaret an impromptu visit on his way back from a Scottish holiday. His arrival, which catches the family by surprise, allows us to see the drawing room as it ordinarily is, in what Veblen would call its 'backstage' state, not specially arranged for the eye of the visitor. Margaret admits Lennox but, startled and disconcerted, leaves him alone for a moment, just long enough for him to 'read' the scene and for us to read his reading of it:

> When she had left the room, he began in his scrutinizing way to look about him. The little drawing-room was looking its best in the streaming light of the morning sun. The middle window in the bow was opened, and clustering roses and the scarlet honeysuckle came peeping round the corner; the small lawn was gorgeous with verbenas and geraniums of all bright colours. But the very brightness outside made the colours within seem poor and faded. The carpet was far from new; the chintz had been often washed; the whole apartment was smaller and shabbier than he had expected, as background and frame-work for Margaret, herself so queenly. He took up one of the books lying on the table; it was the *Paradiso* of Dante, in the proper old Italian binding of white vellum and gold; by it lay a dictionary, and some words copied out in Margaret's hand-writing. They were a dull list of words, but somehow he liked looking at them. He put them down with a sigh.
>
> 'The living is evidently as small as she said. It seems strange, for the Beresfords belong to a good family.' (55)

The order in which Gaskell presents the features of the scene – the garden outside, the shabby furnishings of the room as a whole, and the volume of Dante on the table – progressively narrows the visual focus, but it also serves to frame the images of dimness, wornness, and enclosure with those of brightness, vitality, and openness. The room may be small, the interior light dim, and the chintz faded, but the window opening onto the sunlit, paradisal garden – bright Nature – is answered by the white and gold *Paradiso*: bright Culture. The framing suggests that 'cultivation,' in both the literal and the figurative senses, opens out the domestic scene and makes the worn furniture irrelevant. At the same time, all three features of the scene speak of respect for the past and of the value of being rooted in a particular place. The faded chintz, the elegantly bound book, and the mature garden, where the family can pick their own unforbidden fruit, have accrued value through time. Henry is socially conservative – whatever Mr Hale's reasons for leaving the church, he would be offended by the scandal[24] – but he is not fully responsive to the aesthetic value of what is old. The very shabbiness of the 'dear old Helstone chintz-curtains and chair covers' (119), a shabbiness that for the reader is a sign of the family's unmaterialistic values and the heroine's domestic contentment, means for him only that her father has not been particularly successful in his career. There are different kinds of vitality here: the efficiency and drive that will bring Henry professional success are contrasted by Gaskell with the kind of inner life that comes from mental culture and reverence for continuity and stability. Leaving Henry alone in the drawing room is a deft way not only of putting it before the reader for the first time but also of implying Margaret's transcendence of and obliviousness to the shabbiness that she is never used to focalize.

The gold and white volume of the *Paradiso*, on which the eye comes finally to rest, is a suggestive detail. The luxurious physical format of the volume as well as the foreign content give it some of the force of the Indian shawls in the opening vignette – it is an object 'rich and strange' against a plain English background – but this object speaks not of a dangerous, alien territory but of European high culture. The study of Dante aligns Margaret with her father in their literary taste (Italian is the 'feminine' equivalent of Latin, recommended as the language in which women might study the classics in translation),[25] while the vocabulary list in Margaret's (presumably elegant) handwriting dramatizes, as is never done of Mr Thornton's literary pursuits, the patient effort such study takes. The chastely elegant gold and white of the book not only produce a spot of cool purity in the scene (and a contrast to the rather garish flowers outside the window) but also tend to associate the attractive text with its pale and elegant reader. Since Henry's eye lights on the open book just as he is thinking about the incongruity between 'queenly' Margaret and her shabby 'back-ground,' the volume becomes metonymically linked with the heroine herself. The expensive binding of the Dante also suggests that the family, who put what money they have into fine books, have a 'proper' hierarchy of values, which Henry, disappointed by the modest scale on which they live, cannot appreciate. Gaskell has so thoroughly spiritualized the physical features of the room as to make Henry's reaction seem anticlimactic and vulgar. Though he and Margaret seem to have certain genteel tastes in common – during the walk they take together, Margaret sketches picturesque vignettes of local life and Lennox sketches Margaret – his response to Margaret's home has made clear, even before she returns to the room, his unworthiness to succeed in his suit.

The gap in taste between Henry and Margaret is articulated again at the end of the meal that Mrs Hale has put before her unexpected guest. Mr Hale wants a pear from his garden for desert. His wife is distressed – has she not prepared a proper collation of 'biscuits and marmalade, and what not, all arranged in formal order on the sideboard'?[26] – but she is peripheral to the triangulated encounter involving the other three characters. Lennox, cultivating a pastoral pose, speaks for doing what comes naturally:

> 'I propose that we adjourn into the garden and eat them there,' said Mr Lennox. 'Nothing is so delicious as so set one's teeth into the crisp, juicy fruit, warm and scented by the sun. The worst is, the wasps are impudent enough to dispute it with one, even at the very crisis and summit of enjoyment.' (59)

Lennox will later speak of the 'refined and simple hospitality' (467) he received at the Thorntons, but the rather condescending tone in which he does it shows that he himself is not quite simple enough fully to appreciate their refinement. His praise of nature, with its Paterian idiom and Keatsian imagery, its evocation of strenuous delight, and its coded allusion to sexual enjoyment, is in fact highly artificial. There is a certain kind of energy here – a verbal energy, a witty sophistication – but also the suggestion of affectation and decadence. The young man's parade of his powers – his lusty appetite, his strong teeth – evokes the older man's inevitable response:

> 'I shall arm myself with a knife ... the days of eating fruit so primitively as you describe are over with me. I must pare it and quarter it before I can enjoy it.' (59)

The retort, while it shows up Lennox's pose of golden-age machismo, at the same time hints at the real inertia that is Mr Hale's most definitive characteristic, the enervation which, in the moral crisis he is shortly to precipitate, will quickly develop into virtual paralysis.

While the men talk, the woman serves. Responding with alacrity to her father's command – 'Run, Margaret, and gather some' (59) – Margaret picks the pears and presents them prettily on a beet-root leaf, 'which threw up their brown gold colour admirably' (59). The tension between nature and culture so self-consciously addressed by the two men is resolved in her emblematic assemblage, which brings the two principles together in an elegantly simple presentation.[27] Her offering shows a woman's taste finessing 'issues' and achieving the gracious equilibrium that the sophisticated males evade. Though Margaret may not, by vulgar Fanny Thornton's criteria, be an 'accomplished' young lady, within the home she is a kind of artist, defined not by what she covets, possesses, or consumes – Margaret herself is not depicted eating the pears – but by what she creates and offers to others. The edible still life she composes grounds her good taste in those household offices that a woman is called upon to perform and to beautify. The plate of pears is a kind of visual oxymoron: easily read as an emblem for Margaret's own ripe nubility, it also dramatizes what she has to offer the family. The episode makes a point of her genuine simplicity, both aesthetic and moral. The insinuating eroticism of Lennox's remarks is lost on Margaret, if not perhaps on her father: the sophisticated 'regular London girl''s alertness to sexual signals is replaced in Margaret by the young virgin's purity of mind and the womanly woman's impulse to serve. Lennox is wrong for Margaret because his self-important busy professionalism and somewhat cold ambition close him off to the cultural refinement she exemplifies. The opening chapters of the novel have been felt to be irrelevant,[28] but what they do is carefully set up a hierarchy of tastefulness into which the successful suitor, John Thornton, will have to insert himself when he arrives on the scene.

The Helstone household in the context of the nation as a whole is analogous to the woman's room in the mansion: a small and marginalized but culturally rich space of refinement and aesthetic potential. The class that has formed Margaret, if revitalized by the kind of energy that she herself exemplifies, might be to the society as a whole what the cultivated woman is to the family. But the heroine has to come out of the garden in order to meet the representative of that society, and Gaskell effects her exit by having Mr Hale decide to resign his living and leave Helstone for Milton. Margaret's capacity to organize the move in the best interests of the whole family is matched only by her talent for 'nesting' in whatever space her father can afford.[29] In Milton she is obliged to create a home overnight in an uncongenial environment. The challenge to which she so ably rises allows Gaskell to focus once again on a domestic interior that reflects the simple good taste of her heroine and to set this interior before a man whose worthiness to marry her we are invited to judge. It is in the context of this move, and on the issue of taste rather than of politics, that John Thornton's values and Margaret's are initially juxtaposed.

Like Henry Lennox, Thornton responds both to the heroine and to the room she has shaped. When Margaret meets him, Gaskell again makes a point of her modest unselfconsciousness. Their face-to-face encounter is described first from the point of view of the narrator ('Margaret opened the door and went in with the straight, fearless, dignified presence habitual to her' [99]), next from her point of view ('She felt no awkwardness; she had too much the habits of society for that' [99]), and finally from Thornton's:

> A young lady came forward with frank dignity, – a young lady of a different type to most of those he was in the habit of seeing. Her dress was very plain: a close straw bonnet of the best material and shape, trimmed with white ribbon; a dark silk gown, without any trimming or flounce; a large Indian shawl, which hung about her in long heavy folds, and which she wore as an empress wears her drapery. He did not understand who she was, as he caught the simple, straight, unabashed look, which showed that his being there ... called up no flush of surprise to the pale ivory of the complexion. (99)

The rhetoric, while overdetermined and transparent, is nevertheless quite complex. Margaret wears the 'large,' 'long heavy' Indian shawl 'as an empress wears her drapery': its sheer size establishes once again her queenly 'dignity' and her physical vitality. But under the shawl, which she shortly removes, Margaret is once again dressed with elegant simplicity. The contrast between the 'dark silk' and white ribbon, as well as the act of doffing the shawl, recalls Spenser's Una, who, until she takes it off at the end of the first book of *The Faerie Queene*, wears a black stole over her radiant white gown. Margaret's simplicity of dress ('very plain,' 'without any trimming or flounce') is underscored by a simplicity of manner: her apparent unselfconsciousness – there is 'no flush of surprise' on 'the pale ivory' of her complexion – impresses both Thornton and the narrator. Margaret's demeanour is as 'fearless' and 'unabashed,' as 'frank' and 'straight,' as if there were no reason to be self-conscious about meeting a man.[30] It is characteristic of the way Gaskell blurs physical and moral characteristics that the repeated word 'straight' aligns Margaret's erect posture in that heavy shawl with lack of conventional feminine coyness.[31]

But though the simplicity of manner and of dress is presented as if it is to Margaret's moral credit, it is of course simply the product of her social status and of the class gap between herself and her visitor. The reason that she is unabashed is that she thinks Thornton so far beneath her socially that she does not respond to him as a man at all. Gaskell mystifies class difference in terms of the aesthetics of simplicity while at the same time investing female modesty and sexual purity with the glamour of Petrarchan hauteur. In this text so imbued with Carlylean erotics of power, Thornton's wry assurance to his mother that there can be no question of a romantic relationship between them, since 'she held herself aloof from me as if she had been queen, and I her humble, unwashed vassal' (117), is a sure signal that that relationship will punctually develop. Thornton's intense response to Margaret's sense of superiority – his observation of the 'haughty curve' of her cheek and the 'quiet maiden freedom' of her 'cold serene' gaze, his sense of her 'proud indifference,' the way 'she seemed to assume some kind of rule over him at once' (99) – eroticizes class difference.[32] In the face of her cool beauty, Thornton learns to feel like 'a great rough fellow.' Equally important, perhaps, given the premises of this novel, he learns something about wallpaper.

Thornton has already, indeed, with what might be called prevenient taste, had an uneasy sense that there may be something not quite right with 'the atrocious blue and pink paper' (98) – 'a certain vulgarity in it ... had struck him at the time of his looking it over' (100). Only Margaret's judgment is needed to confirm his intuition. Predictably, Margaret opts for a quieter and smaller pattern, repudiating 'the taste that loves ornament, however bad, more than the plainness and simplicity which are of themselves the framework of elegance' (98). The narrative voice thus endorses her judgment. Though from time to time the reader is invited to question Margaret's little snobberies – we sense, for example, that when she condemns the Gormans as 'shoppy' (50) she will have to learn to redefine her terms – it is made clear that this is not one of the times. There is ornament and there is ornament. Gaskell's readers are expected to know the difference between bright colour and complicated pattern on a priceless Indian shawl and on cheap, mass-produced wallpaper.

For at least a decade before the publication of *North and South* social critics had been expressing the anxiety that the forthright, utilitarian English character was producing a nation without taste – a nation dependent on France, in fact, for patterns in such goods as wallpaper and textiles – and that English manufactures were suffering as a result.[33]

No doubt relevant to Gaskell's wallpaper episode was the establishment in 1853 of the Department of Science and Art, to 'diffuse' taste throughout English society, with the aim of refining the products of British industry. Advancing the principle that 'simplicity and truth must indeed be the first canons of art,' the Department ruled that wallpaper 'must be treated as a background, to display the furniture and other objects in the room; the decoration must be subdued and unobtrusive, not inviting special attention by strongly pronounced contrasts either of form or colour.'[34] The wallpaper in the Hale drawing room really is 'hideous' (101), we are expected to recognize, and we are expected to exclaim, with Margaret, '"What taste!"' (98).

This is what Mr Thornton is learning to do. A sociologist might see him as an upwardly mobile young man, eager to assimilate the preferences of his social betters, who is studying to rise into their class. But no such cynicism is invited by Gaskell's narrative. On the contrary: Margaret's 'proper' taste in wallpaper is a reliable sign of her feeling for domestic harmony and comfort and Thornton's appreciation of it a reliable sign of his readiness to take what she has to give.[35] His potential to rise to Margaret's cultural level is suggested less by his interest in Homer, which always remains rather theoretical, than by his responsiveness to her aesthetic standards in domestic interiors.[36] Evidently, Thornton already possesses the aesthetic instincts it was the Department of Art's purpose to 'diffuse' among manufacturers: like so many heroines of romance, he has the natural taste that only requires cultivation. This manufacturer requires not a government-sponsored art course, but simply more exposure to Margaret.

Margaret can bemoan the wallpaper, but her father cannot persuade the landlord to change it. But what he 'did not care to do for a Reverend Mr Hale, unknown, in Milton, he was only too glad to do at the one short sharp remonstrance of Mr Thornton, the wealthy manufacturer' (103). The authority over men that will become so prominent a feature of Thornton's character is first illustrated in his decisive handling of the wallpaper crisis. The suggestion is that Mr Thornton, the man who can get things done, will be a better husband than Mr Hale, and that a woman with Margaret's taste deserves a man who can support and enforce it. The alliance between Thornton's financial capital and Margaret's cultural capital would seem to point to a new class that will combine both.[37]

Where has John Thornton acquired his interest in Homer? we might wonder. And where has he developed taste in wallpaper? Studying

Homer is a way of resuming the education interrupted by his family's
financial ruin, for Thornton came from a home with some cultural pretensions and had to be taken out of school only because his father went
bankrupt. Despite a demeanour that makes Frederick take him for a
tradesman, Thornton was, apparently, solidly middle-class until his early
teens. There is a peculiar ambiguity, in fact, about the family's class position. Mrs Hale, noticing the piece of fine old lace that Mrs Thornton
wears, assumes that she is from old money,[38] yet the novel posits her as
one of Arnold's philistines *avant la lettre*, narrowly focused on the 'one
thing needful.'[39] Evidently Gaskell could not allow her heroine to fall in
love with a mere working man, but at the same time she needs to use
Thornton's narrow mother to exemplify the kind of vulgar taste from
which it is Margaret's role to rescue her future husband. When Margaret
suggests that her son's study of classics might broaden a 'mind too long
directed to one object' (159), Mrs Thornton retorts, in terms calculated
to make the reader cringe, 'Having many interests does not suit the life
of a Milton manufacturer. It is, or ought to be, enough for him to have
one great desire, and to bring all the purposes of his life to bear on the
fulfilment of that' (160). More graphically than Arnold but no less insistently, Gaskell associates such narrowness of focus with bad taste. She
positions the Thornton women, steely Mrs Thornton and enervated
Fanny, as foils to Margaret, and the Thornton mansion with its showy
vulgarity as the antithesis of all the values, domestic and aesthetic, exemplified by the heroine.

The home from which John Thornton comes, a mansion that directly
adjoins the factory itself, is an ugly showcase for the family's puritanism
and prosperity. We get our first glimpse of the 'grim handsomely-fur-
nished dining-room' as the narrator introduces Mrs Thornton mending
a tablecloth:

> There was not a book about the room, with the exception of Matthew
> Henry's Bible Commentaries, six volumes of which lay in the centre of the
> massive side-board, flanked by a tea-urn on one side, and a lamp on the
> other. In some remote apartment, there was exercise upon the piano going
> on. Someone was practising up a morceau de salon, playing it very rapidly.
> (116)

Some time later Margaret, arriving unexpectedly on the day of the riot,
happens to see the Thornton's drawing room (as Lennox saw the
Hales') as it looks when only the family is at home:

It seemed as though no one had been in it since the day when the furniture
was bagged up with as much care as if the house was to be overwhelmed
with lava, and discovered a thousand years hence. The walls were pink and
gold; the pattern on the carpet represented bunches of flowers on a light
ground, but it was carefully covered up in the centre by a linen drugget,
glazed and colourless. The window-curtains were lace; each chair and sofa
had its own particular veil of netting, or knitting. Great alabaster groups
occupied every flat surface, safe from dust under their glass shades. In the
middle of the room, right under the bagged-up chandelier, was a large cir-
cular table, with smartly-bound books arranged at regular intervals round
the circumference of the polished surface, like gaily-coloured spokes of a
wheel. Everything reflected light, nothing absorbed it. The whole room
had a painfully spotted, spangled, speckled look about it, which impressed
Margaret so unpleasantly that she was hardly conscious of the peculiar
cleanliness required to keep everything so white in such an atmosphere, or
of the trouble that must be willingly expended to secure that effect of icy,
snowy discomfort. Wherever she looked there was evidence of care and
labour, but not care and labour to procure ease, to help on habits of tran-
quil home employment; solely to ornament, and then to preserve ornament from dirt or destruction. (157)

The 'care and labour' to protect costly objects, potentially a sign of arriviste anxiety, are here aligned merely with emotional fridigity and moral
arrogance. In this context, 'ornament' is a thoroughly pejorative word.
Is it improbable or inevitable that a man brought up in such an environment, a man, moreover, who has spent every minute of his time since
boyhood founding a factory and working to pay off his father's debt,
would sense the vulgarity of a gaudy wallpaper pattern or be highly susceptible to the charm of more cultivated aesthetic standards?

Thornton seems never to have noticed the deficiencies in his
mother's taste up to this point, but all it takes is exposure to Margaret to
awaken him to a higher set of aesthetic values. Entering the (repapered)
drawing room of the Hales' cramped, potentially depressing rented
house, he instantly feels the contrast with the 'handsome, ponderous'
drawing room of his mother twice, 'twenty times as fine; not one quarter
as comfortable':

Here were no mirrors, not even a scrap of glass to reflect the light, and
answer the same purpose as water in a landscape; no gilding; a warm, sober
breadth of colouring, well relieved by the dear old Helstone chintz-curtains

and chair covers. An open davenport stood in the window opposite the door; in the other there was a stand, with a tall white china vase, from which drooped wreaths of English ivy, pale-green birch and copper-coloured beech-leaves. Pretty baskets of work stood about in different places: and books, not cared for on account of their bindings solely, lay on one table, as if recently put down. Behind the door was another table decked out for tea, with a white table-cloth, on which flourished the cocoa-nut cakes, and a basket piled with oranges and ruddy American apples, heaped on leaves. (119–20)[40]

Thornton is focalizing this scene, but the old Helstone chintzes are not 'dear' to him, and in the narrator's voice, which takes over and interprets what he sees, we hear several subtly different discourses, all carrying value judgments. The passage is replete with positive associations of various kinds: the metaphorical phrase 'warm sober breadth' to describe the colours of the room – visually vague but evocative of psychological balance and amplitude; the interior-design language to describe the flower stand, with its 'tall china vase, from which drooped wreaths of English ivy' (this could be the caption to a vignette from Loudon's *Suburban Gardener and Villa Companion*); the still life with oranges and 'ruddy American apples,' suggesting both simple luxury and rude health; the graceful vertical lines of the 'tall white vase' and drooping ivy, easily associated with the tall, slim heroine herself (Thornton feels that the room is 'of a piece with' her [120]); the no-cost but pleasing arrangements of subtly coloured leaves; the domestic purity (the white tablecloth, which Margaret may very well have ironed); and the hospitality (we know that she has made the coconut cakes herself). Gaskell's way of filling a domestic interior with objects irradiated by desire anticipates the language of the advertising age and of the shelter magazine. To complete the picture and focus our eyes on the vital centre of this gracious home, Gaskell has Margaret, as Thornton enters, lighting the lamp, which throws 'a pretty light into the centre of the dusky room, from which with country habits, they did not exclude the night-skies, and the outer darkness of air' (119). Improbably, despite the dust of which Mrs Hale constantly complains and from which Mrs Thornton has to protect her furniture, in this room, as in the drawing room at Helstone, the windows are kept open, suggesting not just a taste for light and air but a receptivity to what goes on outside, an openness to nature and to people. Good taste is here assimilated to emotional and intellectual receptivity, domestic comfort, and genuine hospitality. Though

Margaret does not feel especially welcoming to Thornton himself at this moment, her ability to create an inviting environment in an inferior rented space and his readiness to respond to its charm signal clearly that it is over his home that she is destined eventually to reign.

Gaskell puts the attractiveness of this room rather transparently on display, but there is no suggestion that the Hales are doing so. The 'care and labour' Mrs Thornton spends on her drawing room are underlined, but the work it would take both to construct such a pleasant space in the unprepossessing lodgings the Hales have been able to afford and to keep it looking like this is almost entirely erased, and with it any sense that they are deliberately trying to make an impression.[41] Margaret has, to be sure, baked for her guests, but the room is otherwise just what it would be for the family: there are 'pretty baskets of work ... in different places' and the books lie 'as if recently put down.'[42] The contrast with the Thorntons' drawing room, as vulgar when it is unveiled for public display as it is repellent when only the family is at home, could not be more pointed. On the evening of Mrs Thornton's famous dinner party, the room's showiness assaults the eye: 'Every cover was taken off, and the apartment blazed forth in yellow silk damask and a brilliantly-flow-ered carpet' – 'Every corner seemed filled up with ornament, until it became a weariness to the eye' (213–14). The menu is equally weari-some: 'Margaret, with her London cultivated taste, felt the number of delicacies to be oppressive; one half of the quantity would have been enough, and the effect lighter and more elegant' (213). Margaret also takes exception to the female guests, who, she later complains to her father, talked exclusively about their possessions: 'they took nouns that were signs of things which gave evidence of wealth – housekeepers, under-gardeners, extent of glass, valuable lace, diamonds, and all such things; and each one formed her speech so as to bring them all in, in the prettiest accidental manner possible' (221). It is made clear that poor John Thornton, who 'might have imagined, and had the capability to relish' society that does not depend on 'an exchange of superb meals' (213), is direly in need of an alternative to this kind of conspicuous con-sumption and competitive display. The alternative is constructed by an alternative set of nouns, the signs of things that give evidence of domes-tic taste: chinz, china, books, baskets, oranges, apples, decorative green-ery, and coconut cakes.

How Margaret will negotiate the social life in which her marriage into such a family will involve her is tactfully omitted from the text. The taste gap that makes social intercourse with Mrs Thornton and her friends so exasperating to Margaret is presumably not going to disappear with her marriage.[43] At the end of the novel, the focus is on Thornton's industrial 'family' rather than his biological one: the question of Margaret's relationship with Thornton's mother and sister is displaced by the issue of her influence on his relationship with his employees. Good taste serves as a signal by which chosen spirits recognize one another, but it cannot redeem those who do not recognize it when they see it. The work that it cannot accomplish Gaskell tactfully omits.

For her part, Margaret, abhors display of any kind. She does not display her home; she does not, we are asked to believe, even think of displaying herself. Though she is the cynosure of all eyes, particularly male – drawing the explicit notice of Higgins, Dr Donaldson, Horsfall, Mr Slickson, and almost every other man in the novel – Margaret is nevertheless presented as 'so unconscious of herself' at the Thornton dinner party 'that she never thought whether she was left unnoticed or not' (215), '"so busy listening!"' (221) to the men's conversation that she never notices that she is the only woman in the room. To feel herself promiscuously observed – as during the riot, or after the interview with the detective of police, which evokes a nightmarish vision of a 'cloud of faces' and the 'unwinking glare of many eyes' (248–9) – is the most tormenting of insults to her modesty. The one person, other than the servant Dixon, whom Margaret snaps at in the whole course of the novel is her cousin, and it is because of Edith's 'coarseness' in setting her up as 'an attraction to the house' (499).

The problem is perhaps that Gaskell displays rather too often, for our admiration, her heroine's unwillingness to be put on display.[44] The novel is itself thoroughly implicated in the display it condemns, and the most conspicuous status symbol of all is the heroine herself.[45] It is Gaskell as much as Mrs Thornton who asks us to look, to aspire, to covet: to fix our eyes on Margaret's 'slow movements, in her soft muslin gown' (251); on her 'round white flexile throat rising out of the full, yet lithe figure' (100) or 'curved outwards like a swan's' (394);[46] on the 'slow deep breathing [which] dilated her thin and beautiful nostrils' (240), 'the fine-grained skin, the oval cheek, the rich outline of her mouth, its corners deep set in dimples' (251), the 'ruffled, luxuriant hair' (240);[47] on 'the round white arms, and taper hands, laid lightly across each other but perfectly motionless in their pretty attitude' (215). Those hands get a lot of attention not only from Thornton, who watches as 'her round taper fingers flew in and out of her sewing' (416) and who is

fascinated when Mr Hale takes 'her little finger and thumb in his masculine hand' to make them 'serve as sugar-tongs' (120), but also from Frederick, who fondly dismisses his sister as 'a little awkward, good-for-
nothing pair of hands' (312) when she tries to light a fire; from Edith,
who thanks her 'dainty-fingered' (298) cousin for an embroidered baby
cap; and from Mr Bell, who remembers Margaret in her grief 'with bent
head and folded hands' (442).[48] Veblen theorizes the prestige of 'delicate and diminutive hands' by arguing that, in a society where 'conspicuous leisure' is a means of testifying to social status, a wife visibly
incapable of useful activity is a status symbol.[49] The gap between Margaret's willingness to try to make a fire and her inability to do it with her
exquisite but unpractised 'good-for-nothing' hands again illustrates
Gaskell's wariness about involving her heroine in actual work. There is a
curious blind spot in Gaskell's rhetoric here. Since a point is made of
the synecdochic term 'hands' to refer to the factory operatives – Thornton, though he knows that Margaret 'does not like to hear the men
called "hands"' (166), also knows that the term accurately expresses
their vulnerability in the marketplace ('he had head as well as hands,
while they had only hands,' 196) – it seems at least tactless to insist on
the middle-class lady's hands as signs of gentle blood and breeding.

But any political implications the word might have are thoroughly
erased in a series of gently sexy moments:

> She had a bracelet on one taper arm, which would fall down over her
> round wrist. Mr Thornton watched the re-placing of this troublesome orna-
> ment ... it fascinated him to see her push it up impatiently, until it tight-
> ened her soft flesh; and then to mark the loosening – the fall. (120)

'Tightened,' 'soft flesh,' 'loosening,' 'fall': the language is teasingly suggestive even for today's readers – no doubt more so for Gaskell's contemporaries, for whom soft, plumpish arms had a still more piquant
appeal.[50] Mr Thornton is the focalizer here, but his male gaze is filtered
through the voice of the woman writer, whose insistent emphasis on
female purity and female power to enthrall and abash spiritualizes the
fashion notes:

> Margaret's black hair was too thick to be plaited; it needed rather to be
> twisted round and round, and have its fine silkiness compressed into mas-
> sive coils, that encircled her head like a crown, and then were gathered
> into a large spiral knot behind. She kept its weight together by two large

coral pins, like small arrows for length. Her white silk sleeves were looped up with strings of the same material, and on her neck, just below the base of her curved and milk-white throat, there lay heavy coral beads. (212)[51]

The rhetoric turns here, as it often does, on the tension between the erotic luxuriance of the heroine's body and the twisting, compressing, tightening, encircling, coiling, knotting, pinning, and looping that bind that body to produce an emblem of queenly and virginal dignity.[52] Though she is not to be valued, like Mrs Thornton's showy books, merely for her binding, Margaret is as richly and elegantly bound as her own copy of Dante: altogether she is a most refined cultural production. The paradox of female modesty, as Poovey points out, is that it whets desire;[53] its danger is that it may be overlooked entirely. Gaskell, in the figure of Margaret, creates a wish-fulfillment fantasy: a 'proper lady' with effortless and innocent erotic allure.

Gaskell, displaying Margaret as conspicuously as Aunt Shaw displays the shawls her husband acquired or as Mrs Thornton displays her son's prosperity, makes clear how effective Margaret will be in displaying what her husband will provide. Thornton himself feels, when he first sees Margaret in evening clothes, that 'such elegance of attire was so befitting her noble figure and lofty serenity of countenance, that she ought to go always thus apparelled' (215): we take the point that he will be only too ready thus to apparel her. His mother reinforces this impression, gloomily foreseeing that to 'John's wife ... all household plenty and comfort, all purple and fine linen, honour, love, obedience, troops of friends, would all come as naturally as jewels on a king's robe' (210).[54] The opening vignette suggests Margaret's fitness to receive tribute, and the novel continues to imply that this lady of refined taste would be the fitting partner for a man able to finance that taste in the manner she deserves.

It is a commonplace of materialist social analysis that the middle-class wife contributes to the working of competitive capitalism in a number of different ways. Gaskell rather markedly exempts her heroine from the crudest. The ambitious or materialistic woman may simply urge her husband to provide handsomely for her. It is made very clear that this is just what Margaret will not do. Unlike her discontented mother, Margaret, rather than pressuring Thornton to succeed financially, will probably suggest that he put the welfare of his workers ahead of his own profit. But there are less direct ways in which a wife can spur her husband's efforts. She can create in the home a space of domestic contentment that motivates his labour[55] and of moral purity that sanctifies it; she can become 'the ceremonial consumer of the goods which he produces,'[56] displaying his earning power in the clothes that she wears and the home that she furnishes; she herself can function as the reward of his efforts.[57] The novel cannot admit that its heroine is herself the kind of status object that it repudiates, but it is too infatuated with Margaret, too eager itself to shower her with ornament, not to make clear what a fine ornament she will be for an industrialist who makes good. The conspicuous way in which Margaret herself is displayed undercuts Gaskell's critique of conspicuous consumption, but the contradiction is blurred by the way she has used 'good taste' to spiritualize class, style, and beauty. Margaret is such an effective figure for Gaskell's purposes for the same reason that she will be such an effective testimony to Thornton's material success: because in her spiritual and ethical values she apparently transcends the material.

As the quintessential English gentlewoman, Margaret is presented as the one for whom all of England's work, at home and abroad, is being done, the cultural product that justifies it. The men of the class of manufacturers and exporters to which Thornton belongs will, as their names become known 'in the East and in the West' – 'in foreign countries and faraway seas' (448) – become the successors of General Shaw's generation, and their women the recipients of the world's bounty. The proper reward of northern industriousness is posited as the southern culture that Margaret represents; her proper reward is the wealth that trade and industry create. Ruskin was to observe that the production of a gentleman, 'much more a lady,' is well purchased at the cost of 'much contributed life' of the working classes.[58] A novel that claims spiritual superiority for the heroine uses the discourse of taste to imply her worthiness for material reward and to endorse the economic system which, whatever problems it may create for the workers, produces the surpluses to adorn her.

If the world's goods should be laid at her feet, so also should the Englishman's reverence. Almost obsessively, Margaret is compared to royalty.[59] The narrator describes the Indian shawl as the 'garb of a princess' (39) and Margaret as sweeping out of the room with 'the noiseless grace of an offended princess' (394), noting that the heavy hair that 'encircle[s] her head' is 'like a crown' (212). The characters, particularly the men, are ready to pick up the metaphor:[60] Dr Donaldson, who muses 'What a queen she is!' (174); the police inspector, who is 'abashed by her regal composure' (345); her godfather Mr Bell, who hopes to find Camaralzaman at Oxford to marry this 'Princess Badoura' (417); Henry Lennox, less abashed than aroused by 'her Zenobia ways,' who insists that 'she has the making of a Cleopatra in her, if only she were a little more pagan' (505). Margaret herself may speak for common humanity, arguing that in God's eyes we are all one, but the language in which her regal demeanour is described suggests we are by no means equal. Gender difference is naturalized and in turn is used to naturalize class difference. A refined lady, the text suggests, has a superiority that every man instinctively acknowledges, and these men express their recognition of it in a metaphor that implies and endorses the reverence of one class for another. The Carlylean message is clear: it is not only a necessity but a pleasure for the 'inferior' to acknowledge genuine superiority.

Almost all of the characters in this novel are sorted out morally in terms of their ability to recognize Margaret's excellence. All the men admire her; so, too, do the working-class women, particularly Dixon, who enjoys being bullied by this chip off the Beresford block and sees Margaret's readiness to rebuke her as reassuring evidence of 'the good old Beresford blood' (178). Mary Poovey and Elizabeth Langland have pointed out that the 'servant problem' was also a problem for the self-construction of the Victorian lady.[61] Gaskell finesses this problem by having the servants with whom Margaret personally has to deal virtually worship her. There are servant problems in Milton – two or three girls are tried out in the Hale household and found wanting, including 'Mary Higgins, the slatternly younger sister' of Bessy (143) – but it is Dixon who has to handle them, not Margaret. No confrontation between Margaret and this kind of unsatisfactory employee is ever dramatized for Gaskell's reader, and it is made clear that the problems the Hales encounter finding suitable household help derive from deficiencies in the young women themselves and have nothing to do with the lack of managerial skills on the employer's part. In this novel, the servants' main task is simply to respond appropriately to Margaret. The lesser servants at Helstone confirm this principle by flunking the test. When Margaret, 'very pale and quiet,' remains perfectly 'calm and collected' at the end of a harrowing day supervising the packing, Charlotte and the cook, interpreting her well-bred reticence as indifference, 'settled it between them that she was not likely to care much for Helstone, having been so long in London.' Their inability to decode correctly what to a middle-class reader is easily recognizable as stoical self-control marks a class gap that is constructed as a lack of insight and refinement on the part of the servants, who 'could not understand how her heart was aching all the time' (89).

Though Margaret is sympathetic to working people and argues that the classes should relate to one another on a person-to-person basis, her own relationships with working women most vividly dramatize the gap between the classes.[62] It is in Bessy Higgins that the idea of working-class reverence is most transparently played out, and played out in specifically aesthetic terms.

Bessy thirsts for beauty in a drab and painful life and fixes her desire on two objects: the heavenly city as described in Revelation, and Margaret herself with 'that face – as bright and as strong as the angel I dream of' (188). Margaret is uneasy when Bessy insists that she had dreamt of her before she met her, 'looking w' yo'r clear steadfast eyes out o' th' darkness, wi' yo'r hair blown off from yo'r brow, and going out like rays round yo'r forehead, which was just as smooth and straight as it is now' (200–1). She is distressed not only by Bessy's effusive compliments but by what she evidently regards as her unwholesomely visionary, even superstitious, orientation towards the Bible. But Bessy's vision of Margaret as an angel seems scarcely a delusion: indeed, after her mother's death, the narrator will describe Margaret as 'a strong angel of comfort' (316) to her father and brother. And the image of Margaret that Bessy constructs – 'coming swiftly towards me, wi' yo'r hair blown back wi' the very swiftness o' the motion, just like the way it grows, a little standing off like; and the white shining dress on yo've getten to wear' (201) – merely complements what we have already heard again and again about the heroine's refinement, vitality, and 'glamour' (391).[63] Though Bessy's remarks are somewhat feverish, her admiration is not unjustified. In short, one of Bessy's main functions in the novel is to serve as yet another focalizer of the excellence of the heroine. Margaret is a narcissistic fantasy, a fantasy of class as well as of gender. She has the innate superiority that women would like to think men instinctively reverence in women and that the middle class would like to think the working class instinctively reverence in their 'superiors.'

Bessy's obsession with the prospect of seeing Margaret in white silk has a particularly ironic inflection in a novel about the textile industry, a novel, too, in which a point is made of the difficulty of getting servants. From the eighteenth century on, people fretted about maintaining sartorial distinction between the classes, and servants, particularly women, who inherited their employers' cast-off clothing were uneasily satirized as a threat to this distinction.[64] By the middle of the nineteenth century, the manufacture of cheap textiles had inflected this old anxiety in a new way. It is impossible to hire servants now, Mrs Beeton remarks in her book on household management, because 'the introduction of cheap silks and cottons, and, still more recently, those ambiguous 'materials' and tweeds, have removed the landmarks between the mistress and her maid, between the master and his man.'[65] It is cheap cotton that Mr Thornton is manufacturing, to Mrs Hale's regret: it is one thing, she says, to associate with Mr Gorman, who 'made carriages for half the gentry of the county,' quite another to meet a cotton manufacturer socially, for, 'but these factory people, who on earth wears cotton that can afford linen?' (80). Bessy's mystified adoration of Margaret, a Carlylean 'hero-ine-worship' that apparently precludes envy, is a reassuring model in the face of a cheaply dressed working-class population that might respond less benignly than she to the sartorial gap that separates them from their betters. In *Mary Barton* Gaskell had looked squarely at the bitter resent-ment the luxurious life of the employers might evoke in the workers, and in *North and South*, too, Bessy's father speaks angrily about the employers' profits and extravagance. In view of the threat of such well-motivated and plausible hostility, the notion that the angelic purity of a lady like Margaret might block a working woman's covetous response to fine clothing is a reassuring one.[66] We never hear what Bessy herself wears, nor of any attempt on her part to beautify her own pathetic home. Apparently, within her own environment Bessy is below the threshold of taste: all she needs is enough taste to respond to the tastefulness of Mar-garet. The desire to look at Margaret displaces the desire to look like her, and the white silk, utterly out of reach for a member of Bessy's class,[67] is deployed as a sign not of the socioeconomic gap between Bessy and Mar-garet but of Margaret's simple refinement and her innate superiority to the young woman who is so willing to adore her.

Poovey points out that desire must be both evoked and controlled so as to enable, by limiting, the competitiveness upon which capitalism depends. It is the function of the middle-class mother to instill 'habits of industry' in her son and thus sanction competitiveness as 'an integral part of the individual.' It is the function of the middle-class wife to con-trol desire, both in her own class and in the working class: in her own class, not only by controlling her own sexual desire, but by anchoring that of her husband; in the working class, by setting an example to her servants, in such a way as 'to contain desire rather than inspire it.'[68] The fantasy that Bessy represents is well explained by Poovey's model. Bessy is a working-class woman, but since she is not Margaret's servant, Margaret is not called upon to control her desire by direct discipline, in the context of an employer–employee relationship. Rather, she 'anchors' Bessy's desire as the wife anchors the desire of her husband: by her voice, her body, and her clothing, which become the objects of Bessy's quasi-erotic gaze. Since Bessy perceives her own desire as fixed in Margaret herself rather than in the material possessions that endow her with glamour, and since she is made to read Margaret's personal appearance as an emblem of spiritual purity rather than of economic position, the question of envying Margaret's wardrobe does not enter the picture.

Yet Gaskell's own writing is calculated to evoke exactly the consumer desire that she erases in Bessy. The problem is that Gaskell is all too effective in infusing material objects, including the body and dress of her own heroine, with spiritual and social value: precisely, in fetishizing them. A fair wage for the working man – the fair wage that the novel imagines it is possible for men of good will to arrive at – is evidently not a wage that would enable his wife and daughters to wear white silk or read Dante in a white and gold binding. Yet if the interior of a household like the Hales' indeed embodies such fine values, why should the worker not want them? If the middle-class lady's tasteful gowns endow her with such spiritual prestige, why should the worker's wife not dream of looking like her? In the just economy implied by Gaskell, the employee would have enough to satisfy his basic needs, but the desire her discourse arouses does not stop at basic needs. Hers is the language of consumer fantasy, almost the language of advertising. If working people are educated, as the novel urges, and then offered images that attribute to clothes, interiors, women, the power to radiate purity and comfort and moral repose, then what the employer considers enough will never be enough, patient explanation of the realities of the market will not quell their discontent, and wholesome dining-hall meals will become the least of their priorities. The fantasy of disinterested taste, Bessy's as well as Margaret's, is another way of repressing anxiety about a society fragmented by competing interests.

In the scenes between Bessy and Margaret, the focus is on Margaret's body. Bessy's is almost invisible, even though she is dying a slow and horrible death before Margaret's eyes. Indeed, the two 'good' working-class characters in this novel, Bessy and her father, exist mainly as voices – as discourse.[69] The term 'class racism' is usually used to refer to the contempt excited by the bodies produced by the material circumstances of the poor.[70] Gaskell expresses no such hostility and for the most part tastefully averts her eyes from the working-class body.[71] If there is class racism in her discourse, it is 'positive' racism: she preserves the gap between classes not by degrading the one at the bottom but by exalting the one at the top. The fact that Bessy's physical debility derives largely from the material circumstances of her life is made clear – indeed, it is part of the overt social message of the novel – but it is not allowed to undercut the mystified suggestion that Margaret's beauty and energy are natural emanations of her more refined and developed spirit. Margaret is almost a different species from Bessy, and Gaskell uses Bessy herself to make this point. Though the novel argues for those bonds that link all human beings as equals before God, much of its rhetoric also implies a natural, quasi-racial distinction between the classes.

The issue of Bessy's taste in biblical narrative reinforces this distinction. Understandably enough, considering her personal situation, Bessy is obsessed with the promises of Revelation, her imagination permeated with apocalyptic imagery. She herself is able to articulate why this part of the Bible appeals to her: she explains to Margaret that dramatizing herself as 'one of those doomed to die by the falling of a star from heaven' (186) makes her able to 'bear pain and sorrow better.' Margaret gently discourages Bessy's fascination with such material, on grounds that are not fully spelled out but that would seem to have something to do with aesthetics and with the notion of simplicity. Margaret is apparently repelled by Bessy's theology, and her response – 'Nay, Bessy – think!' – is gentle but peremptory: she insists that 'God does not willingly afflict' and that Bessy should not 'dwell so much on the prophecies, but read the clearer parts of the Bible' (187). It is not entirely clear why Margaret wants to insist that individual suffering cannot be part of God's plan. One might feel, too, that her pedagogical authority has been weakened by the dubious analogy she has just drawn between Bessy's suffering and her own: her assertion that 'God is just' on the grounds that the middle classes suffer too – that her own mother is also dying. Gaskell, as always, tries to be fair, allowing Bessy to speak with a good deal of force: persuasively to defend her taste in biblical imagery (Revelation offers her visions 'so far different fro' the dreary world' and language so sonorous that it is 'as good as an organ' [187]); allowing her, even, in a really startling moment, to imply that Margaret may be damned for her wealth ('But if yo' ask me to cool yo'r tongue wi' th' tip of my finger, I'll come across the great gulf to yo'' [202]).[72] But Margaret is always given the last word. Here she retorts that the fact 'that some of us have been beggars here, and some of us have been rich' is not what matters and that 'we shall not be judged by that poor accident, but by our faithful follow-ing of Christ' (202), and we are not invited to repudiate her doctrine or judge her advice to Bessy as unkind or misguided. Margaret's offer to come and read to her 'some of my favourite chapters' (187) is presented as a praiseworthy attempt to encourage in this working girl a more cen-tral and wholesome taste in biblical reading.

Margaret evidently prefers doctrine to narrative. Though the Hales are supposed to be great readers, we are not told a great deal about Mar-garet's literary tastes. Beyond Dante's *Paradiso* and the Bible, no individ-ual title or author is ever mentioned. We are told that Margaret's home is full of books, 'not cared for on account of their bindings solely' (120), but their bindings are all we know of them, and if the Hales are not using these volumes as a sign of culture, Gaskell is certainly doing so on their behalf (indeed, the single volume whose contents are identified, the Dante, *is* described in terms of its binding and is never mentioned again after the volume has served as an icon of tastefulness). We do know that Margaret has no use for people who talk about art 'in a merely sensuous way ... instead of allowing themselves to learn what it has to teach' (497), and we have some evidence that when she goes to books, as she does when grieving over her lie to the police detective, it is for moral guidance and inspiration. We gain some sense of what her favourite Bible chapters might be on the night of her mother's funeral, 'when, without a word of preparation' Margaret comforts her father by reciting from memory '"Let not your heart be troubled" ... and ... all that chapter of unspeakable consolation' (317) and when, during the funeral, she repeats to him 'all the noble verses of holy comfort, or texts expressive of faithful resignation, that she could remember' (338). But the gap between her taste and Bessy's is more graphically suggested by Bessy's own plea, just before her death: 'Read me not a sermon chapter, but a story chapter: they've pictures in them, which I see when my eyes are shut. Read about the New Heavens, and the New Earth; and m'appen I'll forget this' (260). Margaret's objection to Revelation may in fact have something to do with those stories and pictures. The prob-lem is not really that Bessy's apocalyptic fantasies are false and certainly not that they are irrelevant, but simply that they are a little vulgar.[73] They are characterized by all the qualities that mark off working-class taste in religious expression from middle-class taste: over-emphasis as opposed to restraint, ornament as opposed to purity, concreteness as opposed to generalization and abstraction, desire as opposed to obligation. Bessy's taste for narrative is the mark of an undeveloped sensibility 'greedy' for the concrete. Margaret's challenge to this taste is one of the means Gaskell uses to suggest the aesthetic decorum of the novel's own 'pure,' mainstream ethical Christian teaching: to mark it off, in its 'stately simplicity,' from the more colourful, more ornamented, more affective kind of religious discourse.

Gaskell herself was a Unitarian but did not of course address herself primarily to Unitarians.[74] Rather, she is employing a broadly ethical Christian rhetoric that would appeal to a wide cross-section of readers and that would, in its 'purity,' register as distinct from Bessy's concrete language. The simplicity of Margaret's Christian teaching is constructed by selecting what Unitarians and Anglicans could have in common and by distinguishing the middle-class Church from working-class radical Dissent. In other words, it is not universal at all, but rather the end product of a number of competing systems. But the politics of this process is repressed by the way in which the simplicity of Margaret's belief, purged of narrative and imagery, is aligned with the simplicity of her aesthetic style.

Although Gaskell has a stake she cannot abandon in the difference between a woman and a lady, man-to-man communication remains a possible dream in this novel. The relationships between men develop by means of the exchange of ideas. John Thornton learns to talk to Higgins and listen to him, and though his solution to the problem of the relationship between capital and labour may not be satisfactory, it is an attempt to formulate a basis for some kind of equality. Thornton and Higgins are presented, however implausibly, as having comparable access to linguistic competence. Though he may not grasp economic theory in the abstract, Higgins expresses himself just as pithily and forcefully as his employer. If the masters will listen, Gaskell implies, the workers can speak; if the masters will speak, the workers can understand. This optimistic scenario is, however, belied and deconstructed by the treatment of Bessy. Bessy cannot, and does not really want to, speak the same language as Margaret: the one she has found answers her needs better than mainstream Christian moral rhetoric. The kind of man-to-man communication the novel wants to believe in depends on unmediated, undifferentiated access to language that Bessy's linguistic investments already suggest is unlikely.

Up to this point I have been concerned with the ways in which the heroine's good taste marks her off from or aligns her with the other characters and with the implications of these distinctions for Gaskell's political and social vision. But the aestheticization of the heroine also shapes the more narrowly discursive sections of the novel: the way specific social and political issues are handled. If simplicity is the mark of good taste in interior decoration, wardrobe, personal style, and biblical rhetoric, it is also, the novel in the end suggests, the mark of correctness in ethical opinion. The way Gaskell contrives to give Margaret the last word in the moral debate is thoroughly informed by the sense of her 'stately simplicity.'

The aestheticization of the heroine shapes, I would argue, the handling of one of the weakest parts of the novel, the episode in which Margaret lies to the detective of police about being at the railway station with her brother Frederick. This incident, which causes a misunderstanding between her and Thornton and keeps them apart until the final pages, is primarily a plot device, and one that Gaskell, perhaps because she was rushed, handles rather carelessly, losing her grip on some of the details.[75] Even more unsatisfactory, though, is the overwrought and mystified way in which Margaret's lie is treated. Margaret has a perfectly good ethical motive for concealing the truth, if it is assumed – as she does assume – that protecting Frederick, despite his scuffle with a thoroughly unsavoury character who later dies, is the right thing to do. Though as it turns out, in a coincidence to which Margaret seems to impute profoundly moral significance, that her lie was unnecessary, it might not have been, and taking this means towards the end of preserving her brother from hanging seems not only justified but prudent.[76] But Margaret condemns herself in the most absolute terms for denying that she was at the railway station, not because she has obstructed justice – the social dimension of her act does not seem to be the issue for her – but simply because she has betrayed some rather mystified standard of decontextualized personal purity. She concludes that in future, if confronted with a similar decision, she would let her brother take his chances:

> If all the world spoke, acted, or kept silence with intent to deceive, – if dearest interests were at stake, and dearest lives in peril, – if no one should ever know her truth or her falsehood to measure out their honour or contempt for her by, straight alone where she stood, in the presence of God, she prayed that she might have strength to speak and act the truth for evermore. (502)

The solution, she now feels, would have been frankly to defy the police to find out about Frederick while daring 'bravely to tell the truth as regarded herself' (358).

The emphasis on self is significant. The way the whole episode is handled – in particular, the interrogation of Margaret by the detective of police, which focuses almost theatrically on the heroine as a visual figure – makes clear that it is not the safety of Frederick or the justice of his cause but the vision of Margaret's own eroticized wholeness and integrity that is at stake. The question is who has *seen* Margaret at the station. Those who do see her notice and remember her: Thornton, of course, but also the grocer's assistant, who, when she is illuminated by 'the full light of the flaring gas' inside the station (331), earns 'a proud look of offended dignity' for his 'somewhat impertinent stare of undisguised admiration' (332), as well as the station master, who recalls her as 'remarkably handsome' (344). When the detective comes to Margaret's home to question her, the narrator, articulating what he focalizes, lingers with the usual fascination on the heroine's 'proud face,' with 'no change of colour, or darker shadow of guilt,' on the 'great gloomy eyes' of 'some creature brought to bay,' on the 'glassy-dreamlike stare,' the 'regal composure,' the stillness of 'some great Egyptian statue' (345). The sentence Margaret mechanically repeats – 'I was not there' – keeps the focus firmly on this 'I': the other players in the scene are hustled off-stage while the physically and morally isolated heroine stands alone. Alone but not whole, for she has betrayed her single-hearted self.[77]

The text has as great a stake as Margaret in her transparent one-ness. The name Margaret means 'the Pearl,' as Mr Bell reminds us (418); Thornton, feeling the contrast between her gaze and the 'wandering eyes' (215) of his sister Fanny, traces 'the one lovely haughty curve' (100) of her face and is fascinated by her 'large soft eyes that looked forth steadily at one object' (215),[78] and, in his disturbing dream, he identifies Margaret with Spenser's Una. It is significant, though, that the allusion enters the novel just at the moment when her unity begins to split and his dream records that split. Thornton, who has come to believe that Margaret has a lover, dreams that she comes dancing invitingly towards him – 'this figure of Margaret – with all Margaret's character taken out of it, as completely as if some evil spirit had got possession of her form' – so that 'when he wakened he felt hardly able to separate the Una from the Duessa' (411). The dream is wrong, of course – Margaret is no Duessa – but the image of the unified self splitting into two nevertheless points to what is happening to her psychologically at this point.[79]

It is under the pressure of this crisis that the heroine, as it were, comes apart and looks at herself in a newly self-conscious way. In a book from her father's library, she finds a passage that mirrors 'her present state of acute self-abasement' (426) – a passage in which the woman writer splits herself into two, apostrophizes her heart ('blind, impudent creature') in the second person ('Come now, my poor heart') and uses the plural pronoun to refer to her composite self ('there we are fallen into the ditch ... let us arise ... set out again ... be on our guard with God's help' [426, translated 537n1]). It is at this point, too, that the imagery of Margaret's statuesque erectness begins to alternate with that of her supine collapse.[80] Margaret has become a fallen woman: 'Trusting to herself, she had fallen' (502). Though paradoxically, this means standing alone with a new kind of self-knowledge – 'She stood face to face at last with her sin. She knew it for what it was' (502) – it also involves a metaphorical collapse before Thornton: 'Mr Thornton, above all people, on whom she had looked down from her imaginary heights till now! She suddenly found herself at his feet, and was strangely distressed by her fall' (356). Margaret becomes obsessed with the awareness that 'Mr Thornton had seen her close to Outwood station' and that 'she stood as a liar in his eyes' (355), tormented with 'the thought of how he must be looking upon her with contempt,' with the conviction that she is 'degraded and abased in Mr Thornton's sight' (358), 'abased in his eyes' (385).[81] The specular language is insistent. Even as she asserts a new kind of isolation and independence, vowing to tell the truth even 'if no one should ever know,' she sees herself as seen by a male focalizer: abased (in suggestively erotic terms, fallen) before Thornton, standing 'straight alone' for judgment 'in the presence of God' (502).

The spiritual crisis is said to give Margaret a new sense of individual responsibility. Having learned that 'what other people may think of the rightness or wrongness is nothing in comparison to my own deep knowledge, my innate conviction, that it was wrong' (487), having 'learnt, in those solemn hours of thought, that she herself must one day answer for her own life, and what she had done with it' (508), she is able to take 'her life into her own hands' and renegotiate with her Aunt Shaw the terms under which she is to live in their house, earning 'the right to follow her own ideas of duty' and move freely about the city, apparently doing some kind of charity work. Gaskell in fact uses the episode to segue, awkwardly and perfunctorily, into a consideration of 'that most difficult problem for women, how much was to be utterly merged in obedience to authority, and how much might be set apart for freedom in working' (508). But the theme of female independence is less memorable and convincing than the eroticized scenario of virginal purity beleaguered and tormented.[82] The overwrought way in which what might seem to us a justifiable prevarication is treated betrays the stake the text has in the fantasy of the intact immaculate female, even as the language makes clear the specular nature of that fantasy. The episode takes the shape that it does because of the way in which the text aestheticizes and eroticizes both the visual and spiritual 'simplicity' of the heroine.[83]

The theme of wholeness, unity, and simplicity also underlies the debate about economic and social justice conducted by a number of the characters and has much to do with the way that debate is set up and resolved – or dismissed. Gaskell tries hard to be fair to both sides and to register the full range of opinions.[84] Every character has a point of view – or, better perhaps, every point of view has a character. Readers of the novel are left, however, with the impression that the middle-class position has been validated,[85] for it turns out that though a range of voices is heard, some voices are more equal than others. The novel makes a sharp distinction between masculine and feminine points of view, emphatically underwriting the polarized vision of natural gender, but in the end the masculine is accommodated to the feminine, Thornton moves towards Margaret, the view of common humanity is endorsed, and the many are folded into the one. The idea of the whole, of the one, of simplicity upon which the heroine is constructed also informs the economic and ethical debate and determines its resolution – or rather, the erasure or co-opting of dissident points of view. The simplicity of the heroine rubs off, as it were, on the arguments to which she contributes and pushes the novel towards a conclusion which has more aesthetic neatness than political plausibility.

The characters' discussion is premised upon some of the axioms of Carlyle and grounded in Carlylean simplicities (if this is not an oxymoron).[86] We hear, for example, about the duty that lies nearest you. Margaret, after the misunderstanding with Thornton, berates herself for her inability to pull herself together, in spite of 'the "One step's enough for me," – in spite of the one plain duty of devotion to her father' (429); Higgins develops the idea more fully and politically, his homely idiom tastefully inflected by the Book of Common Prayer:

> 'When I see the world going all wrong at this time o' day, bothering itself wi' things it knows nought about, and leaving undone all the things that lie in disorder close at its hand – why, I say, leave a' this talk about religion alone, and set to work on what yo' see and know. That's my creed. It's simple.' (133)[87]

The fact that one's immediate duty may be anything but simple – that when the decent, earnest individuals in the novel do turn their attention to current problems, they are unable to come up with any very satisfactory answer as to what to do about them – does not apparently undercut the rhetorical resonance of such remarks. All the morally positive characters use the words 'simple' and 'simplicity' at key moments, implying that what is right is simple, and what is simple is right. Bell comforts Margaret, distressed about her lie, that 'the veriest idiot who obeys his own simple law of right ... is wiser and stronger than I' (430); Thornton in his grief begs his mother to speak to him in such a way as to 'make me feel some of the pious simplicity of my childhood' (517); more significantly, Margaret judges her behaviour on the occasion of the riot: 'It was right and simple, and true to save where she could save' (257).

The notion of simple rightness is most fully expressed in the discourse of Margaret, who repeatedly intervenes in the men's debate in order to bring them back to first principles.[88] Though admitting to Thornton that she is no 'political economist like you' (165), she never hesitates to insert herself into the conversation: her assertiveness, justifiable even by some conduct books of the time, is not apparently as unconventional as a modern reader might imagine[89] and is fully legitimized by her articulation of the pure Christian teaching with which it is woman's duty to keep man in touch. With Socratic innocence, Margaret gets to the heart of every problem. She asks Thornton, for example, why he cannot do what he eventually decides he ought to do: simply explain to his workers the reasons he has to expect that trade will be bad. She states, in lucidly Carlylean terms and in a single sentence, the central paradox of the capitalist economy – 'I see two classes dependent on each other in every possible way, yet each evidently regarding the interest of the other as opposed to their own' (165). She makes clear to Thornton, again in Carlylean terms, 'why you should not do what you like with your own' (164),[90] admitting that although there is 'no human law' preventing employers from exploiting their workers, 'there are passages in the Bible which would rather imply – to me, at least – that they neglected their duties as stewards if they did so' (165). Margaret's own idiom is, indeed, often vaguely biblical. She teaches by parable, in little vignettes that have the flavour of Christlike simplicity, analysing the issue of strikes, for example, in language that evokes the imagery of reaping and sowing[91] – 'if the people struck ... the seed would not be sown, the hay got in, the corn reaped ... and where would the money

come from to pay the labourers' wages?' (181), and, more problem-
atically, putting in play, with her accusation that Thornton treats
his employees like children and her account of the untaught child of
Nuremberg, the analogy between family and class relations. The analogy
is itself a simplification, and, as many critics have pointed out, an ideologically loaded displacement.[92] It is Margaret, too, who first expresses
the notion of common humanity which will do so much work in the
novel. When Thornton says he has no right to influence his men outside
of working hours merely because he is their employer, she replies, 'not
in the least because of your labour and capital positions ... but because
you are a man, dealing with a set of men over whom you have ...
immense power.' As Carlyle pointed out, and Margaret reiterates, 'God
has made us so that we must be mutually dependent' (169). Margaret
seems thoroughly acquainted with Carlyle's thought, though, no doubt
to keep her from seeming too much of a bluestocking, Gaskell does not
assert that she has ever read him. Indeed, she is made to state explicitly
that 'Cromwell is no hero of mine' (171), in order, no doubt, to purge
Carlyle's teaching of his ideological and rhetorical excesses and transmit
its simple essence.

The moral simplicity Margaret postulates is highly gendered. She sees
her defence of the helpless during the strike as 'a woman's work' (247),
insisting to Thornton that she was 'merely guided by womanly instinct'
(254) and that 'any woman, worthy of the name of woman, would come
forward to shield, with her reverenced helplessness, a man in danger
from the violence of numbers' (253). A woman who sees moral issues in
their simplicity is, it is suggested, likely to see them clearly.[93] Margaret is
following a similar womanly instinct, presumably, when she helps
Boucher's family, and we are to admire her for her compassion. Gaskell
does take care to point out that the simple human response may, by utilitarian standards and within the existing economic system, prove in the
end to be inhumane. Margaret may be right to abort the police attack
on the strikers, but supplying them with food, as her father points out,
could prolong the strike and cause greater suffering in the long run.
The problems Gaskell is discussing have no simple solution, and on one
level she acknowledges this. Yet in the last analysis moral simplicity is
always allowed to trump the more complex political arguments. Margaret and her father, despite Higgins's passionate and coherent defence of
the Union, nevertheless cling to the vision of a larger union, humanity
united in a single glorious body:

'Your Union it itself would be beautiful, glorious, – it would be Christianity itself – if it were but for an end which affected the good of all, instead of that merely of one class as opposed to another.' (296)

The chapter ends with the three of them, 'Margaret the Churchwoman, her father the Dissenter, Higgins the Infidel' (297), kneeling together in prayer. That this mystified vision of the union of all allows Gaskell to evade the serious contemplation of more disturbing and radical solutions to the problems she puts before us is not a new point to make, but what I want to draw attention to is the way the aesthetic of the text as a whole endorses the vision. Though the struggle to articulate the right relationship between classes is inconclusive, the model of unity is allowed to trump that of class antagonism, partly by invoking the authority of Christianity, but also by aligning this authority with the aesthetic prestige which has accrued to the notion of simplicity and one-ness.

John Thornton, the pragmatic industrialist, cannot be shown as espousing, in the same rather visionary way as the Hales, the dream of a unified society. Though Thornton agrees with Margaret that in theory 'my interests are identical with those of my workpeople and vice versa' (166), he also believes that it is only 'on some future day – in some millennium – in Utopia' that 'this unity may be brought into practice' (167). But as the romantic hero, Thornton has to be aligned with simplicity if he is to be paired off with the heroine. The dining-hall plan that he comes up with at the end of the novel, particularly his decision to eat with his employees, is another move in constructing this simplicity. Eating, as Mr Bell points out, is an act that unites us all, and eating with the men has perhaps even a faintly eucharistic association; certainly it follows up on the model of society as a family that the Hales have introduced. The simplicity that supposedly characterizes it, however, is the product of a rather elaborate ruse. It is Thornton who comes up with what is presumably a sensible plan of saving money by buying in bulk. When Higgins 'found fault with every detail of my plan' (445), Thornton, not wishing to interfere 'with the independence of my men' [note 'my'], drops it. Then, he says, 'when suddenly, this Higgins came to me and graciously signified his approval of a scheme so nearly the same as mine, that I might fairly have claimed it' (445), Thornton, subduing his irritation at not being given credit for the idea, 'coolly took the part assigned to me' (445). This elaborate, paternalistic,[94] and condescending game is supposed to express his respect for the men's autonomy, but it certainly does not signal the transcendence of class divisions.

Indeed, when he refuses Bell's offer of ten pounds to give the men a feast on the grounds that such an act of charity would '[spoil] the simplicity of the whole thing' (446), the simplicity he is referring to is not the unity of employer and employee but the clarity of the line that separates them. Even this degree of 'simplicity' depends on manipulation and on the collusion of middle-class men who talk behind the backs (and over the heads) of the workers they want to help. Both Thornton's realistic sense of the gap between himself and his employees and his investment in individual autonomy preclude any easy vision of a truly simple social order. Yet his very use of the *word* 'simplicity' serves, in some slightly mystified way, as a guarantee of his good moral taste and essential purity of intention.

'Simplicity' is a word Thornton uses often and a value he strongly espouses. He admits with regret, for example, that the 'sense of justice' of the first-generation capitalist 'and his simplicity, were often utterly smothered' (124). He challenges Margaret to say whether those who have most deeply influenced her have not done so just by being 'simple, true men, taking up their duty' (170). Thornton himself, of course, is just such a man: his taste for simplicity is a sign of his manliness, an aspect of his honourable, straightforward nature. The word 'man' has both erotic and class implications. When Margaret tells Thornton 'you are a man,' she is thinking of his moral obligations as a captain of industry, not of his passionate virility, but the noun, echoing through the novel, comes quickly to suggest that virility to the reader. The word 'man' is one on which Thornton himself likes to meditate: he objects, he tells Margaret, to the word 'gentleman,' preferring 'the full simplicity of the noun 'man' and the adjective 'manly'' because they denote a man 'not merely with regard to his fellow-men, but in relation to himself, – to life – to time – to eternity' (218).[95] But this very remark, suggesting at once his male forcefulness, his impatience with affectation, and his refined attention to the nuances of language, makes clear that Thornton is what he denies. It takes a gentleman to object to the word 'gentleman' in language like this. Just as it is his objection to the word 'gentleman' that proves he is one, so it is his willingness to pretend that he and his employees are simply all 'true men' together that makes clear his right to authority over them.

Mr Hale wondered if Thornton had been inspired in his early struggles by 'the recollection of the heroic simplicity of the Homeric life' (127). Though Thornton dismisses the suggestion with a smile, the image of the epic hero sticks, giving Gaskell's captain of industry a classical, and classy, inflection. The notion of simplicity is mobilized both to endorse the vision of a truly unified social body and to suggest the ineluctable superiority of those vital and attractive bodies whose union will consummate it. A taste for stately simplicity – in clothing, interiors, nature, women, language, and industrial relations – is the mark of those refined and at the same time heroic individuals who are worthy to lead society into the future. In a willed and conspicuous oversimplification, the union of Margaret and Thornton both displaces and adumbrates the social union otherwise unachieved in the novel.

*Middlemarch*, like *North and South*, features a female protagonist who is introduced in terms of her elegantly simply clothing. Dorothea is a more modern kind of heroine than Margaret Hale, insofar as she is made to confront the 'woman question' to which Gaskell alludes only in passing (even if she does end up in almost the same position, as a supportive wife to a somewhat déclassé husband). Yet Gaskell and Eliot construct their radiant heroines in rather the same way. *Middlemarch* indeed opens with a vignette that could have been modelled on chapter 1 of *North and South*: the 'jewel scene,' where once again the simple purity of the heroine's austere dress is complemented by rich, bright, costly colour. To be sure, the tone that Eliot takes towards Dorothea is, at least in the first few pages of the novel, amusedly objective and detached. Unlike Gaskell, Eliot refuses to ignore or repress the labour that goes into producing luxury goods for the wealthy – she has Dorothea reflect about the cost in human suffering of the gems she admires – and, unlike Margaret's, Dorothea's simple costume is given a deflationary sociological explanation. As has often been pointed out, however, this detached tone is soon dropped, and in the novel as a whole Eliot will develop the 'feminine mystique' of Dorothea rather in the way Gaskell develops Margaret's. While Margaret is defined by the 'stately simplicity' that inflects every aspect of the novel, Dorothea is characterized by radiant 'consistency,' a notion equally important in the shaping of *Middlemarch*.

In both Gaskell's novel and Eliot's, the taste of the manufacturing class is used as a way of constructing the idealized, more genteel heroine. But Gaskell gives a much more positive picture of her Captain of Industry than Eliot does of the Vincys and the Plymdales. Having been criticized for her unsympathetic treatment of the employer in *Mary Barton*, Gaskell writes *North and South* to right the balance, and if there are certain inconsistencies in her portrait of Thornton – inconsistencies that testify no doubt to her own class prejudices – she nevertheless treats him with respect and sympathy, putting before the reader the by-no-means-simple issues that such a manufacturer would face. If we set Mr Thornton against Mr Vincy, the ribbon manufacturer in *Middlemarch*, Eliot's comparative hostility towards the business and manufacturing classes becomes apparent. Though Vincy and Thornton face rather different financial and commercial problems – Eliot is dealing with an earlier period and different labour conditions – the business setbacks that Vincy does encounter are used not to invite sympathy for his plight or to throw light on wider economic issues but simply to motivate his changing attitudes towards the conspicuous consumption of his children Fred and Rosamond. Mr Vincy indeed is used by Eliot as he is used by his family, chiefly to provide financial support for their style of life, which is represented as just as bright and banal as the ribbons he manufactures. The female Vincys function like the female Thorntons, primarily as foils to the heroine, and the mechanical or conventional kinds of uniformity that characterize them, associated as they are with commerce and commodification (as well as with evangelical religion), are set against the 'consistency' exemplified by the heroine. In the following chapter I shall argue that anxiety about commodification and mass production in *Middlemarch* inflects Eliot's investment in the notion of organic unity of character, and that this unity is figured in Dorothea's style, which is represented as an expression of her essential selfhood. Condescension to the manufacturing class is, I shall argue, one way of manufacturing a heroine like Dorothea Brooke.

# 7 The Importance of Being Consistent: Culture and Commerce in *Middlemarch*

'Consistency' is a word that turns up all the time in nineteenth-century moral discourse. To be accused of 'inconsistency' is no light charge: it implies a fundamental lack of moral seriousness. Hester Chapone recommends that her young readers 'acquire habits of constancy and steadiness,' for 'without them there can be no regularity or consistency of action or character.' J.C. Loudon says that rather than being tempted to purchase a house beyond one's means it is 'more manly and consistent' to calculate from the outset what one can afford. Hannah More refers to the 'character of a man of sense, of which consistency is the most unequivocal proof.' Elizabeth Gaskell thanks Charles Eliot Norton for his letter of advice to her daughter Meta, 'especially all that part relating to consistency of character.' Hardy's Jude Fawley accuses himself of inconsistency when he finds himself on his knees reciting Horace's invocation to Diana: 'strange forgetfulness ... in one who wished ... to be a Christian divine.'[1] Being consistent is as important as being earnest; indeed, one quality involves the other. So common is the term in this period as to raise the suspicion that the notion of 'consistency' is a defensive reaction against the threat to coherent subjectivity posed by what is perceived as a fragmenting social environment.

George Eliot seemed to her contemporaries notable for her own consistency, which her readers over the decades continued to attribute both to her texts and to her persona. Richard Simpson in 1863, for example, praises her insight into character:

> The first requisite in a character is a distinct individuality – not an external consistency which makes a gardener talk of flowers, and a dairy-woman of

cheeses; nor an arbitrary signalment which distinguishes him by an out-ward badge, like a habit of sniffing, or of saying '*for* to do' a thing; but an internal consistency, which represents the person as the endogenous growth of a central life, putting forth its own natural fruit under the stimu-lating or depressing influence of circumstance.[2]

As Eliot adopts organicist models of community from thinkers like Spencer,[3] so she also adopts the organicist model of Romantic subjectiv-ity, and Simpson's metaphors replicate Eliot's emphasis on 'organic' unity and wholeness of character, the subjective coherence that is the basis of consistent moral vision. Consistency was also attributed to Eliot's methods – Robert Laing in 1873 praises 'the consistent patience and infinite pains with which our authoress works'[4] – and to her thought – in 1884 a critic noting 'the close relation of her teaching to that of Comte, Darwin, Lewes, and Spencer,' remarks that their doctrines, 'when passed through the alembic of her mind ... attain a consistency and a unity hardly to be found' in the original works themselves.[5] Eliot would no doubt have been pleased by these observations, for consistency is a quality she imputes to her most idealized characters. When in the Pre-lude to *Middlemarch* the narrator describes the fate of ardent dreamers born into an unheroic era and laments the 'mere inconsistency and formlessness' (3) of their moral careers – or what would look like 'inconsistency and formlessness to common eyes' – it is in order to alter that 'common' way of looking. Eliot, more percipient, will demonstrate that a psyche that appears inconsistent 'to common eyes' may be unified in ways that the superficial observer cannot understand: specifically, that Dorothea Brooke, whose extreme religious feelings make her seem 'inconsistent' to her unsympathetic neighbours, in fact possesses the luminous consistency worthy of a moral heroine.

The notion of consistency shapes not only the characterization but also the structure of *Middlemarch*. The importance of being consistent is spelled out, in a way that can only be called relentlessly consistent, in the narratives of the two 'split' characters, Lydgate and Bulstrode, who are torn between two opposing sets of values and destroyed by the clash between them. The still more scattered characters – the dilettantes Fred Vincy, Will Ladislaw, and Mr Brooke – are also consistently dealt with. The two unworthy suitors are saved by the love of consistent women, who inspire them to abandon their wayward tastes and habits and get focused;[6] Mr Brooke – perhaps the most inconsistent figure in fiction, a character who seems to impersonate just the linguistic dispersal that

Neil Hertz says we use polarity to repress – is allowed, since he is a comic minor character, to remain an ineffectual loose end.[7] Rosamond Vincy, persistent rather than consistent, serves as a foil to Dorothea Brooke, whose unity and consistency are the keynote of her characterization, while the sturdy members of the Garth family are all, in their different ways, consistency personified. The novel's insistence on the dangers of doubleness is unique – in no other Eliot text do we find so many examples of the same theme – and the sheer repetition speaks to an anxiety about organic selfhood that *Middlemarch* seems especially to express (or to generate).

The consistency of the integrated psyche is replicated in the dense verbal texture of the novel. *Middlemarch*, despite its length, is a minutely patterned and highly unified 'web,' woven together with parallels, analogues, and echoes into an intricate network of details. The process of reading this substantial text, remembering the details, and linking them into meaningful sets is an analogue of the coherent subjectivity in which Eliot is determined to believe: the reader, in 'comprehending' the narrative, models the process that enables the fully evolved characters to achieve coherence in their own psyches.[8] We are expected, for example, to remember Dorothea's early objection to the word 'fond' when over six hundred pages later she confesses her fondness for Will Ladislaw, to whom she has now engaged, and to reflect that Dorothea's 'two love choices' have led her to change her mind both about the value of 'fondness' and about the right tone to take towards Celia's somewhat vulgar choice of diction.[9] The reader's ability to connect the two details and draw this conclusion models the 'deep' consistency that makes the heroine capable of such change. In Eliot's novels only characters who are already consistent in this deep way – who demand from their lives the coherence and cohesion of an Eliot novel – can undergo the moral transformation the author demands of them.

To illustrate the intricacy of Eliot's web as well as to make clear that the consistency in which Eliot is interested always has an aesthetic dimension, I begin with the smallest possible detail: the feather in Harriet Bulstrode's hat.

An awareness of the serious value the period assigned to 'consistency' is needed to pick up the full comedy of the scene in which Mrs Plymdale and a group of Harriet Bulstrode's acquaintances discuss her probable reaction to the news of her husband's disgrace. The story of Bulstrode's past and Raffles's blackmail has just made its way across town, and the women wonder whether Harriet can have heard it. Mrs Tom Toller opines that she has not, since 'she was with her girls at church yesterday, and they had new Tuscan bonnets,' adding snidely that Harriet's 'own had a feather in it. I have never seen that her religion made any difference in her dress' (545). Mrs Plymdale, 'a little stung' because she is Harriet's particular friend as well as her co-religionist, retorts defensively: 'She wears very neat patterns always ... And that feather I know she got dyed a pale lavender on purpose to be consistent. I must say it of Harriet that she wishes to do right' (545). Q.D. Leavis asserts that the 'consistency of dress' referred to here is not a matter of colour coordination for the sake of aesthetic effect, but rather of evangelical sobriety and austerity, 'lavender being a shade of conventional mourning and therefore not a colour.'[10] Whereas a worldly woman would dye a feather for motives of fashion, an evangelical woman does it for reasons of principle.[11] Harriet Bulstrode does both: she chooses a hat with a feather to display their prosperity and then orders it dyed lavender to display their evangelical allegiance: a tiny (though not trivial) analogy to the split in her husband's life. The joke is in the word 'consistent,' not only because Harriet's stance is the reverse of consistent but also because, whether Mrs Plymdale is thinking of elegance or righteousness or the saving gap between them, her use of such a lofty word to refer to the colour of a feather is an incongruity that dramatizes the moral vacuum out of which she speaks. If dyeing her feather lavender is the way Harriet's desire to 'do right' is manifested in the minds of Mrs Plymdale and her ilk, none of them have the authority to sit in judgment on the Bulstrodes.

The reference to Harriet's costume belongs to a set of scenes having to do with the donning and doffing of emblematic garments and ornaments. The first occurs only five pages or so after this bit of gossip, when Harriet does find out about the scandal and demonstrates just the consistency that her friend claims for her, though not in the way she means. Though up to this point her 'phrases and habits were an odd patchwork' (550), Harriet sticks by her husband and 'with one leap of her heart' (549) commits herself to her new, ruined life. She is consistent in the most literal sense of the word (the root is the Latin *sistere*, to take a position, to stay in the same place), and this genuine consistency also has its sartorial expression: Harriet '[takes] off all her ornaments,' '[puts] on a plain black gown,' '[brushes] her hair down and [puts] on a plain bonnet-cap, which made her look suddenly like an early Methodist' (550). There is nothing unselfconscious about this gesture: like the decorous feather, Harriet Bulstrode's new garb is intended to be observed by 'all spectators visible and invisible' (550) as a sign of her renewed loyalty. As before, Harriet presents herself as an exemplary object, but this time she is making an authentically moral statement. The 'religion' that counts to her credit is not her evangelical Christianity but the sympathy Eliot espouses as a humanist ideal.[12] By renouncing her carefully chosen wardrobe and embracing a straitened existence at her husband's side, Harriet Bulstrode demonstrates the authentic consistency that is one of the principal values of *Middlemarch*.

As has been pointed out, this incident too is part of a larger pattern. Mrs Bulstrode's gesture contrasts with her niece Rosamond's frigid response to her own husband's ruin, her begrudging surrender of the jewels Lydgate had given her. Behind all of these moments is the jewel scene involving Dorothea and her sister in the first chapter, where Dorothea, though refusing to wear any of their mother's jewellery, keeps the gorgeous emerald for herself, and Celia, naturally enough, accuses her of being 'inconsistent.' This youthful, rather self-righteous act of renunciation is in turn put in perspective by the much more painful renunciation demanded of Dorothea later on, when she comes to believe that Will Ladislaw is in love with Rosamond Vincy. After the 'backstage' scene in her blue boudoir in which Dorothea wrestles with her grief and undergoes the epiphanic revelation at the window,[13] she decides to return to Rosamond's and attempt to reach out to her. As a sign of her new commitment to others, she asks her maid Tantripp to bring her a dress of lighter mourning.[14] Like Harriet Bulstrode though in reverse – re-entering the world rather than withdrawing from it – Dorothea selects garments not because they are consistent with each other or with social convention but because they are a sign of a new moral commitment. Tantripp's criteria for finding this decision 'consistent' are, like Mrs Plymdale's, purely conventional – 'three folds at the bottom of your skirt and a plain quilling in your bonnet,' she says approvingly, 'is what's consistent for a second year' (578) – but her very superficiality teaches the reader how to read Dorothea's gesture correctly. Unlike Harriet, Dorothea does not think of her costume as a sign to be observed by 'spectators visible and invisible' or decoded by her acquaintances: this is a private, existential gesture. But her change of clothing makes her a visual emblem of the kind of consistency that matters: the ardent desire to act nobly that has motivated her from the beginning.

Nor do the connections stop here. Mrs Plymdale's remark about neat patterns and dyed-to-match feathers asks to be linked with yet another set of details in *Middlemarch*, those that document the commercial involvements of the Bulstrode/Vincy/Plymdale circle. Mr Plymdale and Mr Vincy are both in the yard-goods business, and Eliot makes clear that the taste displayed by their wives and daughters is the taste of a particular class, a class whose vulgarity is subjected to consistent irony. When the narrator introduces Dorothea by establishing her 'connections' as 'unquestionably good' precisely because 'if you inquired backward for a generation or two, you would not find any yard-measuring or parcel-tying forefathers' (5), Eliot is ironizing the snobbery expressed in such judgments; yet in the characterization of the Bulstrode/Vincy group she herself exploits the same stereotypes. Mr Vincy, who sells ribbons made for him by what Mrs Cadwallader calls 'the wretched handloom weavers in Tipton and Freshitt,' is dismissed by this lady as 'one of those who suck the life out of' them (239), and though Mrs Cadwallader is a snob, her thumbnail vignette of the Vincy family 'so fair and sleek' (239) at Featherstone's funeral is in line with what we already know about them. The narrator tells us that when Mr Vincy 'was disappointed in a market for his silk braids, he swore at the groom' (250). Vincy in turn attributes Mr Plymdale's handsome contributions to their church to the profits of bad workmanship: to his use of 'those blue and green dyes ... from the Brassing manufactory' that 'rot the silk' (96). By associating vivid colour, sartorial self-display, and questionable commercial practices, Eliot makes the same link between moral inadequacy and philistine vulgarity that we have learned to expect in the nineteenth-century novel from Burney and Austen on.[15] Eliot draws attention to Rosamond's snobbishness, her contempt for the young men she knows who 'could speak on no subject with striking knowledge, except perhaps the dyeing and carrying trades' (197), but in her own representation of the Vincy-Plymdale set she assumes a similar set of values on the part of the reader.

This yard-goods imagery frames the characterization of Harriet's niece, a young woman who is 'beguiled by attractive merchandise' (71) and who, though she imagines herself immeasurably superior to her family and the other natives of Middlemarch, in fact shares their aesthetic assumptions. Rosamond Vincy, 'who had excellent taste in costume, with that nymph-like figure and pure blondness which give the largest range to choice in the flow and colour of drapery' (71), is characterized by her taste for expensive, delicately or richly coloured fabrics and ornamental trimmings, attracting Lydgate with a dress that seemed 'to be made out of the faintest blue sky' (118), presiding over his tea table 'in her cherry-coloured dress with swansdown trimming' (340), and complacently anticipating Dorothea's admiration of 'her pale-blue dress of a fit and fashion so perfect that no dressmaker could look at it without emotion' (316). The middle-class Middlemarch household represented by the Vincys is founded on the gender contract described by Veblen: the man of the family provides the money, the women combine to spend it with conspicuous tastefulness. Rosamond is used to being liberally supported by her father and assisted in her project of consumption by her mother and a network of other female providers and supporters. The income that Mr Vincy has made marketing items produced by the 'wretched hand-loom weavers' allows his daughter to order her trousseau linen hand-sewn by her cousin Mary Garth, whose needlework, says Rosamond with airy malice, is 'the nicest thing I know about Mary' (252), and who is at Rosamond's disposal – as the weavers are at her father's – because of financial need (her own father being not a questionable merchant but a principled man of 'business'). That the outfitting of the middle-class young lady is a labour-intensive process and that most of the labour is done by women, well-established themes in the more strident kind of Victorian social criticism, is understatedly handled by Eliot. Rosamond, who wants 'to have all my cambric frilling double-hemmed' and knows that 'it takes a long time' (252), is perfectly willing to put off the date of her wedding to Lydgate until Mary can finish her task and she herself can amass the requisite collection of clothing and household goods, though she yields to her fiancé's importunities when it occurs to her that she can foist much of the labour upon her mother. In the Vincy set, women work together on the project of vicarious consumption, exploiting their less fortunate sisters if necessary, to assemble, exhibit, and assess the display of the goods provided by men, and their wardrobes are the signs of their husbands' prosperity and indulgence as well as of their own consistent effort. In her portrait of a bourgeois household on the make, Eliot anticipates Veblen: her critique of Rosamond is precisely in line with his insights.

Like her aunt Bulstrode, Rosamond becomes associated with co-ordinated multiplicity: items in matching sets. As Mary sardonically observes, her cousin 'can't be married without this handkerchief ... Because this is one of a dozen, and without it there would only be eleven' (292). The emphasis on enumeration and multiplicity is in line with Eliot's critique of the Vincys' materialism. The persona that Rosamond carefully constructs is likewise a conventional set: a set of tastes and talents, as laboriously assembled as her wardrobe, as emptily complete as her even dozen of handkerchiefs. At Mrs Lemon's school she has acquired the accomplishments that will mark her as 'the irresistible woman for the doomed man of that date' (198), and the narrator suggests both her commitment to the project and the banality of the result in a series of itemized lists:

> Her singing was less remarkable, but also well trained, and sweet to hear as a chime perfectly in tune. It is true she sang 'Meet me by moonlight,' and 'I've been roaming;' for mortals must share the fashions of their time, and none but the ancients can be always classical. But Rosamond could also sing 'Black-eyed Susan' with effect, or Haydn's canzonets, or 'Voi, che sapete,' or 'Batti, batti' – she only wanted to know what her audience liked. (119)

'Perfectly in tune' herself with conventional expectations, aware of her market, diligent in her efforts to turn herself into a cliché of contemporary feminine charm, Rosamond becomes before her marriage even more 'active in sketching her landscape and market-carts and portraits of friends, in practising her music ... read[ing] the best novels, and even the second best' (124), exhibiting 'always that combination of correct sentiments, music, dancing, drawing, elegant note-writing, private album for extracted verse, and perfect blond loveliness' (198) that she assumes her audience expects.

Rosamond considers herself eminently consistent, and in one sense she is. Single-minded in her goals from the time we first meet her until the end of the novel, she never, as she charmingly informs Lydgate, deviates from what she chooses to do.[16] But her stubbornness is the very opposite of the consistency attributed to Dorothea. Gillian Beer notes the double relevance of the quotation from Spenser's sonnet in praise of constancy that serves as the epigraph for chapter 37: the quotation, ironic if applied to the demeanour of Rosamond in chapter 36, will be recuperated for 'a fuller meaning' if applied to Dorothea in chapter 37 itself.[17] Eliot represents Dorothea in terms of radiant wholeness,[18] while the lists by which Rosamond is constructed have the effect, like the blazon, of dividing her up into parts. These lists are an inventory, summing up her stock in trade. Rosamond is presented as a manufactured item, a made-to-order product, and her taste, the taste of a successful manufacturer's daughter, is a medium of exchange, a form of cultural capital.[19] Like her father, Rosamond is in the market, and what she has to sell is her carefully cultivated image, in which so much of her own effort and many of the family's resources have been invested.[20]

The taste of women like Harriet Bulstrode and Rosamond Vincy is predictable because it expresses not their personal distinction but their membership in a middle-class provincial 'set.' The assumption behind the sociological method of characterization that constructs Rosamond – the assumption that all taste is an expression of social class – is articulated by her brother Fred in the scene in which Rosamond objects to their unsophisticated mother's idiom. When Mrs Vincy accuses her daughter of being 'tetchy' with her brothers, Rosamond echoes her wording in her retort ('Not tetchy, mamma: you never hear me speak in an unladylike way' [73]); but when her mother complains of her turning down 'the pick' of the town's young men, Rosamond, complacent enough about the tribute to her sexual power to ignore the vulgarity of the idea itself, has the leisure to observe that 'the pick' is 'rather a vulgar expression' of it (73). She herself would say 'the best of them' (73); Mrs Vincy, finding this 'just as plain and common,' would opt instead for 'the most superior young men' (73). Enter Fred, to observe that 'there are so many superior teas and sugars now' that 'superior is getting to be shopkeeper's slang,' and to articulate a generalization surprisingly theoretical for a somewhat dunder-headed young man, a generalization that governs Eliot's own depiction of this family: 'All choice of words is slang. It marks a class' (73). No doubt parroting a notion he has picked up at college, Fred provocatively characterizes what his sister calls 'correct English' (73) as merely 'the slang of prigs who write histories and essays' (74).

Fred's analysis might seem admirably relativistic and objective, but its relativism is, so to speak, only relative. The awareness that taste is produced by social class does not preclude judgments of taste as better or worse: on the contrary, as there are more and less refined classes, there are more and less refined tastes, as both Fred and Eliot make clear. The distinctions Fred makes are to be neither taken as simply belonging to Eliot nor dismissed just because it is he who makes them. The reader is invited to evaluate the characters' linguistic choices in this scene, in light of Fred's insight though not entirely in line with his criteria, precisely by bringing to them a sophisticated sense of the way social class has produced them. We are expected to rank Mrs Vincy's colloquial but unselfconscious 'tetchy' and 'pick' above her affectedly genteel 'superior.' We are asked to prefer Rosamond's 'simple and plain' word choice to either, while realizing that Rosamond – a mimic, 'clever with that sort of cleverness which catches every tone except the humorous' (117), who watches Lydgate for 'the slightest hint that anything was not ... in the very highest taste' (200) – is also perhaps merely parroting a principle she has heard. We are also expected to judge Fred, for his power to generalize, as intellectually superior to the women, who never rise above particularities, but to note the tactlessness, indeed vulgarity, of his own objection to 'shopkeepers' slang,' since the education that has enabled both him and his sister to critique their mother's language has been financed by trade. The Vincy family represents a class on its way up, and all its members' 'individual' opinions are shaped simply by how far they have climbed and by what means. Recognizing taste as a product of class does not preclude judgments about vulgarity. This sketch, dissecting with sociological precision the variants in the class that produced Rosamond, exemplifies both the condescension that shapes Eliot's depiction of the whole Vincy family and also her reliance on the good taste of her implied reader to pick up the nuances that produce such subtle class distinctions.

Taste is both individual and universal, the product at once of personal choice and of group consensus. Eliot turns this paradox into a double bind for the characters she satirizes. Insofar as the taste of women like Harriet Bulstrode and Rosamond Vincy expresses the standards of the group, it is banal. Eliot makes clear that these people, though they are different from one another, have no true individuality but are all thoroughly conventional. On the other hand, insofar as their aesthetic choices involve time and effort, they signal unworthy priorities and moral triviality. In *Middlemarch*, the more energy characters spend on aesthetic choice, the less individual they are. The taste of those who think themselves notably tasteful is a marker both of their mediocrity and of their conventionality. Eliot's heroine, on the other hand, who never thinks about dress at all – who finds herself unable to 'reconcile the anxieties of a spiritual life involving eternal consequences, with a keen interest in guimp and artificial protrusions of drapery' (6) – is stunningly distinguished, not only in her beauty (and her wardrobe) but also in her moral nature. In this respect she lines up in an unexpected way with Lydgate, a character who is like Dorothea not only in his ardent idealism but also in the offhand elegance with which he wears his clothes, but who is otherwise pointedly inconsistent in his values.

Lydgate fully recognizes the mediocrity of the set to which Rosamond belongs: the fatuity of Ned Plymdale and his *Keepsake*, the 'tinge of unpretentious, inoffensive vulgarity in Mrs Vincy' (117). This vulgarity is presently illustrated by her not so inoffensive remark about the wedding gift Sir Godwin might be expected to give her daughter: 'I should think he would do something handsome. A thousand or two can be nothing to a baronet' (261). It is a Jane-Austenish moment, and Lydgate, who has already felt that he is 'descending a little in relation to Rosamond's family' (256), imagines that his beloved, 'that exquisite creature,' suffers, like Elizabeth Bennet in *Pride and Prejudice*, 'in the same kind of way' as he does from her mother's crudity (256). Conscious of his superiority to his own family, Lydgate is ready to impute the same exceptionality to her. What he fails to realize however is that Rosamond is more like the people from whom she dissociates herself than she is like him. She shares Mrs Lemon's sense of what a woman should be, her mother's assumptions about the standard of living she deserves, and, indeed, Ned's interest in the *Keepsake* volume. Whereas Lydgate, with no access to the backstage scenes that reveal to us her complicity with their values, sees her relatives in rather novelistic terms as her foils, giving 'more effect to Rosamond's refinement' (117), in fact she is very much like them. He sees in Rosamond the superiority that confirms his own superiority to the group to which she belongs, but we see his taste for her as a sign that he shares her vulgarity, despite his aristocratic background and his claims to intellectual distinction.

Indeed, Lydgate is vulnerable to Rosamond's blandishments and incapable of recognizing her real nature because he has bad taste in women. When the narrator observes that the 'distinction of mind which belonged to his intellectual ardour did not penetrate his feeling and judgement about furniture or women' (111), the point is made not only that women are a species of furniture in his mind but also that there is a fundamental split in his character. An idealist about his profession, Lydgate is a materialist in regard to both women and furniture of the inanimate kind. He takes a refined style of life for granted – 'it had never occured to him that he should live in any other than what he would have called an ordinary way' (255) – and a decorative and soothing spouse is part of the domestic scenario he imagines. The narrator insists that this sense of entitlement is also a form of 'vulgarity,' drawing attention to 'the vulgarity of [his] feeling that there would be incompatibility in his furniture not being of the best' (112). Like Rosamond's, Lydgate's taste is a class marker, a product of the aristocratic background to which he is otherwise loftily indifferent, and when they marry their complementary assumptions about the kind of goods they require combine to induce them to live beyond their means:

> Rosamond, accustomed from her childhood to an extravagant household, thought that good housekeeping consisted simply in ordering the best of everything – nothing else 'answered;' and Lydgate supposed that 'If things

were done at all, they must be done properly' – he did not see how they
were to live otherwise. (429)

His aristocratic sense of entitlement jibes with her family's habits of conspicuous consumption to produce the bankruptcy for which they are
both responsible.

Yet their attitudes to material luxury, though equally attributed (Fred-
like) to class background, are not equally condemned. It is true that the
'careless refinement' (68) that marks Lydgate's manner, his 'careless
politeness of conscious superiority' (197), evokes a certain irony. Lydgate, the third major figure in *Middlemarch* who is characterized by his
taste in clothing, is a man with an 'air of inbred distinction' whose
'clothes hung well upon him' (111) and who seems to wear 'the right
clothes ... by a certain natural affinity, without ever having to think
about them' (197). The elegance is in the detail: Mary Garth, taking
'inventory' of his attractions ('heavy eyebrows, thick dark hair, large
solid white hands' [85]) in a list that subliminally links him, as a stock
gender stereotype, with his bride, also observes his 'exquisite cambric
pocket-handkerchief' (85). Yet it is detail to which he himself seems
indifferent. Lydgate buys a house as he buys shirts and handkerchiefs,
'in an episodic way, very much as he gave orders to his tailor for every
requisite of perfect dress, without any notion of being extravagant'
(255), and without much selective attention. Like Rosamond, he orders
items in sets, but while Rosamond counts her handkerchiefs by dozens,
Lydgate takes it as 'a matter of course that he had abundance of fresh
garments' and 'naturally' orders them 'in sheaves' (429–30). Such 'careless refinement' is by no means naturalized by Eliot, who, distinguishing
subtly between the different ways of buying in complete sets, makes
clear that Lydgate's style of consumption derives from abundant cultural and material resources and is aligned with 'that personal pride and
unreflecting egoism which I have already called commonness' (255).
She makes the point that though his taste for 'superior' commodities is
inconsistent with his 'French social theories,' it is his very access to the
former that makes him open to the latter:

> We may handle even extreme opinions with impunity while our furniture,
> our dinner-giving, and preference for armorial bearings in our own case,
> link us indissolubly with the established order. And Lydgate's tendency was
> not toward extreme opinions: he would have liked no barefooted doc-
> trines, being particular about his boots. (255)

He is also particular about the aesthetics of the dinner table. Lydgate's taste in china is associated with his attitude to servants: he takes for granted not only 'green glasses for hock' but also 'excellent waiting at table' (255), and purchases a set of expensive china on the assumption that 'one must hire servants who will not break things' (258). Servants are simply part of the domestic machinery that must run smoothly if it is to deliver to Lydgate the refined satisfactions that he expects. In this respect they are like wives. The set-of-china motif links Lydgate's complacency about his own prospective household with his distaste for that of the local practitioner Wrench. Contemplating the aesthetic deficiencies of this domestic scene – 'the doors all open, the oil-cloth worn, the children in soiled pinafores, and lunch lingering in the form of bones, black-handled knives and willow-pattern' (260) – Lydgate comforts himself with the thought that 'Wrench had a wretched lymphatic wife who made a mummy of herself indoors in a large shawl' (260). His callousness about what Mrs Wrench has to contend with is consistent with his shortsighted admiration for Rosamond, whom he sees as a pure product of nature, with little sense of the effort that has gone into her self-presentation.

Lydgate's demand for 'the best' in purchasable commodities is, then, associated with what the narrator tells us is a kind of 'vulgarity,' of 'commonness' – not only with pride and arrogance but also with a certain contempt for other people. But the paradoxical flavour of this assertion – the narrator's emphasis on his vulgarity, as if vulgarity were not a trait one would 'naturally' attribute to someone of his social background – demonstrates the rigour of Eliot's moral judgment while it also back-handedly relativizes it. For after all, as the narrator's emphasis itself implies, this is vulgarity with a difference. There is indeed a certain inconsistency in Eliot's presentation of Lydgate in that some of his assumptions about material goods are ones we are invited to share. Consistent with his carelessness, for example, are his respect for intellectuality and his contempt for conspicuous consumption. As a dinner guest Lydgate 'would have despised any ostentation of expense; his profession had familiarized him with all grades of poverty, and he cared much for those who suffered hardships' (255). Though he 'hated ugly crockery' (258), he would 'have behaved perfectly at a table where the sauce was served in a jug with a handle off' and 'remembered nothing about a grand dinner except that a man was there who talked well' (255). Qualifying the suggestion that his carelessness is an affectation is the implication that, while he has picked up a sense of entitlement from his family background, at some 'deeper' level Lydgate himself is essentially indifferent to merely material surroundings. His carelessness about material goods is also linked with his ardent generosity towards Rosamond. Whatever we are told about his tastes, Lydgate apparently lives in a very simple way until he has to set up housekeeping for her. If he thinks of his wife as 'furniture,' it is for her nevertheless that he purchases furniture, and it is only on her behalf that he regrets having to sell it.

Paradoxically, the split in Lydgate endows his sartorial elegance with a certain innocence. The very lack of connection between Lydgate's lofty ideals and his habits of consumption, though reliably ominous in a novel so committed to organic wholeness of character, exempts him from the meanness of actually thinking about what he consumes. For a gentleman, 'the ordinary way of living' and 'every requisite of perfect dress' are established by convention. Good taste does not require of an Englishman, indeed it positively precludes, individual choice. Lydgate's taste for the best, precisely because it is group taste, does not require him to spend time or effort on the objects he purchases. There is no sense that in furnishing his wardrobe Lydgate needs even for an instant to focus his mind upon particulars. For a woman of the same period, on the other hand, dressing in conventional good taste would take a good deal of individual judgment and effort. In differentiating between the Vincy and Lydgate styles of consumption – in her negative characterization of middle-class women who think about their dress and her somewhat more indulgent treatment of Lydgate – Eliot focuses on the effects of class while ignoring the constraints of gender. An aristocratic gentleman may be above such details; a woman of any class cannot be. Yet Rosamond and her set are satirized for thinking about what they wear, whereas Dorothea is exalted by her indifference to her wardrobe. That this set of moral valences is not always consistent – that it contributes to the mystified construction of the heroine as above the material concerns of everyday life – is borne out by almost every scene in which Dorothea appears as a visual figure.[21]

Like *North and South*, *Middlemarch* opens with a tableau displaying the heroine in all the austere glamour of her sober dress. While Margaret Hale's simple garb is summarily explained by the death of an anonymous relative, the Brooke sisters' is accounted for by a more nuanced and extended account of the 'mixed conditions' that produced it:

> The pride of being ladies had something to do with it: the Brooke connections, though not exactly aristocratic, were unquestionably 'good'; if you

inquired backward for a generation or two, you would not find any yard-measuring or parcel-tying forefathers – anything lower than an admiral or a clergyman; and there was even an ancestor discernible as a Puritan gentleman who served under Cromwell, but afterwards conformed, and managed to come out of all political troubles as the proprietor of a respectable family estate. Young women of such birth, living in a quiet country-house, and attending a village church hardly larger than a parlour, naturally regarded frippery as the ambition of a huckster's daughter. Then there was well-bred economy, which in those days made show in dress the first item to be deducted from, when any margin was required for expenses more distinctive of rank. (5)

It is made perfectly clear, not only that the kind of quiet elegance that characterizes Dorothea's wardrobe is the product of complex social and cultural forces over which she has no control, but also that one has to have been deeply implicated in material acquisition in order to rise 'above' it in this way: that the Brooke estate was acquired by a time-server; that elegantly inconspicuous dress may actually be a side effect of conspicuous consumption when it is required to allow the purchase of items 'more distinctive of rank.'

What the passage also adumbrates, however, is how the heroine's good taste will be produced in the novel itself by a process of differentiation and how the 'frippery' of the 'huckster's daughter' Rosamond Vincy is going to be used to set off the plain dress of the heroine. The snobbery of the narrator's formulation is associated in a surprisingly personal way with the heroine herself. We are told that such young women as Dorothea and Celia '*naturally* regarded frippery' – not 'naturally *would regard* it' – 'as the ambition of a huckster's daughter.' It is a remarkable assertion that not only, with whatever degree of saving irony, naturalizes class snobbery but also flirts with attributing it to the Brooke sisters. The slippery generalization implies that Dorothea and Celia might 'naturally' regard not only 'frippery' but the 'huckster's daughter' herself – whom of course they would not 'know' socially – with the kind of automatic disdain that this distinction implies. Though the Dorothea we become acquainted with cannot be imagined thinking about her social 'inferiors' in this way, Eliot stops just short of attributing the snobbery by which Rosamond is constructed by the text to the heroine herself as well as to the class that produced her. As sociological analysis, this is perfectly plausible: it would indeed be 'natural' for such young women, however well-meaning and good-hearted, to absorb some of the prejudices of their class. But such parochial prejudices are never, once the novel gets under way, shown influencing the notably independent-minded Dorothea, who consistently transcends them (and who, when she does eventually come face to face with the huckster's daughter, is in no state to register the 'frippery' Rosamond hopes might impress her). The passage is a remarkably sceptical and detached introduction to the young woman we have already been prepared to perceive as a kind of Saint Theresa, as well as a knowing contextualization of the simple glamour a novelistic heroine must possess. Aristocratic Beauty is demystified by the astringent application of novelistic Truth, the kind of truth a writer in the realist mode can bring to bear on social and historical context.

The assumption that the heroine's sartorial taste is to be understood as a sign of her individual nature is apparently qualified not only by the sociological framing but also by the fact that the two sisters dress alike and are introduced together. The socioeconomic factors Eliot has listed are said to act on both the sisters, though not precisely in the same way, to account for the style they have in common. Dorothea and Celia seem not so much to have chosen their garments as to have had them chosen for them by their nationality, religion, place of residence, family income, and social position. Yet though they are linked, in this admirably poised opening paragraph, by the similarity of their basic costume, by the second page of the novel, where Dorothea's religious scruples are first mentioned, a strenuous process of differentiation has already begun, and by the end of the chapter Celia has been firmly assigned the position of foil to the heroine, and Dorothea's taste has begun to serve as a sign of her own essential character.

The split begins of course in the scene in which the two girls divide their mother's jewels. Celia, who suggests inventorying the jewellery with a view to wearing it, is eager to abandon the sartorial simplicity hitherto prescribed for her and is morally placed as not-the-heroine by her interest in how she looks. Dorothea on the other hand responds even more strongly than Celia to the gems, but on grounds that have nothing to do with personal adornment. Attracted to their pure glowing colour with an intensity that suggests a capacity for sensuous response of which she is not fully aware, Dorothea rationalizes her pleasure in terms of the biblical associations of the jewels ('spiritual emblems in the Revelation of St John' (10), attempting to 'justify her delight in the colours by merging them in her mystic religious joy,' and then censors it with a Ruskinian compunction about the 'miserable men' who 'find such things, and work at them, and sell them!' (10). Her difference from her conventionally feminine sister (and her status as heroine) is confirmed by her lack of personal vanity on the one hand and her moral and aesthetic responsiveness on the other.

Despite the qualification to which she instantly subjects it, Dorothea's delight in the beauty of the jewels is a moment of emotion as pure and intense as their colour. It is startling to realize that this moment is the only dramatized example of positive aesthetic choice – choice of an object, that is, as opposed to a human being – in the entire novel. There is in *Middlemarch* a consistent pattern of de-selection, of the repudiation of the aesthetic artifact, on the part of a whole range of characters. As has often been pointed out, Dorothea is pointedly hostile to a range of aesthetic products – refusing to wear jewellery, responding with distaste or incomprehension to painting, oppressed by Rome, distressed by nude statues, and appalled by the red Christmas decorations in the Vatican – but other characters are equally dismissive. Casaubon is blind to the beauties of Rome, recommends *Cupid and Psyche* in frigid terms that make clear he is not in the least moved by it, and cannot stand music of any kind. Lydgate makes fun of the *Keepsake* but has left off reading more serious literature. Will Ladislaw, the artist, objects to the idea of capturing Dorothea's beauty on canvas, mocks the allegorical mode of painting exemplified by his Nazarene friend Naumann, has little use either for his own efforts or his friend's, and judges the supposed Guido, praised by the auctioneer Trumbull, to be almost worthless. Celia Brooke, who does object to Dorothea's dark clothing and insists on removing her widow's cap, is as blind to any aesthetic effect more abstract than personal appearance as her sister is to Casaubon's white mole. Celia's gesture produces a typical *Middlemarch* vignette, focusing our attention on Dorothea as a visual object, a noble and arresting contrast to the lesser female figure who serves as her foil. Indeed, Dorothea herself is the only legitimate object of aesthetic attention in the novel. She is also the only character who exercises aesthetic choice, the only one swept away by pure aesthetic delight. It is the moment when she does so that first establishes her essential nature.

As this scene unfolds, Eliot slides away the detached sociological mode of discourse that characterized the opening paragraph. The biblical associations Dorothea makes with the gems and her concern for miserable miners are no doubt explicable, though they are not explained, by her Christian upbringing, but nothing we are told about her environment or education accounts for her intense response to pure colour and light, which asks to be read simply as an emanation of her essential nature. It is only when 'the sun passing beyond a cloud sent a bright beam over the table' that Dorothea, 'under a new current of feeling, as sudden as the gleam,' feels 'how deeply colours seem to penetrate one, like scent' and perceives them as 'fragments of heaven' (10). The shift in tone is as sudden as the sunbeam. Metaphor replaces metonymy, analogy replaces class analysis, as Eliot shifts from the notion of taste as a class marker to the suggestion that Dorothea's flash of feeling is a sign of her 'deep,' sweet, non-contingent selfhood, abstracted from historical particularity (like the pure colour of the gem), inward (like the gleam at its heart), and responsive (like the gem to the sun's rays). If the jewels are 'fragments of heaven,' the responsive human soul, galvanized and penetrated by the divine 'gleam,' is, by analogy, a fragment of the divine nature. As a visual tableau, a word painting, this is a kind of Protestant Neo-Platonic Annunciation, with the sunlight coming through the window to light up the gems and penetrate Dorothea, selecting her out as blessed among women by means of her own act of selection. Despite the immaturity and adolescent self-dramatization of her somewhat theoretical moral stance, despite her condescension to Celia and her lack of self-understanding in the scene as a whole, Dorothea is identified as a member of the elect by this impulse of delight.[22] The emerald's brilliance is 'consistent,' not with the colour scheme of the costume she might wear it with, but rather with Dorothea's own 'gemlike' (201) beauty and the 'inward fire' (10) of her spirit, which, directed at Celia, is 'not without a scorching quality' (10), but which will burn steadily throughout the novel. A chapter that begins with the knowing subversion of the very notion of individual taste concludes with a scene that foregrounds Dorothea's intensely personal aesthetic response as a transparent sign of her illuminated spirit.

The spiritualization is facilitated by the rapid transition from the ring in which the emerald is set, to the emerald itself, to the colour of the emerald. It is important that Dorothea be moved by abstract colour and light, uncontaminated by problematic imagery. Ecstatic response to colour is as much a Ruskinian value as concern for the welfare of the worker, and, though Eliot herself identified truth to nature as Ruskin's essential moral insight, she no doubt also knew the exercises in pure colour that he set for his pupils.[23] But it is Eliot rather than her character who has been reading Ruskin: there is no sense that Dorothea's instinctive impulse of joy is a product of her education. The coloured light that penetrates her with joy – the actual colour of the emerald, as opposed to the gem itself or the piece of jewellery in which it is set – precedes culture and language, though it is presently mediated by them. An emblem of pure origin, it is immaterial, non-representational, and uncommodifiable. The contentless image of light at which she gazes spiritualizes Dorothea, lifts her out of the world of feminine sartorial display, and gives her, if only for a moment, an emblematic quality. As Dorothea gazes at the emerald, we contemplate Dorothea-looking-at-the-emerald, the first of a series of tableaux that offer her as a figure to be interpreted by the awakened reader. The vignette, an image fit for a genre painting, is the first of several to turn Dorothea herself into a moral emblem.[24]

To be sure, the aesthetic impulse is promptly framed and moralized, not only by Dorothea herself, who questions 'the purity of her own feeling and speech' (11) in retaining the emerald for herself, but also by Celia, who 'thought that her sister was going to renounce the ornaments, as in consistency she ought to do' (10) – 'that Dorothea was inconsistent: either she should have taken her full share of the jewels, or, after what she had said, she should have renounced them altogether' (11). But though Celia has a point, Dorothea is not essentially inconsistent, as Eliot shortly makes clear. Ten pages later the word 'inconsistency' is picked up and its inaccuracy made clear. Dorothea's idealism startles and offends her neighbours:

> The intensity of her religious disposition, the coercion it exercised over her life, was but one aspect of a nature altogether ardent, theoretic, and intellectually consequent: and with such a nature, struggling in the bands of a narrow teaching, hemmed in by a social life which seemed nothing but a labyrinth of petty courses, a walled-in maze of small paths that led no whither, the outcome was sure to strike others as at once exaggeration and inconsistency. (21)

But these 'others' of course are wrong: it is their own moral vacuity that has forced Dorothea into what look like exaggerated responses. Pointing out their error gives Eliot an opportunity to enrich the meaning of the authentic consistency that Dorothea exhibits to the more discriminating observer.

The almost submerged metaphors here equate stasis and movement, progress in time with stability in place. The 'con*sequent*' nature – the nature that *follows out* its own premises – is also the unchanging nature, the 'con*sistent*' nature that takes its stand and does not move. The sequential layeredness of Dorothea's response to the emerald – the way her initial, theoretical judgment about the jewels is qualified by a sudden, more spontaneous 'gleam' of feeling – implies a receptiveness that Celia lacks, a capacity for illumination of which the light at the heart of the emerald is an emblem. Her evolving, even contradictory response to the jewels is consistent with her own unfolding, 'intellectually consequent' nature, in which impulses and ideals must struggle with one another to form a nervous, organic whole, but it originates in a steady inner light – a consistent depth and intensity of response – that will characterize her from the first page to the last. From the point of view of the other characters who observe her, Dorothea's actions and decisions will continue to seem inconsistent, but their very incomprehension suggests that the heroine possesses an essential self distinct from these actions and decisions.

The way Dorothea dresses is as expressive of her inner consistency as Rosamond's inventoried trousseau is of her specular dispersal. After the first pages of the novel we are never again invited to submit Dorothea's wardrobe to sociological analysis but rather constrained to read her taste in clothes, as Mrs Plymdale reads Harriet Bulstrode's, as manifesting excellence of character. Indeed, though Eliot can ask us to smile at the conventional language by which the novelistic heroine is constructed, she is also ready to exploit it for her own purposes. When Dorothea reassures Celia that even though she herself would not wear a cross as an ornament, she would not think it wicked for Celia to wear one, she rather smugly deploys an invidious metaphor to account for her own higher standards: 'Souls have complexions too: what will suit one will not suit another' (9). But though her condescension is ironized here, irony quickly collapses into adulation, and the effusive rhetoric with which Dorothea's own complexion is later described – pale, but 'with a bloom like a Chiny rose' (352), to quote the worshipful Tantripp – does tend to make it, like her wardrobe, an emblem of her soul, and to differentiate Celia's soul from hers.

Aristocratic refinement of toilette is now to be understood as an outward and visible sign of Dorothea's spiritual distinction. Ellen Moers has pointed out, in her comparison of Dorothea to Mme de Staël's Corinne, that Eliot's heroine is not only given a 'stunning' wardrobe, she is typically pictured making a grand entrance.[25] On her first documented public appearance after her marriage, there was, we are told,

> an agreeable image of serene dignity when she came into the drawing-room in her silver-grey dress – the simple lines of her dark hair parted over her brow and coiled massively behind. (65)

Realism promptly slides into sublimity:

> Sometimes when she was in company, there seemed to be as complete an
> air of repose about her as if she had been a picture of Santa Barbara look-
> ing out from her tower into the clear air. (65)

Dorothea is a speaking picture, a moral emblem that teaches without
her having to utter a word. The comparison of the image to a picture
conveys the sense of the stillness – the *sistere* in 'consistent' – that is often
associated with this bride of quietness, the pause in the narrative that
implies not only her own inner repose but also the arrested attention of
an impressed focalizer. Though this impression of 'repose' is immediately qualified, 'these intervals of quietude' serving merely to make 'the
energy of her speech and emotion the more remarked when some outward appeal had touched her,' the impression of stillness sticks to Dorothea, as does the suggestion that she is there to be observed – by the
narrator and the reader even more than by the characters around her –
made to stand still so that we will have time to take her all in. Unlike
Rosamond, however (and Rosamond's literary progenitors – Lady Wishfort, for example, in *The Way of the World*) Dorothea never assumes a picturesque pose deliberately, but rather has it imposed upon her by her
author, who constructs her as a visual work of art worthy of our aesthetic
as well as moral contemplation.

   This author is ambiguously represented within the text. Indeed, there
is a peculiar instability in the narrative voice in many of the descriptions
of Dorothea. Who exactly 'remarks' the energy of Dorothea's speech?
The passive 'remarked' implies, without actually asserting, that Dorothea is the object of the group's attention. Or is it only the narrator
who is so fascinated by her beauty? Certainly it is not her husband:
Casaubon, who cannot perceive Dorothea's quality, is never used to
focalize his wife. Often the gazer is Will Ladislaw – indeed, Eliot sometimes qualifies the impression of the narrator's own 'fondness' for Dorothea by attributing it to Will, whose besotted adoration can be lightly
ironized – but Will is not present at this particular gathering. The per-
spectival fuzziness here manages to imply both that Dorothea is visibly
superior to everyone around her and that only the instructed eye of the
tasteful observer – the eye of someone cultivated enough to appreciate
the allusion to Santa Barbara – can appreciate her excellence. That eye
will select her among all the other figures in the room, pick her out
from the background precisely as a satisfying aesthetic object, choose

her (as Rosamond always imagines herself being chosen) as ineffably superior to everyone around her. The selection of Dorothea is the only kind of aesthetic choice, other than Dorothea's own choice of the emerald, that is either dramatized or endorsed in *Middlemarch*. It is a taste for Dorothea that the author aims to cultivate in her reader.

Despite her consistently striking appearance, it is never suggested that Dorothea spends a moment's thought on her costume. Indeed, in her first public appearance at the evening party in chapter 10, the narrator remarks that the simplicity of her hairstyle is 'in keeping with the entire absence from her manner and expression of all search after mere effect' (65), and there is no hint that this complete unselfconsciousness is ever qualified. Like Harriet Bulstrode, Dorothea is a moral emblem, but unlike Harriet she is unaware of the attention she attracts and indifferent to the clothes she wears. How then does she manage to be so consistently elegant?

In the Vincy circle, individual costume is a group project: the women dress for each other, in anticipation of the collective critique. Rosamond's mother evidently not only gives her a sense of entitlement, she helps her in practical ways, while Mrs Lemon schools her in fashion as well as in 'extras, such as the getting in and out of a carriage' (71). Dorothea, who belongs to no such female community and who does not have a mother, must choose her clothes for herself. She has no trouble mothering Celia in this respect: she is perfectly aware of how to accessorize her sister's wardrobe ('There, Celia! You can wear that with your Indian muslin. But this cross you must wear with your dark dresses' [9]). Yet we are never invited to believe she thinks like this on her own behalf, or that she is aware of the 'mere effect' that she herself produces.

It goes without saying that Dorothea is never shown looking in a mirror. What Barbara Hardy identifies as a mirroring moment, Dorothea's contemplation of the portrait of Will's mother and her empathy with another victim of an unhappy marriage, erases narcissism in the assertion of fellow-feeling.[26] Except at the moment when she asks Tantripp to bring her lighter mourning, Dorothea is never shown as selecting, much less donning, garments, only as throwing them impetuously off.[27] Indeed, she is never depicted involved in any domestic or personal task at all: she is consistently exempted from all the mundane decisions a woman would have to make in putting together the distinctive costumes in which we always see her. We are told that Dorothea would regularly 'drive into Middlemarch alone, on little errands of shopping or charity such as occur to every lady of any wealth when she lives within three miles of a town' (315), but we are given no sense of what those little errands might be. Jane Austen would tell us: it is to select ribbons for a hat. Though Lewes complained that in Austen's novels we do not know what people look like, we do know what they are buying. Eliot on the other hand tells us in considerable detail what Dorothea looks like, but the process by which she manages to look like this is completely elided from the text. Her wardrobe, like her voice – or like the spark at the heart of the emerald – is to be understood as a kind of spontaneous emanation of her inner excellence.[28]

There is a class element here, a mystified valorization of the 'careless refinement' that had earlier been identified as aristocratic. Because the characters' personal styles are constructed by means of the careful/careless binary and because Eliot cannot have Dorothea thinking about her clothes as Rosamond does, she ends up willy-nilly aligning her with the offhand Lydgate: her unmindful glamour is a mystified version of his perhaps studiedly careless elegance. It is suggestive that the two noblest characters in the novel both happen to be of 'good blood.' The fact that Dorothea and Lydgate transcend their class – that they are notably superior to and misunderstood by the other members of their families – is consistent with the liberal intellectual's claim to be 'above' class interests;[29] but the way Dorothea's sartorial style, which is initially linked to her class background, is then used as a sign of her *individual* excellence suggests that Eliot was not entirely immune to the aristocratic glamour that she also ironizes. The difference, though, is that whereas Lydgate's clothing would, in its very perfection, be perfectly conventional, Dorothea's is supposedly highly individualized, marking her out as unlike any other woman in the world. Dorothea's intuitive tastefulness, a sign of her election, needs to be separated from any active process of decision making which could make it an expression of her will. In a novel that is all about choices, the heroine's dress is a reliable emblem of her spiritual excellence precisely because she is not felt to have chosen it.

The unselfconscious glamour of the heroine, however, creates a certain problem with the moral organization of the novel. Eliot insists that Dorothea in her suffering is exemplary: that there are many other Dorotheas whose lives are being blighted by our prejudices. As Dorothea learns to sympathize with Rosamond as the universal suffering wife, so are we asked to sympathize with Dorothea as the universal frustrated woman. Yet all the aesthetic energy in the novel is directed towards demonstrating that Dorothea Brooke is unique. While Eliot's heroine may be morally representative, insofar as she stands for the many women who cannot put their ideals into practice, she is certainly not physically representative. But the relationship between the quality for which she is typical (frustrated idealism) and the quality in which she is utterly unique (aesthetic perfection) is muddled in that one is presented as the product of the other. Sympathizing with this radiant heroine is not at all like learning to sympathize with limited and unattractive personalities like Casaubon and Bulstrode. Eliot is endeavouring to produce both a reader who feels a charitable bond with common humanity in its universal suffering and a reader whose taste will be satisfied only by a Dorothea, and there is a tension between her ethics and her aesthetics.

The uniqueness of the heroine is consistently developed by visual contrast: contrast with her physical setting and with the other women in the novel, many of whom are carefully positioned to serve as her foils. That Dorothea's personal style is anachronistic has often been pointed out: 'archaic' in a modern setting, she is youthful and vital in an antique one.[30] She is characteristically described as if in a painting, standing out against a background that is older or darker or in some way baser than she. As Will waits for her arrival at the Lowick church, for example, his eyes scan 'the group of rural faces which made the congregation from year to year within the white-washed walls and dark old pews' until his beloved appears silhouetted 'on this quaint background, walking up the short aisle in her white beaver bonnet and grey cloak' (346). When he visits her in the library for the first time after the Roman trip, Eliot has her posed studiedly against a background that is not only dark in colour but associated with antique learning and with her husband's dry researches:

> She seated herself on a dark ottoman with the brown books behind her, looking in her plain dress of some thin woollen-white material, without a single ornament on her besides her wedding-ring, as if she were under a vow to be different from all other women. (266)

A similar contrast between dimness and brightness, youth and age, informs the much more erotic vignette of Dorothea, back from her honeymoon to Lowick 'in the middle of January,' entering her blue-green boudoir like the star of a theatrical production making her first appearance on stage:

> The bright fire of dry oak-boughs burning on the dogs seemed an incongruous renewal of life and glow – like the figure of Dorothea herself as she entered carrying the red-leather cases containing the cameos for Celia.

> She was glowing from her morning toilette as only healthful youth can glow: there was gem-like brightness on her coiled hair and in her hazel eyes; there was warm red life in her lips. (201)

Recognizing this as a 'backstage' moment in Goffman's sense underscores Eliot's idealization of her heroine: Dorothea backstage is as good and beautiful as she is in public. Her red-blooded 'glow' here is almost explicitly sexual, and as the description is elaborated the erotic feeling is heightened:

> Her throat had a breathing whiteness above the differing white of the fur which itself seemed to wind about her neck and cling down her blue-grey pelisse with a tenderness gathered from her own, a sentient commingled innocence which kept its loveliness against the crystalline purity of the outdoor snow. (201)

There seems to be an autoerotic embrace going on here, and as sonneteering comparisons proliferate and Dorothea becomes associated both with snow and with fire (and thus also differentiated from both), the syntax itself threatens to break down. The semiotics in this passage are as problematic as the narrator's warmth is striking. Swansdown on Rosamond's cherry-coloured gown is a sign, apparently, of her vanity: snowy-white fur on Dorothea's pelisse, on the other hand, is a sign of ... what? The somewhat hackneyed rhetoric illustrates just the kind of linguistic paradox of which Eliot can be so aware. Just as 'we can so seldom declare what a thing is, except by saying it is something else,'[31] so also it is impossible to say a thing is different without saying it is the same: impossible to claim that your heroine is uniquely lovely without using the same kind of language that has been used for centuries to make the same claim for a crowd of literary ladies.[32] The very strenuousness with which Eliot insists on Dorothea's difference threatens to turn her into just the kind of cliché that Rosamond strives to become, albeit a cliché from a 'higher' genre: from the sonnet as shaped by Petrarchan Neo-Platonism, associated with great male writers of the past, rather than from romance fiction, associated with contemporary women readers and silly lady novelists.

The distinction between high and mass culture – and between the past, which is associated with aesthetic excellence, and the present, characterized by the cheap and the transitory – is a consistent motif of

Dorothea's characterization. Though Dorothea sounds almost like a contemporary fashion plate in her fur-trimmed pelisse – and though none of the characters in the novel, whatever they think of her eccentricities in behaviour, ever mention oddity of dress, but on the contrary consistently emphasize her distinguished appearance – Eliot repeatedly suggests that Dorothea's clothing is anti-fashionable, vaguely archaic, and for that reason more elegant and dignified. The very first sentence of the novel, which claims that 'Miss Brooke had that kind of beauty which seems to be thrown into relief by poor dress,' subliminally suggests, by the metaphor of relief sculpture, austere and presumably monotone classicalities. Critics have remarked on the comparison between Dorothea and the Madonna ('Her hand and wrist were so finely formed that she could wear sleeves not less bare of style than those in which the blessed Virgin appeared to Italian painters' [5]) and have often cited the simile that follows:[33]

> Her plain garments ... by the side of provincial fashion gave her the impressiveness of a fine quotation from the Bible, – or from one of our elder poets, – in a paragraph of to-day's newspaper. (5)

Eliot dissociates Dorothea's wardrobe from the fragmentary newspaper paragraph, a product of modern technologies as well as modern discourses, and aligns it with equally fragmentary but richly signifying 'touchstones' of high culture, quotations that are timeless in an Arnoldian way, and with texts that are apparently not produced at all but rather divinely or poetically inspired: the Bible, or one of 'our elder poets.' The first-person 'our' associates the reader with the narrator's hierarchy of values. 'We,' apparently, are a group of cultivated readers who, understanding ourselves as inheritors of the great poetry of the past, naturally disdain the prose and the opinions of mere contemporary journalists (rather as the stuffier Middlemarchers disdain Will Ladislaw). The passage implies that Dorothea is too fine ever to be at home in the world of the daily newspaper – precisely the world in which at the end of the novel, as Will's wife, she will find herself. Her costume is represented as more like poetic inspiration than journalistic production: an emanation rather than a systematic composition, timeless like the utterance of genius rather than time-bound like journalism or indeed like serial publication in parts. By polarizing 'high' and 'low' writing as a means of characterizing her heroine, Eliot implies a kind of snobbery that other elements in the novel seem to repudiate and that could even ironize her own literary project, which must owe as much to contemporary journalism as to sacred text.

There is a similar inconsistency in the metaphor Eliot later uses to describe Will's feeling of possessiveness about Dorothea:

> Do we not shun the street version of a fine melody? – or shrink from the news that the rarity – some bit of chiselling or engraving perhaps – which we have dwelt on even with exultation in the trouble it has cost us to snatch glimpses of it, is really not an uncommon thing, and may be obtained as an everyday possession? (344)

This is not Will's metaphor: it is the narrator, interpreting Will's jealous feeling, who describes Dorothea in terms of a melody, a carving, an engraving – an artifact the limited access to which helps to produce its value. The metaphor quickly acquires a life of its own. While it is one thing to feel that the value of one's mistress is lowered if anyone can have access to her, it is a rather different thing to object to the nuances of a 'fine melody' being coarsened and cheapened by a 'street version.' And it is something else again to begrudge to others access, by means of mass production, to a work of art not thereby denied to 'us,' on the grounds that the difficulty in glimpsing it was part of its value for 'us.' To admit that the tasteful object is a commodity constructed by scarcity is to agree precisely with Bourdieu: to demystify the notion of taste itself, upon which the effect of this particular metaphor, as well as so much else in the novel, depends.

It is also an awkward image to apply to one's heroine. By associating Dorothea with high (but also low) art, the analogy commodifies her. But the notion that she is an artwork one might not only glimpse, evaluate, and select, but, if cheapened, purchase and possess is an even more startling suggestion. The grotesque notion of a 'street version' of Dorothea does not help, suggesting as it does prostitution in the literal rather than the figurative sense. The initial analogy between Dorothea and gem stones might suggest that she has a price beyond rubies, certainly not that she is connected with the modern marketplace. Rosamond is a made-for-the-market article: she is precisely 'produced' to a pattern, by a process that Eliot makes very visible. To imply that 'Dorotheas' as well as 'Rosamonds' could be produced (and in various versions, some cheaper and more available than others) functions as a rather tactless reminder that Dorothea too is a product manufactured and marketed within a system of printing and publication that makes the cultural artifact available to a wide readership and turns out items not dependent on physical scarcity for their cultural appeal.

Dorothea's anachronistic difference continues to generate contradictions in the two most calculated tableaux in the novel: the view of her in the Vatican museum, focalized by Will Ladislaw and Alfred Naumann, and the scene in which Dorothea accidentally intrudes on Rosamond with Will Ladislaw – not exactly focalized by Will. These are set pieces, designed to present the reader with 'a fine bit of antithesis' (140) between a classic and a modern figure. At the Lydgates', Dorothea in timeless white makes a striking contrast to Rosamond in her fashionable blue gown; at the Vatican, in her prim Quakerish costume, she makes an equally striking contrast to the ancient statue of Ariadne ('formerly known as the Cleopatra') reclining in loose and sexy 'drapery.' Here we approach Dorothea as an unidentified visual figure, from the point of view of the two would-be artists, who arrive at the spot

> where the reclining Ariadne, then called the Cleopatra, lies in the marble voluptuousness of her beauty, the drapery folding round her with a petal-like ease and tenderness. They were just in time to see another figure standing against a pedestal near the reclining marble: a breathing blooming girl, whose form, not shamed by the Ariadne, was clad in Quakerish grey drapery; her long cloak, fastened at the neck, was thrown backward from her arms, and one beautiful ungloved hand pillowed her cheek, pushing somewhat backward the white beaver bonnet which made a sort of halo to her face around the simply braided dark-brown hair. (140)

Dorothea's contemporary yet austere dress is a sign not of fashion consciousness – it is conspicuously non-fashionable – but of an evolved, troubled, Christian (or post-Christian) spirituality. Naumann proposes a reading of this tableau:

> 'There lies antique beauty, not corpse-like even in death, but arrested in the complete contentment of its sensuous perfection: and here lies beauty in its breathing life, with the consciousness of Christian centuries in its bosom.' (140)

In her fusion of physical beauty and modern *angst*, Dorothea is an emblem replete with cultural meaning: an unhappy, if not unravished, bride; an Arnoldian incarnation of sweetness and light. Though the men's impression of her is going to be corrected in the next chapter by the narrative of the events that brought her there, Naumann is not merely wrong: for once his insistence on allegorizing has found an adequate object. His commentary makes Dorothea into a 'social figure' in Cottom's sense, a tragic incarnation of the modern spirit, suspended between the sweetness of a sentimentalized past and the light of an envisioned future.[34] As usual, however, Dorothea has no idea that she is being observed. She is 'not looking at the sculpture, probably not thinking of it: her large eyes were fixed dreamily on a streak of sunlight which fell across the floor' (140). The metaphoric suggestion that she is looking for light is perhaps less important than the implication that she has no idea what a striking picture she makes.

Dorothea has been so carefully posed by her author that it is not surprising that Naumann proposes painting a picture of her. Will's repudiation of this suggestion allows Eliot to get the best of both worlds. His assertion that such beauty cannot be captured in a visual medium has been recognized as an allusion to Lessing's *Laokoön*; he feels that Dorothea's beauty transcends the detailed and specific representation that was dismissed by the Romantics as base and mechanical:[35]

> 'Language gives a fuller image, which is all the better for being vague. After all, the true seeing is within; and painting stares at you with an insistent imperfection. I feel that especially about representations of women. As if a woman were a mere coloured superficies! You must wait for movement and tone. There is a difference in their very breathing: they change from moment to moment. – This woman whom you have just seen, for example: how would you paint her voice, pray? But her voice is much diviner than anything you have seen of her.' (142)

But Eliot has already provided, in language not at all vague, a full and notably static account of the 'coloured superficies' of Dorothea, who gets the benefit of her author's documentation of her costume as well as of Naumann's interpretation of her spirit and Will's assertion of her unrepresentability. While Eliot characteristically uses figurative language to suggest the general effect Dorothea has on the viewer – the job that Lessing says poetry, as opposed to painting, is peculiarly fitted to do – she also takes pains to tell us specifically what her heroine is wearing. The reproduction of 'coloured superficies' is justified because these 'superficies' are just as reliable a sign of Dorothea's 'divine' nature as the mellifluous voice Will rhapsodizes about.

This is not the first reference to Dorothea's voice, or the last. Will has responded to it before, and Caleb Garth waxes lyrical about it, in a simile surprisingly high-cultural for a man of his tastes and education: 'a voice like music. Bless me! it reminds me of bits in the Messiah – "and straightway there appeared a multitude of the heavenly host, praising God and saying"' (402). As Moers tartly remarks, Dorothea's voice apparently teaches, yet without content.[36] This is just criticism, and it calls attention to how inarticulate and intellectually naive Dorothea remains for a young woman who, however sketchy her education, has in the past been inspired by theological texts and supposedly yearns after knowledge and wisdom. Though she is depicted applying herself to abstruse tomes she cannot master, Dorothea is never shown simply reading,[37] and she expresses herself in language that remains simple, almost childlike. Wary of abstraction and philosophical generalization, she has worked out 'a belief of my own' (286) and emphatically does not want to know of what discourses it is constructed: 'Please not to call it by any name ... You will say it is Persian, or something geographical' (286). The suggestion is that Dorothea's moral insight, like her wardrobe, is an unmediated expression of her individual excellence and that situating it historically would – to use Will's metaphor – breathe on its crystal and cloud it. By evading the fact that even such a 'personal' philosophy must of necessity locate the philosopher at a point in time and in a nexus of inherited discourses, Dorothea joins her author in repudiating the relativistic, sociological language by which she was originally constructed as well as in evading the necessity of translating aestheticized moral feeling into any coherent course of action.

Dorothea's voice is a spontaneous emanation of her spirit, like the light in the heart of the emerald: its mere music is as significant an expression of her inner nature as the words she utters. We might contrast this effortless emanation of the spirit to the laborious learning that produced *Middlemarch*. Daniel Cottom would say that this heroine in whom Truth is identified with Beauty impersonates Eliot's flight from philosophical theory and what she called 'opinion.' Like the 'social figure' of 'the individual,' which Cottom argues is the mere negation of social and historical causality, Dorothea has to remain empty of content while radiant with apparent meaningfulness. Dorothea's inability to find a vocation is not just a reflection of social fact, it is a discursive necessity.

She has to remain an empty sign if she is to comprehend and recuperate the past and point to the future.[38] Will Ladislaw's romantic assertion that Dorothea, though unable to 'produce a poem,' is essentially a poet because she *is* a poem (166) is ironized by her naive commonsense response, yet the novel positions her rather in the same way.

The scene in the Vatican Museum continues the polarizing process begun in chapter 1, the process by which Dorothea is defined visually as well as morally against other female figures.[39] As foil to Dorothea, Celia is soon eclipsed by Rosamond Vincy. Since Eliot cannot have Dorothea and Rosamond actually meet until near the end of the novel – realistically, because ladies like the Brookes would not receive the Vincy women socially, and structurally, because the interaction between the two characters when they do occur needs to stand out in climactic contrast to what has gone before – she establishes their utter difference at the beginning by suggesting that to choose Rosamond is actively to repudiate Dorothea. There is a reiterated 'choice of Hercules' paradigm that polarizes the women both visually and morally: Chicheley cannot simply admire Rosamond, he must make the point that he does not think much of Dorothea; Lydgate cannot simply fall for Rosamond, he has to be shown contemplating Dorothea's style of beauty and rejecting it. But by setting Dorothea up so consistently in opposition not only to Rosamond but to 'all other women' (266), identifying her as 'not-Rosamond,' 'not-cliché,' Eliot empties out the very category by which her heroine is defined. When the lover in Shakespeare's sonnet declares that 'my mistress' eyes are nothing like the sun' and goes on to enumerate the ways in which she differs from the conventional beauty, the implication is that this woman is unique and the poet uniquely discriminating in his preference for her. But an anti-blazon is still a blazon, and as he ticks off the list of features his mistress does not possess it becomes clear that she is less a person than a rhetorical figure, a product of pure polarity. By insisting so pointedly on Dorothea's difference from Rosamond, Eliot draws attention to this paradox. If there is something theoretical about Dorothea's unity, her wholeness, her moral consistency, it is partly because this unity is dependent for its construction on its demonic double.

The way this works is most dramatically illustrated in the scene in which Dorothea, coming to sympathize with Rosamond about Lydgate's plight, happens upon a tête-à-tête between Rosamond and Will. We are invited to see the moment when Rosamond's 'drawing-room door open[s] and Dorothea enter[s]' as highly theatrical: 'By the present audience of two persons, no dramatic heroine could have been expected with more interest than Mrs Casaubon' (316). But this audience of two are not the focalizers of the tableau that follows. Rosamond quickly becomes not an observer but one of the two figures to be observed, and Will is 'too much occupied with the presence of the one woman to reflect on the contrast between the two' (316). It is not the characters but the reader who is asked to be the 'calm observer' and moral interpreter of the contrast between the two exemplary female figures.

Yet the narrator's own tone is by no means calm. Even though the passage begins with the recognition that the difference between the costumes of the two women is partly a matter of difference in class – that it is 'a sort of contrast not infrequent in country life when the habits of the different ranks were less blent than now' – the narrative voice insists nevertheless that we read Dorothea's dress as an emblem of her purity and simplicity:

> Let those who know, tell us exactly what stuff it was that Dorothea wore in those days of mild autumn – that thin white woollen stuff soft to the touch and soft to the eye. It always seemed to have been lately washed, and to smell of the sweet hedges – was always in the shape of a pelisse with sleeves hanging all out of fashion. Yet if she had entered before a still audience as Imogene or Cato's daughter, the dress might have seemed right enough: the grace and dignity were in her limbs and neck; and about her simply parted hair and candid eyes the large round poke which was then in the fate of women, seemed no more odd as a head-dress than the gold trencher we call a halo. (316)

Who exactly is speaking here? Apparently someone who would customarily be close enough to catch the scent of Dorothea's gown and intimate enough to touch it. It sounds like a lover, yet it does not seem to be Will who is making the comparison with Imogen or Cato's daughter, and it certainly is not he who asks to be told 'exactly what stuff it was in those days': the question is retrospective, and the rhetorical appeal here – 'Let those who know, tell us' – calls attention to itself by its oddity. Though it has some of the force of 'What men or gods are these?' this is not quite a rhetorical question, but no more than Keats's question does it await an answer. It does not mean 'Name that fabric' – it is not a question about the textiles produced in 1832 (Eliot has created the effect she wants with 'thin white woollen stuff,' and that is all we need to know about what Dorothea's dress is made of) – but rather something like 'Let those who once knew her testify of their experience.' This lyric intrusion is so unusual in tone, so unexpectedly personal and intimate, and so hyperbolic in its figures of speech that it is curious even in the context of the admiration customarily evoked by Dorothea. It is at least as striking and unexpected as the famous injunction to pay due attention to the sorrows of Casaubon at the beginning of chapter 29. If, as the narrator there complained, we care more for blooming young complexions than grumpy old men, it is surely partly because of passages like this, which only intensify at the end of the novel when the grumpy old man has been disposed of.[40]

By making Dorothea suddenly into an almost legendary figure from the past, a figure about whom testimony can be taken, and a character who evidently recalls the lost youth of whoever it is that is speaking, the phrase paradoxically makes us aware of the forty-year gap between the publication of *Middlemarch* and the passing of the first Reform Bill and yet suspends the heroine in a timeless present. Eliot provides the flavour of a historical moment so that the image of Dorothea can transcend it. Yet Dorothea in her white garment cannot in fact rise above her historical moment. On the contrary, she is very much of it: she is simply the 'fashion type' familiar to the Victorians, the type that Mary Anne Schimmelpenninck calls 'sublime.'[41] That the sartorial sublime is a product of uneasiness about the commodification of female beauty is suggested by the context into which Dorothea in her white robe is so theatrically inserted.

The paean to Dorothea herself is promptly capped by an overdetermined contrast between her and Rosamond:

> They were both tall, and their eyes were on a level; but imagine Rosamond's infantine blondness and wondrous crown of hair-plaits, with her pale-blue dress of a fit and fashion so perfect that no dressmaker could look at it without emotion, a large embroidered collar which it was to be hoped all beholders would know the price of, her small hands duly set off with rings, and that controlled self-consciousness of manner which is the expensive substitute for simplicity. (316)

The implied addressee has shifted again: now it is not someone who knew Dorothea and can 'tell us' what she used to wear but rather someone who needs to be commanded to 'imagine' Rosamond's appearance and then instructed how to interpret it. But the lesson is too insistent. It makes too clear that Rosamond's costume needs to be represented as the frippery of a huckster's daughter so that Dorothea can look so otherworldly beside her. Taste is always differential: vulgarity is needed to set it off, and Eliot has already linked Rosamond's vulgarity with social class. Ironically, it is just as Dorothea is appealing to Rosamond in recognition of the suffering that unites them that Eliot demonstrates how utterly different the two women are in quality. The one character in the novel we are not called upon to sympathize with is Rosamond. There are limits to Eliot's doctrine of universal sympathy. Dorothea may reach out to Rosamond in a burst of fellow-feeling, but Eliot's reader is made to remain a 'calm observer' of the difference between them.

Both the colour and the lustre of the women's costumes structure the epigraph to this chapter: the pseudo-fragment, in imitation of Browning, implicitly comparing Dorothea and Rosamond to two figurines.[42] The description of the living Dorothea is monochrome, relieved only by the imaginary gold of a metaphoric halo, while Rosamond's blue dress is set off by a merely material crown ('her wondrous crown of hair-plaits' of 'infantine blonde'), as her small hands are by rings. Beside Dorothea's woollen robe, her costume seems to shine and glitter. The figurines described in the epigraph are polarized along the same lines. 'Dorothea' comes first:

> This figure hath high price; 'twas wrought with love
> Ages ago in finest ivory;
> Nought modish in it, pure and noble lines
> Of generous womanhood that fits all time.

'Rosamond' follows, with five lines to Dorothea's four (the vendor perhaps noticing that he has caught the buyer's interest?):

> That too is costly ware; majolica
> Of deft design, to please a lordly eye:
> The smile, you see, is perfect – wonderful
> As mere Faience! a table ornament
> To suit the richest mounting. (315)

The consistency of the contrast is neat if rather relentless. Not only is the Rosamond figure made out of a cheap, common material – 'mere Faience,' which is worthless until it is 'worked up,' brightly painted, and glazed – it is also described as a 'table ornament,' recalling both

Rosamond's decorative appearance at Lydgate's tea table and the suggestion that he chose her rather as he chose his china. The phrase 'the richest mounting' evokes Rosamond's demand to be handsomely maintained and recalls the jewellery Lydgate gave her. The way the figures have been shaped is also appropriate to the way the women's characters have been formed: 'Rosamond' moulded, suggesting her suave, ductile personality; 'Dorothea' carved, evoking fine but decisive strokes of the knife. Unlike clay, ivory was once a living substance; less brittle and more valuable than majolica, it is more likely to survive into the future. 'Dorothea' teaches, a speaking picture embodying 'generous womanhood'; 'Rosamond' merely delights, pleasing the covetous eye. The monochrome 'purity' of the ivory and its lack of 'modishness' are what we would expect of a Dorothea figurine.

But would we expect a Dorothea figurine at all? The conceit itself is disconcerting. While Rosamond constructs herself as an ornament, as an object of the male gaze, Dorothea emphatically does not. Rosamond is frankly for sale to the highest bidder – she will shortly be described with the word 'expensive' ('expensive substitute for simplicity') – whereas from the first page of the novel Dorothea is supposedly exempt from the taint of trade, both literally and figuratively. The metaphor that is intended emphatically to differentiate the two women instead equates them in an unexpected way. It puts them on display, offers them for sale, as one man, the vendor, commends his wares to the 'lordly gaze' of another. The way the dramatic monologue implies collusion between two men – one displays the beauties of two women and invites the other to choose between them – has an element of the grotesque, even the salacious. The vendor recalls Browning's unsavoury collectors – the Duke in 'My Last Duchess,' who also displays a woman as an art object, and the Bishop in 'The Bishop Orders His Tomb – men whose lust for objects is associated or equated with illicit or exploitative relationships with women. But the pairing of two women and the idea of buying and selling them are added touches, putting the vendor in the position of a pimp. The Lilliputian scale of the female figures, along with their rigid immobility, implies their helplessness before the male gaze. The epigraph repeats the 'choice of Hercules' scenario already developed in several different keys in the novel but in a way that renders it unexpectedly gross and grotesque. The verse is an imitation of Browning, but it is a demonic parody of the discourse of the narrative voice itself.

The suggestion is that the potential buyer, who is probably not really 'lordly' – this is no doubt the vendor's flattery – is also not highly discriminating. The merchant rather quickly moves from the simpler figurine, which has apparently failed to hold the customer's attention, to the more elaborate one, and as his manner becomes more flattering – the smile on the face of the majolica figure transferring itself both to the seller who praises it and to the customer whose eye is evidently caught by the painted face – he couches his appeal more frankly in terms of money and status. The 'huckster' himself perfectly knows the relative aesthetic value of the two objects, but he is prepared for a customer who does not and is equally willing to sell tasteful or vulgar goods, as long as he makes a sale. Taken out of context, this sharp, cynical piece of characterization is a skillful little vignette, but considered in terms of the wider analogy Eliot has so studiedly set up it makes some odd identifications. The real connoisseur – the one who would not need to be told that 'Dorothea' is more valuable than 'Rosamond' – is not present in the text: it is the reader, whose taste for the 'superior' commodity has been cultivated from the first pages of the novel. And the vendor to this consumer is – who but the author herself, who quite literally offers them both for sale?

This peculiar introduction to an equally arresting episode tends, not despite but because of its overdetermined contrasts, to deconstruct the polarity between the women in which Eliot has such a stake. It acknowledges that Dorothea, like the figurines, has indeed become an ornament – an ornament of Eliot's text. She has become a figure whose function is to arrest the gaze, to announce that it is 'the best' on the market, the most 'superior' article, the object of choice for the consumer who is convinced (like Lydgate) that nothing but the best will do. It is a tactless reminder that Eliot's investment in Dorothea's physical loveliness not only problematizes the insistence on her heroine's uniqueness and originality but naturalizes the construction of woman as the object of the male gaze and of men's evaluation and assessment.[43]

Not only is the linking to Dorothea of the marketing imagery hitherto connected with Rosamond decidedly incongruous, the analogy that situates Eliot herself in the position of the one who produces the two figures for sale implies her own financial motivation in a disconcerting way. While 'if [Dorothea] had written a book, she must have done it as Saint Theresa did, under the command of an authority that constrained her conscience' (64), Eliot writes as well to make a living: indeed the negotiations between Lewes and Blackwood about the novel way in which *Middlemarch* was to be sold and marketed would have kept its commercial aspect very present in her mind.[44] There is a very real sense in which Eliot is manufacturing a certain kind of female beauty as a commodity: deferring to the very cultural expectations that she identifies as inhibiting women's full development, and indeed suggesting that a woman, no matter how distinguished her mind or soul, has to be physically beautiful to be interesting as a heroine. Norman Feltes has suggested that the idealization of Lydgate is Eliot's defence against or repression of her own commercial motivation.[45] That the spiritualization of Dorothea serves a similar purpose is suggested by the metaphor which momentarily deconstructs it.

The notion of consistency means so much to Victorian moralists because it confirms the sovereignty of individual subjectivity, the self-containedness and independence of individual moral life, not constructed by social discourse, at a moment when the possibility of understanding subjectivity in terms of the humanist concept of 'character' was coming under threat. Eliot, deeply invested in this vision of integrity, aims at a similar kind of consistency in her novel, weaving innumerable strands together into a single reverberating whole and then topping it up with several sets of 'instructions for reading' intended to drive the reader down a single interpretative path. The firm moral framing of the narrative – the narrator's interventions, the overdetermined ironies, the titles of chapters and books, and the epigraphs – is designed to nail down or net in meaning. The aesthetic effect however is the opposite of the simplicity we are asked to adore in Dorothea. Eliot's prose is more like Rosamond Vincy's costume than like Dorothea Brooke's: fully thought out, elaborately trimmed, thoughtfully accessorized, designed to produce an effect both of copia and of fastidious coordination. But the very exhaustiveness of Eliot's method can work against her. As she ranges for 'textual braid,' 'guimp,' and 'trimmings' (6) to enrich her text, loose threads pull in various directions. The more Eliot insists on the consistency of Dorothea, the more clearly her heroine emerges as an inconsistent construction, an inevitably self-contradictory effect of the discourse in which she is embedded, and as a defence against those features of contemporary life that make individual consistency impossible.

The Victorian investment in 'consistency,' which is usually a matter of knowing what you believe in and sticking firmly to your principles, is, like its valorization of wholeness and unity of character, no doubt a defence against the social and intellectual pressures that seemed to militate against both stable selfhood and assured moral commitment. Like her contemporaries who find the term 'consistency' an ever-apposite buzzword, Eliot is responding with a kind of desperate organicism to the threat to subjectivity posed not only by intellectual challenges to faith but also by the pressures of commodification and capitalism at the time. It is worth noting how limited is her optimism in the face of this threat. An organically unified individual is possible still to imagine; an organic society is not. There is no consistent community in *Middlemarch* to which the consistent individual could be creatively connected, nor is it suggested that any amount of 'reform' is likely to produce one in the near future. Dorothea's exceptionality impresses and inspires, but in the end it can do nothing to alter the destructive energies of Middlemarch.[46] To the degree that the exceptional individual is radiantly consistent, she is marked off from rather than integrated into the society apparently so much in need of her idealism. The aesthetics of the text, which places this woman, who is a figure from romance (visually at least and no doubt morally as well), against a community that is given a sociologically 'realistic' treatment, signals the gap in Eliot's project to which Daniel Cottom has called attention. It is emblematic not only of Dorothea's exceptionality but also of the way she is marooned in history that she is so often posed alone and alienated against a background hostile or indifferent to humanist values of which her beauty is a mystified emblem.

It takes a period like the present, when the very notion of coherent subjectivity has come under question, for the work that 'consistency' has to do in *Middlemarch* to draw itself to the reader's attention. Eagleton argues that to become a work of art the physical object had first to become a commodity, and the way that Eliot constructs her heroine as a defence against commodification provides a test case for his argument. Adorno sees modern art as valuable only insofar as it encodes within itself the reality of its commodification – insofar as 'it provides an implicit critique of the conditions which produce it' by acknowledging 'how deeply it is compromised by what it opposes.' But, he says, for the text 'to press this logic too far' – that is, to represent itself frankly as pure commodity – would be 'to undermine its authenticity.' It is the tension that is productive: 'it is this internal slippage or hiatus within the art work,' Adorno argues, 'which provides the very source of its critical power.'[47] By his criteria, it is Eliot's inability to construct an autonomous, perfect text with no loose ends that gives the novel the power it has to testify against the conditions under which she produced it.

# Conclusion

My study concludes with *Middlemarch*, a high Victorian text still deeply invested in the notion of 'moral taste.' Attempting to illustrate what patterns will emerge if we take tastefulness as seriously as did the nineteenth century, and convinced that the only way to do that is to look closely at its shaping influence on individual texts, I have necessarily limited myself to a small number of authors and to the high Victorian period.

Other novelists who could well have been included in such a discussion will come immediately to mind. Dickens might well have a whole chapter, and so might Anthony Trollope, who consistently invokes aesthetic feeling and the perfect taste of characters like Glencora Palliser[1] in the defence of what has been taken to be a conservative agenda, though more ironically and skeptically than has often been recognized. Disraeli and the Young England movement invite analysis, which might be complemented by a study of the High Anglican aesthetic as disseminated to children. I would have liked to include a discussion of Elizabeth Sewell's *Amy Herbert* (1844), a juvenile novel addressed to Anglican girls, which not only rewrites *Mansfield Park* and anticipates *Jane Eyre* but also makes central use of a number of the devices I have identified (the starry-sky scenario, the woman's room, and the landscape prospect) in the service of a gentrified Anglican quietism.

Wider topics also invite investigation. Aesthetic judgments consistently underpin judgments about nationality and race in the period. I have glanced at this issue in my discussion of the beauty tips of Mrs Alexander Walker and in the chapter on Charlotte Brontë, but while their judgments are unusually overt and violent, they are far from uncommon. It would be useful to look at the way both Disraeli and Trollope use the discourse of taste in the construction, for example, of characters like the Duke of Sidonia, who, though represented as a supremely cultivated gentleman who has 'exhausted all the sources of human knowledge,' introduces himself to Coningsby prosaically enough by praising the English 'national dish' of bacon and eggs ('How much better than an omelette or a greasy olla, that they would give us in a posada! 'Tis a wonderful country this England!'),[2] or Ferdinand Lopez, the mysterious financier in *The Prime Minister*, 'the sort of man whitewashed of all prejudices, who wouldn't mind whether he ate horseflesh or beef if horseflesh were as good as beef, and never had an association in his life.'[3] Indeed the way taste for food is lined up with other kinds of tastefulness would be a promising topic: I had at one point planned a chapter called 'Grease,' drawing on Bourdieu's analysis of the way dietary choices are associated, in France, not only with body type but with styles of articulation. Ferdinand Lopez, the man without associations, invites a focused investigation of the theory of associationism itself: its omnipresence in the nineteenth-century discourses of subjectivity, its link with aesthetic feeling on the one hand and with the emerging science of psychoanalysis on the other. (My article on associationism in Austen represents some preliminary thinking about this topic that could not be fitted into this study.) The Victorian use of the past is another promising line of investigation. It would be useful, in thinking about the construction of taste, to move beyond Victorian medievalism and Victorian bardolatry to consider other authors, like Spenser, whose relevance to Scott and Gaskell has been suggested here, and Pope, whose vignette of Belinda at her toilet table no doubt informs the novelistic Victorian 'boudoir' as significantly if not as self-consciously as it does the modernist reinterpretation of this topos by Eliot in *The Waste Land*.[4]

These roads not taken invite future consideration. What I want to do in these final pages instead is glance forward to what happens to the theme of tastefulness in the last quarter of the century, specifically to the split between what might be called sociological relativism, in Thomas Hardy's *Jude the Obscure, The Mayor of Casterbridge*, and *A Laodicean* and George Gissing's *New Grub Street*, and aestheticism, represented by Henry James's *The Awkward Age*. These novels all continue to draw on topoi used by Scott in *Waverley* in 1814, though in parodic ways that testify to the breakdown of the discourse in the face of cultural change.

The century, as my selection constructs it, begins and ends with narratives that focus on male characters reading works they love. Against the image of aristocratic Waverley devouring 'feminine' romances, we have three working-class men – Hardy's Jude Fawley, Gissing's Edmund Reardon and Harold Biffen – studying the virile classics. But while Waverley's reading paradoxically ends by making a man of him, helping him to understand his society and find a place in it, Hardy's and Gissing's characters are isolated and eventually destroyed by the aspirations engendered by their love of books.

Like *Waverley*, *Jude the Obscure* and *New Grub Street* define their protagonists partly by means of bibliographies. Jude's solitary studies produce a single ecstatic moment when, inspired by the rising moon, he falls on his knees by the side of the road to recite lines from Horace's 'Carmen Saeculare' (29). But all this does is make him reflect that he should be spending less time on pagan texts and more on Christian. From then on, the books he studies are rather grimly listed either as bibliographical items, complete with information about editions (Caesar, Horace, and Virgil in 'old Delphin editions,' 'Clarke's Homer,' 'the Gospels and Epistles in Griesbach's text'); as an academic inventory, 'a mental estimate of ... progress thus far' ('I have read two books of the Iliad, besides being pretty familiar with passages such as the speech of Phoenix in the ninth book, the fight of Hector and Ajax in the fourteenth ... '), or, at the other extreme, as the 'voices' of Christminster, disembodied male voices of Culture speaking to him across the ages (28, 30–2, 67). Both the idealizing of the masculine voices of high culture and the self-conscious inventorying of the contents of one's mind and bookshelf are the signs of the autodidact with a fraught investment in his hard-won achievement.

The contrast between the education of Scott's protagonist and that of Hardy's and Gissing's earnest young men perfectly illustrates Bourdieu's distinction between cultural and educational capital. It would be counterproductive for Scott to specify in what edition Waverley reads Spenser: the point is that he simply picks up whatever his family owns. It is precisely because the books he finds in the family library connect him to generations of prosperous if not necessarily cultivated ancestors that they will in time connect him to other members of his social class, and it is because Jude and Reardon lack such ancestors that theirs never will. The educational capital of Jude, Reardon, and Biffen, the learning laboriously acquired on their own by young men who have no social background to support their intellectual tastes, does not help them tap into the network that they would need to succeed. As clearly as any sociological text, Hardy and Gissing demonstrate that it is not what one knows but how one comes to know it, not what one loves but the society in which one learns to love it, that makes one register as 'tasteful' with those who can reward taste. The aesthetic response of Hardy's and Gissing's doomed antiheroes is just as ardent, just as sincere, as Waverley's, but without the recognition of an influential other who apprehends their literary taste as a synecdochic sign of a cultural whole, not only does it fail to produce the subjective coherence that taste is supposed to confer, it alienates them from society rather than integrating them into it. And whatever Reardon thinks, this is not just because they live in a period of debased mass culture. A taste for the classics would even in such a society continue to work on any of these men's behalf if they had acquired it in the right way: that is, if it functioned as the sign of a privileged social background.

The feminization of the tasteful but déclassé writer is signalled by the way he is characterized by a topos previously applied to women, the description of the room as a sign of interior culture. The only room in *New Grub Street* that we enter along with a character, the only room set up by the author as itself worthy of attention, is the room of Harold Biffen, Reardon's even less successful friend. The fact that we enter it along with Reardon is in line with the traditional topos, for Reardon is indeed Biffen's one true love. The Greek motif in the novel hints, if not at homosexual, at least at homosocial devotion between these men, and like the lover in the traditional text this voyeur is characterized by his unique ability to appreciate the rich subjectivity to which the room testifies. But unlike Waverley or Edmund Bertram, Reardon will never be able to support his beloved's beautiful mind because he himself has no money or social power. Biffen's room is put before us in all its pathetic detail, complete with low ceiling, cracked plaster, empty grate, 'weedy carpet,' wobbly table, 'small wash-hand-stand,' and 'chair-bedstead,' the climax of the description being, as is conventional, the signs of culture: 'There was no bookcase, but a few hundred battered volumes were arranged some on the floor and some on a rough chest' (241). These are the volumes – 'all my classics, with years of scribbling in the margins!' (471) – that go up in smoke when the house burns down. The scenario is repeated when Harold, after Reardon's death, takes Amy to visit 'Reardon's poor room at Islington,' where her tears evoke a 'passionate tenderness' (523) in Biffen that eventually leads to his suicide. We see the influence of Zola and the naturalist program in the depressing detail and doomed outcome, but the scenario itself is a convention that goes as far back as Radcliffe. True taste may be visible in the same old way to those capable of recognizing it, but its signs lead nowhere in the absence of a social power structure that supports it.

Gissing's treatment of the female characters in these novels is also a self-conscious demystification of established novelistic stereotypes. The figure in *New Grub Street* who is recognized by society as tasteful in just the way that Veblen had in mind – the woman who is set up both to stimulate her husband's economic productivity and brilliantly to display the results of his labour – is Amy Reardon Milvain, whose personal appearance and style make her the perfect consort for an ambitious writer. In the characterization of Amy, Gissing distinguishes sharply between aesthetic and moral refinement. Amy is physically beautiful and dresses tastefully, but this limited good taste is not a sign of moral or spiritual excellence. Gissing makes clear that personal beauty and a taste for art by no means have to go together. Amy is aesthetically rather unresponsive. Though initially willing to indulge Reardon in his enthusiasm for classical verse, when their marriage sours she ceases to counterfeit attention: 'most of the things which were Reardon's supreme interests lost their value for her' (397). She is intelligent, and her life experiences have made her particularly interested in sociology and given her the 'impulse to occupy herself with a kind of reading alien to Reardon's sympathies': 'solid periodicals,' articles on 'themes of social science' – 'anything that savoured of newness and boldness in philosophic thought' (397). Acquainted second hand with the arguments of such topical thinkers as Spencer and Darwin, Amy becomes 'a typical woman of the new time, the woman who has developed concurrently with journalistic enterprise' (398). Her mindset is associated with cool, somewhat hard opportunism, and her intellectual interests represented not as culture but merely as an alert and never disinterested response to the world around her.

Yet Amy will always register as highly tasteful within her expanding social set, for two reasons. The first is that she deliberately chooses as husbands men who impress others, particularly other women, as distinguished:

> One of her strongest motives in marrying [Reardon] was the belief that he would achieve distinction ... no degree of distinction in her husband would be of much value to her unless she had the pleasure of witnessing its effect upon others: she must shine with reflected light before an admiring assembly. (163)

By positing an equality between the sexes that Veblen cannot yet envision – by imagining a female character with her own set of desires – Gissing makes clear that it is not only woman who functions as prestigious possession: a husband can just as easily be objectified by a wife with her own game to play. Reardon's initial success as a novelist does pay off for Amy in this way, as is made clear by the admiration of her friend Edith Carter, who is ready to claim both the author and his wife as glamorous acquaintances. When Amy marries Jasper Milvain, however, she finds her true role: that of the 'matchless wife' who helps her husband professionally by attracting 'clever and worthy people' to their first modest home – who indeed 'would attract men of taste to a very much poorer abode' (547). Amy consciously and willingly chooses the role that Veblen implies is forced upon women by a barbaric culture, and she does it for her own advantage as much as for his.

As Gissing makes clear, Amy's charismatic personal presence has little to do with character, much less virtue: the second reason she registers as tasteful is that she happens to have the right type of beauty. Slender, strong, erect, with 'ruddy gold' hair that, as the hair of Victorian heroines is so apt to do, 'made a superb crown to the beauty of her small, refined head,' she has a sculptural quality, with sharply curved lips and 'a magnificently clear-cut bust': 'one thought, in looking at her, of the newly-finished head which some honest sculptor has wrought with his own hand from the marble block; there was a suggestion of "planes" and of the chisel' (78–9). The text's Greek motif ironizes even her appearance: Amy is utterly indifferent to purity of metre, but her fortune is made by purity of line. Her dress, 'unpretending in fashion and colour, but of admirable fit' (79), sounds exactly like that of the classic Victorian heroine, and her carriage testifies to the kind of 'ladylike' status in which Gissing himself seems to have a considerable investment:[5]

> She walked well; you saw that her foot, however gently, was firmly planted. When she seated herself, her posture was instantly graceful, and that of one who is indifferent to support for the back. (79)

Amy has in short the natural 'grace' that Castiglione and Montesquieu admire,[6] and although it is grace in the narrowest sense of the word – merely physical grace – it testifies, to those within her social world, to her distinction. But Gissing makes clear that this grace is an accident of nature: Amy has simply been born with a fashionable body type and with the physical energy to live up to it. 'Not a day of illness in her life,' says her mother (95): the 'bright young eyes' so admired by Reardon, which 'seemed to bid defiance to all the years to come' (96), express the optimism and confidence that accompany such vigour. Her mother's indulgence has given her a sense of entitlement, so that Amy, with the imposing presence of a Dorothea Brooke,[7] is also much like Margaret Hale in her haughtiness and pride, with 'a nature which resents any form of humiliation' (487). But such pride is not mystified by Gissing as it is by Gaskell: associated with her hardness of heart, her inability to fully repent of the way she has treated her husband, it is a Darwinian quality, which marks her not as a spiritual aristocrat but simply as a survivor. An unhappy marriage leaves her style not only unscathed but enhanced. Finding her true mate only after a false start is represented as a positive advantage for Amy, who by the time she graces Milvain's table has become a type of mature elegance:

> Amy looked her years to the full, but her type of beauty ... was independent of youthfulness ... at forty, at fifty, she would be one of the stateliest of dames. When she bent her head towards the person with whom she spoke, it was an act of queenly favour. Her words were uttered with just enough deliberation to give them the value of an opinion; she smiled with a delicious shade of irony; her glance intimated that nothing could be too subtle for her understanding. (547)

Nothing has suggested that Amy has a particularly subtle mind: her intellectual sophistication is largely an illusion, a matter of style. But it impresses her guests and satisfies her husband. The novel concludes with a parodic allusion to the Lydgate/Rosamond relationship from *Middlemarch*. Amy is just the decorative and supportive wife Lydgate imagined – 'Go to the piano, dear, and play me something,' requests her husband (550) – and Jasper is completely satisfied: 'So Amy first played, and then sang, and Jasper lay back in dreamy bliss' (551). In *New Grub Street* only characters without real taste are granted a happy ending.

Gissing's construction of character is programmatic: he has a theory, a theory not unlike Bourdieu's, and he devises characters and situations to illustrate it. The result is somewhat predictable. His irreverent system of values may *épater* but cannot long surprise the reader once his ideological agenda is grasped. Hardy, more bemused by women but equally skeptical about tastefulness, offers what is in some ways a more interesting critique of the discourse.

Tastefulness, to be sure, is usually a quality neither of Hardy's female characters nor of their characterization. Women writers such as Brontë, Gaskell, and Eliot, unwilling to admit the stake they have in mere physical beauty, rationalize their heroine's appeal by defining it in terms of taste and connecting it with moral excellence. Thomas Hardy labours under no such constraint: he has no inhibitions against admiring physical beauty in women, and as a result his description of the female body is quite literally tasteless, in the sense that taste is not the issue. Even when he describes fashionable clothes, like Bathsheba Everdene's svelte riding costume, in prose that sounds like a fashion-plate description, the point is not to characterize her sartorial taste but simply to dramatize her effect on the male imagination.

The only point at which taste in clothing as an explicit issue contributes to Hardy's female characterization is in his treatment of Elizabeth Jane in *The Mayor of Casterbridge*, a not very sexy young woman who in some ways is Hardy's alter ego. An episode in her story line offers a disenchanted view of the limits of sartorial 'consistency.' When Elizabeth Jane's standard of living suddenly goes up, she hesitates to change her style of dress, because it seems to her 'inconsistent with her past life to blossom gaudily the moment she had become possessed of money' (96). But when her father presents her with a box of gloves, he initiates a process that takes on a life of its own:

> She wanted to wear them, to show her appreciation of his kindness, but she had no bonnet that would harmonize. As an artistic indulgence she thought she would have such a bonnet. When she had a bonnet that would go with the gloves she had no dress that would go with the bonnet. It was now absolutely necessary to finish; she ordered the requisite article; and found that she had no sunshade to go with the dress. In for a penny in for a pound; she bought the sunshade; and the whole structure was at last complete. (96)

The moral drawn by the narrator – 'nothing is more insidious than the evolution of wishes from mere fancies, and of wants from mere wishes' (96) – tolerantly condemns Elizabeth Jane and frivolous female desire, but this is just the desire constructed and exploited by merchandisers in order to ensure that buying one item involves buying the whole set. Her public's reception of her transformation is also pointedly ironic. Elizabeth Jane's sartorial consistency is existential inconsistency, but it is just that inconsistency that piques the admiration of Casterbridge society:

> Everybody was attracted, and some said that her bygone simplicity was the art that conceals art, the 'delicate imposition' of Rochefoucauld; she had produced an effect, a contrast; and it had been done on purpose. As a mat-

ter of fact this was not true, but it had its result; for as soon as Casterbridge thought her artful it thought her worth notice. (96)

In this context, the gratuitous allusion to Rochefoucauld functions as a self-reflexive irony. Hardy's own class position makes him both skeptical about the conventional indices of middle-class tastefulness and anxious to appropriate the signs of high culture, and this kind of name-dropping is an example of the same anxiety that motivates his characters at this point in the narrative.

Hardy has an equally wry (and perhaps equally self-referential) view of Elizabeth Jane's aspirations to gentility. Henchard's daughter does not realize she is socially and culturally deficient until she is harassed by her father about her handwriting and diction – bullied by him, not tutored by him as the Victorian maiden was supposed to be. Henchard is cruel to her not only because he believes her not to be his biological child but also because he feels humiliated by his own lack of refinement: he is projecting onto her an anxiety about a rough-and-readiness that will eventually combine with other factors to cost him the respect of his customers. Thus browbeaten, Elizabeth Jane struggles to acquire some belated educational capital, but she fails to impress her father, who does not realize what efforts she has made until he enters her room just as she is preparing to leave his house for Lucetta's. The woman's-room topos functions here precisely in the orthodox way, to illustrate to the male voyeur on whom a woman's happiness and material security depend that she has the cultivated interiority that merits support. But the outcome is not as happy as in Radcliffe and Scott:

> He entered the house, and, seeing that all her things had not yet been brought down, went up to her room to look on. He had never been there since she had occupied it. Evidences of her care, of her endeavours for improvement, were visible all around, in the form of books, sketches, maps, and little arrangements for tasteful effects. Henchard had known nothing of these efforts. (146)

The woman's room traditionally testifies to unity, both psychological and aesthetic, but here there is only fragmentation: it is clear that Elizabeth Jane has been able to pull together only disconnected scraps of information, and it is only when her room is being taken apart that we enter it for the first time. As we expect in Hardy's novels, Henchard's illumination comes just 'ten minutes too late': he asks her to stay but she refuses, and the result, ultimately, is his own death. Elizabeth Jane herself to be sure eventually succeeds: that is, she succeeds in securing the financial support of a decent and prosperous man – a man however who is capable of romantic feeling only towards the shallower, less morally fastidious Lucetta. Unlike Rose Bradwardine's, Elizabeth Jane's tastefulness never becomes the luminous sign of an adorable desirability but merely expresses the anxiety about social decorum that fits her to be the second wife of the practical, conventional Farfrae.

Elizabeth Jane is a limited character, a rare bird among Hardy's heroines because she is not erotically fascinating. Hardy's very detachment from her enables him to critique the discourse by which the Victorian heroine is constructed. A perhaps more suggestive, because less controlled, characterization is that of Paula Power in *A Laodicean.* The woman's-room topos is particularly congenial to Hardy's voyeuristic imagination, and it is not surprising that, in a narrative involving two architects roaming around a woman's estate, he uses it not once but twice: more or less conventionally near the beginning of the novel when George Somerset, given the run of the place for his architectural researches, stumbles upon Paula's private apartment; considerably less conventionally when Somerset's rival Havill peeps at Paula herself in pink flannel doing her gymnastic exercises. Out of control though the second scene may seem, Hardy no doubt intends a programmatic parallel: while the base Havill is aroused by Paula's body, the true hero, Somerset, is intrigued in the usual way by her spirit. Whatever their artistic merits, however, both episodes are socially suggestive and insightful. The scene in the gymnasium makes clear that new possibilities of self-development for women are going to create a new kind of female sexuality and new erotic tastes in men. The athletic woman's body and her own enjoyment of it – for Paula, unaware she is being looked at, is having a wonderful time – may liberate her in some ways but will also put her into yet another scopic box.

Though in comparison with this flagrantly voyeuristic scene, Somerset's entrance into Paula's 'sleeping chamber' seems tame if a little creepy, in the end it is only slightly less peculiar. The room contains almost all the conventional signs of personal culture:

It was a pretty place, and seemed to have been hastily fitted up. In a corner, overhung by a blue and white canopy of silk, was a little cot, hardly large enough to impress the character of a bedroom upon the old place. Upon a counterpane lay a parasol and a silk neckerchief. On the other side of the room was a tall mirror of startling newness, draped like the bedstead, in blue and white. Thrown at random on the floor was a pair of satin slippers that would have fitted Cinderella. A dressing-gown lay across a settee; and opposite, upon a small easy-chair in the same blue and white livery, were a Bible, the *Baptist Magazine*, Wardlaw on Infant Baptism [Paula had been flirting with the idea of being baptized], Walford's County Families, and the *Court Journal*. On and over the mantelpiece were knickknacks of various descriptions, and photographic portraits of the artistic, scientific, and literary celebrities of the day. (66–7)

Instead of the harmony, the unified sensibility to which the woman's room usually points, this description emphasizes incongruity. Paula has conventional feminine tastes, as demonstrated by the dainty blue and white motif and the mirror, but she is also tuned in to the outside world in a scattershot and slightly opportunistic way. In the anteroom Somerset has already noticed 'popular papers and periodicals ... not only English, but from Paris, Italy, and America ... books from a London circulating library, paper-covered light literature in French and choice Italian, and the latest monthly reviews.' He has also noticed that 'between the two windows stood the telegraph apparatus' (66).

This fascinating machine is characterized by Hardy with surprising intensity. A lithely phallic intruder, its wire penetrates Paula's personal space more gracefully yet more violently than the earnest, rather morose Somerset ever manages to do. Its aesthetic incongruity merely adds a piquant hint of attack and profanation:

From the poles amid the trees it leaped across the moat, over the girdling wall, and thence by a tremendous stretch towards a tower which might have been the keep where, to judge by sound, it vanished through an arrow-slit into the interior. (52)

As so often in Hardy, there is a weirdly somatic undercurrent to the figurative language. The entity penetrated is a static, 'hoary,' 'girdled' body, a 'fossil of feudalism,' the penetrating wire a swift, vital, arrow-like 'machine.' It is not clear whether the fertilization that results is a good thing, promoting 'cosmopolitan views and the intellectual and moral kinship of all mankind,' or a bad, bringing with it 'the modern fever and fret which consumes people before they can grow old' (52), but there is the suggestion that independent, individualistic Paula is both electrified and in an odd way feminized by her enthusiasm for connection. It turns out for the most part to be a sexual rather than cultural connection, however. Paula uses the telegraph not as a way of communicating with modern Europe but as a leash that she can twitch to summon Somerset to her side: this, Somerset reflects, is the machine 'whose wire had been the means of bringing him hither' (66). The telegraph is as out of place in the castle as is her imperious sexual *maistrie* in the context of the usual woman's-room ethos.

The heterogeneity of the castle's architectural styles is equally suggestive, if ultimately ambiguous. The architectural material is not well integrated into the narrative, but what Hardy does with it is intriguing. It is because Paula aspires to taste, because she is interested in the history of style and has some feeling for aesthetic values, that she will perpetrate a historical blunder when she tacks a Greek court onto her medieval castle. It is interesting that what stops her is a heritage-industry kind of aesthetic correctness. Her project is attacked in a letter to the editor, 'professedly written by a dispassionate person solely in the interests of art,' who complains that she is about to insert into the middle of 'that ancient pile ... a monstrous travesty of some Greek temple' that will render the building 'a complete ruin' (133). Public opinion is represented for Paula by the newspaper, a medium that expresses however not mass values but conservative ones, a haut-bourgeois sentimentality about images of the national past – or can plausibly be made to testify, for the letter of course is a fake, planted by the unscrupulous Havill to induce Paula to reopen the competition with his rival. Havill doesn't know much about his profession, at least about architectural history – he is bluffing when he claims that the perpendicular style is undercut – but he does know enough about the discourse of taste to realize that such an old-buffer letter could register as authentic in this provincial setting. Were it not that his destiny is being shaped by Hardy, who has willed a happy ending for Somerset, such savvy might get him further than genuine scholarship seems likely to get Somerset, whose attempt to cultivate Paula's knowledge of undercutting – a truly weird replay of the *maître-de-sa-maîtresse* convention – does not particularly advance his courtship. When Somerset guides Paula's fingers into the hollow of the stone, it is an erotic moment (at least for Somerset), but it is not part of the systematic process of cultural awakening facilitated by the conventional male tutor. The novel itself is a collection of moments rather than a coherent aesthetic structure, and while this may be the result simply of its conditions of composition – Hardy was very ill when he was writing it – it does convey something about the disconnectedness of culture at the moment when established conventions for constructing subjectivity were beginning to look empty and factitious.

Paula seems to be less impressed by Somerset's tutoring than by Havill's letter, as a result of which she decides to go for 'synchronism' and abandon the idea of a Greek court. This is presumably to be understood as a good thing. Yet simply to live in an ancient building is to be 'unsynchronic.' Paula's bedroom, with its blue and white draperies, is just as anomalous an addition to the castle as a Greek court, if a less public one: all she can do is in effect camp in this castle in a room whose style has nothing to do with the style of any of its parts. But then the styles of its parts have nothing to do with each other: the building's elements are of different historical periods. It is such temporal layering that has produced its 'organic' growth over the centuries, as every generation has added what it needs. Houses thus constructed had prestige, as testifying to family continuity and organic rootedness – such prestige that this kind of historical evolution was faked.[8] No doubt as the castle was added to over the centuries, the last layer always looked anachronistic at the moment when it was built. To be sure, a Greek court, an addition not in the contemporary vernacular style but tacked on as an inauthentic revival, would be doubly anachronistic. Yet as time passed it would also no doubt become romantic, if only as testifying to an 'authentic' period feeling: that is, genuine Victorian enthusiasm for fake Greek courts. 'Authenticity' itself is an illusion, and a frankly illusionistic folly is perhaps less objectionable, because less deceptive, than the kind of restoration that can fool people. When Paula declares that she would 'prefer an honest patch to ... make-believe ... Saxon relics' on the grounds that 'in time to come, when ... those stones have become stained like the rest, people will be deceived' (98) – a scruple Hardy himself endorses in his non-fiction writings – she is in a sense legitimizing the court, which will certainly not deceive people, even when she is not around to explain it. The way the whole issue is developed makes clear that no generation, particularly not this one, can really connect with the past, but it also suggests that Somerset's rather smug obsession with historical accuracy, which at times seems to function as a sign of his cultivated taste, is just as sterile as Havill's opportunistic fictions. Life is too short, Paula's reference to her own death might make us feel, to worry about the aesthetic purity of our pleasures or the architectural confusions of the next generation.

As it turns out, no addition Paula makes will have time to acquire the patina of age, since the castle is burnt down by the illegitimate son of the actual heir. The symbolism makes clear that this is the end of the line for the aristocracy, a moment of historical rupture, which inevitably produces ruptured people. On the last page of the novel Paula has lost the castle, and it cannot be said that she possesses herself. Paula is torn: she wants both the social status that came with the castle (that she partly purchased but would have to confirm by marrying into the family and getting the name) but she also wants the freedom to live her life unhampered by the lifestyle this status would impose. The wistful tone of her final remark does not augur well for her marriage to Somerset, but both characters are so wooden and unattractive that it is hard to worry much about their future. The question the novel raises is not whether these two are going to live happily ever after, rarely an option in Hardy's world, but whether Paula is the type who will survive in a new age. In fact she does seem to be a survivor. A Sue Bridehead whose hang-ups do not hang her up but simply push her to experiment with various modes of feeling, she is the willful consumer of the next century, an unfocused and somewhat scatty but consistent egotist who is going to do her best to have it all. The castle is gone, but the incoherent subjectivity to which it points has a long future. The novel foreshadows the emergence of a new consumer subjectivity and posits the self as *bricolage* – as constructed of bits and pieces of culture and media. Paula Power is not a very likeable character and her portrait is not well realized, but it is nevertheless prescient. There is a sense in which Paula tells us as much about the decades to come as Amy Milvain or as the more celebrated, and much more skilfully constructed, Sue.

She certainly tells us more about the future than Henry James's Nanda Brookenham, the poignant heroine of *The Awkward Age*, whose fate is to be defined by her author as well as by the characters within her fictional world in terms of the conventional heroine of the past. James invites us to read Nanda in terms not only of Victorian values but of Victorian fictional conventions. Like Rose Bradwardine or Fanny Price, Nanda is installed in a limited, elevated space and tutored by a man who supplies her with books and works out a curriculum for her; like Fanny she is conspicuously sidelined while the life of the household goes on without her; more surprisingly, like the indulged heroines of Elizabeth Braddon, whose fiction James despised, she will eventually be liberally, even extravagantly, supported by a wealthy older man who finds his splendid old house empty without her. The way James handles the room-with-a-view topos is a brilliantly ambiguous rerun of an ideologically loaded device.

'Van' Vanderbank, who as Nanda's potential suitor is bound by the rules of fiction to enter and evaluate her private apartment, draws attention to the parody when he compares his hostess, 'perched in your tower or what do you call it? – your bower' with 'flowers and pictures and ... books and birds' (282), to the typical heroine of nineteenth-century fiction. The broad differences are obvious, and obviously ironic. We know that Mrs Brook, so complacent about having given her thoroughly modern daughter a room of her own, simply wants to get her out of the way, and we take the point that modern society can no longer either shelter a young woman effectively nor find a place for her outside the home. But every detail of the scene is equally meaningful. The woman's-room device has been called 'coy,'[9] and its coyness is systematically exposed by James's point-by-point deconstruction of the traditional topos. James's phrase 'that chamber of comfort' sounds like an allusion to *Mansfield Park*,[10] and what is said of Nanda is close to what is said of Fanny: 'that chamber of comfort in which so much of her life had lately been passed, the redecorated and rededicated room, upstairs, in which she had enjoyed a due measure both of solitude and society' (281). But 'due measure' is dry understatement: there is never any pretence here, as there seems to be in Austen's text, that such isolation could be satisfying. We enter the room only to see Nanda out of it, and the question is whether her exit is an Easter resurrection, a rising from the tomb that is left empty behind her, or an entry into a considerably more gothic situation.

Van's entry is played against the traditional entry of the voyeur. The very fact that a young man has no problem gaining access to a young woman's private room – that Van does not need to be sponsored by a parent, that Nanda is free to receive whomever she chooses and requires only a servant to function as her usher – testifies to the social contamination that makes Van unable to marry her. There is no Aggie-like faux innocence or Rose-like unselfconsciousness on Nanda's part about his visit. Unlike the conventional heroine, who is always supposed to be 'taken by surprise,' as Lady Wishfort puts it,[11] Nanda frankly prepares both herself and the room for inspection, paying special attention to those emblematic books, altering 'repeatedly for five minutes the positions of various volumes, transferr[ing] to tables those that were on shelves and rearrang[ing] shelves with an eye to the effect of backs ... flagrantly engaged throughout indeed in the study of effect' (281). It is obvious to Van, who knows exactly how Nanda feels about him, that this is a carefully prepared stage set: he remarks on the room's studied air, though he pretends to believe that 'of course' she has done it for Longdon rather than for himself (284). James has all the conventional details, and they are all parodic. There are the portraits – photographic portraits, at this date – which, whether or not they include Nanda's family (their subjects are not specified), do not testify to her secure situation in a loving home. Neither here nor in fact anywhere in the novel, so full of allusions to photographs and portraiture, is there a photograph of that famous grandmother Nanda is supposed to resemble, and while the absence of such a portrait is a structural requirement, Nanda's displacement of her grandmother being precisely the issue,[12] her inability to connect with women who have gone before her (as Dorothea Brooke, for example, imaginatively does with the portrait of Ladislaw's unlucky grandmother) underscores her isolation in a world of men who define her in terms of their own needs.

Nanda's photographs are arranged so that Van will notice them, 'highly prepared, with small intense faces each, that happened in every case to be turned to the door' (281). But what they chiefly do is put Van himself under scrutiny: every eye is turned towards him, including his own. The face-in-the-mirror element of the conventional topos is cleverly replicated here by Van's own photographic image, which, surprised to see him come in, 'visibly widen[s] his gaze at the opening of the door' (281). Nanda wants Van to see, in his picture, evidence that she loves him, but all it makes him see is himself. The mirroring photo is an emblem of the intense self-consciousness that aborts any meaningful communication between these two at this critical moment. Van, desperately uncomfortable, cannot help looking at himself and listening to himself, as he commits a final act of what he knows is great cruelty.

In his anguished babbling, Van is made to canvass one by one the other stock features of the topos. He remarks on the view his hostess must have from this height: 'You quite hang over the place, you know – the great wicked city, the wonderful London sky and the monuments looming through' (283). But neither of them can look out that window. Miserable Van has eyes and ears only for his own performance – 'or am I again,' he asks, 'only muddling up my Zola?' (283). And there is no 'prospect' in London for Nanda: she cannot, like an enlightened Dorothea Brooke at the famous moment when she decides to try to save Rosamond, look out into a world in which there might be a moral role for her. On the contrary, her windows are covered with blinds, which she carefully adjusts, turning her back on them to greet her visitor. It is not a link with London that Nanda desires, but the love of her sunny beloved, and unlike Dorothea she is never going to get it.[13] The rooms of Emily St Aubert and Fanny Price face east, suggesting illumination in the morning of life, and it is early in the morning when Dorothea has the moment of epiphanic feeling that sends her to Rosamond, but Apollonian Van talks not of sunrise but of sunset ('You must have the sunsets – haven't you?' [283]) – which, though an ominous difference, does at least suggest that the room faces west and would get the afternoon sun that James can so resonantly evoke.[14] But Van has made yet another blunder: 'No – what am I talking about? Of course you look north' (283). The fact that this north-facing chamber is not a choice space – that like Fanny Price's, it is a room that nobody else wants – is the least of its layered ironies.

Nanda's books, especially her set of 'the British Poets' (285), are equally dubious symbols. These volumes may not be 'cared for on account of their bindings solely,' as Gaskell puts it, but the bindings are what Van comments on: 'Where did you learn so much about bindings?' (283). If Nanda had in fact even chosen the bindings, her expertise would testify to the kind of cultural capital that might redeem her a bit in Van's eyes. But he knows that it was Longdon not Nanda who had the books bound. All Nanda can ever aim at is educational capital, which always has a flavour of belatedness. She does not lack moral insight: alert, sensitive, and highly intelligent, she has learned to negotiate, with clear eyes and with a generous heart, the complex environment she has been born into. Her knowingness could be read as another kind of 'capital' – as a set of positive skills, rather than as the sinister stain Longdon and Van make it to be, and it arguably looks all the more vital and real when set against the academic course of study that Longdon seems to be offering her in exchange. The set of British Poets is just the kind of material Waverley arranged to have sent to Rose, but there are far too many volumes in this set: if this is a joke,[15] it is not clear at whose expense. 'What an awfully jolly lot of books,' says Van, 'have you read them all?' (282–3). His admission, delivered with disingenuous ruefulness, that he himself, involved as he is in real life, has little time to read, recalls Gaskell's Henry Lennox, affecting to regret the busy professional life of 'real law work' that precludes aesthetic otium. But if Van has too little leisure, Nanda, he feels, will have too much. Unmarried, she will be in the position of those women considered as particularly in need of 'resources,' and Van is alluding to this traditional discourse when he remarks that 'You're laying up treasure' (282). The biblical language with which he spiritualizes the financial metaphor is appallingly ironic in view of the financial manoeuvring, the attempt by Longdon to purchase Van himself as a 'treasure' for Nanda, that has been going on behind the scenes. But like Camilla's uncle in Burney's novel, Nanda may be getting too much too late. The books seem a poor replacement for what she is losing.

Like Fanny, Nanda will be tutored by someone she loves, but unlike Edmund Bertram, her tutor will never become a lover.[16] Will she blossom under London's cultivation? The flowers in Nanda's room – 'awfully good ones – where did you get them?' (283) – are of course from Longdon's estate, and Nanda assures him that Longdon is an expert gardener and his garden is a feast, 'like a dinner in a house where the person – the person of the house – thoroughly knows and cares' (284). Will this purely aesthetic diet be enough for Nanda, or will she, like Lucy Snowe, find herself starving? Is Longdon her saviour or the 'old demon' (284) Van calls him? Longdon's estate Beccles is supposed to represent real culture, but partly because it is not grounded, as is Mansfield Park, in a specific economic system, however unsavoury – because the basis of his wealth is not spelled out – it remains somewhat unreal, a purely aesthetic space. Nanda is part of Longdon's aesthetic vision, another art work, while she is dependent upon him for her upkeep: a somewhat gothic situation if, as has been suggested, 'Gothic terror in woman's fiction is unremittingly economic.'[17] That the ending of this novel is disturbingly ambiguous is a commonplace of criticism. It is James's brilliant parody of what had looked like an exhausted convention that helps cause the disturbance.

These examples make clear that by the end of the century the novelistic codes that defined taste for so many decades are beginning to look merely conventional and that the set of conventions is beginning to come apart and some of its elements to be recognized as having more to do with material factors such as money, class, and biological inheritance than with spiritual excellence. It is not that the claim to innate superiority cannot be made, but it cannot be made in just the same way. Other elements, however, persist, albeit in an altered form. Nanda Brookenham's fastidiousness about dress – the 'extreme freshness' of her personal appearance, of which we have also just been reminded (281) – is a sign that functions just as it would in Brontë, to suggest her essential purity. Nanda is indeed a traditional 'heroine,' with the simplicity and luminous presence of a Dorothea Brooke, even if her moral insight has to be represented, like Edith Dombey's, as a vivid sense of her own contamination: the steadiness with which she confronts her destiny is a 'consistency' as poignant as any Eliot could imagine.

Nevertheless, the polarities of purity and contamination, altruism and self-interest, coherence and fragmentation on which these five novels turn announce a cultural shift. Nanda is also an anachronism, not in her degradation but in her clear superiority to everyone around her. When the kind of estate to which she is doomed to retire has had its day, when international modernism renders parochial the Englishness celebrated from Austen to James, culture can no longer so clearly be situated in the middle-class appropriation of English aristocratic images and practices, and old-fashioned heroines are not so readily constructed. Yet signs of tastefulness do continue to signal moral seriousness in imaginative literature up to the present day. Though Bourdieu's critics are probably right in arguing that there is no longer any single set of aesthetic values that have the breadth and resilience of those that inform nineteenth-century moral/aesthetic discourse, 'moral taste' still registers, at least in fiction.

Indeed, the taste for the Victorian novel itself becomes a familiar novelistic motif. Anita Brookner's Ruth Weiss, for example, whose life has 'been ruined by literature,' fails to get the happy ending that Dickens's novels promise the domestic angel, but she functions as such an angel nevertheless when her deracinated parents undergo a moral collapse, and her taste in literature tells the reader from the very first sentence of the novel that she will have the strength of character to do so.[18] Mordecai Richler's adolescent Kate Panofsky exasperates her mother by sticking with *Middlemarch* instead of setting the table for her parents' dinner party, but Kate's ability, while continuing to be loyal to both of them, to extricate herself from the mess they make of their marriage is adumbrated by her ability to immerse herself in the trials of Dorothea Brooke.[19] Their literary taste endows both heroines not only with moral stature but also with a touch of class. The nineteenth-century novel is of course an inevitable resource for authors seeking models of ethically engaged subjectivity. But a taste for Dickens or Eliot implies, in these modern heroines, more than just virtuous character: it is also a mark of intellectual and cultural distinction. Allusions such as these make clear that the idealized Englishness celebrated by Jane Austen has not to this day lost its semiotic prestige. The conventions examined in this study persist, often in attenuated or popular form, to shape perceptions and evoke judgments, and for this reason alone they are worth our attention.

# Notes

## Introduction

1 *Camilla,* 658–9, 912, 645.
2 *The Prime Minister,* chap. 16, 176.
3 Letter cited by Karl, 108.
4 Charles Darwin, 205.
5 On cultural consumption and consumerism, for example, see Rappaport, Cvetkovich, and Brewer; on colour, Gage, Ball, Garfield, and Pastoureau; on architecture, Lubbock and Wigley; on language, Olivia Smith and Mugglestone; on theatre and fashion, Joel Kaplan and Stowell.
6 Eagleton, 3.
7 Shaftesbury asserts that 'to philosophize ... is but to carry good breeding a step higher. For the accomplishment of breeding is to learn whatever is decent in company or beautiful in arts, and the sum of philosophy is to learn what is just in society and beautiful in nature and the order of the world'; both 'the well-bred man' and the philosopher 'aim at what is excellent, aspire to a just taste and carry in view the model of what is beautiful and becoming' (407).
8 Hutcheson, xv.
9 See Home, xiii.
10 Alison, 2.435.
11 Alison, 2.437.
12 Akenside, 3.605 and 3.626–7.
13 Alison, 2.443.
14 Burke, 26 and 22.
15 Reynolds, 202.
16 Loudon, 'Of Taste,' 45.

17 *Ladies Cabinet* (1844), cited by Calder, 115, and Waters, 20.
18 Tuite's word, in her discussion of how Austen's novels appropriate aristo-cratic status symbols and imbue them with middle-class values.
19 Eagleton, 9.
20 Joyce, 212.
21 Eagleton, 9.
22 Eagleton, 19.
23 Markman Ellis, 136.
24 See Armstrong.
25 Siskin, 12. See Siskin, also Lynch, 1–20, on the emergence of 'deep' charac-ters at the end of the century; Richardson, 305n73, and Henderson, 1–2, on criticism's recent focus on depth.
26 Cottom points out that the working classes were characterized as violent even when their actions were notably restrained, as a means, he argues, of establishing middle class authority (*Social Figures*, 34, 40–7).
27 Burke, 23.
28 De Bruyn, 42.
29 Burke, 22.
30 Burke, 20.
31 De Bruyn, 51–3.
32 Scott, *Waverley*, 111; Blair, 338; Gerard, pt. 2, sec. 3, 95 (italics in original).
33 Enfield, 104–6. Tom has to memorize passages from *The Speaker* when he has flubbed his Latin translation (Eliot, *Mill on the Floss*, bk. 2, chap. 3, 146).
34 *Faerie Queene*, 3.5.51.5 and 6.Proem.4.3–4. The young hunter Tristram is also described as an opening flower (*Faerie Queene*, 6.2.35.7–9).
35 'He who has grace finds grace,' says Castiglione, bk. 1, sec. 24, 41. The refer-ence is to the notion of prevenient grace, which in Reformation theology is 'the grace of God which precedes repentance and conversion, predisposing the heart to seek God, previously to any desire or motion on the part of the recipient' (*OED*). The virtue of courtesy in Book 6 of Spenser's *The Faerie Queene* is associated with the three graces and with grace in the theological sense. The mysterious gratuitousness of grace is underlined by Montesquieu, who in the subsection entitled '*Du je ne sais quoi*' discusses 'grace naturelle' (1253–4), and by Burke, who, describing the 'magic of grace ... what is called its *je ne scai quoi*' (102), is apparently borrowing from Montesquieu.
36 Castiglione, 1.14.28.
37 Castiglione, 1.14.29.
38 Akenside, bk. 3, ll. 535–44.
39 Akenside, bk. 3, ll. 578–81.
40 Burke, 18–20.

41 Megill suggests that historical thought itself originates in the early eigh-teenth-century attempts to define taste, which forced philosophers to acknowledge that human responses differ in different times and places.

42 Ruskin says that many flowers 'are stained with vulgar, vicious, or discordant colour' but happily not those 'of temperate climates' (15.418). On dahlias see chapter 4, note 17.

43 *Mansfield Park*, 244.

44 Cottom, *Civilized Imagination*, 16. In this study he is talking about the aristoc-racy in the eighteenth century; but in his analysis of a later period and a dif-ferent system – Victorian capitalism – he asserts that the notion of noble or superior souls functions to make the social hierarchy, which now is supposed to emerge as a result of free competition, seem 'an effect of human nature' (*Social Figures*, 11). Evidently, any system that depends on the acquiescence of those at the bottom can use the hypothesis of innate superiority to make the good fortune of those at the top seem natural.

45 The term 'pedagod' is Neill's, 100.

46 *The Old Manor House*, 161, 166, 289, 382.

47 Originally from Rousseau, 540–1.

48 Richardson discusses 'the fantasy of absolute control over a woman by attempting to engineer her very subjectivity' (182, 193–4, 196, 203). For a discussion of Edmund Bertram's tutoring of Fanny Price as Foucauldian dis-cipline, see Stewart, 134.

49 *Sybil*, 300.

50 Thus the discourse of 'natural taste' works along with the notion of vocation, which erases the labour both of the man of letters and of the housewife: see Poovey, *Uneven Developments*, 76–7 and passim.

51 Veblen, 48.

52 Goffman, *Presentation of Self*, 34.

53 *Mill on the Floss*, bk. 1, chap. 3; Veblen, 110, 50.

54 Veblen, 43

55 Veblen, 53, 59.

56 Veblen, 358, 356, 362.

57 Veblen, 75.

58 Veblen, 141.

59 Veblen, 390.

60 Veblen, 53.

61 Veblen, 58.

62 Goffman, *Presentation of Self*, 70.

63 Bal, 92.

64 Goffman, *Presentation of Self*, 70.

65 Goffman, *Presentation of Self*, 18.
66 Goffman, *Presentation of Self*, 72.
67 Goffman, *Presentation of Self*. 75.
68 Goffman, *Interaction Ritual*, 44–5.
69 Judith Butler, *Bodies That Matter*, 15.
70 Judith Butler, *Gender Trouble*, xv.
71 Judith Butler, *Gender Trouble*, 67.
72 Judith Butler, *Gender Trouble*, xv.
73 Judith Butler, *Gender Trouble*, xxv.
74 See Bourdieu on the distinction between *bouche* and *gueule* (*Language*, 86–7) .
75 Judith Butler, *Bodies That Matter*, 241.
76 Bourdieu has been described as 'resolutely pre-Freudian' (Robbins, 171).
77 Bourdieu, *Distinction*, 282.
78 Bourdieu, *Language*, 55.
79 Bourdieu, *Distinction*, 22.
80 Bourdieu, *State Nobility*, 318.
81 Bourdieu, *Distinction*, 3.
82 Bourdieu, *Distinction*, 68.
83 Bourdieu, *Language*, 83–4.
84 Bourdieu is also eager to debunk the notion of the 'eye' of the art critic, insisting with Burke (though not for Burke's reasons) that rapid judgment, though it may look innate and instinctive, is always the product of occulted learning. On the three 'linked ideologies' dissected by Bourdieu – the ideology of the fresh eye, the ideology of the charismatic artist, and the ideology of natural taste – see Fowler, 43 and passim.
85 Bourdieu, *Distinction*, 29.
86 Bourdieu, *Distinction*, 5, 53–5, and passim.
87 Bourdieu, *Distinction*, 227–8.
88 Bourdieu, *Language*, 43, quoting Comte.
89 Bourdieu, *Language*, 43.
90 Bourdieu, 'Concluding Remarks,' 266, is here quoting Kant.
91 Bourdieu, 'Concluding Remarks,' 266.
92 *Mansfield Park*, 139.
93 Bourdieu, *Distinction*, 66.
94 Bourdieu, *Distinction*, 330–1.
95 Bourdieu, *Language*, 63.
96 Bourdieu, *Language*, 69.
97 Bourdieu, *Language*,124–5.
98 On habitus, see Bourdieu, *Distinction*, chap. 3 and passim.
99 Bourdieu, *Distinction*, 175.

100 Bourdieu says that Sartre's 'body-for-others' should be understood not as a generic, universal body but as the body constructed by the gaze of the socially powerful at a 'receiver' who recognizes his own categorization (*Distinction*, 207).

101 Robbins, 174; Fowler, 3.

102 Robbins, 8; for a survey of opposing opinions, see Fowler, 9.

103 Calhoun, 70–2; Robbins, 175; Lash, 206–10.

104 Bourdieu, *Language*, 122.

105 Bourdieu, *Distinction*, 56.

106 Bourdieu, *Distinction*, 251.

107 Bourdieu, *Language*, 260n23.

108 Bourdieu, *Distinction*, 218.

109 Bourdieu, 'Concluding Remarks,' 273. See also *Distinction*, 232, on goods that seem to 'go together.'

110 Fowler, 27.

111 Halle says that appreciating 'high' art like abstract painting does not in fact take a lot of education: that the rich see very much what the poor see in abstract art and do not like it much better, 131.

112 Zolberg, 199. Bourdieu has also been criticized for ignoring gender issues (Krais), youth culture and the popular media (Fowler, 155), the critical potential of serious art (Fowler, 11), and the community-building potential of style (Lash, 206), and for actively participating in the very game of prestige that he critiques. Robbins complains that since reading *Distinction* is a means of gaining distinction, the book is politically dysfunctional (129). For a feminist defence of Bourdieu, see Moi.

113 Charles Riley, 4–21.

114 Bourdieu, *Distinction*, 56.

115 Bourdieu, *Distinction*, 491.

116 Gerard, pt. 1, sec. 3, 41.

117 Alison, 1.302, 304.

118 Mill, 2.246, 354–5.

119 Knight, bk. 1, ll. 181–4; bk. 1, ll. 94–5; bk. 1, l. 166; bk. 3, ll. 317–42; Gilpin, 110.

120 Knight, 3.234, 1.285; Repton, 34.

121 'Architectural Masks,' 1.199–200 in Hynes ed.; *Tess of the d'Urbervilles*, 66–7.

122 Mrs Alexander Walker, 284–6.

123 Mrs Alexander Walker, 432.

124 Mrs Alexander Walker, 134–5.

125 Mrs Alexander Walker, 429–30.

126 Sarah Ellis, 111.

127 Mrs Alexander Walker, 432.
128 Mrs Alexander Walker, 301.
129 Ribeiro, 131.
130 Ribeiro, 130.
131 Evans, 25, citing Marshall Canrobert.
132 Burn, 27.
133 Noël Riley, 58.
134 Eden, 127.
135 Lathrop, 29.
136 Lynn Linton, 305.
137 Braddon, *Aurora Floyd*, 132.
138 Charles Riley cites Ruskin as an individual in whom the quarrel between line and colour plays out in a particularly intense way (5.)
139 Chapter 7 of 'The Laws of Fésole,' *Works*, 15.414–39. Ruskin vehemently opposed the associationist theory of colour, asserting for example that 'whatever is good for human life is also made beautiful in human sight, not by "association of ideas" but by the appointment of God' (15.422).
140 Ruskin, 14.289–90. After her death Saint Dorothea sent down a basket of roses from Paradise: see Ruskin, 14.290n.
141 'Coloured' in both senses of the word: both dark-skinned and gorgeously costumed.
142 On the perennial appeal of 'simplicity' in architectural discourse, see Forty, 250.
143 The phrase is Neill's, applied to Emma (99).

**1. The Discourse of Taste in *Waverley***

1 Critics who have discussed *Waverley* in terms of the *Bildungsroman* include Hart, 14–31; Jane Millgate, *Walter Scott*; Shaw; and Duncan.
2 Rousseau, *Émile*, 3.211, 4.282–8; Wordsworth, *Prelude*, bk. 5; Eliot, *Mill on the Floss*, bk. 4, chap. 3; and Thomas Hardy, *Jude the Obscure*, pt. 1, chap. 5, and pt. 2, chap. 1.
3 Maggie's reading in *The Mill on the Floss*, for example, and Lyndall's reading in Olive Schreiner's *The Story of an African Farm* strongly differentiate them from their society's feminine stereotypes.
4 Richardson, 8.
5 Jane Millgate argues that it is Waverley's very romance commitments that enable his maturation. *Walter Scott*, 35, 39, 57.
6 See Ferris. My argument builds on but qualifies the contention of Ferris, 99–100, and Duncan, 62–7, that Waverley is a type of female reader.

7 This is Scott's phrase to describe himself as a youth.

8 Scott is implying precisely the distinction Bourdieu makes between cultural capital and educational capital, e.g., *Distinction*, 66.

9 The aesthetic disposition 'unites all those who are a product of similar conditions while distinguishing them from all others' (Bourdieu, *Distinction*, 56). A contemporary reader comments on Scott's 'perpetual allusion to the English and Latin classics' as demonstrating 'no common share of scholarship and of taste.' Ferris cites this quotation from the *British Critic* in support of her assertion that the narrative has 'the authority of a very specific kind of male writing' because of the way it weaves in 'a constant strain of allusion to the entire European literary canon, notably to the classics' (85).

10 *Iliad*, 9.553–65.

11 *Paradise Lost*, 1.103; *Inferno*, 3.112–20; *Aeneid*, 6.109–18.

12 See Duncan's argument, which turns, in part, on the tension in *Waverley* between androgyny as cultivation and androgyny as emasculation (72 and passim).

13 For another view of Scott's anxiety about circulation, see Henderson's discussion of *The Heart of Midlothian*, a brilliant close reading that does not, however, escape the depth/non-depth binary she intends to challenge.

14 Welsh notes the Waverley hero's dependence for his identity on written documents, 'frequently subject to loss or discovery in dreams,' attributing the nightmarish situations in which the hero tends to get involved to his participation in a contract society: see *Hero of the Waverley Novels*, 103.

15 'Taste is what brings together things and people that go together' (Bourdieu, *Distinction*, 241). See Welsh on the Waverley hero as gentleman and 'ideal *member* of society,' particularly his discussion of honour, in *Hero of the Waverley Novels*, 24, 134–54; see also Hart, 19–31, and Duncan on Waverley's relationships with father figures.

16 Shaw notes this 'strange metamorphosis,' accounting for it as 'intended to symbolize the brief efflorescence of the Jacobite cause' (184).

17 On Bourdieu's concept of 'habitus,' see Introduction.

18 Duncan, focusing on the moment when Waverley looks in the mirror, works out the implications of this narcissism (65).

19 Colley attributes the lack of support for the Jacobites in 1745 largely to the commercial anxiety of both these groups (77–85).

20 Arguing that Scott participated in the discursive project of 'Improvement,' a process that marginalized the Highlands and doomed the region to be supported by tourism, Womack refers to Scott himself as speaking 'for the practical future' (165).

21 Gilpin for example makes the characteristic distinction between Englishness,

the Picturesque, liberty, and 'nature,' on the one hand, and continental formality, despotism, and 'art' on the other: 'Among the peculiar features of
English landscape, may be added the embellished garden, and park-scene.
In other countries the environs of great houses are yet under the direction of
formality. The wonder-working hand of art, with it's regular cascades, spouting fountains, flights of terraces, and other atchievements, have still possession of the gardens of kings, and princes. In England alone the model of
nature is adopted' (9). The distaste for Versailles was already conventional:
Kames called it 'a lasting monument of a taste the most depraved' (Home,
429).

22 Gilpin, 62. Liu observes that 'The garden of liberalism was Richmond and
Stowe versus Versailles' (104).

23 Burke, 19.

24 See Bourdieu, *Distinction*, 175.

25 Welsh's discussion of the way in which characters of lower rank compete with
and parody the protagonists is relevant here: see *Hero of the Waverley Novels*,
178–90.

26 Welsh remarks that, unlike the dark hero, who is morally weak or even dia-
bolic, the dark heroine is immune to criticism (*Hero of the Waverley Novels*,
48).

27 Jane Millgate registers the ambiguity in her characterization, seeing Flora
both as 'a victim of her own idealizing imagination,' who has altered the glen
'not so much to deceive as to heighten what she sees as the essential qualities
of the scene,' but also as one of the pair who have 'deliberately fostered and
even partly created' the glamour of Glennaquoich (*Walter Scott*, 49).

28 Garside, whose theme is the unreliability of perception and understanding
in Waverley, points out that 'we can only guess at its contents' (667).

29 Watson, 130.

30 See Garside, 670; Shaw, 184–85; Jane Millgate, *Walter Scott*, 44–8.

31 Shaw, 185.

32 Duncan discusses Donald Bean Lean as an Autolycus or trickster figure who
parodies the satanic ambition of Fergus and contaminates the romance of
Jacobitism with 'a sort of natural politics of self–interest' (78). I argue that
Donald parodies Flora in the same way.

33 There is a slight grammatical bobble here that adds to the ambiguity of the
assertion: that is, the adverbial use of an adjective phrase. The narrator refers
to the 'delight and awe with which [Waverley] approached her, like a fair
enchantress of Boiardo or Ariosto' (106). Since 'like a fair enchantress' must
modify 'her,' the sense is suspended between 'Waverley approached her *as if
she were* an enchantress,' which tends to attribute the metaphor to him, and

'Waverley approached her, and she was like an enchantress,' which gives it to the narrator. Kiely, arguing for Scott's own investment in the romance he intermittently ironizes, points out that 'it is Scott who likens his hero to a knight and who calls the place "a land of romance"' (144).

34  Duncan points to the ambiguity – 'At the same time Flora is not herself an Acrasia or Alcina but a pure woman' (82) – but does not account for it.

35  Garside, focusing on the name Poussin, identifies Flora's landscaping as a version of 'the "ideal" beauties of Franco-Italian landscape painting,' which he points out were already going out of style in Scotland in favour of 'a more individualist, natural, "impressionistic" school' with which Scott sympathized (674, 681n21): that is, evidently, a school influenced by the Picturesque ideal. But Scott first wrote not 'Poussin' but 'Claude,' and changed the noun only when it was pointed out to him that Claude was notoriously bad as a painter of the human figure (see *Waverley*, 106 and 436n106.14). Womack points out that the Claude/Rosa pairing is a commonplace of Picturesque writing (75), and it is clearly the Picturesque that Scott had in mind here rather than the 'refinement' of the Italian school. The allusion to Claude pairs the scene with Waverley's visit to Donald Bean Lean's cave, where he expects 'to meet a stern, gigantic, ferocious figure, such as Salvator would have chosen to be the central object of a group of banditti' (*Waverley*, 80). Jane Millgate mentions the Picturesque aspect of the landscape (*Walter Scott*, 47–9).

36  Gilpin describes spots where 'a cleft pine is thrown across a chasm,' leaving the dismayed traveller in a quandary: 'Return, he dare not – for he knows what a variety of terrors he has already passed. – Yet if his foot slip, or the plank on which he rests, give way; he will find his death, and his grave together; and never more be heard of' (1.188); Knight in *The Landscape* refers in a list of appropriate rustic ornaments to 'the prostrate tree, or rudely propt-up beam / That leads the path across the foaming stream' (bk. 2, ll. 238–9).

37  Price, pt. 1, chap. 2, 18.

38  Price, pt. 1, chap. 3, 54, and pt. 1, chap. 2, 21.

39  Price, pt. 1. chap. 2,18.

40  Price, pt. 2, chap. 6, 107, and pt. 2, chap. 1, 198. See Jones on the titillation and ultimate frustration of the male voyeur, which she argues expresses anxiety about masculinity at a moment when women are becoming threatening.

41  Knight, bk. 1, ll. 215 and 218. The 'bursting' may be moral as well as material: Winnington's epigraph to this text asserts that Knight's readers will hail the hour when 'trammel'd nature' will again be free to 'burst luxuriant into liberty' (xiv).

42 Price, pt. 1, chap. 4, 86.
43 Price, pt. 1, chap. 3, 57. Garside alludes to 'the implicit Toryism in 'picturesque' theory,' to which he asserts Scott was 'not averse' (681n14). Jones
   argues that while the particular controversy dramatized the antagonism
   between 'Burkean and Picturesque politics,' there was a 'deeper ideological
   alliance' between them, 'based on class allegiance and 'Country' values'
   (126–7).
44 Price, pt. 2, chap. 1, 192n; and pt. 2, chap. 2, 216.
45 Sidney Robinson cites these two quotations (79).
46 Knight, Preface, 104.
47 The association between Picturesque theory and Foxite liberalism has been
   well documented: see Liu, 103–13, and Sidney Robinson, 79–80. Whether
   Scott's readers would remember the debate in 1814 is not clear. Repton in
   1816 thinks that 'So many years have now elapsed since the controversy
   between Mr. Knight and Mr. Price on the subject of landscape gardening'
   that his own readers may have forgotten it (33n).
48 Barrell suggests that the Picturesque perspective had become the 'transcendent viewing-position which had through the eighteenth century been
   regarded as the perquisite of the gentleman' (*Birth of Pandora*, cited in
   Copley and Garside, 8).
49 Gilpin was born in 1724. If we imagine Flora as in her middle twenties in
   1745, she is about the same age as Gilpin. Waverley supposed that Flora 'is
   two years older than I am,' and Rose, who is seventeen, seems to him 'much
   younger' than Flora (see *Waverley*, 255, 40, 377).
50 See Duncan, who argues that in the Waverley novels the dark heroine
   'donates her own magic' to the domestic space in which the male protagonist will end up (70–1). Levine notes that 'what Flora describes here is what
   Scott himself, at Abbotsford, was trying to achieve' (*Realistic Imagination*, 84).
51 See Welsh, *Hero of the Waverley Novels*, especially chapter 4, on the inheritance
   of property in the Waverley novels, and Colley on the importance of cross-
   border marriages in the formation of a British ruling class (158–9).
52 Though with Waverley's money: the sum is what Talbot paid for Brerewood
   Lodge, the estate Waverley inherited from his mother.
53 Colley's account of the reconstruction in the 1780s of Braham Castle, a
   fortress-like mansion damaged by the English army in 1725, recalls Scott's
   description of the restoration of Tully-Veolan (see Colley, 158–9; *Waverley*,
   333–4).
54 Duncan, 70.
55 See Makdisi, who argues that '*Waverley* does not so much order the various
   historical narratives aurrounding the Clearances as suppress them' (80).

Trumpener discusses *Guy Mannering* as Scott's response to Clearances, comparing it to Austen's *Mansfield Park* as illuminating 'the workings of the imperialist unconscious' (184).

56 Duncan, 90.

57 Tuite defines kitsch as the bourgeois appropriation of aristocratic images and decries what she calls 'heritage-industry' nostalgia, which she sees as sinister because it depoliticizes the periods it 'restores' and forgets the class exploitation that enabled the construction of the buildings it sentimentalizes.

58 Colley documents the new interest on the part of English landowners in purchasing estates on the Celtic fringe, even, by the 1820s, in the Highlands (158). On the link between Scott and the Highlands as a holiday destination, see Womack, 140–65. Duncan, who draws attention to Scott's own reliance on English capital (54–5), describes Waverley at the end of the novel as 'the donor of renewed historical possibility in the form of capital and political connection' (98). Makdisi points out that Scott drastically speeds up the process of returning the Jacobite properties to their previous owners, which in reality did not take place until 1784, and explains the 'quasi-magical restoration' of Tully-Veolan in terms of the mediation of Talbot, which he says purifies it 'by an almost ritualistic passage through the modern economic system of the market' (77, 93).

59 On Scott's too-pat happy endings, see Welsh, 100, 154, and passim, and Ferris, who says that they 'cooperate with ... literary expectations, although they do so with some irony by ... assuming their own predictability' (131). Levine, with his sense of the 'sentimental self-mockery' with which 'Scott enacts the movement the whole novel will confirm,' was one of the first to emphasize the self-referential aspect of *Waverley*: 'The narrative endorses the ineffectual romanticism of Waverley and Scott, just as history (with some help from Scott) has sentimentally romanticized highland life' (*Realistic Imagination*, 84). See also Kerr, who sees the novels as parodying the satisfactions Scott provides; Burgess, who reads the later novels (though not *Waverley*) as evincing an uneasiness with the Hanoverian legitimacy that they apparently endorse; and Duncan, 60–2. The feminization of the endings – the way they extract the hero from public history and fold him into a private, domestic space – is examined by Duncan and Burgess.

60 On the eighteenth-century formulation of the relationship between portraiture and history painting, which was considered the nobler genre, see Barrell, *Political Theory of Painting*.

61 Critics who have discussed the painting include Garside, 677; Levine, *Realistic Imagination*, 104–5; Shaw, 186; Makdisi, 97; Kerr, 19–21; and Watson, 133. The

consensus is that it is an ironic mirror-text, an unreliable aestheticization with self-reflexive force: with whatever degree of self-consciousness, 'an allegorical restatement of *Waverley*'s own production of the past' (Makdisi, 97).

62  On Scott's distrust of the pictorial 'moment,' see Ferris, 220–2, and Butterworth, who deal with the discussion between Peter Pattieson and the painter Dick Tinto in *The Bride of Lammermoor*; also Eric Walker's discussion of 'The Laird's Jock,' 69–73. The limitation of the painter to a single moment out of time is a theme of art critics: e.g., Reynolds: 'A Painter ... has but one sentence to utter, one moment to exhibit' (120). Scott was evidently well acquainted with such debates: see note 76 to chapter 3, below.

63  In its elegiac feeling and some of its details it is recalled in chapter 35 of *Rob Roy*, where MacGregor's followers make their farewell appearance in a column behind him.

64  Bourdieu, *Distinction*, 71.

65  There is of course an anachronism here: the painting is done soon after 1745 but in the style of Raeburn, who was not born until 1756. The figure of Fergus is said to be based on Col. Alastair Macdonnell and Scott's conception of his character inspired by Raeburn's portrait of him: see Andrew Williams and Brown, 47.

66  *Mill on the Floss*, book 5, chap. 4.

67  The painting is thus eminently tasteful by the standards of Reynolds, who held that the portrait ought to fuse the recognizable individual with the ideal type: see *Discourses*, 103, 105–6, 118, 120–1.

68  Scott is seen either as critiquing the inevitable falsification of history, for example by Kerr, or participating in it: see Watson on Kerr, 133n25.

## 2. A Room with a Viewer: The Evolution of a Victorian Topos

1  For example, Phineas Finn's interview with Lady Laura Standish, who, like Flora, has political ambitions (Trollope, *Phineas Finn*, chaps 14 and 15), and Frank Greystock's with Lizzy Eustace at Portray, which, like Scott's, has Spenserian echoes (Trollope, *The Eustace Diamonds*, chaps 21, 22, 26). Maggie Tulliver's transgressive meeting with Philip Wakem in the Red Deeps (*Mill on the Floss*, bk. 5, chap. 1) may also allude to *Waverley*: parallels include the artfully wild natural setting, the initiatory ambience, the troubled, unconsummated erotic feeling, and the brunette protagonist (Maggie, who identifies with Scott's dark heroines but quite lacks Flora's sophistication and rhetorical control).

2  The parallels between the two spaces have been noted by Jane Millgate, *Walter Scott*, 42, 48–9. Fergus does not actually initiate Waverley into Flora's

glen – in keeping with Flora's more active role, it is Flora herself who decides to invite Waverley there – but she is acting under the auspices of her brother, who has urged that Flora recite her translation of Mac-Murrough's song.

3 *Awkward Age* 283.

4 For an extended treatment of 'accomplishments,' see Moler, 109–54. Marilyn Butler observes that the critique of accomplishments is a staple of the novel of female education (220–1).

5 Drawing on the model of triangulated desire postulated by René Girard, Sedgwick points out that women are often used in the plots of Victorian novels as a means through which men connect with each other.

6 I am drawing on Fletcher's distinction between temple and labyrinth in *The Faerie Queene* (25–8 and passim). Duncan, who deals in detail with *Waverley*'s Spenserian context, also points out the similarity between Rose's room and Flora's glen (80).

7 See Introduction, 10–11.

8 My argument about the woman's-room view complements and qualifies that of Barrell, who demonstrates that the eminence from which the viewer surveys the landscape is the spatial equivalent of the power to abstract and generalize that differentiates gentlemen both from women and from the vulgar ('Public Prospect,' 19), and that of Labbé, who bases her remarks on Barrell's arguments (ix–xii). In novels by both men and women throughout the century, women sometimes do in fact command a prospect view (I shall discuss those focalized by Rose Bradwardine, Emily St Aubert, and Emma Woodhouse), though their ability to do so is by virtue of the social status conferred upon them by men.

9 Jane Millgate argues that the focalization here is Waverley's, since the view 'seems to speak more of Edward's heightened sensibility than of Rose's' (43). On the use of the word ekphrasis to refer to a description of landscape, see Crawford, 139–40. Barrell points out that in a period when to 'display a correct taste in landscape was a valuable social accomplishment, quite as much as to sing well or to write a correct letter,' the habit of 'conceiv[ing] a landscape as a pictorial composition' shaped the locodescriptions of poets. He argues, for example, that Thomson's syntactical structure is 'invented to imitate the response of the *eye* to the landscape it looks over' (see *Idea of Landscape*, 5, 6, 27).

10 'The use of both these arts [music and drawing] is more for yourself than others: it is but seldom that a private person has leisure or application enough to gain any high degree of excellence in them; and your own family are perhaps the only persons who would not much rather be entertained by the performance of a professor than by yours' (Chapone, *Letters* 8, 119).

11  'L'Allegro,' line 137. The gendering of words and music is traditional: e.g., Richard Barnfield's 'To His Friend Master R.L., in Praise of Music and Poetry' (a poem attributed to Shakespeare in the *Passionate Pilgrim* of 1599). The two arts are described as siblings: 'If music and sweet poetry agree / As they must needs (the sister and the brother).' Words consistently trump music in contemporary constructions of the feminine: e.g., in Radcliffe's *The Romance of the Forest*, where Adeline's poetry is a more adequate response to the sublime than Clara La Luc's pencil (chap. 18) or her lute playing (chap. 16), which become associated with irresponsible self-indulgence. The contrast between polished execution and sensibility is also conventional: cf. Radcliffe's description of Clara's singing: 'She knew nothing of the intricacies of execution; her airs were simple, and her style equally so, but she soon gave them a touching expression, inspired by the sensibility of her heart, which seldom left those of her hearers unaffected' (chap. 16).

12  As Pettit points out in her review of Kathryn King's study of Jane Barker, the virtues of a room of one's own were already being extolled by Barker's fictional heroine Galesia in 1723. Galesia's room is quite different from Rose's: a shabby garret space without the usual signs of tasteful feminine activity, it is defined simply by its view out over the roofs of London. This prospect, often compared to Jane Eyre's view from the leads at Thornfield, evokes Galesia's satire of corrupt English institutions, though King suggests that it signals her 'desire for connection ... with a world of books, buildings, laws ... the "symbolic order"' (King, cited by Pettit).

13  It is true that Rose does emerge from her apartment to act on Waverley's behalf, but she is either offstage at these moments or in disguise, so that neither Waverley nor the reader knows who she is. Scott evidently felt that dramatizing her 'outside' activities more fully would compromise the impression of chaste enclosure upon which his picture of idealized femininity is based.

14  Recent critics have emphasized the escape from history at the end of *Waverley*, the retreat into a feminized domestic sphere and the ways in which 'Scott's ... conclusions ... feminize and enclose the plot they type as romance, highlighting the contingency of its solution-narratives and insulating it from the political history it resolves' (Burgess, 197; also see Duncan).

15  See Bradbrook, who cites the heroines' care of their plants (106).

16  *Kenilworth* 46–7; *Romance of the Forest* 156–7 and 163–4.

17  The reviewer of Ruskin's *The Elements of Drawing* asserts for example that 'A man who does not draw may almost be said not to see' (Paget, 38).

18  The allusion is to Poovey's *Proper Lady*, to which my argument is indebted at this point.

19 Langland, 85.

20 Though Poovey argues in *Uneven Developments* that in *David Copperfield* the notion of vocation is used to erase the labour involved in both Agnes's housekeeping and David's novel writing, I would suggest that, in contrast to Dora's self-indulgent play, David's activity does register as serious work.

21 Landseer's pictures were often reproduced in Berlin woolwork. See Noël Riley, 59.

22 Theorists of consumerism argue that 'traditional old-style hedonists wanted control over the *objects*; the modern consumer wants control over the *meaning* of the objects' (Copeland, 93). The transition has clearly already taken place in *Coningsby*.

23 As mentioned above, the carceral boudoir is already in Radcliffe and Scott. On 'demonic modulation,' see Frye, 156–7, 196, and passim.

24 See Sedgwick, who does not however discuss the Dombey–Carker relationship.

25 The metaphor Nunokawa has analysed, the notion of woman as the only property that lasts, is ironized by such plots.

26 For a fuller discussion of Edith's commodification and prostitution, see Waters, 49–52.

27 The *vanitas* is a particular kind of still-life painting that displays a set of objects chosen as emblems of the brevity and vanity of material existence.

28 The heroine/hag figure is a staple of romance: for example, Duessa robed and disrobed in *Faerie Queene*, 1.2.13, 1.2.40–1, and 1.8.45–8; Frankenstein's dream of embracing the beautiful Elizabeth, only to find he is holding the maggot-ridden body of his dead mother (Shelley, chap. 5); the transformation of Ayesha in Rider Haggard's *She*, chap. 26. In the more realistic text, the figure is split into two characters.

29 As critics have read the flight of Quentin in *The Sound and the Fury* (Michael Millgate, 103).

30 For a sympathetic treatment of Edith Dombey and her double Alice, see John, 215–28, who describes both women as possessed of 'thoughtful integrity,' as 'true to a hidden self, a self driven underground by the social restrictions on the behavior of women' (221).

31 Cvetkovich in her discussion of *Lady Audley's Secret* connects consumer culture and commodity fetishism with female madness. Her analysis however does not consider the note of cupidity here or account for the downright zestful treatment of consumerism in *Aurora Floyd*. See Matus: 'The very specific inventory of lavish, material treasures in her bedroom titillates the reader with a feast of conspicuous consumption as it suggests that Lady Aud-

ley's beauty, ornamentality, and apparent conformity are purchased and rewarded by such prizes' (200).

32 Skilton, editor of the Oxford edition of the novel, wonders why the narrator points out that it was old-fashioned to do needlework, suggesting that Lady Audley is adopting a style of activity that Sir Michael would be at home with (450n118). Perhaps we are to read her fashionable sketch as a deliberate attempt to defer to what she knows is his mediocre taste. In opportunistically parodying the taste of the class she is trying to join, she would be like Becky Sharp.

33 Becky will not admit to Amelia that she does not have a lock of her son's hair (see *Vanity Fair*, 637–8).

34 *Lady Audley's Secret* also owes much to *Bleak House*, with Robert Audley playing Mr Tulkinghorn to Lady Audley's Lady Dedlock and Phoebe combining the functions of the French maid Hortense and Jenny the brickmaker's wife, both of whom dress up as Lady Dedlock.

35 Matus, 190–200.

36 Men like Mellish were believed to contribute to the decline of English painting: see Atkinson on the market for 'pleasing commonplace' in painting, shaped by 'wealthy manufacturers' who frequent art exhibitions to purchase 'showy pictures, to hang on the walls of their dining and drawing rooms' (155).

37 Aurora's pork-pie hat is what would today be called her 'signature' accessory. Fashion quickly becomes so predictable that some kind of piquantly conventional eccentricity is needed to signal 'individuality': shelter magazines often refer to a homeowner's 'signature collection of enamel snuff-boxes,' for example.

38 Chase and Levenson argue that Braddon's novel is a defence of the newly independent woman – a daydream about 'the sublime imperial woman who nevertheless belongs to the right sort' (i.e., the genteel class) – and assert that 'the labor of the novel is to channel the heroine's will into a defense of the union between old family and new money' (211) so as to allow women the same freedom of marital choice as men. This seems a somewhat complacent reading of the consumer fantasy that the novel endorses.

39 Chase and Levenson, arguing that between 1835 and 1865 'domestic life itself was impelled towards acts of exposure and display,' focus on myth-making texts, like Dickens's novels, that celebrate the 'triumphs of privacy,' and on scandals that undercut the myth. Although they do not mention the 'house-tour' simulated by Braddon (and endorsed by J.C. Loudon), their argument is relevant to this topos.

### 3. Resources and Performance: *Mansfield Park* and *Emma*

1 Volume 2, chap. 18.
2 Critics who have applied Bourdieu's terms to Austen include Copeland, who observes that 'Austen trades heavily in cultural capital, one of the pseudo-gentry's most important notes of exchange,' explains Bourdieu's distinction between cultural and educational capital, and comments on the cultural capital of Jane Fairfax (107–9), and Tuite, who notes how Austen 'relates social mobility to cultural capital' (10).
3 The parallel between Emma and Mrs Elton is a critical commonplace; the echo of 'resources' is remarked by Booth, 247, and Pickrel, 301–2.
4 Michaelson, identifying the function of reading Austen's dialogue aloud, suggests that it helped her readers learn to speak (182) – and presumably how not to speak.
5 Cicero, 215.
6 Chesterfield, letter of 4 October O.S. 1746, 15–16.
7 Chesterfield, letter of 11 December O.S. 1749, 38.
8 Tuite, 144.
9 *Camilla*, bk. 1, chap. 1, 10, and bk. 1, chap. 4, 34.
10 'Resource' was evidently something of a buzzword in contemporary discourse about women's occupations. Bob Stuart, Cherry Wilkinson's destined husband in Barrett's parodic *The Heroine*, describes the perfect woman: 'When solitary, she should have the power of contemplation, and if her needle broke, she should be capable of finding resource in a book' (letter 12, 113). On the link between *The Heroine* and *Emma*, see Kirkham, *Jane Austen, Feminism and Fiction*, 129–31. Thomas Gisborne asks: 'What resource, what possible occupation, except cards? To the unfurnished mind, none' (cited by Bradbrook, 37). Sydney Smith, reviewing Thomas Broadhurst's *Advice to Young Ladies on the Improvement of the Mind* (1808), argues that 'the object is, to give children resources that will endure as long as life endures' (306).
11 *Camilla*, bk. 1, chap. 7, 52.
12 In fact Mrs Elton's very emphasis suggests that Selina's estate is probably not secluded enough: fast-growing maples have no doubt been planted in order to hide the house from the road.
13 Genlis, 2.233 and 251.
14 Copeland argues that 'Gothic terror in woman's fiction is unremittingly economic' (36).
15 See Wilt.
16 Edith Dombey laments that 'I have not an accomplishment or grace that might have been a resource to me, but it has been paraded and vended to

enhance my value' (Dickens, *Dombey and Son,* 856); the narrator of *Little Women* explains that during the week when the March girls decide to neglect their household duties, Amy March 'fared worst of all, for her resources were small; and, when her sisters left her to amuse and care for herself, she soon found that accomplished and important little self a great burden' (Alcott, 110–11).

17 *Camilla,* bk. 1, chap. 6, 46.

18 Bermingham points out that accomplishments were usually abandoned after marriage ('Aesthetics of Ignorance,' cited by Michaelson, 123).

19 Neill says the novel is about how people are to be ranked and finds *Emma* 'violently discriminatory' (87, 99–100, 110). Dole, who also finds *Emma* a snob, nevertheless recognizes that Austen endorses class distinction (67). The most penetrating recent study of Austen's treatment of social mobility is that of Tuite, who analyses the 'marriage plot of upward female mobility, where a bourgeois female subject is elevated into an aristocratic class which is at once the ultimate object of desire and reward for this exemplary form of bourgeois subjectivity and desperately in need of reform and renovation through this exemplary bourgeois female subject' (10).

20 Hazlitt, 157.

21 For a discussion of Edmund's guidance as Foucauldian 'discipline,' see Stewart, 134. Tuite notes that the instruction of a young woman by her father or a member of the clergy was a middle-class ideal (109).

22 Woman's situation was compared to slavery by feminists of the period: see Kirkham, 'Feminist Irony,' 243; also Claudia Johnson, 107–8; Neill, 8, 84–5.

23 Kirkham argues that Austen, by emphasizing the drawbacks of Fanny's physical weakness, is critiquing the sentimentalization of feminine delicacy: see *Jane Austen, Feminism and Fiction,* 103–5. Her argument is intriguing, yet I feel that Austen's intention is not so clear-cut: even as she critiques the social stereotype, she exploits the imagery of pristine delicacy and refinement. See also note 66 below.

24 Critics who idealize the room include Schneider; Tave, 200; Duckworth, 73–4. But Barbara Hardy also points out that it is 'no pure retreat' (30), and others have noticed the way Fanny is invaded, e.g., Morgan, 135.

25 Austen's novels contain demonized characters like Mary Crawford, Augusta Elton, and even Harriet Smith, who voice the cynicism or satire that the novel dramatizes but disavows: on Mary, see Q.D. Leavis, 57; Lerner, 27–8; Neill, 71, 78; Lanser, 76–7; on Mrs Elton, Neill, 105.

26 The necklace episode has been widely discussed, pro (see Lascelles, 136–7, on its mock-epic charm) and con (Marilyn Butler, on its 'crude' symbolism,

246), and Fanny's distress about wearing Henry's chain sometimes condemned as priggish and ungracious (Gard, 135; Waldron, 104). In Fanny's
defence, it helps to visualize what Mary hoped to bring about: the spectacle
of Fanny, at her coming-out party, marked with a sign that she herself is
unable to read.

27 It is a commonplace of criticism that *Mansfield Park* 'resolutely disturbs the
usual gratifying decorum by which good manners, good appearance, good
taste in the arts, intelligence, and liveliness and charm accompany, while not
being identical with, good people': Gard, 123.

28 Neill, 100.

29 E.g., in Radcliffe's *The Romance of the Forest*, where La Luc points out the planets and stars to Adeline and Clara, observing that 'no study ... so much en-
larges the mind, or impresses it with so sublime and idea of the Deity, as that
of astronomy. When the imagination launches into the regions of space, and
contemplates the innumerable worlds which are scattered through it, we are
lost in astonishment and awe' (275).

30 This reversal of roles supports Kirkham's argument that Austen constructs
her heroines in opposition to the degrading stereotypes current in the culture: 'Feminist Irony,' 117–27. On the other hand, Waldron sees Fanny as an
answer to the over-idealized heroine of evangelical fiction. Critics tend to
approach Fanny either thus – as a *caractère à thèse*, a figure constructed by
Austen to advance an argument – or as a 'case,' an emotionally damaged
human being with diagnosable pathologies.

31 E.g., Gard, 148; but Lanser points out she did not invent it (74).

32 A number of critics have pointed out the theatricality of this moment and of
others that make Fanny the focus of attention, moments that seem anomalous in the light of the anti-theatrical emphasis of the novel as a whole: see
Marshall; Yeazell, *Fictions of Modesty*, 151; Neill, 80; Gard, 137. As Yeazell says,
'even an antitheatrical novel is inevitably dramatic': the problem of how
to display the modest heroine is solved in similar ways in any number of
fictions.

33 Italics mine. The topic of 'improvement' has been thoroughly canvassed,
beginning with Duckworth, who explains the novel's opposition to it in
terms of Austen's Burkean conservatism. On the analogy with self-improvement, see Donoghue, who notes the analogy between the character of the
person and the 'character' of the estate (52–3), and Tuite, who points out
that self-culture is the one kind of improvement against which the novel does
not take a stand (109).

34 Italics mine.

35 See Daniels, *Field of Vision*, 83; Crawford, 5, 66, and passim.; also chapter 4. In

his last book, published in1816, Repton himself was to inveigh against mere size: 'the quantity of acres attached does not make a place large or small'; 'There is no error so common as the mistaking of greatness of dimensions for greatness of character': see *Fragments*, 83, 40.

36 It is because Brown was 'bred a gardener,' Price implies, condemning his design for Blenheim, that 'he formed his style (or rather his plan) upon the model of a parterre, and transferred its minute beauties ... to the great scale of nature'; 'his mind having never been prepared, by a study of the great masters of landscape, for a more enlarged one of nature; finding no invention, no resources within himself, he copied what he had most seen and most admired – his own little works' (Price, pt. 2, chap. 1, 188–9, and pt. 2, chap. 3, 266).

37 Responding to the site is what the Picturesque gardener was supposed to do. The fact that the formula is still used today in shelter magazines – 'I listened to the house and it told me what it wanted' – suggests its function in mystifying ownership of property. See Kurt, 86 and 87.

38 Miller accounts for Henry's attractiveness in terms of his 'narratability,' his resistance to the closure that the novelist will eventually have to impose on him (20–5).

39 Fleishman says that Henry is 'a Romantic actor, like Kean as contemporaries describe him' and cites Hazlitt and Keats on 'negative capability'; Gay sees him as a Garrick (99). Duckworth finds Henry's 'Protean' quality sinister (65); Fleishman points out that 'although desirable for the artist, such a lack of determinate selfhood is dangerous to the moral personality' (49). Kirkham makes a similar point: that there is a difference between 'the kinds of responsibility appropriate to art on the one hand, and to ... daily life' on the other, and that, although Fanny's and Edmund's ability to respond to acting is a measure of their 'true sensibility,' 'her admiration for Crawford the actor, is always contrasted with her dislike of Crawford the man': *Jane Austen, Feminism and Fiction*, 108, 109. I am not sure that either Fanny's responses or the reader's are so neatly polarized. Gay identifies Henry as the Vice figure partly on the basis of his 'changefulness' (100–1). John Hardy finds the ability to act 'the sign of a character not sufficiently grounded in itself' (77). Gard, however, who believes that most readers like the Crawfords, says that the Shakespeare episode 'puts acting in a pleasanter light' (139).

40 Kirkham argues that Edmund corrects Henry's sexist 'Englishman' and 'man' by substituting 'one' and 'we': *Jane Austen, Feminism and Fiction*, 114. But this exaggerates the tension between the two men at this point. Edmund's praise of Henry is so effusive that his pronouns do not sound like a rebuke of Henry's word choice.

41 Bourdieu's remarks about symbolic appropriation and about Comte's 'linguistic communism' explain the disingenuousness of this kind of claim: see Introduction.

42 See Neill, 101–4, on the class resonances of idealized 'Englishness' in Austen.

43 Edwards notices the management of point of view in this scene (60).

44 Fleishman makes this point (24–5).

45 Enfield describes oral reading as an 'accomplishment' (ix) and concludes by claiming that 'the study of polite literature' produces 'the Accomplished and Happy Man' (xliii). Michaelson documents Austen's knowledge of the elocution movement (122–34, 149, 195) and demonstrates 'how tightly connected were the discourses on various kinds of display – accomplishments, reading aloud, theater, and speech' (128).

46 Michaelson points out that women read aloud only to other women but were frequently subjected to what she calls 'patriarchal' reading by men (156). Fanny stops reading as soon as the men enter the room.

47 The words again are Enfield's, who urges in his preface: 'What a man has hourly occasion to do, should be done well. Every private company, and almost every public assembly, afford opportunities of remarking the difference between a just and graceful, and a faulty and unnatural elocution' (ix).

48 Variety in spoken delivery is highly valued by Enfield, who insists on it throughout his two prefatory essays and organizes his anthology into subsections to allow for a wide range of voices and tones. Enfield's emphasis on 'the freedom, ease, and variety of just elocution' (xxv) sounds like Austen's description of Henry's performance. Michaelson points out that Henry's selection of 'beauties' follows the set-up of elocution anthologies like Enfield's (175). It is in Enfield's *The Speaker* that Tom would have found 'My name is Norval' (46), and Antony's speeches mourning Caesar (321–2), and Henry no doubt includes among his selections from *Henry VIII* the passage Enfield entitles 'Wolsey and Cromwell' (312–13): 'Farewell, a long farewell to all my greatness.'

49 Robinson's *An Essay on the Composition of a Sermon* (1778) is a popular translation of Jean Claude's *Traité de la composition d'un sermon* (1688); the quoted passage is from Robinson's extensive and influential notes to the translation (1.466–7). The quotation continues: 'The best method seems to be that, which the most popular and pious preachers use. They study till they thoroughly understand the subject. They habitually feel it. They retire ten minutes before preaching, and in fervent prayer to God, possess their souls with a full idea of the importance of the matter, on which they are going to treat. They go from prayer to the pulpit, as Moses went down from the mount from

God to speak to the people.' I am grateful to my colleague Dan White for drawing my attention to this quotation.

50 Duckworth points out that Henry seems to be echoing Blair's remark that since clergymen deal in commonplaces they need excellent execution, but that Blair also supports Edmund by valuing text over style (68). Michaelson also comments on Blair's emphasis on personal character and ethos over technique (184–5). Indeed, such handbooks of rhetoric, while recommending 'artificial rules,' exercise and practice, consistently call for a balance between content and technique: Enfield for example warns the senator, barrister, and preacher who make their living talking to beware of assuming 'the character of a Spouter' (xxv–xxvi).

51 Enfield, ix.

52 The word 'harangue' itself had a theatrical connotation and was less pejorative than it is today. Kames declares that 'dancing affords great opportunities for displaying grace; and haranguing still more': see Home, 159. Book V in Enfield's *The Speaker* is entitled 'Orations and Harangues.'

53 Said; Claudia Johnson, 96; Stewart, 122–34; Neill, 8, 88–9 and passim. See Fleishman, 35–8, and Trumpener, 180–5, on the social and economic changes that might have impinged upon Sir Thomas's fortunes at this point.

54 The remark is seen by Fleishman as demonstrating Fanny's 'willingness to identify with the fortunes of the family' (39), by Stewart, in terms of her 'wish to please Sir Thomas' (122); Claudia Johnson says there is no reason to assume Fanny is critical of slavery (107); Neill suggests that Edmund's assumption is that his father 'would have explained methods and procedures he would have felt no need to justify' (88); Tuite argues that Fanny is anything but subversive: 'the text nervously overcompensates for the impertinence of Fanny's question to Sir Thomas by staging a slavish display of her desire for his approval' (117). See Neill's comments on the problematic 'taciturnity' of the novel on the issue of slavery (89).

55 See Litvak, 'The Infection of Acting' and *Caught in the Act*, and Marshall.

56 Neill, 94.

57 That these are the conservative values of Scott and Burke has often been pointed out: see Fleishman, 17 and 32; Neill, 80; and Tuite, 119–24. Tuite argues that Fanny's declaration 'proleptically announces her entitlement to the house and contents of Mansfield Park. It is this landless but *appreciative* female subjectivity which Austen's fiction teaches the aristocracy, in turn, to appreciate as the mark of the cultural, social and political complicity which enables class compromise for mutual gain' (141).

58 On Mansfield Park as an ideal, see Duckworth, 45 and Marilyn Butler, 229, 239–45. Dole, responding to more recent criticism, can still assert that in

spite of its 'internal problems, the traditional estate provides a worthier exemplum of proper living that [*sic*] any available alternative – as Fanny recognizes in Portsmouth' (64). Neill suggests that Fanny over-identifies with what he considers a thoroughly sinister place because of her insecure status as a woman and an outsider (74) and makes essentially the same point about Emma's approval of Donwell Abbey. Neill eschews speculation about authorial intention, but his argument implicitly applies to Austen herself, whose enthusiasm for such establishments might be attributed to her own similar situation. Tuite comments on 'the conflicted effect of Austen's involvement in a paternal, landed aristocratic culture and her commitment to upward social mobility for landless gentry or bourgeois women' (10).

59 Tave, 204.

60 Tuite persuasively argues, however, that Austen displaces onto Mary what might plausibly be Fanny's wish for Tom's death: 'The compensatory fantasy of spiritual inheritance sublates the death wish' (130).

61 Kotzebue, 10. Moler points out that Fanny does in fact acquire accomplishments (149–54). On the parallels between *Mansfield Park* and *Lovers' Vows*, see Claudia Johnson, 109–10; Musselwhite, 29 and passim.

62 Stewart points out that in *Mansfield Park* 'all the status that women possess derives from men, while morally approved action is that which directly supports the father's power and extends his interest' (13): for 'while' she might say 'hence.' Deborah Kaplan, explaining why the women of Austen's circle bought into the ideology of domesticity even while resisting some of its claims, points out that 'marriage was the only option that enabled women of the lesser gentry to secure their social status economically' (21). Kaplan hypothesizes that Austen herself was content to have remained single but demonstrates that she was unhappy with her economic dependence on men: see 125–30, 80–1, 126–30.

63 Neill, 87.

64 E.g., Claudia Johnson, who compares it to the gratitude expected of slaves (107–8).

65 Gard, 140.

66 Marilyn Butler says Fanny's physical weakness is a counterpoint to her inner strength (248); Wiltshire argues that it is a critique of the patriarchy that has rendered her hysterical: see *Jane Austen and the Body*, 70. See also note 26.

67 Fleishman says that Fanny is too critical of her parents (50) and that the lower middle class are so burdened that they are unable to love (93); see also Neill, 72, and Musselwhite, 31. Marilyn Butler however points out that the low-life sequence is a cliché of the anti-Jacobin novel (244).

68 Critics who have commented on the incestuous nature of the ending include

Claudia Johnson, 116–19; Neill, 91, who emphasizes its creepiness; Tuite, 98–126, who argues that endogamy 'symptomatizes both a desire and fear of self-enclosure' on the part of a defensive social class (100); and Watson, who suggests that 'the radical potential of female sexuality can best be contained by keeping it in the family' (92–3).

69 Indeed, Musselwhite implies that she does when he argues that Austen has stolen Kotzebue's radical plot and deodorized it. In *Lovers' Vows* there really is a crossing of class borders: Amelia is a daughter of a poor but honest farmer. Fanny's elevation into what is after all a close branch of her own family is only 'radical' if we are induced to read her as belonging to a much lower class. Musselwhite's readiness to do this suggests that we are, and it confirms the strategic value of the demonization he objects to.

70 Morgan, who reads the novel as a narrative of moral growth and identifies 'the process of character development' as its subject, emphasizes the change in Fanny, asserting that her virtues are not those she was born with and that she is 'without natural gifts' (164–5); Kirkham says that Fanny is constructed as the opposite of the heroines Wollstonecraft dismisses as 'born immaculate': 'Feminist Irony,' 240. Duckworth points out that her excellence can be neither genetic nor a result of education (72). Tuite, in support of her argument about Austen's investment in patriarchal structures, insists on Fanny's 'deficient nature,' which she inherits from 'the deficient maternal nature of the Ward bloodline' (109) – 'the natural impurity and defect of the matrilineal relation of both Ward aunts' (117). But I cannot agree with her, since this supposedly impure bloodline produces the two 'good seeds' who are innately refined. The point I think is that Fanny's superiority is not a matter of inheritance at all, but a mystified construction, borrowed from fairy tales and the 'natural taste' discourse, which is used to rationalize a very limited kind of social mobility.

71 Dale, 69; Neill, 107–8.

72 Siskin, 141. On Harriet's stupidity, see for example Morgan, 34; Marilyn Butler, 267; Ginsburg, 121.

73 Emma eventually realizes that Harriet needs the 'security, stability, and improvement' that Martin will provide and the home he will give her, which is 'retired enough for safety' – moral safety, evidently: 'She would never be led into temptation, nor left for it to find her out' (379). This judgment cannot be dismissed merely by arguing that it is filtered through Emma's consciousness.

74 The rules for charades can be articulated: see Selwyn, 286–7. Harriet's inability to intuit the principles Selwyn systematically outlines is one element in Austen's construction of her as fundamentally stupid.

75 Emma's indifference to the rules is a mark of her social status: an example of
'condescension' in Bourdieu's sense (see Introduction), it signals the class
superiority that, though acknowledged on the first page of the novel, cannot
be cited by Austen in her heroine's defence. Hence Austen's instinct to displace the sociological explanation of Emma's *sprezzatura* with the *moral* picture of her affection for her family. On the possible unreliability of Austen's
narrators, see for example Lascelles, 102; Nardin, 9; Dole, 68.

76 In *Guy Mannering* (chapter 50) Scott alludes to Timanthes when he describes
Dominie Sampson as sinking into his chair and spreading his handkerchief
over his face 'to serve, as I suppose, for the Grecian painter's veil' (573). The
anecdote was a commonplace in eighteenth-century art criticism, cited by
Lessing and Reynolds among others (see Barrell, *Political Theory of Painting*,
112), and Scott seems to take for granted that his readers would be familiar
with it. As Reynolds points out, Timanthes' is a solution that can be used only
once: 'whoever does it a second time, will not only want novelty, but be justly
suspected of using artifice to evade difficulties' (Discourse #8, 227).

77 On mere 'mechanic' imitation, see Reynolds, 104, 122, 169, and174.

78 Lascelles points out that Austen's female characters never exhibit the 'disagreeable silliness' of romance-reader heroines like Barrett's Cherry Wilkinson (*The Heroine*), who have the 'perverse conviction that they are themselves
heroic figures' (69). In *Emma* Austen splits the romanticizing female reader
into two, making Emma the author of tales about other 'heroines' and displacing the disagreeable silliness onto Mrs Elton. See also note 86 below. Fry
asserts that Emma is no female Quixote or romance addict and that she recognizes the limitations of Radcliffe (135).

79 Marilyn Butler observes that 'Harriet shows bad taste when she prefers
Elton's poetry to Martin's prose' (266); see also Knoepflmacher; Barbara
Hardy, *Reading of Jane Austen*, 161; Burrows, 30.

80 See Ginsburg, who argues that social mixing is used in Austen to reaffirm
class distinction by making the main characters fully conscious of the values
they have always held.

81 Page points out that he never speaks (141, 161).

82 See Dole, 72, on Martin's appearance at Donwell Abbey in the film.

83 Marilyn Butler asserts that Emma knows the letter is good and the charade
poor but 'in every case [her] self-will suppresses the conclusion her reason
has just reached on the basis of evidence' (266). My point is that what is
operating is taste not reason, and what Butler calls 'evidence' is nothing so
objective but simply aesthetic judgment. See Cunningham, 323, on Emma's
willful misreading of the letter.

84 It has been pointed out that Emma is often right in her judgments: e.g.,

Tave, 240–1; Duckworth, 148; Gard, 177; Waldron, 126. Litvak in 'Reading Characters,' locating this rightness in her refusal of the right/wrong polarity, erases a pattern that is important to the meaning of the novel, which expresses belief in objective fact and in the value of deferring to it. Watson objects to Litvak's attempt to recuperate Austen as rebelling against moral fixity: 'misreading or deliberately suppressing her ideological choices seems both patronizing and dishonest' (95n35).

85  Harding calls this the story of 'the child brought up in humble circumstances whose inborn nature fits her for better things' and points out that this theme 'is frankly parodied and deflated in the story of Harriet Smith' (21); Fry notes Harriet's 'conventional foundling-status' (131). Moler traces the parallels between Austen's novel and romantic novels of the period and their parodies (155–85).

86  Kirkham argues persuasively that Miss Taylor is constructed by Austen to undercut the stereotype of the irresponsible governess, particularly as illustrated in Barrett's *The Heroine*, on which she believes *Emma* is partly based (*Jane Austen, Feminism and Fiction*, 131). I see the bad-governess function reappearing, however, in the person of Emma herself.

87  Claudia Johnson characterizes this as the 'tale of guilty passion' (137). Watson sees the 'epistolary plot' as 'a narrative of forbidden desire modeled upon *La Nouvelle Héloïse*' (94), and also 'an adulterous triangle of desire highly reminiscent of Helen Maria Williams's *Julia*' (98).

88  Knoepflmacher points out that *georgos* means 'the farmer' (655); Duckworth observes that he is always at work (155).

89  Marilyn Butler, 272.

90  Litvak, 'Reading Characters,' 762. Kirkham on the other hand sees Knightley as a feminist ideal because of the respect he shows for women (*Jane Austen, Feminisn and Fiction*, 128), whereas Neill, acknowledging his charm, accuses Emma (and Austen) of creating an idealized fantasy figure (103–4).

91  Gard, 164.

92  *Emma*, 189. Marilyn Butler argues that there is no reason to take Mr Knightley's characterization of Miss Bates at the moment when he is criticizing Emma's impertinence as the last word (270). The reader is allowed to see faults in Miss Bates that Emma does not remark on or Mr Knightley observe: see Garson, 'Associationism,' 98.

93  'Maria Edgeworth has her (French, of course) Marmontel prefer the English sense in the near contemporary *Ormond*, 1817 – so the topic must have been current' (Gard, 158). Gard cites Page, who notes that such discussion of the shades of meaning of words in translation was common in Austen's day.

94 That his judgment is based on jealousy is a commonplace: e.g., Tave, 236; Kirkham, *Jane Austen, Feminism and Fiction*, 133; Gard, 168.

95 In Genlis's *Adelaide and Theodore*, Adelaide expects to live with her mother, and her fiancé agrees to this scheme (1.252–2).

96 Marilyn Butler, 265; see also Burrows's statistical analysis (192). Knoepflmacher links the brevity of this exchange to that of Martin's letter (643).

97 Maples spring up quickly and are hard to eradicate, since the root grows sideways and the stem breaks easily at ground level. According to Spenser, the maple is 'seeldom inward sound' (*Faerie Queene*, 1.1.9.9). According to J.C. Loudon, the maple is a secondary tree, suitable for planting near water and in churchyards (*Villa Companion*, 599–600). Maple Grove is near Bristol, and since this was a slaving port the suggestion is that Selina's husband has profited from the slave trade: see Kirkham, *Jane Austen, Feminism and Fiction*, 132; Baum, 6. This suggestion throws a somewhat positive light back on Sir Thomas, who is at least obliged to travel and take personal risks, in contrast with Selina's husband, who (perhaps) merely profits from the trade. In *Emma* the symbol of the house is split in two, the association with slavery going to Maple Grove, the positive associations to Donwell.

98 Claudia Johnson, 71; Gard, 172; Gay, 142; Barrett, 149, letter 17. Ida and Glorvina were heroines of contemporary romantic novels.

99 See Neill on Austen's 'English Ideology,' 105–6.

100 Duckworth points out the parallel with Pemberley (175). Within this novel, Emma is like Mrs Elton and Harriet in that she assesses the home her husband will provide for her, though she does not realize it and they do.

101 Tuite cites Austen's description of Pemberley as an example of her 'embourgeoisement' of the aristocratic aesthetic (139–47).

102 This moment has been much discussed: see Trilling; Marilyn Butler, 272–3; Thompson, 39; and Deborah Kaplan, 196–203, on Austen's acceptance of patriarchal land ownership; John Hardy, 102, and Neill, 106–8, on Emma's snobbishness; and Tuite on the link between the heroine's capacity for aesthetic response and her material entitlement (139–41). Tuite discusses *Pride and Prejudice* and *Mansfield Park*, but her remarks are equally relevant to *Emma*.

103 Fry, who points out that both landscape and society are 'gently stratified' at the end of the novel, also remarks on Emma's 'taste for closed prospects' (140, 138) – a taste explained by Barrell in terms of the influence of landscape painting (*Idea of Landscape*, 32) and by Crawford in terms of the debates about enclosure, which associated containment with productivity. On the 1824 *Encyclopaedia Britannica*'s identification of 'well-fenced, well-cultivated fields' with 'Beauty,' see Garson, 'Associationism,' 86.

104 Neill says that Knightley's 'claims to both property and gentility are ancient, so that no one can "see the join"' (110). The name of Donwell Abbey makes clear that it was originally church property: the implied contrast is between responsible Protestant stewardship and the clerical indolence of the Roman Catholic monastic orders.

105 Neill, 89.

106 Predictably, strong exception has been taken to this speech, especially to the word 'furniture,' by a number of critics, including Langland, 226. Knightley's retort needs to be read however in the context of the novel's systematic if understated indication of the right attitude to take to servants. Austen consistently constructs her characters in terms of the notion of excess and defect: in *Emma*, for example, Mr Weston represents the excess of sociability, John Knightley the defect. The issue of the proper attitude towards servants is addressed in the same way: if Mrs Elton is defective in her consideration for her servants, whose names she claims she cannot remember, Mr Woodhouse, who urges the abandonment of a proposed outing to Randals because he does not want to bother James the coachman, is excessive. The implications of this patterning are thoroughly paternalistic: the fact that not knowing one's servants' names is vulgar implies that knowing them would redeem the relationship. But it does suggest that Austen takes for granted that 'gentlemen and ladies' are 'furnished' with servants and is not inviting us to condemn Knightley, whose attitude to the people who work for or with him is always presented as exemplary. Oddly, Langland, though she objects to Knightley's remark, does not otherwise deal with the servants in this novel.

107 Eagleton's remark on the different ways the world presents itself to producer and consumer is relevant here: 'From the standpoint of consumption, the world is uniquely ours': the subject finds himself 'center[ed] … in the sphere of values' rather than decentered in the 'realm of things' (92).

108 See Litvak ('Reading Characters,' 765), who calls the letter 'comically nitpicking' and says Emma tries to mitigate its reductiveness.

109 Fergus, who assumes that the reader shares Emma's initial judgment, comments on this pattern of reversal (140–1).

110 Wiltshire quotes this remark of Johnson's to support the argument that Austen uses Mary Crawford's uncharacteristically self-incriminating letters to destroy her character: see *Recreating Jane Austen*, 103–4. The quotation is equally apposite to Frank's performance.

111 Knoepflmacher makes this point, noting that a reader trained to 'prefer brevity to circumlocution' will find Frank's prose distasteful (654) and concludes that Knightley is right in his critique. Watson refers to Frank's

'unscrupulous rhetoric of feeling' (101) and considers the letter 'as a test of the reader's resistance to his blandishments' (100).

112 'In Memory of W.B. Yeats,' line 36, 197.

113 Langland's theme is the real social power exercised by ladies: she cites Lady Cumnor in Gaskell's *Wives and Daughters*, who by taking Molly's side is able to change her social destiny. Emma's patronage of Harriet does not however produce effects of this kind: Emma does not succeed in 'selling' Harriet to the man Emma wishes would marry her. It would be consistent with Langland's argument to submit, as she does about Dorothea Brooke in *Middlemarch*, that Austen erases the actual social power a woman like her heroine would have – shows her not being able to do what she thinks she can do (and what in real life she would be able to do) – and that this colludes with patriarchal condescension to 'idle,' 'useless' woman. But this is not the line she takes. Rather, she draws attention to Emma's shrewdness about how signs really work in the new social world (225–6). Those who point out that Emma does no real harm include Waldron, 116; Thompson, 42; and Claudia Johnson, 130.

114 Ironically, Elton might have bettered himself had he deferred to Emma's wishes, as Mr Collins does to Lady Catherine de Burgh's in *Pride and Prejudice*.

115 Watson rationalizes this paradox by stating that Austen realizes 'there is simply no stopping people like Mrs Elton' and adds 'nor will Jane Fairfax's rescue from the hands of the Smallridge family prevent the Smallridges and their ilk from eventually acquiring cultural capital for themselves – from people like Jane Fairfax, only less fortunate' (109). This is a very astute remark, but what interests me is that we never see this happen. Copeland argues that Knightley's shrewdness (about, for example, how far Harriet will rise), his 'practical assessments of social mobility,' make him the novel's hero (109). But the point is that he stops with assessing. His insight never taints his courtesy to everyone he encounters. He communicates his assessment only to Emma, and, as Copeland also points out, he mixes easily with the Coxes. This yoking of refined standards and nuanced observation on the one hand and open sociability on the other is yet another feature that marks Knightley as the fantasy construction that some critics have seen him to be.

116 Repton, 68–9.

### 4. The Improvement of the Estate: J.C. Loudon and Some Spaces in Dickens

1 Daniels, 96. On Repton's anguished response to what he saw as the decay of the established gentry after 1800, see Daniels, 82–4.

2 The lines have been translated: 'that jog there, / Spoiling my property line as it does' (Horace, bk. 2, satire 6, ll. 8–9, 81). The allusion was a commonplace: see Lord Chesterfield's letter of 18 November O.S. 1748 (87). For Naboth, see 1 Kings 21.

3 Pope, Epistle 3: 'To Allen Lord Bathurst,' lines 81–2. On the 'happy-man' topos, see Røstvig.

4 Crawford, 4, 86, 170, 191.

5 Cited by Bermingham, *Landscape and Ideology*, 13. Crawford cites similar remarks by Bradley in 1726 and Mason in 1770 (179–80).

6 Bermingham, 13.

7 Book 4, chap. 2.

8 As indeed does Repton when he describes the improvement of his own little property with 'before' and 'after' pictures in Fragment 36, 'Hare Street,' though notoriously he 'improves' the view by screening out the objectionable items (and people) in this public scene.

9 Noël Riley, 35. Loudon published *The Gardener's Magazine* (1826–43), where much of the material subsequently reprinted in the *Villa Companion* first appeared, and also edited the *Architectural Magazine* (1834–9), where he was first to publish Ruskin. See the biographical essay in Matthew and Harrison, eds, 34.475–7.

10 On the purchase of Gad's Hill and Dickens's improvements, see Edgar Johnson, 441–5, 487, 507, 571.

11 Loudon, *Villa Companion*, 728, also 164 and 445; Edgar Johnson, fig. 83.

12 Dickens, *Letters*, 6.43.

13 *The Landscape Gardening and Landscape Architecture of the Late Humphry Repton.*

14 Daniels, 99.

15 Loudon defines the four rates (34–7).

16 See Crawford, 70 and 74–5, on 'appropriation.' Jones notes that the Picturesque style functions to 'minimize precisely those "formal separations of property" that enable the development of the garden in the first place' (121).

17 The giant dahlia quickly acquired working-class associations: Morris refers to 'Tony Weller's fellow coachmen, each sporting a ceremonial dahlia' as they celebrate Weller's coming into his wife's property (Morris, 34; *Pickwick Papers*, 872).

18 Crawford, 202.

19 See Jordan on the pretence of building in stages (108).

20 See p. 223. Condemning waxworks, Coleridge asserts: 'If there be likeness to nature without any check of difference, the result is disgusting, and the more complete the delusion, the more loathsome the effect' (220).

21  See Introduction.

22  See Mary Shelley, *Frankenstein* (1818).

23  Noël Riley notes, in Loudon's designs for furniture, the same contradiction between 'undisciplined' ornament and a theoretical regard for unity (*Victorian Design*, 56).

24  Loudon's gardenesque style, 'unambiguously charming,' was a huge success, becoming 'a model for all classes of polite society, from suburban villa owners to landed aristocrats' (Daniels, 99).

25  Elsewhere, Loudon traces the taste for irregularity in architecture to Uvedale Price (see *Encyclopaedia*, 774), who – though Loudon does not say so – made explicit the link between the Picturesque style in gardening and English liberal values (see chapter 1 above).

26  The phrase is Lord Kames's, almost a century before Loudon: 'In gardening as well as architecture, simplicity ought to be the governing taste. Profuse ornamentation hath no better effect than to confound the eye, and to prevent the object from making an impression as one entire whole. An artist destitute of genius for capital beauties is naturally prompted to supply the defect by crowding his plan with slight embellishments: hence in a garden, triumphal arches, Chinese houses, temples, obelisks, cascades, fountains, without end; and in a building, pillars, vases, statues, and a profusion of carved work. Thus, some women, defective in taste, are apt to overcharge every part of their dress with ornament' (Home, 424). Schor cites this passage to document the perennial association of ornament and fussy detail with the feminine (20).

27  The piety is a bit perfunctory: Loudon is quoting another writer.

28  Crawford, 204.

29  Crawford, 28–34.

30  Chase and Levenson, citing the section 'Families and Households' in the 1851 census, note the definition of the 'household as a social pyramid – a complex of relations, by no means all biological, that receive their coherence only from the form-giving power of the "householder, master, husband, or father"' (4). Such a pyramid could scarcely be more clearly evoked than by Loudon's description of the household at its gardening tasks.

31  Recommending the scarlet runner for fourth-rate gardens, Loudon points out that, although it produces an excellent, nutritious 'farinaceous' food easily digested by children, this plant was originally cultivated for its flowers (198). The implication I think is that even the fourth-rate gardener hard-pressed enough financially to depend upon his garden to feed his family has access to floral beauty that considerably wealthier individuals have rightly appreciated.

32 'Our French Watering-Place,' 154 and 156.

33 *Bleak House* and Ruskin's *The Nature of Gothic* were more or less contemporaneous. Dickens began *Bleak House* in the fall of 1851; the first number was published in March 1852, and the serial ran for the next eighteen months until the end of August 1853; the novel was published in book form in 1853. The first volume of *Stones of Venice* was published in 1851; the second, which contains *The Nature of Gothic*, in 1853. Before beginning *Bleak House* Dickens had however read Ruskin's *The Seven Lamps of Architecture* (1849), which anticipated many of the ideas in *The Nature of Gothic*: see Edgar Johnson, 514. The chapter 'The Lamp of Memory' is particularly relevant to Dickens, emphasizing as it does that the domestic home should be built to last for generations and regarded with grateful reverence by the builder's descendants who inherit it.

34 This description has been characterized by Musselwhite as 'wallpaper' – 'the most trivial kind of banal artifice' – and cited as an unpleasant example of Dickens's mature style, the 'official-author' voice which, Musselwhite argues, testifies to the novelist's self-commodification (see 206–8, 220). He seems not to register the parodic tone of this passage – the text's distaste for Carker's conventional tastefulness.

35 Is she more? Waters suggests that 'there is the vague suggestion that in "taming" this murderess to be his housekeeper, Mr Jaggers has also fashioned a mistress for himself' (172).

36 Loudon, 137.

37 Loudon in 1837 considered that one great advantage of suburban living was access to the 'provision, entertainment, and recreation' of the city (29), but by the late 1850s and early 1860s those who could afford to were moving to the fashionable suburbs away from poverty and crime (see Morris, 106).

38 Welsh sees Wemmick's activities as anticipating the hobby work of 'today's suburbanite,' both resulting from 'the increasing separation of [the worker's] home from his economic function in the city' (see *City of Dickens*, 143–4).

39 Loudon, 107.

40 Critics who have discussed cannibalism in Dickens include Marlow, Stone, Houston, and Waters, 87. Houston deals briefly with the pig motif (164–5) but does not mention Wemmick's pig.

41 Carlyle, 'Chartism,' *Selected Writings*, 171.

42 Engels, 124.

43 Mayhew, 377.

44 Morris draws attention to the tone of condescension in which Dickens addressed the working-class members of his audience at an 1853 banquet in

his honour in Birmingham, pointing out 'the conflicting currents of desire and aggression' he exhibited towards the class from which he had come (1).

45 See Ruskin, 18.437. The same assumption lies behind Matthew Arnold's professed hope of abolishing classes by raising the general level of culture (79).

46 The ideological manoeuvre has not lost its power: the Australian film *The Castle* works in precisely the same way, ironizing, though in a 'heart-warming' way, the working-class characters whose comically modest dwelling provides them with all they can desire. See Sitch.

47 In the context of her overall argument that in Dickens's novels working-class voices, expressing positive energies, engage dialogically with more conservative discourses, Morris argues that in the late 1850s and early 1860s the dominant classes used 'consumer persuasion' to keep the poor in their place, placating them with the 'dream of consumer plenitude' (111). She identifies the consumer in *Great Expectations* as Pip and sees Wemmick as representing the 'dialogic challenge' to the protagonist's consumer dreams. While agreeing that the pair are dialogically connected, I would query this reading. It is Wemmick not Pip who feels himself in a state of 'plenitude' that is linked with the possession of material objects. Morris distinguishes between consumerism and 'Wemmick's inventive pleasure in a self-made-domestic lifestyle' (114). Such hobby activity is not however an alternative to consumerism, but, like other kinds of 'grooming' of one's property, a branch of it: indeed, the do-it-yourself ethos calls upon the hobbyist to invest even more time and attention in his possessions.

48 Morris alludes suggestively but perfunctorily to the Boffins: their story, she says, 'recognizes the function of consumerism, but without the critical focus of *Great Expectations*' (132); their 'consumer delight,' depicted 'as an imaginative expansive reaction to their earlier life of unremitting drudgery, is part of the text's positive underwriting of desire for transformation in the poor. Only as the novel progresses does escape into consumer luxury become the substitute for genuine transformative energy' (140n10).

### 5. Charlotte Brontë: Sweetness and Colour

1 Tayler documents, for example, the contrasts Brontë draws between the victimized 'Marys' and the aggressively intellectual 'Zenobia' women of genius and between the 'children of bondage' and the 'children of the heavenly Jerusalem' (112–14, 123–4).

2 Lonoff points out that Brontë consistently gave a Protestant twist to her version of texts Heger assigned her, responding with particular intensity to narratives about strangers in strange lands or sensitive individuals in an

unsympathetic society (lxi–lxii), and that under Heger's influence she developed a new antithetical style (lxxi).

3  On Brontë's 'new elaborate use of metaphor' and her personified abstractions, see Lonoff, xxxvii–xxxviii. Shuttleworth links some of these personifications with Brontë's interest in phrenology, which understood the faculties of the mind as in conflict with one another (52, 56–8). On Hypochondria, considered an organic illness at the time, see Shuttleworth, 141, 235, 273n23. Boumelha reads the figures of speech in *Villette* in the light of Beer's hypothesis that the female self, 'conceived in resistance to plot,' needs to express itself in what escapes plot, that is, in figurative language (Boumelha, 105).

4  Clarke-Beattie notes that in *Villette* 'the language of what really happened never achieves the ontological priority over figurative language that we expect of realism' (829, cited by Boumelha, 106). On other characters in *Jane Eyre* as fragments or projections of Jane, see Chase, 66–9; Boumelha, 76.

5  Brontë, 'Emma,' 319–20.

6  Weissman, 84.

7  The definitive treatment of Brontë's relationship to these two systems is that of Shuttleworth, 59–62, who concludes that Brontë draws mainly on phrenology, since in physiognomy Jane's and Rochester's plain appearance would signal bad character (170). I see rather an unsystematic fusion of both systems.

8  See for example Sadoff, 131–47.

9  Both Crimsworth and Frances seem to be facets of Brontë herself (Ewbank, 157).

10  Shuttleworth, citing the allusion to Orestes that associates the mother with sexual disgust, accounts for his venom in terms of his need to exorcize his romantic attachment to his aristocratic mother (130). This is perhaps unnecessarily ingenious. The contempt for all the women whose style must repel the hero if he is to adore the heroine is a consistent feature of Brontë's novels and does not need to be accounted for in individual cases.

11  The most notorious example of racism is of course the characterization of Bertha Mason, whose association with other 'coloured' women – that is, women in brightly coloured costumes – I have discussed elsewhere ('Alice Munro and Charlotte Brontë,' 788–94). As the issue of taste is not relevant to Bertha, I do not deal with her here.

12  Shuttleworth argues that Brontë's emphasis on the neatness and cleanliness of her heroines was a defence against prevailing medical ideas that associated women with sexual filth (74). Tayler points out that Brontë was self-conscious about her own thin hair (209).

13 Crimsworth's claim that in Frances he has not one wife but two has been read positively and negatively: she has been seen as successfully combining love and vocation or as 'split apart' by 'the opposing needs of the male characters': see Tayler, 166, and Boumelha, 53.

14 Brontë also wrote a poem on this subject: see *Poems*, ed. Winnifrith, 254–5, and *The Professor*, 278n132.

15 Gilbert and Gubar, 328–9.

16 Poovey, *Uneven Developments*, 139.

17 Rigby [Lady Eastlake], 164, cited by Poovey, *Uneven Developments*, 135. Poovey takes Lady Eastlake's remark to refer to 'the gap between Jane's professed innocence and the sexual knowledge the author insinuates in the language and action of the novel,' but the context makes clear that sexual knowledge is not what Lady Eastlake means at all: rather, her point is the contrast between her own hostile response to Jane and the response of the characters whose compliments Jane records.

18 Shuttleworth, 149, 10. She asserts that Crimsworth, like Jane and Rochester, 'derives pleasure' from this game, which confirms 'the sense of possession of an interiorized self' (136; also 172, 245). The point of the game however is ultimately to lose it.

19 Jane is 'united to Rochester by their shared readerly skills' (Shuttleworth, 173).

20 On traditional emblems in *Jane Eyre*, see Lee.

21 See for example Sewell, chap. 10, 120. The type is satirized in Edgeworth's 'Mlle Panache,' an essay evidently known by Brontë, who uses the name for an obnoxious school-mistress in *Villette* (504).

22 *Early Writings*, 1.86.

23 *Early Writings*, 1.286n2.

24 *High Life*, 9 and 20.

25 *High Life*, 41: Brontë likes the phrase, and the lips in these paintings really are brilliant coral.

26 *High Life*, plate 6.

27 Tayler points out that Brontë's 'Marys' usually die. Mary Rivers of course does not die but marries a clergyman, while her sister Diana marries a naval captain, their choice of mates sustaining the contrast on which these figures are based. Since both sisters do eventually marry, both their names end up signalling the balance between flesh and spirit ('Mary' virgin/mother, 'Diana' celibate/wife).

28 Armstrong, 204.

29 Lanser cites this remark of Jane's in pursuit of her argument that in Brontë's work a female 'authoritative voice ... belongs ... only to white educated Christian Englishwomen of the middle class' (192).

30 Because he represents vocation, whereas Rochester offers domesticity, according to Tayler, 177.

31 See Jane Millgate's 'Narrative Distance.' It is now conventional to deplore the 'domestication of desire' at the end of the novel (Boumelha, 29). Tayler for example argues that in order to preserve her vocation the female artist has to 'withdraw from the web of relationships, the ethos of caring' (301).

32 Julia was a popular name for heroines of romantic novels at the end of the eighteenth century.

33 Helen is persecuted however by a woman, Miss Scatcherd, not by a man, a difference that further disguises the theme of heterosexual rivalry implied in the hair-cutting episode.

34 Tayler identifies the theme of 'women deserted by the withdrawing father-god' in Brontë's work, explaining it in biographical terms (111, 231). Boumelha in her more political reading sees Jane as 'turned back to the patriarchal determinations of kinship and inheritance' when she realizes that she cannot get what she needs from the powerless mother (64). The Rosamond figure, the indulged, beautifully dressed daughter, returns in *Villette* in Paulina Mary Home, originally called Rosa and eventually dismissed as an 'ultimately trivial creature' (Tayler, 230, 234). In *Jane Eyre*, where we find the originary and more complicated version of the oedipal triangle, the split father figure (Brocklehurst/St John) is a clergyman, and the protagonist, initially tormented by him, is at last able to torment him, using as her weapon his own appetite for her rival.

35 This point is made by Boumelha, who argues that 'Nature' is 'invoked ... to underwrite ... class' (73).

36 Shuttleworth, 178.

37 Tayler sees him as a muse (177–9); Thormahlen, while recognizing his deficiencies as a Christian, concludes that he finds salvation (212–28).

38 Judith Williams makes this point (51–2), and Thormahlen endorses it (205).

39 The fact that Mrs Reed dies refusing to forgive Jane makes her eventual destination clear. Whether or not the Brontës believed in hell, the novel does.

40 Patrick Brontë was of the opinion that highly intelligent women were not attractive to men, and Tayler argues that Brontë's work was shaped by this anxiety (111–14).

41 Lonoff notes that Brontë's labour on 'Athens Saved by Poetry' was comparable to Lucy's when she was preparing this essay (352–3). She suggests that, like M. Paul, Heger might have believed that his pupil knew Greek and Latin (354).

42 Lonoff says that 'only the titles seem to link these compositions' and notes that there is no rebellion in Brontë's own essay (121, 214).

43 Paulina has been read as Brontë's vision of what she herself might have been (Tayler 208, 229–32; Parkin-Gounelas, 35).

44 Brontë's characterization of colour recalls Picturesque discourse, which defines primary colours as vulgar and associates refinement of taste with a preference for subtle blended colours that change with the light and with atmospheric conditions: see Introduction.

45 Formerly understood in terms of Lucy's repression (e.g., Gilbert and Gubar, 426), the nun is now most often read as a semiotic cipher: e.g., Crosby: 'the nun "is" nothing ... The nun is an excess, a remainder left over in the division of meaning' (709, cited by Boumelha, 104). Yeazell reads the figure in specular terms: 'Take away the promise of the lover's gaze and the modest Englishwoman may dangerously resemble a buried nun' (*Fictions of Modesty*, 176). See also Gilbert and Gubar, 432.

46 Shuttleworth attributes the period's emphasis on self-control and self-regulation to a pervading anxiety about mental illness (23, 33–6, and passim).

47 The biblical allusion that is the basis of so much of Brontë's figurative language is exhaustively discussed by Tayler.

48 Bourdieu's analysis of disgust is relevant to the way Lucy links greedy eating with other kinds of bad taste: 'The denial of lower, coarse, venal, servile – in a word, natural – enjoyment, which constitutes the sacred sphere of culture, implies an affirmation of the superiority of those who can be satisfied with the sublimated, refined, disinterested, gratuitous, distinguished pleasures forever closed to the profane' (*Distinction*, 7).

49 Chocolate is recommended to women who wish to gain weight by Mrs Alexander Walker (170–1), who takes for granted that thinness, which she supposes to be caused by the drying effects of passion (146), is 'hideous' (168).

50 In her discussion of the Cleopatra, Matus establishes the link between fat and prostitution in medical discourse (138–9).

51 My reference is to Miller, who connects 'cure' – Austen's word, applied to Mary Crawford – with closure in *Mansfield Park* (20–3).

52 On Vashti see Gilbert and Gubar, 399–400; Boumelha, 109, 116; Matus, 145–8. Cf. Scott's allusion to 'Queen Vashti, not Queen Esther – the bold and commanding, not the retiring beauty' (*Redgauntlet*, 286).

53 Shuttleworth believes that Dr John's judgment of Vashti in terms of the conventional norms of female behaviour earns Lucy's contempt: 'His verdict underscores, for Lucy, his indifference to the inner movement of female experience' (238). But Lucy simply records his judgment without comment, and it is just as possible that she is gratified by it. When a Brontë heroine dis-

agrees with another character, she tends to make her disagreement clear to the reader; when she records a remark without comment, it is often because it is to her credit.

54 Thormählen points out that the proposed union of Lucy and M. Paul is the only example of a successful 'mixed marriage' she knows of in the fiction of the period (35–7).

55 Tayler notes that this figure is 'charged with the imagery of Revelation' (237). Such comparisons were current at the time: Thormählen cites an anonymous 1824 sermon referring to the Roman Catholic Church as 'the Mother of Harlots' (27). On Brontë's probable early reading of at least the first book of *The Faerie Queene*, see *Early Writings*, vol. 2, part 1, 232n51.

56 Thormählen disputes the suggestion that Brontë's repudiation of Catholicism masked an attraction to it, arguing that her hostility to it was not excessive by contemporary standards (37). Shuttleworth connects anti-Catholicism with anxiety about confession and female sexuality and notes that the Papal Aggression was frequently discussed in the Leeds newspapers (40–1, 224–7). See also Clark-Beattie.

57 For Kucich, it is the blocking that creates the desire. But *Villette* qualifies Kucich's contention that repression in the Victorian novel is consistently used for private, psychological gain rather than for public, social benefit: in the service of enhanced, deepened subjectivity rather than in the service of others. Though Lucy's self-repression certainly does others no good, and though it no doubt 'deepens' and in a way enhances her nature, Brontë knows that it does not offer pure subjective gain: it can also distort one's personality and skews one's life chances.

### 6. *North and South*: 'Stately Simplicity'

1 O'Farrell notices the tendency to have Margaret strike poses (70).

2 Furbank cannot believe she does not. He asserts that her 'bright amused look' is intended to 'make it plain that the shawls were not her own idea, and thus that the thought that she might be admired in them has never crossed her mind' (53). Furbank's discussion of what he calls Margaret's (and Gaskell's) 'mendacity' points to some of the work that the notion of simplicity has to do in this novel.

3 See Gaskell's advice to her daughter Marianne in *Letters*, 153, 752, 755, 836, 208. Mrs Hale dislikes Milton because the poor are dirty, 'the rich ladies over-dressed, and not a man that she saw, high or low, had his clothes made to fit him' (448).

4 The way 'Margaret's special quality is created by contrast with other women'

(Bodenheimer, 63) has often been noticed. On her superiority to her parents, see Rubenius, 15–17, and David, 13.

5 Margaret is decked with flowers and coral, but no gems. This is not just a sign of genteel poverty, as David suggests (22), but part of the semiotics by which she is defined. Mrs Alexander Walker suggests that flowers are the appropriate ornament for young girls because they 'decorate the system of life, which is exuberant only in the young,' whereas jewels should be reserved for older women (392). Walker offers paired colour plates illustrating the 'Different Character of Ornament': a young girl in ruffled white and flowers opposite a young matron in purple velvet and jewelled earring, tiara, bracelets, sleeves, and belt. I shall quote Walker liberally in the notes to this chapter, since her *Female Beauty* is an excellent gloss on Gaskell's representation of her female characters, suggesting both its conventional nature and the anxieties it negotiates.

6 The *Lady's Newspaper* of 1847 observed that 'shawls were never more in favour than during the present winter.' By 1850 'A fine shawl was ... a much-prized, much-desired acquisition.' See Buck, 107.

7 Buck, 106.

8 Cunnington, 432.

9 Bermingham, 'Picturesque,' 103.

10 Porter, *Thaddeus of Warsaw*, 280.

11 Scott, *Saint Ronan's Well*, 191. Gaskell may have had this particular episode in mind as she wrote the opening scene of *North and South*. The tableau in which Scott's heroine Clara Mowbray is involved is from *A Midsummer Night's Dream* (Clara, because of her height, representing Helena). Gaskell works an allusion to the same play into her opening paragraph, in the simile comparing Edith to Titania. Clara's statuesque, 'immovable' pose (191) and abstracted manner recall attitudes assumed by Margaret. There is also the issue of display: Clara's dastardly brother has insisted she wear the shawl as he shows her off to the man he intends her to marry; and Margaret too is displayed, albeit in a less sinister way, to a prospective suitor to whom she is indifferent.

12 Disraeli, *Coningsby*, 270; *Sybil*, 224; Gaskell, *Wives and Daughters*, 401, 577; Edgar Wright, 'Elizabeth Cleghorn Gaskell,' 175.

13 Bermingham also makes the point, equally relevant to *North and* South, that 'the industrialization of the British cotton industry destroyed not only native hand-weaving but also the indigenous cotton industries of India' ('Picturesque,' 96). There is a sustained 'textile motif' in this novel. O'Farrell comments on textile manufacture in relation to Fanny Thornton's manufactured blush (60–3). Other such images suggest Margaret's refinement (e.g., the

baby bonnet she embroiders for Edith's child, 298). See also notes 42 and 48 below.

14 *Saint Ronan's Well*, 192.

15 See Schor, 124; Harman, 54; Colby, 48.

16 See Brownstein, 109, whose observation that the heroine also may have a charming 'defect' that differentiates her from the conventional beauty (164) is also relevant to Margaret.

17 Schor, 124.

18 On symbolic appropriation, see Introduction.

19 The tension between the industrial plot and the love story has been criticized from the beginning (see Oliphant, 560). The consensus is that the novel fails the political challenge it sets itself because Gaskell folds the public back into the private. Schor and Harman, contesting this reading and insisting on the importance of Margaret's emergence into the public arena and of her brief period of independence, summarize the opposing arguments (see Schor, 225–6n2; Harman, 52–3).

20 Brontë's influence on *North and South* was recognized immediately: Oliphant, assessing novels influenced by Brontë's 'furious love-making,' traces the 'passion for *strength*' even 'further back than *Jane Eyre*,' to Carlyle's *Heroes and Hero-worship*, 557–9. See also Dodsworth, 14–15, and Gérin, 152.

21 See Mrs Walker's warnings about the damage done to female health and beauty by the habit of sleeping during the daytime (152).

22 The housework itself has an aesthetic dimension: Margaret is involved in the care of refined textiles and in the preparation and presentation of sweet food. Rubenius documents Gaskell's disapproval of idleness in women, contrasting Margaret's housework in Milton with her enforced idleness at her cousins' at the end of the novel (123–5); Colby also comments approvingly on Margaret's willingness to work (51). Nevertheless, as Langland points out, middle-class women were expected to supervise servants, not labour physically themselves: Langland cites Mrs Ellis's disparaging comments about women who develop a taste for actual cooking and cleaning (Langland, 72; Ellis, 41). Gaskell apparently feels some anxiety that physical work might degrade her heroine in the reader's eyes: that it will – as Schor says it does – 'blur those [class] distinctions' (147). But she takes care to see that they are not blurred, partly by means of the very assertion that Schor cites ('I am myself a born and bred lady through it all' [115]), partly by thoroughly aestheticizing Margaret's earliest expressions of physical energy.

23 Cottom's discussion of Wordsworth's leech-gatherer, denied his own subjectivity in order to become an object for the poetic imagination, is relevant to the sketching expedition, where one of the picturesque subjects is a crippled

old man (see Cottom, *Civilized Imagination*, 44). I take Gaskell to be applying Cottom's critique to Margaret.

24 He will later, to Bell's disgust, refer in disparaging terms to 'her father's conduct' as though Mr Hale had done something immoral (466).

25 Chapone advises her niece to read Virgil in Annibal Caro's translation, since 'the idiom of the Latin and Italian languages being more alike, it is, I believe, much closer, yet preserves more of the spirit of the original than the English translation' (153). Blair calls Italian the most perfect modern language (88). See Rubenius on the similarities between *North and South* and Henry Fothergill Chorley's *Pomfret* (1845), which include the heroine's study of Dante (247–52). Ruskin believed that 'each book ... that a young girl touches should be bound in white vellum' (Harrison, 44).

26 In a novel, anxiety about the impression one's 'backstage' space would create is the mark of the mediocre, overly conventional character. The noble soul, on the other hand, is serenely indifferent – but then her 'backstage' space consistently testifies to her excellence.

27 Beeton advises that fruit should be 'tastefully' arranged with leaves (#1598). Bourdieu cites Schopenhauer on good and bad taste in still-life painting: 'Painted fruit is yet admissible, because we may regard it as the further development of the flower, and as a beautiful product of nature in form and colour, without being obliged to think of it as eatable,' but the depiction of 'oysters, herrings, crabs, bread and butter, beer, wine, and so forth ... is altogether to be condemned' (see Bourdieu, *Distinction*, 487; Schopenhauer, 1.3.40.269). In her depiction of the Hales' food Gaskell always stays within Schopenhauer's parameters.

28 E.g., Dodsworth, 10–12; O'Farrell, 58–9.

29 Newton says that Margaret's 'achievement is to turn a series of houses into homes' (165).

30 On Margaret's pallor, see O'Farrell, 63. A pale complexion had long been associated with a range of mental and spiritual qualities (see Alison on pallor as a sign of 'Purity, Fineness, Gaiety,' 2.222; 'Gentleness, Tenderness' and 'Debility,' 2.225; 'Grief ... Sensibility ... or Study,' 2.240).

31 Furbank objects that Margaret is anything but 'straight' (51).

32 Cvetkovich's analysis of the fetishization of Laura Fairlie in Collins's *The Woman in White* is equally relevant to Margaret. She points out that Walter Hartright 'reads the signs of [Laura's] position as if they emanated naturally from her body rather than being a function of her social position' (76), an effect that Bourdieu calls 'charisma.' Those noting the relationship between 'character' and socioeconomic position include Newton, who complains that Gaskell represents Edith's idleness and languor as an expression of her indi-

vidual character rather than as the products of the middle-class woman's situation of economic dependency (173), and O'Farrell, who observes that Mrs Thornton resents Fanny 'for having become the very daughter she has encouraged her to be, the frivolous possession by which industry would show its accession to gentility but which by its very existence violates industry's utilitarian values' (61).

33　See Noël Riley, 9–11. Even a writer whose main topic is music rehearses this familiar complaint (see Peel, 130–1).

34　Atkinson, 153 and 159–60, in his review of Gardner's *On Colour, and on the Necessity for a General Diffusion of Taste among All Classes.* Among its programs, the Department provided drawing lessons for working-class boys, with the hope that, if the mechanic did not become an artist, he might nevertheless 'be made the more humanized mechanic' (157). Atkinson notes that, as a result of the efforts of this Department, it was by 1860 commonly acknowledged that ornament must not violate 'the dictates of reason and common sense' but be 'consonant with utilitarian uses' (153). 'The fantastic, the extravagant, and the monstrous may now be said to have had its day ... Already carpets loaded with mountains of fruit and of flowers are out of fashion ... Carpets should be quiet in design and negative in colour' (159), and wallpaper should provide a neutral background. The Department was set up just before the publication of *Hard Times,* and both Dickens in that novel and Gaskell in *North and South* raise the issue of wallpaper design in a way that suggests that they are responding to the promulgation of this official aesthetic, though in very different ways.

　　Some critics who comment on the wallpaper episode simply accept Gaskell's aesthetic judgment (see for example Edgar Wright, *Mrs Gaskell,* 137–8; Lansbury, 107). O'Farrell has a sharper sense of the ideological work done by aesthetics, though she does not take up the topic of taste in detail: see note 38 below.

35　Gaskell's signs are always reliable. Gallagher, *Industrial Reformation,* and Schor, arguing that Gaskell problematizes the system of signification on which she also relies, exaggerate the novel's indeterminacy. The facts cited to support this argument – that the characters sometimes have trouble communicating with one another, that Margaret is exposed to a new vocabulary (Schor), that Mr Hale objects to Margaret's use of figurative language, and that some character's concepts are based on private associations (Gallagher) – do not add up to a critique of referentiality. Schor's assertion that the romance genre undercuts its own assumptions also seems to me implausible, failing to take account of what Furbank calls the 'curious and special "heroine style"' in which Margaret is consistently described (51).

36 Lucas, praising Gaskell's insight into the way class identity is formulated by the defensive reactions of the dominated class who need to 'disparage what they are excluded from' (196), deals insightfully with Mrs Thornton's defiant philistinism but does not take account of her son's readiness to adopt Margaret's aesthetic standards.

37 As it transpires, as a result of the strike and Thornton's subsequent bankruptcy, both kinds of capital have to come from Margaret. The novel was completed in haste, and its ending was probably shaped by a number of factors, including the need to conclude the serial quickly and perhaps the influence of *Jane Eyre*, which might have suggested the proud-man-brought-low scenario that allows the bride to contribute materially to the marriage. But if Thornton needs Margaret's money at this particular point, we are allowed to believe that he will use it to make more, and that their marriage will fuse the industrialist's financial power with the finer tastes of a gentler class. Newton points out that when they marry, Margaret will lose control over the money she has brought into the marriage (168). The compensatory fantasy Gaskell hints at is that the rich man will want to give his wife whatever she desires.

38 Gallagher assumes that the lace has been purchased (see *Industrial Reformation*, 182). I am not so sure: the signs that suggest the hero's class position seem to be mixed – indeed, incoherent. David points out that although Thornton impersonates the kind of 'prudence, forethought, and self-denial' that the working classes were urged to cultivate, he himself is by no means a 'common workman,' and that his project is to restore, not establish, the family name (17–18). O'Farrell argues that in having her heroine fall in love with a working man, 'Gaskell negotiates a collapse of class categories that also and nevertheless makes her nervous' (64). I think that she is right and that this nervousness manifests itself in the ambiguity about the precise social status of the Thornton family as well as in other ways that I attempt to document.

39 See Arnold, 'Porro Unum Est Necessarium,' 138–52. *North and South* of course predates *Culture and Anarchy*; but the phrase 'the one thing needful' was already current in social criticism (e.g., Carlyle, *Past and Present*, 217). The source is Luke 10.42.

40 Mrs Thornton's drawing room has been discussed by O'Farrell as 'an index by which aesthetics plot a narrative of class' (62). The contrast between the Thornton and Hale drawing rooms has been discussed by Edgar Wright, *Mrs Gaskell*, 138; Lansbury, 107; and David, 23–5; see also Lucas, 198.

41 Goffman's observation that 'to furnish a house so that it will express simple, quiet dignity' can take a great deal of busy effort is relevant to many of Gaskell's idealized interiors, which are represented as emanations of the

family's character rather than as the result of 'backstage' planning and labour (see *Presentation of Self*, 32).

42 These look almost like stage props designed by Gaskell to balance genteel 'work' – i.e., women's needlework – against cultivated leisure: cf. Walter Besant on the 'fiction in genteel families that the ladies of the house never did anything serious or serviceable after dinner ... Therefore if the girls were at the moment engaged upon any useful work – they crammed it under the sofa, and pretended to be reading a book' (11, cited by Goffman, *Presentation of Self*, 111).

43 David draws attention to the unresolved tension and the 'essential class differences' between Margaret and Mrs Thornton (22), suggesting that wherever Thornton and Margaret decide to live, it will presumably not be with his mother. Rubenius points out that there are very few positive mother–daughter relationships in Gaskell's fiction (198n2). Margaret's rather inadequate mother is eventually out of the picture, but her mother-in-law looks like a survivor.

44 Harman argues that Margaret is subjected to the gaze when she emerges into the public arena (67–8). But even within the domestic environment, she is consistently on display. Harman's public/private polarity blurs the scopic investment Gaskell has in her heroine throughout the novel.

45 Gaskell's over-identification with her heroine has often been noticed. Furbank accuses Gaskell of 'fibbing' about her own 'guilty secret': that in daydreaming about her heroine she is daydreaming about herself (51); see also Craik, 127; Gérin, 152; O'Farrell, 70.

46 The slightly grotesque emphasis on the length of Margaret's neck is interestingly glossed by Mrs Walker, who says that the Frenchwoman uses neck frills 'because her neck, which may be relatively long, is black and skinny, and presents the horrible *cordes au cou*, or stringy neck, caused by passion, crying, shrieking, loud talking, etc., – the Englishwoman, whose neck may be relatively short, round, polished and white, absurdly adopts the same disguises, and leaves herself as little neck as a pig!' (428–9).

47 'A luxuriant head of hair is the most beautiful ornament a female can possess' (Mrs Walker, 245).

48 'White well-shaped hands have always been much admired. Needlework, writing, drawing and music, afford ladies many opportunities of exhibiting the beauty of their arms, the whiteness of their hands, and the shape and cleanliness of their nails' (Mrs Walker, 226).

49 Veblen, 148.

50 'There is nothing more pleasing, nothing more charming, than a well-shaped beautiful arm, but at the same time, there is nothing so rare,' says

Mrs Walker (338). Women are warned that 'the bracelet is a very dangerous ornament to wear; for if it embellish a pretty arm, it draws too much attention to one of defective form' (394): 'The arm is frequently thin and too small in relation to the body; and still more frequently, when its size is proportionate, the arm is flat and fleshless, and the veins are visible. In either case, the arm should not be exposed more than can be avoided' (339). Walker recommends the use, 'under the sleeves of the dress,' of 'skin-coloured sleeves, wadded or padded so as to render the arm of necessary dimensions; and the padding is doubled, to conceal the elbow if it be too sharp' (339).

51 Mrs Walker, writing on 'Gathering the Hair Up into a Knot,' makes the point that Roman and Greek ladies, who 'always took care to unite simplicity with beauty' (406), favoured this style: 'There is nothing more simple than the twist ... arranged like a crown on the top of the head' (415).

52 The loose/bound polarity is traditional in the construction of erotic but pure femininity: e.g., Belphoebe in Spenser, *Faerie Queene*, 2.3.26–20.

53 Poovey, *Proper Lady and the Woman Writer*, 21.

54 Mrs Thornton's phrasing evokes the biblical allusion, common in conduct literature, to the virtuous woman who is characterized by the care of, and adornment by, luxurious textiles: e.g., 'She is not afraid of the snow for her household, for all her household are clothed with scarlet. She maketh herself coverings of tapestry; her clothing is silk and purple. Her husband is known in the gates, where he sitteth among the elders of the land' (Winslow, 20, citing Proverbs 31.21–3). The allusion to *Macbeth* subliminally associates Mrs Thornton with Lady Macbeth as an overambitious woman who pushes her man into sterile activity.

55 'A woman may make a man's home delightful, and may thus increase his motives for virtuous exertion' (Sandford, 6).

56 Veblen, 83. Roberts, who cites Veblen, also quotes an 1847 article on a wife's duty to display her husband's wealth.

57 Veblen, 53–83; Poovey, *Proper Lady and the Woman Writer*, 10; *Uneven Developments*, 114–15.

58 Ruskin argues that a gentleperson is 'a great production; a better production than most statues; being beautifully coloured as well as shaped, and plus all the brains; a glorious thing to look at, a wonderful thing to talk to' ('Of King's Treasuries,' 18.107–8, Ruskins's note to paragraph 30).

59 O'Farrell notes the 'national symbolics' of this sustained metaphor (70).

60 O'Farrell observes that Margaret's statuesque body 'is repeatedly noticed by characters *in* the text' as well as '*by* the text' (70); Nord notices that 'the narrator repeatedly inhabits the position of the male gaze' (176).

61 Conduct books emphasized the importance of such command: e.g., Pennington points out the necessity of checking 'the first appearance of ... impertinence, by a reprimand sufficiently severe to prevent a repetition of it' (36). Poovey argues that the middle-class woman had to deal effectively with her servants or risk exposing the economic exploitation upon which household service was based (*Uneven Developments*, 115). Langland points out that the ability to manage servants was an essential mark of middle-class womanhood and suggests that the management skills thus gained may have empowered early feminists. She analyses the mystification of the servant/employer relationship in the Victorian novel but does not discuss *North and South*. Gaskell's representation of Dixon, so complacent about being chided by her superior, naturalizes class distinction in just the way Langland documents. On Margaret's disciplining of Dixon, see Pike, 89.

62 I cannot agree with Bodenheimer that Gaskell's narrative 'continually dismantles the hierarchical structure of class' (67). On the contrary: the erotics of the narrative reinstall hierarchies that the social-theory debates partly challenge.

63 'In moving forward the hair falls back, and in very swift motion floats upon the air behind; hence, by association of ideas, when the hair is made to retire from the cheeks, it gives an intimation of the youthful agility of the person' (Erasmus Darwin, 83). Margaret is alternately seen in statuesque repose and in swift, spiritualized movement.

64 'The well-dressed serving-maid remained the whipping girl for vague social ills throughout the century' (Buck, 111).

65 Beeton, #2153.

66 David finds Bessy a 'tedious and taxing' character (37), partly because of her 'sycophantic' admiration of Margaret, yet David's own emphasis on the mythopoeic function of the industrial novel – its tendency to offer hopeful fantasies as an imagined solution to intractable problems (12, 20, 34, 39) – adequately accounts for Bessy's reverence for middle-class taste and culture. The fantasy of working-class awe of the fine lady is ironized by Dickens's Jenny Wren, the doll's dressmaker, who says that when the society ladies whose clothes she copies see her observing them, 'I dare say they think I am wondering and admiring with all my eyes and heart' (*Our Mutual Friend*, 496). See also Langland on the protection afforded to the lady visitor by her refined dress and the 'power of class' of which it was the sign (157).

67 On the maintenance of white garments in a rural working-class home, see Thomas Hardy's *Tess of the d'Urbervilles*, 40–1. Bessy's capacity to admire a simple white costume differentiates her from the supposedly vulgar working-class woman: the gorgeous dress of Braddon's Aurora Floyd impresses the

Yorkshire servants, 'whose uncultivated tastes were a great deal more disposed to recognize splendour of colour than purity of form' (132).

68  Poovey, *Uneven Developments*, 114–15.

69  Cvetkovich argues that the nineteenth-century novel, by depicting the working-class body, illuminates the evils of capitalism as effectively as do Marxist
exposés of factory conditions: 'The worker's physical exploitation is only one
sensational symptom of the effect of the capitalist system of social relations'
(11). The fetishization of Margaret's body and erasure of Bessy's is a negative
example that nevertheless confirms Cvetkovich's paradigm.

70  See Bourdieu on 'bodily hexis' (*Distinction*, 190–1, 474, and passim).

71  The exception of course is the horrible image of Boucher in death.

72  The allusion to the story of Dives and Lazarus also occurs in *Mary Barton*,
where, it has been argued, Gaskell uses it to condemn the desire for revenge
(Wheeler, 53–7). Bessy's remark, which testifies to her willingness to forgive
Margaret as an individual while anticipating the damnation of employers as a
class, is not so clearly repudiated: like many of the employees' complaints in
*North and South*, it is allowed to stand unanswered.

73  The status of the Book of Revelation among the cultivated can be glossed by
a passage from *Middlemarch*, where Dorothea Brooke, attempting to assess
the relative merits of Tyke and Farebrother for the chaplaincy of Bulstrode's
fever hospital, muses: 'I have been looking into a volume of sermons by Mr
Tyke: such sermons would be of no use at Lowick – I mean, about imputed
righteousness and the prophecies in the Apocalypse' (363). Her objection
can be construed as Lansbury construes Margaret's (106), in terms of an
emphasis on practical morality, but it also has a class note. As his name suggests, Tyke is no gentleman, and his dissenting Christianity, like Bulstrode's,
functions as a mark of his low social origins as well as of his intellectual narrowness and religious hypocrisy.

   Lansbury buys into the novel's judgment on what she calls Bessy's 'wild
rhapsodies,' accounting for Margaret's distaste in terms of her abhorrence of
Bessy's 'belief that the measure of her suffering on earth will correspond precisely to the measure of her joys in heaven' (109). But this distorts Bessy's
statements, which have nothing to do with weighing and measuring.

74  Gaskell, of a Dissenting family, was raised in a religion of 'charity and hope'
with a 'social practical' emphasis (Gérin, 14, 41). She married a Unitarian
minister but in an Anglican church, and had no prejudice against attending
Anglican services, finding the liturgy 'beautiful and impressive' (see Gérin,
304; *Letters*, 860). She believed in an afterlife of some kind, wishing she were
with her dead child Willie 'in that light' (Gérin, 56, citing *Letters*, 111).

75  Furbank points out the contradictions about what Margaret knew and when

434 Notes to pages 320–2

she knew it. Since she is said to realize in chapter 39 that Thornton 'must take Frederick for some lover,' Furbank calls her subsequent assertion to Bell (in chapter 46) that she has 'never thought anything of that kind' an 'untruth' – though his own word 'muddle' is perhaps more just. Margaret's failure to excuse herself to Thornton is also badly motivated. Margaret assures Mrs Thornton that, though she will not explain her conduct, 'I have not acted in the unbecoming way you apprehended': precisely what she might have said to Thornton himself, who would have been only too ready to believe her. She explains to Bell why she did not confide in Thornton: 'was I to tell him the secrets of our family, involving, as they seemed to do, the chances or poor Frederick's entire exculpation?' (She cannot say 'safety,' since she knew at a much earlier point in the narrative that Frederick had left England even *before* the lie was told.) She adds, 'Fred's last words had been to enjoin me to keep his visit a secret from all'; yet on the very next page she requests Mr Bell, at his earliest opportunity, to 'tell him the whole circumstances' (see Furbank, 52 and 54; *North and South*, 357, 400, 453, and 485–6).

76 Colby, pointing out that Margaret lies to protect not herself but a family member, believes that 'Gaskell clearly intends for the reader to sympathize with Margaret' and endorse her lie (55). Sympathize with her dilemma, no doubt: yet Margaret's overwrought horror at her fall from purity is also endorsed by the text.

77 Trodd, documenting the contemporary assumption that a middle-class family is justified in protecting its privacy from the intrusion of a working-class policeman, nevertheless comments on 'the confusion of the writing' here, the 'failure to direct the reader coherently in the scene,' which she takes to be a sign of Gaskell's moral uneasiness: 'it is not clear to the reader what Margaret's disdain [of the policeman] is supposed to express' (37).

78 Furbank detects another lie here. Margaret's steady gaze on this occasion is directed at Fanny, whose conversation is said to interest her deeply; but since 'everyone agrees how boring Fanny is,' this cannot be true (53).

79 On the Una/Duessa image, see also Stoneman, 136, and Terence Wright, 113–14. In *Wives and Daughters* Cynthia Gibson is compared to Duessa (699).

80 O'Farrell, arguing that Gaskell seeks, in the swoon, a somatic sign more authentic than the blush, deals with the erotics of the two related scenes: Margaret's interview with the police inspector and her later collapse (75–6).

81 A number of critics have based arguments on these contradictions. David points out how the lie helps Gaskell fudge her economic critique: 'Margaret changes her views of commerce because she has lied,' feeling herself as dishonoured as she had previously made Thornton out to be (46). Gallagher

argues along the same line that 'the heroine and the narrator both seem to believe that Margaret has lost her right to question the ethics of industrial society because he has failed to maintain her private moral integrity' (*Industrial Reformation*, 176). Gallagher points out that, though Margaret's lie is made into 'the central ethical problem' of the novel (175), Thornton is not upset by it. Spencer makes the same point, arguing Gaskell is trying to 'show how Margaret's motives are inevitably misunderstood in a world that sees only *man*'s honour as truthfulness, women's being chastity' (93). Schor sees Margaret's failure to explain the truth to Thornton as another example of the 'thematics of inappropriate speech' (146). What these critics take as purposeful irony or thematic emphasis I see as part of the overall muddle in this episode, muddle inflected by the mystification of Margaret's exemplary wholeness.

82 Harman emphasizes this theme (73–5), but, as Nord points out, 'the narrative only hints obliquely at this activity and never describes Margaret's experience of it' (172).

83 What attitude we are invited to take towards Margaret's investment in her own moral purity has been the object of some debate among critics who find it unmotivated and excessive. Stoneman argues that since the important lie in the novel is the one Margaret tells to herself – since her repression of her love for Thornton, induced by excessive modesty, is itself 'an unacknowledged lie' – 'her real lie at the railroad station ... attracts disproportionate guilt' (129). The guilt does indeed seem disproportionate, yet I cannot agree with Stoneman that Gaskell is developing a systematic critique of the ethic of feminine modesty (129–37). Spencer notices similar contradictions, but does not make clear whether the problem lies in Margaret's misguided perceptions or in the 'ideological constraints' under which Gaskell worked (93). I am arguing that the novel has a mystified investment in the image of outraged virginal womanhood, that this image is an element of the wider aesthetic by which Margaret is constructed, and that her dismay is supposed to be a mark of her superfineness, not a critique of her surrender to ideology.

84 Gaskell has been defended for her honest attempt to confront insoluble problems: see David, 6–7; Stoneman, 126, 134; and Schor, who argues that the novel critiques its own genre. Bodenheimer's summary is fair: 'Gaskell allows the ideal of saving womanhood to stand, but she renders dramatically the action and passion that it fails to account for' (66).

85 Most readers take the novel to suggest that 'the middle class ... deserves to remain in control of things' (David, 44): e.g., Newton, 166; Pike, 82–3.

86 The entire discussion of industrial issues is framed in Carlylean terms. Themes and motifs include: Mr Hale's wonder at the magical power of the

industrial machinery (cf. *Past and Present*, 272–3; all page references in this note are to *P&P* unless otherwise indicated); Thornton's talk of doing battle not against his employees but against 'ignorance and improvidence' and intransigent matter (162, 191, 272–3); the metaphor of the captain or soldier who puts himself at risk for the good of others – an image that links the novel's 'Captain of Industry' (267–73), Thornton, with Higgins and with Margaret's brother Frederick (181 and passim); the terms 'chivalry' (191–3, 268–70) and 'heroism,' which derive from this metaphor; the vision of a global commercial empire (170); Thornton's emphasis on the need to discipline and control his employees (248–9); the idealization of the 'sharp' master who earns the respect of those he dominates (104–5); the ideas that cultivating good personal relations with one's workers may be 'an excellent investment,' ensuring their docility and loyalty (276), and that the interests of the employer and the worker are linked (277); the emphasis on social isolation as the worst kind of suffering (271, 282); the issue of industrial legislation that hampers the manufacturer – an issue about which Carlyle, like the novel, is of two minds (207–8, 261–2); key catch-phrases like 'doing what you like with your own' (11, 59, 181), 'one thing needful' (217), and 'buying in the cheapest market and selling in the dearest' (11, 162, 191, 272–3); a number of local but specific allusions, for example, to Thor (273), to the Teutonic character (*Heroes*, 265), to Cromwell (the subject of lecture 6 of *Heroes*), to the proverb that 'No man is a hero to his valet' (introduced in *Heroes*, 411, and picked up in *P&P*, 31 and 149–50 ); the actual title of *Past and Present* (cf. *North and South*, 414); the criteria by which Higgins judges the employers' real religious beliefs (72–3, 147–8, 203, 267); even Margaret's complaint about the lack of 'serious' conversation in Edith's smart set (152–3). (Others are noted in the text below.) All the morally serious characters express themselves in terms of Carlylean ideas, including Higgins, who is presumably not to be taken as having read Carlyle's work.

87 'Most true it is, as a wise man teaches us, that "Doubt of any sort cannot be removed except by Action." On which ground, too, let him who gropes painfully in darkness or uncertain light, and prays vehemently that the dawn may ripen into day, lay this other precept well to heart, which to me was of invaluable service: "*Do the Duty which lies nearest thee*, which thou knowest to be a Duty! Thy second Duty will already have become clearer"' (*Sartor Resartus*, 148; see also *Past and Present*, 230).

88 Craik characterizes her arguments as 'simplistic' and says that they 'will not answer' with Higgins and Thornton, 'whose arguments she cannot refute' (119). Her arguments are indeed simplistic, yet there is no suggestion that Gaskell invites us to condemn them as such.

89 More, for example, who in 'Thoughts on Conversation' warns young women not to try to be witty and recommends a pointed silence as often the best way of directing a conversation, nevertheless insists that there is no 'necessity or propriety' in concealing the knowledge one possesses (277). She urges 'girls [to] endeavour to habituate themselves to a custom of observing, thinking, and reasoning' (284): 'she who is accustomed to give a due arrangement to her thoughts, to reason justly on common affairs, and judiciously to deduce effects from their causes, will be a better logician than some of those who claim the name because they have studied the art' (285). In 'True and False Meekness,' More asserts that there are times when a young woman has a positive duty to speak up: 'She who hears innocence maligned without vindicating it, falsehood asserted without contradicting it, or religion profaned without resenting it, is not gentle but wicked' (312). Margaret's spunky discourse always falls within More's guidelines.

90 The phrase was a commonplace; see for example More: 'There is another popular but unfounded axiom respecting the use of wealth, that "a man may do what he will with his own." Christianity denies this assertion' ('England's Best Hope,' 45). The difference is that both Carlyle (*Past and Present*, 11) and Margaret are referring to human beings rather than money.

91 As well as the chapter headings in *Hard Times*, which was serialized just before *North and South* in *Household Words*.

92 Newton asserts that Margaret believes society should be a family (165), and this does not seem far off the mark. Following Gallagher's *Industrial Reformation*, however, it has become a commonplace of criticism that the novel rejects the parent–child metaphor (e.g., Elliott, 44n26). Since this opinion is now orthodoxy, it is worth examining the argument on which it is based.

Gallagher argues that Gaskell rejects not only 'the family-society metaphor' but 'metaphors in general,' on the grounds that Mr Hale begs Margaret 'don't go into similes' (167–8). But Hale, who is here objecting not to the metaphor of family but to what promises to be a mixed metaphor comparing the working man to a rock, merely seems embarrassed at his daughter's volubility and assertiveness. Certainly he cannot be against figurative language in general, because he himself has just picked up and refined the parenthood metaphor introduced by his daughter, suggesting that the workers should be treated not as children but as adolescents, whose parent wisely 'humours the desire for independent action, so as to become the friend and adviser when his absolute rule shall cease' (168).

The critical debate is blurred by the tendency to collapse two distinct meanings of 'child.' A child is both 'an individual below the age of puberty' and 'a person of whom one is the parent.' The Hales deny that the employees are children in the first sense but imply that that they are children in the second sense. The gist of the Hales' remarks is that Thornton is *in loco parentis* in relation to his employees and that he should treat them not as young children but as growing youths who will one day be grown (there is an implicit threat here). It is misleading to say that the Hales object to the 'despotic authority' implied in the parent metaphor (Gallagher, *Industrial Reformation*, 167), because the purpose of Mr Hale's qualification of the metaphor is precisely to sever the association between parenthood and *despotic* authority. Neither of the Hales denies that Thornton has legitimate authority over his employees, and neither rejects the metaphor of fatherhood.

It is true that Thornton, in this scene at least, does reject the responsibility implied by the paternal metaphor, but the grounds on which he does so point to his future acceptance of it. He defends himself on this occasion by arguing that, unlike a parent, he does not have, or seek, any influence over his workers out of factory hours. But once his conscience has been awakened, he finds a way of exerting precisely such influence: in his dining-hall scheme. Helping his employers to partake of wholesome communal dinners the preparation of which they themselves organize is indeed a way of inserting his middle-class values into their after-work lives, particularly since he is often invited to join them. The analogy with domestic ritual is obvious.

A contemporary source for the parental metaphor is offered by Pike, 85. Carlyle in *Past and Present* also uses the metaphor of family, referring to the working classes as sisters (210), sons, and brothers (100, 149, 270), and to the employing and employed classes as a married couple who cannot divorce (277).

93 Many readers take the novel's message to be 'that womanly values should be adopted in the public world that men control, and by men themselves' (Spencer, 94–5; see also Newton, 165; Harsh, 17–46; Bodenheimer, 66). I contend, in addition, that 'womanly values' are represented as 'simple' in a way that associates them with other signs of purity and elegance and thus provides aesthetic endorsement of their authority.

94 'Paternalism' has become a contested term in criticism of this novel. I stand by my use of it here. The argument that the novel does not endorse paternalism is based partly on its supposed rejection of the metaphor of family relations: but see note 92. Bodenheimer, who denies that the novel is paternalistic, summarizes the arguments of those who contend that it is (57–8).

95 Again Gaskell seems to be remembering Carlyle's *Past and Present*, e.g., his remarks on Abbot Samson: 'The great antique heart: how like a child's in its simplicity, like a man's in its earnest solemnity and depth! Heaven's splen-

dour over his head, Hell's darkness under his feet. A great Law of Duty, high as these two Infinitudes, dwarfing all else, annihilating all else'; on man and his work: 'Spinning Cotton ... founding Cities ... tilling Canaan ... man is ever man; the missionary of Unseen Powers ... Brother, thou art a Man, I think ... thou hast verily a Soul in thee ... Go or stand, in what time, in what place we will, are there not Immensities, Eternities over us, around us, in us?' (*Past and Present*, 118–19 and 226–7).

## 7. The Importance of Being Consistent: Culture and Commerce in *Middlemarch*

1 Chapone, 129–30; Loudon, *Villa Companion*, 33; More, 'Thoughts,' 2.278; Gaskell, *Letters*, 640, Thomas Hardy, *Jude the Obscure*, 29.
2 'Richard Simpson on George Eliot,' in Carroll, ed., 237.
3 Kucich, 25.
4 *Quarterly Review* 134 (1873): 184–5, cited by Harvey in Barbara Hardy, ed., *Middlemarch: Critical Approaches*, 137.
5 'George Eliot Moralist and Thinker,' *Round Table Series II* (1884): 3, cited by Myers, 1.
6 Miller replicates Eliot's conceptual categories when he explains why Will is reformed by Dorothea: 'The consistency of Dorothea's character offers so strong and simple a unity that it virtually commands imitation by one whose life has been programmatically dispersive' (172).
7 Hertz argues that it is more reassuring to represent a self split in two by narcissistic doubling than to deal with a more indeterminate 'self-dispersion' in language, which undermines the 'possibilities of the consistency of the self.' Miller points out that humour characters do not require closure (41).
8 My allusion is to Cottom's discussion of Eliot as a liberal intellectual whose determinedly apolitical stance mystifies her thinking. Cottom argues that Eliot aims to 'comprehend' the totality of social phenomena, in both senses of the word: to understand them and to master and contain them (see *Social Figures*, 25, 54–6, 70–1, 125, 179).
9 Oldfield sees 'fond' as one of the signs of the plight of Dorothea, condemned to use language unworthy of her feelings (80).
10 Q.D. Leavis, 1.330–1.
11 Cf. Eliot's comment in 'Silly Novels' on the recently converted woman: 'She thinks as much of her dress as before, but she adopts a more sober choice of colours and patterns' (315).
12 Carroll refers to her forgiveness as 'George Eliot's own version of imputed righteousness' (*Conflict of Interpretations*, 262).
13 This scene is yet another variation on the 'woman's-room' scenario, with the

significant pictures on its walls – the portraits of Casaubon's mother and his aunt, who turns out to be Ladislaw's grandmother – and its even more significant window. The two scenes of self-surrender that take place in this room – the scenes in which Dorothea decides to make her dying husband the promise he demands and to reach out to her rival Rosamond – lead to her escape from the sterile world that the room represents. The window functions in the usual way, to suggest the heroine's creative connection with the world outside, but here it is integrated with developments in the plot. It is looking out the window, seeing the labourers who are going to work in the morning and suddenly feeling that 'she was a part of that involuntary, palpitating life' (478), that makes Dorothea decide to attempt to help Rosamond (and which thus leads eventually to her reconciliation with Will).

14 Barbara Hardy notes the parallels between Harriet's and Rosamond's reaction to their husbands' disgrace and between Harriet's and Dorothea's change of costume (*Novels of George Eliot*, 102–4).

15 Myers identifies 'the themes of nobility and commonness' in *Middlemarch* (187); Langland notes the use of plain dress as a mark of gentility and of frippery as a sign of vulgarity (36), pointing out that 'the dialectic of nature and artifice also grounds an opposition between nobility and commonness' (190).

16 Carroll points out that Rosamond is the one really unified figure in the novel and is so 'formidable' precisely because 'her world-view is coherent and her life undivided' (*Conflict of Interpretations*, 268).

17 Beer, 197–8.

18 There is a cluster of 'whole's in chapters 76, 77, and 80, as the novel moves towards closure: the narrator's reference to being 'seen and judged in the wholeness of our character' (558); Dorothea's offer to use her money to make Lydgate's life 'quite whole and well again' (561); her sense of her relationship with Will as 'one that was whole and without blemish' (566); of her life 'that might have been whole enough without him' (576); of his failure to offer her 'the whole price of her heart' (576). The repetition makes clear how much work the word has to do in constructing the vision of subjectivity in which Eliot needs to believe.

19 Cf. the epigraph to chapter 10 of *Daniel Deronda*: 'What woman should be? Sir, consult the taste / Of marriageable men ... Our daughters must be wives, / And to be wives must be what men will choose: / Man's taste is woman's test' (132).

20 Blake points out that Rosamond is 'as "industrious" in her way as other characters' (301).

21 Those who have complained about the idealization of Dorothea include F.R. Leavis, who calls her Eliot's 'day-dream ideal self' and complains of Eliot's

'unqualified self-identification' with her heroine (74–5); Moers, who cites the influence of *Corinne*; and Myers, who points out how improbably innocent she remains (130–1). On the degree of irony to which she is subjected, see Barbara Hardy, *Novels of George Eliot*, 164; Lerner, 251–7; and McSweeney, who finds Eliot's treatment of Dorothea 'inconsistent or ambivalent' (101).

22 McSweeney observes that the capacity for fellow-feeling is like grace, an unexplained 'given' of Dorothea's nature (27–8).

23 Ruskin asserts that we should make lace, cut jewels, or invest in luxury goods that do not sustain life – 'substances valued only for their appearance and rarity (as gold and jewels)' – when people are in need, though he does add that jewels at least are not perishable and that 'splendid dress' may be unselfish: see 'A Joy Forever,' 16.38 and 51. Ruskin also points out that religious painters delight to depict gems: e.g., 26.174 and 195. On Eliot's response to Ruskin, see Wiesenfarth, 365–71; Witemeyer, 16–17, 156, and passim.

24 Witemeyer relates Eliot's tableaux to various types of genre painting, including the conversation piece and the problem picture (110–22).

25 Moers, 343.

26 Barbara Hardy, *Novels of George Eliot*, 122–3.

27 Harvey makes this point (166).

28 See Bermingham on the notion of a woman's dress as an unmediated expression of her essential nature ('Picturesque,' 106–13). The construction of Dorothea is also a perfect example of what Bourdieu calls the 'charismatic ideology': see Introduction.

29 Cottom, *Social Figures*, xiv, 22–5, and 38–9.

30 'Archaic' is Welsh's word ('Knowledge in *Middlemarch*,' 239; 'The Later Novels,' 65). Jan Gordon notes that she is often 'seen in relief against some background that looms large and which places her ... in the shadows of an historical epic frieze' and locates her in relation to a mystified notion of origin (95). See also Cottom on quotation (*Social Figures*, 54, 179).

31 *Mill on the Floss*, bk. 2, chap. 1, 124.

32 O'Farrell, in her discussion of the problem of using the blush as a transparent sign of authentic character, makes an analogous point. Dorothea, she points out, is said not to blush, but in fact she blushes quite often in the novel. Eliot's desire to differentiate her blushes from those of Celia and Rosamond – to insist that '*these* blushes ... *mean* something' – 'registers her own irritation with a blush that has been debased and robbed of expressivity by convention' (121). The discursive problem however is a more general one. It is not just the blush but all the traits and topoi by which the idealized woman is represented that inevitably come to seem nothing more than conventional.

33 Lerner argues that the comparison to the Virgin Mary 'sets up a view of Dorothea that, through all the shifts of emphasis, is never abandoned' (251). Welsh notes that the reference to the newspaper 'immediately registers the archaism of the character and opposes her to the print culture of the nineteenth century' ('Knowledge in *Middlemarch*,' 239). The most authoritative and wide-ranging treatment of the Madonna metaphor is given by Matus, 213–48.

34 Cottom argues that the liberal intellectual, in flight from the political realities of the present, looks to a sentimentalized past and idealizes a socially harmonious future, which will arrive only when the mass of society evolves towards the intellectual's level of mental cultivation (*Social Figures*, 28–30, 37, 81–5, 159–73).

35 See Wiesenfarth, 270–1; Witemeyer, 41–2; Matus, 229–31.

36 Moers, 343. Myers points out that Eliot assigns Dorothea her own most charming quality (239). Cf. the musical and inspiring voice of Disraeli's Sybil Gerard (*Sybil*, 66, 175, 194, 360).

37 She is said to have 'favourite books' – Herodotus, Pascal, *The Christian Year* (347–8) – but they are mentioned only when they fail to hold her attention.

38 Cottom argues that it is because Eliot is so determinedly apolitical that she is at a loss to suggest any specific course of action (*Social Figures*, 185). The 'individual' of liberal intellectual discourse is, Cottom argues, an 'empty' figure – 'an abstract negation of class divisions, aristocratic traditions, and social history' (72; see also 67–80, 130–40). On Eliot's attitude to 'opinion,' see 175–9.

39 Witemeyer calls attention to Eliot's habit of pairing female figures (90–1). Dorothea cannot be shown with Mary Garth because their semiotics clash. In Mary physical homeliness signals moral beauty, so she will be set side by side with Rosamond and the gap between them moralized. Since in Dorothea however physical beauty signals moral beauty, to bring the two women into the same space would make Mary's homeliness unreadable.

40 Lerner points out that Eliot's attack on the reader for being more sympathetic to Dorothea than to Casaubon is 'unfair ... in so far as the prejudice in favour of "young skins that look blooming in spite of trouble" is one which Eliot herself has fostered' (261).

41 See Bermingham's discussion of the theories of Schimmelpenninck, the author of *Theory on the Classification of Beauty and Deformity* (1815) and the posthumous *The Principles of Beauty as Manifested in Nature, Art, and Human Character* (1859), who classified the beauty of both man-made and natural

objects into three universal types – the sublime, the sentimental, and the sprightly – and developed an analysis of female fashion types based on this threefold classification (Bermingham, 'Picturesque,' 108–11). This kind of system was an established trope in 'beauty' discourse of the period (see Kanner, 1.126). Dickens seems to be parodying it in his characterization of Harold Skimpole's three daughters, 'the Beauty daughter,' 'the Sentiment daughter,' and 'the Comedy daughter,' who are coiffed and dressed to correspond to their type, in *Bleak House*, chap. 43, 454.

42 Kitchel identifies it as by Eliot, 'though the Browning tone is quite obvious' (40n81).

43 Beaty documents Lewes's efforts to secure the most profitable method of publication (44). On the novelist as prostitute, see Gallagher, 'George Eliot and *Daniel Deronda*'; Lanser, 87. Cottom asserts that Eliot's 'technique of aesthetic purity and exclusivity' renders her novels commodity fetishes (*Social Figures*, 106). One might say that she produces novels that in their appeal to the knowing connoisseur are like the ivory figurine she idealizes.

44 As is well known, *Middlemarch*'s status as a commodity text had a direct impact on the way it was composed and shaped. After Lewes had negotiated with Blackwood the system of publishing in parts, 'Eliot would write a novel that accommodated such specifications': the decision 'was not merely a publishing decision, but one related to composition, to shaping, to patterning the novel' (Karl, 479). Eliot also agreed with Lewes's proposal, suggested to him by an enthusiastic reader, to publish a collection of 'sayings' from her work, which came out under the title *Wise, Witty and Tender Sayings in Prose and Verse Selected from the Works of George Eliot* in December 1871. See Karl, 479–83.

45 Feltes argues that Eliot, though herself an ambitious professional, fails to tell the story of the professionalization of medicine in the period when Lydgate was developing his practice and thus idealizes his vocation (49–56).

46 Kucich, pursuing his argument that repression in these novels is inward-looking rather than communitarian, suggests that when she visits Rosamond 'her actions ... do nothing to make us feel that she has opened herself to others' but rather 'confirm the remoteness of Dorothea, and the private exaltation of her desire' (168). Whatever melioration takes place in the novel is 'beyond human consciousness and intentionality' rather than the result of focused individual effort: Dorothea's sympathy for Rosamond and Lydgate, Kucich suggests, is scarcely more efficacious than her cottage project (169–70).

47 Gunster, 349, quoting Adorno.

**Conclusion**

1 Kate Vavasour, reluctant to serve as bridesmaid along with a group of aristocratic ladies at her cousin Alice's wedding, is reassured, 'Glencora will not
   desert you. You can't conceive what taste she has' (*Can You Forgive Her?*
   chap. 79, 493).
2 *Coningsby*, bk. 4, chap. 10, 232, and bk. 3, chap. 1, 127–8.
3 *The Prime Minister*, chap. 16, 183.
4 Indeed, the first scene in 'A Game of Chess,' with its luxurious boudoir, its
   disregarded jewellery, its mirror, its picture, its birds, its duplicated 'voyeurs,'
   its focus on taste ('high' and debased), and its themes of penetration and
   escape, invites comparison not only with its poetic precursors but also with
   the woman's-room topos as developed in the novel.
5 Compare his description of Virginia Madden in *The Odd Women*, in her plain,
   even shabby costume: 'Yet Virginia could not have been judged anything but
   a lady. She wore her garments as only a lady can (the position and movement
   of the arms has much to do with this), and had the step never to be acquired
   by a person of vulgar instincts' (17).
6 Cf. Monica Madden in *The Odd Women*, who is said to have 'native elegance'
   (11).
7 Gissing's characters' relationships parody those in *Middlemarch* in many particulars. Marian Yule is also like Dorothea in that her life is blighted by a
   moribund scholar, though unlike Eliot's heroine she is allowed no escape.
8 See chapter 4, 191.
9 Gard, 128.
10 Fanny's room is called 'this nest of comforts' (174).
11 Congreve, 3.1.53.
12 If there were a photograph of Lady Julia, the illusoriness of Longdon's vision
    of Nanda would be measurable. The degree to which Nanda is 'really' like
    her grandmother has to be kept open so that the status of the ideal can
    remain the issue. Ginsburg's analysis of how the novel both depends on and
    deconstructs the notion of an art (and an ideal past) that can transcend time
    and money is relevant to this issue (193).
13 Blackall points out that the comparison of Van to Phoebus connects him
    with Hugo's Captain Phoebus, hopelessly loved by Esmerelda. It also links
    him to sunny Will Ladislaw, a parallel that ominously puts Longdon in the
    position of Casaubon. The surnames of Nanda Brookenham and Dorothea
    Brooke invite comparison with Eliot's novel.
14 E.g., in the first paragraph of *Portrait of a Lady*.
15 'James is pulling the reader's leg' (*Awkward Age*, 323n3).

16 One hopes – but see Ginsburg, 189.

17 Copeland, 36. Of course the fact that gothic terror is always economic does not mean that economic pressure is always gothic, but when such pressure is combined with isolation in a man's house in the country the gothic note sounds in the background.

18 Brookner, 1. Ruth's professional immersion not in the Victorian novel but in French naturalism, which provides her with a disenchanted view of social causation more reflective of her own experience, helps construct the same contrast as does *New Grub Street* between 'classic' literature and sordid modern life.

19 Richler, 133–5.

# Bibliography

Addison, Joseph, Richard Steele, and others. *The Spectator.* Edited by Gregory Smith. Introduced by Peter Smithers. 4 vols. London: J.M. Dent; New York: E.P. Dutton, 1945.

Akenside, Mark. 'The Pleasures of Imagination.' *The Poetical Works of Mark Akenside.* Edited by Robin Dix. Madison, Teaneck: Fairleigh Dickinson University Press; London: Associated University Presses, 1996.

Alcott, Louisa May. *Little Women.* Edited and introduced by Elaine Showalter. Notes by Siobhan Kilfeather and Vinca Showalter. New York: Penguin, 1989.

Alison, Archibald. *Essays on the Nature and Principles of Taste.* 4th ed. 2 vols. Edinburgh: printed by George Ramsay for Archibald Constable; London: Longman, Hurst, Rees, Ormes, and Brown, 1815.

Armstrong, Nancy. *Desire and Domestic Fiction: A Political History of the Novel.* Oxford: Oxford University Press, 1987.

Arnold, Matthew. Culture and Anarchy *and Other Writings.* Edited by Stefan Collini. Cambridge: Cambridge University Press, 1993.

Atkinson, J.B. 'The Diffusion of Taste among All Classes a National Necessity' [review]. *Blackwoods* 87 (February 1860): 151–61.

Austen, Jane. *Emma.* Edited and introduced by Lionel Trilling. Boston: Houghton Mifflin, 1957.

– *Mansfield Park.* Edited and introduced by Tony Tanner. Harmondsworth, Middlesex: Penguin, 1966.

Bakhtin, M.M. 'Forms of Time and Chronotope in the Novel.' *The Dialogic Imagination: Four Essays.* Edited by Michael Holquist. Translated by Caryl Emerson and Michael Holquist, 84–258. Austin: University of Texas Press, 1981.

Bal, Mieke. *Narratology: Introduction to the Theory of Narrative.* Translated by Christine van Boheemen. Toronto: University of Toronto Press, 1985, 1997.

Ball, Philip. *Bright Earth: Art and the Invention of Color.* London: Penguin, 2001.

Barrell, John. *The Birth of Pandora and the Division of Knowledge*. Philadelphia: University of Pennsylvania Press, 1992.

– *The Idea of Landscape and the Sense of Place, 1730–1840: An Approach to the Poetry of John Clare*. Cambridge: Cambridge University Press, 1972.

– *The Political Theory of Painting from Reynolds to Hazlitt*. New Haven, CT: Yale University Press, 1986.

– 'The Public Prospect and the Private View: The Politics of Taste in Britain.' In Pugh, ed., *Reading Landscape*, 19–40.

Barrett, Eaton Stannard. *The Heroine*. Introduced by Michael Sadleir. London: Elkin Mathews and Marrot, 1927. Printed from the 3rd edition, 1815.

Barthes, Roland. *The Fashion System*. Translated by Matthew Ward and Richard Howard. New York: Hill and Wang, 1983.

Baum, Joan. *Mind-Forg'd Manacles: Slavery and the English Romantic Poets*. North Haven, CT: Archon, 1994.

Beaty, Jerome. Middlemarch *from Notebook to Novel: A Study of George Eliot's Creative Method*. Urbana: University of Illinois Press, 1960.

Beer, Gillian. *George Eliot*. Brighton, Sussex: Harvester, 1986.

Beeton, Isabella Mary. *The Book of Household Management*. London: Beeton, 1861; facsimile reproduction. London: Jonathan Cape, 1968.

Bermingham, Ann. 'The Aesthetics of Ignorance: The Accomplished Woman in the Culture of Connoisseurship.' *The Oxford Art Journal* 16.2 (1993): 3–20.

– *Landscape and Ideology: The English Rustic Tradition, 1740–1860*. Berkeley: University of California Press, 1986.

– 'The Picturesque and Ready-to-Wear Femininity.' In Copley and Garside, eds, *The Politics of the Picturesque*, 81–119.

Besant, Walter. 'Fifty Years Ago.' *The Graphic Jubilee Number* 35 (20 June 1887): 2–30.

Blackall, Jean Frantz. 'Literary Allusion as Imaginative Event in *The Awkward Age*.' *Modern Fiction Studies* 26 (1980): 179–97.

Blair, Hugh. *Letters on Rhetoric and Belles Lettres*. (1783). Facsimile reprint of 1819 ed. Introduced by Charlotte Downey. Delmar, NY: Scholars' Facsimiles and Reprints, 1993.

Blake, Kathleen. '*Middlemarch* and the Woman Question.' *Nineteenth-Century Fiction* 31 (1976): 285–312.

Bodenheimer, Rosemarie. *The Politics of Story in Victorian Social Fiction*. Ithaca, NY: Cornell University Press, 1988.

Booth, Wayne. *The Rhetoric of Fiction*. 2nd ed. Chicago: University of Chicago Press, 1983.

Boumelha, Penny. *Charlotte Brontë*. Hemel Hempstead, Hertfordshire: Harvester Wheatsheaf, 1990.

Bourdieu, Pierre. 'Concluding Remarks: For a Sociogenetic Understanding of Intellectual Works.' In Calhoun, LiPuma, and Postone, *Bourdieu*, 262–75.

– *Distinction: A Social Critique of the Judgement of Taste*. Translated by Richard Nice. Cambridge, MA: Harvard University Press, 1984.

– *Language and Symbolic Power*. Edited and introduced by John B. Thompson. Translated by Gino Raymond and Matthew Adamson. Cambridge, MA: Harvard University Press, 1991.

– *The State Nobility: Elite Schools in the Field of Power*. Translated by Lauretta C. Clough. Cambridge: Polity, 1996.

Bradbrook, Frank W. *Jane Austen and Her Predecessors*. Cambridge: Cambridge University Press, 1966.

Braddon, Mary Elizabeth. *Aurora Floyd*. Edited and introduced by P.D. Edwards. Oxford: Oxford University Press, 1996.

– *Lady Audley's Secret*. Edited and introduced by David Skilton. Oxford: Oxford University Press, 1987.

Brewer, John. *The Pleasures of the Imagination: English Culture in the Eighteenth Century*. London: Harper Collins, 1997.

Brontë, Charlotte. *Charlotte Brontë's* High Life in Verdopolis*: A Story from the Glass Town Saga*. With facsimile illustrations. Edited and introduced by Christine Alexander. London: British Library, 1995.

– *An Edition of the Early Writings of Charlotte Brontë*. Edited by Christine Alexander. 2 vols. Vol. 2 in 2 parts. Oxford: Basil Blackwell for the Shakespeare Head Press, 1983. Vol.1: *The Glass Town Saga, 1826–32*. Vol. 2: *The Rise of Angria, 1833–1834*.

– 'Emma.' In *The Professor*, 303–25.

– *Jane Eyre*. Edited by Jane Jack and Margaret Smith. Oxford: Clarendon Press, 1969; revised edition, 1975.

– *The Poems of Charlotte Brontë*. Edited by Tom Winnifrith. Oxford: Oxford University Press, 1984.

– *The Professor*. Edited by Margaret Smith and Herbert Rosengarten. Introduced by Herbert Rosengarten. Oxford: Clarendon Press, 1987.

– *Villette*. Edited by Margaret Smith and Herbert Rosengarten. Introduced by Margaret Smith. Oxford: Oxford University Press, 1990.

Brontë, Charlotte, and Emily Brontë. *The Belgian Essays: Charlotte Brontë and Emily Brontë*. Edited and translated by Sue Lonoff. New Haven, CT: Yale University Press, 1996.

Brookner, Anita. *A Start in Life*. London: Jonathan Cape, 1983.

Brownstein, Rachel M. *Becoming a Heroine: Reading about Women in Novels.* New York: Viking, 1982.

Buck, Anne. *Victorian Costume and Costume Accessories.* London: Herbert Jenkins, 1961.

Buckley, Jerome H., ed. *The Worlds of Victorian Fiction.* Cambridge, MA: Harvard University Press, 1975.

Burgess, Miranda J. *British Fiction and the Production of Social Order, 1740–1830.* Cambridge: Cambridge University Press, 2000.

Burke, Edmund. *On Taste. On the Sublime and Beautiful. Reflections on the French Revolution. A Letter to a Noble Lord.* Vol. 25 of The Harvard Classics. Edited by Charles W. Eliot. New York: Collier, 1909.

Burn, William. *The Age of Equipoise: A Study of the Mid-Victorian Generation.* London: Allen and Unwin, 1974.

Burney, Frances. *Camilla, or A Picture of Youth.* Edited and introduced by Edward A. Bloom and Lillian D. Bloom. Oxford: Oxford University Press, 1972.

Burrows, J.F. *Computation into Criticism: A Study of Jane Austen's Novels and an Experiment in Method.* Oxford: Clarendon Press, 1987.

Butler, Judith. *Bodies That Matter: On the Discursive Limits of 'Sex.'* New York: Routledge, 1993.

– *Gender Trouble: Feminism and the Subversion of Identity.* New York: Routledge, 1990; reprint with new preface, 1999.

Butler, Marilyn. *Jane Austen and the War of Ideas.* Oxford: Clarendon Press, 1975.

Butterworth, Daniel S. 'Tinto, Pattieson and the Theories of Pictorial and Dramatic Representation in Scott's *Bride of Lammermoor.*' *South Atlantic Review* 56 (1991): 1–15.

Calder, Jenni. *The Victorian Home.* London: Batsford, 1977.

Calhoun, Craig. 'Habitus, Field, and Capital: The Question of Historical Specificity.' In Calhoun, LiPuma and Postone, eds, *Bourdieu*, 61–88.

Calhoun, Craig, Edward LiPuma, and Moishe Postone, eds. *Bourdieu: Critical Perspectives.* Cambridge: Polity, 1993.

Carlyle, Thomas. *On Heroes and Hero Worship.* In *Sartor Resartus; On Heroes and Hero Worship.* Introduced by W.H. Hudson. London: Dent; New York: Dutton, 1956.

– *Past and Present.* Edited, introduced, and annotated by Richard D. Altick. Boston: Houghton Mifflin, 1965.

– *Sartor Resartus.* Edited, introduced, and annotated by Kerry McSweeney and Peter Sabor. Oxford: Oxford University Press, 1987.

– *Thomas Carlyle: Selected Writings.* Edited and introduced by Alan Shelston. Harmondsworth, Middlesex: Penguin, 1971.

Carroll, David. *George Eliot and the Conflict of Interpretations: A Reading of the Novels.* Cambridge: Cambridge University Press, 1992.

Carroll, David, ed. *George Eliot: The Critical Heritage.* London: Routledge and Kegan Paul, 1971.

Castiglione, Baldesar. *The Book of the Courtier* (1528). Translated by Charles S. Singleton. New York: Anchor Books/Doubleday, 1959.

Chapone, Hester. *Letters on the Improvement of the Mind.* 1773; London: H. and G. Mozley, 1800.

Chase, Karen. *Eros and Psyche: The Representation of Personality in Charlotte Brontë, Charles Dickens and George Eliot.* New York: Methuen, 1984.

Chase, Karen, and Michael Levenson. *The Spectacle of Intimacy: A Public Life for the Victorian Family.* Princeton, NJ: Princeton University Press, 2000.

Chesterfield, Lord. *Lord Chesterfield's Letters to His Son and Others.* Introduced by R.K. Root. London: J.M. Dent; New York: E.P. Dutton, 1929.

Cicero, Marcus Tullius. *Selected Works.* Translated and introduced by Michael Grant. Harmondsworth, Middlesex: Penguin, 1971.

Clark-Beattie, Rosemary. 'Fables of Rebellion: Anti-Catholicism and the Structure of *Villette*.' *English Literary History* (1986): 821–47.

Colby, Robin B. *'Some Appointed Work to Do': Women and Vocation in the Fiction of Elizabeth Gaskell.* Westport, CT: Greenwood Press, 1995.

Coleridge, S.T. 'On Poesy and Art.' *The Literary Remains of Samuel Taylor Coleridge.* Collected and edited by Henry Nelson Coleridge, 216–30. London: William Pickering, 1836; New York: AMS Press, 1967.

Coliey, Linda. *Britons: Forging the Nation, 1701–1837.* New Haven, CT: Yale University Press, 1992.

Congreve, William. *The Way of the World.* Edited by Brian Gibbons. London: A. and C. Black, 1971.

Copeland, Edward. *Women Writing about Money: Women's Fiction in England, 1790–1820.* Cambridge: Cambridge University Press, 1995.

Copley, Stephen, and Peter Garside, eds. *The Politics of the Picturesque: Literature, Landscape and Aesthetics since 1770.* Cambridge: Cambridge University Press, 1994.

Correa, Delia da Sousa. *George Eliot, Music and Victorian Culture.* Houndmills, Basingstoke: Palgrave Macmillan, 2003.

Cottom, Daniel. *The Civilized Imagination: A Study of Ann Radcliffe, Jane Austen, and Sir Walter Scott.* Cambridge: Cambridge University Press, 1985.

– *Social Figures: George Eliot, Social History, and Literary Representation.* Foreword by Terry Eagleton. Minneapolis: University of Minnesota Press, 1987.

Craik, W.A. *Elizabeth Gaskell and the English Provincial Novel.* London: Methuen, 1975.

Crawford, Rachel. *Poetry, Enclosure, and the Vernacular Landscape, 1700–1830.* Cambridge: Cambridge University Press, 2002.

Crosby, Christina. 'Charlotte Brontë's Haunted Text.' *Studies in English Literature* 24 (1984): 701–15.

Cunningham, Valentine. *In the Reading Gaol: Postmodernity, Texts, and History.* Oxford: Blackwell, 1994.

Cunnington, C. Willett. *Handbook of English Costume in the Nineteenth Century.* 3rd ed. London: Faber and Faber, 1970.

Cvetkovich, Ann. *Mixed Feelings: Feminism, Mass Culture, and Victorian Sensationalism.* New Brunswick, NJ: Rutgers University Press, 1992.

Daniels, Stephen. 'Humphry Repton and the Improvement of the Estate.' In Daniels, *Fields of Vision,* 80–111.

Daniels, Stephen, ed. *Fields of Vision: Landscape Imagery and National Identity in England and the United States.* Cambridge: Polity, 1993.

Darwin, Charles. *Darwin: A Norton Critical Edition.* 2nd ed. Edited by Philip Appleman. New York: W.W. Norton, 1979.

Darwin, Erasmus. *A Plan for the Conduct of Female Education in Boarding Schools.* Derby, 1797. Yorkshire: S.R. Publishers; New York: Johnson Reprint Corporation, 1968.

David, Dierdre. *Fictions of Resolution in Three Victorian Novels:* North and South, Our Mutual Friend, Daniel Deronda. London: Macmillan, 1981.

De Bruyn, Frans. 'Edmund Burke's Natural Aristocrat: The "Man of Taste" as a Political Ideal.' *Eighteenth-Century Life* 11.2 (1987): 41–60.

Dickens, Charles. *Bleak House.* Introduced by Morton Dauwen Zabel. Boston: Houghton Mifflin, 1956.

– *Dombey and Son.* Edited by Peter Fairclough. Introduced by Raymond Williams. Harmondsworth, Middlesex: Penguin, 1970; reprint 1985.

– *Great Expectations.* Introduced by Earle Davis. New York: Rinehart, 1948.

– *Hard Times.* Edited and introduced by David Craig. Harmondsworth, Middlesex: Penguin, 1969.

– *The Letters of Charles Dickens.* Edited by Graham Storey, Kathleen Tillotson, and Nina Burgis. Oxford: Clarendon Press, 1988.

– 'Our French Watering-Place.' In Pascoe, *Charles Dickens,* 152–63.

– *Our Mutual Friend.* Edited and introduced by Stephen Gill. Harmondsworth, Middlesex: Penguin, 1971.

– *The Posthumous Papers of the Pickwick Club.* Edited and introduced by Robert L. Patten. Harmondsworth, Middlesex: Penguin, 1972.

– *A Tale of Two Cities.* Oxford: Oxford University Press, 1988.

Disraeli, Benjamin. *Coningsby, or The New Generation.* Oxford: Oxford University Press, 1982.

– *Sybil, or The Two Nations.* Edited Sheila M. Smith. Oxford: Oxford University Press, 1981.

Dodsworth, Martin. Introduction to *North and South* by Elizabeth Gaskell, 7–26. Harmondsworth: Penguin, 1970.

Dole, Carol M. 'Austen, Class, and the American Market.' In Troost and Greenfield, eds, *Jane Austen in Hollywood*, 58–77.

Donoghue, Denis. 'A View of *Mansfield Park.*' In Southam, *Critical Essays on Jane Austen*, 39–59.

Duckworth, Alistair M. *The Improvement of the Estate: A Study of Jane Austen's Novels.* Baltimore: Johns Hopkins University Press, 1971.

Duncan, Ian. *Modern Romance and Transformations of the Novel: The Gothic, Scott, Dickens.* Cambridge: Cambridge University Press, 1992.

Eagleton, Terry. *The Ideology of the Aesthetic.* Oxford: Basil Blackwell, 1990.

Eastlake, Lady. See Elizabeth Rigby.

Eden, Emily. *Up the Country: Letters Written to Her Sister from the Upper Provinces of India.* Introduced by Edward Thompson. Oxford University Press, 1930; reprint London: Curzon Press, 1978.

Edgeworth, Maria. 'Mlle Panache.' *The Parent's Assistant, or Stories for Children.* Introduced by Christina Edgeworth Colvin, 187–8. New York: Garland, 1976.

Edwards, Thomas R. 'The Difficult Beauty of *Mansfield Park.*' *Nineteenth-Century Fiction* 20 (1965): 51–67.

Eliot, George. *Daniel Deronda.* Edited and introduced by Barbara Hardy. Harmondsworth, Middlesex: Penguin, 1967.

– *Middlemarch.* Edited, introduced, and annotated by Gordon S. Haight. Boston: Houghton Mifflin, 1956.

– *The Mill on the Floss.* Edited, introduced, and annotated by Gordon S. Haight. Boston: Houghton Mifflin, 1961.

– 'Silly Novels by Lady Novelists.' In *Selected Critical Writings.* Edited by Rosemary Ashton, 296–321. Oxford: Oxford University Press, 1992.

Elliott, Dorice Williams. 'The Female Visitor and the Marriage of Classes in Gaskell's *North and South.*' *Nineteenth-Century Literature* 49 (1994): 21–49.

Ellis, Markman. *The Politics of Sensibility.* Cambridge: Cambridge University Press, 1996.

Ellis, Sarah Stickney. *The Women of England: Their Social Duties, and Domestic Habits.* 12th ed. London and Paris: Fisher, 1839.

Enfield, William. *The Speaker: or, Miscellaneous Pieces, Selected from the Best English Writers, and Disposed under Proper Heads, with a View to Facilitate the Improvement of Youth in Reading and Speaking* (1774). London: Printed by Andrew Wilson for J. Johnson, 1808.

Engels, Friedrich. *The Condition of the Working Class in England from Personal Observation and Authentic Sources.* Introduced by Eric Hobsbawm. London: Granada, 1969.

Evans, Joan. *The Victorians.* London: Cambridge University Press, 1966.

Ewbank, Inga-Stina. *Their Proper Sphere: A Study of the Brontë Sisters as Early-Victorian Female Novelists.* Cambridge, MA: Harvard University Press, 1966.

Feltes, N.N. 'One Round of a Long Ladder: Gender, Profession, and the Production of *Middlemarch.*' In *Modes of Production of Victorian Novels,* 36–56. Chicago: University of Chicago Press, 1986.

Fergus, Jan. *Jane Austen and the Didactic Novel:* Northanger Abbey, Sense and Sensibility, *and* Pride and Prejudice. Totowa, NJ: Barnes and Noble, 1983.

Ferris, Ina. *The Achievement of Literary Authority: Gender, History, and the Waverley Novels.* Ithaca, NY: Cornell University Press, 1991.

Fleishman, Avrom. *A Reading of* Mansfield Park: *An Essay in Critical Synthesis.* Minneapolis: University of Minnesota Press, 1967.

Fletcher, Angus. *The Prophetic Moment: An Essay on Spenser.* Chicago: University of Chicago Press, 1971.

Forty, Adrian. *Words and Buildings: A Vocabulary of Modern Architecture.* New York: Thames and Hudson, 2000.

Fowler, Bridget. *Pierre Bourdieu and Cultural Theory: Critical Investigations.* London: Sage, 1997.

Fry, Paul. 'Georgic Comedy: The Fictive Territory of Jane Austen's *Emma.*' *Studies in the Novel* 11 (1979): 129–46.

Frye, Northrop. *Anatomy of Criticism: Four Essays.* Princeton, NJ: Princeton University Press, 1957.

Furbank, P.N. 'Mendacity in Mrs Gaskell.' *Encounter* 40 (June 1973): 51–5.

Gage, John. *Colour and Culture: Practice and Meaning from Antiquity to Abstraction.* Singapore: Thames and Hudson, 1993.

Gallagher, Catherine. 'George Eliot and *Daniel Deronda:* The Prostitute and the Jewish Question.' In Yeazell, ed, *Sex, Politics, and Science in the Nineteenth-Century Novel,* 39–62.

– *The Industrial Reformation of English Fiction: Social Discourse and Narrative Form 1832–1867.* Chicago: University of Chicago Press, 1985.

Gard, Roger. *Jane Austen's Novels: The Art of Clarity.* New Haven, CT: Yale University Press, 1992.

Garfield, Simon. *Mauve: How One Man Invented a Colour That Changed the World.* London: Faber and Faber, 2001.

Garside, P.D. 'Waverley's Pictures of the Past.' *English Literary History* 44 (1977): 659–82.

Garson, Marjorie. 'Alice Munro and Charlotte Brontë.' *University of Toronto Quarterly* 69 (2000): 783–825.

- 'Associationism and the Dialogue in *Emma.*' *Eighteenth-Century Fiction* 10 (1997): 79–100.

Gaskell, Elizabeth. *The Letters of Mrs. Gaskell.* Edited by J.A.V. Chapple and Arthur Pollard. Manchester: Manchester University Press, 1966.

- *North and South.* Introduced by Martin Dodsworth. Harmondsworth, Middlesex: Penguin, 1970.

- *Wives and Daughters.* Edited by Frank Glover Smith. Introduced by Laurence Lerner. Harmondsworth, Middlesex: Penguin, 1969.

Gay, Penny. *Jane Austen and the Theatre.* Cambridge: Cambridge University Press, 2002.

Genlis, Stephanie Felicité Ducrest de St Aubin. *Adelaide and Theodore; or Letters on Education.* 3 vols. London: for Bathurst and for Cadell, 1783.

Gerard, Alexander. *An Essay on Taste* (1759). *Together with Observations Concerning the Imitative Nature of Poetry.* Facs. rep. of 3rd ed. 1780. Introduced by Walter J. Hipple, Jr. Gainesville, FL: Scholars' Facsimiles and Reprints, 1963.

Gérin, Winifred. *Elizabeth Gaskell: A Biography.* Oxford: Clarendon Press, 1976.

Gilbert, Sandra M., and Susan Gubar. *The Madwoman in the Attic: The Woman Writer and the Nineteenth-Century Literary Imagination.* New Haven, CT: Yale University Press, 1979.

Gilpin, William. *Observations, Relative Chiefly to Picturesque Beauty, Made in the Year 1772, On Several Parts of England; particularly the Mountains, and Lake of Cumberland, and Westmoreland.* London: R. Blamire, 1786. Facsimile reprint, New York: Woodstock, 1996.

Ginsburg, Michal Peled. *Economies of Change: Form and Transformation in the Nineteenth-Century Novel.* Stanford, CA: Stanford University Press, 1996.

Gissing, George. *New Grub Street.* Notes Bernard Bergonzi. Harmondsworth, Middlesex: Penguin, 1968.

- *The Odd Women.* London, New York: W.W. Norton, 1977.

Goffman, Erving. *Interaction Ritual: Essays on Face-to-Face Behaviour.* 1967; Harmondsworth, Middlesex: Penguin, 1972.

- *The Presentation of Self in Everyday Life.* 1956; revised and expanded for Anchor edition. Garden City, NY: Doubleday, 1959.

Gordon, Jan B. 'George Eliot's Crisis of the Antecedent.' In Smith, *George Eliot,* 124–51.

Gunster, Shane. *Capitalizing Culture: Critical Theory for Cultural Studies.* Toronto: University of Toronto Press, 2004.

Halle, David. 'The Audience for Abstract Art: Class, Culture, and Power.' In Lamont and Fournier, eds, *Cultivating Differences,* 131–51.

Harding, D.W. *Regulated Hatred and Other Essays on Jane Austen.* Edited by Monica Lawlor. London: Athlone Press, 1998.

Hardy, Barbara, ed. Middlemarch: *Critical Approaches to the Novel*. London: Athlone Press, 1967.

– *The Novels of George Eliot: A Study in Form*. London: Athlone Press, 1959.

– *A Reading of Jane Austen*. London: Peter Owen, 1975.

Hardy, John. *Jane Austen's Heroines: Intimacy in Human Relationships*. London: Routledge and Kegan Paul, 1984.

Hardy, Thomas. *The Complete Poetical Works of Thomas Hardy*. Edited by Samuel Hynes. 5 vols. Oxford: Clarendon Press, 1982.

– *Jude the Obscure*. Edited by Norman Page. New York: W.W. Norton, 1978.

– *A Laodicean*. Introduced by Barbara Hardy. Annotated by Ernest Hardy. London: Macmillan, 1975.

– *The Mayor of Casterbridge*. Edited and introduced by Dale Kramer. Oxford: Oxford University Press, 1987.

– *Tess of the d'Urbervilles*. Introduced by P.N. Furbank. London: Macmillan, 1974.

Harman, Barbara Leah. *The Feminine Political Novel in Victorian England*. Charlottesville: University Press of Virginia, 1998.

Harrison, Jane Ellen. *Reminiscences of a Student's Life*. London: Hogarth Press, 1925.

Harsh, Constance D. *Subversive Heroines: Feminist Resolutions of Social Crisis in the Condition-of-England Novel*. Ann Arbor: University of Michigan Press, 1994.

Hart, Francis R. *Scott's Novels: The Plotting of Historic Survival*. Charlottesville: University Press of Virginia, 1966.

Harvey, W.J. 'Criticism of the Novel: Contemporary Reception.' In Barbara Hardy, ed, *Middlemarch*, 125–47.

Hazlitt, William. 'On Vulgarity and Affectation.' *Table Talk*. Edited by M. Maclean, 156–68. London: J.M. Dent; New York: E.P. Dutton, 1961.

Henderson, Andrea K. *Romantic Identities: Varieties of Subjectivity, 1774–1830*. Cambridge: Cambridge University Press, 1996.

Hertz, Neil. 'Recognizing Casaubon.' *Glyph* 6 (1979): 24–41.

Home, Henry (Lord Kames). *Elements of Criticism*. 1761. 11th ed. London: B. Blake, 13 Bell Yard, Temple Bar, 1839.

Horace. *The Complete Works of Horace* (*Quintus Horatius Flaccus*). Translated and annotated by Charles E. Passage. New York: Frederick Ungar, 1983.

Houston, Gail Turley. *Consuming Fictions: Gender, Class, and Hunger in Dickens's Novels*. Carbondale: Southern Illinois University Press, 1994.

Hutcheson, Francis. *An Essay on the Nature and Conduct of the Passions and Affections*. 1728. Facsimile reprint Menton, Yorkshire: Scolar Press, 1972.

James, Henry. *The Awkward Age*. Edited, introduction, and notes by Ronald Blythe; additional notes by Patricia Crick. Harmondsworth, Middlesex: Penguin, 1987.

John, Juliet. *Dickens's Villains: Melodrama, Character, Popular Culture.* Oxford: Oxford University Press, 2001.

Johnson, Claudia L. *Jane Austen: Women, Politics and the Novel.* Chicago: University of Chicago Press, 1988.

Johnson, Edgar. *Charles Dickens: Tragedy and Triumph.* 1952; revised and abridged edition, New York: Viking, 1977.

Jones, Vivien. '"The Coquetry of Nature": Politics and the Picturesque in Women's Fiction.' In Copley and Garside, *The Politics of the Picturesque,* 120–44.

Jordan, R. Furneaux. *Victorian Architecture.* Harmondsworth, Middlesex: Penguin, 1966.

Joyce, James. *A Portrait of the Artist as a Young Man.* Harmondsworth, Middlesex: Penguin, 1960.

Kames, Lord. *See* Home, Henry (Lord Kames).

Kanner, Barbara. *Women in English Social History, 1800–1914: A Guide to Research.* 3 vols. New York: Garland, 1987–90.

Kaplan, Deborah. *Jane Austen among Women.* Baltimore: Johns Hopkins University Press, 1992.

Kaplan, Joel H. and Sheila Stowell. *Theatre and Fashion: Oscar Wilde to the Suffragettes.* Cambridge: Cambridge University Press, 1994.

Karl, Frederick R. *George Eliot: Voice of a Century. A Biography.* New York: W.W. Norton, 1995.

Kemp, Edward. *How to Lay Out a Garden.* Reprint from the 2nd London edition. New York: John Wiley, 1860.

Kerr, James. *Fiction against History: Scott as Storyteller.* Cambridge: Cambridge University Press, 1989.

Kiely, Robert. *The Romantic Novel in England.* Cambridge, MA: Harvard University Press, 1972.

Kirkham, Margaret. 'Feminist Irony and the Priceless Heroine of *Mansfield Park.*' In Todd, *Jane Austen,* 231–47.

– *Jane Austen, Feminism and Fiction.* Sussex: Harvester; Totawa, NJ: Barnes and Noble, 1983.

Kitchel, Anna Theresa. *Quarry for Middlemarch.* Berkeley: University of California Press; London: Cambridge University Press, 1950.

Knight, Richard Payne. *The Landscape, a Didactic Poem in Three Books Addressed to Uvedale Price, Esq.* 2nd ed. London: R. Bulmer, 1795.

Knoepflmacher, U.C. 'The Importance of Being Frank: Character and Letter-Writing in *Emma.' Studies in English Literature* 7 (1967): 639–58.

Kotzebue, August von. *Lovers' Vows.* Adapted by Elizabeth Inchbald. London: printed for G.G. and J. Robinson, Pater-Noster-Row, 1798. Facsimile reprint, Oxford: Woodstock, 1990.

Krais, Beate. 'Gender and Symbolic Violence: Female Oppression in the Light of Pierre Bourdieu's Theory of Social Practice.' In Calhoun, LiPuma, and Postone, *Bourdieu*, 156–77.

Kucich, John. *Repression in Victorian Fiction*. Berkeley: University of California Press, 1987.

Kurt, June. 'The Deep Seduction.' *House Beautiful* 127.9 (September 1995): 84–9.

Labbé, Jacqueline M. *Romantic Visualities: Landscape, Gender and Romanticism*. Macmillan: St Martin's, 1998.

Lamont, Michèle and Marcel Fournier, eds. *Cultivating Differences: Symbolic Boundaries and the Making of Inequality*. Chicago: University of Chicago Press, 1992.

Langland, Elizabeth. *Nobody's Angels: Middle-Class Women and Domestic Ideology in Victorian Culture*. Ithaca, NY: Cornell University Press, 1995.

Lansbury, Coral. *Elizabeth Gaskell: The Novel of Social Crisis*. London: Paul Elek; New York: Barnes and Noble, 1975.

Lanser, Susan Sniader. *Fictions of Authority: Women Writers and Narrative Voice*. Ithaca, NY: Cornell University Press, 1992.

Lascelles, Mary. *Jane Austen and Her Art*. Oxford: Clarendon Press; London: Humphrey Milford, 1939.

Lash, Scott. 'Pierre Bourdieu: Cultural Economy and Social Change.' In Calhoun, LiPuma, and Postone, *Bourdieu*, 193–211.

Lathrop, George Parsons. 'An Echo of Passion.' *Atlantic Monthly* 49 (1882): 17–80, 163–79.

Leavis, F.R. *The Great Tradition: George Eliot, Henry James, Joseph Conrad*. 1948; London: Chatto and Windus, 1960.

Leavis, Q.D. *Collected Essays*. Collected and edited by G. Singh. Cambridge: Cambridge University Press, 1983–. Vol. 1: *The Englishness of the English Novel*, 1983. Vol. 3: *The Novel of Religious Controversy*, 1989.

Lee, Hermione. 'Emblems and Enigmas in *Jane Eyre*.' *English* 30 (1981): 233–55.

Lerner, Laurence. *The Truthtellers: Jane Austen, George Eliot, D.H. Lawrence*. New York: Schocken, 1967.

Levine, George, ed. *The Cambridge Companion to George Eliot*. Cambridge: Cambridge University Press, 2001.

– *The Realistic Imagination: English Fiction from Frankenstein to Lady Chatterley*. Chicago: University of Chicago Press, 1981.

Litvak, Joseph. *Caught in the Act: Theatricality in the Nineteenth-Century English Novel*. Berkeley: University of California Press, 1992.

– 'The Infection of Acting: Theatricals and Theatricality in *Mansfield Park*.' *English Literary History* 53 (1986): 331–55.

– 'Reading Characters: Self, Society, and Text in *Emma.*' *Modern Language Assoca-
tion of America Publications* 100 (1985): 763–73.

Liu, Alan. *Wordsworth: The Sense of History.* Stanford, CA: Stanford University
Press, 1989.

Lonoff, Sue. See Brontë, Charlotte, and Emily Brontë, *The Belgian Essays.*

Loudon, John Claudius. *An Encyclopaedia of Cottage, Farm, and Villa Architecture
and Furniture.* London: Longman, Rees, Orme, Brown, Greene, and Longmans, 1834.

– *The Suburban Gardener and Villa Companion.* London: Longman, Orme, Brown,
Green, and Longmans; Edinburgh: W. Black, 1838. Facsimile reprint, New
York: Garland, 1982

– 'Of Taste, Chiefly in Regard to Scenery and Architecture.' In *A Treatise on Forming, Improving and Managing Country Residences.* 2 vols, vol. 1, part 2, 15–51. London: Longman, Rees, and Orme, Pater-Noster-Row, by C. Whittingham, 1806.

Lubbock, Jules. *The Tyranny of Taste: The Politics of Architecture and Design in Britain, 1550–1960.* New Haven, CT: Yale University Press, 1995.

Lucas, John. 'Mrs. Gaskell and Brotherhood.' In *Tradition and Tolerance in Nineteenth-Century Fiction: Critical Essays on Some English and American Novels.* Edited
by David Howard, John Lucas, and John Goode, 141–205. London: Routledge and Kegan Paul, 1966.

Lynch, Deidre Shauna. *The Economy of Character: Novels, Market Culture, and the
Business of Inner Meaning.* Chicago: University of Chicago Press, 1998.

Lynn Linton, Eliza. 'On the Side of the Maids.' *Cornhill* 29 (March 1874):
298–307.

Makdisi, Saree. *Romantic Imperialism: Universal Empire and the Culture of Modernity.*
Cambridge: Cambridge University Press, 1998.

Marlow, James E. 'English Cannibalism: Dickens after 1859.' *Studies in English
Literature* 23 (1983): 647–66.

Marshall, David. 'True Acting and the Language of Real Feeling: *Mansfield Park.*'
*Yale Journal of Criticism* 3.1 (Fall 1989): 87–106.

Matthew, H.C.G. and Brian Harrison, eds. *The Oxford Dictionary of National Biography: From the Earliest Times to the Year 2000.* New York: Oxford University
Press, 2004.

Matus, Jill. *Unstable Bodies: Victorian Representations of Sexuality and Maternity.*
Manchester: Manchester University Press, 1995.

Mayhew, Henry. *London Labour and the London Poor.* Selected and introduced by
Victor Neuburg. Harmondsworth, Middlesex: Penguin, 1985.

McSweeney, Kerry. *Middlemarch.* London: George Allen and Unwin, 1984.

Megill, Allan. 'Aesthetic Theory and Historical Consciousness in the Eighteenth
Century.' *History and Theory* 17 (1978): 30–62.

Michaelson, Patricia Howell. *Speaking Volumes: Women, Reading, and Speech in the Age of Austen*. Stanford, CA: Stanford University Press, 2002.

Mill, James. *Analysis of the Phenomena of the Human Mind*. 2nd ed. (1869). 2 vols. New York: Augustus M. Kelley, 1967.

Miller, D.A. *Narrative and Its Discontents: Problems of Closure in the Traditional Novel*. Princeton, NJ: Princeton University Press, 1981.

Millgate, Jane. 'Narrative Distance in *Jane Eyre*: The Relevance of the Pictures.' *Modern Language Review* 63 (1968): 315–19.

– '*Waverley:* Romance as Education.' In *Walter Scott: The Making of the Novelist*, 35–57. Toronto: University of Toronto Press, 1984.

Millgate, Michael. *The Achievement of William Faulkner*. New York: Random House; London: Constable, 1966.

Moers, Ellen. 'Performing Heroinism: The Myth of Corinne.' In Buckley, *The Worlds of Victorian Fiction*, 319–50.

Moi, Toril. 'Appropriating Bourdieu: Feminist Theory and Pierre Bourdieu's Sociology of Culture.' *New Literary History* 22 (1991): 1017–49.

Moler, Kenneth L. *Jane Austen's Art of Allusion*. Lincoln: University of Nebraska Press, 1968.

Montesquieu, Charles de Secondat, Baron de. 'Essai sur le Goût dans les choses de la nature et de l'art.' In *Oeuvres Complètes de Montesquieu*. Edited and annotated by Roger Caillois, vol. 2, 1240–63. Paris: Librarie Gallimard, 1951.

More, Hannah. 'England's Best Hope.' *Works*, 11:38–53.

– 'Thoughts on Conversation.' *Works*, 6: 277–87.

– 'Thoughts on the Manners of the Great.' *Works*, 2:239–82.

– 'True and False Meekness.' *Works*, 6: 309–15.

– *The Works of Hannah More*. 11 vols. London: Henry G. Bohn, 1853.

Morgan, Susan. *In the Meantime: Character and Perception in Jane Austen's Fiction*. Chicago: University of Chicago Press, 1980.

Morris, Pam. *Dickens's Class Consciousness: A Marginal View*. New York: St Martin's, 1991.

Mugglestone, Lynda. *'Talking Proper': The Rise of Accent as a Social Symbol*. 2nd ed. Oxford: Oxford University Press, 2003.

Musselwhite, David E. *Partings Welded Together: Politics and Desire in the Nineteenth-Century English Novel*. London: Methuen, 1987.

Myers, William. *The Teaching of George Eliot*. Leicester: Leicester University Press, 1984.

Nardin, Jane. *Those Elegant Decorums: The Concept of Propriety in Jane Austen's Novels*. Albany: State University of New York Press, 1973.

Neill, Edward. *The Politics of Jane Austen*. Houndmills, Basingstoke: Macmillan, 1999.

Newton, Judith Lowder. *Women, Power, and Subversion: Social Strategies in British Fiction, 1778–1860*. Athens: University of Georgia Press, 1981.

Nord, Deborah Epstein. *Walking the Victorian Streets: Women, Representation, and the City*. Ithaca, NY: Cornell University Press, 1995.

Nunokawa, Jeff. *The Afterlife of Property: Domestic Security and the Victorian Novel*. Princeton, NJ: Princeton University Press, 1994.

O'Farrell, Mary Ann. *Telling Complexions: The Nineteenth-Century English Novel and the Blush*. Durham, NC: Duke University Press, 1997.

Oldfield, Derek. 'The Language of the Novel: The Character of Dorothea.' In Barbara Hardy, ed., *Middlemarch*, 63–86.

Oliphant, Margaret. 'Modern Novelists – Great and Small.' *Blackwoods* 77 (May 1855): 554–68.

Page, Norman. *The Language of Jane Austen*. Oxford: Basil Blackwell, 1972.

Paget, John. 'Elements of Drawing.' [Review of Ruskin's *Elements of Drawing*.]. *Blackwoods* 87 (January 1860): 32–44.

Parkin-Gounelas, Ruth. *Fictions of the Female Self: Charlotte Brontë, Olive Schreiner, Katherine Mansfield*. Houndmills, Basingstoke: Macmillan, 1991.

Pascoe, David, ed. *Charles Dickens: Selected Journalism, 1850–1870*. London: Penguin, 1997.

Pastoureau, Michel. *Blue: The History of a Color*. Translated by Markus I. Cruse. Princeton, NJ: Princeton University Press, 2001.

Payne Knight, Richard. See Knight.

Peel, Jonathan. 'Taste and Music in England.' *Blackwoods* 53 (January 1843): 127–40.

Pennington, Sarah. *A Mother's Advice to Her Absent Daughters* (1817). New York: Garland, 1986.

Pettit, Clare. 'Room of Her Own: Jane Barker, Jacobite, Satirist and Hack.' [Review of Kathryn King's *Jane Barker, Exile: A Literary Career, 1675–1715*.] *Times Literary Supplement* 6 April 2001: 5.

Pickrel, Paul. 'Lionel Trilling and *Emma*: A Reconsideration.' *Nineteenth-Century Fiction* 40 (1985): 297–311.

Pike, E. Holly. *Family and Society in the Works of Elizabeth Gaskell*. New York: Peter Lang, 1995.

Poovey, Mary. *The Proper Lady and the Woman Writer: Ideology as Style in the Works of Mary Wollstonecraft, Mary Shelley, and Jane Austen*. Chicago: University of Chicago Press, 1984.

– *Uneven Developments: The Ideological Work of Gender in Mid-Victorian England*. Chicago: University of Chicago Press, 1988.

Pope, Alexander. *The Poems of Alexander Pope*. A one-volume edition of the Twickenham text with selected annotations. Edited by John Butt. London: Methuen, 1963.

Porter, Jane. *Thaddeus of Warsaw.* London: George Virtue, 1845.

Price, Uvedale. *An Essay on the Picturesque, as Compared with the Sublime and the Beautiful; and, on the Use of Studying Pictures, for the Purpose of Improving Real Landscapes.* London: J. Robson, 1794.

Pugh, Simon, ed. *Reading Landscape: Country – City – Capital.* Manchester: Manchester University Press, 1990.

Radcliffe, Ann. *The Mysteries of Udolpho: A Romance Interspersed with Some Pieces of Poetry.* Edited and introduced by Bonamy Dobrée. Notes by Frederick Garber. Oxford: Oxford University Press, 1970.

– *The Romance of the Forest.* Edited and introduced by Chloë Chard. Oxford: Oxford University Press, 1986.

Rappaport, Erika Diane. *Shopping for Pleasure: Women in the Making of London's West End.* Princeton, NJ: Princeton University Press, 2000.

Repton, Humphry. *Fragments on the Theory and Practice of Landscape Gardening* (1816). New York and London: Garland, 1982.

– *The Landscape Gardening and Landscape Architecture of the Late Humphry Repton, Esq.* Edited, introduced, and annotated by John Claudius Loudon. London: Longman; Edinburgh: A. and C. Black, 1840.

Reynolds, Joshua. *Discourses.* Edited, introduction, and notes by Pat Rogers. Harmondsworth, Middlesex: Penguin, 1992.

Ribeiro, Aileen. *Dress and Morality.* New York: Holmes and Meier, 1986.

Richardson, Alan. *Literature, Education, and Romanticism: Reading as Social Practice, 1780–1832.* Cambridge: Cambridge University Press, 1994.

Richler, Mordecai. *Barney's Version.* Toronto: Vintage (Random House), 1998.

Rigby, Elizabeth (Lady Eastlake). '*Vanity Fair* – and *Jane Eyre.*' *Quarterly Review* 84 (December 1848): 153–85.

Riley, Charles A. *Color Codes: Modern Theories of Color in Philosophy, Painting and Architecture, Literature, Music, and Psychology.* Hanover, NH: University Press of New England, 1995.

Riley, Noël. *Victorian Design Source Book.* Oxford: Phaidon, 1989.

Robbins, Derek. *The Work of Pierre Bourdieu: Recognizing Society.* Buckingham: Open University Press, 1991.

Roberts, Helene E. 'The Exquisite Slave: The Role of Clothes in the Making of the Victorian Woman.' *Signs* (1977): 554–67.

Robinson, Robert. *An Essay on the Composition of a Sermon.* 2 vols. Cambridge, 1778. Translation of Jean Claude's *Traité de la composition d'un sermon.* Amsterdam, 1688.

Robinson, Sidney K. *Inquiry into the Picturesque.* Chicago: Chicago University Press, 1991.

Røstvig, Maren-Sofie. *The Happy Man: Studies in the Metamorphoses of a Classical*

*Ideal, 1600–1700.* Oslo: Akademisk Forlag, 1952. 2nd ed., Norwegian Universities Press, 1962.

Rousseau, Jean-Jacques. *Émile.* Paris: Garnier, 1951.

Rubenius, Aina. *The Woman Question in Mrs. Gaskell's Life and Works.* Upsala: University of Upsala Press; Cambridge, MA: Harvard University Press, 1950; reissued New York: Russell and Russell, 1973.

Ruskin, John. *The Works of John Ruskin.* Edited and annotated by E.T. Cook and Alexander Wedderburn. 39 vols. London: George Allen; New York: Longmans Green, 1903–11.

Sadoff, Dianne F. *Monsters of Affection: Dickens, Eliot, and Brontë.* Baltimore: Johns Hopkins University Press, 1982.

Said, Edward W. *Culture and Imperialism.* New York: Knopf, 1993.

Sandford, Mrs John. *Woman in Her Social and Domestic Character.* Bound with Hubbard Winslow, *Woman as She Should Be.* 2nd London ed. Boston: Otis, Broaders, 1838.

Schneider, Sister M. Lucy. 'The Little White Attic and the East Room: Their Function in *Mansfield Park.*' *Modern Philology* 63 (1966): 227–35.

Schopenhauer, Arthur. *The World as Will and Idea.* Translated by R.B. Haldane and J. Kemp. London: Routledge and Kegan Paul, 1883.

Schor, Hilary M. *Scheherezade in the Marketplace: Elizabeth Gaskell and the Victorian Novel.* Oxford: Oxford University Press, 1992.

Scott, Sir Walter. *Guy Mannering.* Edited by Peter Garside. Edinburgh: Edinburgh University Press, 1999.

– *Kenilworth: A Romance.* Edited by J.H. Alexander. Edinburgh: Edinburgh University Press, 1993.

– *Redgauntlet.* Edited by G.A.M. Wood with David Hewitt. Edinburgh: Edinburgh University Press; New York: Columbia University Press, 1997.

– *Saint Ronan's Well.* Edited by Mark Weinstein. Edinburgh: Edinburgh University Press; New York: Columbia University Press, 1995.

– *Waverley; or, 'Tis Sixty Years Since.* Edited by Claire Lamont. Oxford: Clarendon Press, 1981.

Sedgwick, Eve Kosofsky. *Between Men: English Literature and Male Homosocial Desire.* New York: Columbia University Press, 1985.

Selwyn, David. *Jane Austen and Leisure.* London: Hambledon Press, 1999.

Sewell, Elizabeth M. *Amy Herbert.* 1844; London: Longmans Green, 1906.

Shaftesbury, Anthony Ashley Cooper, Earl of. *Characteristics of Men, Manners, Opinions, Times.* Edited by Lawrence Klein. Cambridge: Cambridge University Press, 1999.

Shaw, Harry E. *The Forms of Historical Fiction: Sir Walter Scott and His Successors.* Ithaca, NY: Cornell University Press, 1983.

Shuttleworth, Sally. *Charlotte Brontë and Victorian Psychology.* Cambridge: Cambridge University Press, 1996.

Siskin, Clifford. *The Historicity of Romantic Discourse.* Oxford: Oxford University Press, 1988.

Sitch, Rob, director. *The Castle.* Los Angeles, CA: Miramax, 1997.

Smith, Anne, ed. *George Eliot: Centenary Essays and an Unpublished Fragment.* London: Vision, 1980.

Smith, Charlotte. *The Old Manor House.* Edited and introduced by Anne Henry Ehrenpreis. London: Oxford University Press, 1969.

Smith, Olivia. *The Politics of Language, 1791–1819.* Oxford: Clarendon Press, 1984.

Smith, Sydney. 'Female Education.' *Edinburgh Review* 15 (January 1810): 299–315.

Southam, B.C., ed. *Critical Essays on Jane Austen.* London: Routledge and Kegan Paul, 1968.

Spencer, Jane. *Elizabeth Gaskell.* Houndmills, Basingstoke: Macmillan, 1993.

Spenser, Edmund. *Spenser: Poetical Works.* Edited and annotated by J.C. Smith and E. De Selincourt; introduced by E. De Selincourt. London: Oxford University Press, 1912.

Stewart, Maaja. *Domestic Realities and Imperial Fiction: Jane Austen's Novels in Eighteenth-Century Contexts.* Athens: University of Georgia Press, 1993.

Stone, Ian. 'The Contents of the Kettles: Charles Dickens, John Rae and Cannibalism on the 1845 Franklin Expedition.' *Dickensian* 83 (1987): 7–16.

Stoneman, Patsy. *Elizabeth Gaskell.* Brighton, Sussex: Harvester, 1987.

Tave, Stuart M. *Some Words of Jane Austen.* Chicago: University of Chicago Press, 1973.

Tayler, Irene. *Holy Ghosts: The Male Muses of Emily and Charlotte Brontë.* New York: Columbia University Press, 1990.

Thackeray, William Makepiece. *Vanity Fair: A Novel without a Hero.* Edited, introduced, and annotated by Geoffrey and Kathleen Tillotson. Boston: Houghton Mifflin, 1963.

Thompson, James. *Between Self and World: The Novels of Jane Austen.* University Park: Pennsylvania State University Press, 1988.

Thormahlen, Marianne. *The Brontës and Religion.* Cambridge: Cambridge University Press, 1999.

Todd, Janet, ed. *Jane Austen: New Perspectives.* New York: Holmes and Meier, 1983.

Trilling, Lionel. Introduction to Austen, *Emma*, v–xxvi. Boston: Houghton Mifflin, 1975.

Trodd, Anthea. *Domestic Crime in the Victorian Novel.* New York: St Martin's, 1989.

Trollope, Anthony. *Can You Forgive Her?* Harmondsworth, Middlesex: Penguin, 1972.

– *The Prime Minister.* Harmondsworth, Middlesex: Penguin, 1993.

Troost, Linda, and Sayre Greenfield, eds. *Jane Austen in Hollywood.* 2nd ed. Lexington: University Press of Kentucky, 2001.

Trumpener, Katie. *Bardic Nationalism: The Romantic Novel and the British Empire.* Princeton, NJ: Princeton University Press, 1997.

Tuite, Clara. *Romantic Austen: Sexual Politics and the Literary Canon.* Cambridge: Cambridge University Press, 2002.

Veblen, Thorstein. *The Theory of the Leisure Class.* New York: B.W. Huebsch, 1918.

Waldron, Mary. *Jane Austen and the Fiction of Her Time.* Cambridge: Cambridge University Press, 1999.

Walker, Mrs Alexander. *Female Beauty, as Preserved and Improved by Regimen, Cleanliness and Dress.* Medical information revised by Sir Anthony Carlisle. Illustrated by J.W. Wright and E.T. Parris. London: Thomas Hurst, 1837.

Walker, Eric G. *Scott's Fiction and the Picturesque.* Salzburg: University of Salzburg, 1982.

Waters, Catherine. *Dickens and the Politics of the Family.* Cambridge: Cambridge University Press, 1997.

Watson, Nicola J. *Revolution and the Form of the British Novel, 1790–1825: Intercepted Letters, Interrupted Seductions.* Oxford: Clarendon Press, 1994.

Weissman, Judith. *Half Savage and Hardy and Free: Women and Rural Radicalism in the Nineteenth-Century Novel.* Middleton, CT: Wesleyan University Press, 1987.

Welsh, Alexander. *The City of Dickens.* Oxford: Clarendon Press, 1971. Reprinted Cambridge, MA: Harvard University Press, 1986.

– *The Hero of the Waverley Novels, with New Essays on Scott.* Princeton, NJ: Princeton University Press, 1992.

– 'Knowledge in *Middlemarch*.' In *George Eliot and Blackmail*, 216–58. Cambridge, MA: Harvard University Press, 1985.

– 'The Later Novels.' In Levine, *The Cambridge Companion to George Eliot*, 57–75.

Wheeler, Michael. *The Art of Allusion in Victorian Fiction.* London: Macmillan, 1979.

Wiesenfarth, Joseph. '*Middlemarch*: The Language of Art.' *Modern Language Association of America Publications* 97 (1982): 363–77.

Wigley, Mark. *White Walls, Designer Dresses: The Fashioning of Modern Architecture.* Cambridge, MA.: MIT Press, 1995.

Williams, Andrew Gibbon, and Andrew Brown. *The Bigger Picture: A History of Scottish Art.* London: BBC Books, 1993.

Williams, Judith. *Perception and Expression in the Novels of Charlotte Brontë*. Ann Arbor: UMI Research Press, 1988.

Wilt, Judith. 'The Powers of the Instrument, or Jane, Frank, and the Pianoforte.' *Persuasions* 5 (December 1983): 41–7.

Wiltshire, John. *Jane Austen and the Body: 'The Picture of Health.'* Cambridge: Cambridge University Press, 1992.

– *Recreating Jane Austen*. Cambridge: Cambridge University Press, 2001.

Winslow, Rev. Hubbard. *Woman as She Should Be*. Bound with Mrs John Sandford, *Woman in Her Social and Domestic Character*. 2nd London ed. Boston: Otis, Broaders, 1838.

Witemeyer, Hugh. *George Eliot and the Visual Arts*. New Haven, CT: Yale University Press, 1979.

Womack, Peter. *Improvement and Romance: Constructing the Myth of the Highlands*. Houndmills, Basingstoke: Macmillan, 1989.

Wright, Edgar. 'Elizabeth Cleghorn Gaskell.' In *Victorian Novelists before 1885*. Edited by Ira B. Nadel and William E. Fredeman. Vol. 21 in *Dictionary of Literary Biography*. Detroit: Gale, 1983.

– *Mrs. Gaskell: The Basis for Reassessment*. London: Oxford University Press, 1965.

Wright, Terence. *Elizabeth Gaskell: 'We Are Not Angels.'* Houndmills, Basingstoke: Macmillan, 1995.

Yeazell, Ruth Bernard. *Fictions of Modesty: Woman and Courtship in the English Novel*. Chicago: University of Chicago Press, 1991.

– ed. *Sex, Politics, and Science in the Nineteenth-Century Novel*. Baltimore: Johns Hopkins University Press, 1986.

Zolberg, Vera L. 'Barrier or Leveller? The Case of the Art Museum.' In Lamont and Fournier, *Cultivating Differences*, 187–209.

# Index

Italicized page numbers indicate the most concentrated discussion of a topic.